# Your Literacy Standards at a Glance

Indexes Cross-Referencing Your State Standards with the Common Core appear at the front of the book.

Specific strands and standards are listed for each state.

Each state and grade level is listed at the top for easy reference.

The gist of each standard is succinctly summarized.

This column shows where to find instructional guidance for each standard.

## Indexes Cross-Referencing Your State Standards

### Alaska, Grade 6

| Alaska Strand/Standard | Focus of Alaska Standard | For More Information |
|---|---|---|
| **Reading Literature** | | |
| RL.1 | Cite textual evidence to support analysis of what the text says explicitly as well as inferences drawn from the text | R1 pp. 6–11 |
| RL.2 | Determine the theme or central idea of a text and how it is conveyed through particular details; provide an objective summary | R2 pp. 12–19 |
| RL.3 | Describe how a particular plot unfolds in a series of episodes as well as how the characters respond or change | R3 pp. 20–25 |
| RL.4 | Determine the meaning of words and phrases as they are used in a text, including figurative and connotative meanings | R4 pp. 26–33 |
| RL.5 | Analyze how a particular sentence, chapter, scene, or stanza fits into the overall structure of a text and contributes to the development of the characters, theme, setting, or plot | R5 pp. 34–39 |
| RL.6 | Determine an author's purpose and explain how an author develops the point of view of the narrator or speaker in a text | R6 pp. 40–47 |
| RL.7 | Compare and contrast the experience of reading a story, drama, or poem to listening to or viewing an audio, video, or live version of the text | R7 pp. 48–55 |
| RL.8 | NA | |
| RL.9 | Compare and contrast texts in different forms or genres in terms of their approaches to similar themes and topics | R9 pp. 64–71 |
| RL.10 | Read and comprehend literature of appropriate complexity independently with proficiency | R10 pp. 72–77 |
| **Reading Informational Text** | | |
| RI.1 | Cite textual evidence to support analysis of what the text says explicitly as well as inferences drawn from the text | R1 pp. 6–11 |
| RI.2 | Determine a central idea of a text and how it is conveyed through particular details; provide an objective summary | R2 pp. 12–19 |
| RI.3 | Analyze in detail how a key individual, event, or idea is introduced, illustrated, and elaborated in a text | R3 pp. 20–25 |
| RI.4 | Determine the meaning of words and phrases as they are used in a text, including figurative, connotative, and technical meanings | R4 pp. 26–33 |
| RI.5 | Analyze how a particular sentence, chapter, or section fits into the overall structure of a text and contributes to the development of the ideas | R5 pp. 34–39 |
| RI.6 | Determine an author's point of view or purpose in a text and explain how it is conveyed in the text | R6 pp. 40–47 |
| RI.7 | Integrate information presented in different media or formats as well as in words to develop a coherent understanding of a topic or issue | R7 pp. 48–55 |
| RI.8 | Trace and evaluate the argument and specific claims that are supported by reasons and evidence from claims that are not | R8 pp. 56–63 |
| RI.9 | Compare and contrast one author's presentation of events with that of another | R9 pp. 64–71 |
| RI.10 | Read and comprehend appropriately complex literary nonfiction, informational, and functional texts independently and proficiently | R10 pp. 72–77 |

(Continued)

| Alaska Strand/Standard | Focus of Alaska Standard | For More Information |
|---|---|---|
| **Writing** | | |
| W.1 | Write arguments to support claims with clear reasons and relevant evidence | W1 pp. 82–89 |
| W.2 | Write informative/explanatory texts to examine a topic and convey ideas, concepts, and information clearly | W2 pp. 90–99 |
| W.3 | Use narrative writing to develop real or imagined experiences or events using effective technique, descriptive details, and well-structured event sequences | W3 pp. 100–109 |
| W.4 | Produce writing in which the development, organization, and style are appropriate to the task, purpose, and audience | W4 pp. 110–115 |
| W.5 | Develop and strengthen writing as needed by planning, revising, editing, rewriting, or trying a new approach | W5 pp. 116–121 |
| W.6 | Use technology to produce and publish writing as well as to interact with others; demonstrate keyboarding skills | W6 pp. 122–127 |
| W.7 | Conduct short research projects to answer a question, drawing on several sources and refocusing the inquiry when appropriate | W7 pp. 128–133 |
| W.8 | Gather information from print and digital sources; assess the credibility of sources; quote or paraphrase while avoiding plagiarism and providing basic bibliographic information | W8 pp. 134–139 |
| W.9 | Draw evidence from literary or informational texts to support analysis, reflection, and research | W9 pp. 140–147 |
| W.10 | Write routinely over extended and shorter time frames for a range of tasks, purposes, and audiences | W10 pp. 148–153 |
| **Speaking and Listening** | | |
| SL.1 | Engage effectively in a range of collaborative discussions with diverse partners, building on others' ideas and expressing their own clearly | SL1 pp. 158–163 |
| SL.2 | Interpret information presented in diverse media and formats and explain how it contributes to a topic, text, or issue under study | SL2 pp. 164–169 |
| SL.3 | Delineate a speaker's argument and specific claims, distinguishing claims that are supported by reasons and evidence from claims that are not | SL3 pp. 170–175 |
| SL.4 | Present claims and findings, sequencing ideas logically and using descriptions, facts, or details to accentuate main ideas or themes; use appropriate eye contact, adequate volume, and clear pronunciation | SL4 pp. 176–181 |
| SL.5 | Include multimedia components and visual displays in presentations to clarify information | SL5 pp. 182–187 |
| SL.6 | Adapt speech to a variety of contexts and tasks, demonstrating command of formal English when appropriate | SL6 pp. 188–193 |
| **Language** | | |
| L.1 | Demonstrate command of the conventions of standard English grammar and usage when writing or speaking | L1 pp. 198–203 |
| L.2 | Demonstrate command of the conventions of standard English capitalization, punctuation, and spelling when writing | L2 pp. 204–209 |
| L.3 | Use knowledge of language and its conventions when writing, speaking, reading, or listening | L3 pp. 210–215 |
| L.4 | Determine or clarify the meaning of unknown and multiple-meaning words and phrases, choosing flexibly from an array of strategies | L4 pp. 216–221 |
| L.5 | Demonstrate understanding of figurative language, word relationships, and nuances in word meanings | L5 pp. 222–227 |
| L.6 | Acquire and use accurately general academic, and domain-specific words and phrases | L6 pp. 228–233 |
| **Reading History/Social Studies** | | |
| RH.1 | Cite textual evidence to support analysis of primary and secondary sources | R1 pp. 6–11 |
| RH.2 | Determine the central ideas or information of a primary or secondary source; provide an objective summary | R2 pp. 12–19 |
| RH.3 | Identify key steps in a text's description of a process related to history/social studies | R3 pp. 20–25 |
| RH.4 | Determine the meaning of words and phrases as they are used in a text, including vocabulary specific to history/social studies | R4 pp. 26–33 |
| RH.5 | Describe how a text presents information | R5 pp. 34–39 |
| RH.6 | Identify aspects of a text that reveal an author's point of view or purpose | R6 pp. 40–47 |
| RH.7 | Integrate visual information with other information in print and digital texts | R7 pp. 48–55 |
| RH.8 | Distinguish among fact, opinion, and reasoned judgment in a text | R8 pp. 56–63 |

Shaded bands highlight the overarching strands.

Each standard under the strand is specifically called out.

Each section begins with a restatement of the official anchor standards as they appear in the actual Common Core State Standards document.

College and Career Readiness Anchor Standards for

# *Reading 6–8*

The grades 6–12 standards on the following pages define what students should understand and be able to do by the end of each grade. They correspond to the College and Career Readiness (CCR) anchor standards by number. The CCR and grade-specific standards are necessary complements—the former providing broad standards, the latter providing additional specificity—that together define the skills and understandings that all students must demonstrate.

**Key Ideas and Details**

1. Read closely to determine what the text says explicitly and to make logical inferences from it; cite specific textual evidence when writing or speaking to support conclusions drawn from the text.
2. Determine central ideas or themes of a text and analyze their development; summarize the key supporting details and ideas.
3. Analyze how and why individuals, events, and ideas develop and interact over the course of a text.

**Craft and Structure**

4. Interpret words and phrases as they are used in a text, including determining technical, connotative, and figurative meanings, and analyze how specific word choices shape meaning or tone.
5. Analyze the structure of texts, including how specific sentences, paragraphs, and larger portions of the text (e.g., a section, chapter, scene, or stanza) relate to one another and the whole.
6. Assess how point of view or purpose shapes the content and style of a text.

**Integration of Knowledge and Ideas**

7. Integrate and evaluate content presented in diverse formats and media, including visually and quantitatively, as well as in words.*
8. Delineate and evaluate the argument and specific claims in a text, including the validity of the reasoning as well as the relevance and sufficiency of the evidence.
9. Analyze how two or more texts address similar themes or topics to build knowledge or to compare the approaches the authors take.

**Range of Reading and Level of Text Complexity**

10. Read and comprehend complex literary and informational texts independently and proficiently.

**Note on Range and Content of Student Reading**

To become college and career ready, students must grapple with works of exceptional craft and thought whose range extends across genres, cultures, and centuries. Such works offer profound insights into the human condition and serve as models for students' thinking and writing. Along with high-quality contemporary works, these texts should be chosen from among seminal U.S. documents, the classics of American literature, and the timeless dramas of Shakespeare. Through wide and deep reading of literature and literary nonfiction of steadily increasing sophistication, students gain a reservoir of literary and cultural knowledge, references, and images; the ability to evaluate intricate arguments; and the capacity to surmount the challenges posed by complex texts.

* Please consult the full Common Core State Standards document (and all updates and appendices) at http://www.corestandards.org/ELA-Literacy. See "Research to Build Knowledge" in the Writing section and "Comprehension and Collaboration" in the Speaking and Listening section for additional standards relevant to gathering, assessing, and applying information from print and digital sources.

Source: Copyright © 2010. National Governors Association Center for Best Practices and Council of Chief State School Officers. All rights reserved.

College and Career Readiness Anchor Standards for

# *Reading*

The College and Career Readiness (CCR) anchor standards are the same for all middle and high school students, regardless of subject area or grade level. What varies is the specific content at each grade level, most notably the level of complexity of the texts, skills, and knowledge at each subsequent grade level in each disciplinary domain. The guiding principle here is that the core reading skills should not change as students advance; rather, the level at which they learn and can perform those skills should increase in complexity as students move from one grade to the next.

**Key Ideas and Details**

This first strand of reading standards emphasizes students' ability to identify key ideas and themes in a text, whether literary, informational, primary, or foundational and whether in print, graphic, quantitative, or mixed media formats. The focus of this first set of standards is on *reading to understand*, during which students focus on *what* the text says. The premise is that students cannot delve into the deeper (implicit) meaning of any text if they cannot first grasp the surface (explicit) meaning of that text. Beyond merely identifying these ideas, readers must learn to see how these ideas and themes, or the story's characters and events, develop and evolve over the course of a text. Such reading demands that students know how to identify, evaluate, assess, and analyze the elements of a text for their importance, function, and meaning within the text.

**Craft and Structure**

The second set of standards builds on the first, focusing not on *what* the text says but *how* it says it, the emphasis here being on analyzing how texts are made to serve a function or achieve a purpose. These standards ask readers to examine the choices the author makes in words and sentence and paragraph structure and how these choices contribute to the meaning of the text and the author's larger purpose. Inherent in the study of craft and structure is how these elements interact with and influence the ideas and details outlined in the first three standards.

**Integration of Knowledge and Ideas**

This third strand might be summed up as *reading to extend or deepen one's knowledge* of a subject by comparing what a range of sources have said about it over time and across different media. In addition, these standards emphasize the importance of being able to read the arguments; that is, they look at how to identify the claims the texts make and evaluate the evidence used to support those claims regardless of the media. Finally, these standards ask students to analyze the choice of means and medium the author chooses and the effect those choices have on ideas and details. Thus, if a writer integrates words, images, and video in a mixed media text, readers should be able to examine how and why the author did that for stylistic and rhetorical purposes.

**Range of Reading and Level of Text Complexity**

The Common Core State Standards document itself offers the most useful explanation of what this last standard means in  footnote titled "Note on range and content of student reading," which accompanies the reading standards:

To become college and career ready, students must grapple with works of exceptional craft and thought whose range extends across genres, cultures, and centuries. Such works offer profound insights into the human condition and serve as models for students' own thinking and writing. Along with high-quality contemporary works, these texts should be chosen from among seminal U.S. documents, the classics of American literature, and the timeless dramas of Shakespeare. Through wide and deep reading of literature and literary nonfiction of steadily increasing sophistication, students gain a reservoir of literary and cultural knowledge, references, and images; the ability to evaluate intricate arguments; and the capacity to surmount the challenges posed by complex texts. (CCSS 2010, p. 35)

On the facing page, a user-friendly "translation" of each standard gives you a fuller sense of the big picture and big objectives as you consider how it relates to your state's standards.

Built-in tabs facilitate navigation.

Bold type spotlighting what's different across grade spans specifically identifies what students must learn within each class and across subjects.

On this page you'll find accessible translations of the standards at your left so you can better grasp what they mean.

The actual CCSS Anchor Standard is included for easy reference.

The specific strand situates you within the larger context of the standards.

The emphasis now is on what students should do, utilizing the same grade-level and subject-area structure at your left.

Comprehension questions are included for helping students master thinking moves and skills behind each standard; all can be adapted to a range of class texts and topics or to needs specific to your particular state standards.

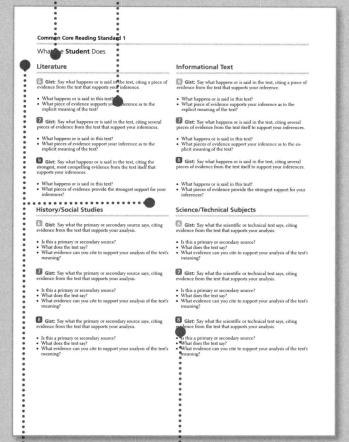

Horizontal and vertical views enable you to consider how the standards change across grade levels for a given subject or down a given grade level in all subjects.

Standards for each discipline are featured on a single page for easy cross-departmental collaboration.

The right-hand page utilizes the very same cross-discipline and grade-level format to provide two distinct visual paths for understanding the standards.

"Gist" sections provide plain-English synopses of the standards so you can put them to immediate use.

Featured on a separate page are specific teaching techniques for realizing each standard. Applicable to all subjects across grades 6–8, these strategies focus on what works in the classroom, based on Jim's own experience and recent content-area research.

**To teach students how to "read closely," do the following:**

- Provide students access to the text—via tablet or photocopy—so they can annotate it as directed.
- Model close reading for students by thinking aloud as you go through the text with them or displaying your annotations on a tablet via an LCD projector; show them how to examine a text by scrutinizing its words, sentence structures, or any other details needed to understand its explicit meaning.
- Display the text via tablet or computer as you direct students' attention—by highlighting, circling, or otherwise drawing their attention—to specific words, sentences, or paragraphs that are essential to the meaning of the text; as you do this, ask them to explain what a word means or how it is used in that sentence, or how a specific sentence contributes to the meaning of the larger text.
- Pose questions—about words, actions, or details—that require students to look closely at the text for answers.

**To get students to determine "what the text says explicitly," do the following:**

- Ask students to "say what it says"—not what it means, since the emphasis here is on its literal meaning.
- Offer students an example of what it means to read explicitly and support your inferences with evidence; then tell them what a passage explicitly says, and ask them to find evidence inside the text to support their statement about its meaning.
- Give students several pieces of evidence and ask them to determine what explicit idea in the text the evidence supports.

**To develop students' ability to "cite specific textual evidence," do the following:**

- Offer them a set of samples of evidence of different degrees of specificity and quality to evaluate, requiring

them to choose the one that is best and provide a rationale for their choice.
- Show students how you would choose evidence from the text to support your inference; discuss with them the questions you would ask to arrive at that selection.

**To "make logical inferences," ask students to do the following:**

- Take what they *learn* (from the text about this subject) to what they already *know* (about that subject); then *confirm* that their reasoning is sound by finding evidence that supports their inferences.
- Think aloud (with your guidance) about the process and how they make such inferences, and then have students find and use evidence to support their inferences.

**To find the textual evidence "that most strongly supports _____," do the following:**

- Create with your students—through collaborative groups or class discussion—a list of different pieces of evidence they might cite; together, develop and apply criteria by which to evaluate the different pieces to identify those which would offer the strongest, most effective support; then ask them to apply these same criteria to new evidence they find themselves as they read the rest of this article or another.

**To help your English Language Learners, try this one strategy:**

- Repeat the process used to make such inferences, verbally labeling each step as you demonstrate it; then ask them to demonstrate their ability to do it on their own or with your prompting. Post the steps (e.g., "Inferences = What You Know + What You Learned") with an example on a poster or handout they can reference on their own as needed.

*Notes*

You can record notes here as you prepare to teach. Additional copies can be made if you'd like to adapt the pages to your school's instructional planning processes.

A dedicated academic
vocabulary section
offers a quick-reference
glossary of key words
and phrases for each
standard.

In this last worksheet,
you can record your final
teaching plan.

**Common Core Reading Standard 1**

**Academic Vocabulary:** Key Words and Phrases

**Analysis of primary and secondary sources:** Primary sources are those accounts recorded from people who witnessed or participated in the event themselves; these sources include journals, letters, and oral history recordings; secondary sources are those written by others *based on* primary sources and the opinions of scholars past and present.

**Cite specific textual evidence:** All claims, assertions, or arguments about what a text means or says require evidence from within the text itself, not the reader's opinion or experience; students should be able to quote or refer to a specific passage from the text to support their idea.

**Conclusions drawn from the text:** Readers take a group of details (different findings, series of events, related examples) and draw from them an insight or understanding about their meaning or importance within the passage or the text as a whole.

**Evidence that most strongly supports an analysis:** Evidence in general includes facts, data, quotations, and any other sources of data to support the claims writers make; in this case, however, it refers to only that evidence that "most strongly supports an analysis." Such evidence would typically be more precise, specific, and effective in its ability to back up one's analysis.

**Explicitly:** This refers to anything clearly stated in great or precise detail; it may suggest factual information or literal meaning, though not necessarily the case.

**Informational text:** These include nonfiction texts from a range of sources and written for a variety of purposes, everything from essays to advertisements, historical documents to op/ed pieces. Informational texts include written arguments as well as infographics.

**Literature:** This refers to fiction, poetry, drama, and graphic stories but also artworks such as master paintings or works by preeminent photographers.

**Logical inferences [drawn from the text]:** To infer, readers add what they *learned* from the text to what they already *know* about the subject; however, for the inference to be "logical," it must be based on evidence *from the text.*

**Primary and secondary sources:** *Primary sources* are those documents—letters, journals, oral histories, and the like—recorded by those who participated in or observed the events firsthand; *secondary sources* are those articles that draw on such primary sources and others to examine or explain events authors did not witness themselves.

**Read closely (close reading):** This refers to reading that emphasizes not only surface details but the deeper meaning and larger connections between words, sentences, and the full text; it also demands scrutiny of craft, including arguments and style used by the author.

**Several pieces of textual evidence:** Evidence is described above; this phrase refers to the act of including evidence not from several *different* texts but different pieces of textual evidence—a number of quotations, some data, several specific examples, for example—from *one* text the student is reading.

**Support analysis:** This is related to "citing textual evidence." This phrase requires readers to back up their claims about what a text says with evidence, such as examples, details, or quotations.

**Text:** In its broadest meaning, a text is whatever one is trying to read: a poem, essay, or article; in its more modern sense, a text can also be an image, an artwork, speech, or multimedia format such as a website, film, or social media message, such as a Tweet.

**Textual evidence:** Not all evidence is created equal; students need to choose those examples or quotations that provide the best example of what they are saying or most compelling quotation to support their assertion.

Clearly worded entries
define each word or
phrase according to the
particular way it is used
in the respective standard.

*Planning to Teach*
What to Do—and How

# Your Literacy Standards Companion, Grades 6–8

# YOUR LITERACY STANDARDS COMPANION, GRADES 6–8

## What They Mean and How to Teach Them

**Jim Burke**

resources.corwin.com/literacycompanion6-8

Name: _____

Department: _____

Learning Team: _____

FOR INFORMATION:

Corwin

A SAGE Company

2455 Teller Road

Thousand Oaks, California 91320

(800) 233-9936

www.corwin.com

SAGE Publications Ltd.

1 Oliver's Yard

55 City Road

London EC1Y 1SP

United Kingdom

SAGE Publications India Pvt. Ltd.

B 1/I 1 Mohan Cooperative Industrial Area

Mathura Road, New Delhi 110 044

India

SAGE Publications Asia-Pacific Pte. Ltd.

3 Church Street

#10-04 Samsung Hub

Singapore 049483

Publisher and Senior Program Director: Lisa Luedeke

Editorial Development Manager: Julie Nemer

Editorial Assistant: Nicole Shade

Production Editor: Melanie Birdsall

Copy Editors: Codi Bowman and Deanna Noga

Typesetter: C&M Digitals (P) Ltd.

Proofreaders: Scott Oney and Theresa Kay

Cover Designer: Scott Van Atta

Interior Designer: Auburn Associates, Inc.

Marketing Manager: Rebecca Eaton

Copyright © 2017 by Corwin

National Governors Association Center for Best Practices, Council of Chief State School Officers, Common Core State Standards, English Language Arts Standards. Publisher: National Governors Association Center for Best Practices, Council of Chief State School Officers, Washington, DC. Copyright 2010. For more information, visit http://www.corestandards.org/ELA-Literacy.

Printed in the United States of America

ISBN 978-1-5063-8553-2

This book is printed on acid-free paper.

17 18 19 20 21 10 9 8 7 6 5 4 3 2 1

# Contents

Visit the companion website at
**resources.corwin.com/literacycompanion6-8**
for downloadable versions of the
Indexes Cross-Referencing Your State Standards.

*Note:* For the complete Common Core standards document, please visit corestandards.org.

# Introduction

# Turning Standards Into Daily Teaching

*People can't live with change if there's not a changeless core inside them. The key to the ability to change is a changeless sense of who you are, what you are about, and what you value.*

—Stephen Covey

## Moving Forward—Together

An excellent education should not be an accident; it should be a right, though nowhere in the U.S. Constitution or any of our other founding documents do we find that right listed. Across the nation, state academic standards address that omission and challenge us all—administrators and teachers, parents and children, politicians and the public at large, professors and student teachers—to commit ourselves anew to the success of our children and our country.

In my nearly 25 years in education, I have been involved with many efforts to develop standards. I have had the honor of sitting alongside some of our country's greatest educational innovators and leaders to help develop the College Board's Pre-AP English Language Arts Framework, the National Board for Professional Teaching Standards for Adolescent Literacy, the National Council of Teachers of English Language Arts Standards, the framework for the Advanced Placement English Literature and Composition, the California Standards for English Language Arts, and, to the extent that such books serve as a form of literacy standards, the Holt McDougal 6–12 language arts textbooks. But the standards movement today is different: it comes with a level of support, a degree of commitment from leaders at all levels of government and business, and a sense of urgency that the other efforts could not or cannot claim.

There is a sense that we are all at some crucial inflection point in our national story, one that provides an opportunity we must not squander if our children are to help make this story we are trying to write about our country come true. I am often struck, listening to my mother-in-law, who has lived with us for many years, by her description of the country during the Depression and World War II, both of which she endured while living in the house she now shares with us. Almost any story she tells conveys a sense of shared commitment to the good of the community and country, that vital sense of mission that everyone was in it together, even—or especially—when the work was difficult and demanded some sacrifice.

It is not just the country and students that stand to benefit from the new commitment to standards, but teachers, too, for as Calkins, Ehrenworth, and Lehman

(2012) argue, teaching to standards can "deepen the reading skills of adults as well." It is this same sense of mutual benefit that Carol Jago (2005) calls to mind in her allusion to the old U.S. Navy watchword of "one hand for the ship, one hand for yourself" (p. 101), because everything I have done to better understand and implement the standards has only made me more aware of my teaching, and improved it, by making it more "intentional [and challenging me to] establish an environment conducive for learning by setting objectives, reinforcing effort, and providing recognition" (Kendall, 2011, p. 28).

Arthur Applebee (2013), in writing more specifically about the Common Core State Standards, offered a detailed analysis that illustrates and confirms "that aligning our teaching [to standards] does not mean we need to abandon all that we have learned about effective curriculum and instruction." Applebee spends much of this journal article analyzing lessons from my own class, which I described in *What's the Big Idea? Question-Driven Units to Motivate Reading, Writing, and Thinking* (Burke, 2010). In his analysis, Applebee notes the following:

> Burke's lessons are quite overtly aligned to standards. Rather than teaching to the tests, these lessons focus on engaging students in cognitively and linguistically challenging tasks in the course of which they will gain the knowledge and skills that the standards require.

> Units with the richness and imagination of those that Burke describes in *What's the Big Idea?* reflect a coming together of the wisdom of practice with the best of current research and theory on the teaching of English language arts. Such teaching does not offer the simple prescriptions that guide classrooms that focus curriculum and instruction more directly on the standards and the tests that accompany them. But the paradox is that by not teaching to the test, students in classrooms like Burke's will do better on tests in general, and at the same time develop the knowledge and skills to do well in other contexts of schooling, life and work. And schools will be much more interesting places to be, for teachers and students alike. (p. 33)

## A Brief Orientation to *Your Literacy Standards Companion, Grades 6–8*

One cannot benefit from or use a standards document that demands more time than a teacher or administrator has each day; thus, I seek here to share with you, my fellow educators, these indispensable resources: concise translations of the standards I currently use in my classroom in California, the Common Core standards, along with detailed correlation indexes showing readers in key non–Common Core states exactly which pages of this book have relevant information for them. I created this book in part for myself, to make my job easier as I plan my lessons every evening, write my books, or prepare the workshops I give around the country.

What I offer you here is a compass of sorts to help you—whether you are an administrator or teacher, department chair or district curriculum supervisor, a professor, or a student teacher training to join us in this richly rewarding enterprise called education—understand and make better use of your standards. Here you will find several features I have designed and refined with the help of many teachers, curriculum supervisors, and superintendents with whom I have met and worked around the country in recent years. Because California has adopted the Common Core standards, these standards are naturally the basis for my plan. Still, I think you'll find the features, in combination with the correlation indexes at the front of this book, will provide you with a working compass to navigate your own state standards.

Additional key features, each developed with you in mind, include the following:

**A one-page overview of *all* the Common Core anchor standards.** The anchor standards form the spine that holds the K–12 ELA standards together. The anchor standards encompass each aspect of English Language Arts: reading, writing, speaking and listening, and language. Beginning in kindergarten and running through grade 12, each grade-specific standard builds incrementally to college and career readiness. If you are in a non–Common Core state, your state standards will be different in specifics, but their purpose and organization are similar. Designed for quick reference, this one-page document offers all users an overview—a place where you can get the lay of the land, no matter what state you're in or what grade you teach.

**Side-by-side anchor standards translation.** How do anchor standards translate to the classroom? The anchor standards for each category—reading, writing, speaking and listening, and language—appear at the start of each section as a two-page spread with the original Common Core anchor standards on the left and, on the right, their matching translations in more accessible, classroom-friendly language. While the specifics of your standards may differ, you'll undoubtedly find the real-world explications relevant and useful to your situation.

**A new user-friendly format for each standard.** Instead of the four reading standard domains—literature, informational, social studies, and science and technical subjects—spread throughout the Common Core State Standards document, here you will find the first reading standard for grades 6–8 and the four different domains, for example, all on one page. This allows you to use the book to see at a glance what Reading Standard 1 looks like in grades 6–8 across different text types and subject areas, but also, equally important, shows you what that same informational text standard looks like across grade levels from 6–8 to be sure your curriculum honors the challenge to increase complexity as students move from grade to grade. If you are in a non–Common Core state, the indexes cross-referencing your state standards will point you to the relevant pages.

**Parallel translation/what students do.** Each standard opens to a two-page spread that has the original Common Core standards on the left (all gathered on that one page for each standard) and a parallel translation of each standard mirrored on the right in more accessible language (referred to on these pages as the "Gist") so you can concentrate on how to *teach* the standards instead of how to understand them, for while they are admirably concise in their original form, they are, nonetheless, remarkably dense texts once you start trying to grasp exactly what they say. These Gist pages align themselves with the original Common Core, so you can move between the two without turning a page as you think about what they mean and how to teach them. Also, beneath each translation of a standard appears a brief but carefully developed list of questions you can teach your students to ask as a way for them to meet that standard. These are meant to be very practical questions students can ask themselves or which you, in the course of teaching them, can pose. Note also that the more advanced requirements added to the 6–8 grade standards are **bolded** for emphasis, quick reference, and ease of use. Again, if you are in a non–Common Core state, the indexes cross-referencing your state standards will direct you to the pages directly relevant to you.

**Instructional techniques/what the teacher does.** These methods and activities, based on current literacy research, offer teachers across subject areas specific, if concise, suggestions for how to teach that specific standard, the activities specifically linked to the demands of the standard.

**Academic vocabulary: key words and phrases.** Each standard comes with a unique glossary since words used in more than one standard have a unique meaning in each. Any word or phrase that seemed a source of possible confusion is defined in some detail.

**Planning notes/teaching notes.** Each standard offers two pages designed to give you a place to transition your curriculum over to your new standards or to make notes about what to teach and how. These pages can serve as a place to capture ideas for yourself or for grade-level teams, departments, schools, and district curriculum offices or for students, teachers, and their professors in a methods class at the university. They can also be copied for additional planning.

## How to Use This Book

As each school or department has its own culture, I am reluctant to say what you should do or how you should use *Your Literacy Standards Companion*. Still, a few ideas suggest themselves, which you should adapt, adopt, or avoid as you see fit:

- Provide all teachers in a department or school with a copy to establish a common text to work from and refer to throughout your planning and instructional design work.
- Bring your *Companion* to all meetings for quick reference or planning with colleagues in the school or your department or grade-level team.
- Use your *Companion* to aid in the transition from what you were doing to what you will be doing, treating the planning pages that accompany each standard as a place to note what you do.
- Begin or end meetings with a brief but carefully planned sample lesson or instructional connection, asking one or more colleagues in the school or department

to present and lead a discussion of how it might apply to other classes, grade levels, or subject areas.

- Use the *Companion* in conjunction with your professional learning community (PLC) to add further cohesion and consistency between all your ideas and plans.
- Begin slowly, proceed incrementally, giving it first to key instructional leaders— department chairs, instructional coaches, PLC, or other team leaders—to figure out how best to roll it out to the larger faculty or integrate into teams examining student work or creating new standards-aligned units.

## Accepting the Invitation

When I began teaching in the late 1980s, I asked my new department chair what I would be teaching. He smiled and handed me a single sheet of paper with a list of titles on it and wished me luck (always making time to help me if I had questions). Years later, many districts, mine included, had thick binders, binders so heavy with so many standards that they were all ignored since they did not come with the time to read and think about how to teach them. Now we have a new set of standards, which come just as a large group of teachers will retire, leaving an equally large group of new teachers feeling a bit up the river without a paddle, as the saying goes. This book is meant to be that oar or a map you or your faculty or colleagues can use to guide you through the curriculum (which derives from the words *current* and *course*).

These new standards offer me a view of the territory I have crossed to arrive here, having been the first in my family to graduate from college. In a section titled "A Country Called School" from my book *School Smarts: The Four Cs of Academic Success* (Burke, 2004), I wrote of my experience of being a student:

Learning is natural; schooling is not. Schools are countries to which we send our children, expecting these places and the people who work there to help draw out and shape our children into the successful adults we want them to become. As with travel to other countries, however, people only truly benefit from the time spent there to the extent that they can and do participate. If someone doesn't know the language, the customs, the culture—well, that person will feel like the outsider they are. As Gerald Graff, author of *Clueless in Academe* (2003) puts it, "schooling takes students who are perfectly street-smart and exposes them to the life of the mind in ways that make them feel dumb" (p. 2).

This is precisely how I felt when I arrived at college. I lacked any understanding of the language. The culture of academics confused me. The conventions that governed students' behaviors and habits were invisible to me. Those who thrived in school seemed to have been born into the culture, have heard the language all their life, and knew inherently what mattered, what was worth paying attention to, how much effort was appropriate. Teachers somehow seemed to expect that we all came equipped with the same luggage, all of which contained the necessary tools and strategies that would ensure our success in their classes and, ultimately, school. It wasn't so. (p. 1)

When I enrolled in a community college all those years ago, I was placed in a remedial writing class, highlighted whole chapters of textbooks, and had no idea what to say or how to enter class discussions. School extended an invitation to me then that I did not know at first how to accept, so disoriented was I by its demands. Across the country, new state standards extend a similar invitation—and challenge—to us all, teachers and administrators, and all others engaged in the very serious business of educating middle and high school students. It is an invitation I have already accepted on behalf of my students and myself.

Reading these standards, I am reminded of a passage from a wonderful book by Magdalene Lampert (2001) titled *Teaching Problems and the Problems of Teaching*. In that book, she has a chapter titled "Teaching Students to Be People Who Study in School," in which she says of students not unlike the one I was and many of those I teach:

> Some students show up at school as "intentional learners"—people who are already interested in doing whatever they need to do to learn academic subjects— they are the exception rather than the rule. Even if they are disposed to study, they probably need to learn how. But more fundamental than knowing how is developing a sense of oneself as a learner that makes it socially acceptable to engage in academic work. The goal of school is not to turn all students into people who see themselves as professional academics, but to enable all of them to include a disposition toward productive study of academic subjects among the personality traits they exhibit while they are in the classroom. If the young people who come to school do not see themselves as learners, they are not going to act like learners even if that would help them to be successful in school. It is the teacher's job to help them change their sense of themselves so that studying is not a self-contradictory activity. (p. 265)

Lampert's statement goes to the core of our work as teachers and these standards, as well. The work ahead will be difficult, as nearly all important work is, because it often asks more of us than we knew we had to give, yet doing the work will give us the strength we need to succeed in the future we are called to create for ourselves and our country. The word "education" stems from the Latin word *educare*, meaning to draw out that which is within, to lead. This is what we must do. I offer you this book to help you do that work and wish you all the strength and patience your two hands can hold.

## References

Applebee, A. (2013). Common Core State Standards: The promise and the peril in a national palimpsest. *English Journal, 103*(1), 25–33.

Burke, J. (2004). *School smarts: The four Cs of academic success.* Portsmouth, NH: Heinemann.

Burke, J. (2010). *What's the big idea? Question-driven units to motivate reading, writing, and thinking.* Portsmouth, NH: Heinemann.

Calkins, L., Ehrenworth, M., & Lehman, C. (2012). *Pathways to the common core: Accelerating achievement.* Portsmouth, NH: Heinemann.

Graff, G. (2003). *Clueless in academe: How schooling obscures the life of the mind.* New Haven, CT: Yale University Press.

Jago, C. (2005). *Papers, papers, papers: An English teacher's survival guide.* Portsmouth, NH: Heinemann.

Kendall, J. (2011). *Understanding common core state standards.* Alexandria, VA: Association for Supervision and Curriculum Development.

Lampert, M. (2001). *Teaching problems and the problems of teaching.* New Haven, CT: Yale University Press.

## Reading

### Key Ideas and Details

1. Read closely to determine what the text says explicitly and to make logical inferences from it; cite specific textual evidence when writing or speaking to support conclusions drawn from the text.

2. Determine central ideas or themes of a text and analyze their development; summarize the key supporting details and ideas.

3. Analyze how and why individuals, events, and ideas develop and interact over the course of a text.

### Craft and Structure

4. Interpret words and phrases as they are used in a text, including determining technical, connotative, and figurative meanings, and analyze how specific word choices shape meaning or tone.

5. Analyze the structure of texts, including how specific sentences, paragraphs, and larger portions of the text (e.g., a section, chapter, scene, or stanza) relate to each other and the whole.

6. Assess how point of view or purpose shapes the content and style of a text.

### Integration of Knowledge and Ideas

7. Integrate and evaluate content presented in diverse formats and media, including visually and quantitatively, as well as in words.

8. Delineate and evaluate the argument and specific claims in a text, including the validity of the reasoning as well as the relevance and sufficiency of the evidence.

9. Analyze how two or more texts address similar themes or topics to build knowledge or to compare the approaches the authors take.

### Range of Reading and Level of Text Complexity

10. Read and comprehend complex literary and informational texts independently and proficiently.

## Writing

### Text Types and Purposes*

1. Write arguments to support claims in an analysis of substantive topics or texts, using valid reasoning and relevant and sufficient evidence.

2. Write informative/explanatory texts to examine and convey complex ideas and information clearly and accurately through the effective selection, organization, and analysis of content.

3. Write narratives to develop real or imagined experiences or events using effective technique, well-chosen details, and well-structured event sequences.

### Production and Distribution of Writing

4. Produce clear and coherent writing in which the development, organization, and style are appropriate to task, purpose, and audience.

5. Develop and strengthen writing as needed by planning, revising, editing, rewriting, or trying a new approach.

6. Use technology, including the Internet, to produce and publish writing and to interact and collaborate with others.

### Research to Build and Present Knowledge

7. Conduct short as well as more sustained research projects based on focused questions, demonstrating understanding of the subject under investigation.

8. Gather relevant information from multiple print and digital sources, assess the credibility and accuracy of each source, and integrate the information while avoiding plagiarism.

9. Draw evidence from literary or informational texts to support analysis, reflection, and research.

### Range of Writing

10. Write routinely over extended time frames (time for research, reflection, and revision) and shorter time frames (a single sitting or a day or two) for a range of tasks, purposes, and audiences.

## Speaking and Listening

### Comprehension and Collaboration

1. Prepare for and participate effectively in a range of conversations and collaborations with diverse partners, building on others' ideas and expressing their own clearly and persuasively.

2. Integrate and evaluate information presented in diverse media and formats, including visually, quantitatively, and orally.

3. Evaluate a speaker's point of view, reasoning, and use of evidence and rhetoric.

### Presentation of Knowledge and Ideas

4. Present information, findings, and supporting evidence such that listeners can follow the line of reasoning and the organization, development, and style are appropriate to task, purpose, and audience.

5. Make strategic use of digital media and visual displays of data to express information and enhance understanding of presentations.

6. Adapt speech to a variety of contexts and communicative tasks, demonstrating command of formal English when indicated or appropriate.

## Language

### Conventions of Standard English

1. Demonstrate command of the conventions of standard English grammar and usage when writing or speaking.

2. Demonstrate command of the conventions of standard English capitalization, punctuation, and spelling when writing.

### Knowledge of Language

3. Apply knowledge of language to understand how language functions in different contexts, to make effective choices for meaning or style, and to comprehend more fully when reading or listening.

### Vocabulary Acquisition and Use

4. Determine or clarify the meaning of unknown and multiple-meaning words and phrases by using context clues, analyzing meaningful word parts, and consulting general and specialized reference materials, as appropriate.

5. Demonstrate understanding of figurative language, word relationships, and nuances in word meanings.

6. Acquire and use accurately a range of general academic and domain-specific words and phrases sufficient for reading, writing, speaking, and listening at the college and career readiness level; demonstrate independence in gathering vocabulary knowledge when considering a word or phrase important to comprehension or expression.

*Source:* Designed by Jim Burke. Visit www.englishcompanion.com for more information.

*Note:* For the complete Common Core standards document, please visit corestandards.org.

*These broad types of writing include many subgenres. See Appendix A for definitions of key writing types.

## Reading

### Key Ideas and Details

1. Read closely to determine what the text says explicitly and to make logical inferences from it; cite specific textual evidence when writing or speaking to support conclusions drawn from the text.

2. Determine central ideas or themes of a text and analyze their development; summarize the key supporting details and ideas.

3. Analyze how and why individuals, events, or ideas develop and interact over the course of a text.

### Craft and Structure

4. Interpret words and phrases as they are used in a text, including determining technical, connotative, and figurative meanings, and analyze how specific word choices shape meaning or tone.

5. Analyze the structure of texts, including how specific sentences, paragraphs, and larger portions of the text (e.g., a section, chapter, scene, or stanza) relate to each other and the whole.

6. Assess how point of view or purpose shapes the content and style of a text.

### Integration of Knowledge and Ideas

7. Integrate and evaluate content presented in diverse formats and media, including visually and quantitatively, as well as in words.

8. Delineate and evaluate the argument and specific claims in a text, including the validity of the reasoning as well as the relevance and sufficiency of the evidence.

9. Analyze how two or more texts address similar themes or topics in order to build knowledge or to compare the approaches the authors take.

### Range of Reading and Level of Text Complexity

10. Read and comprehend complex literary and informational texts independently and proficiently.

## Writing

### Text Types and Purposes*

1. Write arguments to support claims in an analysis of substantive topics or texts using valid reasoning and relevant and sufficient evidence.

2. Write informative/explanatory texts to examine and convey complex ideas and information clearly and accurately through the effective selection, organization, and analysis of content.

3. Write narratives to develop real or imagined experiences or events using effective technique, well-chosen details, and well-structured event sequences.

### Production and Distribution of Writing

4. Produce clear and coherent writing in which the development, organization, and style are appropriate to task, purpose, and audience.

5. Develop and strengthen writing as needed by planning, revising, editing, rewriting, or trying a new approach.

6. Use technology, including the Internet, to produce and publish writing and to interact and collaborate with others.

### Research to Build and Present Knowledge

7. Conduct short as well as more sustained research projects based on focused questions, demonstrating understanding of the subject under investigation.

8. Gather relevant information from multiple print and digital sources, assess the credibility and accuracy of each source, and integrate the information while avoiding plagiarism.

9. Draw evidence from literary or informational texts to support analysis, reflection, and research.

### Range of Writing

10. Write routinely over extended time frames (time for research, reflection, and revision) and shorter time frames (a single sitting or a day or two) for a range of tasks, purposes, and audiences.

Source: Designed by Jim Burke. Visit www.englishcompanion.com for more information.

Note: For the complete Common Core standards document, please visit corestandards.org.

*These broad types of writing include many subgenres. See Appendix A for definitions of key writing types.

# Indexes Cross-Referencing Your State Standards

Available for download at **resources.corwin.com/literacycompanion6-8**

## Alaska, Grade 6

| Alaska Strand/Standard | Focus of Alaska Standard | For More Information |
|---|---|---|
| **Reading Literature** | | |
| RL.1 | Cite textual evidence to support analysis of what the text says explicitly as well as inferences drawn from the text | R1 pp. 6–11 |
| RL.2 | Determine the theme or central idea of a text and how it is conveyed through particular details; provide an objective summary | R2 pp. 12–19 |
| RL.3 | Describe how a particular plot unfolds in a series of episodes as well as how the characters respond or change | R3 pp. 20–25 |
| RL.4 | Determine the meaning of words and phrases as they are used in a text, including figurative and connotative meanings | R4 pp. 26–33 |
| RL.5 | Analyze how a particular sentence, chapter, scene, or stanza fits into the overall structure of a text and contributes to the development of the characters, theme, setting, or plot | R5 pp. 34–39 |
| RL.6 | Determine an author's purpose and explain how an author develops the point of view of the narrator or speaker in a text | R6 pp. 40–47 |
| RL.7 | Compare and contrast the experience of reading a story, drama, or poem to listening to or viewing an audio, video, or live version of the text | R7 pp. 48–55 |
| RL.8 | NA | |
| RL.9 | Compare and contrast texts in different forms or genres in terms of their approaches to similar themes and topics | R9 pp. 64–71 |
| RL.10 | Read and comprehend literature of appropriate complexity independently with proficiency | R10 pp. 72–77 |
| **Reading Informational Text** | | |
| RI.1 | Cite textual evidence to support analysis of what the text says explicitly as well as inferences drawn from the text | R1 pp. 6–11 |
| RI.2 | Determine a central idea of a text and how it is conveyed through particular details; provide an objective summary | R2 pp. 12–19 |
| RI.3 | Analyze in detail how a key individual, event, or idea is introduced, illustrated, and elaborated in a text | R3 pp. 20–25 |
| RI.4 | Determine the meaning of words and phrases as they are used in a text, including figurative, connotative, and technical meanings | R4 pp. 26–33 |
| RI.5 | Analyze how a particular sentence, chapter, or section fits into the overall structure of a text and contributes to the development of the ideas | R5 pp. 34–39 |
| RI.6 | Determine an author's point of view or purpose in a text and explain how it is conveyed in the text | R6 pp. 40–47 |
| RI.7 | Integrate information presented in different media or formats as well as in words to develop a coherent understanding of a topic or issue | R7 pp. 48–55 |
| RI.8 | Trace and evaluate the argument and specific claims that are supported by reasons and evidence from claims that are not | R8 pp. 56–63 |
| RI.9 | Compare and contrast one author's presentation of events with that of another | R9 pp. 64–71 |
| RI.10 | Read and comprehend appropriately complex literary nonfiction, informational, and functional texts independently and proficiently | R10 pp. 72–77 |

*(Continued)*

| Alaska Strand/Standard | Focus of Alaska Standard | For More Information |
|---|---|---|
| **Writing** | | |
| W.1 | Write arguments to support claims with clear reasons and relevant evidence | W1 pp. 82–89 |
| W.2 | Write informative/explanatory texts to examine a topic and convey ideas, concepts, and information clearly | W2 pp. 90–99 |
| W.3 | Use narrative writing to develop real or imagined experiences or events using effective technique, descriptive details, and well-structured event sequences | W3 pp.100–109 |
| W.4 | Produce writing in which the development, organization, and style are appropriate to the task, purpose, and audience | W4 pp. 110–115 |
| W.5 | Develop and strengthen writing as needed by planning, revising, editing, rewriting, or trying a new approach | W5 pp. 116–121 |
| W.6 | Use technology to produce and publish writing as well as to interact with others; demonstrate keyboarding skills | W6 pp. 122–127 |
| W.7 | Conduct short research projects to answer a question, drawing on several sources and refocusing the inquiry when appropriate | W7 pp. 128–133 |
| W.8 | Gather information from print and digital sources; assess the credibility of sources; quote or paraphrase while avoiding plagiarism and providing basic bibliographic information | W8 pp. 134–139 |
| W.9 | Draw evidence from literary or informational texts to support analysis, reflection, and research | W9 pp. 140–147 |
| W.10 | Write routinely over extended and shorter time frames for a range of tasks, purposes, and audiences | W10 pp. 148–153 |
| **Speaking and Listening** | | |
| SL.1 | Engage effectively in a range of collaborative discussions with diverse partners, building on others' ideas and expressing their own clearly | SL1 pp. 158–163 |
| SL.2 | Interpret information presented in diverse media and formats and explain how it contributes to a topic, text, or issue under study | SL2 pp. 164–169 |
| SL.3 | Delineate a speaker's argument and specific claims, distinguishing claims that are supported by reasons and evidence from claims that are not | SL3 pp. 170–175 |
| SL.4 | Present claims and findings, sequencing ideas logically and using descriptions, facts, or details to accentuate main ideas or themes; use appropriate eye contact, adequate volume, and clear pronunciation | SL4 pp. 176–181 |
| SL.5 | Include multimedia components and visual displays in presentations to clarify information | SL5 pp. 182–187 |
| SL.6 | Adapt speech to a variety of contexts and tasks, demonstrating command of formal English when appropriate | SL6 pp. 188–193 |
| **Language** | | |
| L.1 | Demonstrate command of the conventions of standard English grammar and usage when writing or speaking | L1 pp. 198–203 |
| L.2 | Demonstrate command of the conventions of standard English capitalization, punctuation, and spelling when writing | L2 pp. 204–209 |
| L.3 | Use knowledge of language and its conventions when writing, speaking, reading, or listening | L3 pp. 210–215 |
| L.4 | Determine or clarify the meaning of unknown and multiple-meaning words and phrases, choosing flexibly from an array of strategies | L4 pp. 216–221 |
| L.5 | Demonstrate understanding of figurative language, word relationships, and nuances in word meanings | L5 pp. 222–227 |
| L.6 | Acquire and use accurately general academic, and domain-specific words and phrases | L6 pp. 228–233 |
| **Reading History/Social Studies** | | |
| RH.1 | Cite textual evidence to support analysis of primary and secondary sources | R1 pp. 6–11 |
| RH.2 | Determine the central ideas or information of a primary or secondary source; provide an objective summary | R2 pp. 12–19 |
| RH.3 | Identify key steps in a text's description of a process related to history/social studies | R3 pp. 20–25 |
| RH.4 | Determine the meaning of words and phrases as they are used in a text, including vocabulary specific to history/social studies | R4 pp. 26–33 |
| RH.5 | Describe how a text presents information | R5 pp. 34–39 |
| RH.6 | Identify aspects of a text that reveal an author's point of view or purpose | R6 pp. 40–47 |
| RH.7 | Integrate visual information with other information in print and digital texts | R7 pp. 48–55 |
| RH.8 | Distinguish among fact, opinion, and reasoned judgment in a text | R8 pp. 56–63 |

| Alaska Strand/Standard | Focus of Alaska Standard | For More Information |
|---|---|---|
| **Reading History/Social Studies** | | |
| RH.9 | Analyze the relationship between a primary and secondary source on the same topic | R9 pp. 64–71 |
| RH.10 | Read and comprehend history/social studies texts of appropriate complexity independently with proficiency | R10 pp. 72–77 |
| **Reading Science/Technical Subjects** | | |
| RST.1 | Cite textual evidence to support analysis of science and technical texts | R1 pp. 6–11 |
| RST.2 | Determine the central ideas or conclusions of a text; provide an objective summary | R2 pp. 12–19 |
| RST.3 | Follow precisely a multistep procedure when carrying out experiments, taking measurements, or performing technical tasks | R3 pp. 20–25 |
| RST.4 | Determine the meaning of symbols, key terms, and other domain-specific words and phrases | R4 pp. 26–33 |
| RST.5 | Analyze the structure an author uses to organize a text, including how the major sections contribute to the whole | R5 pp. 34–39 |
| RST.6 | Analyze the author's purpose in providing an explanation, describing a procedure, or discussing an experiment | R6 pp. 40–47 |
| RST.7 | Integrate quantitative or technical information expressed in words with a version of the information expressed visually | R7 pp. 48–55 |
| RST.8 | Distinguish among facts, reasoned judgment based on research findings, and speculation in a text | R8 pp. 56–63 |
| RST.9 | Compare and contrast the information gained from experiments, simulations, video, or multimedia sources with that gained from reading a text on the same topic | R9 pp. 64–71 |
| RST.10 | Read and comprehend appropriately complex science/technical texts independently and proficiently | R10 pp. 72–77 |
| **Writing History/Social Studies and Science/Technical Subjects** | | |
| WHST.1 | Write arguments based on discipline-specific content | W1 pp. 82–89 |
| WHST.2 | Write informative/explanatory texts including the narration of historical events, scientific procedures/experiments, or technical processes | W2 pp. 90–99 |
| WHST.3 | NA | |
| WHST.4 | Produce writing in which the development, organization, and style are appropriate to the task, purpose, and audience | W4 pp. 110–115 |
| WHST.5 | Develop and strengthen writing as needed by planning, revising, editing, rewriting, or trying a new approach | W5 pp. 116–121 |
| WHST.6 | Use technology to produce and publish writing as well as to interact with others; demonstrate keyboarding skills | W6 pp. 122–127 |
| WHST.7 | Conduct short research projects to answer a question, drawing on several sources and refocusing the inquiry when appropriate | W7 pp. 128–133 |
| WHST.8 | Gather information from print and digital sources; assess the credibility of sources; quote or paraphrase while avoiding plagiarism and providing basic bibliographic information | W8 pp. 134–139 |
| WHST.9 | Draw evidence from informational texts to support analysis, reflection, and research | W9 pp. 140–147 |
| WHST.10 | Write routinely over extended and shorter time frames for a range of tasks, purposes, and audiences | W10 pp. 148–153 |

# Alaska, Grade 7

| Alaska Strand/Standard | Focus of Alaska Standard | For More Information |
|---|---|---|
| **Reading Literature** | | |
| RL.1 | Cite several pieces of textual evidence to support analysis of what the text says explicitly as well as inferences drawn from the text | R1 pp. 6–11 |
| RL.2 | Determine the theme or central idea of a text and analyze its development; provide an objective summary of the text | R2 pp. 12–19 |

*(Continued)*

| Alaska Strand/Standard | Focus of Alaska Standard | For More Information |
|---|---|---|
| **Reading Literature** | | |
| RL.3 | Analyze how particular elements of a story or drama interact | R3 pp. 20–25 |
| RL.4 | Determine the meaning of words and phrases as they are used in a text, including figurative and connotative meanings | R4 pp. 26–33 |
| RL.5 | Analyze how a drama's or poem's form or structure contributes to its meaning | R5 pp. 34–39 |
| RL.6 | Analyze author's purpose and how an author develops and contrasts the points of view of different characters or narrators in a text | R6 pp. 40–47 |
| RL.7 | Compare and contrast a written story, drama, or poem to its audio, filmed, staged, or multimedia version | R7 pp. 48–55 |
| RL.8 | NA | |
| RL.9 | Compare and contrast a fictional portrayal of a time, place, or character and a historical account of the same period | R9 pp. 64–71 |
| RL.10 | Read and comprehend literature of appropriate complexity independently with proficiency | R10 pp. 72–77 |
| **Reading Informational Text** | | |
| RI.1 | Cite several pieces of textual evidence to support analysis of what the text says explicitly as well as inferences drawn from the text | R1 pp. 6–11 |
| RI.2 | Determine the central idea and subtopics in a text and analyze their development; provide an objective summary of the text | R2 pp. 12–19 |
| RI.3 | Analyze the interactions between individuals, events, and ideas in a text | R3 pp. 20–25 |
| RI.4 | Determine the meaning of words and phrases as they are used in a text, including figurative, connotative, and technical meanings | R4 pp. 26–33 |
| RI.5 | Analyze the structure an author uses to organize a text, including how the major sections contribute to the whole | R5 pp. 34–39 |
| RI.6 | Determine an author's point of view or purpose in a text and analyze how the author distinguishes his or her position from that of others | R6 pp. 40–47 |
| RI.7 | Compare and contrast a text to an audio, video, or multimedia version of the text | R7 pp. 48–55 |
| RI.8 | Trace and evaluate the argument and specific claims in a text, assessing whether the reason is sound and the evidence is relevant and sufficient | R8 pp. 56–63 |
| RI.9 | Analyze how two or more authors writing about the same topic shape their presentations of key information | R9 pp. 64–71 |
| RI.10 | Read and comprehend appropriately complex literary nonfiction, informational, and functional texts independently and proficiently | R10 pp. 72–77 |
| **Writing** | | |
| W.1 | Write arguments to support claims with clear reasons and relevant evidence | W1 pp. 82–89 |
| W.2 | Write informative/explanatory texts to examine a topic and convey ideas, concepts, and information clearly | W2 pp. 90–99 |
| W.3 | Write narratives to develop real or imagined experiences or events using effective technique, descriptive details, and well-structured event sequences | W3 pp. 100–109 |
| W.4 | Produce writing in which the development, organization, and style are appropriate to the task, purpose, and audience | W4 pp. 110–115 |
| W.5 | Develop and strengthen writing as needed by planning, revising, editing, rewriting, or trying a new approach | W5 pp. 116–121 |
| W.6 | Use technology to produce and publish writing, link to and cite sources; interact and collaborate with others | W6 pp. 122–127 |
| W.7 | Conduct short research projects to answer a question, drawing on several sources and additional related questions for further investigation | W7 pp. 128–133 |
| W.8 | Gather information from print and digital sources; assess the credibility of sources; quote or paraphrase while avoiding plagiarism and following a standard format for citation | W8 pp. 134–139 |
| W.9 | Draw evidence from literary or informational texts to support analysis, reflection, and research | W9 pp. 140–147 |
| W.10 | Write routinely over extended and shorter time frames for a range of tasks, purposes, and audiences | W10 pp. 148–153 |

| Alaska Strand/Standard | Focus of Alaska Standard | For More Information |
|---|---|---|
| **Speaking and Listening** | | |
| SL.1 | Engage effectively in a range of collaborative discussions with diverse partners, building on others' ideas and expressing their own clearly | SL1 pp. 158–163 |
| SL.2 | Analyze the main ideas and supporting details presented in diverse media and formats and explain how the ideas clarify a topic, text, or issue under study | SL2 pp. 164–169 |
| SL.3 | Delineate a speaker's argument and specific claims evaluating the soundness of the reasoning and the relevance and sufficiency of the evidence | SL3 pp. 170–175 |
| SL.4 | Present claims and findings, emphasizing salient points in a focused coherent manner; use appropriate eye contact, adequate volume, and clear pronunciation | SL4 pp. 176–181 |
| SL.5 | Include multimedia components and visual displays in presentations to clarify claims and findings | SL5 pp. 182–187 |
| SL.6 | Adapt speech to a variety of contexts and tasks, demonstrating command of formal English when appropriate | SL6 pp. 188–193 |
| **Language** | | |
| L.1 | Demonstrate command of the conventions of standard English grammar and usage when writing or speaking | L1 pp. 198–203 |
| L.2 | Demonstrate command of the conventions of standard English capitalization, punctuation, and spelling when writing | L2 pp. 204–209 |
| L.3 | Use knowledge of language and its conventions when writing, speaking, reading, or listening | L3 pp. 210–215 |
| L.4 | Determine or clarify the meaning of unknown and multiple-meaning words and phrases, choosing flexibly from an array of strategies | L4 pp. 216–221 |
| L.5 | Demonstrate understanding of figurative language, word relationships, and nuances in word meanings | L5 pp. 222–227 |
| L.6 | Acquire and use accurately general academic, and domain-specific words and phrases | L6 pp. 228–233 |
| **Reading History/Social Studies** | | |
| RH.1 | Cite textual evidence to support analysis of primary and secondary sources | R1 pp. 6–11 |
| RH.2 | Determine the central ideas or information of a primary or secondary source; provide an objective summary | R2 pp. 12–19 |
| RH.3 | Identify key steps in a text's description of a process related to history/social studies | R3 pp. 20–25 |
| RH.4 | Determine the meaning of words and phrases as they are used in a text, including vocabulary specific to history/social studies | R4 pp. 26–33 |
| RH.5 | Describe how a text presents information | R5 pp. 34–39 |
| RH.6 | Identify aspects of a text that reveal an author's point of view or purpose | R6 pp. 40–47 |
| RH.7 | Integrate visual information with other information in print and digital texts | R7 pp. 48–55 |
| RH.8 | Distinguish among fact, opinion, and reasoned judgment in a text | R8 pp. 56–63 |
| RH.9 | Analyze the relationship between a primary and secondary source on the same topic | R9 pp. 64–71 |
| RH.10 | Read and comprehend history/social studies texts of appropriate complexity independently with proficiency | R10 pp. 72–77 |
| **Reading Science/Technical Subjects** | | |
| RST.1 | Cite textual evidence to support analysis of science and technical texts | R1 pp. 6–11 |
| RST.2 | Determine the central ideas or conclusions of a text; provide an objective summary | R2 pp. 12–19 |
| RST.3 | Follow precisely a multistep procedure when carrying out experiments, taking measurements, or performing technical tasks | R3 pp. 20–25 |
| RST.4 | Determine the meaning of symbols, key terms, and other domain-specific words and phrases | R4 pp. 26–33 |
| RST.5 | Analyze the structure an author uses to organize a text, including how the major sections contribute to the whole | R5 pp. 34–39 |
| RST.6 | Analyze the author's purpose in providing an explanation, describing a procedure, or discussing an experiment | R6 pp. 40–47 |
| RST.7 | Integrate quantitative or technical information expressed in words with a version of the information expressed visually | R7 pp. 48–55 |
| RST.8 | Distinguish among facts, reasoned judgment based on research findings, and speculation in a text | R8 pp. 56–63 |

*(Continued)*

| Alaska Strand/Standard | Focus of Alaska Standard | For More Information |
|---|---|---|
| **Reading Science/Technical Subjects** | | |
| RST.9 | Compare and contrast the information gained from experiments, simulations, video, or multimedia sources with that gained from reading a text on the same topic | R9 pp. 64–71 |
| RST.10 | Read and comprehend appropriately complex science/technical texts independently and proficiently | R10 pp. 72–77 |
| **Writing History/Social Studies and Science/Technical Subjects** | | |
| WHST.1 | Write arguments based on discipline-specific content | W1 pp. 82–89 |
| WHST.2 | Write informative/explanatory texts including the narration of historical events, scientific procedures/experiments, or technical processes | W2 pp. 90–99 |
| WHST.3 | NA | |
| WHST.4 | Produce writing in which the development, organization, and style are appropriate to the task, purpose, and audience | W4 pp. 110–115 |
| WHST.5 | Develop and strengthen writing as needed by planning, revising, editing, rewriting, or trying a new approach | W5 pp. 116–121 |
| WHST.6 | Use technology to produce and publish writing as well as to interact with others; demonstrate keyboarding skills | W6 pp. 122–127 |
| WHST.7 | Conduct short research projects to answer a question, drawing on several sources and refocusing the inquiry when appropriate | W7 pp. 128–133 |
| WHST.8 | Gather information from print and digital sources; assess the credibility of sources; quote or paraphrase while avoiding plagiarism and providing basic bibliographic information | W8 pp. 134–139 |
| WHST.9 | Draw evidence from informational texts to support analysis, reflection, and research | W9 pp. 140–147 |
| WHST.10 | Write routinely over extended and shorter time frames for a range of tasks, purposes, and audiences | W10 pp. 148–153 |

# Alaska, Grade 8

| Alaska Strand/Standard | Focus of Alaska Standard | For More Information |
|---|---|---|
| **Reading Literature** | | |
| RL.1 | Cite the textual evidence that most strongly supports an analysis of what the text says explicitly as well as inferences drawn from the text | R1 pp. 6–11 |
| RL.2 | Determine a theme or central idea of a text and analyze its development, including its relationship to the characters, setting, and plot; provide an objective summary of the text | R2 pp. 12–19 |
| RL.3 | Analyze how particular lines of dialogue or incidents in a story or drama propel the action, reveal aspects of a character, or provoke a decision | R3 pp. 20–25 |
| RL.4 | Determine the meaning of words and phrases as they are used in a text, including figurative and connotative meanings | R4 pp. 26–33 |
| RL.5 | Compare and contrast the structure of two or more texts and analyze how the differing structure of each contributes to its meaning and style | R5 pp. 34–39 |
| RL.6 | Analyze author's purpose and how differences in the points of view of the characters and the audience or reader create such effects as suspense or humor | R6 pp. 40–47 |
| RL.7 | Analyze the extent to which a filmed or live production of a story or drama stays faithful or departs from the text or script | R7 pp. 48–55 |
| RL.8 | NA | |
| RL.9 | Analyze how a modern work of fiction draws on themes, patterns of events, or character types from traditional stories, describing how the material is rendered new | R9 pp. 64–71 |
| RL.10 | Read and comprehend literature of appropriate complexity independently with proficiency | R10 pp. 72–77 |

| Alaska Strand/Standard | Focus of Alaska Standard | For More Information |
|---|---|---|
| **Reading Informational Text** | | |
| RI.1 | Cite the textual evidence that most strongly supports an analysis of what the text says explicitly as well as inferences drawn from the text | R1 pp. 6–11 |
| RI.2 | Determine the central idea and subtopics of a text and analyze their development, including the relationship to supporting ideas; provide an objective summary of the text | R2 pp. 12–19 |
| RI.3 | Analyze how a text makes connections among distinctions between individuals, ideas, or events | R3 pp. 20–25 |
| RI.4 | Determine the meaning of words and phrases as they are used in a text, including figurative, connotative, and technical meanings | R4 pp. 26–33 |
| RI.5 | Analyze the structure of a specific paragraph in a text, including the role of particular sentences in developing and refining a key concept | R5 pp. 34–39 |
| RI.6 | Determine an author's point of view or purpose in a text and analyze how the author acknowledges and responds to conflicting evidence or viewpoints | R6 pp. 40–47 |
| RI.7 | Evaluate the advantages and disadvantages of using different mediums to present a particular topic or idea | R7 pp. 48–55 |
| RI.8 | Delineate and evaluate the argument and specific claims in a text, assessing whether the reason is sound and the evidence is relevant and sufficient | R8 pp. 56–63 |
| RI.9 | Analyze a case in which two or more texts provide conflicting information on the same topic | R9 pp. 64–71 |
| RI.10 | Read and comprehend appropriately complex literary nonfiction, informational, and functional texts independently and proficiently | R10 pp. 72–77 |
| **Writing** | | |
| W.1 | Write arguments to support claims with clear reasons and relevant evidence | W1 pp. 82–89 |
| W.2 | Write informative/explanatory texts to examine a topic and convey ideas, concepts, and information clearly | W2 pp. 90–99 |
| W.3 | Use narrative writing to develop real or imagined experiences or events using effective technique, descriptive details, and well-structured event sequences | W3 pp. 100–109 |
| W.4 | Produce writing in which the development, organization, and style are appropriate to the task, purpose, and audience | W4 pp. 110–115 |
| W.5 | Develop and strengthen writing as needed by planning, revising, editing, rewriting, or trying a new approach | W5 pp. 116–121 |
| W.6 | Use technology to produce and publish writing, link to and cite sources; interact and collaborate with others | W6 pp. 122–127 |
| W.7 | Conduct short research projects to answer a question, drawing on several sources and additional related questions for further investigation | W7 pp. 128–133 |
| W.8 | Gather information from print and digital sources; assess the credibility of sources; quote or paraphrase while avoiding plagiarism and following a standard format for citation | W8 pp. 134–139 |
| W.9 | Draw evidence from literary or informational texts to support analysis, reflection, and research | W9 pp. 140–147 |
| W.10 | Write routinely over extended and shorter time frames for a range of tasks, purposes, and audiences | W10 pp. 148–153 |
| **Speaking and Listening** | | |
| SL.1 | Engage effectively in a range of collaborative discussions with diverse partners, building on others' ideas and expressing their own clearly | SL1 pp. 158–163 |
| SL.2 | Analyze the purpose of information presented in diverse media and formats and evaluate the motives behind its presentation | SL2 pp. 164–169 |
| SL.3 | Delineate a speaker's argument and specific claims evaluating the soundness of the reasoning and the relevance and sufficiency of the evidence | SL3 pp. 170–175 |
| SL.4 | Present claims and findings, emphasizing salient points in a focused coherent manner; use appropriate eye contact, adequate volume, and clear pronunciation | SL4 pp. 176–181 |
| SL.5 | Integrate multimedia and visual displays into presentations to clarify information, strengthen claims, and add interest | SL5 pp. 182–187 |
| SL.6 | Adapt speech to a variety of contexts and tasks, demonstrating command of formal English when appropriate | SL6 pp. 188–193 |

*(Continued)*

| Alaska Strand/Standard | Focus of Alaska Standard | For More Information |
|---|---|---|
| **Language** | | |
| L.1 | Demonstrate command of the conventions of standard English grammar and usage when writing or speaking | L1 pp. 198–203 |
| L.2 | Demonstrate command of the conventions of standard English capitalization, punctuation, and spelling when writing | L2 pp. 204–209 |
| L.3 | Use knowledge of language and its conventions when writing, speaking, reading, or listening | L3 pp. 210–215 |
| L.4 | Determine or clarify the meaning of unknown and multiple-meaning words and phrases, choosing flexibly from an array of strategies | L4 pp. 216–221 |
| L.5 | Demonstrate understanding of figurative language, word relationships, and nuances in word meanings | L5 pp. 222–227 |
| L.6 | Acquire and use accurately general academic, and domain-specific words and phrases | L6 pp. 228–233 |
| **Reading History/Social Studies** | | |
| RH.1 | Cite textual evidence to support analysis of primary and secondary sources | R1 pp. 6–11 |
| RH.2 | Determine the central ideas or information of a primary or secondary source; provide an objective summary | R2 pp. 12–19 |
| RH.3 | Identify key steps in a text's description of a process related to history/social studies | R3 pp. 20–25 |
| RH.4 | Determine the meaning of words and phrases as they are used in a text, including vocabulary specific to history/social studies | R4 pp. 26–33 |
| RH.5 | Describe how a text presents information | R5 pp. 34–39 |
| RH.6 | Identify aspects of a text that reveal an author's point of view or purpose | R6 pp. 40–47 |
| RH.7 | Integrate visual information with other information in print and digital texts | R7 pp. 48–55 |
| RH.8 | Distinguish among fact, opinion, and reasoned judgment in a text | R8 pp. 56–63 |
| RH.9 | Analyze the relationship between a primary and secondary source on the same topic | R9 pp. 64–71 |
| RH.10 | Read and comprehend history/social studies texts of appropriate complexity independently with proficiency | R10 pp. 72–77 |
| **Reading Science/Technical Subjects** | | |
| RST.1 | Cite textual evidence to support analysis of science and technical texts | R1 pp. 6–11 |
| RST.2 | Determine the central ideas or conclusions of a text; provide an objective summary | R2 pp. 12–19 |
| RST.3 | Follow precisely a multistep procedure when carrying out experiments, taking measurements, or performing technical tasks | R3 pp. 20–25 |
| RST.4 | Determine the meaning of symbols, key terms, and other domain-specific words and phrases | R4 pp. 26–33 |
| RST.5 | Analyze the structure an author uses to organize a text, including how the major sections contribute to the whole | R5 pp. 34–39 |
| RST.6 | Analyze the author's purpose in providing an explanation, describing a procedure, or discussing an experiment | R6 pp. 40–47 |
| RST.7 | Integrate quantitative or technical information expressed in words with a version of the information expressed visually | R7 pp. 48–55 |
| RST.8 | Distinguish among facts, reasoned judgment based on research findings, and speculation in a text | R8 pp. 56–63 |
| RST.9 | Compare and contrast the information gained from experiments, simulations, video, or multimedia sources with that gained from reading a text on the same topic | R9 pp. 64–71 |
| RST.10 | Read and comprehend appropriately complex science/technical texts independently and proficiently | R10 pp. 72–77 |
| **Writing History/Social Studies and Science/Technical Subjects** | | |
| WHST.1 | Write arguments based on discipline-specific content | W1 pp. 82–89 |
| WHST.2 | Write informative/explanatory texts including the narration of historical events, scientific procedures/experiments, or technical processes | W2 pp. 90–99 |
| WHST.3 | NA | |
| WHST.4 | Produce writing in which the development, organization, and style are appropriate to the task, purpose, and audience | W4 pp. 110–115 |

| Alaska Strand/Standard | Focus of Alaska Standard | For More Information |
|---|---|---|
| **Writing History/Social Studies and Science/Technical Subjects** | | |
| WHST.5 | Develop and strengthen writing as needed by planning, revising, editing, rewriting, or trying a new approach | W5 pp. 116–121 |
| WHST.6 | Use technology to produce and publish writing as well as to interact with others; demonstrate keyboarding skills | W6 pp. 122–127 |
| WHST.7 | Conduct short research projects to answer a question, drawing on several sources and refocusing the inquiry when appropriate | W7 pp. 128–133 |
| WHST.8 | Gather information from print and digital sources; assess the credibility of sources; quote or paraphrase while avoiding plagiarism and providing basic bibliographic information | W8 pp. 134–139 |
| WHST.9 | Draw evidence from informational texts to support analysis, reflection, and research | W9 pp. 140–147 |
| WHST.10 | Write routinely over extended and shorter time frames for a range of tasks, purposes, and audiences | W10 pp. 148–153 |

# Arizona, Grade 6

| Arizona Strand/Standard | Focus of Arizona Standard | For More Information |
|---|---|---|
| **Reading Literature** | | |
| RL.1 | Cite textual evidence to support analysis of what the text says explicitly as well as inferences drawn from the text | R1 pp. 6–11 |
| RL.2 | Determine the theme or central idea of a text and how it is conveyed through particular details; provide an objective summary | R2 pp. 12–19 |
| RL.3 | Describe how a particular plot unfolds in a series of episodes as well as how the characters respond or change | R3 pp. 20–25 |
| RL.4 | Determine the meaning of words and phrases as they are used in a text, including figurative and connotative meanings | R4 pp. 26–33 |
| RL.5 | Analyze how a particular sentence, chapter, scene, or stanza fits into the overall structure of a text and contributes to the development of the theme, setting, or plot | R5 pp. 34–39 |
| RL.6 | Explain how an author develops the point of view of the narrator or speaker in a text | R6 pp. 40–47 |
| RL.7 | Compare and contrast the experience of reading a story, drama, or poem to listening to or viewing an audio, video, or live version of the text | R7 pp. 48–55 |
| RL.8 | NA | |
| RL.9 | Compare and contrast texts in different forms or genres in terms of their approaches to similar themes and topics | R9 pp. 64–71 |
| RL.10 | Read and comprehend literature of appropriate complexity independently with proficiency | R10 pp. 72–77 |
| **Reading Informational Text** | | |
| RI.1 | Cite textual evidence to support analysis of what the text says explicitly as well as inferences drawn from the text | R1 pp. 6–11 |
| RI.2 | Determine a central idea of a text and how it is conveyed through particular details; provide an objective summary | R2 pp. 12–19 |
| RI.3 | Analyze in detail how a key individual, event, or idea is introduced, illustrated, and elaborated in a text | R3 pp. 20–25 |
| RI.4 | Determine the meaning of words and phrases as they are used in a text, including figurative, connotative, and technical meanings | R4 pp. 26–33 |
| RI.5 | Analyze how a particular sentence, chapter, scene, or section fits into the overall structure of a text and contributes to the development of the ideas | R5 pp. 34–39 |
| RI.6 | Determine an author's point of view or purpose in a text and explain how it is conveyed in the text | R6 pp. 40–47 |

*(Continued)*

| Arizona Strand/Standard | Focus of Arizona Standard | For More Information |
|---|---|---|
| **Reading Informational Text** | | |
| RI.7 | Integrate information presented in different media or formats as well as in words to develop a coherent understanding of a topic or issue | R7 pp. 48–55 |
| RI.8 | Trace and evaluate the argument and specific claims, distinguishing claims that are supported by reasons and evidence from claims that are not | R8 pp. 56–63 |
| RI.9 | Compare and contrast one author's presentation of events with that of another | R9 pp. 64–71 |
| RI.10 | Read and comprehend appropriately complex literary nonfiction, informational, and functional texts independently and proficiently | R10 pp. 72–77 |
| **Writing** | | |
| W.1 | Write arguments to support claims with clear reasons and relevant evidence | W1 pp. 82–89 |
| W.2 | Write informative/explanatory texts to examine a topic and convey ideas, concepts, and information clearly | W2 pp. 90–99 |
| W.3 | Write narratives to develop real or imagined experiences or events using effective technique, descriptive details, and well-structured event sequences | W3 pp. 100–109 |
| W.4 | Produce writing in which the development, organization, and style are appropriate to the task, purpose, and audience | W4 pp. 110–115 |
| W.5 | Develop and strengthen writing as needed by planning, revising, editing, rewriting, or trying a new approach | W5 pp. 116–121 |
| W.6 | Use technology to produce and publish writing as well as to interact with others; demonstrate keyboarding skills | W6 pp. 122–127 |
| W.7 | Conduct short research projects to answer a question, drawing on several sources and refocusing the inquiry when appropriate | W7 pp. 128–133 |
| W.8 | Gather information from print and digital sources; assess the credibility of sources; quote or paraphrase while avoiding plagiarism and providing basic bibliographic information | W8 pp. 134–139 |
| W.9 | Draw evidence from literary or informational texts to support analysis, reflection, and research | W9 pp. 140–147 |
| W.10 | Write routinely over extended and shorter time frames for a range of tasks, purposes, and audiences | W10 pp. 148–153 |
| **Speaking and Listening** | | |
| SL.1 | Engage effectively in a range of collaborative discussions with diverse partners, building on others' ideas and expressing their own clearly | SL1 pp. 158–163 |
| SL.2 | Interpret information presented in diverse media and formats and explain how it contributes to a topic, text, or issue under study | SL2 pp. 164–169 |
| SL.3 | Delineate a speaker's argument and specific claims that are supported by reasons and evidence from claims that are not | SL3 pp. 170–175 |
| SL.4 | Present claims and findings, sequencing ideas logically and using descriptions, facts, or details to accentuate main ideas or themes; use appropriate eye contact, adequate volume, and clear pronunciation | SL4 pp. 176–181 |
| SL.5 | Include multimedia components and visual displays in presentations to clarify information | SL5 pp. 182–187 |
| SL.6 | Adapt speech to a variety of contexts and tasks, demonstrating command of formal English when appropriate | SL6 pp. 188–193 |
| **Language** | | |
| L.1 | Demonstrate command of the conventions of standard English grammar and usage when writing or speaking | L1 pp. 198–203 |
| L.2 | Demonstrate command of the conventions of standard English capitalization, punctuation, and spelling when writing | L2 pp. 204–209 |
| L.3 | Use knowledge of language and its conventions when writing, speaking, reading, or listening | L3 pp. 210–215 |
| L.4 | Determine or clarify the meaning of unknown and multiple-meaning words and phrases, choosing flexibly from an array of strategies | L4 pp. 216–221 |
| L.5 | Demonstrate understanding of figurative language, word relationships, and nuances in word meanings | L5 pp. 222–227 |
| L.6 | Acquire and use accurately general academic, and domain-specific words and phrases | L6 pp. 228–233 |

| Arizona Strand/Standard | Focus of Arizona Standard | For More Information |
|---|---|---|
| **Reading History/Social Studies** | | |
| RH.1 | Cite textual evidence to support analysis of primary and secondary sources | R1 pp. 6–11 |
| RH.2 | Determine the central ideas or information of a primary or secondary source; provide an objective summary | R2 pp. 12–19 |
| RH.3 | Identify key steps in a text's description of a process related to history/social studies | R3 pp. 20–25 |
| RH.4 | Determine the meaning of words and phrases as they are used in a text, including vocabulary specific to history/social studies | R4 pp. 26–33 |
| RH.5 | Describe how a text presents information | R5 pp. 34–39 |
| RH.6 | Identify aspects of a text that reveal an author's point of view or purpose | R6 pp. 40–47 |
| RH.7 | Integrate visual information with other information in print and digital texts | R7 pp. 48–55 |
| RH.8 | Distinguish among fact, opinion, and reasoned judgment in a text | R8 pp. 56–63 |
| RH.9 | Analyze the relationship between a primary and secondary source on the same topic | R9 pp. 64–71 |
| RH.10 | Read and comprehend history/social studies texts of appropriate complexity independently with proficiency | R10 pp. 72–77 |
| **Reading Science/Technical Subjects** | | |
| RST.1 | Cite textual evidence to support analysis of science and technical texts | R1 pp. 6–11 |
| RST.2 | Determine the central ideas or conclusions of a text; provide an objective summary | R2 pp. 12–19 |
| RST.3 | Follow precisely a multistep procedure when carrying out experiments, taking measurements, or performing technical tasks | R3 pp. 20–25 |
| RST.4 | Determine the meaning of symbols, key terms, and other domain-specific words and phrases | R4 pp. 26–33 |
| RST.5 | Analyze the structure an author uses to organize a text, including how the major sections contribute to the whole | R5 pp. 34–39 |
| RST.6 | Analyze the author's purpose in providing an explanation, describing a procedure, or discussing an experiment | R6 pp. 40–47 |
| RST.7 | Integrate quantitative or technical information expressed in words with a version of the information expressed visually | R7 pp. 48–55 |
| RST.8 | Distinguish among facts, reasoned judgment based on research findings, and speculation in a text | R8 pp. 56–63 |
| RST.9 | Compare and contrast the information gained from experiments, simulations, video, or multimedia sources with that gained from reading a text on the same topic | R9 pp. 64–71 |
| RST.10 | Read and comprehend appropriately complex science/technical texts independently and proficiently | R10 pp. 72–77 |
| **Writing History/Social Studies and Science/Technical Subjects** | | |
| WHST.1 | Write arguments based on discipline-specific content | W1 pp. 82–89 |
| WHST.2 | Write informative/explanatory texts including the narration of historical events, scientific procedures/experiments, or technical processes | W2 pp. 90–99 |
| WHST.3 | NA | |
| WHST.4 | Produce writing in which the development, organization, and style are appropriate to the task, purpose, and audience | W4 pp. 110–115 |
| WHST.5 | Develop and strengthen writing as needed by planning, revising, editing, rewriting, or trying a new approach | W5 pp. 116–121 |
| WHST.6 | Use technology to produce and publish writing as well as to interact with others; demonstrate keyboarding skills | W6 pp. 122–127 |
| WHST.7 | Conduct short research projects to answer a question, drawing on several sources and refocusing the inquiry when appropriate | W7 pp. 128–133 |
| WHST.8 | Gather information from print and digital sources; assess the credibility of sources; quote or paraphrase while avoiding plagiarism and providing basic bibliographic information | W8 pp. 134–139 |
| WHST.9 | Draw evidence from informational texts to support analysis, reflection, and research | W9 pp. 140–147 |
| WHST.10 | Write routinely over extended and shorter time frames for a range of tasks, purposes, and audiences | W10 pp. 148–153 |

# Arizona, Grade 7

| Arizona Strand/Standard | Focus of Arizona Standard | For More Information |
|---|---|---|
| **Reading Literature** | | |
| RL.1 | Cite several pieces of textual evidence to support analysis of what the text says explicitly as well as inferences drawn from the text | R1 pp. 6–11 |
| RL.2 | Determine the theme or central idea of a text and analyze its development; provide an objective summary of the text | R2 pp. 12–19 |
| RL.3 | Analyze how particular elements of a story or drama interact | R3 pp. 20–25 |
| RL.4 | Determine the meaning of words and phrases as they are used in a text, including figurative and connotative meanings | R4 pp. 26–33 |
| RL.5 | Analyze how a drama's or poem's form or structure contributes to its meaning | R5 pp. 34–39 |
| RL.6 | Analyze how an author develops and contrasts the points of view of different characters or narrators in a text | R6 pp. 40–47 |
| RL.7 | Compare and contrast a written story, drama, or poem to its audio, filmed, staged, or multimedia version | R7 pp. 48–55 |
| RL.8 | NA | |
| RL.9 | Compare and contrast a fictional portrayal of a time, place, or character and a historical account of the same period | R9 pp. 64–71 |
| RL.10 | Read and comprehend literature of appropriate complexity independently with proficiency | R10 pp. 72–77 |
| **Reading Informational Text** | | |
| RI.1 | Cite several pieces of textual evidence to support analysis of what the text says explicitly as well as inferences drawn from the text | R1 pp. 6–11 |
| RI.2 | Determine two or more central ideas in a text and analyze their developments; provide an objective summary of the text | R2 pp. 12–19 |
| RI.3 | Analyze the interactions between individuals, events, and ideas in a text | R3 pp. 20–25 |
| RI.4 | Determine the meaning of words and phrases as they are used in a text, including figurative, connotative, and technical meanings | R4 pp. 26–33 |
| RI.5 | Analyze the structure an author uses to organize a text, including how the major sections contribute to the whole | R5 pp. 34–39 |
| RI.6 | Determine an author's point of view or purpose in a text and analyze how the author distinguishes his or her position from that of others | R6 pp. 40–47 |
| RI.7 | Compare and contrast a text to an audio, video, or multimedia version of the text | R7 pp. 48–55 |
| RI.8 | Trace and evaluate the argument and specific claims in a text, assessing whether the reason is sound and the evidence is relevant and sufficient | R8 pp. 56–63 |
| RI.9 | Analyze how two or more authors writing about the same topic shape their presentations of key information | R9 pp. 64–71 |
| RI.10 | Read and comprehend appropriately complex literary nonfiction, informational, and functional texts independently and proficiently | R10 pp. 72–77 |
| **Writing** | | |
| W.1 | Write arguments to support claims with clear reasons and relevant evidence | W1 pp. 82–89 |
| W.2 | Write informative/explanatory texts to examine a topic and convey ideas, concepts, and information clearly | W2 pp. 90–99 |
| W.3 | Write narratives to develop real or imagined experiences or events using effective technique, descriptive details, and well-structured event sequences | W3 pp. 100–109 |
| W.4 | Produce writing in which the development, organization, and style are appropriate to the task, purpose, and audience | W4 pp. 110–115 |
| W.5 | Develop and strengthen writing as needed by planning, revising, editing, rewriting, or trying a new approach | W5 pp. 116–121 |
| W.6 | Use technology to produce and publish writing, link to and cite sources; interact and collaborate with others | W6 pp. 122–127 |

| Arizona Strand/Standard | Focus of Arizona Standard | For More Information |
|---|---|---|
| **Writing** | | |
| W.7 | Conduct short research projects to answer a question, drawing on several sources and generating additional related questions for further investigation | W7 pp. 128–133 |
| W.8 | Gather information from print and digital sources; assess the credibility of sources; quote or paraphrase while avoiding plagiarism and following a standard format for citation | W8 pp. 134–139 |
| W.9 | Draw evidence from literary or informational texts to support analysis, reflection, and research | W9 pp. 140–147 |
| W.10 | Write routinely over extended and shorter time frames for a range of tasks, purposes, and audiences | W10 pp. 148–153 |
| **Speaking and Listening** | | |
| SL.1 | Engage effectively in a range of collaborative discussions with diverse partners, building on others' ideas and expressing their own clearly | SL1 pp. 158–163 |
| SL.2 | Analyze the main ideas and supporting details presented in diverse media and formats and explain how the ideas clarify a topic, text, or issue under study | SL2 pp. 164–169 |
| SL.3 | Delineate a speaker's argument and specific claims evaluating the soundness of the reasoning and the relevance and sufficiency of the evidence | SL3 pp. 170–175 |
| SL.4 | Present claims and findings, emphasizing salient points in a focused coherent manner; use appropriate eye contact, adequate volume, and clear pronunciation | SL4 pp. 176–181 |
| SL.5 | Include multimedia components and visual displays in presentations to clarify claims and findings | SL5 pp. 182–187 |
| SL.6 | Adapt speech to a variety of contexts and tasks, demonstrating command of formal English when appropriate | SL6 pp. 188–193 |
| **Language** | | |
| L.1 | Demonstrate command of the conventions of standard English grammar and usage when writing or speaking | L1 pp. 198–203 |
| L.2 | Demonstrate command of the conventions of standard English capitalization, punctuation, and spelling when writing | L2 pp. 204–209 |
| L.3 | Use knowledge of language and its conventions when writing, speaking, reading, or listening | L3 pp. 210–215 |
| L.4 | Determine or clarify the meaning of unknown and multiple-meaning words and phrases, choosing flexibly from an array of strategies | L4 pp. 216–221 |
| L.5 | Demonstrate understanding of figurative language, word relationships, and nuances in word meanings | L5 pp. 222–227 |
| L.6 | Acquire and use accurately general academic, and domain-specific words and phrases | L6 pp. 228–233 |
| **Reading History/Social Studies** | | |
| RH.1 | Cite textual evidence to support analysis of primary and secondary sources | R1 pp. 6–11 |
| RH.2 | Determine the central ideas or information of a primary or secondary source; provide an objective summary | R2 pp. 12–19 |
| RH.3 | Identify key steps in a text's description of a process related to history/social studies | R3 pp. 20–25 |
| RH.4 | Determine the meaning of words and phrases as they are used in a text, including vocabulary specific to history/social studies | R4 pp. 26–33 |
| RH.5 | Describe how a text presents information | R5 pp. 34–39 |
| RH.6 | Identify aspects of a text that reveal an author's point of view or purpose | R6 pp. 40–47 |
| RH.7 | Integrate visual information with other information in print and digital texts | R7 pp. 48–55 |
| RH.8 | Distinguish among fact, opinion, and reasoned judgment in a text | R8 pp. 56–63 |
| RH.9 | Analyze the relationship between a primary and secondary source on the same topic | R9 pp. 64–71 |
| RH.10 | Read and comprehend history/social studies texts of appropriate complexity independently with proficiency | R10 pp. 72–77 |
| **Reading Science/Technical Subjects** | | |
| RST.1 | Cite textual evidence to support analysis of science and technical texts | R1 pp. 6–11 |
| RST.2 | Determine the central ideas or conclusions of a text; provide an objective summary | R2 pp. 12–19 |
| RST.3 | Follow precisely a multistep procedure when carrying out experiments, taking measurements, or performing technical tasks | R3 pp. 20–25 |

*(Continued)*

| Arizona Strand/Standard | Focus of Arizona Standard | For More Information |
|---|---|---|
| **Reading Science/Technical Subjects** | | |
| RST.4 | Determine the meaning of symbols, key terms, and other domain-specific words and phrases | R4 pp. 26–33 |
| RST.5 | Analyze the structure an author uses to organize a text, including how the major sections contribute to the whole | R5 pp. 34–39 |
| RST.6 | Analyze the author's purpose in providing an explanation, describing a procedure, or discussing an experiment | R6 pp. 40–47 |
| RST.7 | Integrate quantitative or technical information expressed in words with a version of the information expressed visually | R7 pp. 48–55 |
| RST.8 | Distinguish among facts, reasoned judgment based on research findings, and speculation in a text | R8 pp. 56–63 |
| RST.9 | Compare and contrast the information gained from experiments, simulations, video, or multimedia sources with that gained from reading a text on the same topic | R9 pp. 64–71 |
| RST.10 | Read and comprehend appropriately complex science/technical texts independently and proficiently | R10 pp. 72–77 |
| **Writing History/Social Studies and Science/Technical Subjects** | | |
| WHST.1 | Write arguments based on discipline-specific content | W1 pp. 82–89 |
| WHST.2 | Write informative/explanatory texts including the narration of historical events, scientific procedures/experiments, or technical processes | W2 pp. 90–99 |
| WHST.3 | NA | |
| WHST.4 | Produce writing in which the development, organization, and style are appropriate to the task, purpose, and audience | W4 pp. 110–115 |
| WHST.5 | Develop and strengthen writing as needed by planning, revising, editing, rewriting, or trying a new approach | W5 pp. 116–121 |
| WHST.6 | Use technology to produce and publish writing as well as to interact with others; demonstrate keyboarding skills | W6 pp. 122–127 |
| WHST.7 | Conduct short research projects to answer a question, drawing on several sources and refocusing the inquiry when appropriate | W7 pp. 128–133 |
| WHST.8 | Gather information from print and digital sources; assess the credibility of sources; quote or paraphrase while avoiding plagiarism and providing basic bibliographic information | W8 pp. 134–139 |
| WHST.9 | Draw evidence from informational texts to support analysis, reflection, and research | W9 pp. 140–147 |
| WHST.10 | Write routinely over extended and shorter time frames for a range of tasks, purposes, and audiences | W10 pp. 148–153 |

# Arizona, Grade 8

| Arizona Strand/Standard | Focus of Arizona Standard | For More Information |
|---|---|---|
| **Reading Literature** | | |
| RL.1 | Cite the textual evidence that most strongly supports an analysis of what the text says explicitly as well as inferences drawn from the text | R1 pp. 6–11 |
| RL.2 | Determine the theme or central idea of a text and analyze its development, including its relationship to the characters, setting, and plot; provide an objective summary of the text | R2 pp. 12–19 |
| RL.3 | Analyze how particular lines of dialogue or incidents in a story or drama propel the action, reveal aspects of a character, or provoke a decision | R3 pp. 20–25 |
| RL.4 | Determine the meaning of words and phrases as they are used in a text, including figurative and connotative meanings | R4 pp. 26–33 |
| RL.5 | Compare and contrast the structure of two or more texts and analyze how the differing structure of each contributes to its meaning and style | R5 pp. 34–39 |
| RL.6 | Analyze how differences in the points of view of the characters and the audience or reader create such effects as suspense or humor | R6 pp. 40–47 |

| Arizona Strand/Standard | Focus of Arizona Standard | For More Information |
|---|---|---|
| **Reading Literature** | | |
| RL.7 | Analyze the extent to which a filmed or live production of a story or drama stays faithful or departs from the text or script | R7 pp. 48–55 |
| RL.8 | NA | |
| RL.9 | Analyze how a modern work of fiction draws on themes, patterns of events, or character types from traditional stories, describing how the material is rendered new | R9 pp. 64–71 |
| RL.10 | Read and comprehend literature of appropriate complexity independently with proficiency | R10 pp. 72–77 |
| **Reading Informational Text** | | |
| RI.1 | Cite the textual evidence that most strongly supports an analysis of what the text says explicitly as well as inferences drawn from the text | R1 pp. 6–11 |
| RI.2 | Determine the central idea of a text and analyze its development, including its relationship to supporting ideas; provide an objective summary of the text | R2 pp. 12–19 |
| RI.3 | Analyze how a text makes connections among and distinctions between individuals, ideas, or events | R3 pp. 20–25 |
| RI.4 | Determine the meaning of words and phrases as they are used in a text, including figurative, connotative, and technical meanings | R4 pp. 26–33 |
| RI.5 | Analyze the structure of a specific paragraph in a text, including the role of particular sentences in developing and refining a key concept | R5 pp. 34–39 |
| RI.6 | Determine an author's point of view or purpose in a text and analyze how the author acknowledges and responds to conflicting evidence or viewpoints | R6 pp. 40–47 |
| RI.7 | Evaluate the advantages and disadvantages of using different mediums to present a particular topic or idea | R7 pp. 48–55 |
| RI.8 | Delineate and evaluate the argument and specific claims in a text, assessing whether the reason is sound and the evidence is relevant and sufficient | R8 pp. 56–63 |
| RI.9 | Analyze a case in which two or more texts provide conflicting information on the same topic | R9 pp. 64–71 |
| RI.10 | Read and comprehend appropriately complex literary nonfiction, informational, and functional texts independently and proficiently | R10 pp. 72–77 |
| **Writing** | | |
| W.1 | Write arguments to support claims with clear reasons and relevant evidence | W1 pp. 82–89 |
| W.2 | Write informative/explanatory texts to examine a topic and convey ideas, concepts, and information clearly | W2 pp. 90–99 |
| W.3 | Write narratives to develop real or imagined experiences or events using effective technique, descriptive details, and well-structured event sequences | W3 pp. 100–109 |
| W.4 | Produce writing in which the development, organization, and style are appropriate to the task, purpose, and audience | W4 pp. 110–115 |
| W.5 | Develop and strengthen writing as needed by planning, revising, editing, rewriting, or trying a new approach | W5 pp. 116–121 |
| W.6 | Use technology to produce and publish writing, link to and cite sources; interact and collaborate with others | W6 pp. 122–127 |
| W.7 | Conduct short research projects to answer a question, drawing on several sources and generating additional related questions for further investigation | W7 pp. 128–133 |
| W.8 | Gather information from print and digital sources; assess the credibility of sources; quote or paraphrase while avoiding plagiarism and following a standard format for citation | W8 pp. 134–139 |
| W.9 | Draw evidence from literary or informational texts to support analysis, reflection, and research | W9 pp. 140–147 |
| W.10 | Write routinely over extended and shorter time frames for a range of tasks, purposes, and audiences | W10 pp. 148–153 |
| **Speaking and Listening** | | |
| SL.1 | Engage effectively in a range of collaborative discussions with diverse partners, building on others' ideas and expressing their own clearly | SL1 pp. 158–163 |
| SL.2 | Analyze the purpose of information presented in diverse media and formats and evaluate the motives behind its presentation | SL2 pp. 164–169 |

*(Continued)*

| Arizona Strand/Standard | Focus of Arizona Standard | For More Information |
|---|---|---|
| **Speaking and Listening** | | |
| SL.3 | Delineate a speaker's argument and specific claims evaluating the soundness of the reasoning and the relevance and sufficiency of the evidence and identifying when irrelevant evidence is introduced | SL3 pp. 170–175 |
| SL.4 | Present claims and findings, emphasizing salient points in a focused coherent manner; use appropriate eye contact, adequate volume, and clear pronunciation | SL4 pp. 176–181 |
| SL.5 | Integrate multimedia components and visual displays into presentations to clarify information, strengthen claims and findings, and add interest | SL5 pp. 182–187 |
| SL.6 | Adapt speech to a variety of contexts and tasks, demonstrating command of formal English when appropriate | SL6 pp. 188–193 |
| **Language** | | |
| L.1 | Demonstrate command of the conventions of standard English grammar and usage when writing or speaking | L1 pp. 198–203 |
| L.2 | Demonstrate command of the conventions of standard English capitalization, punctuation, and spelling when writing | L2 pp. 204–209 |
| L.3 | Use knowledge of language and its conventions when writing, speaking, reading, or listening | L3 pp. 210–215 |
| L.4 | Determine or clarify the meaning of unknown and multiple-meaning words and phrases, choosing flexibly from an array of strategies | L4 pp. 216–221 |
| L.5 | Demonstrate understanding of figurative language, word relationships, and nuances in word meanings | L5 pp. 222–227 |
| L.6 | Acquire and use accurately general academic, and domain-specific words and phrases | L6 pp. 228–233 |
| **Reading History/Social Studies** | | |
| RH.1 | Cite textual evidence to support analysis of primary and secondary sources | R1 pp. 6–11 |
| RH.2 | Determine the central ideas or information of a primary or secondary source; provide an objective summary | R2 pp. 12–19 |
| RH.3 | Identify key steps in a text's description of a process related to history/social studies | R3 pp. 20–25 |
| RH.4 | Determine the meaning of words and phrases as they are used in a text, including vocabulary specific to history/social studies | R4 pp. 26–33 |
| RH.5 | Describe how a text presents information | R5 pp. 34–39 |
| RH.6 | Identify aspects of a text that reveal an author's point of view or purpose | R6 pp. 40–47 |
| RH.7 | Integrate visual information with other information in print and digital texts | R7 pp. 48–55 |
| RH.8 | Distinguish among fact, opinion, and reasoned judgment in a text | R8 pp. 56–63 |
| RH.9 | Analyze the relationship between a primary and secondary source on the same topic | R9 pp. 64–71 |
| RH.10 | Read and comprehend history/social studies texts of appropriate complexity independently with proficiency | R10 pp. 72–77 |
| **Reading Science/Technical Subjects** | | |
| RST.1 | Cite textual evidence to support analysis of science and technical texts | R1 pp. 6–11 |
| RST.2 | Determine the central ideas or conclusions of a text; provide an objective summary | R2 pp. 12–19 |
| RST.3 | Follow precisely a multistep procedure when carrying out experiments, taking measurements, or performing technical tasks | R3 pp. 20–25 |
| RST.4 | Determine the meaning of symbols, key terms, and other domain-specific words and phrases | R4 pp. 26–33 |
| RST.5 | Analyze the structure an author uses to organize a text, including how the major sections contribute to the whole | R5 pp. 34–39 |
| RST.6 | Analyze the author's purpose in providing an explanation, describing a procedure, or discussing an experiment | R6 pp. 40–47 |
| RST.7 | Integrate quantitative or technical information expressed in words with a version of the information expressed visually | R7 pp. 48–55 |
| RST.8 | Distinguish among facts, reasoned judgment based on research findings, and speculation in a text | R8 pp. 56–63 |
| RST.9 | Compare and contrast the information gained from experiments, simulations, video, or multimedia sources with that gained from reading a text on the same topic | R9 pp. 64–71 |
| RST.10 | Read and comprehend appropriately complex science/technical texts independently and proficiently | R10 pp. 72–77 |

| Arizona Strand/Standard | Focus of Arizona Standard | For More Information |
|---|---|---|
| **Writing History/Social Studies and Science/Technical Subjects** | | |
| WHST.1 | Write arguments based on discipline-specific content | W1 pp. 82–89 |
| WHST.2 | Write informative/explanatory texts including the narration of historical events, scientific procedures/experiments, or technical processes | W2 pp. 90–99 |
| WHST.3 | NA | |
| WHST.4 | Produce writing in which the development, organization, and style are appropriate to the task, purpose, and audience | W4 pp. 110–115 |
| WHST.5 | Develop and strengthen writing as needed by planning, revising, editing, rewriting, or trying a new approach | W5 pp. 116–121 |
| WHST.6 | Use technology to produce and publish writing as well as to interact with others; demonstrate keyboarding skills | W6 pp. 122–127 |
| WHST.7 | Conduct short research projects to answer a question, drawing on several sources and refocusing the inquiry when appropriate | W7 pp. 128–133 |
| WHST.8 | Gather information from print and digital sources; assess the credibility of sources; quote or paraphrase while avoiding plagiarism and providing basic bibliographic information | W8 pp. 134–139 |
| WHST.9 | Draw evidence from informational texts to support analysis, reflection, and research | W9 pp. 140–147 |
| WHST.10 | Write routinely over extended and shorter time frames for a range of tasks, purposes, and audiences | W10 pp. 148–153 |

# Arkansas, Grade 6

| Arkansas Strand/Standard | Focus of Arkansas Standard | For More Information |
|---|---|---|
| **Reading Literature** | | |
| RL.1 | Cite textual evidence to support analysis of what the text says explicitly as well as inferences drawn from the text | R1 pp. 6–11 |
| RL.2 | Examine a text; determine the theme or central idea and how it is conveyed through particular details; provide an objective summary | R2 pp. 12–19 |
| RL.3 | Describe how a particular plot unfolds in a series of episodes as well as how the characters respond or change | R3 pp. 20–25 |
| RL.4 | Determine the meaning of words and phrases as they are used in a text, including figurative and connotative meanings | R4 pp. 26–33 |
| RL.5 | Analyze how a particular sentence, chapter, scene, or stanza fits into the overall structure of a text and contributes to the development of the theme, setting, or plot | R5 pp. 34–39 |
| RL.6 | Explain how an author develops the point of view and/or perspective of the narrator or speaker in a text | R6 pp. 40–47 |
| RL.7 | Compare and contrast the experience of reading a story, drama, or poem to listening to or viewing an audio, video, or live version of the text | R7 pp. 48–55 |
| RL.8 | NA | |
| RL.9 | Compare and contrast texts in different forms or genres in terms of their approaches to similar themes and topics | R9 pp. 64–71 |
| RL.10 | Read and comprehend literature of appropriate complexity independently with proficiency | R10 pp. 72–77 |
| **Reading Informational Text** | | |
| RI.1 | Cite textual evidence to support analysis of what the text says explicitly as well as inferences drawn from the text | R1 pp. 6–11 |
| RI.2 | Examine a text; determine a central idea and how it is conveyed through particular details; provide an objective summary | R2 pp. 12–19 |

*(Continued)*

| Arkansas Strand/Standard | Focus of Arkansas Standard | For More Information |
|---|---|---|
| **Reading Informational Text** | | |
| RI.3 | Analyze in detail how a key individual, event, or idea is introduced, illustrated, and elaborated in a text | R3 pp. 20–25 |
| RI.4 | Determine the meaning of words and phrases as they are used in a text, including figurative, connotative, and technical meanings | R4 pp. 26–33 |
| RI.5 | Analyze how a particular sentence, chapter, scene, or section fits into the overall structure of a text and contributes to the development of the ideas | R5 pp. 34–39 |
| RI.6 | Determine an author's point of view, perspective, and/or purpose in a text and explain how it is conveyed in the text | R6 pp. 40–47 |
| RI.7 | Integrate information presented in different media or formats as well as in words to develop a coherent understanding of a topic or issue | R7 pp. 48–55 |
| RI.8 | Trace and evaluate the argument and specific claims that are supported by reasons and evidence from claims that are not | R8 pp. 56–63 |
| RI.9 | Compare and contrast one author's presentation of events with that of another | R9 pp. 64–71 |
| RI.10 | Read and comprehend appropriately complex literary nonfiction, informational, and functional texts independently and proficiently | R10 pp. 72–77 |
| **Writing** | | |
| W.1 | Write arguments to support claims with clear reasons and relevant evidence | W1 pp. 82–89 |
| W.2 | Write informative/explanatory texts to examine a topic and convey ideas, concepts, and information clearly | W2 pp. 90–99 |
| W.3 | Write narratives to develop real or imagined experiences or events using effective technique, descriptive details, and well-structured event sequences | W3 pp. 100–109 |
| W.4 | Produce writing in which the development, organization, and style are appropriate to the task, purpose, and audience | W4 pp. 110–115 |
| W.5 | Develop and strengthen writing as needed by planning, revising, editing, rewriting, or trying a new approach | W5 pp. 116–121 |
| W.6 | Use technology to produce and publish writing as well as to interact with others; demonstrate keyboarding skills | W6 pp. 122–127 |
| W.7 | Conduct short research projects to answer a question, drawing on several sources and refocusing the inquiry when appropriate | W7 pp. 128–133 |
| W.8 | Gather information from print and digital sources; assess the credibility of sources; quote or paraphrase while avoiding plagiarism and providing basic bibliographic information | W8 pp. 134–139 |
| W.9 | Draw evidence from literary or informational texts to support analysis, reflection, and research | W9 pp. 140–147 |
| W.10 | Write routinely over extended and shorter time frames for a range of tasks, purposes, and audiences | W10 pp. 148–153 |
| **Speaking and Listening** | | |
| SL.1 | Engage effectively in a range of collaborative discussions with diverse partners, building on others' ideas and expressing their own clearly | SL1 pp. 158–163 |
| SL.2 | Interpret information that is gained by means other than reading and explain how it contributes to a topic, text, or issue under study | SL2 pp. 164–169 |
| SL.3 | Describe precisely a speaker's argument and specific claims, distinguishing claims that are supported by reasons and evidence from claims that are not | SL3 pp. 170–175 |
| SL.4 | Present claims and findings, sequencing ideas logically and using descriptions, facts, or details to accentuate main ideas or themes; use appropriate eye contact, adequate volume, and clear pronunciation | SL4 pp. 176–181 |
| SL.5 | Include multimedia components and visual displays in presentations to clarify information | SL5 pp. 182–187 |
| SL.6 | Adapt speech to a variety of contexts and tasks, demonstrating command of formal English when appropriate | SL6 pp. 188–193 |
| **Language** | | |
| L.1 | Demonstrate command of the conventions of standard English grammar and usage when writing or speaking | L1 pp. 198–203 |
| L.2 | Demonstrate command of the conventions of standard English capitalization, punctuation, and spelling when writing | L2 pp. 204–209 |

| Arkansas Strand/Standard | Focus of Arkansas Standard | For More Information |
|---|---|---|
| **Language** | | |
| L.3 | Use knowledge of language and its conventions when writing, speaking, reading, or listening | L3 pp. 210–215 |
| L.4 | Determine or clarify the meaning of unknown and multiple-meaning words and phrases, choosing flexibly from an array of strategies | L4 pp. 216–221 |
| L.5 | Demonstrate understanding of figurative language, word relationships, and nuances in word meanings | L5 pp. 222–227 |
| L.6 | Acquire and use accurately general academic, and domain-specific words and phrases | L6 pp. 228–233 |

# Arkansas, Grade 7

| Arkansas Strand/Standard | Focus of Arkansas Standard | For More Information |
|---|---|---|
| **Reading Literature** | | |
| RL.1 | Cite several pieces of textual evidence to support analysis of what the text says explicitly as well as inferences drawn from the text | R1 pp. 6–11 |
| RL.2 | Examine a text; determine the theme or central idea and analyze its development; provide an objective summary of the text | R2 pp. 12–19 |
| RL.3 | Analyze how particular elements of a story or drama interact | R3 pp. 20–25 |
| RL.4 | Determine the meaning of words and phrases as they are used in a text, including figurative and connotative meanings | R4 pp. 26–33 |
| RL.5 | Analyze how particular elements of a drama or poem fit into the overall structure and contribute to its meaning | R5 pp. 34–39 |
| RL.6 | Analyze how an author develops and contrasts the points of view and/or perspectives of different characters or narrators in a text | R6 pp. 40–47 |
| RL.7 | Compare and contrast a written story, drama, or poem to its audio, filmed, staged, or multimedia version | R7 pp. 48–55 |
| RL.8 | NA | |
| RL.9 | Compare and contrast a fictional portrayal of a time, place, or character and a historical account of the same period | R9 pp. 64–71 |
| RL.10 | Read and comprehend literature of appropriate complexity independently with proficiency | R10 pp. 72–77 |
| **Reading Informational Text** | | |
| RI.1 | Cite several pieces of textual evidence to support analysis of what the text says explicitly as well as inferences drawn from the text | R1 pp. 6–11 |
| RI.2 | Examine a text; determine two or more central ideas and analyze their developments; provide an objective summary of the text | R2 pp. 12–19 |
| RI.3 | Analyze the interactions between individuals, events, and ideas in a text | R3 pp. 20–25 |
| RI.4 | Determine the meaning of words and phrases as they are used in a text, including figurative, connotative, and technical meanings | R4 pp. 26–33 |
| RI.5 | Analyze the structure an author uses to organize a text, including how the major sections contribute to the whole | R5 pp. 34–39 |
| RI.6 | Determine an author's point of view, perspective, and/or purpose in a text and analyze how the author distinguishes his or her position from that of others | R6 pp. 40–47 |
| RI.7 | Compare and contrast a text to an audio, video, or multimedia version of the text | R7 pp. 48–55 |
| RI.8 | Trace and evaluate the argument and specific claims in a text, assessing whether the reason is sound and the evidence is relevant and sufficient | R8 pp. 56–63 |
| RI.9 | Analyze how two or more authors writing about the same topic shape their presentations of key information | R9 pp. 64–71 |
| RI.10 | Read and comprehend appropriately complex literary nonfiction, informational, and functional texts independently and proficiently | R10 pp. 72–77 |

*(Continued)*

| Arkansas Strand/Standard | Focus of Arkansas Standard | For More Information |
|---|---|---|
| **Writing** | | |
| W.1 | Write arguments to support claims with clear reasons and relevant evidence | W1 pp. 82–89 |
| W.2 | Write informative/explanatory texts to examine a topic and convey ideas, concepts, and information clearly | W2 pp. 90–99 |
| W.3 | Write narratives to develop real or imagined experiences or events using effective technique, descriptive details, and well-structured event sequences | W3 pp. 100–109 |
| W.4 | Produce writing in which the development, organization, and style are appropriate to the task, purpose, and audience | W4 pp. 110–115 |
| W.5 | Develop and strengthen writing as needed by planning, revising, editing, rewriting, or trying a new approach | W5 pp. 116–121 |
| W.6 | Use technology to produce and publish writing, link to and cite sources; interact and collaborate with others | W6 pp. 122–127 |
| W.7 | Conduct short research projects to answer a question, drawing on several sources and additional related questions for further investigation | W7 pp. 128–133 |
| W.8 | Gather information from print and digital sources; assess the credibility of sources; quote or paraphrase while avoiding plagiarism and following a standard format for citation | W8 pp. 134–139 |
| W.9 | Draw evidence from literary or informational texts to support analysis, reflection, and research | W9 pp. 140–147 |
| W.10 | Write routinely over extended and shorter time frames for a range of tasks, purposes, and audiences | W10 pp. 148–153 |
| **Speaking and Listening** | | |
| SL.1 | Engage effectively in a range of collaborative discussions with diverse partners, building on others' ideas and expressing their own clearly | SL1 pp. 158–163 |
| SL.2 | Analyze the main ideas and supporting details that are gained by means other than reading and explain how the ideas clarify a topic, text, or issue under study | SL2 pp. 164–169 |
| SL.3 | Determine a speaker's argument and specific claims evaluating the soundness of the reasoning and the relevance and sufficiency of the evidence | SL3 pp. 170–175 |
| SL.4 | Present claims and findings, emphasizing salient points in a focused coherent manner; use appropriate eye contact, adequate volume, and clear pronunciation | SL4 pp. 176–181 |
| SL.5 | Include multimedia components and visual displays in presentations to clarify claims and findings | SL5 pp. 182–187 |
| SL.6 | Adapt speech to a variety of contexts and tasks, demonstrating command of formal English when appropriate | SL6 pp. 188–193 |
| **Language** | | |
| L.1 | Demonstrate command of the conventions of standard English grammar and usage when writing or speaking | L1 pp. 198–203 |
| L.2 | Demonstrate command of the conventions of standard English capitalization, punctuation, and spelling when writing | L2 pp. 204–209 |
| L.3 | Use knowledge of language and its conventions when writing, speaking, reading, or listening | L3 pp. 210–215 |
| L.4 | Determine or clarify the meaning of unknown and multiple-meaning words and phrases, choosing flexibly from an array of strategies | L4 pp. 216–221 |
| L.5 | Demonstrate understanding of figurative language, word relationships, and nuances in word meanings | L5 pp. 222–227 |
| L.6 | Acquire and use accurately general academic, and domain-specific words and phrases | L6 pp. 228–233 |

# Arkansas, Grade 8

| Arkansas Strand/Standard | Focus of Arkansas Standard | For More Information |
|---|---|---|
| **Reading Literature** | | |
| RL.1 | Cite the textual evidence that most strongly supports an analysis of what the text says explicitly as well as inferences drawn from the text | R1 pp. 6–11 |
| RL.2 | Examine a text; determine the theme or central idea and analyze its development, including its relationship to the characters, setting, and plot; provide an objective summary of the text | R2 pp. 12–19 |
| RL.3 | Analyze how particular lines of dialogue or incidents in a story or drama propel the action, reveal aspects of a character, or provoke a decision | R3 pp. 20–25 |
| RL.4 | Determine the meaning of words and phrases as they are used in a text, including figurative and connotative meanings | R4 pp. 26–33 |
| RL.5 | Compare and contrast the structure of two or more texts and analyze how the differing structure of each contributes to its meaning and style | R5 pp. 34–39 |
| RL.6 | Analyze how differences in the points of view and/or perspectives of the characters and the audience or reader create such effects as suspense or humor | R6 pp. 40–47 |
| RL.7 | Analyze the extent to which a filmed or live production of a story or drama stays faithful or departs from the text or script | R7 pp. 48–55 |
| RL.8 | NA | |
| RL.9 | Analyze how a modern work of fiction draws on themes, patterns of events, or character types from traditional stories, describing how the material is rendered new | R9 pp. 64–71 |
| RL.10 | Read and comprehend literature of appropriate complexity independently with proficiency | R10 pp. 72–77 |
| **Reading Informational Text** | | |
| RI.1 | Cite the textual evidence that most strongly supports an analysis of what the text says explicitly as well as inferences drawn from the text | R1 pp. 6–11 |
| RI.2 | Examine a text; determine the central idea and analyze its development, including its relationship to supporting ideas; provide an objective summary of the text | R2 pp. 12–19 |
| RI.3 | Analyze how a text makes connections among distinctions between individuals, ideas, or events | R3 pp. 20–25 |
| RI.4 | Determine the meaning of words and phrases as they are used in a text, including figurative, connotative, and technical meanings | R4 pp. 26–33 |
| RI.5 | Analyze the structure of a specific paragraph in a text, including the role of particular sentences in developing and refining a key concept | R5 pp. 34–39 |
| RI.6 | Determine an author's point of view, perspective, and/or purpose in a text and analyze how the author acknowledges and responds to conflicting evidence or viewpoints | R6 pp. 40–47 |
| RI.7 | Evaluate the advantages and disadvantages of using different mediums to present a particular topic or idea | R7 pp. 48–55 |
| RI.8 | Analyze and evaluate the argument and specific claims in a text, assessing whether the reason is sound and the evidence is relevant and sufficient | R8 pp. 56–63 |
| RI.9 | Analyze a case in which two or more texts provide conflicting information on the same topic | R9 pp. 64–71 |
| RI.10 | Read and comprehend appropriately complex literary nonfiction, informational, and functional texts independently and proficiently | R10 pp. 72–77 |
| **Writing** | | |
| W.1 | Write arguments to support claims with clear reasons and relevant evidence | W1 pp. 82–89 |
| W.2 | Write informative/explanatory texts to examine a topic and convey ideas, concepts, and information clearly | W2 pp. 90–99 |

*(Continued)*

| Arkansas Strand/Standard | Focus of Arkansas Standard | For More Information |
|---|---|---|
| **Writing** | | |
| W.3 | Write narratives to develop real or imagined experiences or events using effective technique, descriptive details, and well-structured event sequences | W3 pp. 100–109 |
| W.4 | Produce writing in which the development, organization, and style are appropriate to the task, purpose, and audience | W4 pp. 110–115 |
| W.5 | Develop and strengthen writing as needed by planning, revising, editing, rewriting, or trying a new approach | W5 pp. 116–121 |
| W.6 | Use technology to produce and publish writing, link to and cite sources; interact and collaborate with others | W6 pp. 122–127 |
| W.7 | Conduct short research projects to answer a question, drawing on several sources and generating additional related questions for further investigation | W7 pp. 128–133 |
| W.8 | Gather information from print and digital sources; assess the credibility of sources; quote or paraphrase while avoiding plagiarism and following a standard format for citation | W8 pp. 134–139 |
| W.9 | Draw evidence from literary or informational texts to support analysis, reflection, and research | W9 pp. 140–147 |
| W.10 | Write routinely over extended and shorter time frames for a range of tasks, purposes, and audiences | W10 pp. 148–153 |
| **Speaking and Listening** | | |
| SL.1 | Engage effectively in a range of collaborative discussions with diverse partners, building on others' ideas and expressing their own clearly | SL1 pp. 158–163 |
| SL.2 | Analyze the purpose of information presented in diverse media and formats and evaluate the motives behind its presentation | SL2 pp. 164–169 |
| SL.3 | Examine a speaker's argument and specific claims evaluating the soundness of the reasoning and the relevance and sufficiency of the evidence and identifying when irrelevant evidence is introduced | SL3 pp. 170–175 |
| SL.4 | Present claims and findings, emphasizing salient points in a focused coherent manner; use appropriate eye contact, adequate volume, and clear pronunciation | SL4 pp. 176–181 |
| SL.5 | Integrate multimedia and visual displays into presentations to clarify information, strengthen claims and findings, and add interest | SL5 pp. 182–187 |
| SL.6 | Adapt speech to a variety of contexts and tasks, demonstrating command of formal English when appropriate | SL6 pp. 188–193 |
| **Language** | | |
| L.1 | Demonstrate command of the conventions of standard English grammar and usage when writing or speaking | L1 pp. 198–203 |
| L.2 | Demonstrate command of the conventions of standard English capitalization, punctuation, and spelling when writing | L2 pp. 204–209 |
| L.3 | Use knowledge of language and its conventions when writing, speaking, reading, or listening | L3 pp. 210–215 |
| L.4 | Determine or clarify the meaning of unknown and multiple-meaning words and phrases, choosing flexibly from an array of strategies | L4 pp. 216–221 |
| L.5 | Demonstrate understanding of figurative language, word relationships, and nuances in word meanings | L5 pp. 222–227 |
| L.6 | Acquire and use accurately general academic, and domain-specific words and phrases | L6 pp. 228–233 |

# Colorado, Grade 6

| Colorado Strand/Standard | Focus of Colorado Standard | For More Information |
|---|---|---|
| **Oral Expression and Listening** | | |
| 1 | Successful group discussions require planning and participation by all | SL1 pp. 158–163<br>SL4 pp. 176–181<br>SL5 pp. 182–187<br>SL6 pp. 188–193 |
| **Reading for All Purposes** | | |
| 1 | Understanding the meaning within different types of literature depends on properly analyzing literary components | R1 pp. 6–11<br>R2 pp. 12–19<br>R3 pp. 20–25<br>R5 pp. 34–39<br>R6 pp. 40–47<br>R9 pp. 64–71<br>R10 pp. 72–77 |
| 2 | Organizing structure to understand and analyze factual information | R1 pp. 6–11<br>R2 pp. 12–19<br>R3 pp. 20–25<br>R5 pp. 34–39<br>R6 pp. 40–47<br>R8 pp. 56–63<br>R9 pp. 64–71<br>R10 pp. 72–77 |
| 3 | Word meanings are determined by how they are designed and how they are used in context | R4 pp. 26–33 |
| **Writing and Composition** | | |
| 1 | Writing literary genres for intended audiences and purposes requires ideas, organization, and voice | W3 pp. 100–109<br>W4 pp. 110–115<br>W5 pp. 116–121 |
| 2 | Writing informational and persuasive genres for intended audiences and purposes require ideas, organization, and voice develop | W1 pp. 82–89<br>W2 pp. 90–99<br>W4 pp. 110–115<br>W5 pp. 116–121 |
| 3 | Specific editing for grammar, usage, and mechanics, and clarity gives writing its precision and legitimacy | L1 pp. 198–203<br>L2 pp. 204–209 |
| **Research and Reasoning** | | |
| 1 | Individual and group research projects require obtaining information on a topic from a variety of sources and organizing it for presentation | W7 pp. 128–133<br>W8 pp. 134–139<br>W9 pp. 140–147 |
| 2 | Assumptions can be concealed, and require identification and evaluation | W8 pp. 134–139<br>SL3 pp. 170–175 |
| 3 | Monitoring the thinking of self and others is a disciplined way to maintain awareness | W6 pp. 122–127<br>SL4 pp. 176–181 |

# Colorado, Grade 7

| Colorado Strand/Standard | Focus of Colorado Standard | For More Information |
|---|---|---|
| **Oral Expression and Listening** | | |
| 1 | Formal presentations require preparation and effective delivery | SL4 pp. 176–181<br>SL5 pp. 182–187<br>SL6 pp. 188–193 |
| 2 | Small and large group discussions rely on active listening and the effective contributions of all participants | SL1 pp. 158–163<br>SL2 pp. 164–169<br>SL3 pp. 170–175 |
| **Reading for All Purposes** | | |
| 1 | Literary elements, characteristics, and ideas are interrelated and guide the comprehension of literary and fictional texts | R1 pp. 6–11<br>R2 pp. 12–19<br>R3 pp. 20–25<br>R5 pp. 34–39<br>R6 pp. 40–47<br>R9 pp. 64–71<br>R10 pp. 72–77 |
| 2 | Informational and persuasive texts are summarized and evaluated | R1 pp. 6–11<br>R2 pp. 12–19<br>R3 pp. 20–25<br>R5 pp. 34–39<br>R6 pp. 40–47<br>R8 pp. 56–63<br>R9 pp. 64–71<br>R10 pp. 72–77 |
| 3 | Purpose, tone, and meaning in word choices influence literary, persuasive, and informational texts | R4 pp. 26–33 |
| **Writing and Composition** | | |
| 1 | Composing literary and narrative texts that incorporate a range of stylistic devices demonstrates knowledge of genre features | W3 pp. 100–109<br>W4 pp. 110–115<br>W5 pp. 116–121 |
| 2 | Organization is used when composing informational and persuasive texts | W1 pp. 82–89<br>W2 pp. 90–99<br>W4 pp. 110–115<br>W5 pp. 116–121 |
| 3 | Editing writing for grammar, usage, mechanics, and clarity improves written work | L1 pp. 198–203<br>L2 pp. 204–209 |
| **Research and Reasoning** | | |
| 1 | Answering a research question logically begins with obtaining and analyzing information from a variety of sources | W7 pp. 128–133<br>W8 pp. 134–139<br>W9 pp. 140–147 |
| 2 | Logical information requires documented sources | W8 pp. 134–139<br>SL3 pp. 170–175 |
| 3 | Reasoned material is evaluated for its quality using both its logic and its use of a medium | W6 pp. 122–127<br>SL4 pp. 176–181<br>SL5 pp. 182–187 |

# Colorado, Grade 8

| Colorado Strand/Standard | Focus of Colorado Standard | For More Information |
|---|---|---|
| **Oral Expression and Listening** | | |
| 1 | Communication skills and interviewing techniques are required to gather information and to develop and deliver oral presentations | SL1 pp. 158–163<br>SL4 pp. 176–181<br>SL6 pp. 188–193 |
| 2 | A variety of response strategies clarifies meaning or messages | SL2 pp. 164–169<br>SL3 pp. 170–175 |
| **Reading for All Purposes** | | |
| 1 | Quality comprehension and interpretation of literary texts demand self-monitoring and self-assessment | R1 pp. 6–11<br>R2 pp. 12–19<br>R5 pp. 34–39<br>R6 pp. 40–47<br>R9 pp. 64–71<br>R10 pp. 72–77 |
| 2 | Quality comprehension and interpretation of informational and persuasive texts demand self-monitoring and self-assessment | R1 pp. 6–11<br>R2 pp. 12–19<br>R3 pp. 20–25<br>R6 pp. 40–47<br>R8 pp. 56–63<br>R9 pp. 64–71<br>R10 pp. 72–77 |
| 3 | Context, grammar, and word choice influence the understanding of literary, persuasive, and informational texts | R3 pp. 20–25<br>R4 pp. 26–33<br>R5 pp. 34–39 |
| **Writing and Composition** | | |
| 1 | Stylistic devices and descriptive details in literary and narrative texts are organized for a variety of audiences and purposes and evaluated for quality | W3 pp. 100–109<br>W4 pp. 110–115<br>W5 pp. 116–121 |
| 2 | Ideas and supporting details in informational and persuasive texts are organized for a variety of audiences and purposes and evaluated for quality | W1 pp. 82–89<br>W2 pp. 90–99<br>W4 pp. 110–115<br>W5 pp. 116–121 |
| 3 | Editing writing for grammar, usage, mechanics, and clarity is an essential trait of a well-written document | L1 pp. 198–203<br>L2 pp. 204–209 |
| **Research and Reasoning** | | |
| 1 | Individual research projects begin with information obtained from a variety of sources, and is organized, documented, and presented using logical procedures | W7 pp. 128–133<br>W8 pp. 134–139<br>W9 pp. 140–147 |
| 2 | Common fallacies and errors occur in reasoning | SL3 pp. 170–175 |
| 3 | Quality reasoning relies on supporting evidence in media | SL4 pp. 176–181<br>SL5 pp. 182–187 |

| Florida Strand/Standard | Focus of Florida Standard | For More Information |
|---|---|---|
| **Reading Literature** | | |
| RL.1.1 | Cite textual evidence to support analysis of what the text says explicitly as well as inferences drawn from the text | R1 pp. 6–11 |
| RL.1.2 | Determine the theme or central idea of a text and how it is conveyed through particular details; provide an objective summary | R2 pp. 12–19 |
| RL.1.3 | Describe how a particular plot unfolds in a series of episodes as well as how the characters respond or change | R3 pp. 20–25 |
| RL.2.4 | Determine the meaning of words and phrases as they are used in a text, including figurative and connotative meanings | R4 pp. 26–33 |
| RL.2.5 | Analyze how a particular sentence, chapter, scene, or stanza fits into the overall structure of a text and contributes to the development of the theme, setting, or plot | R5 pp. 34–39 |
| RL.2.6 | Explain how an author develops the point of view of the narrator or speaker in a text | R6 pp. 40–47 |
| RL.3.7 | Compare and contrast the experience of reading a story, drama, or poem to listening to or viewing an audio, video, or live version of the text | R7 pp. 48–55 |
| RL.3.8 | NA | |
| RL.3.9 | Compare and contrast texts in different forms or genres in terms of their approaches to similar themes and topics | R9 pp. 64–71 |
| RL.4.10 | Read and comprehend literature of appropriate complexity independently with proficiency | R10 pp. 72–77 |
| **Reading Informational Text** | | |
| RI.1.1 | Cite textual evidence to support analysis of what the text says explicitly as well as inferences drawn from the text | R1 pp. 6–11 |
| RI.1.2 | Determine a central idea of a text and how it is conveyed through particular details; provide an objective summary | R2 pp. 12–19 |
| RI.1.3 | Analyze in detail how a key individual, event, or idea is introduced, illustrated, and elaborated in a text | R3 pp. 20–25 |
| RI.2.4 | Determine the meaning of words and phrases as they are used in a text, including figurative, connotative, and technical meanings | R4 pp. 26–33 |
| RI.2.5 | Analyze how a particular sentence, chapter, scene, or section fits into the overall structure of a text and contributes to the development of the ideas | R5 pp. 34–39 |
| RI.2.6 | Determine an author's point of view or purpose in a text and explain how it is conveyed in the text | R6 pp. 40–47 |
| RI.3.7 | Integrate information presented in different media or formats as well as in words to develop a coherent understanding of a topic or issue | R7 pp. 48–55 |
| RI.3.8 | Trace and evaluate the argument and specific claims that are supported by reasons and evidence from claims that are not | R8 pp. 56–63 |
| RI.3.9 | Compare and contrast one author's presentation of events with that of another | R9 pp. 64–71 |
| RI.4.10 | Read and comprehend appropriately complex literary nonfiction, informational, and functional texts independently and proficiently | R10 pp. 72–77 |
| **Writing** | | |
| W.1.1 | Write arguments to support claims with clear reasons and relevant evidence | W1 pp. 82–89 |
| W.1.2 | Write informative/explanatory texts to examine a topic and convey ideas, concepts, and information clearly | W2 pp. 90–99 |
| W.1.3 | Write narratives to develop real or imagined experiences or events using effective technique, descriptive details, and well-structured event sequences | W3 pp. 100–109 |
| W.2.4 | Produce writing in which the development, organization, and style are appropriate to the task, purpose, and audience | W4 pp. 110–115 |
| W.2.5 | Develop and strengthen writing as needed by planning, revising, editing, rewriting, or trying a new approach | W5 pp. 116–121 |
| W.2.6 | Use technology to produce and publish writing as well as to interact with others; demonstrate keyboarding skills | W6 pp. 122–127 |

| Florida Strand/Standard | Focus of Florida Standard | For More Information |
|---|---|---|
| **Writing** | | |
| W.3.7 | Conduct short research projects to answer a question, drawing on several sources and refocusing the inquiry when appropriate | W7 pp. 128–133 |
| W.3.8 | Gather information from print and digital sources; assess the credibility of sources; quote or paraphrase while avoiding plagiarism and providing basic bibliographic information | W8 pp. 134–139 |
| W.3.9 | Draw evidence from literary or informational texts to support analysis, reflection, and research | W9 pp. 140–147 |
| W.4.10 | Write routinely over extended and shorter time frames for a range of tasks, purposes, and audiences | W10 pp. 148–153 |
| **Speaking and Listening** | | |
| SL.1.1 | Engage effectively in a range of collaborative discussions with diverse partners, building on others' ideas and expressing their own clearly | SL1 pp. 158–163 |
| SL.1.2 | Interpret information presented in diverse media and formats and explain how it contributes to a topic, text, or issue under study | SL2 pp. 164–169 |
| SL.1.3 | Delineate a speaker's argument and specific claims that are supported by reasons and evidence from claims that are not | SL3 pp. 170–175 |
| SL.2.4 | Present claims and findings, sequencing ideas logically and using descriptions, facts, or details to accentuate main ideas or themes; use appropriate eye contact, adequate volume, and clear pronunciation | SL4 pp. 176–181 |
| SL.2.5 | Include multimedia components and visual displays in presentations to clarify information | SL5 pp. 182–187 |
| SL.2.6 | Adapt speech to a variety of contexts and tasks, demonstrating command of formal English when appropriate | SL6 pp. 188–193 |
| **Language** | | |
| L.1.1 | Demonstrate command of the conventions of standard English grammar and usage when writing or speaking | L1 pp. 198–203 |
| L.1.2 | Demonstrate command of the conventions of standard English capitalization, punctuation, and spelling when writing | L2 pp. 204–209 |
| L.2.3 | Use knowledge of language and its conventions when writing, speaking, reading, or listening | L3 pp. 210–215 |
| L.3.4 | Determine or clarify the meaning of unknown and multiple-meaning words and phrases, choosing flexibly from an array of strategies | L4 pp. 216–221 |
| L.3.5 | Demonstrate understanding of figurative language, word relationships, and nuances in word meanings | L5 pp. 222–227 |
| L.3.6 | Acquire and use accurately general academic, and domain-specific words and phrases | L6 pp. 228–233 |
| **Reading History/Social Studies** | | |
| RH.1.1 | Cite textual evidence to support analysis of primary and secondary sources | R1 pp. 6–11 |
| RH.1.2 | Determine the central ideas or information of a primary or secondary source; provide an objective summary | R2 pp. 12–19 |
| RH.1.3 | Identify key steps in a text's description of a process related to history/social studies | R3 pp. 20–25 |
| RH.2.4 | Determine the meaning of words and phrases as they are used in a text, including vocabulary specific to history/social studies | R4 pp. 26–33 |
| RH.2.5 | Describe how a text presents information | R5 pp. 34–39 |
| RH.2.6 | Identify aspects of a text that reveal an author's point of view or purpose | R6 pp. 40–47 |
| RH.3.7 | Integrate visual information with other information in print and digital texts | R7 pp. 48–55 |
| RH.3.8 | Distinguish among fact, opinion, and reasoned judgment in a text | R8 pp. 56–63 |
| RH.3.9 | Analyze the relationship between a primary and secondary source on the same topic | R9 pp. 64–71 |
| RH.4.10 | Read and comprehend history/social studies texts of appropriate complexity independently with proficiency | R10 pp. 72–77 |
| **Reading Science/Technical Subjects** | | |
| RST.1.1 | Cite textual evidence to support analysis of science and technical texts | R1 pp. 6–11 |
| RST.1.2 | Determine the central ideas or conclusions of a text; provide an objective summary | R2 pp. 12–19 |

*(Continued)*

| Florida Strand/Standard | Focus of Florida Standard | For More Information |
|---|---|---|
| **Reading Science/Technical Subjects** | | |
| RST.1.3 | Follow precisely a multistep procedure when carrying out experiments, taking measurements, or performing technical tasks | R3 pp. 20–25 |
| RST.2.4 | Determine the meaning of symbols, key terms, and other domain-specific words and phrases | R4 pp. 26–33 |
| RST.2.5 | Analyze the structure an author uses to organize a text, including how the major sections contribute to the whole | R5 pp. 34–39 |
| RST.2.6 | Analyze the author's purpose in providing an explanation, describing a procedure, or discussing an experiment | R6 pp. 40–47 |
| RST.3.7 | Integrate quantitative or technical information expressed in words with a version of the information expressed visually | R7 pp. 48–55 |
| RST.3.8 | Distinguish among facts, reasoned judgment based on research findings, and speculation in a text | R8 pp. 56–63 |
| RST.3.9 | Compare and contrast the information gained from experiments, simulations, video, or multimedia sources with that gained from reading a text on the same topic | R9 pp. 64–71 |
| RST.4.10 | Read and comprehend appropriately complex science/technical texts independently and proficiently | R10 pp. 72–77 |
| **Writing History/Social Studies, Science and Technical Subjects** | | |
| WHST.1.1 | Write arguments based on discipline-specific content | W1 pp. 82–89 |
| WHST.1.2 | Write informative/explanatory texts including the narration of historical events, scientific procedures/experiments, or technical processes | W2 pp. 90–99 |
| WHST.1.3 | NA | |
| WHST.2.4 | Produce writing in which the development, organization, and style are appropriate to the task, purpose, and audience | W4 pp. 110–115 |
| WHST.2.5 | Develop and strengthen writing as needed by planning, revising, editing, rewriting, or trying a new approach | W5 pp. 116–121 |
| WHST.2.6 | Use technology to produce and publish writing as well as to interact with others; demonstrate keyboarding skills | W6 pp. 122–127 |
| WHST.3.7 | Conduct short research projects to answer a question, drawing on several sources and refocusing the inquiry when appropriate | W7 pp. 128–133 |
| WHST.3.8 | Gather information from print and digital sources; assess the credibility of sources; quote or paraphrase while avoiding plagiarism and providing basic bibliographic information | W8 pp. 134–139 |
| WHST.3.9 | Draw evidence from informational texts to support analysis, reflection, and research | W9 pp. 140–147 |
| WHST.4.10 | Write routinely over extended and shorter time frames for a range of tasks, purposes, and audiences | W10 pp. 148–153 |

# Florida, Grade 7

| Florida Strand/Standard | Focus of Florida Standard | For More Information |
|---|---|---|
| **Reading Literature** | | |
| RL.1.1 | Cite several pieces of textual evidence to support analysis of what the text says explicitly as well as inferences drawn from the text | R1 pp. 6–11 |
| RL.1.2 | Determine the theme or central idea of a text and analyze its development; provide an objective summary of the text | R2 pp. 12–19 |
| RL.1.3 | Analyze how particular elements of a story or drama interact | R3 pp. 20–25 |
| RL.2.4 | Determine the meaning of words and phrases as they are used in a text, including figurative and connotative meanings | R4 pp. 26–33 |
| RL.2.5 | Analyze how a drama's or poem's form or structure contributes to its meaning | R5 pp. 34–39 |
| RL.2.6 | Analyze how an author develops and contrasts the points of view of different characters or narrators in a text | R6 pp. 40–47 |
| RL.3.7 | Compare and contrast a written story, drama, or poem to its audio, filmed, staged, or multimedia version | R7 pp. 48–55 |

| Florida Strand/Standard | Focus of Florida Standard | For More Information |
|---|---|---|
| **Reading Literature** | | |
| RL.3.8 | NA | |
| RL.3.9 | Compare and contrast a fictional portrayal of a time, place, or character and a historical account of the same period | R9 pp. 64–71 |
| RL.4.10 | Read and comprehend literature of appropriate complexity independently with proficiency | R10 pp. 72–77 |
| **Reading Informational Text** | | |
| RI.1.1 | Cite several pieces of textual evidence to support analysis of what the text says explicitly as well as inferences drawn from the text | R1 pp. 6–11 |
| RI.1.2 | Determine two or more central ideas in a text and analyze their developments; provide an objective summary of the text | R2 pp. 12–19 |
| RI.1.3 | Analyze the interactions between individuals, events, and ideas in a text | R3 pp. 20–25 |
| RI.2.4 | Determine the meaning of words and phrases as they are used in a text, including figurative, connotative, and technical meanings | R4 pp. 26–33 |
| RI.2.5 | Analyze the structure an author uses to organize a text, including how the major sections contribute to the whole | R5 pp. 34–39 |
| RI.2.6 | Determine an author's point of view or purpose in a text and analyze how the author distinguishes his or her position from that of others | R6 pp. 40–47 |
| RI.3.7 | Compare and contrast a text to an audio, video, or multimedia version of the text | R7 pp. 48–55 |
| RI.3.8 | Trace and evaluate the argument and specific claims in a text, assessing whether the reason is sound and the evidence is relevant and sufficient | R8 pp. 56–63 |
| RI.3.9 | Analyze how two or more authors writing about the same topic shape their presentations of key information | R9 pp. 64–71 |
| RI.4.10 | Read and comprehend appropriately complex literary nonfiction, informational, and functional texts independently and proficiently | R10 pp. 72–77 |
| **Writing** | | |
| W.1.1 | Write arguments to support claims with clear reasons and relevant evidence | W1 pp. 82–89 |
| W.1.2 | Write informative/explanatory texts to examine a topic and convey ideas, concepts, and information clearly | W2 pp. 90–99 |
| W.1.3 | Write narratives to develop real or imagined experiences or events using effective technique, descriptive details, and well-structured event sequences | W3 pp. 100–109 |
| W.2.4 | Produce writing in which the development, organization, and style are appropriate to the task, purpose, and audience | W4 pp. 110–115 |
| W.2.5 | Develop and strengthen writing as needed by planning, revising, editing, rewriting, or trying a new approach | W5 pp. 116–121 |
| W.2.6 | Use technology to produce and publish writing, link to and cite sources; interact and collaborate with others | W6 pp. 122–127 |
| W.3.7 | Conduct short research projects to answer a question, drawing on several sources and generating additional related questions for further investigation | W7 pp. 128–133 |
| W.3.8 | Gather information from print and digital sources; assess the credibility of sources; quote or paraphrase while avoiding plagiarism and following a standard format for citation | W8 pp. 134–139 |
| W.3.9 | Draw evidence from literary or informational texts to support analysis, reflection, and research | W9 pp. 140–147 |
| W.4.10 | Write routinely over extended and shorter time frames for a range of tasks, purposes, and audiences | W10 pp. 148–153 |
| **Speaking and Listening** | | |
| SL.1.1 | Engage effectively in a range of collaborative discussions with diverse partners, building on others' ideas and expressing their own clearly | SL1 pp. 158–163 |
| SL.1.2 | Analyze the main ideas and supporting details presented in diverse media and formats and explain how the ideas clarify a topic, text, or issue under study | SL2 pp. 164–169 |
| SL.1.3 | Delineate a speaker's argument and specific claims evaluating the soundness of the reasoning and the relevance and sufficiency of the evidence | SL3 pp. 170–175 |
| SL.2.4 | Present claims and findings, emphasizing salient points in a focused coherent manner; use appropriate eye contact, adequate volume, and clear pronunciation | SL4 pp. 176–181 |

*(Continued)*

| Florida Strand/Standard | Focus of Florida Standard | For More Information |
|---|---|---|
| **Speaking and Listening** | | |
| SL.2.5 | Include multimedia components and visual displays in presentations to clarify claims and findings | SL5 pp. 182–187 |
| SL.2.6 | Adapt speech to a variety of contexts and tasks, demonstrating command of formal English when appropriate | SL6 pp. 188–193 |
| **Language** | | |
| L.1.1 | Demonstrate command of the conventions of standard English grammar and usage when writing or speaking | L1 pp. 198–203 |
| L.1.2 | Demonstrate command of the conventions of standard English capitalization, punctuation, and spelling when writing | L2 pp. 204–209 |
| L.2.3 | Use knowledge of language and its conventions when writing, speaking, reading, or listening | L3 pp. 210–215 |
| L.3.4 | Determine or clarify the meaning of unknown and multiple-meaning words and phrases, choosing flexibly from an array of strategies | L4 pp. 216–221 |
| L.3.5 | Demonstrate understanding of figurative language, word relationships, and nuances in word meanings | L5 pp. 222–227 |
| L.3.6 | Acquire and use accurately general academic, and domain-specific words and phrases | L6 pp. 228–233 |
| **Reading History/Social Studies** | | |
| RH.1.1 | Cite textual evidence to support analysis of primary and secondary sources | R1 pp. 6–11 |
| RH.1.2 | Determine the central ideas or information of a primary or secondary source; provide an objective summary | R2 pp. 12–19 |
| RH.1.3 | Identify key steps in a text's description of a process related to history/social studies | R3 pp. 20–25 |
| RH.2.4 | Determine the meaning of words and phrases as they are used in a text, including vocabulary specific to history/social studies | R4 pp. 26–33 |
| RH.2.5 | Describe how a text presents information | R5 pp. 34–39 |
| RH.2.6 | Identify aspects of a text that reveal an author's point of view or purpose | R6 pp. 40–47 |
| RH.3.7 | Integrate visual information with other information in print and digital texts | R7 pp. 48–55 |
| RH.3.8 | Distinguish among fact, opinion, and reasoned judgment in a text | R8 pp. 56–63 |
| RH.3.9 | Analyze the relationship between a primary and secondary source on the same topic | R9 pp. 64–71 |
| RH.4.10 | Read and comprehend history/social studies texts of appropriate complexity independently with proficiency | R10 pp. 72–77 |
| **Reading Science/Technical Subjects** | | |
| RST.1.1 | Cite textual evidence to support analysis of science and technical texts | R1 pp. 6–11 |
| RST.1.2 | Determine the central ideas or conclusions of a text; provide an objective summary | R2 pp. 12–19 |
| RST.1.3 | Follow precisely a multistep procedure when carrying out experiments, taking measurements, or performing technical tasks | R3 pp. 20–25 |
| RST.2.4 | Determine the meaning of symbols, key terms, and other domain-specific words and phrases | R4 pp. 26–33 |
| RST.2.5 | Analyze the structure an author uses to organize a text, including how the major sections contribute to the whole | R5 pp. 34–39 |
| RST.2.6 | Analyze the author's purpose in providing an explanation, describing a procedure, or discussing an experiment | R6 pp. 40–47 |
| RST.3.7 | Integrate quantitative or technical information expressed in words with a version of the information expressed visually | R7 pp. 48–55 |
| RST.3.8 | Distinguish among facts, reasoned judgment based on research findings, and speculation in a text | R8 pp. 56–63 |
| RST.3.9 | Compare and contrast the information gained from experiments, simulations, video, or multimedia sources with that gained from reading a text on the same topic | R9 pp. 64–71 |
| RST.4.10 | Read and comprehend appropriately complex science/technical texts independently and proficiently | R10 pp. 72–77 |
| **Writing History/Social Studies, Science and Technical Subjects** | | |
| WHST.1.1 | Write arguments based on discipline-specific content | W1 pp. 82–89 |
| WHST.1.2 | Write informative/explanatory texts including the narration of historical events, scientific procedures/experiments, or technical processes | W2 pp. 90–99 |
| WHST.1.3 | NA | |

| Florida Strand/Standard | Focus of Florida Standard | For More Information |
|---|---|---|
| **Writing History/Social Studies, Science and Technical Subjects** | | |
| WHST.2.4 | Produce writing in which the development, organization, and style are appropriate to the task, purpose, and audience | W4 pp. 110–115 |
| WHST.2.5 | Develop and strengthen writing as needed by planning, revising, editing, rewriting, or trying a new approach | W5 pp. 116–121 |
| WHST.2.6 | Use technology to produce and publish writing as well as to interact with others; demonstrate keyboarding skills | W6 pp. 122–127 |
| WHST.3.7 | Conduct short research projects to answer a question, drawing on several sources and refocusing the inquiry when appropriate | W7 pp. 128–133 |
| WHST.3.8 | Gather information from print and digital sources; assess the credibility of sources; quote or paraphrase while avoiding plagiarism and providing basic bibliographic information | W8 pp. 134–139 |
| WHST.3.9 | Draw evidence from informational texts to support analysis, reflection, and research | W9 pp. 140–147 |
| WHST.4.10 | Write routinely over extended and shorter time frames for a range of tasks, purposes, and audiences | W10 pp. 148–153 |

# Florida, Grade 8

| Florida Strand/Standard | Focus of Florida Standard | For More Information |
|---|---|---|
| **Reading Literature** | | |
| RL.1.1 | Cite the textual evidence that most strongly supports an analysis of what the text says explicitly as well as inferences drawn from the text | R1 pp. 6–11 |
| RL.1.2 | Determine the theme or central idea of a text and analyze its development, including its relationship to the characters, setting, and plot; provide an objective summary of the text | R2 pp. 12–19 |
| RL.1.3 | Analyze how particular lines of dialogue or incidents in a story or drama propel the action, reveal aspects of a character, or provoke a decision | R3 pp. 20–25 |
| RL.2.4 | Determine the meaning of words and phrases as they are used in a text, including figurative and connotative meanings | R4 pp. 26–33 |
| RL.2.5 | Compare and contrast the structure of two or more texts and analyze how the differing structure of each contributes to its meaning and style | R5 pp. 34–39 |
| RL.2.6 | Analyze how differences in the points of view of the characters and the audience or reader create such effects as suspense or humor | R6 pp. 40–47 |
| RL.3.7 | Analyze the extent to which a filmed or live production of a story or drama stays faithful or departs from the text or script | R7 pp. 48–55 |
| RL.3.8 | NA | |
| RL.3.9 | Analyze how a modern work of fiction draws on themes, patterns of events, or character types from traditional stories, describing how the material is rendered new | R9 pp. 64–71 |
| RL.4.10 | Read and comprehend literature of appropriate complexity independently with proficiency | R10 pp. 72–77 |
| **Reading Informational Text** | | |
| RI.1.1 | Cite the textual evidence that most strongly supports an analysis of what the text says explicitly as well as inferences drawn from the text | R1 pp. 6–11 |
| RI.1.2 | Determine the central idea of a text and analyze its development, including its relationship to supporting ideas; provide an objective summary of the text | R2 pp. 12–19 |
| RI.1.3 | Analyze how a text makes connections among distinctions between individuals, ideas, or events | R3 pp. 20–25 |
| RI.2.4 | Determine the meaning of words and phrases as they are used in a text, including figurative, connotative, and technical meanings | R4 pp. 26–33 |
| RI.2.5 | Analyze the structure of a specific paragraph in a text, including the role of particular sentences in developing and refining a key concept | R5 pp. 34–39 |
| RI.2.6 | Determine an author's point of view or purpose in a text and analyze how the author acknowledges and responds to conflicting evidence or viewpoints | R6 pp. 40–47 |

*(Continued)*

| Florida Strand/Standard | Focus of Florida Standard | For More Information |
|---|---|---|
| **Reading Informational Text** | | |
| RI.3.7 | Evaluate the advantages and disadvantages of using different mediums to present a particular topic or idea | R7 pp. 48–55 |
| RI.3.8 | Delineate and evaluate the argument and specific claims in a text, assessing whether the reason is sound and the evidence is relevant and sufficient | R8 pp. 56–63 |
| RI.3.9 | Analyze a case in which two or more texts provide conflicting information on the same topic | R9 pp. 64–71 |
| RI.4.10 | Read and comprehend appropriately complex literary nonfiction, informational, and functional texts independently and proficiently | R10 pp. 72–77 |
| **Writing** | | |
| W.1.1 | Write arguments to support claims with clear reasons and relevant evidence | W1 pp. 82–89 |
| W.1.2 | Write informative/explanatory texts to examine a topic and convey ideas, concepts, and information clearly | W2 pp. 90–99 |
| W.1.3 | Write narratives to develop real or imagined experiences or events using effective technique, descriptive details, and well-structured event sequences | W3 pp. 100–109 |
| W.2.4 | Produce writing in which the development, organization, and style are appropriate to the task, purpose, and audience | W4 pp. 110–115 |
| W.2.5 | Develop and strengthen writing as needed by planning, revising, editing, rewriting, or trying a new approach | W5 pp. 116–121 |
| W.2.6 | Use technology to produce and publish writing, link to and cite sources; interact and collaborate with others | W6 pp. 122–127 |
| W.3.7 | Conduct short research projects to answer a question, drawing on several sources and generating additional related questions for further investigation | W7 pp. 128–133 |
| W.3.8 | Gather information from print and digital sources; assess the credibility of sources; quote or paraphrase while avoiding plagiarism and following a standard format for citation | W8 pp. 134–139 |
| W.3.9 | Draw evidence from literary or informational texts to support analysis, reflection, and research | W9 pp. 140–147 |
| W.4.10 | Write routinely over extended and shorter time frames for a range of tasks, purposes, and audiences | W10 pp. 148–153 |
| **Speaking and Listening** | | |
| SL.1.1 | Engage effectively in a range of collaborative discussions with diverse partners, building on others' ideas and expressing their own clearly | SL1 pp. 158–163 |
| SL.1.2 | Analyze the purpose of information presented in diverse media and formats and evaluate the motives behind its presentation | SL2 pp. 164–169 |
| SL.1.3 | Delineate a speaker's argument and specific claims evaluating the soundness of the reasoning and the relevance and sufficiency of the evidence and identifying when irrelevant evidence is introduced | SL3 pp. 170–175 |
| SL.2.4 | Present claims and findings, emphasizing salient points in a focused coherent manner; use appropriate eye contact, adequate volume, and clear pronunciation | SL4 pp. 176–181 |
| SL.2.5 | Integrate multimedia and visual displays into presentations to clarify information, strengthen claims and findings, and add interest | SL5 pp. 182–187 |
| SL.2.6 | Adapt speech to a variety of contexts and tasks, demonstrating command of formal English when appropriate | SL6 pp. 188–193 |
| **Language** | | |
| L.1.1 | Demonstrate command of the conventions of standard English grammar and usage when writing or speaking | L1 pp. 198–203 |
| L.1.2 | Demonstrate command of the conventions of standard English capitalization, punctuation, and spelling when writing | L2 pp. 204–209 |
| L.2.3 | Use knowledge of language and its conventions when writing, speaking, reading, or listening | L3 pp. 210–215 |
| L.3.4 | Determine or clarify the meaning of unknown and multiple-meaning words and phrases, choosing flexibly from an array of strategies | L4 pp. 216–221 |
| L.3.5 | Demonstrate understanding of figurative language, word relationships, and nuances in word meanings | L5 pp. 222–227 |
| L.3.6 | Acquire and use accurately general academic, and domain-specific words and phrases | L6 pp. 228–233 |

| Florida Strand/Standard | Focus of Florida Standard | For More Information |
|---|---|---|
| **Reading History/Social Studies** | | |
| RH.1.1 | Cite textual evidence to support analysis of primary and secondary sources | R1 pp. 6–11 |
| RH.1.2 | Determine the central ideas or information of a primary or secondary source; provide an objective summary | R2 pp. 12–19 |
| RH.1.3 | Identify key steps in a text's description of a process related to history/social studies | R3 pp. 20–25 |
| RH.2.4 | Determine the meaning of words and phrases as they are used in a text, including vocabulary specific to history/social studies | R4 pp. 26–33 |
| RH.2.5 | Describe how a text presents information | R5 pp. 34–39 |
| RH.2.6 | Identify aspects of a text that reveal an author's point of view or purpose | R6 pp. 40–47 |
| RH.3.7 | Integrate visual information with other information in print and digital texts | R7 pp. 48–55 |
| RH.3.8 | Distinguish among fact, opinion, and reasoned judgment in a text | R8 pp. 56–63 |
| RH.3.9 | Analyze the relationship between a primary and secondary source on the same topic | R9 pp. 64–71 |
| RH.4.10 | Read and comprehend history/social studies texts of appropriate complexity independently with proficiency | R10 pp. 72–77 |
| **Reading Science/Technical Subjects** | | |
| RST.1.1 | Cite textual evidence to support analysis of science and technical texts | R1 pp. 6–11 |
| RST.1.2 | Determine the central ideas or conclusions of a text; provide an objective summary | R2 pp. 12–19 |
| RST.1.3 | Follow precisely a multistep procedure when carrying out experiments, taking measurements, or performing technical tasks | R3 pp. 20–25 |
| RST.2.4 | Determine the meaning of symbols, key terms, and other domain-specific words and phrases | R4 pp. 26–33 |
| RST.2.5 | Analyze the structure an author uses to organize a text, including how the major sections contribute to the whole | R5 pp. 34–39 |
| RST.2.6 | Analyze the author's purpose in providing an explanation, describing a procedure, or discussing an experiment | R6 pp. 40–47 |
| RST.3.7 | Integrate quantitative or technical information expressed in words with a version of the information expressed visually | R7 pp. 48–55 |
| RST.3.8 | Distinguish among facts, reasoned judgment based on research findings, and speculation in a text | R8 pp. 56–63 |
| RST.3.9 | Compare and contrast the information gained from experiments, simulations, video, or multimedia sources with that gained from reading a text on the same topic | R9 pp. 64–71 |
| RST.4.10 | Read and comprehend appropriately complex science/technical texts independently and proficiently | R10 pp. 72–77 |
| **Writing History/Social Studies, Science and Technical Subjects** | | |
| WHST.1.1 | Write arguments based on discipline-specific content | W1 pp. 82–89 |
| WHST.1.2 | Write informative/explanatory texts including the narration of historical events, scientific procedures/experiments, or technical processes | W2 pp. 90–99 |
| WHST.1.3 | NA | |
| WHST.2.4 | Produce writing in which the development, organization, and style are appropriate to the task, purpose, and audience | W4 pp. 110–115 |
| WHST.2.5 | Develop and strengthen writing as needed by planning, revising, editing, rewriting, or trying a new approach | W5 pp. 116–121 |
| WHST.2.6 | Use technology to produce and publish writing as well as to interact with others; demonstrate keyboarding skills | W6 pp. 122–127 |
| WHST.3.7 | Conduct short research projects to answer a question, drawing on several sources and refocusing the inquiry when appropriate | W7 pp. 128–133 |
| WHST.3.8 | Gather information from print and digital sources; assess the credibility of sources; quote or paraphrase while avoiding plagiarism and providing basic bibliographic information | W8 pp. 134–139 |
| WHST.3.9 | Draw evidence from informational texts to support analysis, reflection, and research | W9 pp. 140–147 |
| WHST.4.10 | Write routinely over extended and shorter time frames for a range of tasks, purposes, and audiences | W10 pp. 148–153 |

# Georgia, Grade 6

| Georgia Strand/Standard | Focus of Georgia Standard | For More Information |
|---|---|---|
| **Reading Literature** | | |
| RL.1 | Cite textual evidence to support analysis of what the text says explicitly as well as inferences drawn from the text | R1 pp. 6–11 |
| RL.2 | Determine a theme of a text and how it is conveyed through particular details; provide an objective summary | R2 pp. 12–19 |
| RL.3 | Describe how a particular plot unfolds in a series of episodes as well as how the characters respond or change | R3 pp. 20–25 |
| RL.4 | Determine the meaning of words and phrases as they are used in a text, including figurative and connotative meanings | R4 pp. 26–33 |
| RL.5 | Analyze how a particular sentence, chapter, scene, or stanza fits into the overall structure of a text and contributes to the development of the theme, setting, or plot | R5 pp. 34–39 |
| RL.6 | Explain how an author develops the point of view of the narrator or speaker in a text | R6 pp. 40–47 |
| RL.7 | Compare and contrast the experience of reading a story, drama, or poem to listening to or viewing an audio, video, or live version of the text | R7 pp. 48–55 |
| RL.8 | NA | |
| RL.9 | Compare and contrast texts in different forms or genres in terms of their approaches to similar themes and topics | R9 pp. 64–71 |
| RL.10 | Read and comprehend literature of appropriate complexity independently with proficiency | R10 pp. 72–77 |
| **Reading Informational Text** | | |
| RI.1 | Cite textual evidence to support analysis of what the text says explicitly as well as inferences drawn from the text | R1 pp. 6–11 |
| RI.2 | Determine a central idea of a text and how it is conveyed through particular details; provide an objective summary | R2 pp. 12–19 |
| RI.3 | Analyze in detail how a key individual, event, or idea is introduced, illustrated, and elaborated in a text | R3 pp. 20–25 |
| RI.4 | Determine the meaning of words and phrases as they are used in a text, including figurative, connotative, and technical meanings | R4 pp. 26–33 |
| RI.5 | Analyze how a particular sentence, chapter, scene, or section fits into the overall structure of a text and contributes to the development of the ideas | R5 pp. 34–39 |
| RI.6 | Determine an author's point of view or purpose in a text and explain how it is conveyed in the text | R6 pp. 40–47 |
| RI.7 | Integrate information presented in different media or formats as well as in words to develop a coherent understanding of a topic or issue | R7 pp. 48–55 |
| RI.8 | Trace and evaluate the argument and specific claims that are supported by reasons and evidence from claims that are not | R8 pp. 56–63 |
| RI.9 | Compare and contrast one author's presentation of events with that of another | R9 pp. 64–71 |
| RI.10 | Read and comprehend appropriately complex literary nonfiction, informational, and functional texts independently and proficiently | R10 pp. 72–77 |
| **Writing** | | |
| W.1 | Write arguments to support claims with clear reasons and relevant evidence | W1 pp. 82–89 |
| W.2 | Write informative/explanatory texts to examine a topic and convey ideas, concepts, and information clearly | W2 pp. 90–99 |
| W.3 | Write narratives to develop real or imagined experiences or events using effective technique, descriptive details, and well-structured event sequences | W3 pp. 100–109 |
| W.4 | Produce writing in which the development, organization, and style are appropriate to the task, purpose, and audience | W4 pp. 110–115 |
| W.5 | Develop and strengthen writing as needed by planning, revising, editing, rewriting, or trying a new approach | W5 pp. 116–121 |
| W.6 | Use technology to produce and publish writing as well as to interact with others | W6 pp. 122–127 |
| W.7 | Conduct short research projects to answer a question, drawing on several sources and refocusing the inquiry when appropriate | W7 pp. 128–133 |

| Georgia Strand/Standard | Focus of Georgia Standard | For More Information |
|---|---|---|
| **Writing** | | |
| W.8 | Gather information from print and digital sources; assess the credibility of sources; quote or paraphrase while avoiding plagiarism and providing basic bibliographic information | W8 pp. 134–139 |
| W.9 | Draw evidence from literary or informational texts to support analysis, reflection, and research | W9 pp. 140–147 |
| W.10 | Write routinely over extended and shorter time frames for a range of tasks, purposes, and audiences | W10 pp. 148–153 |
| **Speaking and Listening** | | |
| SL.1 | Engage effectively in a range of collaborative discussions with diverse partners, building on others' ideas and expressing their own clearly | SL1 pp. 158–163 |
| SL.2 | Interpret information presented in diverse media and formats and explain how it contributes to a topic, text, or issue under study | SL2 pp. 164–169 |
| SL.3 | Delineate a speaker's argument and specific claims that are supported by reasons and evidence from claims that are not | SL3 pp. 170–175 |
| SL.4 | Present claims and findings, sequencing ideas logically and using descriptions, facts, or details to accentuate main ideas or themes; use appropriate eye contact, adequate volume, and clear pronunciation | SL4 pp. 176–181 |
| SL.5 | Include multimedia components and visual displays in presentations to clarify information | SL5 pp. 182–187 |
| SL.6 | Adapt speech to a variety of contexts and tasks, demonstrating command of formal English when appropriate | SL6 pp. 188–193 |
| **Language** | | |
| L.1 | Demonstrate command of the conventions of standard English grammar and usage when writing or speaking | L1 pp. 198–203 |
| L.2 | Demonstrate command of the conventions of standard English capitalization, punctuation, and spelling when writing | L2 pp. 204–209 |
| L.3 | Use knowledge of language and its conventions when writing, speaking, reading, or listening | L3 pp. 210–215 |
| L.4 | Determine or clarify the meaning of unknown and multiple-meaning words and phrases, choosing flexibly from an array of strategies | L4 pp. 216–221 |
| L.5 | Demonstrate understanding of figurative language, word relationships, and nuances in word meanings | L5 pp. 222–227 |
| L.6 | Acquire and use accurately general academic, and domain-specific words and phrases | L6 pp. 228–233 |
| **Reading History/Social Studies** | | |
| RH.1 | Cite textual evidence to support analysis of primary and secondary sources | R1 pp. 6–11 |
| RH.2 | Determine the central ideas or information of a primary or secondary source; provide an objective summary | R2 pp. 12–19 |
| RH.3 | Identify key steps in a text's description of a process related to history/social studies | R3 pp. 20–25 |
| RH.4 | Determine the meaning of words and phrases as they are used in a text, including vocabulary specific to history/social studies | R4 pp. 26–33 |
| RH.5 | Describe how a text presents information | R5 pp. 34–39 |
| RH.6 | Identify aspects of a text that reveal an author's point of view or purpose | R6 pp. 40–47 |
| RH.7 | Integrate visual information with other information in print and digital texts | R7 pp. 48–55 |
| RH.8 | Distinguish among fact, opinion, and reasoned judgment in a text | R8 pp. 56–63 |
| RH.9 | Analyze the relationship between a primary and secondary source on the same topic | R9 pp. 64–71 |
| RH.10 | Read and comprehend history/social studies texts of appropriate complexity independently with proficiency | R10 pp. 72–77 |
| **Reading Science/Technical Subjects** | | |
| RST.1 | Cite textual evidence to support analysis of science and technical texts | R1 pp. 6–11 |
| RST.2 | Determine the central ideas or conclusions of a text; provide an objective summary | R2 pp. 12–19 |
| RST.3 | Follow precisely a multistep procedure when carrying out experiments, taking measurements, or performing technical tasks | R3 pp. 20–25 |
| RST.4 | Determine the meaning of symbols, key terms, and other domain-specific words and phrases | R4 pp. 26–33 |

*(Continued)*

| Georgia Strand/Standard | Focus of Georgia Standard | For More Information |
|---|---|---|
| **Reading Science/Technical Subjects** | | |
| RST.5 | Analyze the structure an author uses to organize a text, including how the major sections contribute to the whole | R5 pp. 34–39 |
| RST.6 | Analyze the author's purpose in providing an explanation, describing a procedure, or discussing an experiment | R6 pp. 40–47 |
| RST.7 | Integrate quantitative or technical information expressed in words with a version of the information expressed visually | R7 pp. 48–55 |
| RST.8 | Distinguish among facts, reasoned judgment based on research findings, and speculation in a text | R8 pp. 56–63 |
| RST.9 | Compare and contrast the information gained from experiments, simulations, video, or multimedia sources with that gained from reading a text on the same topic | R9 pp. 64–71 |
| RST.10 | Read and comprehend appropriately complex science/technical texts independently and proficiently | R10 pp. 72–77 |
| **Writing History/Social Studies and Science/Technical Subjects** | | |
| WHST.1 | Write arguments based on discipline-specific content | W1 pp. 82–89 |
| WHST.2 | Write informative/explanatory texts including the narration of historical events, scientific procedures/experiments, or technical processes | W2 pp. 90–99 |
| WHST.3 | NA | |
| WHST.4 | Produce writing in which the development, organization, and style are appropriate to the task, purpose, and audience | W4 pp. 110–115 |
| WHST.5 | Develop and strengthen writing as needed by planning, revising, editing, rewriting, or trying a new approach | W5 pp. 116–121 |
| WHST.6 | Use technology to produce and publish writing as well as to interact with others; demonstrate keyboarding skills | W6 pp. 122–127 |
| WHST.7 | Conduct short research projects to answer a question, drawing on several sources and refocusing the inquiry when appropriate | W7 pp. 128–133 |
| WHST.8 | Gather information from print and digital sources; assess the credibility of sources; quote or paraphrase while avoiding plagiarism and providing basic bibliographic information | W8 pp. 134–139 |
| WHST.9 | Draw evidence from informational texts to support analysis, reflection, and research | W9 pp. 140–147 |
| WHST.10 | Write routinely over extended and shorter time frames for a range of tasks, purposes, and audiences | W10 pp. 148–153 |

# Georgia, Grade 7

| Georgia Strand/Standard | Focus of Georgia Standard | For More Information |
|---|---|---|
| **Reading Literature** | | |
| RL.1 | Cite several pieces of textual evidence to support analysis of what the text says explicitly as well as inferences drawn from the text | R1 pp. 6–11 |
| RL.2 | Determine a theme of a text and analyze its development; provide an objective summary of the text | R2 pp. 12–19 |
| RL.3 | Analyze how particular elements of a story or drama interact | R3 pp. 20–25 |
| RL.4 | Determine the meaning of words and phrases as they are used in a text, including figurative and connotative meanings | R4 pp. 26–33 |
| RL.5 | Analyze how a drama's or poem's form or structure contributes to its meaning | R5 pp. 34–39 |
| RL.6 | Analyze how an author develops and contrasts the points of view of different characters or narrators in a text | R6 pp. 40–47 |
| RL.7 | Compare and contrast a written story, drama, or poem to its audio, filmed, staged, or multimedia version | R7 pp. 48–55 |
| RL.8 | NA | |
| RL.9 | Compare and contrast a fictional portrayal of a time, place, or character and a historical account of the same period | R9 pp. 64–71 |
| RL.10 | Read and comprehend literature of appropriate complexity independently with proficiency | R10 pp. 72–77 |

| Georgia Strand/Standard | Focus of Georgia Standard | For More Information |
|---|---|---|
| **Reading Informational Text** | | |
| RI.1 | Cite several pieces of textual evidence to support analysis of what the text says explicitly as well as inferences drawn from the text | R1 pp. 6–11 |
| RI.2 | Determine two or more central ideas in a text and analyze their developments; provide an objective summary of the text | R2 pp. 12–19 |
| RI.3 | Analyze the interactions between individuals, events, and ideas in a text | R3 pp. 20–25 |
| RI.4 | Determine the meaning of words and phrases as they are used in a text, including figurative, connotative, and technical meanings | R4 pp. 26–33 |
| RI.5 | Analyze the structure an author uses to organize a text, including how the major sections contribute to the whole | R5 pp. 34–39 |
| RI.6 | Determine an author's point of view or purpose in a text and analyze how the author distinguishes his or her position from that of others | R6 pp. 40–47 |
| RI.7 | Compare and contrast a text to an audio, video, or multimedia version of the text | R7 pp. 48–55 |
| RI.8 | Trace and evaluate the argument and specific claims in a text, assessing whether the reason is sound and the evidence is relevant and sufficient | R8 pp. 56–63 |
| RI.9 | Analyze how two or more authors writing about the same topic shape their presentations of key information | R9 pp. 64–71 |
| RI.10 | Read and comprehend appropriately complex literary nonfiction, informational, and functional texts independently and proficiently | R10 pp. 72–77 |
| **Writing** | | |
| W.1 | Write arguments to support claims with clear reasons and relevant evidence | W1 pp. 82–89 |
| W.2 | Write informative/explanatory texts to examine a topic and convey ideas, concepts, and information clearly | W2 pp. 90–99 |
| W.3 | Write narratives to develop real or imagined experiences or events using effective technique, descriptive details, and well-structured event sequences | W3 pp. 100–109 |
| W.4 | Produce writing in which the development, organization, and style are appropriate to the task, purpose, and audience | W4 pp. 110–115 |
| W.5 | Develop and strengthen writing as needed by planning, revising, editing, rewriting, or trying a new approach | W5 pp. 116–121 |
| W.6 | Use technology to produce and publish writing, link to and cite sources; interact and collaborate with others | W6 pp. 122–127 |
| W.7 | Conduct short research projects to answer a question, drawing on several sources and generating additional related questions for further investigation | W7 pp. 128–133 |
| W.8 | Gather information from print and digital sources; assess the credibility of sources; quote or paraphrase while avoiding plagiarism and following a standard format for citation | W8 pp. 134–139 |
| W.9 | Draw evidence from literary or informational texts to support analysis, reflection, and research | W9 pp. 140–147 |
| W.10 | Write routinely over extended and shorter time frames for a range of tasks, purposes, and audiences | W10 pp. 148–153 |
| **Speaking and Listening** | | |
| SL.1 | Engage effectively in a range of collaborative discussions with diverse partners, building on others' ideas and expressing their own clearly | SL1 pp. 158–163 |
| SL.2 | Analyze the main ideas and supporting details presented in diverse media and formats and explain how the ideas clarify a topic, text, or issue under study | SL2 pp. 164–169 |
| SL.3 | Delineate a speaker's argument and specific claims evaluating the soundness of the reasoning and the relevance and sufficiency of the evidence | SL3 pp. 170–175 |
| SL.4 | Present claims and findings, emphasizing salient points in a focused coherent manner; use appropriate eye contact, adequate volume, and clear pronunciation | SL4 pp. 176–181 |
| SL.5 | Include multimedia components and visual displays in presentations to clarify claims and findings | SL5 pp. 182–187 |
| SL.6 | Adapt speech to a variety of contexts and tasks, demonstrating command of formal English when appropriate | SL6 pp. 188–193 |

*(Continued)*

| Georgia Strand/Standard | Focus of Georgia Standard | For More Information |
|---|---|---|
| **Language** | | |
| L.1 | Demonstrate command of the conventions of standard English grammar and usage when writing or speaking | L1 pp. 198–203 |
| L.2 | Demonstrate command of the conventions of standard English capitalization, punctuation, and spelling when writing | L2 pp. 204–209 |
| L.3 | Use knowledge of language and its conventions when writing, speaking, reading, or listening | L3 pp. 210–215 |
| L.4 | Determine or clarify the meaning of unknown and multiple-meaning words and phrases, choosing flexibly from an array of strategies | L4 pp. 216–221 |
| L.5 | Demonstrate understanding of figurative language, word relationships, and nuances in word meanings | L5 pp. 222–227 |
| L.6 | Acquire and use accurately general academic, and domain-specific words and phrases | L6 pp. 228–233 |
| **Reading History/Social Studies** | | |
| RH.1 | Cite textual evidence to support analysis of primary and secondary sources | R1 pp. 6–11 |
| RH.2 | Determine the central ideas or information of a primary or secondary source; provide an objective summary | R2 pp. 12–19 |
| RH.3 | Identify key steps in a text's description of a process related to history/social studies | R3 pp. 20–25 |
| RH.4 | Determine the meaning of words and phrases as they are used in a text, including vocabulary specific to history/social studies | R4 pp. 26–33 |
| RH.5 | Describe how a text presents information | R5 pp. 34–39 |
| RH.6 | Identify aspects of a text that reveal an author's point of view or purpose | R6 pp. 40–47 |
| RH.7 | Integrate visual information with other information in print and digital texts | R7 pp. 48–55 |
| RH.8 | Distinguish among fact, opinion, and reasoned judgment in a text | R8 pp. 56–63 |
| RH.9 | Analyze the relationship between a primary and secondary source on the same topic | R9 pp. 64–71 |
| RH.10 | Read and comprehend history/social studies texts of appropriate complexity independently with proficiency | R10 pp. 72–77 |
| **Reading Science/Technical Subjects** | | |
| RST.1 | Cite textual evidence to support analysis of science and technical texts | R1 pp. 6–11 |
| RST.2 | Determine the central ideas or conclusions of a text; provide an objective summary | R2 pp. 12–19 |
| RST.3 | Follow precisely a multistep procedure when carrying out experiments, taking measurements, or performing technical tasks | R3 pp. 20–25 |
| RST.4 | Determine the meaning of symbols, key terms, and other domain-specific words and phrases | R4 pp. 26–33 |
| RST.5 | Analyze the structure an author uses to organize a text, including how the major sections contribute to the whole | R5 pp. 34–39 |
| RST.6 | Analyze the author's purpose in providing an explanation, describing a procedure, or discussing an experiment | R6 pp. 40–47 |
| RST.7 | Integrate quantitative or technical information expressed in words with a version of the information expressed visually | R7 pp. 48–55 |
| RST.8 | Distinguish among facts, reasoned judgment based on research findings, and speculation in a text | R8 pp. 56–63 |
| RST.9 | Compare and contrast the information gained from experiments, simulations, video, or multimedia sources with that gained from reading a text on the same topic | R9 pp. 64–71 |
| RST.10 | Read and comprehend appropriately complex science/technical texts independently and proficiently | R10 pp. 72–77 |
| **Writing History/Social Studies and Science/Technical Subjects** | | |
| WHST.1 | Write arguments based on discipline-specific content | W1 pp. 82–89 |
| WHST.2 | Write informative/explanatory texts including the narration of historical events, scientific procedures/experiments, or technical processes | W2 pp. 90–99 |
| WHST.3 | NA | |
| WHST.4 | Produce writing in which the development, organization, and style are appropriate to the task, purpose, and audience | W4 pp. 110–115 |
| WHST.5 | Develop and strengthen writing as needed by planning, revising, editing, rewriting, or trying a new approach | W5 pp. 116–121 |
| WHST.6 | Use technology to produce and publish writing as well as to interact with others; demonstrate keyboarding skills | W6 pp. 122–127 |

| Georgia Strand/Standard | Focus of Georgia Standard | For More Information |
|---|---|---|
| **Writing History/Social Studies and Science/Technical Subjects** | | |
| WHST.7 | Conduct short research projects to answer a question, drawing on several sources and refocusing the inquiry when appropriate | W7 pp. 128–133 |
| WHST.8 | Gather information from print and digital sources; assess the credibility of sources; quote or paraphrase while avoiding plagiarism and providing basic bibliographic information | W8 pp. 134–139 |
| WHST.9 | Draw evidence from informational texts to support analysis, reflection, and research | W9 pp. 140–147 |
| WHST.10 | Write routinely over extended and shorter time frames for a range of tasks, purposes, and audiences | W10 pp. 148–153 |

# Georgia, Grade 8

| Georgia Strand/Standard | Focus of Georgia Standard | For More Information |
|---|---|---|
| **Reading Literature** | | |
| RL.1 | Cite the textual evidence that most strongly supports an analysis of what the text says explicitly as well as inferences drawn from the text | R1 pp. 6–11 |
| RL.2 | Determine a theme and/or central idea of a text and analyze its development, including its relationship to the characters, setting, and plot; provide an objective summary of the text | R2 pp. 12–19 |
| RL.3 | Analyze how particular lines of dialogue or incidents in a story or drama propel the action, reveal aspects of a character, or provoke a decision | R3 pp. 20–25 |
| RL.4 | Determine the meaning of words and phrases as they are used in a text, including figurative and connotative meanings | R4 pp. 26–33 |
| RL.5 | Compare and contrast the structure of two or more texts and analyze how the differing structure of each contributes to its meaning and style | R5 pp. 34–39 |
| RL.6 | Analyze how differences in the points of view of the characters and the audience or reader create such effects as suspense or humor | R6 pp. 40–47 |
| RL.7 | Analyze the extent to which a filmed or live production of a story or drama stays faithful or departs from the text or script | R7 pp. 48–55 |
| RL.8 | NA | |
| RL.9 | Analyze how a modern work of fiction draws on themes, patterns of events, or character types from traditional stories, describing how the material is rendered new | R9 pp. 64–71 |
| RL.10 | Read and comprehend literature of appropriate complexity independently with proficiency | R10 pp. 72–77 |
| **Reading Informational Text** | | |
| RI.1 | Cite the textual evidence that most strongly supports an analysis of what the text says explicitly as well as inferences drawn from the text | R1 pp. 6–11 |
| RI.2 | Determine the central idea of a text and analyze its development, including its relationship to supporting ideas; provide an objective summary of the text | R2 pp. 12–19 |
| RI.3 | Analyze how a text makes connections among distinctions between individuals, ideas, or events | R3 pp. 20–25 |
| RI.4 | Determine the meaning of words and phrases as they are used in a text, including figurative, connotative, and technical meanings | R4 pp. 26–33 |
| RI.5 | Analyze the structure of a specific paragraph in a text, including the role of particular sentences in developing and refining a key concept | R5 pp. 34–39 |
| RI.6 | Determine an author's point of view or purpose in a text and analyze how the author acknowledges and responds to conflicting evidence or viewpoints | R6 pp. 40–47 |
| RI.7 | Evaluate the advantages and disadvantages of using different mediums to present a particular topic or idea | R7 pp. 48–55 |
| RI.8 | Delineate and evaluate the argument and specific claims in a text, assessing whether the reason is sound and the evidence is relevant and sufficient | R8 pp. 56–63 |
| RI.9 | Analyze a case in which two or more texts provide conflicting information on the same topic | R9 pp. 64–71 |
| RI.10 | Read and comprehend appropriately complex literary nonfiction, informational, and functional texts independently and proficiently | R10 pp. 72–77 |

*(Continued)*

| Georgia Strand/Standard | Focus of Georgia Standard | For More Information |
|---|---|---|
| **Writing** | | |
| W.1 | Write arguments to support claims with clear reasons and relevant evidence | W1 pp. 82–89 |
| W.2 | Write informative/explanatory texts to examine a topic and convey ideas, concepts, and information clearly | W2 pp. 90–99 |
| W.3 | Write narratives to develop real or imagined experiences or events using effective technique, descriptive details, and well-structured event sequences | W3 pp. 100–109 |
| W.4 | Produce writing in which the development, organization, and style are appropriate to the task, purpose, and audience | W4 pp. 110–115 |
| W.5 | Develop and strengthen writing as needed by planning, revising, editing, rewriting, or trying a new approach | W5 pp. 116–121 |
| W.6 | Use technology to produce and publish writing, link to and cite sources; interact and collaborate with others | W6 pp. 122–127 |
| W.7 | Conduct short research projects to answer a question, drawing on several sources and generating additional related questions for further investigation | W7 pp. 128–133 |
| W.8 | Gather information from print and digital sources; assess the credibility of sources; quote or paraphrase while avoiding plagiarism and following a standard format for citation | W8 pp. 134–139 |
| W.9 | Draw evidence from literary or informational texts to support analysis, reflection, and research | W9 pp. 140–147 |
| W.10 | Write routinely over extended and shorter time frames for a range of tasks, purposes, and audiences | W10 pp. 148–153 |
| **Speaking and Listening** | | |
| SL.1 | Engage effectively in a range of collaborative discussions with diverse partners, building on others' ideas and expressing their own clearly | SL1 pp. 158–163 |
| SL.2 | Analyze the purpose of information presented in diverse media and formats and evaluate the motives behind its presentation | SL2 pp. 164–169 |
| SL.3 | Delineate a speaker's argument and specific claims evaluating the soundness of the reasoning and the relevance and sufficiency of the evidence and identifying when irrelevant evidence is introduced | SL3 pp. 170–175 |
| SL.4 | Present claims and findings, emphasizing salient points in a focused coherent manner; use appropriate eye contact, adequate volume, and clear pronunciation | SL4 pp. 176–181 |
| SL.5 | Integrate multimedia components and visual displays into presentations to clarify information, strengthen claims and findings, and add interest | SL5 pp. 182–187 |
| SL.6 | Adapt speech to a variety of contexts and tasks, demonstrating command of formal English when appropriate | SL6 pp. 188–193 |
| **Language** | | |
| L.1 | Demonstrate command of the conventions of standard English grammar and usage when writing or speaking | L1 pp. 198–203 |
| L.2 | Demonstrate command of the conventions of standard English capitalization, punctuation, and spelling when writing | L2 pp. 204–209 |
| L.3 | Use knowledge of language and its conventions when writing, speaking, reading, or listening | L3 pp. 210–215 |
| L.4 | Determine or clarify the meaning of unknown and multiple-meaning words and phrases, choosing flexibly from an array of strategies | L4 pp. 216–221 |
| L.5 | Demonstrate understanding of figurative language, word relationships, and nuances in word meanings | L5 pp. 222–227 |
| L.6 | Acquire and use accurately general academic, and domain-specific words and phrases | L6 pp. 228–233 |
| **Reading History/Social Studies** | | |
| RH.1 | Cite textual evidence to support analysis of primary and secondary sources | R1 pp. 6–11 |
| RH.2 | Determine the central ideas or information of a primary or secondary source; provide an objective summary | R2 pp. 12–19 |

| Georgia Strand/Standard | Focus of Georgia Standard | For More Information |
|---|---|---|
| **Reading History/Social Studies** | | |
| RH.3 | Identify key steps in a text's description of a process related to history/social studies | R3 pp. 20–25 |
| RH.4 | Determine the meaning of words and phrases as they are used in a text, including vocabulary specific to history/social studies | R4 pp. 26–33 |
| RH.5 | Describe how a text presents information | R5 pp. 34–39 |
| RH.6 | Identify aspects of a text that reveal an author's point of view or purpose | R6 pp. 40–47 |
| RH.7 | Integrate visual information with other information in print and digital texts | R7 pp. 48–55 |
| RH.8 | Distinguish among fact, opinion, and reasoned judgment in a text | R8 pp. 56–63 |
| RH.9 | Analyze the relationship between a primary and secondary source on the same topic | R9 pp. 64–71 |
| RH.10 | Read and comprehend history/social studies texts of appropriate complexity independently with proficiency | R10 pp. 72–77 |
| **Reading Science/Technical Subjects** | | |
| RST.1 | Cite textual evidence to support analysis of science and technical texts | R1 pp. 6–11 |
| RST.2 | Determine the central ideas or conclusions of a text; provide an objective summary | R2 pp. 12–19 |
| RST.3 | Follow precisely a multistep procedure when carrying out experiments, taking measurements, or performing technical tasks | R3 pp. 20–25 |
| RST.4 | Determine the meaning of symbols, key terms, and other domain-specific words and phrases | R4 pp. 26–33 |
| RST.5 | Analyze the structure an author uses to organize a text, including how the major sections contribute to the whole | R5 pp. 34–39 |
| RST.6 | Analyze the author's purpose in providing an explanation, describing a procedure, or discussing an experiment | R6 pp. 40–47 |
| RST.7 | Integrate quantitative or technical information expressed in words with a version of the information expressed visually | R7 pp. 48–55 |
| RST.8 | Distinguish among facts, reasoned judgment based on research findings, and speculation in a text | R8 pp. 56–63 |
| RST.9 | Compare and contrast the information gained from experiments, simulations, video, or multimedia sources with that gained from reading a text on the same topic | R9 pp. 64–71 |
| RST.10 | Read and comprehend appropriately complex science/technical texts independently and proficiently | R10 pp. 72–77 |
| **Writing History/Social Studies and Science/Technical Subjects** | | |
| WHST.1 | Write arguments based on discipline-specific content | W1 pp. 82–89 |
| WHST.2 | Write informative/explanatory texts including the narration of historical events, scientific procedures/experiments, or technical processes | W2 pp. 90–99 |
| WHST.3 | NA | |
| WHST.4 | Produce writing in which the development, organization, and style are appropriate to the task, purpose, and audience | W4 pp. 110–115 |
| WHST.5 | Develop and strengthen writing as needed by planning, revising, editing, rewriting, or trying a new approach | W5 pp. 116–121 |
| WHST.6 | Use technology to produce and publish writing as well as to interact with others; demonstrate keyboarding skills | W6 pp. 122–127 |
| WHST.7 | Conduct short research projects to answer a question, drawing on several sources and refocusing the inquiry when appropriate | W7 pp. 128–133 |
| WHST.8 | Gather information from print and digital sources; assess the credibility of sources; quote or paraphrase while avoiding plagiarism and providing basic bibliographic information | W8 pp. 134–139 |
| WHST.9 | Draw evidence from informational texts to support analysis, reflection, and research | W9 pp. 140–147 |
| WHST.10 | Write routinely over extended and shorter time frames for a range of tasks, purposes, and audiences | W10 pp. 148–153 |

# Indiana, Grade 6

| Indiana Strand/Standard | Focus of Indiana Standard | For More Information |
|---|---|---|
| **Reading Literature** | | |
| RL.1 | Read and comprehend literature of appropriate complexity independently with proficiency | R10 pp. 72–77 |
| RL.2.1 | Cite textual evidence to support analysis of what the text says explicitly as well as inferences drawn from the text | R1 pp. 6–11 |
| RL.2.2 | Determine how the theme or central idea of a text is conveyed through particular details; provide an objective summary | R2 pp. 12–19 |
| RL.2.3 | Explain how a plot unfolds in a series of episodes as well as how the characters respond or change | R3 pp. 20–25 |
| RL.3.1 | Analyze how a particular sentence, chapter, scene, or stanza fits into the overall structure of a text and contributes to the development of the theme, setting, or plot | R5 pp. 34–39 |
| RL.3.2 | Explain how an author develops the point of view of the narrator or speaker in a text | R6 pp. 40–47 |
| RL.4.1 | Compare and contrast the experience of reading a story, drama, or poem to listening to or viewing an audio, video, or live version of the text | R7 pp. 48–55 |
| RL.4.2 | Compare and contrast works of literature in different forms or genres in terms of their approaches to similar themes and topics | R9 pp. 64–71 |
| **Reading Nonfiction** | | |
| RN.1 | Read and comprehend appropriately complex literary nonfiction, informational, and functional texts independently and proficiently | R10 pp. 72–77 |
| RN.2.1 | Cite textual evidence to support analysis of what the text says explicitly as well as inferences drawn from the text | R1 pp. 6–11 |
| RN.2.2 | Determine how a central idea of a text is conveyed through particular details; provide an objective summary | R2 pp. 12–19 |
| RN.2.3 | Analyze in detail how a key individual, event, or idea is introduced, illustrated, and elaborated in a text | R3 pp. 20–25 |
| RN.3.2 | Analyze how a particular sentence, chapter, scene, or section fits into the overall structure of a text and contributes to the development of the ideas | R5 pp. 34–39 |
| RN.3.3 | Determine an author's perspective or purpose in a text and explain how it is conveyed in the text | R6 pp. 40–47 |
| RN.4.1 | Trace and evaluate the argument and specific claims, distinguishing claims that are supported by reasons and evidence from claims that are not | R8 pp. 56–63 |
| RN.4.2 | Integrate information presented in different media or formats as well as in words to develop a coherent understanding of a topic or issue | R7 pp. 48–55 |
| RN.4.3 | Compare and contrast one author's presentation of events with that of another | R9 pp. 64–71 |
| **Reading Vocabulary** | | |
| RV.1 | Acquire and use accurately general academic, and domain-specific words and phrases | L6 pp. 228–233 |
| RV.2.1 | Use context to determine or clarify the meaning of unknown and multiple-meaning words and phrases | L4 pp. 216–221 |
| RV.2.2 | Use the relationship between particular words to better understand each of the words | L5 pp. 222–227 |
| RV.2.3 | Distinguish among the connotations of words with similar denotations | L5 pp. 222–227 |
| RV.2.4 | Use common Greek or Latin affixes and roots as clues to the meaning of a word | L4 pp. 216–221 |
| RV.2.5 | Consult reference materials to find the pronunciation of a word or determine or clarify its meaning | L4 pp. 216–221 |
| RV.3.1 | Determine the meaning of words and phrases as they are used in literature, including figurative and connotative meanings | R4 pp. 26–33 |
| RV.3.2 | Determine the meaning of words and phrases as they are used in a nonfiction text, including figurative, connotative, and technical meanings | R4 pp. 26–33 |
| RV.3.3 | Interpret figures of speech in context | L5 pp. 222–227 |
| **Writing** | | |
| W.1 | Write routinely over extended and shorter time frames for a range of tasks, purposes, and audiences | W10 pp. 148–153 |
| W.3.1 | Write arguments to support claims with clear reasons and relevant evidence | W1 pp. 82–89 |

| Indiana Strand/Standard | Focus of Indiana Standard | For More Information |
|---|---|---|
| **Writing** | | |
| W.3.2 | Write informative/explanatory texts to examine a topic and convey ideas, concepts, and information clearly | W2 pp. 90–99 |
| W.3.3 | Write narratives to develop real or imagined experiences or events using effective technique, descriptive details, and well-structured event sequences | W3 pp. 100–109 |
| W.4 | Apply the writing process to develop, draft, revise, rewrite, try a new approach, and edit to produce writing that is clear and coherent; use technology to produce, publish, and update writing | W5 pp. 116–121 W6 pp. 122–127 |
| W.5 | Conduct research assignments to build knowledge about the process and the topics | W7 pp. 128–133 W8 pp. 134–139 |
| W.6.1 | Demonstrate command of the conventions of standard English grammar and usage | L1 pp. 198–203 |
| W.6.2 | Demonstrate command of the conventions of standard English capitalization, punctuation, and spelling | L2 pp. 204–209 |
| **Speaking and Listening** | | |
| SL.1 | Listen actively and adjust the use of spoken language to communicate effectively with a variety of audiences and for a variety of purposes | SL6 pp. 188–193 |
| SL.2.1 | Engage effectively in a range of collaborative discussions with diverse partners, building on others' ideas and expressing their own clearly | SL1 pp. 158–163 |
| SL.2.2 | Elaborate and reflect on ideas under discussion by identifying specific evidence | SL1 pp. 158–163 |
| SL.2.3 | Follow rules for considerate discussions | SL1 pp. 158–163 |
| SL.2.4 | Pose and respond to questions by making comments that contribute to the discussion | SL1 pp. 158–163 |
| SL.2.5 | Demonstrate understanding of multiple perspectives through reflection and paraphrasing | SL1 pp. 158–163 |
| SL.3.1 | Interpret information presented in diverse media and formats and explain how it contributes to a topic, text, or issue under study | SL2 pp. 164–169 |
| SL.3.2 | Delineate a speaker's argument and specific claims that are supported by reasons and evidence from claims that are not | SL3 pp. 170–175 |
| SL.4.1 | Present claims and findings, sequencing ideas logically and using descriptions, facts, or details to accentuate main ideas or themes; use appropriate eye contact, adequate volume, and clear pronunciation | SL4 pp. 176–181 |
| SL.4.2 | Include multimedia components and visual displays in presentations to clarify information | SL5 pp. 182–187 |
| **History/Social Studies** | | |
| LH.1.1 | Read and comprehend history/social studies texts of appropriate complexity | R10 pp. 72–77 |
| LH.1.2 | Write routinely for a range of discipline-specific tasks, purposes, and audiences | W10 pp. 148–153 |
| LH.2.1 | Cite textual evidence to support analysis of primary and secondary sources | R1 pp. 6–11 |
| LH.2.2 | Determine the central ideas or information of a primary or secondary source; provide an objective summary | R2 pp. 12–19 |
| LH.2.3 | Identify key steps in a text's description of a process related to history/social studies | R3 pp. 20–25 |
| LH.3.1 | Determine the meaning of words and phrases, including vocabulary describing political, social, or economic aspects of history/social studies | R4 pp. 26–33 |
| LH.3.2 | Describe how a text presents information | R5 pp. 34–39 |
| LH.3.3 | Identify aspects of a text that reveal an author's point of view or purpose | R6 pp. 40–47 |
| LH.4.1 | Integrate visual information with other information in print and digital texts | R7 pp. 48–55 |
| LH.4.2 | Distinguish among fact, opinion, and reasoned judgment in a text | R8 pp. 56–63 |
| LH.4.3 | Analyze the relationship between a primary and secondary source on the same topic | R9 pp. 64–71 |
| LH.5.1 | Write arguments based on discipline-specific content | W1 pp. 82–89 |
| LH.5.2 | Write informative/explanatory texts including the narration of historical events, scientific procedures/experiments, or technical processes | W2 pp. 90–99 |
| LH.6.1 | Produce clear and coherent writing in which the development, organization, and style are appropriate to task, purpose, and audience; develop and strengthen writing as needed by planning, revising, editing, rewriting, or trying a new approach | W4 pp. 110–115 W5 pp. 116–121 |

(Continued)

| Indiana Strand/Standard | Focus of Indiana Standard | For More Information |
|---|---|---|
| **History/Social Studies** | | |
| LH.6.2 | Use technology to produce and publish writing as well as to interact with others; demonstrate keyboarding skills | W6 pp. 122–127 |
| LH.7.1 | Conduct short research projects to answer a question, drawing on several sources and refocusing the inquiry when appropriate | W7 pp. 128–133 |
| LH.7.2 | Gather information from print and digital sources; assess the credibility of sources; quote or paraphrase while avoiding plagiarism and providing basic bibliographic information | W8 pp. 134–139 |
| LH.7.3 | Draw evidence from informational texts to support analysis, reflection, and research | W9 pp. 140–147 |
| **Science/Technical Subjects** | | |
| LST.1.1 | Read and comprehend science/technical texts of appropriate complexity | R10 pp. 72–77 |
| LST.1.2 | Write routinely for a range of discipline-specific tasks, purposes, and audiences | W10 pp. 148–153 |
| LST.2.1 | Cite textual evidence to support analysis of science and technical texts | R1 pp. 6–11 |
| LST.2.2 | Determine the central ideas or conclusions of a text; provide an objective summary | R2 pp. 12–19 |
| LST.2.3 | Follow precisely a multistep procedure when carrying out experiments, taking measurements, or performing technical tasks | R3 pp. 20–25 |
| LST.3.1 | Determine the meaning of symbols, key terms, and other domain-specific words and phrases | R4 pp. 26–33 |
| LST.3.2 | Analyze the structure an author uses to organize a text, including how the major sections contribute to the whole | R5 pp. 34–39 |
| LST.3.3 | Analyze the author's purpose in providing an explanation, describing a procedure, or discussing an experiment | R6 pp. 40–47 |
| LST.4.1 | Integrate quantitative or technical information expressed in words with a version of the information expressed visually | R7 pp. 48–55 |
| LST.4.2 | Distinguish among facts, reasoned judgment based on research findings, and speculation in a text | R8 pp. 56–63 |
| LST.4.3 | Compare and contrast the information gained from experiments, simulations, video, or multimedia sources with that gained from reading a text on the same topic | R9 pp. 64–71 |
| LST.5.1 | Write arguments focused on discipline-specific content | W1 pp. 82–89 |
| LST.5.2 | Write informative/explanatory texts including the narration of historical events, scientific procedures/experiments, or technical processes | W2 pp. 90–99 |
| LST.6.1 | Produce clear and coherent writing in which the development, organization, and style are appropriate to task, purpose, and audience; develop and strengthen writing as needed by planning, revising, editing, rewriting, or trying a new approach | W4 pp. 110–115 W5 pp. 116–121 |
| LST.6.2 | Use technology to produce and publish writing as well as to interact with others; demonstrate keyboarding skills | W6 pp. 122–127 |
| LST.7.1 | Conduct short research projects to answer a question, drawing on several sources and refocusing the inquiry when appropriate | W7 pp. 128–133 |
| LST.7.2 | Gather information from print and digital sources; assess the credibility of sources; quote or paraphrase while avoiding plagiarism and providing basic bibliographic information | W8 pp. 134–139 |
| LST.7.3 | Draw evidence from informational texts to support analysis, reflection, and research | W9 pp. 140–147 |

# Indiana, Grade 7

| Indiana Strand/Standard | Focus of Indiana Standard | For More Information |
|---|---|---|
| **Reading Literature** | | |
| RL.1 | Read and comprehend literature of appropriate complexity independently with proficiency | R10 pp. 72–77 |
| RL.2.1 | Cite several pieces of textual evidence to support analysis of what the text says explicitly as well as inferences drawn from the text | R1 pp. 6–11 |
| RL.2.2 | Analyze the development of the theme or central idea of a text; provide a detailed summary of the text | R2 pp. 12–19 |
| RL.2.3 | Analyze the interaction of elements in a work of literature | R3 pp. 20–25 |

| Indiana Strand/Standard | Focus of Indiana Standard | For More Information |
|---|---|---|
| **Reading Literature** | | |
| RL.3.1 | Analyze how a work of literature's structural elements contribute to its meaning and plot | R5 pp. 34–39 |
| RL.3.2 | Analyze how an author develops and contrasts the points of view of different characters or narrators in a text | R6 pp. 40–47 |
| RL.4.1 | Compare and contrast a written story, drama, or poem to its audio, filmed, staged, or multimedia version | R7 pp. 48–55 |
| RL.4.2 | Compare and contrast a fictional portrayal of a time, place, or character and a historical account of the same period | R9 pp. 64–71 |
| **Reading Nonfiction** | | |
| RN.1 | Read and comprehend appropriately complex literary nonfiction, informational, and functional texts independently and proficiently | R10 pp. 72–77 |
| RN.2.1 | Cite several pieces of textual evidence to support analysis of what the text says explicitly as well as inferences drawn from the text | R1 pp. 6–11 |
| RN.2.2 | Analyze the development of two or more central ideas in a text; provide a detailed objective summary of the text | R2 pp. 12–19 |
| RN.2.3 | Analyze the interactions between individuals, events, and ideas in a text | R3 pp. 20–25 |
| RN.3.2 | Analyze the structure an author uses to organize a text, including how the major sections contribute to the whole | R5 pp. 34–39 |
| RN.3.3 | Determine an author's perspective or purpose in a text and analyze how the author distinguishes his or her position from that of others | R6 pp. 40–47 |
| RN.4.1 | Trace and evaluate the argument and specific claims in a text, assessing whether the reason is sound and the evidence is relevant and sufficient | R8 pp. 56–63 |
| RN.4.2 | Compare and contrast a text to an audio, video, or multimedia version of the text | R7 pp. 48–55 |
| RN.4.3 | Analyze how two or more authors writing about the same topic shape their presentations of key information | R9 pp. 64–71 |
| **Reading Vocabulary** | | |
| RV.1 | Acquire and use accurately general academic, and domain-specific words and phrases | L6 pp. 228–233 |
| RV.2.1 | Use context to determine or clarify the meaning of words and phrases | L4 pp. 216–221 |
| RV.2.2 | Use the relationship between particular words to better understand each of the words | L5 pp. 222–227 |
| RV.2.3 | Distinguish among the connotations of words with similar denotations | L5 pp. 222–227 |
| RV.2.4 | Use common Greek or Latin affixes and roots as clues to the meaning of a word | L4 pp. 216–221 |
| RV.2.5 | Consult reference materials to find the pronunciation of a word or determine or clarify its meaning | L4 pp. 216–221 |
| RV.3.1 | Determine the meaning of words and phrases as they are used in literature, including figurative and connotative meanings | R4 pp. 26–33 |
| RV.3.2 | Determine the meaning of words and phrases as they are used in a nonfiction text, including figurative, connotative, and technical meanings | R4 pp. 26–33 |
| RV.3.3 | Interpret figures of speech in context | L5 pp. 222–227 |
| **Writing** | | |
| W.1 | Write routinely over extended and shorter time frames for a range of tasks, purposes, and audiences | W10 pp. 148–153 |
| W.3.1 | Write arguments to support claims with clear reasons and relevant evidence | W1 pp. 82–89 |
| W.3.2 | Write informative/explanatory texts to examine a topic and convey ideas, concepts, and information clearly | W2 pp. 90–99 |
| W.3.3 | Write narratives to develop real or imagined experiences or events using effective technique, descriptive details, and well-structured event sequences | W3 pp. 100–109 |
| W.4 | Apply the writing process to develop, draft, revise, rewrite, try a new approach, and edit to produce writing that is clear and coherent; use technology to produce, publish, and update writing | W5 pp. 116–121 W6 pp. 122–127 |
| W.5 | Conduct research assignments to build knowledge about the process and the topics | W7 pp. 128–133 W8 pp. 134–139 |
| W.6.1 | Demonstrate command of the conventions of standard English grammar and usage | L1 pp. 198–203 |
| W.6.2 | Demonstrate command of the conventions of standard English capitalization, punctuation, and spelling | L2 pp. 204–209 |

*(Continued)*

| Indiana Strand/Standard | Focus of Indiana Standard | For More Information |
|---|---|---|
| **Speaking and Listening** | | |
| SL.1 | Listen actively and adjust the use of spoken language to communicate effectively with a variety of audiences and for a variety of purposes | SL6 pp. 188–193 |
| SL.2.1 | Engage effectively in a range of collaborative discussions with diverse partners, building on others' ideas and expressing their own clearly | SL1 pp. 158–163 |
| SL.2.2 | Elaborate and reflect on ideas under discussion by identifying specific evidence | SL1 pp. 158–163 |
| SL.2.3 | Follow rules for considerate discussions | SL1 pp. 158–163 |
| SL.2.4 | Pose questions that elicit elaboration and respond to questions with relevant observations and ideas | SL1 pp. 158–163 |
| SL.2.5 | Acknowledge new information expressed by others and consider it in relation to one's own views | SL1 pp. 158–163 |
| SL.3.1 | Analyze the main ideas and supporting details presented in diverse media and formats and explain how it contributes to a topic, text, or issue under study | SL2 pp. 164–169 |
| SL.3.2 | Delineate a speaker's argument and specific claims, evaluating the soundness of the reasoning and the relevance and sufficiency of the evidence | SL3 pp. 170–175 |
| SL.4.1 | Present claims and findings, emphasizing salient points in a focused coherent manner; use appropriate eye contact, adequate volume, and clear pronunciation | SL4 pp. 176–181 |
| SL.4.2 | Include multimedia components and visual displays in presentations to clarify claims and findings and emphasize salient points | SL5 pp. 182–187 |
| **History/Social Studies** | | |
| LH.1.1 | Read and comprehend history/social studies texts of appropriate complexity | R10 pp. 72–77 |
| LH.1.2 | Write routinely for a range of discipline-specific tasks, purposes, and audiences | W10 pp. 148–153 |
| LH.2.1 | Cite textual evidence to support analysis of primary and secondary sources | R1 pp. 6–11 |
| LH.2.2 | Determine the central ideas or information of a primary or secondary source; provide an objective summary | R2 pp. 12–19 |
| LH.2.3 | Identify key steps in a text's description of a process related to history/social studies | R3 pp. 20–25 |
| LH.3.1 | Determine the meaning of words and phrases, including vocabulary describing political, social, or economic aspects of history/social studies | R4 pp. 26–33 |
| LH.3.2 | Describe how a text presents information | R5 pp. 34–39 |
| LH.3.3 | Identify aspects of a text that reveal an author's point of view or purpose | R6 pp. 40–47 |
| LH.4.1 | Integrate visual information with other information in print and digital texts | R7 pp. 48–55 |
| LH.4.2 | Distinguish among fact, opinion, and reasoned judgment in a text | R8 pp. 56–63 |
| LH.4.3 | Compare and contrast treatments of the same topic in a primary and secondary source | R9 pp. 64–71 |
| LH.5.1 | Write arguments based on discipline-specific content | W1 pp. 82–89 |
| LH.5.2 | Write informative texts including analyses of historical events | W2 pp. 90–99 |
| LH.6.1 | Produce clear and coherent writing using appropriate reference materials; strengthen writing as needed by planning, revising, editing, rewriting, or trying a new approach | W4 pp. 110–115 W5 pp. 116–121 |
| LH.6.2 | Use technology to produce and publish writing and present the relationship between information and ideas clearly and efficiently | W6 pp. 122–127 |
| LH.7.1 | Conduct short research projects to answer a question, drawing on several sources and refocusing the inquiry when appropriate | W7 pp. 128–133 |
| LH.7.2 | Gather information from multiple sources; assess the credibility of sources; quote or paraphrase while avoiding plagiarism and providing basic bibliographic information | W8 pp. 134–139 |
| LH.7.3 | Draw evidence from informational texts to support analysis, reflection, and research | W9 pp. 140–147 |
| **Science/Technical Subjects** | | |
| LST.1.1 | Read and comprehend science/technical texts of appropriate complexity | R10 pp. 72–77 |
| LST.1.2 | Write routinely for a range of discipline-specific tasks, purposes, and audiences | W10 pp. 148–153 |
| LST.2.1 | Cite textual evidence to support analysis of science and technical texts | R1 pp. 6–11 |
| LST.2.2 | Determine the central ideas or conclusions of a text; provide an objective summary | R2 pp. 12–19 |
| LST.2.3 | Follow precisely a multistep procedure when carrying out experiments, taking measurements, or performing technical tasks | R3 pp. 20–25 |

| Indiana Strand/Standard | Focus of Indiana Standard | For More Information |
|---|---|---|
| **Science/Technical Subjects** | | |
| LST.3.1 | Determine the meaning of symbols, key terms, and other domain-specific words and phrases | R4 pp. 26–33 |
| LST.3.2 | Analyze the structure an author uses to organize a text, including how the major sections contribute to the whole | R5 pp. 34–39 |
| LST.3.3 | Analyze the author's purpose in providing an explanation, describing a procedure, or discussing an experiment | R6 pp. 40–47 |
| LST.4.1 | Integrate quantitative or technical information expressed in words with a version of the information expressed visually | R7 pp. 48–55 |
| LST.4.2 | Distinguish among facts, reasoned judgment based on research findings, and speculation in a text | R8 pp. 56–63 |
| LST.4.3 | Compare and contrast the information gained from experiments, simulations, video, or multimedia sources with that gained from reading a text on the same topic | R9 pp. 64–71 |
| LST.5.1 | Write arguments focused on discipline-specific content | W1 pp. 82–89 |
| LST.5.2 | Write informative texts including scientific procedures/experiments, or technical processes | W2 pp. 90–99 |
| LST.6.1 | Produce clear and coherent writing using appropriate reference materials; strengthen writing as needed by planning, revising, editing, rewriting, or trying a new approach | W4 pp. 110–115 W5 pp. 116–121 |
| LST.6.2 | Use technology to produce and publish writing and present the relationship between information and ideas clearly and efficiently | W6 pp. 122–127 |
| LST.7.1 | Conduct short research projects to answer a question, drawing on several sources and refocusing the inquiry when appropriate | W7 pp. 128–133 |
| LST.7.2 | Gather information from multiple sources; assess the credibility of sources; quote or paraphrase while avoiding plagiarism and providing basic bibliographic information | W8 pp. 134–139 |
| LST.7.3 | Draw evidence from informational texts to support analysis, reflection, and research | W9 pp. 140–147 |

# Indiana, Grade 8

| Indiana Strand/Standard | Focus of Indiana Standard | For More Information |
|---|---|---|
| **Reading Literature** | | |
| RL.1 | Read and comprehend literature of appropriate complexity independently with proficiency | R10 pp. 72–77 |
| RL.2.1 | Cite the textual evidence that most strongly supports an analysis of what the text says explicitly as well as inferences drawn from the text | R1 pp. 6–11 |
| RL.2.2 | Analyze the development of the theme or central idea of a work of literature, including its relationship to the characters, setting, and plot; provide an objective summary of the text | R2 pp. 12–19 |
| RL.2.3 | Analyze how particular lines of dialogue or incidents in a story or drama propel the action, reveal aspects of a character, or provoke a decision | R3 pp. 20–25 |
| RL.3.1 | Compare and contrast the structure of two or more related texts and analyze how the differing structure of each contributes to its meaning and style | R5 pp. 34–39 |
| RL.3.2 | Analyze a particular point of view or cultural experience in a work of world literature | R6 pp. 40–47 |
| RL.4.1 | Analyze the extent to which a filmed or live production of a story or drama stays faithful or departs from the text or script | R7 pp. 48–55 |
| RL.4.2 | Analyze how works of literature draw on and transform earlier texts | R9 pp. 64–71 |
| **Reading Nonfiction** | | |
| RN.1 | Read and comprehend appropriately complex literary nonfiction, informational, and functional texts independently and proficiently | R10 pp. 72–77 |
| RN.2.1 | Cite the textual evidence that most strongly supports an analysis of what the text says explicitly as well as inferences drawn from the text | R1 pp. 6–11 |
| RN.2.2 | Analyze the development of the central idea of a text, including its relationship to supporting ideas; provide an objective summary of the text | R2 pp. 12–19 |

*(Continued)*

| Indiana Strand/Standard | Focus of Indiana Standard | For More Information |
|---|---|---|
| **Reading Nonfiction** | | |
| RN.2.3 | Analyze how a text makes connections among distinctions between individuals, ideas, or events | R3 pp. 20–25 |
| RN.3.2 | Analyze the structure of a specific paragraph in a text, including the role of particular sentences in developing and refining a key concept | R5 pp. 34–39 |
| RN.3.3 | Determine an author's point of view or purpose in a text and analyze how the author acknowledges and responds to conflicting evidence or viewpoints | R6 pp. 40–47 |
| RN.4.1 | Delineate and evaluate the argument and specific claims in a text, assessing whether the reason is sound and the evidence is relevant and sufficient | R8 pp. 56–63 |
| RN.4.2 | Evaluate the advantages and disadvantages of using different mediums to present a particular topic or idea | R7 pp. 48–55 |
| RN.4.3 | Analyze a case in which two or more texts provide conflicting information on the same topic | R9 pp. 64–71 |
| **Reading Vocabulary** | | |
| RV.1 | Acquire and use accurately general academic, and domain-specific words and phrases | L6 pp. 228–233 |
| RV.2.1 | Use context to determine or clarify the meaning of words and phrases | L4 pp. 216–221 |
| RV.2.2 | Use the relationship between particular words to better understand each of the words | L5 pp. 222–227 |
| RV.2.3 | Distinguish among the connotations of words with similar denotations | L5 pp. 222–227 |
| RV.2.4 | Use common Greek or Latin affixes and roots as clues to the meaning of a word | L4 pp. 216–221 |
| RV.2.5 | Select appropriate reference materials to find the pronunciation of a word or determine or clarify its meaning | L4 pp. 216–221 |
| RV.3.1 | Analyze the meaning of words and phrases as they are used in literature, including figurative and connotative meanings | R4 pp. 26–33 |
| RV.3.2 | Determine the meaning of words and phrases as they are used in a nonfiction text, including figurative, connotative, and technical meanings | R4 pp. 26–33 |
| RV.3.3 | Interpret figures of speech in context | L5 pp. 222–227 |
| **Writing** | | |
| W.1 | Write routinely over extended and shorter time frames for a range of tasks, purposes, and audiences | W10 pp. 148–153 |
| W.3.1 | Write arguments to support claims with clear reasons and relevant evidence | W1 pp. 82–89 |
| W.3.2 | Write informative/explanatory texts to examine a topic and convey ideas, concepts, and information clearly | W2 pp. 90–99 |
| W.3.3 | Write narratives to develop real or imagined experiences or events using effective technique, descriptive details, and well-structured event sequences | W3 pp. 100–109 |
| W.4 | Apply the writing process to develop, draft, revise, rewrite, try a new approach, and edit to produce writing that is clear and coherent; use technology to produce, publish, and update writing | W5 pp. 116–121 W6 pp. 122–127 |
| W.5 | Conduct research assignments to build knowledge about the process and the topics | W7 pp. 128–133 W8 pp. 134–139 |
| W.6.1 | Demonstrate command of the conventions of standard English grammar and usage | L1 pp. 198–203 |
| W.6.2 | Demonstrate command of the conventions of standard English capitalization, punctuation, and spelling | L2 pp. 204–209 |
| **Speaking and Listening** | | |
| SL.1 | Listen actively and adjust the use of spoken language to communicate effectively with a variety of audiences and for a variety of purposes | SL6 pp. 188–193 |
| SL.2.1 | Engage effectively in a range of collaborative discussions with diverse partners, building on others' ideas and expressing their own clearly | SL1 pp. 158–163 |
| SL.2.2 | Elaborate and reflect on ideas under discussion by identifying specific evidence | SL1 pp. 158–163 |
| SL.2.3 | Follow rules for considerate discussions and decision-making | SL1 pp. 158–163 |
| SL.2.4 | Pose questions that connect the ideas of several speakers and respond to questions with relevant observations and ideas | SL1 pp. 158–163 |
| SL.2.5 | Acknowledge new information expressed by others and consider it in relation to one's own views | SL1 pp. 158–163 |
| SL.3.1 | Analyze the purpose of information presented in diverse media and formats and evaluate the motives behind its presentation | SL2 pp. 164–169 |

| Indiana Strand/Standard | Focus of Indiana Standard | For More Information |
|---|---|---|
| **Speaking and Listening** | | |
| SL.3.2 | Delineate a speaker's argument and specific claims, evaluating the soundness of the reasoning and the relevance and sufficiency of the evidence | SL3 pp. 170–175 |
| SL.4.1 | Present claims and findings, emphasizing salient points in a focused coherent manner; use appropriate eye contact, adequate volume, and clear pronunciation | SL4 pp. 176–181 |
| SL.4.2 | Integrate multimedia components and visual displays in presentations to clarify claims and findings and emphasize salient points | SL5 pp. 182–187 |
| **History/Social Studies** | | |
| LH.1.1 | Read and comprehend history/social studies texts of appropriate complexity | R10 pp. 72–77 |
| LH.1.2 | Write routinely for a range of discipline-specific tasks, purposes, and audiences | W10 pp. 148–153 |
| LH.2.1 | Cite textual evidence to support analysis of primary and secondary sources | R1 pp. 6–11 |
| LH.2.2 | Determine the central ideas or information of a primary or secondary source; provide an objective summary | R2 pp. 12–19 |
| LH.2.3 | Identify key steps in a text's description of a process related to history/social studies | R3 pp. 20–25 |
| LH.3.1 | Determine the meaning of words and phrases, including vocabulary describing political, social, or economic aspects of history/social studies | R4 pp. 26–33 |
| LH.3.2 | Describe how a text presents information | R5 pp. 34–39 |
| LH.3.3 | Identify aspects of a text that reveal an author's point of view or purpose | R6 pp. 40–47 |
| LH.4.1 | Integrate visual information with other information in print and digital texts | R7 pp. 48–55 |
| LH.4.2 | Distinguish among fact, opinion, and reasoned judgment in a text | R8 pp. 56–63 |
| LH.4.3 | Compare and contrast treatments of the same topic in a primary and secondary source | R9 pp. 64–71 |
| LH.5.1 | Write arguments based on discipline-specific content | W1 pp. 82–89 |
| LH.5.2 | Write informative texts including analyses of historical events | W2 pp. 90–99 |
| LH.6.1 | Produce clear and coherent writing using appropriate reference materials; strengthen writing as needed by planning, revising, editing, rewriting, or trying a new approach | W4 pp. 110–115 W5 pp. 116–121 |
| LH.6.2 | Use technology to produce and publish writing and present the relationship between information and ideas clearly and efficiently | W6 pp. 122–127 |
| LH.7.1 | Conduct short research projects to answer a question, drawing on several sources and refocusing the inquiry when appropriate | W7 pp. 128–133 |
| LH.7.2 | Gather information from multiple sources; assess the credibility of sources; quote or paraphrase while avoiding plagiarism and providing basic bibliographic information | W8 pp. 134–139 |
| LH.7.3 | Draw evidence from informational texts to support analysis, reflection, and research | W9 pp. 140–147 |
| **Science/Technical Subjects** | | |
| LST.1.1 | Read and comprehend science/technical texts of appropriate complexity | R10 pp. 72–77 |
| LST.1.2 | Write routinely for a range of discipline-specific tasks, purposes, and audiences | W10 pp. 148–153 |
| LST.2.1 | Cite textual evidence to support analysis of science and technical texts | R1 pp. 6–11 |
| LST.2.2 | Determine the central ideas or conclusions of a text; provide an objective summary | R2 pp. 12–19 |
| LST.2.3 | Follow precisely a multistep procedure when carrying out experiments, taking measurements, or performing technical tasks | R3 pp. 20–25 |
| LST.3.1 | Determine the meaning of symbols, key terms, and other domain-specific words and phrases | R4 pp. 26–33 |
| LST.3.2 | Analyze the structure an author uses to organize a text, including how the major sections contribute to the whole | R5 pp. 34–39 |
| LST.3.3 | Analyze the author's purpose in providing an explanation, describing a procedure, or discussing an experiment | R6 pp. 40–47 |
| LST.4.1 | Integrate quantitative or technical information expressed in words with a version of the information expressed visually | R7 pp. 48–55 |
| LST.4.2 | Distinguish among facts, reasoned judgment based on research findings, and speculation in a text | R8 pp. 56–63 |

*(Continued)*

| Indiana Strand/Standard | Focus of Indiana Standard | For More Information |
|---|---|---|
| **Science/Technical Subjects** | | |
| LST.4.3 | Compare and contrast the information gained from experiments, simulations, video, or multimedia sources with that gained from reading a text on the same topic | R9 pp. 64–71 |
| LST.5.1 | Write arguments focused on discipline-specific content | W1 pp. 82–89 |
| LST.5.2 | Write informative texts including scientific procedures/experiments, or technical processes | W2 pp. 90–99 |
| LST.6.1 | Produce clear and coherent writing using appropriate reference materials; strengthen writing as needed by planning, revising, editing, rewriting, or trying a new approach | W4 pp. 110–115 W5 pp. 116–121 |
| LST.6.2 | Use technology to produce and publish writing and present the relationship between information and ideas clearly and efficiently | W6 pp. 122–127 |
| LST.7.1 | Conduct short research projects to answer a question, drawing on several sources and refocusing the inquiry when appropriate | W7 pp. 128–133 |
| LST.7.2 | Gather information from multiple sources; assess the credibility of sources; quote or paraphrase while avoiding plagiarism and providing basic bibliographic information | W8 pp. 134–139 |
| LST.7.3 | Draw evidence from informational texts to support analysis, reflection, and research | W9 pp. 140–147 |

# Iowa, Grade 6

| Iowa Strand/Standard | Focus of Iowa Standard | For More Information |
|---|---|---|
| **Reading Literature** | | |
| RL.1 | Cite textual evidence to support analysis of what the text says explicitly as well as inferences drawn from the text | R1 pp. 6–11 |
| RL.2 | Determine the theme or central idea of a text and how it is conveyed through particular details; provide an objective summary | R2 pp. 12–19 |
| RL.3 | Describe how a particular plot unfolds in a series of episodes as well as how the characters respond or change | R3 pp. 20–25 |
| RL.4 | Determine the meaning of words and phrases as they are used in a text, including figurative and connotative meanings | R4 pp. 26–33 |
| RL.5 | Analyze how a particular sentence, chapter, scene, or stanza fits into the overall structure of a text and contributes to the development of the theme, setting, or plot | R5 pp. 34–39 |
| RL.6 | Explain how an author develops the point of view of the narrator or speaker in a text | R6 pp. 40–47 |
| RL.7 | Compare and contrast the experience of reading a story, drama, or poem to listening to or viewing an audio, video, or live version of the text | R7 pp. 48–55 |
| RL.8 | NA | |
| RL.9 | Compare and contrast texts in different forms or genres in terms of their approaches to similar themes and topics | R9 pp. 64–71 |
| RL.10 | Read and comprehend literature of appropriate complexity independently with proficiency | R10 pp. 72–77 |
| **Reading Informational Text** | | |
| RI.1 | Cite textual evidence to support analysis of what the text says explicitly as well as inferences drawn from the text | R1 pp. 6–11 |
| RI.2 | Determine a central idea of a text and how it is conveyed through particular details; provide an objective summary | R2 pp. 12–19 |
| RI.3 | Analyze in detail how a key individual, event, or idea is introduced, illustrated, and elaborated in a text | R3 pp. 20–25 |
| RI.4 | Determine the meaning of words and phrases as they are used in a text, including figurative, connotative, and technical meanings | R4 pp. 26–33 |
| RI.5 | Analyze how a particular sentence, chapter, scene, or section fits into the overall structure of a text and contributes to the development of the ideas | R5 pp. 34–39 |
| RI.6 | Determine an author's point of view or purpose in a text and explain how it is conveyed in the text | R6 pp. 40–47 |

| Iowa Strand/Standard | Focus of Iowa Standard | For More Information |
|---|---|---|
| **Reading Informational Text** | | |
| RI.7 | Integrate information presented in different media or formats as well as in words to develop a coherent understanding of a topic or issue | R7 pp. 48–55 |
| RI.8 | Trace and evaluate the argument and specific claims that are supported by reasons and evidence from claims that are not | R8 pp. 56–63 |
| RI.9 | Compare and contrast one author's presentation of events with that of another | R9 pp. 64–71 |
| RI.10 | Read and comprehend appropriately complex literary nonfiction, informational, and functional texts independently and proficiently | R10 pp. 72–77 |
| **Writing** | | |
| W.1 | Write arguments to support claims with clear reasons and relevant evidence | W1 pp. 82–89 |
| W.2 | Write informative/explanatory texts to examine a topic and convey ideas, concepts, and information clearly | W2 pp. 90–99 |
| W.3 | Write narratives to develop real or imagined experiences or events using effective technique, descriptive details, and well-structured event sequences | W3 pp. 100–109 |
| W.4 | Produce writing in which the development, organization, and style are appropriate to the task, purpose, and audience | W4 pp. 110–115 |
| W.5 | Develop and strengthen writing as needed by planning, revising, editing, rewriting, or trying a new approach | W5 pp. 116–121 |
| W.6 | Use technology to produce and publish writing as well as to interact with others; demonstrate keyboarding skills | W6 pp. 122–127 |
| W.7 | Conduct short research projects to answer a question, drawing on several sources and refocusing the inquiry when appropriate | W7 pp. 128–133 |
| W.8 | Gather information from print and digital sources; assess the credibility of sources; quote or paraphrase while avoiding plagiarism and providing basic bibliographic information | W8 pp. 134–139 |
| W.9 | Draw evidence from literary or informational texts to support analysis, reflection, and research | W9 pp. 140–147 |
| W.10 | Write routinely over extended and shorter time frames for a range of tasks, purposes, and audiences | W10 pp. 148–153 |
| **Speaking and Listening** | | |
| SL.1 | Engage effectively in a range of collaborative discussions with diverse partners, building on others' ideas and expressing their own clearly | SL1 pp. 158–163 |
| SL.2 | Interpret information presented in diverse media and formats and explain how it contributes to a topic, text, or issue under study | SL2 pp. 164–169 |
| SL.3 | Delineate a speaker's argument and specific claims that are supported by reasons and evidence from claims that are not | SL3 pp. 170–175 |
| SL.4 | Present claims and findings, sequencing ideas logically and using descriptions, facts, or details to accentuate main ideas or themes; use appropriate eye contact, adequate volume, and clear pronunciation | SL4 pp. 176–181 |
| SL.5 | Include multimedia components and visual displays in presentations to clarify information | SL5 pp. 182–187 |
| SL.6 | Adapt speech to a variety of contexts and tasks, demonstrating command of formal English when appropriate | SL6 pp. 188–193 |
| **Language** | | |
| L.1 | Demonstrate command of the conventions of standard English grammar and usage when writing or speaking | L1 pp. 198–203 |
| L.2 | Demonstrate command of the conventions of standard English capitalization, punctuation, and spelling when writing | L2 pp. 204–209 |
| L.3 | Use knowledge of language and its conventions when writing, speaking, reading, or listening | L3 pp. 210–215 |
| L.4 | Determine or clarify the meaning of unknown and multiple-meaning words and phrases, choosing flexibly from an array of strategies | L4 pp. 216–221 |
| L.5 | Demonstrate understanding of figurative language, word relationships, and nuances in word meanings | L5 pp. 222–227 |
| L.6 | Acquire and use accurately general academic, and domain-specific words and phrases | L6 pp. 228–233 |

*(Continued)*

| Iowa Strand/Standard | Focus of Iowa Standard | For More Information |
|---|---|---|
| **Reading History/Social Studies** | | |
| RH.1 | Cite textual evidence to support analysis of primary and secondary sources | R1 pp. 6–11 |
| RH.2 | Determine the central ideas or information of a primary or secondary source; provide an objective summary | R2 pp. 12–19 |
| RH.3 | Identify key steps in a text's description of a process related to history/social studies | R3 pp. 20–25 |
| RH.4 | Determine the meaning of words and phrases as they are used in a text, including vocabulary specific to history/social studies | R4 pp. 26–33 |
| RH.5 | Describe how a text presents information | R5 pp. 34–39 |
| RH.6 | Identify aspects of a text that reveal an author's point of view or purpose | R6 pp. 40–47 |
| RH.7 | Integrate visual information with other information in print and digital texts | R7 pp. 48–55 |
| RH.8 | Distinguish among fact, opinion, and reasoned judgment in a text | R8 pp. 56–63 |
| RH.9 | Analyze the relationship between a primary and secondary source on the same topic | R9 pp. 64–71 |
| RH.10 | Read and comprehend history/social studies texts of appropriate complexity independently with proficiency | R10 pp. 72–77 |
| **Reading Science/Technical Subjects** | | |
| RST.1 | Cite textual evidence to support analysis of science and technical texts | R1 pp. 6–11 |
| RST.2 | Determine the central ideas or conclusions of a text; provide an objective summary | R2 pp. 12–19 |
| RST.3 | Follow precisely a multistep procedure when carrying out experiments, taking measurements, or performing technical tasks | R3 pp. 20–25 |
| RST.4 | Determine the meaning of symbols, key terms, and other domain-specific words and phrases | R4 pp. 26–33 |
| RST.5 | Analyze the structure an author uses to organize a text, including how the major sections contribute to the whole | R5 pp. 34–39 |
| RST.6 | Analyze the author's purpose in providing an explanation, describing a procedure, or discussing an experiment | R6 pp. 40–47 |
| RST.7 | Integrate quantitative or technical information expressed in words with a version of the information expressed visually | R7 pp. 48–55 |
| RST.8 | Distinguish among facts, reasoned judgment based on research findings, and speculation in a text | R8 pp. 56–63 |
| RST.9 | Compare and contrast the information gained from experiments, simulations, video, or multimedia sources with that gained from reading a text on the same topic | R9 pp. 64–71 |
| RST.10 | Read and comprehend appropriately complex science/technical texts independently and proficiently | R10 pp. 72–77 |
| **Writing History/Social Studies and Science/Technical Subjects** | | |
| WHST.1 | Write arguments based on discipline-specific content | W1 pp. 82–89 |
| WHST.2 | Write informative/explanatory texts including the narration of historical events, scientific procedures/experiments, or technical processes | W2 pp. 90–99 |
| WHST.3 | NA | |
| WHST.4 | Produce writing in which the development, organization, and style are appropriate to the task, purpose, and audience | W4 pp. 110–115 |
| WHST.5 | Develop and strengthen writing as needed by planning, revising, editing, rewriting, or trying a new approach | W5 pp. 116–121 |
| WHST.6 | Use technology to produce and publish writing as well as to interact with others; demonstrate keyboarding skills | W6 pp. 122–127 |
| WHST.7 | Conduct short research projects to answer a question, drawing on several sources and refocusing the inquiry when appropriate | W7 pp. 128–133 |
| WHST.8 | Gather information from print and digital sources; assess the credibility of sources; quote or paraphrase while avoiding plagiarism and providing basic bibliographic information | W8 pp. 134–139 |
| WHST.9 | Draw evidence from informational texts to support analysis, reflection, and research | W9 pp. 140–147 |
| WHST.10 | Write routinely over extended and shorter time frames for a range of tasks, purposes, and audiences | W10 pp. 148–153 |

# Iowa, Grade 7

| Iowa Strand/Standard | Focus of Iowa Standard | For More Information |
|---|---|---|
| **Reading Literature** | | |
| RL.1 | Cite several pieces of textual evidence to support analysis of what the text says explicitly as well as inferences drawn from the text | R1 pp. 6–11 |
| RL.2 | Determine the theme or central idea of a text and analyze its development; provide an objective summary of the text | R2 pp. 12–19 |
| RL.3 | Analyze how particular elements of a story or drama interact | R3 pp. 20–25 |
| RL.4 | Determine the meaning of words and phrases as they are used in a text, including figurative and connotative meanings | R4 pp. 26–33 |
| RL.5 | Analyze how a drama's or poem's form or structure contributes to its meaning | R5 pp. 34–39 |
| RL.6 | Analyze how an author develops and contrasts the points of view of different characters or narrators in a text | R6 pp. 40–47 |
| RL.7 | Compare and contrast a written story, drama, or poem to its audio, filmed, staged, or multimedia version | R7 pp. 48–55 |
| RL.8 | NA | |
| RL.9 | Compare and contrast a fictional portrayal of a time, place, or character and a historical account of the same period | R9 pp. 64–71 |
| RL.10 | Read and comprehend literature of appropriate complexity independently with proficiency | R10 pp. 72–77 |
| **Reading Informational Text** | | |
| RI.1 | Cite several pieces of textual evidence to support analysis of what the text says explicitly as well as inferences drawn from the text | R1 pp. 6–11 |
| RI.2 | Determine two or more central ideas in a text and analyze their developments; provide an objective summary of the text | R2 pp. 12–19 |
| RI.3 | Analyze the interactions between individuals, events, and ideas in a text | R3 pp. 20–25 |
| RI.4 | Determine the meaning of words and phrases as they are used in a text, including figurative, connotative, and technical meanings | R4 pp. 26–33 |
| RI.5 | Analyze the structure an author uses to organize a text, including how the major sections contribute to the whole | R5 pp. 34–39 |
| RI.6 | Determine an author's point of view or purpose in a text and analyze how the author distinguishes his or her position from that of others | R6 pp. 40–47 |
| RI.7 | Compare and contrast a text to an audio, video, or multimedia version of the text | R7 pp. 48–55 |
| RI.8 | Trace and evaluate the argument and specific claims in a text, assessing whether the reason is sound and the evidence is relevant and sufficient | R8 pp. 56–63 |
| RI.9 | Analyze how two or more authors writing about the same topic shape their presentations of key information | R9 pp. 64–71 |
| RI.10 | Read and comprehend appropriately complex literary nonfiction, informational, and functional texts independently and proficiently | R10 pp. 72–77 |
| **Writing** | | |
| W.1 | Write arguments to support claims with clear reasons and relevant evidence | W1 pp. 82–89 |
| W.2 | Write informative/explanatory texts to examine a topic and convey ideas, concepts, and information clearly | W2 pp. 90–99 |
| W.3 | Write narratives to develop real or imagined experiences or events using effective technique, descriptive details, and well-structured event sequences | W3 pp. 100–109 |
| W.4 | Produce writing in which the development, organization, and style are appropriate to the task, purpose, and audience | W4 pp. 110–115 |
| W.5 | Develop and strengthen writing as needed by planning, revising, editing, rewriting, or trying a new approach | W5 pp. 116–121 |
| W.6 | Use technology to produce and publish writing, link to and cite sources; interact and collaborate with others | W6 pp. 122–127 |

*(Continued)*

| Iowa Strand/Standard | Focus of Iowa Standard | For More Information |
|---|---|---|
| **Writing** | | |
| W.7 | Conduct short research projects to answer a question, drawing on several sources and additional related questions for further investigation | W7 pp. 128–133 |
| W.8 | Gather information from print and digital sources; assess the credibility of sources; quote or paraphrase while avoiding plagiarism and following a standard format for citation | W8 pp. 134–139 |
| W.9 | Draw evidence from literary or informational texts to support analysis, reflection, and research | W9 pp. 140–147 |
| W.10 | Write routinely over extended and shorter time frames for a range of tasks, purposes, and audiences | W10 pp. 148–153 |
| **Speaking and Listening** | | |
| SL.1 | Engage effectively in a range of collaborative discussions with diverse partners, building on others' ideas and expressing their own clearly | SL1 pp. 158–163 |
| SL.2 | Analyze the main ideas and supporting details presented in diverse media and formats and explain how the ideas clarify a topic, text, or issue under study | SL2 pp. 164–169 |
| SL.3 | Delineate a speaker's argument and specific claims evaluating the soundness of the reasoning and the relevance and sufficiency of the evidence | SL3 pp. 170–175 |
| SL.4 | Present claims and findings, emphasizing salient points in a focused coherent manner; use appropriate eye contact, adequate volume, and clear pronunciation | SL4 pp. 176–181 |
| SL.5 | Include multimedia components and visual displays in presentations to clarify claims and findings | SL5 pp. 182–187 |
| SL.6 | Adapt speech to a variety of contexts and tasks, demonstrating command of formal English when appropriate | SL6 pp. 188–193 |
| **Language** | | |
| L.1 | Demonstrate command of the conventions of standard English grammar and usage when writing or speaking | L1 pp. 198–203 |
| L.2 | Demonstrate command of the conventions of standard English capitalization, punctuation, and spelling when writing | L2 pp. 204–209 |
| L.3 | Use knowledge of language and its conventions when writing, speaking, reading, or listening | L3 pp. 210–215 |
| L.4 | Determine or clarify the meaning of unknown and multiple-meaning words and phrases, choosing flexibly from an array of strategies | L4 pp. 216–221 |
| L.5 | Demonstrate understanding of figurative language, word relationships, and nuances in word meanings | L5 pp. 222–227 |
| L.6 | Acquire and use accurately general academic, and domain-specific words and phrases | L6 pp. 228–233 |
| **Reading History/Social Studies** | | |
| RH.1 | Cite textual evidence to support analysis of primary and secondary sources | R1 pp. 6–11 |
| RH.2 | Determine the central ideas or information of a primary or secondary source; provide an objective summary | R2 pp. 12–19 |
| RH.3 | Identify key steps in a text's description of a process related to history/social studies | R3 pp. 20–25 |
| RH.4 | Determine the meaning of words and phrases as they are used in a text, including vocabulary specific to history/social studies | R4 pp. 26–33 |
| RH.5 | Describe how a text presents information | R5 pp. 34–39 |
| RH.6 | Identify aspects of a text that reveal an author's point of view or purpose | R6 pp. 40–47 |
| RH.7 | Integrate visual information with other information in print and digital texts | R7 pp. 48–55 |
| RH.8 | Distinguish among fact, opinion, and reasoned judgment in a text | R8 pp. 56–63 |
| RH.9 | Analyze the relationship between a primary and secondary source on the same topic | R9 pp. 64–71 |
| RH.10 | Read and comprehend history/social studies texts of appropriate complexity independently with proficiency | R10 pp. 72–77 |

| Iowa Strand/Standard | Focus of Iowa Standard | For More Information |
|---|---|---|
| **Reading Science/Technical Subjects** | | |
| RST.1 | Cite textual evidence to support analysis of science and technical texts | R1 pp. 6–11 |
| RST.2 | Determine the central ideas or conclusions of a text; provide an objective summary | R2 pp. 12–19 |
| RST.3 | Follow precisely a multistep procedure when carrying out experiments, taking measurements, or performing technical tasks | R3 pp. 20–25 |
| RST.4 | Determine the meaning of symbols, key terms, and other domain-specific words and phrases | R4 pp. 26–33 |
| RST.5 | Analyze the structure an author uses to organize a text, including how the major sections contribute to the whole | R5 pp. 34–39 |
| RST.6 | Analyze the author's purpose in providing an explanation, describing a procedure, or discussing an experiment | R6 pp. 40–47 |
| RST.7 | Integrate quantitative or technical information expressed in words with a version of the information expressed visually | R7 pp. 48–55 |
| RST.8 | Distinguish among facts, reasoned judgment based on research findings, and speculation in a text | R8 pp. 56–63 |
| RST.9 | Compare and contrast the information gained from experiments, simulations, video, or multimedia sources with that gained from reading a text on the same topic | R9 pp. 64–71 |
| RST.10 | Read and comprehend appropriately complex science/technical texts independently and proficiently | R10 pp. 72–77 |
| **Writing History/Social Studies and Science/Technical Subjects** | | |
| WHST.1 | Write arguments based on discipline-specific content | W1 pp. 82–89 |
| WHST.2 | Write informative/explanatory texts including the narration of historical events, scientific procedures/experiments, or technical processes | W2 pp. 90–99 |
| WHST.3 | NA | |
| WHST.4 | Produce writing in which the development, organization, and style are appropriate to the task, purpose, and audience | W4 pp. 110–115 |
| WHST.5 | Develop and strengthen writing as needed by planning, revising, editing, rewriting, or trying a new approach | W5 pp. 116–121 |
| WHST.6 | Use technology to produce and publish writing as well as to interact with others; demonstrate keyboarding skills | W6 pp. 122–127 |
| WHST.7 | Conduct short research projects to answer a question, drawing on several sources and refocusing the inquiry when appropriate | W7 pp. 128–133 |
| WHST.8 | Gather information from print and digital sources; assess the credibility of sources; quote or paraphrase while avoiding plagiarism and providing basic bibliographic information | W8 pp. 134–139 |
| WHST.9 | Draw evidence from informational texts to support analysis, reflection, and research | W9 pp. 140–147 |
| WHST.10 | Write routinely over extended and shorter time frames for a range of tasks, purposes, and audiences | W10 pp. 148–153 |

# Iowa, Grade 8

| Iowa Strand/Standard | Focus of Iowa Standard | For More Information |
|---|---|---|
| **Reading Literature** | | |
| RL.1 | Cite the textual evidence that most strongly supports an analysis of what the text says explicitly as well as inferences drawn from the text | R1 pp. 6–11 |
| RL.2 | Determine the theme or central idea of a text and analyze its development, including its relationship to the characters, setting, and plot; provide an objective summary of the text | R2 pp. 12–19 |

*(Continued)*

| Iowa Strand/Standard | Focus of Iowa Standard | For More Information |
|---|---|---|
| **Reading Literature** | | |
| RL.3 | Analyze how particular lines of dialogue or incidents in a story or drama propel the action, reveal aspects of a character, or provoke a decision | R3 pp. 20–25 |
| RL.4 | Determine the meaning of words and phrases as they are used in a text, including figurative and connotative meanings | R4 pp. 26–33 |
| RL.5 | Compare and contrast the structure of two or more texts and analyze how the differing structure of each contributes to its meaning and style | R5 pp. 34–39 |
| RL.6 | Analyze how differences in the points of view of the characters and the audience or reader create such effects as suspense or humor | R6 pp. 40–47 |
| RL.7 | Analyze the extent to which a filmed or live production of a story or drama stays faithful or departs from the text or script | R7 pp. 48–55 |
| RL.8 | NA | |
| RL.9 | Analyze how a modern work of fiction draws on themes, patterns of events, or character types from traditional stories, describing how the material is rendered new | R9 pp. 64–71 |
| RL.10 | Read and comprehend literature of appropriate complexity independently with proficiency | R10 pp. 72–77 |
| **Reading Informational Text** | | |
| RI.1 | Cite the textual evidence that most strongly supports an analysis of what the text says explicitly as well as inferences drawn from the text | R1 pp. 6–11 |
| RI.2 | Determine the central idea of a text and analyze its development, including its relationship to supporting ideas; provide an objective summary of the text | R2 pp. 12–19 |
| RI.3 | Analyze how a text makes connections among distinctions between individuals, ideas, or events | R3 pp. 20–25 |
| RI.4 | Determine the meaning of words and phrases as they are used in a text, including figurative, connotative, and technical meanings | R4 pp. 26–33 |
| RI.5 | Analyze the structure of a specific paragraph in a text, including the role of particular sentences in developing and refining a key concept | R5 pp. 34–39 |
| RI.6 | Determine an author's point of view or purpose in a text and analyze how the author acknowledges and responds to conflicting evidence or viewpoints | R6 pp. 40–47 |
| RI.7 | Evaluate the advantages and disadvantages of using different mediums to present a particular topic or idea | R7 pp. 48–55 |
| RI.8 | Delineate and evaluate the argument and specific claims in a text, assessing whether the reason is sound and the evidence is relevant and sufficient | R8 pp. 56–63 |
| RI.9 | Analyze a case in which two or more texts provide conflicting information on the same topic | R9 pp. 64–71 |
| RI.10 | Read and comprehend appropriately complex literary nonfiction, informational, and functional texts independently and proficiently | R10 pp. 72–77 |
| **Writing** | | |
| W.1 | Write arguments to support claims with clear reasons and relevant evidence | W1 pp. 82–89 |
| W.2 | Write informative/explanatory texts to examine a topic and convey ideas, concepts, and information clearly | W2 pp. 90–99 |
| W.3 | Write narratives to develop real or imagined experiences or events using effective technique, descriptive details, and well-structured event sequences | W3 pp. 100–109 |
| W.4 | Produce writing in which the development, organization, and style are appropriate to the task, purpose, and audience | W4 pp. 110–115 |
| W.5 | Develop and strengthen writing as needed by planning, revising, editing, rewriting, or trying a new approach | W5 pp. 116–121 |

| Iowa Strand/Standard | Focus of Iowa Standard | For More Information |
|---|---|---|
| **Writing** | | |
| W.6 | Use technology to produce and publish writing, link to and cite sources; interact and collaborate with others | W6 pp. 122–127 |
| W.7 | Conduct short research projects to answer a question, drawing on several sources and additional related questions for further investigation | W7 pp. 128–133 |
| W.8 | Gather information from print and digital sources; assess the credibility of sources; quote or paraphrase while avoiding plagiarism and following a standard format for citation | W8 pp. 134–139 |
| W.9 | Draw evidence from literary or informational texts to support analysis, reflection, and research | W9 pp. 140–147 |
| W.10 | Write routinely over extended and shorter time frames for a range of tasks, purposes, and audiences | W10 pp. 148–153 |
| **Speaking and Listening** | | |
| SL.1 | Engage effectively in a range of collaborative discussions with diverse partners, building on others' ideas and expressing their own clearly | SL1 pp. 158–163 |
| SL.2 | Analyze the purpose of information presented in diverse media and formats and evaluate the motives behind its presentation | SL2 pp. 164–169 |
| SL.3 | Delineate a speaker's argument and specific claims evaluating the soundness of the reasoning and the relevance and sufficiency of the evidence and identifying when irrelevant evidence is introduced | SL3 pp. 170–175 |
| SL.4 | Present claims and findings, emphasizing salient points in a focused coherent manner; use appropriate eye contact, adequate volume, and clear pronunciation | SL4 pp. 176–181 |
| SL.5 | Integrate multimedia components and visual displays into presentations to clarify information, strengthen claims and findings, and add interest | SL5 pp. 182–187 |
| SL.6 | Adapt speech to a variety of contexts and tasks, demonstrating command of formal English when appropriate | SL6 pp. 188–193 |
| **Language** | | |
| L.1 | Demonstrate command of the conventions of standard English grammar and usage when writing or speaking | L1 pp. 198–203 |
| L.2 | Demonstrate command of the conventions of standard English capitalization, punctuation, and spelling when writing | L2 pp. 204–209 |
| L.3 | Use knowledge of language and its conventions when writing, speaking, reading, or listening | L3 pp. 210–215 |
| L.4 | Determine or clarify the meaning of unknown and multiple-meaning words and phrases, choosing flexibly from an array of strategies | L4 pp. 216–221 |
| L.5 | Demonstrate understanding of figurative language, word relationships, and nuances in word meanings | L5 pp. 222–227 |
| L.6 | Acquire and use accurately general academic, and domain-specific words and phrases | L6 pp. 228–233 |
| **Reading History/Social Studies** | | |
| RH.1 | Cite textual evidence to support analysis of primary and secondary sources | R1 pp. 6–11 |
| RH.2 | Determine the central ideas or information of a primary or secondary source; provide an objective summary | R2 pp. 12–19 |
| RH.3 | Identify key steps in a text's description of a process related to history/social studies | R3 pp. 20–25 |
| RH.4 | Determine the meaning of words and phrases as they are used in a text, including vocabulary specific to history/social studies | R4 pp. 26–33 |
| RH.5 | Describe how a text presents information | R5 pp. 34–39 |

*(Continued)*

| Iowa Strand/Standard | Focus of Iowa Standard | For More Information |
|---|---|---|
| **Reading History/Social Studies** | | |
| RH.6 | Identify aspects of a text that reveal an author's point of view or purpose | R6 pp. 40–47 |
| RH.7 | Integrate visual information with other information in print and digital texts | R7 pp. 48–55 |
| RH.8 | Distinguish among fact, opinion, and reasoned judgment in a text | R8 pp. 56–63 |
| RH.9 | Analyze the relationship between a primary and secondary source on the same topic | R9 pp. 64–71 |
| RH.10 | Read and comprehend history/social studies texts of appropriate complexity independently with proficiency | R10 pp. 72–77 |
| **Reading Science/Technical Subjects** | | |
| RST.1 | Cite textual evidence to support analysis of science and technical texts | R1 pp. 6–11 |
| RST.2 | Determine the central ideas or conclusions of a text; provide an objective summary | R2 pp. 12–19 |
| RST.3 | Follow precisely a multistep procedure when carrying out experiments, taking measurements, or performing technical tasks | R3 pp. 20–25 |
| RST.4 | Determine the meaning of symbols, key terms, and other domain-specific words and phrases | R4 pp. 26–33 |
| RST.5 | Analyze the structure an author uses to organize a text, including how the major sections contribute to the whole | R5 pp. 34–39 |
| RST.6 | Analyze the author's purpose in providing an explanation, describing a procedure, or discussing an experiment | R6 pp. 40–47 |
| RST.7 | Integrate quantitative or technical information expressed in words with a version of the information expressed visually | R7 pp. 48–55 |
| RST.8 | Distinguish among facts, reasoned judgment based on research findings, and speculation in a text | R8 pp. 56–63 |
| RST.9 | Compare and contrast the information gained from experiments, simulations, video, or multimedia sources with that gained from reading a text on the same topic | R9 pp. 64–71 |
| RST.10 | Read and comprehend appropriately complex science/technical texts independently and proficiently | R10 pp. 72–77 |
| **Writing History/Social Studies and Science/Technical Subjects** | | |
| WHST.1 | Write arguments based on discipline-specific content | W1 pp. 82–89 |
| WHST.2 | Write informative/explanatory texts including the narration of historical events, scientific procedures/experiments, or technical processes | W2 pp. 90–99 |
| WHST.3 | NA | |
| WHST.4 | Produce writing in which the development, organization, and style are appropriate to the task, purpose, and audience | W4 pp. 110–115 |
| WHST.5 | Develop and strengthen writing as needed by planning, revising, editing, rewriting, or trying a new approach | W5 pp. 116–121 |
| WHST.6 | Use technology to produce and publish writing as well as to interact with others; demonstrate keyboarding skills | W6 pp. 122–127 |
| WHST.7 | Conduct short research projects to answer a question, drawing on several sources and refocusing the inquiry when appropriate | W7 pp. 128–133 |
| WHST.8 | Gather information from print and digital sources; assess the credibility of sources; quote or paraphrase while avoiding plagiarism and providing basic bibliographic information | W8 pp. 134–139 |
| WHST.9 | Draw evidence from informational texts to support analysis, reflection, and research | W9 pp. 140–147 |
| WHST.10 | Write routinely over extended and shorter time frames for a range of tasks, purposes, and audiences | W10 pp. 148–153 |

# Kansas, Grade 6

| Kansas Strand/Standard | Focus of Kansas Standard | For More Information |
|---|---|---|
| **Reading Literature** | | |
| RL.1 | Cite textual evidence to support analysis of what the text says explicitly as well as inferences drawn from the text | R1 pp. 6–11 |
| RL.2 | Determine the theme or central idea of a text and how it is conveyed through particular details; provide an objective summary | R2 pp. 12–19 |
| RL.3 | Describe how a particular plot unfolds in a series of episodes as well as how the characters respond or change | R3 pp. 20–25 |
| RL.4 | Determine the meaning of words and phrases as they are used in a text, including figurative and connotative meanings | R4 pp. 26–33 |
| RL.5 | Analyze how a particular sentence, chapter, scene, or stanza fits into the overall structure of a text and contributes to the development of the theme, setting, or plot | R5 pp. 34–39 |
| RL.6 | Explain how an author develops the point of view of the narrator or speaker in a text | R6 pp. 40–47 |
| RL.7 | Compare and contrast the experience of reading a story, drama, or poem to listening to or viewing an audio, video, or live version of the text | R7 pp. 48–55 |
| RL.8 | NA | |
| RL.9 | Compare and contrast texts in different forms or genres in terms of their approaches to similar themes and topics | R9 pp. 64–71 |
| RL.10 | Read and comprehend literature of appropriate complexity independently with proficiency | R10 pp. 72–77 |
| **Reading Informational Text** | | |
| RI.1 | Cite textual evidence to support analysis of what the text says explicitly as well as inferences drawn from the text | R1 pp. 6–11 |
| RI.2 | Determine a central idea of a text and how it is conveyed through particular details; provide an objective summary | R2 pp. 12–19 |
| RI.3 | Analyze in detail how a key individual, event, or idea is introduced, illustrated, and elaborated in a text | R3 pp. 20–25 |
| RI.4 | Determine the meaning of words and phrases as they are used in a text, including figurative, connotative, and technical meanings | R4 pp. 26–33 |
| RI.5 | Analyze how a particular sentence, chapter, scene, or section fits into the overall structure of a text and contributes to the development of the ideas | R5 pp. 34–39 |
| RI.6 | Determine an author's point of view or purpose in a text and explain how it is conveyed in the text | R6 pp. 40–47 |
| RI.7 | Integrate information presented in different media or formats as well as in words to develop a coherent understanding of a topic or issue | R7 pp. 48–55 |
| RI.8 | Trace and evaluate the argument and specific claims that are supported by reasons and evidence from claims that are not | R8 pp. 56–63 |
| RI.9 | Compare and contrast one author's presentation of events with that of another | R9 pp. 64–71 |
| RI.10 | Read and comprehend appropriately complex literary nonfiction, informational, and functional texts independently and proficiently | R10 pp. 72–77 |
| **Writing** | | |
| W.1 | Write arguments to support claims with clear reasons and relevant evidence | W1 pp. 82–89 |
| W.2 | Write informative/explanatory texts to examine a topic and convey ideas, concepts, and information clearly | W2 pp. 90–99 |
| W.3 | Write narratives to develop real or imagined experiences or events using effective technique, descriptive details, and well-structured event sequences | W3 pp. 100–109 |
| W.4 | Produce writing in which the development, organization, and style are appropriate to the task, purpose, and audience | W4 pp. 110–115 |
| W.5 | Develop and strengthen writing as needed by planning, revising, editing, rewriting, or trying a new approach | W5 pp. 116–121 |
| W.6 | Use technology to produce and publish writing as well as to interact with others; demonstrate keyboarding skills | W6 pp. 122–127 |

*(Continued)*

| Kansas Strand/Standard | Focus of Kansas Standard | For More Information |
|---|---|---|
| **Writing** | | |
| W.7 | Conduct short research projects to answer a question, drawing on several sources and refocusing the inquiry when appropriate | W7 pp. 128–133 |
| W.8 | Gather information from print and digital sources; assess the credibility of sources; quote or paraphrase while avoiding plagiarism and providing basic bibliographic information | W8 pp. 134–139 |
| W.9 | Draw evidence from literary or informational texts to support analysis, reflection, and research | W9 pp. 140–147 |
| W.10 | Write routinely over extended and shorter time frames for a range of tasks, purposes, and audiences | W10 pp. 148–153 |
| **Speaking and Listening** | | |
| SL.1 | Engage effectively in a range of collaborative discussions with diverse partners, building on others' ideas and expressing their own clearly | SL1 pp. 158–163 |
| SL.2 | Interpret information presented in diverse media and formats and explain how it contributes to a topic, text, or issue under study | SL2 pp. 164–169 |
| SL.3 | Delineate a speaker's argument and specific claims that are supported by reasons and evidence from claims that are not | SL3 pp. 170–175 |
| SL.4 | Present claims and findings, sequencing ideas logically and using descriptions, facts, or details to accentuate main ideas or themes; use appropriate eye contact, adequate volume, and clear pronunciation | SL4 pp. 176–181 |
| SL.5 | Include multimedia components and visual displays in presentations to clarify information | SL5 pp. 182–187 |
| SL.6 | Adapt speech to a variety of contexts and tasks, demonstrating command of formal English when appropriate | SL6 pp. 188–193 |
| **Language** | | |
| L.1 | Demonstrate command of the conventions of standard English grammar and usage when writing or speaking | L1 pp. 198–203 |
| L.2 | Demonstrate command of the conventions of standard English capitalization, punctuation, and spelling when writing | L2 pp. 204–209 |
| L.3 | Use knowledge of language and its conventions when writing, speaking, reading, or listening | L3 pp. 210–215 |
| L.4 | Determine or clarify the meaning of unknown and multiple-meaning words and phrases, choosing flexibly from an array of strategies | L4 pp. 216–221 |
| L.5 | Demonstrate understanding of figurative language, word relationships, and nuances in word meanings | L5 pp. 222–227 |
| L.6 | Acquire and use accurately general academic, and domain-specific words and phrases | L6 pp. 228–233 |
| **Reading History/Social Studies** | | |
| RH.1 | Cite textual evidence to support analysis of primary and secondary sources | R1 pp. 6–11 |
| RH.2 | Determine the central ideas or information of a primary or secondary source; provide an objective summary | R2 pp. 12–19 |
| RH.3 | Identify key steps in a text's description of a process related to history/social studies | R3 pp. 20–25 |
| RH.4 | Determine the meaning of words and phrases as they are used in a text, including vocabulary specific to history/social studies | R4 pp. 26–33 |
| RH.5 | Describe how a text presents information | R5 pp. 34–39 |
| RH.6 | Identify aspects of a text that reveal an author's point of view or purpose | R6 pp. 40–47 |
| RH.7 | Integrate visual information with other information in print and digital texts | R7 pp. 48–55 |
| RH.8 | Distinguish among fact, opinion, and reasoned judgment in a text | R8 pp. 56–63 |
| RH.9 | Analyze the relationship between a primary and secondary source on the same topic | R9 pp. 64–71 |
| RH.10 | Read and comprehend history/social studies texts of appropriate complexity independently with proficiency | R10 pp. 72–77 |
| **Reading Science/Technical Subjects** | | |
| RST.1 | Cite textual evidence to support analysis of science and technical texts | R1 pp. 6–11 |
| RST.2 | Determine the central ideas or conclusions of a text; provide an objective summary | R2 pp. 12–19 |
| RST.3 | Follow precisely a multistep procedure when carrying out experiments, taking measurements, or performing technical tasks | R3 pp. 20–25 |
| RST.4 | Determine the meaning of symbols, key terms, and other domain-specific words and phrases | R4 pp. 26–33 |

| Kansas Strand/Standard | Focus of Kansas Standard | For More Information |
|---|---|---|
| **Reading Science/Technical Subjects** | | |
| RST.5 | Analyze the structure an author uses to organize a text, including how the major sections contribute to the whole | R5 pp. 34–39 |
| RST.6 | Analyze the author's purpose in providing an explanation, describing a procedure, or discussing an experiment | R6 pp. 40–47 |
| RST.7 | Integrate quantitative or technical information expressed in words with a version of the information expressed visually | R7 pp. 48–55 |
| RST.8 | Distinguish among facts, reasoned judgment based on research findings, and speculation in a text | R8 pp. 56–63 |
| RST.9 | Compare and contrast the information gained from experiments, simulations, video, or multimedia sources with that gained from reading a text on the same topic | R9 pp. 64–71 |
| RST.10 | Read and comprehend appropriately complex science/technical texts independently and proficiently | R10 pp. 72–77 |
| **Writing History/Social Studies and Science/Technical Subjects** | | |
| WHST.1 | Write arguments based on discipline-specific content | W1 pp. 82–89 |
| WHST.2 | Write informative/explanatory texts including the narration of historical events, scientific procedures/experiments, or technical processes | W2 pp. 90–99 |
| WHST.3 | NA | |
| WHST.4 | Produce writing in which the development, organization, and style are appropriate to the task, purpose, and audience | W4 pp. 110–115 |
| WHST.5 | Develop and strengthen writing as needed by planning, revising, editing, rewriting, or trying a new approach | W5 pp. 116–121 |
| WHST.6 | Use technology to produce and publish writing as well as to interact with others; demonstrate keyboarding skills | W6 pp. 122–127 |
| WHST.7 | Conduct short research projects to answer a question, drawing on several sources and refocusing the inquiry when appropriate | W7 pp. 128–133 |
| WHST.8 | Gather information from print and digital sources; assess the credibility of sources; quote or paraphrase while avoiding plagiarism and providing basic bibliographic information | W8 pp. 134–139 |
| WHST.9 | Draw evidence from informational texts to support analysis, reflection, and research | W9 pp. 140–147 |
| WHST.10 | Write routinely over extended and shorter time frames for a range of tasks, purposes, and audiences | W10 pp. 148–153 |

# Kansas, Grade 7

| Kansas Strand/Standard | Focus of Kansas Standard | For More Information |
|---|---|---|
| **Reading Literature** | | |
| RL.1 | Cite several pieces of textual evidence to support analysis of what the text says explicitly as well as inferences drawn from the text | R1 pp. 6–11 |
| RL.2 | Determine the theme or central idea of a text and analyze its development; provide an objective summary of the text | R2 pp. 12–19 |
| RL.3 | Analyze how particular elements of a story or drama interact | R3 pp. 20–25 |
| RL.4 | Determine the meaning of words and phrases as they are used in a text, including figurative and connotative meanings | R4 pp. 26–33 |
| RL.5 | Analyze how a drama's or poem's form or structure contributes to its meaning | R5 pp. 34–39 |
| RL.6 | Analyze how an author develops and contrasts the points of view of different characters or narrators in a text | R6 pp. 40–47 |
| RL.7 | Compare and contrast a written story, drama, or poem to its audio, filmed, staged, or multimedia version | R7 pp. 48–55 |
| RL.8 | NA | |

*(Continued)*

| **Reading Literature** | | |
|---|---|---|
| RL.9 | Compare and contrast a fictional portrayal of a time, place, or character and a historical account of the same period | R9 pp. 64–71 |
| RL.10 | Read and comprehend literature of appropriate complexity independently with proficiency | R10 pp. 72–77 |
| **Reading Informational Text** | | |
| RI.1 | Cite several pieces of textual evidence to support analysis of what the text says explicitly as well as inferences drawn from the text | R1 pp. 6–11 |
| RI.2 | Determine two or more central ideas in a text and analyze their developments; provide an objective summary of the text | R2 pp. 12–19 |
| RI.3 | Analyze the interactions between individuals, events, and ideas in a text | R3 pp. 20–25 |
| RI.4 | Determine the meaning of words and phrases as they are used in a text, including figurative, connotative, and technical meanings | R4 pp. 26–33 |
| RI.5 | Analyze the structure an author uses to organize a text, including how the major sections contribute to the whole | R5 pp. 34–39 |
| RI.6 | Determine an author's point of view or purpose in a text and analyze how the author distinguishes his or her position from that of others | R6 pp. 40–47 |
| RI.7 | Compare and contrast a text to an audio, video, or multimedia version of the text | R7 pp. 48–55 |
| RI.8 | Trace and evaluate the argument and specific claims in a text, assessing whether the reason is sound and the evidence is relevant and sufficient | R8 pp. 56–63 |
| RI.9 | Analyze how two or more authors writing about the same topic shape their presentations of key information | R9 pp. 64–71 |
| RI.10 | Read and comprehend appropriately complex literary nonfiction, informational, and functional texts independently and proficiently | R10 pp. 72–77 |
| **Writing** | | |
| W.1 | Write arguments to support claims with clear reasons and relevant evidence | W1 pp. 82–89 |
| W.2 | Write informative/explanatory texts to examine a topic and convey ideas, concepts, and information clearly | W2 pp. 90–99 |
| W.3 | Write narratives to develop real or imagined experiences or events using effective technique, descriptive details, and well-structured event sequences | W3 pp. 100–109 |
| W.4 | Produce writing in which the development, organization, and style are appropriate to the task, purpose, and audience | W4 pp. 110–115 |
| W.5 | Develop and strengthen writing as needed by planning, revising, editing, rewriting, or trying a new approach | W5 pp. 116–121 |
| W.6 | Use technology to produce and publish writing, link to and cite sources; interact and collaborate with others | W6 pp. 122–127 |
| W.7 | Conduct short research projects to answer a question, drawing on several sources and additional related questions for further investigation | W7 pp. 128–133 |
| W.8 | Gather information from print and digital sources; assess the credibility of sources; quote or paraphrase while avoiding plagiarism and following a standard format for citation | W8 pp. 134–139 |
| W.9 | Draw evidence from literary or informational texts to support analysis, reflection, and research | W9 pp. 140–147 |
| W.10 | Write routinely over extended and shorter time frames for a range of tasks, purposes, and audiences | W10 pp. 148–153 |
| **Speaking and Listening** | | |
| SL.1 | Engage effectively in a range of collaborative discussions with diverse partners, building on others' ideas and expressing their own clearly | SL1 pp. 158–163 |
| SL.2 | Analyze the main ideas and supporting details presented in diverse media and formats and explain how the ideas clarify a topic, text, or issue under study | SL2 pp. 164–169 |
| SL.3 | Delineate a speaker's argument and specific claims evaluating the soundness of the reasoning and the relevance and sufficiency of the evidence | SL3 pp. 170–175 |
| SL.4 | Present claims and findings, emphasizing salient points in a focused coherent manner; use appropriate eye contact, adequate volume, and clear pronunciation | SL4 pp. 176–181 |
| SL.5 | Include multimedia components and visual displays in presentations to clarify claims and findings | SL5 pp. 182–187 |
| SL.6 | Adapt speech to a variety of contexts and tasks, demonstrating command of formal English when appropriate | SL6 pp. 188–193 |

| Kansas Strand/Standard | Focus of Kansas Standard | For More Information |
|---|---|---|
| **Language** | | |
| L.1 | Demonstrate command of the conventions of standard English grammar and usage when writing or speaking | L1 pp. 198–203 |
| L.2 | Demonstrate command of the conventions of standard English capitalization, punctuation, and spelling when writing | L2 pp. 204–209 |
| L.3 | Use knowledge of language and its conventions when writing, speaking, reading, or listening | L3 pp. 210–215 |
| L.4 | Determine or clarify the meaning of unknown and multiple-meaning words and phrases, choosing flexibly from an array of strategies | L4 pp. 216–221 |
| L.5 | Demonstrate understanding of figurative language, word relationships, and nuances in word meanings | L5 pp. 222–227 |
| L.6 | Acquire and use accurately general academic, and domain-specific words and phrases | L6 pp. 228–233 |
| **Reading History/Social Studies** | | |
| RH.1 | Cite textual evidence to support analysis of primary and secondary sources | R1 pp. 6–11 |
| RH.2 | Determine the central ideas or information of a primary or secondary source; provide an objective summary | R2 pp. 12–19 |
| RH.3 | Identify key steps in a text's description of a process related to history/social studies | R3 pp. 20–25 |
| RH.4 | Determine the meaning of words and phrases as they are used in a text, including vocabulary specific to history/social studies | R4 pp. 26–33 |
| RH.5 | Describe how a text presents information | R5 pp. 34–39 |
| RH.6 | Identify aspects of a text that reveal an author's point of view or purpose | R6 pp. 40–47 |
| RH.7 | Integrate visual information with other information in print and digital texts | R7 pp. 48–55 |
| RH.8 | Distinguish among fact, opinion, and reasoned judgment in a text | R8 pp. 56–63 |
| RH.9 | Analyze the relationship between a primary and secondary source on the same topic | R9 pp. 64–71 |
| RH.10 | Read and comprehend history/social studies texts of appropriate complexity independently with proficiency | R10 pp. 72–77 |
| **Reading Science/Technical Subjects** | | |
| RST.1 | Cite textual evidence to support analysis of science and technical texts | R1 pp. 6–11 |
| RST.2 | Determine the central ideas or conclusions of a text; provide an objective summary | R2 pp. 12–19 |
| RST.3 | Follow precisely a multistep procedure when carrying out experiments, taking measurements, or performing technical tasks | R3 pp. 20–25 |
| RST.4 | Determine the meaning of symbols, key terms, and other domain-specific words and phrases | R4 pp. 26–33 |
| RST.5 | Analyze the structure an author uses to organize a text, including how the major sections contribute to the whole | R5 pp. 34–39 |
| RST.6 | Analyze the author's purpose in providing an explanation, describing a procedure, or discussing an experiment | R6 pp. 40–47 |
| RST.7 | Integrate quantitative or technical information expressed in words with a version of the information expressed visually | R7 pp. 48–55 |
| RST.8 | Distinguish among facts, reasoned judgment based on research findings, and speculation in a text | R8 pp. 56–63 |
| RST.9 | Compare and contrast the information gained from experiments, simulations, video, or multimedia sources with that gained from reading a text on the same topic | R9 pp. 64–71 |
| RST.10 | Read and comprehend appropriately complex science/technical texts independently and proficiently | R10 pp. 72–77 |
| **Writing History/Social Studies and Science/Technical Subjects** | | |
| WHST.1 | Write arguments based on discipline-specific content | W1 pp. 82–89 |
| WHST.2 | Write informative/explanatory texts including the narration of historical events, scientific procedures/experiments, or technical processes | W2 pp. 90–99 |
| WHST.3 | NA | |
| WHST.4 | Produce writing in which the development, organization, and style are appropriate to the task, purpose, and audience | W4 pp. 110–115 |
| WHST.5 | Develop and strengthen writing as needed by planning, revising, editing, rewriting, or trying a new approach | W5 pp. 116–121 |

*(Continued)*

| Kansas Strand/Standard | Focus of Kansas Standard | For More Information |
|---|---|---|
| **Writing History/Social Studies and Science/Technical Subjects** | | |
| WHST.6 | Use technology to produce and publish writing as well as to interact with others; demonstrate keyboarding skills | W6 pp. 122–127 |
| WHST.7 | Conduct short research projects to answer a question, drawing on several sources and refocusing the inquiry when appropriate | W7 pp. 128–133 |
| WHST.8 | Gather information from print and digital sources; assess the credibility of sources; quote or paraphrase while avoiding plagiarism and providing basic bibliographic information | W8 pp. 134–139 |
| WHST.9 | Draw evidence from informational texts to support analysis, reflection, and research | W9 pp. 140–147 |
| WHST.10 | Write routinely over extended and shorter time frames for a range of tasks, purposes, and audiences | W10 pp. 148–153 |

# Kansas, Grade 8

| Kansas Strand/Standard | Focus of Kansas Standard | For More Information |
|---|---|---|
| **Reading Literature** | | |
| RL.1 | Cite the textual evidence that most strongly supports an analysis of what the text says explicitly as well as inferences drawn from the text | R1 pp. 6–11 |
| RL.2 | Determine the theme or central idea of a text and analyze its development, including its relationship to the characters, setting, and plot; provide an objective summary of the text | R2 pp. 12–19 |
| RL.3 | Analyze how particular lines of dialogue or incidents in a story or drama propel the action, reveal aspects of a character, or provoke a decision | R3 pp. 20–25 |
| RL.4 | Determine the meaning of words and phrases as they are used in a text, including figurative and connotative meanings | R4 pp. 26–33 |
| RL.5 | Compare and contrast the structure of two or more texts and analyze how the differing structure of each contributes to its meaning and style | R5 pp. 34–39 |
| RL.6 | Analyze how differences in the points of view of the characters and the audience or reader create such effects as suspense or humor | R6 pp. 40–47 |
| RL.7 | Analyze the extent to which a filmed or live production of a story or drama stays faithful or departs from the text or script | R7 pp. 48–55 |
| RL.8 | NA | |
| RL.9 | Analyze how a modern work of fiction draws on themes, patterns of events, or character types from traditional stories, describing how the material is rendered new | R9 pp. 64–71 |
| RL.10 | Read and comprehend literature of appropriate complexity independently with proficiency | R10 pp. 72–77 |
| **Reading Informational Text** | | |
| RI.1 | Cite the textual evidence that most strongly supports an analysis of what the text says explicitly as well as inferences drawn from the text | R1 pp. 6–11 |
| RI.2 | Determine the central idea of a text and analyze its development, including its relationship to supporting ideas; provide an objective summary of the text | R2 pp. 12–19 |
| RI.3 | Analyze how a text makes connections among distinctions between individuals, ideas, or events | R3 pp. 20–25 |
| RI.4 | Determine the meaning of words and phrases as they are used in a text, including figurative, connotative, and technical meanings | R4 pp. 26–33 |
| RI.5 | Analyze the structure of a specific paragraph in a text, including the role of particular sentences in developing and refining a key concept | R5 pp. 34–39 |
| RI.6 | Determine an author's point of view or purpose in a text and analyze how the author acknowledges and responds to conflicting evidence or viewpoints | R6 pp. 40–47 |
| RI.7 | Evaluate the advantages and disadvantages of using different mediums to present a particular topic or idea | R7 pp. 48–55 |
| RI.8 | Delineate and evaluate the argument and specific claims in a text, assessing whether the reason is sound and the evidence is relevant and sufficient | R8 pp. 56–63 |
| RI.9 | Analyze a case in which two or more texts provide conflicting information on the same topic | R9 pp. 64–71 |
| RI.10 | Read and comprehend appropriately complex literary nonfiction, informational, and functional texts independently and proficiently | R10 pp. 72–77 |

| Kansas Strand/Standard | Focus of Kansas Standard | For More Information |
|---|---|---|
| **Writing** | | |
| W.1 | Write arguments to support claims with clear reasons and relevant evidence | W1 pp. 82–89 |
| W.2 | Write informative/explanatory texts to examine a topic and convey ideas, concepts, and information clearly | W2 pp. 90–99 |
| W.3 | Write narratives to develop real or imagined experiences or events using effective technique, descriptive details, and well-structured event sequences | W3 pp. 100–109 |
| W.4 | Produce writing in which the development, organization, and style are appropriate to the task, purpose, and audience | W4 pp. 110–115 |
| W.5 | Develop and strengthen writing as needed by planning, revising, editing, rewriting, or trying a new approach | W5 pp. 116–121 |
| W.6 | Use technology to produce and publish writing, link to and cite sources; interact and collaborate with others | W6 pp. 122–127 |
| W.7 | Conduct short research projects to answer a question, drawing on several sources and additional related questions for further investigation | W7 pp. 128–133 |
| W.8 | Gather information from print and digital sources; assess the credibility of sources; quote or paraphrase while avoiding plagiarism and following a standard format for citation | W8 pp. 134–139 |
| W.9 | Draw evidence from literary or informational texts to support analysis, reflection, and research | W9 pp. 140–147 |
| W.10 | Write routinely over extended and shorter time frames for a range of tasks, purposes, and audiences | W10 pp. 148–153 |
| **Speaking and Listening** | | |
| SL.1 | Engage effectively in a range of collaborative discussions with diverse partners, building on others' ideas and expressing their own clearly | SL1 pp. 158–163 |
| SL.2 | Analyze the purpose of information presented in diverse media and formats and evaluate the motives behind its presentation | SL2 pp. 164–169 |
| SL.3 | Delineate a speaker's argument and specific claims evaluating the soundness of the reasoning and the relevance and sufficiency of the evidence and identifying when irrelevant evidence is introduced | SL3 pp. 170–175 |
| SL.4 | Present claims and findings, emphasizing salient points in a focused coherent manner; use appropriate eye contact, adequate volume, and clear pronunciation | SL4 pp. 176–181 |
| SL.5 | Integrate multimedia components and visual displays into presentations to clarify information, strengthen claims and findings, and add interest | SL5 pp. 182–187 |
| SL.6 | Adapt speech to a variety of contexts and tasks, demonstrating command of formal English when appropriate | SL6 pp. 188–193 |
| **Language** | | |
| L.1 | Demonstrate command of the conventions of standard English grammar and usage when writing or speaking | L1 pp. 198–203 |
| L.2 | Demonstrate command of the conventions of standard English capitalization, punctuation, and spelling when writing | L2 pp. 204–209 |
| L.3 | Use knowledge of language and its conventions when writing, speaking, reading, or listening | L3 pp. 210–215 |
| L.4 | Determine or clarify the meaning of unknown and multiple-meaning words and phrases, choosing flexibly from an array of strategies | L4 pp. 216–221 |
| L.5 | Demonstrate understanding of figurative language, word relationships, and nuances in word meanings | L5 pp. 222–227 |
| L.6 | Acquire and use accurately general academic, and domain-specific words and phrases | L6 pp. 228–233 |
| **Reading History/Social Studies** | | |
| RH.1 | Cite textual evidence to support analysis of primary and secondary sources | R1 pp. 6–11 |
| RH.2 | Determine the central ideas or information of a primary or secondary source; provide an objective summary | R2 pp. 12–19 |
| RH.3 | Identify key steps in a text's description of a process related to history/social studies | R3 pp. 20–25 |
| RH.4 | Determine the meaning of words and phrases as they are used in a text, including vocabulary specific to history/social studies | R4 pp. 26–33 |

*(Continued)*

| Kansas Strand/Standard | Focus of Kansas Standard | For More Information |
|---|---|---|
| **Reading History/Social Studies** | | |
| RH.5 | Describe how a text presents information | R5 pp. 34–39 |
| RH.6 | Identify aspects of a text that reveal an author's point of view or purpose | R6 pp. 40–47 |
| RH.7 | Integrate visual information with other information in print and digital texts | R7 pp. 48–55 |
| RH.8 | Distinguish among fact, opinion, and reasoned judgment in a text | R8 pp. 56–63 |
| RH.9 | Analyze the relationship between a primary and secondary source on the same topic | R9 pp. 64–71 |
| RH.10 | Read and comprehend history/social studies texts of appropriate complexity independently with proficiency | R10 pp. 72–77 |
| **Reading Science/Technical Subjects** | | |
| RST.1 | Cite textual evidence to support analysis of science and technical texts | R1 pp. 6–11 |
| RST.2 | Determine the central ideas or conclusions of a text; provide an objective summary | R2 pp. 12–19 |
| RST.3 | Follow precisely a multistep procedure when carrying out experiments, taking measurements, or performing technical tasks | R3 pp. 20–25 |
| RST.4 | Determine the meaning of symbols, key terms, and other domain-specific words and phrases | R4 pp. 26–33 |
| RST.5 | Analyze the structure an author uses to organize a text, including how the major sections contribute to the whole | R5 pp. 34–39 |
| RST.6 | Analyze the author's purpose in providing an explanation, describing a procedure, or discussing an experiment | R6 pp. 40–47 |
| RST.7 | Integrate quantitative or technical information expressed in words with a version of the information expressed visually | R7 pp. 48–55 |
| RST.8 | Distinguish among facts, reasoned judgment based on research findings, and speculation in a text | R8 pp. 56–63 |
| RST.9 | Compare and contrast the information gained from experiments, simulations, video, or multimedia sources with that gained from reading a text on the same topic | R9 pp. 64–71 |
| RST.10 | Read and comprehend appropriately complex science/technical texts independently and proficiently | R10 pp. 72–77 |
| **Writing History/Social Studies and Science/Technical Subjects** | | |
| WHST.1 | Write arguments based on discipline-specific content | W1 pp. 82–89 |
| WHST.2 | Write informative/explanatory texts including the narration of historical events, scientific procedures/experiments, or technical processes | W2 pp. 90–99 |
| WHST.3 | NA | |
| WHST.4 | Produce writing in which the development, organization, and style are appropriate to the task, purpose, and audience | W4 pp. 110–115 |
| WHST.5 | Develop and strengthen writing as needed by planning, revising, editing, rewriting, or trying a new approach | W5 pp. 116–121 |
| WHST.6 | Use technology to produce and publish writing as well as to interact with others; demonstrate keyboarding skills | W6 pp. 122–127 |
| WHST.7 | Conduct short research projects to answer a question, drawing on several sources and refocusing the inquiry when appropriate | W7 pp. 128–133 |
| WHST.8 | Gather information from print and digital sources; assess the credibility of sources; quote or paraphrase while avoiding plagiarism and providing basic bibliographic information | W8 pp. 134–139 |
| WHST.9 | Draw evidence from informational texts to support analysis, reflection, and research | W9 pp. 140–147 |
| WHST.10 | Write routinely over extended and shorter time frames for a range of tasks, purposes, and audiences | W10 pp. 148–153 |

# Louisiana, Grade 6

| Louisiana Strand/Standard | Focus of Louisiana Standard | For More Information |
|---|---|---|
| **Reading Literature** | | |
| RL.1 | Cite textual evidence to support analysis of what the text says explicitly as well as inferences drawn from the text | R1 pp. 6–11 |
| RL.2 | Determine the theme or central idea of a text and how it is conveyed through particular details; provide an objective summary | R2 pp. 12–19 |
| RL.3 | Describe how a particular plot unfolds in a series of episodes as well as how the characters respond or change | R3 pp. 20–25 |
| RL.4 | Determine the meaning of words and phrases as they are used in a text, including figurative and connotative meanings | R4 pp. 26–33 |
| RL.5 | Analyze how a particular sentence, chapter, scene, or stanza fits into the overall structure of a text and contributes to the development of the theme, setting, or plot | R5 pp. 34–39 |
| RL.6 | Explain how an author develops the point of view of the narrator or speaker in a text | R6 pp. 40–47 |
| RL.7 | Compare and contrast the experience of reading a story, drama, or poem to listening to or viewing an audio, video, or live version of the text | R7 pp. 48–55 |
| RL.8 | NA | |
| RL.9 | Compare and contrast texts in different forms or genres in terms of their approaches to similar themes and topics | R9 pp. 64–71 |
| RL.10 | Read and comprehend literature of appropriate complexity independently with proficiency | R10 pp. 72–77 |
| **Reading Informational Text** | | |
| RI.1 | Cite textual evidence to support analysis of what the text says explicitly as well as inferences drawn from the text | R1 pp. 6–11 |
| RI.2 | Determine a central idea of a text and how it is conveyed through particular details; provide an objective summary | R2 pp. 12–19 |
| RI.3 | Analyze in detail how a key individual, event, or idea is introduced, illustrated, and elaborated in a text | R3 pp. 20–25 |
| RI.4 | Determine the meaning of words and phrases as they are used in a text, including figurative, connotative, and technical meanings | R4 pp. 26–33 |
| RI.5 | Analyze how a particular sentence, chapter, scene, or section fits into the overall structure of a text and contributes to the development of the ideas | R5 pp. 34–39 |
| RI.6 | Determine an author's point of view or purpose in a text and explain how it is conveyed in the text | R6 pp. 40–47 |
| RI.7 | Integrate information presented in different media or formats as well as in words to develop a coherent understanding of a topic or issue | R7 pp. 48–55 |
| RI.8 | Trace and evaluate the argument and specific claims, distinguishing claims that are supported by reasons and evidence from claims that are not | R8 pp. 56–63 |
| RI.9 | Compare and contrast one author's presentation of events with that of another | R9 pp. 64–71 |
| RI.10 | Read and comprehend appropriately complex literary nonfiction, informational, and functional texts independently and proficiently | R10 pp. 72–77 |
| **Writing** | | |
| W.1 | Write arguments to support claims with clear reasons and relevant evidence | W1 pp. 82–89 |
| W.2 | Write informative/explanatory texts to examine a topic and convey ideas, concepts, and information clearly | W2 pp. 90–99 |
| W.3 | Write narratives to develop real or imagined experiences or events using effective technique, descriptive details, and well-structured event sequences | W3 pp. 100–109 |
| W.4 | Produce writing in which the development, organization, and style are appropriate to the task, purpose, and audience | W4 pp. 110–115 |
| W.5 | Develop and strengthen writing as needed by planning, revising, editing, rewriting, or trying a different approach | W5 pp. 116–121 |
| W.6 | Use technology to produce and publish writing | W6 pp. 122–127 |

*(Continued)*

| Louisiana Strand/Standard | Focus of Louisiana Standard | For More Information |
|---|---|---|
| **Writing** | | |
| W.7 | Conduct short research projects to answer a question, drawing on several sources and refocusing the inquiry when appropriate | W7 pp. 128–133 |
| W.8 | Gather information from print and digital sources; assess the credibility of sources; quote or paraphrase while avoiding plagiarism and providing basic bibliographic information | W8 pp. 134–139 |
| W.9 | Draw evidence from literary or informational texts to support analysis, reflection, and research | W9 pp. 140–147 |
| W.10 | Write routinely over extended and shorter time frames for a range of tasks, purposes, and audiences | W10 pp. 148–153 |
| **Speaking and Listening** | | |
| SL.1 | Engage effectively in a range of collaborative discussions with diverse partners, building on others' ideas and expressing their own clearly | SL1 pp. 158–163 |
| SL.2 | Interpret information presented in diverse media and formats and explain how it contributes to a topic, text, or issue under study | SL2 pp. 164–169 |
| SL.3 | Delineate a speaker's argument and specific claims that are supported by reasons and evidence from claims that are not | SL3 pp. 170–175 |
| SL.4 | Present claims and findings, sequencing ideas logically and using descriptions, facts, or details to accentuate main ideas or themes; use appropriate eye contact, adequate volume, and clear pronunciation | SL4 pp. 176–181 |
| SL.5 | Include multimedia components and visual displays in presentations to clarify information | SL5 pp. 182–187 |
| SL.6 | Adapt speech to a variety of contexts and tasks, demonstrating command of formal English when appropriate | SL6 pp. 188–193 |
| **Language** | | |
| L.1 | Demonstrate command of the conventions of standard English grammar and usage when writing or speaking | L1 pp. 198–203 |
| L.2 | Demonstrate command of the conventions of standard English capitalization, punctuation, and spelling when writing | L2 pp. 204–209 |
| L.3 | Use knowledge of language and its conventions when writing, speaking, reading, or listening | L3 pp. 210–215 |
| L.4 | Determine or clarify the meaning of unknown and multiple-meaning words and phrases, choosing flexibly from an array of strategies | L4 pp. 216–221 |
| L.5 | Demonstrate understanding of figurative language, word relationships, and nuances in word meanings | L5 pp. 222–227 |
| L.6 | Acquire and use accurately general academic, and domain-specific words and phrases | L6 pp. 228–233 |
| **Reading History/Social Studies** | | |
| RH.1 | Cite textual evidence to support analysis of primary and secondary sources | R1 pp. 6–11 |
| RH.2 | Determine the central ideas or information of a primary or secondary source; provide an objective summary | R2 pp. 12–19 |
| RH.3 | Identify key steps in a text's description of a process related to history/social studies | R3 pp. 20–25 |
| RH.4 | Determine the meaning of words and phrases as they are used in a text, including vocabulary specific to history/social studies | R4 pp. 26–33 |
| RH.5 | Describe how a text presents information | R5 pp. 34–39 |
| RH.6 | Identify aspects of a text that reveal an author's point of view or purpose | R6 pp. 40–47 |
| RH.7 | Integrate visual information with other information in print and digital texts | R7 pp. 48–55 |
| RH.8 | Distinguish among fact, opinion, and reasoned judgment in a text | R8 pp. 56–63 |
| RH.9 | Analyze the relationship between a primary and secondary source on the same topic | R9 pp. 64–71 |
| RH.10 | Read and comprehend history/social studies texts of appropriate complexity independently with proficiency | R10 pp. 72–77 |
| **Reading Science/Technical Subjects** | | |
| RST.1 | Cite textual evidence to support analysis of science and technical texts | R1 pp. 6–11 |
| RST.2 | Determine the central ideas or conclusions of a text; provide an objective summary | R2 pp. 12–19 |
| RST.3 | Follow precisely a multistep procedure when carrying out experiments, taking measurements, or performing technical tasks | R3 pp. 20–25 |

| Louisiana Strand/Standard | Focus of Louisiana Standard | For More Information |
|---|---|---|
| **Reading Science/Technical Subjects** | | |
| RST.4 | Determine the meaning of symbols, key terms, and other domain-specific words and phrases | R4 pp. 26–33 |
| RST.5 | Analyze the structure an author uses to organize a text, including how the major sections contribute to the whole | R5 pp. 34–39 |
| RST.6 | Analyze the author's purpose in providing an explanation, describing a procedure, or discussing an experiment | R6 pp. 40–47 |
| RST.7 | Integrate quantitative or technical information expressed in words with a version of the information expressed visually | R7 pp. 48–55 |
| RST.8 | Distinguish among facts, reasoned judgment based on research findings, and speculation in a text | R8 pp. 56–63 |
| RST.9 | Compare and contrast the information gained from experiments, simulations, video, or multimedia sources with that gained from reading a text on the same topic | R9 pp. 64–71 |
| RST.10 | Read and comprehend appropriately complex science/technical texts independently and proficiently | R10 pp. 72–77 |
| **Writing History/Social Studies and Science/Technical Subjects** | | |
| WHST.1 | Write arguments based on discipline-specific content | W1 pp. 82–89 |
| WHST.2 | Write informative/explanatory texts including the narration of historical events, scientific procedures/experiments, or technical processes | W2 pp. 90–99 |
| WHST.3 | NA | |
| WHST.4 | Produce writing in which the development, organization, and style are appropriate to the task, purpose, and audience | W4 pp. 110–115 |
| WHST.5 | Develop and strengthen writing as needed by planning, revising, editing, rewriting, or trying a new approach | W5 pp. 116–121 |
| WHST.6 | Use technology to produce and publish writing as well as to interact with others; demonstrate keyboarding skills | W6 pp. 122–127 |
| WHST.7 | Conduct short research projects to answer a question, drawing on several sources and refocusing the inquiry when appropriate | W7 pp. 128–133 |
| WHST.8 | Gather information from print and digital sources; assess the credibility of sources; quote or paraphrase while avoiding plagiarism and providing basic bibliographic information | W8 pp. 134–139 |
| WHST.9 | Draw evidence from informational texts to support analysis, reflection, and research | W9 pp. 140–147 |
| WHST.10 | Write routinely over extended and shorter time frames for a range of tasks, purposes, and audiences | W10 pp. 148–153 |

# Louisiana, Grade 7

| Louisiana Strand/Standard | Focus of Louisiana Standard | For More Information |
|---|---|---|
| **Reading Literature** | | |
| RL.1 | Cite several pieces of textual evidence to support analysis of what the text says explicitly as well as inferences drawn from the text | R1 pp. 6–11 |
| RL.2 | Determine a theme or central idea of a text and analyze its development; provide an objective summary of the text | R2 pp. 12–19 |
| RL.3 | Analyze how particular elements of a story or drama interact | R3 pp. 20–25 |
| RL.4 | Determine the meaning of words and phrases as they are used in a text, including figurative and connotative meanings | R4 pp. 26–33 |
| RL.5 | Analyze how the overall structure of a text contributes to its meaning | R5 pp. 34–39 |
| RL.6 | Analyze how an author develops and contrasts the points of view of different characters or narrators in a text | R6 pp. 40–47 |
| RL.7 | Compare and contrast a written story, drama, or poem to its audio, filmed, staged, or multimedia version | R7 pp. 48–55 |

*(Continued)*

| Louisiana Strand/Standard | Focus of Louisiana Standard | For More Information |
|---|---|---|
| **Reading Literature** | | |
| RL.8 | NA | |
| RL.9 | Compare and contrast a fictional portrayal of a time, place, or character and a historical account of the same period | R9 pp. 64–71 |
| RL.10 | Read and comprehend literature of appropriate complexity independently with proficiency | R10 pp. 72–77 |
| **Reading Informational Text** | | |
| RI.1 | Cite several pieces of textual evidence to support analysis of what the text says explicitly as well as inferences drawn from the text | R1 pp. 6–11 |
| RI.2 | Determine two or more central ideas in a text and analyze their developments; provide an objective summary of the text | R2 pp. 12–19 |
| RI.3 | Analyze the interactions between individuals, events, and ideas in a text | R3 pp. 20–25 |
| RI.4 | Determine the meaning of words and phrases as they are used in a text, including figurative, connotative, and technical meanings | R4 pp. 26–33 |
| RI.5 | Analyze the structure an author uses to organize a text, including how the major sections contribute to the whole | R5 pp. 34–39 |
| RI.6 | Determine an author's point of view or purpose in a text and analyze how the author distinguishes his or her position from that of others | R6 pp. 40–47 |
| RI.7 | Compare and contrast a text to an audio, video, or multimedia version of the text | R7 pp. 48–55 |
| RI.8 | Trace and evaluate the argument and specific claims in a text, assessing whether the reason is sound and the evidence is relevant and sufficient | R8 pp. 56–63 |
| RI.9 | Analyze how two or more authors writing about the same topic shape their presentations of key information | R9 pp. 64–71 |
| RI.10 | Read and comprehend appropriately complex literary nonfiction, informational, and functional texts independently and proficiently | R10 pp. 72–77 |
| **Writing** | | |
| W.1 | Write arguments to support claims with clear reasons and relevant evidence | W1 pp. 82–89 |
| W.2 | Write informative/explanatory texts to examine a topic and convey ideas, concepts, and information clearly | W2 pp. 90–99 |
| W.3 | Write narratives to develop real or imagined experiences or events using effective technique, descriptive details, and well-structured event sequences | W3 pp. 100–109 |
| W.4 | Produce writing in which the development, organization, and style are appropriate to the task, purpose, and audience | W4 pp. 110–115 |
| W.5 | Develop and strengthen writing as needed by planning, revising, editing, rewriting, or trying a different approach | W5 pp. 116–121 |
| W.6 | Use technology to produce and publish writing, link to and cite sources; interact and collaborate with others | W6 pp. 122–127 |
| W.7 | Conduct short research projects to answer a question, drawing on several sources and generating additional related questions for further investigation | W7 pp. 128–133 |
| W.8 | Gather information from print and digital sources; assess the credibility of sources; quote or paraphrase while avoiding plagiarism and following a standard format for citation | W8 pp. 134–139 |
| W.9 | Draw evidence from literary or informational texts to support analysis, reflection, and research | W9 pp. 140–147 |
| W.10 | Write routinely over extended and shorter time frames for a range of tasks, purposes, and audiences | W10 pp. 148–153 |
| **Speaking and Listening** | | |
| SL.1 | Engage effectively in a range of collaborative discussions with diverse partners, building on others' ideas and expressing their own clearly | SL1 pp. 158–163 |
| SL.2 | Analyze the main ideas and supporting details presented in diverse media and formats and explain how the ideas clarify a topic, text, or issue under study | SL2 pp. 164–169 |
| SL.3 | Delineate a speaker's argument and specific claims evaluating the soundness of the reasoning and the relevance and sufficiency of the evidence | SL3 pp. 170–175 |
| SL.4 | Present claims and findings, emphasizing salient points in a focused coherent manner; use appropriate eye contact, adequate volume, and clear pronunciation | SL4 pp. 176–181 |

| Louisiana Strand/Standard | Focus of Louisiana Standard | For More Information |
|---|---|---|
| **Speaking and Listening** | | |
| SL.5 | Include multimedia components and visual displays in presentations to clarify claims and findings | SL5 pp. 182–187 |
| SL.6 | Adapt speech to a variety of contexts and tasks, demonstrating command of formal English when appropriate | SL6 pp. 188–193 |
| **Language** | | |
| L.1 | Demonstrate command of the conventions of standard English grammar and usage when writing or speaking | L1 pp. 198–203 |
| L.2 | Demonstrate command of the conventions of standard English capitalization, punctuation, and spelling when writing | L2 pp. 204–209 |
| L.3 | Use knowledge of language and its conventions when writing, speaking, reading, or listening | L3 pp. 210–215 |
| L.4 | Determine or clarify the meaning of unknown and multiple-meaning words and phrases, choosing flexibly from an array of strategies | L4 pp. 216–221 |
| L.5 | Demonstrate understanding of figurative language, word relationships, and nuances in word meanings | L5 pp. 222–227 |
| L.6 | Acquire and use accurately general academic, and domain-specific words and phrases | L6 pp. 228–233 |
| **Reading History/Social Studies** | | |
| RH.1 | Cite textual evidence to support analysis of primary and secondary sources | R1 pp. 6–11 |
| RH.2 | Determine the central ideas or information of a primary or secondary source; provide an objective summary | R2 pp. 12–19 |
| RH.3 | Identify key steps in a text's description of a process related to history/social studies | R3 pp. 20–25 |
| RH.4 | Determine the meaning of words and phrases as they are used in a text, including vocabulary specific to history/social studies | R4 pp. 26–33 |
| RH.5 | Describe how a text presents information | R5 pp. 34–39 |
| RH.6 | Identify aspects of a text that reveal an author's point of view or purpose | R6 pp. 40–47 |
| RH.7 | Integrate visual information with other information in print and digital texts | R7 pp. 48–55 |
| RH.8 | Distinguish among fact, opinion, and reasoned judgment in a text | R8 pp. 56–63 |
| RH.9 | Analyze the relationship between a primary and secondary source on the same topic | R9 pp. 64–71 |
| RH.10 | Read and comprehend history/social studies texts of appropriate complexity independently with proficiency | R10 pp. 72–77 |
| **Reading Science/Technical Subjects** | | |
| RST.1 | Cite textual evidence to support analysis of science and technical texts | R1 pp. 6–11 |
| RST.2 | Determine the central ideas or conclusions of a text; provide an objective summary | R2 pp. 12–19 |
| RST.3 | Follow precisely a multistep procedure when carrying out experiments, taking measurements, or performing technical tasks | R3 pp. 20–25 |
| RST.4 | Determine the meaning of symbols, key terms, and other domain-specific words and phrases | R4 pp. 26–33 |
| RST.5 | Analyze the structure an author uses to organize a text, including how the major sections contribute to the whole | R5 pp. 34–39 |
| RST.6 | Analyze the author's purpose in providing an explanation, describing a procedure, or discussing an experiment | R6 pp. 40–47 |
| RST.7 | Integrate quantitative or technical information expressed in words with a version of the information expressed visually | R7 pp. 48–55 |
| RST.8 | Distinguish among facts, reasoned judgment based on research findings, and speculation in a text | R8 pp. 56–63 |
| RST.9 | Compare and contrast the information gained from experiments, simulations, video, or multimedia sources with that gained from reading a text on the same topic | R9 pp. 64–71 |
| RST.10 | Read and comprehend appropriately complex science/technical texts independently and proficiently | R10 pp. 72–77 |
| **Writing History/Social Studies and Science/Technical Subjects** | | |
| WHST.1 | Write arguments based on discipline-specific content | W1 pp. 82–89 |
| WHST.2 | Write informative/explanatory texts including the narration of historical events, scientific procedures/experiments, or technical processes | W2 pp. 90–99 |

*(Continued)*

| Louisiana Strand/Standard | Focus of Louisiana Standard | For More Information |
|---|---|---|
| **Writing History/Social Studies and Science/Technical Subjects** | | |
| WHST.3 | NA | |
| WHST.4 | Produce writing in which the development, organization, and style are appropriate to the task, purpose, and audience | W4 pp. 110–115 |
| WHST.5 | Develop and strengthen writing as needed by planning, revising, editing, rewriting, or trying a new approach | W5 pp. 116–121 |
| WHST.6 | Use technology to produce and publish writing as well as to interact with others; demonstrate keyboarding skills | W6 pp. 122–127 |
| WHST.7 | Conduct short research projects to answer a question, drawing on several sources and refocusing the inquiry when appropriate | W7 pp. 128–133 |
| WHST.8 | Gather information from print and digital sources; assess the credibility of sources; quote or paraphrase while avoiding plagiarism and providing basic bibliographic information | W8 pp. 134–139 |
| WHST.9 | Draw evidence from informational texts to support analysis, reflection, and research | W9 pp. 140–147 |
| WHST.10 | Write routinely over extended and shorter time frames for a range of tasks, purposes, and audiences | W10 pp. 148–153 |

# Louisiana, Grade 8

| Louisiana Strand/Standard | Focus of Louisiana Standard | For More Information |
|---|---|---|
| **Reading Literature** | | |
| RL.1 | Cite the textual evidence that most strongly supports an analysis of what the text says explicitly as well as inferences drawn from the text | R1 pp. 6–11 |
| RL.2 | Determine the theme or central idea of a text and analyze its development, including its relationship to the characters, setting, and plot; provide an objective summary of the text | R2 pp. 12–19 |
| RL.3 | Analyze how particular lines of dialogue or incidents in a story or drama propel the action, reveal aspects of a character, or provoke a decision | R3 pp. 20–25 |
| RL.4 | Determine the meaning of words and phrases as they are used in a text, including figurative and connotative meanings | R4 pp. 26–33 |
| RL.5 | Compare and contrast the structure of two or more texts and analyze how the differing structure of each contributes to its meaning and style | R5 pp. 34–39 |
| RL.6 | Analyze how differences in the points of view of the characters and the audience or reader create such effects as suspense or humor | R6 pp. 40–47 |
| RL.7 | Analyze the extent to which non-print media connects to or departs from the text or script, evaluating the choices | R7 pp. 48–55 |
| RL.8 | NA | |
| RL.9 | Analyze how a modern work of fiction draws on themes, patterns of events, or character types from traditional stories, describing how the material is rendered new | R9 pp. 64–71 |
| RL.10 | Read and comprehend literature of appropriate complexity independently with proficiency | R10 pp. 72–77 |
| **Reading Informational Text** | | |
| RI.1 | Cite the textual evidence that most strongly supports an analysis of what the text says explicitly as well as inferences drawn from the text | R1 pp. 6–11 |
| RI.2 | Determine the central idea of a text and analyze its development, including its relationship to supporting ideas; provide an objective summary of the text | R2 pp. 12–19 |
| RI.3 | Analyze how a text makes connections among distinctions between individuals, ideas, or events | R3 pp. 20–25 |
| RI.4 | Determine the meaning of words and phrases as they are used in a text, including figurative, connotative, and technical meanings | R4 pp. 26–33 |
| RI.5 | Analyze the structure of a specific paragraph in a text, including the role of particular sentences in developing and refining a key concept | R5 pp. 34–39 |

| Louisiana Strand/Standard | Focus of Louisiana Standard | For More Information |
|---|---|---|
| **Reading Informational Text** | | |
| RI.6 | Determine an author's point of view or purpose in a text and analyze how the author acknowledges and responds to conflicting evidence or viewpoints | R6 pp. 40–47 |
| RI.7 | Evaluate the advantages and disadvantages of using different mediums to present a particular topic or idea | R7 pp. 48–55 |
| RI.8 | Delineate and evaluate the argument and specific claims in a text, assessing whether the reason is sound and the evidence is relevant and sufficient | R8 pp. 56–63 |
| RI.9 | Analyze a case in which two or more texts provide conflicting information on the same topic | R9 pp. 64–71 |
| RI.10 | Read and comprehend appropriately complex literary nonfiction, informational, and functional texts independently and proficiently | R10 pp. 72–77 |
| **Writing** | | |
| W.1 | Write arguments to support claims with clear reasons and relevant evidence | W1 pp. 82–89 |
| W.2 | Write informative/explanatory texts to examine a topic and convey ideas, concepts, and information clearly | W2 pp. 90–99 |
| W.3 | Write narratives to develop real or imagined experiences or events using effective technique, descriptive details, and well-structured event sequences | W3 pp. 100–109 |
| W.4 | Produce writing in which the development, organization, and style are appropriate to the task, purpose, and audience | W4 pp. 110–115 |
| W.5 | Develop and strengthen writing as needed by planning, revising, editing, rewriting, or trying a different approach | W5 pp. 116–121 |
| W.6 | Use technology to produce and publish writing, link to and cite sources; interact and collaborate with others | W6 pp. 122–127 |
| W.7 | Conduct short research projects to answer a question, drawing on several sources and generating additional related questions for further investigation | W7 pp. 128–133 |
| W.8 | Gather information from print and digital sources; assess the credibility of sources; quote or paraphrase while avoiding plagiarism and following a standard format for citation | W8 pp. 134–139 |
| W.9 | Draw evidence from literary or informational texts to support analysis, reflection, and research | W9 pp. 140–147 |
| W.10 | Write routinely over extended and shorter time frames for a range of tasks, purposes, and audiences | W10 pp. 148–153 |
| **Speaking and Listening** | | |
| SL.1 | Engage effectively in a range of collaborative discussions with diverse partners, building on others' ideas and expressing their own clearly | SL1 pp. 158–163 |
| SL.2 | Analyze the purpose of information presented in diverse media and formats and evaluate the motives behind its presentation | SL2 pp. 164–169 |
| SL.3 | Delineate a speaker's argument and specific claims evaluating the soundness of the reasoning and the relevance and sufficiency of the evidence and identifying when irrelevant evidence is introduced | SL3 pp. 170–175 |
| SL.4 | Present claims and findings, emphasizing salient points in a focused coherent manner; use appropriate eye contact, adequate volume, and clear pronunciation | SL4 pp. 176–181 |
| SL.5 | Integrate multimedia and visual displays into presentations to clarify information, strengthen claims and findings, and add interest | SL5 pp. 182–187 |
| SL.6 | Adapt speech to a variety of contexts and tasks, demonstrating command of formal English when appropriate | SL6 pp. 188–193 |
| **Language** | | |
| L.1 | Demonstrate command of the conventions of standard English grammar and usage when writing or speaking | L1 pp. 198–203 |
| L.2 | Demonstrate command of the conventions of standard English capitalization, punctuation, and spelling when writing | L2 pp. 204–209 |
| L.3 | Use knowledge of language and its conventions when writing, speaking, reading, or listening | L3 pp. 210–215 |
| L.4 | Determine or clarify the meaning of unknown and multiple-meaning words and phrases, choosing flexibly from an array of strategies | L4 pp. 216–221 |
| L.5 | Demonstrate understanding of figurative language, word relationships, and nuances in word meanings | L5 pp. 222–227 |
| L.6 | Acquire and use accurately general academic, and domain-specific words and phrases | L6 pp. 228–233 |

*(Continued)*

| Louisiana Strand/Standard | Focus of Louisiana Standard | For More Information |
|---|---|---|
| **Reading History/Social Studies** | | |
| RH.1 | Cite textual evidence to support analysis of primary and secondary sources | R1 pp. 6–11 |
| RH.2 | Determine the central ideas or information of a primary or secondary source; provide an objective summary | R2 pp. 12–19 |
| RH.3 | Identify key steps in a text's description of a process related to history/social studies | R3 pp. 20–25 |
| RH.4 | Determine the meaning of words and phrases as they are used in a text, including vocabulary specific to history/social studies | R4 pp. 26–33 |
| RH.5 | Describe how a text presents information | R5 pp. 34–39 |
| RH.6 | Identify aspects of a text that reveal an author's point of view or purpose | R6 pp. 40–47 |
| RH.7 | Integrate visual information with other information in print and digital texts | R7 pp. 48–55 |
| RH.8 | Distinguish among fact, opinion, and reasoned judgment in a text | R8 pp. 56–63 |
| RH.9 | Analyze the relationship between a primary and secondary source on the same topic | R9 pp. 64–71 |
| RH.10 | Read and comprehend history/social studies texts of appropriate complexity independently with proficiency | R10 pp. 72–77 |
| **Reading Science/Technical Subjects** | | |
| RST.1 | Cite textual evidence to support analysis of science and technical texts | R1 pp. 6–11 |
| RST.2 | Determine the central ideas or conclusions of a text; provide an objective summary | R2 pp. 12–19 |
| RST.3 | Follow precisely a multistep procedure when carrying out experiments, taking measurements, or performing technical tasks | R3 pp. 20–25 |
| RST.4 | Determine the meaning of symbols, key terms, and other domain-specific words and phrases | R4 pp. 26–33 |
| RST.5 | Analyze the structure an author uses to organize a text, including how the major sections contribute to the whole | R5 pp. 34–39 |
| RST.6 | Analyze the author's purpose in providing an explanation, describing a procedure, or discussing an experiment | R6 pp. 40–47 |
| RST.7 | Integrate quantitative or technical information expressed in words with a version of the information expressed visually | R7 pp. 48–55 |
| RST.8 | Distinguish among facts, reasoned judgment based on research findings, and speculation in a text | R8 pp. 56–63 |
| RST.9 | Compare and contrast the information gained from experiments, simulations, video, or multimedia sources with that gained from reading a text on the same topic | R9 pp. 64–71 |
| RST.10 | Read and comprehend appropriately complex science/technical texts independently and proficiently | R10 pp. 72–77 |
| **Writing History/Social Studies and Science/Technical Subjects** | | |
| WHST.1 | Write arguments based on discipline-specific content | W1 pp. 82–89 |
| WHST.2 | Write informative/explanatory texts including the narration of historical events, scientific procedures/experiments, or technical processes | W2 pp. 90–99 |
| WHST.3 | NA | |
| WHST.4 | Produce writing in which the development, organization, and style are appropriate to the task, purpose, and audience | W4 pp. 110–115 |
| WHST.5 | Develop and strengthen writing as needed by planning, revising, editing, rewriting, or trying a new approach | W5 pp. 116–121 |
| WHST.6 | Use technology to produce and publish writing as well as to interact with others; demonstrate keyboarding skills | W6 pp. 122–127 |
| WHST.7 | Conduct short research projects to answer a question, drawing on several sources and refocusing the inquiry when appropriate | W7 pp. 128–133 |
| WHST.8 | Gather information from print and digital sources; assess the credibility of sources; quote or paraphrase while avoiding plagiarism and providing basic bibliographic information | W8 pp. 134–139 |
| WHST.9 | Draw evidence from informational texts to support analysis, reflection, and research | W9 pp. 140–147 |
| WHST.10 | Write routinely over extended and shorter time frames for a range of tasks, purposes, and audiences | W10 pp. 148–153 |

# Maryland, Grade 6

| Maryland Strand/Standard | Focus of Maryland Standard | For More Information |
|---|---|---|
| **Reading Literature** | | |
| RL.1 | Cite textual evidence to support analysis of what the text says explicitly as well as inferences drawn from the text | R1 pp. 6–11 |
| RL.2 | Determine the theme or central idea of a text and how it is conveyed through particular details; provide an objective summary | R2 pp. 12–19 |
| RL.3 | Describe how a particular plot unfolds in a series of episodes as well as how the characters respond or change | R3 pp. 20–25 |
| RL.4 | Determine the meaning of words and phrases as they are used in a text, including figurative and connotative meanings | R4 pp. 26–33 |
| RL.5 | Analyze how a particular sentence, chapter, scene, or stanza fits into the overall structure of a text and contributes to the development of the theme, setting, or plot | R5 pp. 34–39 |
| RL.6 | Explain how an author develops the point of view of the narrator or speaker in a text | R6 pp. 40–47 |
| RL.7 | Compare and contrast the experience of reading a story, drama, or poem to listening to or viewing an audio, video, or live version of the text | R7 pp. 48–55 |
| RL.8 | NA | |
| RL.9 | Compare and contrast texts in different forms or genres in terms of their approaches to similar themes and topics | R9 pp. 64–71 |
| RL.10 | Read and comprehend literature of appropriate complexity independently with proficiency | R10 pp. 72–77 |
| **Reading Informational Text** | | |
| RI.1 | Cite textual evidence to support analysis of what the text says explicitly as well as inferences drawn from the text | R1 pp. 6–11 |
| RI.2 | Determine a central idea of a text and how it is conveyed through particular details; provide an objective summary | R2 pp. 12–19 |
| RI.3 | Analyze in detail how a key individual, event, or idea is introduced, illustrated, and elaborated in a text | R3 pp. 20–25 |
| RI.4 | Determine the meaning of words and phrases as they are used in a text, including figurative, connotative, and technical meanings | R4 pp. 26–33 |
| RI.5 | Analyze how a particular sentence, chapter, scene, or section fits into the overall structure of a text and contributes to the development of the ideas | R5 pp. 34–39 |
| RI.6 | Determine an author's point of view or purpose in a text and explain how it is conveyed in the text | R6 pp. 40–47 |
| RI.7 | Integrate information presented in different media or formats as well as in words to develop a coherent understanding of a topic or issue | R7 pp. 48–55 |
| RI.8 | Trace and evaluate the argument and specific claims that are supported by reasons and evidence from claims that are not | R8 pp. 56–63 |
| RI.9 | Compare and contrast one author's presentation of events with that of another | R9 pp. 64–71 |
| RI.10 | Read and comprehend appropriately complex literary nonfiction, informational, and functional texts independently and proficiently | R10 pp. 72–77 |
| **Writing** | | |
| W.1 | Write arguments to support claims with clear reasons and relevant evidence | W1 pp. 82–89 |
| W.2 | Write informative/explanatory texts to examine a topic and convey ideas, concepts, and information clearly | W2 pp. 90–99 |
| W.3 | Write narratives to develop real or imagined experiences or events using effective technique, descriptive details, and well-structured event sequences | W3 pp. 100–109 |
| W.4 | Produce writing in which the development, organization, and style are appropriate to the task, purpose, and audience | W4 pp. 110–115 |
| W.5 | Develop and strengthen writing as needed by planning, revising, editing, rewriting, or trying a new approach | W5 pp. 116–121 |
| W.6 | Use technology to produce and publish writing as well as to interact with others; demonstrate keyboarding skills | W6 pp. 122–127 |

*(Continued)*

| Maryland Strand/Standard | Focus of Maryland Standard | For More Information |
|---|---|---|
| **Writing** | | |
| W.7 | Conduct short research projects to answer a question, drawing on several sources and refocusing the inquiry when appropriate | W7 pp. 128–133 |
| W.8 | Gather information from print and digital sources; assess the credibility of sources; quote or paraphrase while avoiding plagiarism and providing basic bibliographic information | W8 pp. 134–139 |
| W.9 | Draw evidence from literary or informational texts to support analysis, reflection, and research | W9 pp. 140–147 |
| W.10 | Write routinely over extended and shorter time frames for a range of tasks, purposes, and audiences | W10 pp. 148–153 |
| **Speaking and Listening** | | |
| SL.1 | Engage effectively in a range of collaborative discussions with diverse partners, building on others' ideas and expressing their own clearly | SL1 pp. 158–163 |
| SL.2 | Interpret information presented in diverse media and formats and explain how it contributes to a topic, text, or issue under study | SL2 pp. 164–169 |
| SL.3 | Delineate a speaker's argument and specific claims that are supported by reasons and evidence from claims that are not | SL3 pp. 170–175 |
| SL.4 | Present claims and findings, sequencing ideas logically and using descriptions, facts, or details to accentuate main ideas or themes; use appropriate eye contact, adequate volume, and clear pronunciation | SL4 pp. 176–181 |
| SL.5 | Include multimedia components and visual displays in presentations to clarify information | SL5 pp. 182–187 |
| SL.6 | Adapt speech to a variety of contexts and tasks, demonstrating command of formal English when appropriate | SL6 pp. 188–193 |
| **Language** | | |
| L.1 | Demonstrate command of the conventions of standard English grammar and usage when writing or speaking | L1 pp. 198–203 |
| L.2 | Demonstrate command of the conventions of standard English capitalization, punctuation, and spelling when writing | L2 pp. 204–209 |
| L.3 | Use knowledge of language and its conventions when writing, speaking, reading, or listening | L3 pp. 210–215 |
| L.4 | Determine or clarify the meaning of unknown and multiple-meaning words and phrases, choosing flexibly from an array of strategies | L4 pp. 216–221 |
| L.5 | Demonstrate understanding of figurative language, word relationships, and nuances in word meanings | L5 pp. 222–227 |
| L.6 | Acquire and use accurately general academic, and domain-specific words and phrases | L6 pp. 228–233 |
| **Reading History/Social Studies** | | |
| RH.1 | Cite textual evidence to support analysis of primary and secondary sources | R1 pp. 6–11 |
| RH.2 | Determine the central ideas or information of a primary or secondary source; provide an objective summary | R2 pp. 12–19 |
| RH.3 | Identify key steps in a text's description of a process related to history/social studies | R3 pp. 20–25 |
| RH.4 | Determine the meaning of words and phrases as they are used in a text, including vocabulary specific to history/social studies | R4 pp. 26–33 |
| RH.5 | Describe how a text presents information | R5 pp. 34–39 |
| RH.6 | Identify aspects of a text that reveal an author's point of view or purpose | R6 pp. 40–47 |
| RH.7 | Integrate visual information with other information in print and digital texts | R7 pp. 48–55 |
| RH.8 | Distinguish among fact, opinion, and reasoned judgment in a text | R8 pp. 56–63 |
| RH.9 | Analyze the relationship between a primary and secondary source on the same topic | R9 pp. 64–71 |
| RH.10 | Read and comprehend history/social studies texts of appropriate complexity independently with proficiency | R10 pp. 72–77 |
| **Reading Science/Technical Subjects** | | |
| RST.1 | Cite textual evidence to support analysis of science and technical texts | R1 pp. 6–11 |
| RST.2 | Determine the central ideas or conclusions of a text; provide an objective summary | R2 pp. 12–19 |
| RST.3 | Follow precisely a multistep procedure when carrying out experiments, taking measurements, or performing technical tasks | R3 pp. 20–25 |

| Maryland Strand/Standard | Focus of Maryland Standard | For More Information |
|---|---|---|
| **Reading Science/Technical Subjects** | | |
| RST.4 | Determine the meaning of symbols, key terms, and other domain-specific words and phrases | R4 pp. 26–33 |
| RST.5 | Analyze the structure an author uses to organize a text, including how the major sections contribute to the whole | R5 pp. 34–39 |
| RST.6 | Analyze the author's purpose in providing an explanation, describing a procedure, or discussing an experiment | R6 pp. 40–47 |
| RST.7 | Integrate quantitative or technical information expressed in words with a version of the information expressed visually | R7 pp. 48–55 |
| RST.8 | Distinguish among facts, reasoned judgment based on research findings, and speculation in a text | R8 pp. 56–63 |
| RST.9 | Compare and contrast the information gained from experiments, simulations, video, or multimedia sources with that gained from reading a text on the same topic | R9 pp. 64–71 |
| RST.10 | Read and comprehend appropriately complex science/technical texts independently and proficiently | R10 pp. 72–77 |
| **Writing History/Social Studies and Science/Technical Subjects** | | |
| WHST.1 | Write arguments based on discipline-specific content | W1 pp. 82–89 |
| WHST.2 | Write informative/explanatory texts including the narration of historical events, scientific procedures/experiments, or technical processes | W2 pp. 90–99 |
| WHST.3 | NA | |
| WHST.4 | Produce writing in which the development, organization, and style are appropriate to the task, purpose, and audience | W4 pp. 110–115 |
| WHST.5 | Develop and strengthen writing as needed by planning, revising, editing, rewriting, or trying a new approach | W5 pp. 116–121 |
| WHST.6 | Use technology to produce and publish writing as well as to interact with others; demonstrate keyboarding skills | W6 pp. 122–127 |
| WHST.7 | Conduct short research projects to answer a question, drawing on several sources and refocusing the inquiry when appropriate | W7 pp. 128–133 |
| WHST.8 | Gather information from print and digital sources; assess the credibility of sources; quote or paraphrase while avoiding plagiarism and providing basic bibliographic information | W8 pp. 134–139 |
| WHST.9 | Draw evidence from informational texts to support analysis, reflection, and research | W9 pp. 140–147 |
| WHST.10 | Write routinely over extended and shorter time frames for a range of tasks, purposes, and audiences | W10 pp. 148–153 |

# Maryland, Grade 7

| Maryland Strand/Standard | Focus of Maryland Standard | For More Information |
|---|---|---|
| **Reading Literature** | | |
| RL.1 | Cite several pieces of textual evidence to support analysis of what the text says explicitly as well as inferences drawn from the text | R1 pp. 6–11 |
| RL.2 | Determine the theme or central idea of a text and analyze its development; provide an objective summary of the text | R2 pp. 12–19 |
| RL.3 | Analyze how particular elements of a story or drama interact | R3 pp. 20–25 |
| RL.4 | Determine the meaning of words and phrases as they are used in a text, including figurative and connotative meanings | R4 pp. 26–33 |
| RL.5 | Analyze how a drama's or poem's form or structure contributes to its meaning | R5 pp. 34–39 |
| RL.6 | Analyze how an author develops and contrasts the points of view of different characters or narrators in a text | R6 pp. 40–47 |
| RL.7 | Compare and contrast a written story, drama, or poem to its audio, filmed, staged, or multimedia version | R7 pp. 48–55 |
| RL.8 | NA | |

*(Continued)*

| Maryland Strand/Standard | Focus of Maryland Standard | For More Information |
|---|---|---|
| **Reading Literature** | | |
| RL.9 | Compare and contrast a fictional portrayal of a time, place, or character and a historical account of the same period | R9 pp. 64–71 |
| RL.10 | Read and comprehend literature of appropriate complexity independently with proficiency | R10 pp. 72–77 |
| **Reading Informational Text** | | |
| RI.1 | Cite several pieces of textual evidence to support analysis of what the text says explicitly as well as inferences drawn from the text | R1 pp. 6–11 |
| RI.2 | Determine two or more central ideas in a text and analyze their developments; provide an objective summary of the text | R2 pp. 12–19 |
| RI.3 | Analyze the interactions between individuals, events, and ideas in a text | R3 pp. 20–25 |
| RI.4 | Determine the meaning of words and phrases as they are used in a text, including figurative, connotative, and technical meanings | R4 pp. 26–33 |
| RI.5 | Analyze the structure an author uses to organize a text, including how the major sections contribute to the whole | R5 pp. 34–39 |
| RI.6 | Determine an author's point of view or purpose in a text and analyze how the author distinguishes his or her position from that of others | R6 pp. 40–47 |
| RI.7 | Compare and contrast a text to an audio, video, or multimedia version of the text | R7 pp. 48–55 |
| RI.8 | Trace and evaluate the argument and specific claims in a text, assessing whether the reason is sound and the evidence is relevant and sufficient | R8 pp. 56–63 |
| RI.9 | Analyze how two or more authors writing about the same topic shape their presentations of key information | R9 pp. 64–71 |
| RI.10 | Read and comprehend appropriately complex literary nonfiction, informational, and functional texts independently and proficiently | R10 pp. 72–77 |
| **Writing** | | |
| W.1 | Write arguments to support claims with clear reasons and relevant evidence | W1 pp. 82–89 |
| W.2 | Write informative/explanatory texts to examine a topic and convey ideas, concepts, and information clearly | W2 pp. 90–99 |
| W.3 | Write narratives to develop real or imagined experiences or events using effective technique, descriptive details, and well-structured event sequences | W3 pp. 100–109 |
| W.4 | Produce writing in which the development, organization, and style are appropriate to the task, purpose, and audience | W4 pp. 110–115 |
| W.5 | Develop and strengthen writing as needed by planning, revising, editing, rewriting, or trying a new approach | W5 pp. 116–121 |
| W.6 | Use technology to produce and publish writing, link to and cite sources; interact and collaborate with others | W6 pp. 122–127 |
| W.7 | Conduct short research projects to answer a question, drawing on several sources and additional related questions for further investigation | W7 pp. 128–133 |
| W.8 | Gather information from print and digital sources; assess the credibility of sources; quote or paraphrase while avoiding plagiarism and following a standard format for citation | W8 pp. 134–139 |
| W.9 | Draw evidence from literary or informational texts to support analysis, reflection, and research | W9 pp. 140–147 |
| W.10 | Write routinely over extended and shorter time frames for a range of tasks, purposes, and audiences | W10 pp. 148–153 |
| **Speaking and Listening** | | |
| SL.1 | Engage effectively in a range of collaborative discussions with diverse partners, building on others' ideas and expressing their own clearly | SL1 pp. 158–163 |
| SL.2 | Analyze the main ideas and supporting details presented in diverse media and formats and explain how the ideas clarify a topic, text, or issue under study | SL2 pp. 164–169 |
| SL.3 | Delineate a speaker's argument and specific claims evaluating the soundness of the reasoning and the relevance and sufficiency of the evidence | SL3 pp. 170–175 |
| SL.4 | Present claims and findings, emphasizing salient points in a focused coherent manner; use appropriate eye contact, adequate volume, and clear pronunciation | SL4 pp. 176–181 |
| SL.5 | Include multimedia components and visual displays in presentations to clarify claims and findings | SL5 pp. 182–187 |
| SL.6 | Adapt speech to a variety of contexts and tasks, demonstrating command of formal English when appropriate | SL6 pp. 188–193 |

| Maryland Strand/Standard | Focus of Maryland Standard | For More Information |
|---|---|---|
| **Language** | | |
| L.1 | Demonstrate command of the conventions of standard English grammar and usage when writing or speaking | L1 pp. 198–203 |
| L.2 | Demonstrate command of the conventions of standard English capitalization, punctuation, and spelling when writing | L2 pp. 204–209 |
| L.3 | Use knowledge of language and its conventions when writing, speaking, reading, or listening | L3 pp. 210–215 |
| L.4 | Determine or clarify the meaning of unknown and multiple-meaning words and phrases, choosing flexibly from an array of strategies | L4 pp. 216–221 |
| L.5 | Demonstrate understanding of figurative language, word relationships, and nuances in word meanings | L5 pp. 222–227 |
| L.6 | Acquire and use accurately general academic, and domain-specific words and phrases | L6 pp. 228–233 |
| **Reading History/Social Studies** | | |
| RH.1 | Cite textual evidence to support analysis of primary and secondary sources | R1 pp. 6–11 |
| RH.2 | Determine the central ideas or information of a primary or secondary source; provide an objective summary | R2 pp. 12–19 |
| RH.3 | Identify key steps in a text's description of a process related to history/social studies | R3 pp. 20–25 |
| RH.4 | Determine the meaning of words and phrases as they are used in a text, including vocabulary specific to history/social studies | R4 pp. 26–33 |
| RH.5 | Describe how a text presents information | R5 pp. 34–39 |
| RH.6 | Identify aspects of a text that reveal an author's point of view or purpose | R6 pp. 40–47 |
| RH.7 | Integrate visual information with other information in print and digital texts | R7 pp. 48–55 |
| RH.8 | Distinguish among fact, opinion, and reasoned judgment in a text | R8 pp. 56–63 |
| RH.9 | Analyze the relationship between a primary and secondary source on the same topic | R9 pp. 64–71 |
| RH.10 | Read and comprehend history/social studies texts of appropriate complexity independently with proficiency | R10 pp. 72–77 |
| **Reading Science/Technical Subjects** | | |
| RST.1 | Cite textual evidence to support analysis of science and technical texts | R1 pp. 6–11 |
| RST.2 | Determine the central ideas or conclusions of a text; provide an objective summary | R2 pp. 12–19 |
| RST.3 | Follow precisely a multistep procedure when carrying out experiments, taking measurements, or performing technical tasks | R3 pp. 20–25 |
| RST.4 | Determine the meaning of symbols, key terms, and other domain-specific words and phrases | R4 pp. 26–33 |
| RST.5 | Analyze the structure an author uses to organize a text, including how the major sections contribute to the whole | R5 pp. 34–39 |
| RST.6 | Analyze the author's purpose in providing an explanation, describing a procedure, or discussing an experiment | R6 pp. 40–47 |
| RST.7 | Integrate quantitative or technical information expressed in words with a version of the information expressed visually | R7 pp. 48–55 |
| RST.8 | Distinguish among facts, reasoned judgment based on research findings, and speculation in a text | R8 pp. 56–63 |
| RST.9 | Compare and contrast the information gained from experiments, simulations, video, or multimedia sources with that gained from reading a text on the same topic | R9 pp. 64–71 |
| RST.10 | Read and comprehend appropriately complex science/technical texts independently and proficiently | R10 pp. 72–77 |
| **Writing History/Social Studies and Science/Technical Subjects** | | |
| WHST.1 | Write arguments based on discipline-specific content | W1 pp. 82–89 |
| WHST.2 | Write informative/explanatory texts including the narration of historical events, scientific procedures/experiments, or technical processes | W2 pp. 90–99 |
| WHST.3 | NA | |
| WHST.4 | Produce writing in which the development, organization, and style are appropriate to the task, purpose, and audience | W4 pp. 110–115 |

*(Continued)*

| Maryland Strand/Standard | Focus of Maryland Standard | For More Information |
|---|---|---|
| **Writing History/Social Studies and Science/Technical Subjects** | | |
| WHST.5 | Develop and strengthen writing as needed by planning, revising, editing, rewriting, or trying a new approach | W5 pp. 116–121 |
| WHST.6 | Use technology to produce and publish writing as well as to interact with others; demonstrate keyboarding skills | W6 pp. 122–127 |
| WHST.7 | Conduct short research projects to answer a question, drawing on several sources and refocusing the inquiry when appropriate | W7 pp. 128–133 |
| WHST.8 | Gather information from print and digital sources; assess the credibility of sources; quote or paraphrase while avoiding plagiarism and providing basic bibliographic information | W8 pp. 134–139 |
| WHST.9 | Draw evidence from informational texts to support analysis, reflection, and research | W9 pp. 140–147 |
| WHST.10 | Write routinely over extended and shorter time frames for a range of tasks, purposes, and audiences | W10 pp. 148–153 |

# Maryland, Grade 8

| Maryland Strand/Standard | Focus of Maryland Standard | For More Information |
|---|---|---|
| **Reading Literature** | | |
| RL.1 | Cite the textual evidence that most strongly supports an analysis of what the text says explicitly as well as inferences drawn from the text | R1 pp. 6–11 |
| RL.2 | Determine the theme or central idea of a text and analyze its development, including its relationship to the characters, setting, and plot; provide an objective summary of the text | R2 pp. 12–19 |
| RL.3 | Analyze how particular lines of dialogue or incidents in a story or drama propel the action, reveal aspects of a character, or provoke a decision | R3 pp. 20–25 |
| RL.4 | Determine the meaning of words and phrases as they are used in a text, including figurative and connotative meanings | R4 pp. 26–33 |
| RL.5 | Compare and contrast the structure of two or more texts and analyze how the differing structure of each contributes to its meaning and style | R5 pp. 34–39 |
| RL.6 | Analyze how differences in the points of view of the characters and the audience or reader create such effects as suspense or humor | R6 pp. 40–47 |
| RL.7 | Analyze the extent to which a filmed or live production of a story or drama stays faithful or departs from the text or script | R7 pp. 48–55 |
| RL.8 | NA | |
| RL.9 | Analyze how a modern work of fiction draws on themes, patterns of events, or character types from traditional stories, describing how the material is rendered new | R9 pp. 64–71 |
| RL.10 | Read and comprehend literature of appropriate complexity independently with proficiency | R10 pp. 72–77 |
| **Reading Informational Text** | | |
| RI.1 | Cite the textual evidence that most strongly supports an analysis of what the text says explicitly as well as inferences drawn from the text | R1 pp. 6–11 |
| RI.2 | Determine the central idea of a text and analyze its development, including its relationship to supporting ideas; provide an objective summary of the text | R2 pp. 12–19 |
| RI.3 | Analyze how a text makes connections among distinctions between individuals, ideas, or events | R3 pp. 20–25 |
| RI.4 | Determine the meaning of words and phrases as they are used in a text, including figurative, connotative, and technical meanings | R4 pp. 26–33 |
| RI.5 | Analyze the structure of a specific paragraph in a text, including the role of particular sentences in developing and refining a key concept | R5 pp. 34–39 |
| RI.6 | Determine an author's point of view or purpose in a text and analyze how the author acknowledges and responds to conflicting evidence or viewpoints | R6 pp. 40–47 |
| RI.7 | Evaluate the advantages and disadvantages of using different mediums to present a particular topic or idea | R7 pp. 48–55 |

| Maryland Strand/Standard | Focus of Maryland Standard | For More Information |
|---|---|---|
| **Reading Informational Text** | | |
| RI.8 | Delineate and evaluate the argument and specific claims in a text, assessing whether the reason is sound and the evidence is relevant and sufficient | R8 pp. 56–63 |
| RI.9 | Analyze a case in which two or more texts provide conflicting information on the same topic | R9 pp. 64–71 |
| RI.10 | Read and comprehend appropriately complex literary nonfiction, informational, and functional texts independently and proficiently | R10 pp. 72–77 |
| **Writing** | | |
| W.1 | Write arguments to support claims with clear reasons and relevant evidence | W1 pp. 82–89 |
| W.2 | Write informative/explanatory texts to examine a topic and convey ideas, concepts, and information clearly | W2 pp. 90–99 |
| W.3 | Write narratives to develop real or imagined experiences or events using effective technique, descriptive details, and well-structured event sequences | W3 pp. 100–109 |
| W.4 | Produce writing in which the development, organization, and style are appropriate to the task, purpose, and audience | W4 pp. 110–115 |
| W.5 | Develop and strengthen writing as needed by planning, revising, editing, rewriting, or trying a new approach | W5 pp. 116–121 |
| W.6 | Use technology to produce and publish writing, link to and cite sources; interact and collaborate with others | W6 pp. 122–127 |
| W.7 | Conduct short research projects to answer a question, drawing on several sources and additional related questions for further investigation | W7 pp. 128–133 |
| W.8 | Gather information from print and digital sources; assess the credibility of sources; quote or paraphrase while avoiding plagiarism and following a standard format for citation | W8 pp. 134–139 |
| W.9 | Draw evidence from literary or informational texts to support analysis, reflection, and research | W9 pp. 140–147 |
| W.10 | Write routinely over extended and shorter time frames for a range of tasks, purposes, and audiences | W10 pp. 148–153 |
| **Speaking and Listening** | | |
| SL.1 | Engage effectively in a range of collaborative discussions with diverse partners, building on others' ideas and expressing their own clearly | SL1 pp. 158–163 |
| SL.2 | Analyze the purpose of information presented in diverse media and formats and evaluate the motives behind its presentation | SL2 pp. 164–169 |
| SL.3 | Delineate a speaker's argument and specific claims evaluating the soundness of the reasoning and the relevance and sufficiency of the evidence and identifying when irrelevant evidence is introduced | SL3 pp. 170–175 |
| SL.4 | Present claims and findings, emphasizing salient points in a focused coherent manner; use appropriate eye contact, adequate volume, and clear pronunciation | SL4 pp. 176–181 |
| SL.5 | Integrate multimedia components and visual displays into presentations to clarify information, strengthen claims and findings, and add interest | SL5 pp. 182–187 |
| SL.6 | Adapt speech to a variety of contexts and tasks, demonstrating command of formal English when appropriate | SL6 pp. 188–193 |
| **Language** | | |
| L.1 | Demonstrate command of the conventions of standard English grammar and usage when writing or speaking | L1 pp. 198–203 |
| L.2 | Demonstrate command of the conventions of standard English capitalization, punctuation, and spelling when writing | L2 pp. 204–209 |
| L.3 | Use knowledge of language and its conventions when writing, speaking, reading, or listening | L3 pp. 210–215 |
| L.4 | Determine or clarify the meaning of unknown and multiple-meaning words and phrases, choosing flexibly from an array of strategies | L4 pp. 216–221 |
| L.5 | Demonstrate understanding of figurative language, word relationships, and nuances in word meanings | L5 pp. 222–227 |
| L.6 | Acquire and use accurately general academic, and domain-specific words and phrases | L6 pp. 228–233 |
| **Reading History/Social Studies** | | |
| RH.1 | Cite textual evidence to support analysis of primary and secondary sources | R1 pp. 6–11 |
| RH.2 | Determine the central ideas or information of a primary or secondary source; provide an objective summary | R2 pp. 12–19 |

*(Continued)*

| Maryland Strand/Standard | Focus of Maryland Standard | For More Information |
|---|---|---|
| **Reading History/Social Studies** | | |
| RH.3 | Identify key steps in a text's description of a process related to history/social studies | R3 pp. 20–25 |
| RH.4 | Determine the meaning of words and phrases as they are used in a text, including vocabulary specific to history/social studies | R4 pp. 26–33 |
| RH.5 | Describe how a text presents information | R5 pp. 34–39 |
| RH.6 | Identify aspects of a text that reveal an author's point of view or purpose | R6 pp. 40–47 |
| RH.7 | Integrate visual information with other information in print and digital texts | R7 pp. 48–55 |
| RH.8 | Distinguish among fact, opinion, and reasoned judgment in a text | R8 pp. 56–63 |
| RH.9 | Analyze the relationship between a primary and secondary source on the same topic | R9 pp. 64–71 |
| RH.10 | Read and comprehend history/social studies texts of appropriate complexity independently with proficiency | R10 pp. 72–77 |
| **Reading Science/Technical Subjects** | | |
| RST.1 | Cite textual evidence to support analysis of science and technical texts | R1 pp. 6–11 |
| RST.2 | Determine the central ideas or conclusions of a text; provide an objective summary | R2 pp. 12–19 |
| RST.3 | Follow precisely a multistep procedure when carrying out experiments, taking measurements, or performing technical tasks | R3 pp. 20–25 |
| RST.4 | Determine the meaning of symbols, key terms, and other domain-specific words and phrases | R4 pp. 26–33 |
| RST.5 | Analyze the structure an author uses to organize a text, including how the major sections contribute to the whole | R5 pp. 34–39 |
| RST.6 | Analyze the author's purpose in providing an explanation, describing a procedure, or discussing an experiment | R6 pp. 40–47 |
| RST.7 | Integrate quantitative or technical information expressed in words with a version of the information expressed visually | R7 pp. 48–55 |
| RST.8 | Distinguish among facts, reasoned judgment based on research findings, and speculation in a text | R8 pp. 56–63 |
| RST.9 | Compare and contrast the information gained from experiments, simulations, video, or multimedia sources with that gained from reading a text on the same topic | R9 pp. 64–71 |
| RST.10 | Read and comprehend appropriately complex science/technical texts independently and proficiently | R10 pp. 72–77 |
| **Writing History/Social Studies and Science/Technical Subjects** | | |
| WHST.1 | Write arguments based on discipline-specific content | W1 pp. 82–89 |
| WHST.2 | Write informative/explanatory texts including the narration of historical events, scientific procedures/experiments, or technical processes | W2 pp. 90–99 |
| WHST.3 | NA | |
| WHST.4 | Produce writing in which the development, organization, and style are appropriate to the task, purpose, and audience | W4 pp. 110–115 |
| WHST.5 | Develop and strengthen writing as needed by planning, revising, editing, rewriting, or trying a new approach | W5 pp. 116–121 |
| WHST.6 | Use technology to produce and publish writing as well as to interact with others; demonstrate keyboarding skills | W6 pp. 122–127 |
| WHST.7 | Conduct short research projects to answer a question, drawing on several sources and refocusing the inquiry when appropriate | W7 pp. 128–133 |
| WHST.8 | Gather information from print and digital sources; assess the credibility of sources; quote or paraphrase while avoiding plagiarism and providing basic bibliographic information | W8 pp. 134–139 |
| WHST.9 | Draw evidence from informational texts to support analysis, reflection, and research | W9 pp. 140–147 |
| WHST.10 | Write routinely over extended and shorter time frames for a range of tasks, purposes, and audiences | W10 pp. 148–153 |

# Minnesota, Grade 6

| Minnesota Strand/Standard | Focus of Minnesota Standard | For More Information |
|---|---|---|
| **Reading Literature** | | |
| 4.1.1 | Cite textual evidence to support analysis of what the text says explicitly as well as inferences drawn from the text | R1 pp. 6–11 |
| 4.2.2 | Determine the theme or central idea of a text and how it is conveyed through particular details; provide an objective summary | R2 pp. 12–19 |
| 4.3.3 | Describe how a particular plot unfolds in a series of episodes as well as how the characters respond or change | R3 pp. 20–25 |
| 4.4.4 | Determine the meaning of words and phrases as they are used in a text, including figurative and connotative meanings | R4 pp. 26–33 |
| 4.5.5 | Analyze how a particular sentence, chapter, scene, or stanza fits into the overall structure of a text and contributes to the development of the theme, setting, or plot | R5 pp. 34–39 |
| 4.6.6 | Explain how an author develops the point of view of the narrator or speaker in a text | R6 pp. 40–47 |
| 4.7.7 | Compare and contrast the experience of reading a story, drama, or poem to listening to or viewing an audio, video, or live version of the text | R7 pp. 48–55 |
| 4.8.8 | NA | |
| 4.9.9 | Compare and contrast texts in different forms or genres in terms of their approaches to similar themes and topics | R9 pp. 64–71 |
| 4.10.10 | Read and comprehend literature of appropriate complexity independently with proficiency | R10 pp. 72–77 |
| **Read Informational Texts** | | |
| 5.1.1 | Cite textual evidence to support analysis of what the text says explicitly as well as inferences drawn from the text | R1 pp. 6–11 |
| 5.2.2 | Determine a central idea of a text and how it is conveyed through particular details; provide an objective summary | R2 pp. 12–19 |
| 5.3.3 | Analyze in detail how a key individual, event, or idea is introduced, illustrated, and elaborated in a text | R3 pp. 20–25 |
| 5.4.4 | Determine the meaning of words and phrases as they are used in a text, including figurative, connotative, and technical meanings | R4 pp. 26–33 |
| 5.5.5 | Analyze how a particular sentence, chapter, scene, or section fits into the overall structure of a text and contributes to the development of the ideas | R5 pp. 34–39 |
| 5.6.6 | Determine an author's point of view or purpose in a text and explain how it is conveyed in the text | R6 pp. 40–47 |
| 5.7.7 | Integrate information presented in different media or formats as well as in words to develop a coherent understanding of a topic or issue | R7 pp. 48–55 |
| 5.8.8 | Trace and evaluate the argument and specific claims, distinguishing claims that are supported by reasons and evidence from claims that are not | R8 pp. 56–63 |
| 5.9.9 | Compare and contrast one author's presentation of events with that of another | R9 pp. 64–71 |
| 5.10.10 | Read and comprehend appropriately complex literary nonfiction, informational, and functional texts independently and proficiently | R10 pp. 72–77 |
| **Writing** | | |
| 7.1.1 | Write arguments to support claims with clear reasons and relevant evidence | W1 pp. 82–89 |
| 7.2.2 | Write informative/explanatory texts to examine a topic and convey ideas, concepts, and information clearly | W2 pp. 90–99 |
| 7.3.3 | Write narratives and other creative texts to develop real or imagined experiences or events using effective technique, descriptive details, and well-structured event sequences | W3 pp. 100–109 |
| 7.4.4 | Produce writing in which the development, organization, and style are appropriate to the task, purpose, and audience | W4 pp. 110–115 |
| 7.5.5 | Use a writing process to develop and strengthen writing as needed by planning, revising, editing, rewriting, or trying a new approach | W5 pp. 116–121 |
| 7.6.6 | Use technology to produce and publish writing as well as to interact with others; demonstrate keyboarding skills | W6 pp. 122–127 |

*(Continued)*

| Minnesota Strand/Standard | Focus of Minnesota Standard | For More Information |
|---|---|---|
| **Writing** | | |
| 7.7.7 | Conduct short research projects to answer a question, drawing on several sources and refocusing the inquiry when appropriate | W7 pp. 128–133 |
| 7.8.8 | Gather information from print and digital sources; assess the credibility of sources; quote or paraphrase while avoiding plagiarism and providing basic bibliographic information | W8 pp. 134–139 |
| 7.9.9 | Draw evidence from literary or informational texts to support analysis, reflection, and research | W9 pp. 140–147 |
| 7.10.10 | Write routinely over extended and shorter time frames for a range of tasks, purposes, and audiences | W10 pp. 148–153 |
| **Speaking, Viewing, Listening, and Media Literacy** | | |
| 9.1.1 | Engage effectively in a range of collaborative discussions with diverse partners, building on others' ideas and expressing their own clearly | SL1 pp. 158–163 |
| 9.2.2 | Interpret information presented in diverse media and formats and explain how it contributes to a topic, text, or issue under study | SL2 pp. 164–169 |
| 9.3.3 | Delineate a speaker's argument and specific claims that are supported by reasons and evidence from claims that are not | SL3 pp. 170–175 |
| 9.4.4 | Present claims and findings, sequencing ideas logically and using descriptions, facts, or details to accentuate main ideas or themes; use appropriate eye contact, adequate volume, and clear pronunciation | SL4 pp. 176–181 |
| 9.5.5 | Include multimedia components and visual displays in presentations to clarify information | SL5 pp. 182–187 |
| 9.6.6 | Adapt speech to a variety of contexts and tasks, demonstrating command of formal English when appropriate | SL6 pp. 188–193 |
| 9.7.7 | NA | |
| 9.8.8 | NA | |
| **Language** | | |
| 11.1.1 | Demonstrate command of the conventions of standard English grammar and usage when writing or speaking | L1 pp. 198–203 |
| 11.2.2 | Demonstrate command of the conventions of standard English capitalization, punctuation, and spelling when writing | L2 pp. 204–209 |
| 11.3.3 | Use knowledge of language and its conventions when writing, speaking, reading, or listening | L3 pp. 210–215 |
| 11.4.4 | Determine or clarify the meaning of unknown and multiple-meaning words and phrases, choosing flexibly from an array of strategies | L4 pp. 216–221 |
| 11.5.5 | Demonstrate understanding of figurative language, word relationships, and nuances in word meanings | L5 pp. 222–227 |
| 11.6.6 | Acquire and use accurately general academic, and domain-specific words and phrases | L6 pp. 228–233 |
| **Literacy in History/Social Studies** | | |
| 12.1.1 | Cite textual evidence to support analysis of primary and secondary sources | R1 pp. 6–11 |
| 12.2.2 | Determine the central ideas or information of a primary or secondary source; provide an objective summary | R2 pp. 12–19 |
| 12.3.3 | Identify key steps in a text's description of a process related to history/social studies | R3 pp. 20–25 |
| 12.4.4 | Determine the meaning of words and phrases as they are used in a text, including vocabulary specific to history/social studies | R4 pp. 26–33 |
| 12.5.5 | Describe how a text presents information | R5 pp. 34–39 |
| 12.6.6 | Identify aspects of a text that reveal an author's point of view or purpose | R6 pp. 40–47 |
| 12.7.7 | Integrate visual information with other information in print and digital texts | R7 pp. 48–55 |
| 12.8.8 | Distinguish among fact, opinion, and reasoned judgment in a text | R8 pp. 56–63 |
| 12.9.9 | Analyze the relationship between a primary and secondary source on the same topic | R9 pp. 64–71 |
| 12.10.10 | Read and comprehend history/social studies texts of appropriate complexity independently with proficiency | R10 pp. 72–77 |
| **Reading Science/Technical Subjects** | | |
| 13.1.1 | Cite textual evidence to support analysis of science and technical texts | R1 pp. 6–11 |
| 13.2.2 | Determine the central ideas or conclusions of a text; provide an objective summary | R2 pp. 12–19 |

| Minnesota Strand/Standard | Focus of Minnesota Standard | For More Information |
|---|---|---|
| **Reading Science/Technical Subjects** | | |
| 13.3.3 | Follow precisely a multistep procedure when carrying out experiments, taking measurements, or performing technical tasks | R3 pp. 20–25 |
| 13.4.4 | Determine the meaning of symbols, key terms, and other domain-specific words and phrases | R4 pp. 26–33 |
| 13.5.5 | Analyze the structure an author uses to organize a text, including how the major sections contribute to the whole | R5 pp. 34–39 |
| 13.6.6 | Analyze the author's purpose in providing an explanation, describing a procedure, or discussing an experiment | R6 pp. 40–47 |
| 13.7.7 | Integrate quantitative or technical information expressed in words with a version of the information expressed visually | R7 pp. 48–55 |
| 13.8.8 | Distinguish among facts, reasoned judgment based on research findings, and speculation in a text | R8 pp. 56–63 |
| 13.9.9 | Compare and contrast the information gained from experiments, simulations, video, or multimedia sources with that gained from reading a text on the same topic | R9 pp. 64–71 |
| 13.10.10 | Read and comprehend appropriately complex science/technical texts independently and proficiently | R10 pp. 72–77 |
| **Writing History/Social Studies, Science and Technical Subjects** | | |
| 14.1.1 | Write arguments based on discipline-specific content | W1 pp. 82–89 |
| 14.2.2 | Write informative/explanatory texts including the narration of historical events, scientific procedures/experiments, or technical processes | W2 pp. 90–99 |
| 14.3.3 | NA | |
| 14.4.4 | Produce writing in which the development, organization, and style are appropriate to the task, purpose, and audience | W4 pp. 110–115 |
| 14.5.5 | Develop and strengthen writing as needed by planning, revising, editing, rewriting, or trying a new approach | W5 pp. 116–121 |
| 14.6.6 | Use technology to produce and publish writing as well as to interact with others; demonstrate keyboarding skills | W6 pp. 122–127 |
| 14.7.7 | Conduct short research projects to answer a question, drawing on several sources and refocusing the inquiry when appropriate | W7 pp. 128–133 |
| 14.8.8 | Gather information from print and digital sources; assess the credibility of sources; quote or paraphrase while avoiding plagiarism and providing basic bibliographic information | W8 pp. 134–139 |
| 14.9.9 | Draw evidence from informational texts to support analysis, reflection, and research | W9 pp. 140–147 |
| 14.10.10 | Write routinely over extended and shorter time frames for a range of tasks, purposes, and audiences | W10 pp. 148–153 |

# Minnesota, Grade 7

| Minnesota Strand/Standard | Focus of Minnesota Standard | For More Information |
|---|---|---|
| **Reading Literature** | | |
| 4.1.1 | Cite several pieces of textual evidence to support analysis of what the text says explicitly as well as inferences drawn from the text | R1 pp. 6–11 |
| 4.2.2 | Determine the theme or central idea of a text and analyze its development; provide an objective summary of the text | R2 pp. 12–19 |
| 4.3.3 | Analyze how particular elements of a story or drama interact | R3 pp. 20–25 |
| 4.4.4 | Determine the meaning of words and phrases as they are used in a text, including figurative and connotative meanings | R4 pp. 26–33 |
| 4.5.5 | Analyze how a drama's or poem's form or structure contributes to its meaning | R5 pp. 34–39 |
| 4.6.6 | Analyze how an author develops and contrasts the points of view of different characters or narrators in a text | R6 pp. 40–47 |

*(Continued)*

| Minnesota Strand/Standard | Focus of Minnesota Standard | For More Information |
|---|---|---|
| **Reading Literature** | | |
| 4.7.7 | Compare and contrast a written story, drama, or poem to its audio, filmed, staged, or multimedia version | R7 pp. 48–55 |
| 4.8.8 | NA | |
| 4.9.9 | Compare and contrast a fictional portrayal of a time, place, or character and a historical account of the same period | R9 pp. 64–71 |
| 4.10.10 | Read and comprehend literature of appropriate complexity independently with proficiency | R10 pp. 72–77 |
| **Read Informational Texts** | | |
| 5.1.1 | Cite several pieces of textual evidence to support analysis of what the text says explicitly as well as inferences drawn from the text | R1 pp. 6–11 |
| 5.2.2 | Determine two or more central ideas in a text and analyze their developments; provide an objective summary of the text | R2 pp. 12–19 |
| 5.3.3 | Analyze the interactions between individuals, events, and ideas in a text | R3 pp. 20–25 |
| 5.4.4 | Determine the meaning of words and phrases as they are used in a text, including figurative, connotative, and technical meanings | R4 pp. 26–33 |
| 5.5.5 | Analyze the structure an author uses to organize a text, including how the major sections contribute to the whole | R5 pp. 34–39 |
| 5.6.6 | Determine an author's point of view or purpose in a text and analyze how the author distinguishes his or her position from that of others | R6 pp. 40–47 |
| 5.7.7 | Compare and contrast a text to an audio, video, or multimedia version of the text | R7 pp. 48–55 |
| 5.8.8 | Trace and evaluate the argument and specific claims in a text, assessing whether the reason is sound and the evidence is relevant and sufficient | R8 pp. 56–63 |
| 5.9.9 | Analyze how two or more authors writing about the same topic shape their presentations of key information | R9 pp. 64–71 |
| 5.10.10 | Read and comprehend appropriately complex literary nonfiction, informational, and functional texts independently and proficiently | R10 pp. 72–77 |
| **Writing** | | |
| 7.1.1 | Write arguments to support claims with clear reasons and relevant evidence | W1 pp. 82–89 |
| 7.2.2 | Write informative/explanatory texts to examine a topic and convey ideas, concepts, and information clearly | W2 pp. 90–99 |
| 7.3.3 | Write narratives and other creative texts to develop real or imagined experiences or events using effective technique, descriptive details, and well-structured event sequences | W3 pp. 100–109 |
| 7.4.4 | Produce writing in which the development, organization, and style are appropriate to the task, purpose, and audience | W4 pp. 110–115 |
| 7.5.5 | Use a writing process to develop and strengthen writing as needed by planning, revising, editing, rewriting, or trying a new approach | W5 pp. 116–121 |
| 7.6.6 | Use technology to produce and publish writing, link to and cite sources; interact and collaborate with others | W6 pp. 122–127 |
| 7.7.7 | Conduct short research projects to answer a question, drawing on several sources and generating additional related questions for further investigation | W7 pp. 128–133 |
| 7.8.8 | Gather information from print and digital sources; assess the credibility of sources; quote or paraphrase while avoiding plagiarism and following a standard format for citation | W8 pp. 134–139 |
| 7.9.9 | Draw evidence from literary or informational texts to support analysis, reflection, and research | W9 pp. 140–147 |
| 7.10.10 | Write routinely over extended and shorter time frames for a range of tasks, purposes, and audiences | W10 pp. 148–153 |
| **Speaking, Viewing, Listening, and Media Literacy** | | |
| 9.1.1 | Engage effectively in a range of collaborative discussions with diverse partners, building on others' ideas and expressing their own clearly | SL1 pp. 158–163 |
| 9.2.2 | Analyze the main ideas and supporting details presented in diverse media and formats and explain how the ideas clarify a topic, text, or issue under study | SL2 pp. 164–169 |
| 9.3.3 | Delineate a speaker's argument and specific claims evaluating the soundness of the reasoning and the relevance and sufficiency of the evidence | SL3 pp. 170–175 |
| 9.4.4 | Present claims and findings, emphasizing salient points in a focused coherent manner; use appropriate eye contact, adequate volume, and clear pronunciation | SL4 pp. 176–181 |

| Minnesota Strand/Standard | Focus of Minnesota Standard | For More Information |
|---|---|---|
| **Speaking, Viewing, Listening, and Media Literacy** | | |
| 9.5.5 | Include multimedia components and visual displays in presentations to clarify claims and findings | SL5 pp. 182–187 |
| 9.6.6 | Adapt speech to a variety of contexts and tasks, demonstrating command of formal English when appropriate | SL6 pp. 188–193 |
| 9.7.7 | NA | |
| 9.8.8 | NA | |
| **Language** | | |
| 11.1.1 | Demonstrate command of the conventions of standard English grammar and usage when writing or speaking | L1 pp. 198–203 |
| 11.2.2 | Demonstrate command of the conventions of standard English capitalization, punctuation, and spelling when writing | L2 pp. 204–209 |
| 11.3.3 | Use knowledge of language and its conventions when writing, speaking, reading, or listening | L3 pp. 210–215 |
| 11.4.4 | Determine or clarify the meaning of unknown and multiple-meaning words and phrases, choosing flexibly from an array of strategies | L4 pp. 216–221 |
| 11.5.5 | Demonstrate understanding of figurative language, word relationships, and nuances in word meanings | L5 pp. 222–227 |
| 11.6.6 | Acquire and use accurately general academic, and domain-specific words and phrases | L6 pp. 228–233 |
| **Literacy in History/Social Studies** | | |
| 12.1.1 | Cite textual evidence to support analysis of primary and secondary sources | R1 pp. 6–11 |
| 12.2.2 | Determine the central ideas or information of a primary or secondary source; provide an objective summary | R2 pp. 12–19 |
| 12.3.3 | Identify key steps in a text's description of a process related to history/social studies | R3 pp. 20–25 |
| 12.4.4 | Determine the meaning of words and phrases as they are used in a text, including vocabulary specific to history/social studies | R4 pp. 26–33 |
| 12.5.5 | Describe how a text presents information | R5 pp. 34–39 |
| 12.6.6 | Identify aspects of a text that reveal an author's point of view or purpose | R6 pp. 40–47 |
| 12.7.7 | Integrate visual information with other information in print and digital texts | R7 pp. 48–55 |
| 12.8.8 | Distinguish among fact, opinion, and reasoned judgment in a text | R8 pp. 56–63 |
| 12.9.9 | Analyze the relationship between a primary and secondary source on the same topic | R9 pp. 64–71 |
| 12.10.10 | Read and comprehend history/social studies texts of appropriate complexity independently with proficiency | R10 pp. 72–77 |
| **Reading Science/Technical Subjects** | | |
| 13.1.1 | Cite textual evidence to support analysis of science and technical texts | R1 pp. 6–11 |
| 13.2.2 | Determine the central ideas or conclusions of a text; provide an objective summary | R2 pp. 12–19 |
| 13.3.3 | Follow precisely a multistep procedure when carrying out experiments, taking measurements, or performing technical tasks | R3 pp. 20–25 |
| 13.4.4 | Determine the meaning of symbols, key terms, and other domain-specific words and phrases | R4 pp. 26–33 |
| 13.5.5 | Analyze the structure an author uses to organize a text, including how the major sections contribute to the whole | R5 pp. 34–39 |
| 13.6.6 | Analyze the author's purpose in providing an explanation, describing a procedure, or discussing an experiment | R6 pp. 40–47 |
| 13.7.7 | Integrate quantitative or technical information expressed in words with a version of the information expressed visually | R7 pp. 48–55 |
| 13.8.8 | Distinguish among facts, reasoned judgment based on research findings, and speculation in a text | R8 pp. 56–63 |
| 13.9.9 | Compare and contrast the information gained from experiments, simulations, video, or multimedia sources with that gained from reading a text on the same topic | R9 pp. 64–71 |
| 13.10.10 | Read and comprehend appropriately complex science/technical texts independently and proficiently | R10 pp. 72–77 |

*(Continued)*

| Minnesota Strand/Standard | Focus of Minnesota Standard | For More Information |
|---|---|---|
| **Writing History/Social Studies, Science and Technical Subjects** | | |
| 14.1.1 | Write arguments based on discipline-specific content | W1 pp. 82–89 |
| 14.2.2 | Write informative/explanatory texts including the narration of historical events, scientific procedures/experiments, or technical processes | W2 pp. 90–99 |
| 14.3.3 | NA | |
| 14.4.4 | Produce writing in which the development, organization, and style are appropriate to the task, purpose, and audience | W4 pp. 110–115 |
| 14.5.5 | Develop and strengthen writing as needed by planning, revising, editing, rewriting, or trying a new approach | W5 pp. 116–121 |
| 14.6.6 | Use technology to produce and publish writing as well as to interact with others; demonstrate keyboarding skills | W6 pp. 122–127 |
| 14.7.7 | Conduct short research projects to answer a question, drawing on several sources and refocusing the inquiry when appropriate | W7 pp. 128–133 |
| 14.8.8 | Gather information from print and digital sources; assess the credibility of sources; quote or paraphrase while avoiding plagiarism and providing basic bibliographic information | W8 pp. 134–139 |
| 14.9.9 | Draw evidence from informational texts to support analysis, reflection, and research | W9 pp. 140–147 |
| 14.10.10 | Write routinely over extended and shorter time frames for a range of tasks, purposes, and audiences | W10 pp. 148–153 |

# Minnesota, Grade 8

| Minnesota Strand/Standard | Focus of Minnesota Standard | For More Information |
|---|---|---|
| **Reading Literature** | | |
| 4.1.1 | Cite the textual evidence that most strongly supports an analysis of what the text says explicitly as well as inferences drawn from the text | R1 pp. 6–11 |
| 4.2.2 | Determine the theme or central idea of a text and analyze its development, including its relationship to the characters, setting, and plot; provide an objective summary of the text | R2 pp. 12–19 |
| 4.3.3 | Analyze how particular lines of dialogue or incidents in a story or drama propel the action, reveal aspects of a character, or provoke a decision | R3 pp. 20–25 |
| 4.4.4 | Determine the meaning of words and phrases as they are used in a text, including figurative and connotative meanings | R4 pp. 26–33 |
| 4.5.5 | Compare and contrast the structure of two or more texts and analyze how the differing structure of each contributes to its meaning and style | R5 pp. 34–39 |
| 4.6.6 | Analyze how differences in the points of view of the characters and the audience or reader create such effects as suspense or humor | R6 pp. 40–47 |
| 4.7.7 | Analyze the extent to which a filmed or live production of a story or drama stays faithful or departs from the text or script | R7 pp. 48–55 |
| 4.8.8 | NA | |
| 4.9.9 | Analyze how a modern work of fiction draws on themes, patterns of events, or character types from traditional stories, describing how the material is rendered new | R9 pp. 64–71 |
| 4.10.10 | Read and comprehend literature of appropriate complexity independently with proficiency | R10 pp. 72–77 |
| **Read Informational Texts** | | |
| 5.1.1 | Cite the textual evidence that most strongly supports an analysis of what the text says explicitly as well as inferences drawn from the text | R1 pp. 6–11 |
| 5.2.2 | Determine the central idea of a text and analyze its development, including its relationship to supporting ideas; provide an objective summary of the text | R2 pp. 12–19 |
| 5.3.3 | Analyze how a text makes connections among distinctions between individuals, ideas, or events | R3 pp. 20–25 |
| 5.4.4 | Determine the meaning of words and phrases as they are used in a text, including figurative, connotative, and technical meanings | R4 pp. 26–33 |
| 5.5.5 | Analyze the structure of a specific paragraph in a text, including the role of particular sentences in developing and refining a key concept | R5 pp. 34–39 |

| Minnesota Strand/Standard | Focus of Minnesota Standard | For More Information |
|---|---|---|
| **Read Informational Texts** | | |
| 5.6.6 | Determine an author's point of view or purpose in a text and analyze how the author acknowledges and responds to conflicting evidence or viewpoints | R6 pp. 40–47 |
| 5.7.7 | Evaluate the advantages and disadvantages of using different mediums to present a particular topic or idea | R7 pp. 48–55 |
| 5.8.8 | Delineate and evaluate the argument and specific claims in a text, assessing whether the reason is sound and the evidence is relevant and sufficient | R8 pp. 56–63 |
| 5.9.9 | Analyze a case in which two or more texts provide conflicting information on the same topic | R9 pp. 64–71 |
| 5.10.10 | Read and comprehend appropriately complex literary nonfiction, informational, and functional texts independently and proficiently | R10 pp. 72–77 |
| **Writing** | | |
| 7.1.1 | Write arguments to support claims with clear reasons and relevant evidence | W1 pp. 82–89 |
| 7.2.2 | Write informative/explanatory texts to examine a topic and convey ideas, concepts, and information clearly | W2 pp. 90–99 |
| 7.3.3 | Write narratives or other creative texts to develop real or imagined experiences or events using effective technique, descriptive details, and well-structured event sequences | W3 pp. 100–109 |
| 7.4.4 | Produce writing in which the development, organization, and style are appropriate to the task, purpose, and audience | W4 pp. 110–115 |
| 7.5.5 | Use a writing process to develop and strengthen writing as needed by planning, revising, editing, rewriting, or trying a new approach | W5 pp. 116–121 |
| 7.6.6 | Use technology to produce and publish writing, link to and cite sources; interact and collaborate with others | W6 pp. 122–127 |
| 7.7.7 | Conduct short research projects to answer a question, drawing on several sources and generating additional related questions for further investigation | W7 pp. 128–133 |
| 7.8.8 | Gather information from print and digital sources; assess the credibility of sources; quote or paraphrase while avoiding plagiarism and following a standard format for citation | W8 pp. 134–139 |
| 7.9.9 | Draw evidence from literary or informational texts to support analysis, reflection, and research | W9 pp. 140–147 |
| 7.10.10 | Write routinely over extended and shorter time frames for a range of tasks, purposes, and audiences | W10 pp. 148–153 |
| **Speaking, Viewing, Listening, and Media Literacy** | | |
| 9.1.1 | Engage effectively in a range of collaborative discussions with diverse partners, building on others' ideas and expressing their own clearly | SL1 pp. 158–163 |
| 9.2.2 | Analyze the purpose of information presented in diverse media and formats and evaluate the motives behind its presentation | SL2 pp. 164–169 |
| 9.3.3 | Delineate a speaker's argument and specific claims evaluating the soundness of the reasoning and the relevance and sufficiency of the evidence and identifying when irrelevant evidence is introduced | SL3 pp. 170–175 |
| 9.4.4 | Present claims and findings, emphasizing salient points in a focused coherent manner; use appropriate eye contact, adequate volume, and clear pronunciation | SL4 pp. 176–181 |
| 9.5.5 | Integrate multimedia components and visual displays into presentations to clarify information, strengthen claims and findings, and add interest | SL5 pp. 182–187 |
| 9.6.6 | Adapt speech to a variety of contexts and tasks, demonstrating command of formal English when appropriate | SL6 pp. 188–193 |
| 9.7.7 | NA | |
| 9.8.8 | NA | |
| **Language** | | |
| 11.1.1 | Demonstrate command of the conventions of standard English grammar and usage when writing or speaking | L1 pp. 198–203 |
| 11.2.2 | Demonstrate command of the conventions of standard English capitalization, punctuation, and spelling when writing | L2 pp. 204–209 |
| 11.3.3 | Use knowledge of language and its conventions when writing, speaking, reading, or listening | L3 pp. 210–215 |
| 11.4.4 | Determine or clarify the meaning of unknown and multiple-meaning words and phrases, choosing flexibly from an array of strategies | L4 pp. 216–221 |

*(Continued)*

| Minnesota Strand/Standard | Focus of Minnesota Standard | For More Information |
|---|---|---|
| **Language** | | |
| 11.5.5 | Demonstrate understanding of figurative language, word relationships, and nuances in word meanings | L5 pp. 222–227 |
| 11.6.6 | Acquire and use accurately general academic, and domain-specific words and phrases | L6 pp. 228–233 |
| **Literacy in History/Social Studies** | | |
| 12.1.1 | Cite textual evidence to support analysis of primary and secondary sources | R1 pp. 6–11 |
| 12.2.2 | Determine the central ideas or information of a primary or secondary source; provide an objective summary | R2 pp. 12–19 |
| 12.3.3 | Identify key steps in a text's description of a process related to history/social studies | R3 pp. 20–25 |
| 12.4.4 | Determine the meaning of words and phrases as they are used in a text, including vocabulary specific to history/social studies | R4 pp. 26–33 |
| 12.5.5 | Describe how a text presents information | R5 pp. 34–39 |
| 12.6.6 | Identify aspects of a text that reveal an author's point of view or purpose | R6 pp. 40–47 |
| 12.7.7 | Integrate visual information with other information in print and digital texts | R7 pp. 48–55 |
| 12.8.8 | Distinguish among fact, opinion, and reasoned judgment in a text | R8 pp. 56–63 |
| 12.9.9 | Analyze the relationship between a primary and secondary source on the same topic | R9 pp. 64–71 |
| 12.10.10 | Read and comprehend history/social studies texts of appropriate complexity independently with proficiency | R10 pp. 72–77 |
| **Reading Science/Technical Subjects** | | |
| 13.1.1 | Cite textual evidence to support analysis of science and technical texts | R1 pp. 6–11 |
| 13.2.2 | Determine the central ideas or conclusions of a text; provide an objective summary | R2 pp. 12–19 |
| 13.3.3 | Follow precisely a multistep procedure when carrying out experiments, taking measurements, or performing technical tasks | R3 pp. 20–25 |
| 13.4.4 | Determine the meaning of symbols, key terms, and other domain-specific words and phrases | R4 pp. 26–33 |
| 13.5.5 | Analyze the structure an author uses to organize a text, including how the major sections contribute to the whole | R5 pp. 34–39 |
| 13.6.6 | Analyze the author's purpose in providing an explanation, describing a procedure, or discussing an experiment | R6 pp. 40–47 |
| 13.7.7 | Integrate quantitative or technical information expressed in words with a version of the information expressed visually | R7 pp. 48–55 |
| 13.8.8 | Distinguish among facts, reasoned judgment based on research findings, and speculation in a text | R8 pp. 56–63 |
| 13.9.9 | Compare and contrast the information gained from experiments, simulations, video, or multimedia sources with that gained from reading a text on the same topic | R9 pp. 64–71 |
| 13.10.10 | Read and comprehend appropriately complex science/technical texts independently and proficiently | R10 pp. 72–77 |
| **Writing History/Social Studies, Science and Technical Subjects** | | |
| 14.1.1 | Write arguments based on discipline-specific content | W1 pp. 82–89 |
| 14.2.2 | Write informative/explanatory texts including the narration of historical events, scientific procedures/experiments, or technical processes | W2 pp. 90–99 |
| 14.3.3 | NA | |
| 14.4.4 | Produce writing in which the development, organization, and style are appropriate to the task, purpose, and audience | W4 pp. 110–115 |
| 14.5.5 | Develop and strengthen writing as needed by planning, revising, editing, rewriting, or trying a new approach | W5 pp. 116–121 |
| 14.6.6 | Use technology to produce and publish writing as well as to interact with others; demonstrate keyboarding skills | W6 pp. 122–127 |
| 14.7.7 | Conduct short research projects to answer a question, drawing on several sources and refocusing the inquiry when appropriate | W7 pp. 128–133 |
| 14.8.8 | Gather information from print and digital sources; assess the credibility of sources; quote or paraphrase while avoiding plagiarism and providing basic bibliographic information | W8 pp. 134–139 |
| 14.9.9 | Draw evidence from informational texts to support analysis, reflection, and research | W9 pp. 140–147 |
| 14.10.10 | Write routinely over extended and shorter time frames for a range of tasks, purposes, and audiences | W10 pp. 148–153 |

# Mississippi, Grade 6

| Mississippi Strand/Standard | Focus of Mississippi Standard | For More Information |
|---|---|---|
| **Reading Literature** | | |
| RL.1 | Cite textual evidence to support analysis of what the text says explicitly as well as inferences drawn from the text | R1 pp. 6–11 |
| RL.2 | Determine the theme or central idea of a text and how it is conveyed through particular details; provide an objective summary | R2 pp. 12–19 |
| RL.3 | Describe how a particular plot unfolds in a series of episodes as well as how the characters respond or change | R3 pp. 20–25 |
| RL.4 | Determine the meaning of words and phrases as they are used in a text, including figurative and connotative meanings | R4 pp. 26–33 |
| RL.5 | Analyze how a particular sentence, chapter, scene, or stanza fits into the overall structure of a text and contributes to the development of the theme, setting, or plot | R5 pp. 34–39 |
| RL.6 | Explain how an author develops the point of view of the narrator or speaker in a text | R6 pp. 40–47 |
| RL.7 | Compare and contrast the experience of reading a story, drama, or poem to listening to or viewing an audio, video, or live version of the text | R7 pp. 48–55 |
| RL.8 | NA | |
| RL.9 | Compare and contrast texts in different forms or genres in terms of their approaches to similar themes and topics | R9 pp. 64–71 |
| RL.10 | Read and comprehend literature of appropriate complexity independently with proficiency | R10 pp. 72–77 |
| **Reading Informational Text** | | |
| RI.1 | Cite textual evidence to support analysis of what the text says explicitly as well as inferences drawn from the text | R1 pp. 6–11 |
| RI.2 | Determine a central idea of a text and how it is conveyed through particular details; provide an objective summary | R2 pp. 12–19 |
| RI.3 | Analyze in detail how a key individual, event, or idea is introduced, illustrated, and elaborated in a text | R3 pp. 20–25 |
| RI.4 | Determine the meaning of words and phrases as they are used in a text, including figurative, connotative, and technical meanings | R4 pp. 26–33 |
| RI.5 | Analyze how a particular sentence, chapter, scene, or section fits into the overall structure of a text and contributes to the development of the ideas | R5 pp. 34–39 |
| RI.6 | Determine an author's point of view or purpose in a text and explain how it is conveyed in the text | R6 pp. 40–47 |
| RI.7 | Integrate information presented in different media or formats as well as in words to develop a coherent understanding of a topic or issue | R7 pp. 48–55 |
| RI.8 | Trace and evaluate the argument and specific claims that are supported by reasons and evidence from claims that are not | R8 pp. 56–63 |
| RI.9 | Compare and contrast one author's presentation of events with that of another | R9 pp. 64–71 |
| RI.10 | Read and comprehend appropriately complex literary nonfiction, informational, and functional texts independently and proficiently | R10 pp. 72–77 |
| **Writing** | | |
| W.1 | Write arguments to support claims with clear reasons and relevant evidence | W1 pp. 82–89 |
| W.2 | Write informative/explanatory texts to examine a topic and convey ideas, concepts, and information clearly | W2 pp. 90–99 |
| W.3 | Write narratives to develop real or imagined experiences or events using effective technique, descriptive details, and well-structured event sequences | W3 pp. 100–109 |
| W.4 | Produce writing in which the development, organization, and style are appropriate to the task, purpose, and audience | W4 pp. 110–115 |
| W.5 | Develop and strengthen writing as needed by planning, revising, editing, rewriting, or trying a new approach | W5 pp. 116–121 |
| W.6 | Use technology to produce and publish writing as well as to interact with others; demonstrate keyboarding skills | W6 pp. 122–127 |

*(Continued)*

| Mississippi Strand/Standard | Focus of Mississippi Standard | For More Information |
|---|---|---|
| **Writing** | | |
| W.7 | Conduct short research projects to answer a question, drawing on several sources and refocusing the inquiry when appropriate | W7 pp. 128–133 |
| W.8 | Gather information from print and digital sources; assess the credibility of sources; quote or paraphrase while avoiding plagiarism and providing basic bibliographic information | W8 pp. 134–139 |
| W.9 | Draw evidence from literary or informational texts to support analysis, reflection, and research | W9 pp. 140–147 |
| W.10 | Write routinely over extended and shorter time frames for a range of tasks, purposes, and audiences | W10 pp. 148–153 |
| **Speaking and Listening** | | |
| SL.1 | Engage effectively in a range of collaborative discussions with diverse partners, building on others' ideas and expressing their own clearly | SL1 pp. 158–163 |
| SL.2 | Interpret information presented in diverse media and formats and explain how it contributes to a topic, text, or issue under study | SL2 pp. 164–169 |
| SL.3 | Delineate a speaker's argument and specific claims that are supported by reasons and evidence from claims that are not | SL3 pp. 170–175 |
| SL.4 | Present claims and findings, sequencing ideas logically and using descriptions, facts, or details to accentuate main ideas or themes; use appropriate eye contact, adequate volume, and clear pronunciation | SL4 pp. 176–181 |
| SL.5 | Include multimedia components and visual displays in presentations to clarify information | SL5 pp. 182–187 |
| SL.6 | Adapt speech to a variety of contexts and tasks, demonstrating command of formal English when appropriate | SL6 pp. 188–193 |
| **Language** | | |
| L.1 | Demonstrate command of the conventions of standard English grammar and usage when writing or speaking | L1 pp. 198–203 |
| L.2 | Demonstrate command of the conventions of standard English capitalization, punctuation, and spelling when writing | L2 pp. 204–209 |
| L.3 | Use knowledge of language and its conventions when writing, speaking, reading, or listening | L3 pp. 210–215 |
| L.4 | Determine or clarify the meaning of unknown and multiple-meaning words and phrases, choosing flexibly from an array of strategies | L4 pp. 216–221 |
| L.5 | Demonstrate understanding of figurative language, word relationships, and nuances in word meanings | L5 pp. 222–227 |
| L.6 | Acquire and use accurately general academic, and domain-specific words and phrases | L6 pp. 228–233 |
| **Reading History/Social Studies** | | |
| RH.1 | Cite textual evidence to support analysis of primary and secondary sources | R1 pp. 6–11 |
| RH.2 | Determine the central ideas or information of a primary or secondary source; provide an objective summary | R2 pp. 12–19 |
| RH.3 | Identify key steps in a text's description of a process related to history/social studies | R3 pp. 20–25 |
| RH.4 | Determine the meaning of words and phrases as they are used in a text, including vocabulary specific to history/social studies | R4 pp. 26–33 |
| RH.5 | Describe how a text presents information | R5 pp. 34–39 |
| RH.6 | Identify aspects of a text that reveal an author's point of view or purpose | R6 pp. 40–47 |
| RH.7 | Integrate visual information with other information in print and digital texts | R7 pp. 48–55 |
| RH.8 | Distinguish among fact, opinion, and reasoned judgment in a text | R8 pp. 56–63 |
| RH.9 | Analyze the relationship between a primary and secondary source on the same topic | R9 pp. 64–71 |
| RH.10 | Read and comprehend history/social studies texts of appropriate complexity independently with proficiency | R10 pp. 72–77 |
| **Reading Science/Technical Subjects** | | |
| RST.1 | Cite textual evidence to support analysis of science and technical texts | R1 pp. 6–11 |
| RST.2 | Determine the central ideas or conclusions of a text; provide an objective summary | R2 pp. 12–19 |
| RST.3 | Follow precisely a multistep procedure when carrying out experiments, taking measurements, or performing technical tasks | R3 pp. 20–25 |

| Mississippi Strand/Standard | Focus of Mississippi Standard | For More Information |
|---|---|---|
| **Reading Science/Technical Subjects** | | |
| RST.4 | Determine the meaning of symbols, key terms, and other domain-specific words and phrases | R4 pp. 26–33 |
| RST.5 | Analyze the structure an author uses to organize a text, including how the major sections contribute to the whole | R5 pp. 34–39 |
| RST.6 | Analyze the author's purpose in providing an explanation, describing a procedure, or discussing an experiment | R6 pp. 40–47 |
| RST.7 | Integrate quantitative or technical information expressed in words with a version of the information expressed visually | R7 pp. 48–55 |
| RST.8 | Distinguish among facts, reasoned judgment based on research findings, and speculation in a text | R8 pp. 56–63 |
| RST.9 | Compare and contrast the information gained from experiments, simulations, video, or multimedia sources with that gained from reading a text on the same topic | R9 pp. 64–71 |
| RST.10 | Read and comprehend appropriately complex science/technical texts independently and proficiently | R10 pp. 72–77 |
| **Writing History/Social Studies and Science/Technical Subjects** | | |
| WHST.1 | Write arguments based on discipline-specific content | W1 pp. 82–89 |
| WHST.2 | Write informative/explanatory texts including the narration of historical events, scientific procedures/experiments, or technical processes | W2 pp. 90–99 |
| WHST.3 | NA | |
| WHST.4 | Produce writing in which the development, organization, and style are appropriate to the task, purpose, and audience | W4 pp. 110–115 |
| WHST.5 | Develop and strengthen writing as needed by planning, revising, editing, rewriting, or trying a new approach | W5 pp. 116–121 |
| WHST.6 | Use technology to produce and publish writing as well as to interact with others; demonstrate keyboarding skills | W6 pp. 122–127 |
| WHST.7 | Conduct short research projects to answer a question, drawing on several sources and refocusing the inquiry when appropriate | W7 pp. 128–133 |
| WHST.8 | Gather information from print and digital sources; assess the credibility of sources; quote or paraphrase while avoiding plagiarism and providing basic bibliographic information | W8 pp. 134–139 |
| WHST.9 | Draw evidence from informational texts to support analysis, reflection, and research | W9 pp. 140–147 |
| WHST.10 | Write routinely over extended and shorter time frames for a range of tasks, purposes, and audiences | W10 pp. 148–153 |

# Mississippi, Grade 7

| Mississippi Strand/Standard | Focus of Mississippi Standard | For More Information |
|---|---|---|
| **Reading Literature** | | |
| RL.1 | Cite several pieces of textual evidence to support analysis of what the text says explicitly as well as inferences drawn from the text | R1 pp. 6–11 |
| RL.2 | Determine the theme or central idea of a text and analyze its development; provide an objective summary of the text | R2 pp. 12–19 |
| RL.3 | Analyze how particular elements of a story or drama interact | R3 pp. 20–25 |
| RL.4 | Determine the meaning of words and phrases as they are used in a text, including figurative and connotative meanings | R4 pp. 26–33 |
| RL.5 | Analyze how a drama's or poem's form or structure contributes to its meaning | R5 pp. 34–39 |
| RL.6 | Analyze how an author develops and contrasts the points of view of different characters or narrators in a text | R6 pp. 40–47 |
| RL.7 | Compare and contrast a written story, drama, or poem to its audio, filmed, staged, or multimedia version | R7 pp. 48–55 |

*(Continued)*

| Mississippi Strand/Standard | Focus of Mississippi Standard | For More Information |
|---|---|---|
| **Reading Literature** | | |
| RL.8 | NA | |
| RL.9 | Compare and contrast a fictional portrayal of a time, place, or character and a historical account of the same period | R9 pp. 64–71 |
| RL.10 | Read and comprehend literature of appropriate complexity independently with proficiency | R10 pp. 72–77 |
| **Reading Informational Text** | | |
| RI.1 | Cite several pieces of textual evidence to support analysis of what the text says explicitly as well as inferences drawn from the text | R1 pp. 6–11 |
| RI.2 | Determine two or more central ideas in a text and analyze their developments; provide an objective summary of the text | R2 pp. 12–19 |
| RI.3 | Analyze the interactions between individuals, events, and ideas in a text | R3 pp. 20–25 |
| RI.4 | Determine the meaning of words and phrases as they are used in a text, including figurative, connotative, and technical meanings | R4 pp. 26–33 |
| RI.5 | Analyze the structure an author uses to organize a text, including how the major sections contribute to the whole | R5 pp. 34–39 |
| RI.6 | Determine an author's point of view or purpose in a text and analyze how the author distinguishes his or her position from that of others | R6 pp. 40–47 |
| RI.7 | Compare and contrast a text to an audio, video, or multimedia version of the text | R7 pp. 48–55 |
| RI.8 | Trace and evaluate the argument and specific claims in a text, assessing whether the reason is sound and the evidence is relevant and sufficient | R8 pp. 56–63 |
| RI.9 | Analyze how two or more authors writing about the same topic shape their presentations of key information | R9 pp. 64–71 |
| RI.10 | Read and comprehend appropriately complex literary nonfiction, informational, and functional texts independently and proficiently | R10 pp. 72–77 |
| **Writing** | | |
| W.1 | Write arguments to support claims with clear reasons and relevant evidence | W1 pp. 82–89 |
| W.2 | Write informative/explanatory texts to examine a topic and convey ideas, concepts, and information clearly | W2 pp. 90–99 |
| W.3 | Write narratives to develop real or imagined experiences or events using effective technique, descriptive details, and well-structured event sequences | W3 pp. 100–109 |
| W.4 | Produce writing in which the development, organization, and style are appropriate to the task, purpose, and audience | W4 pp. 110–115 |
| W.5 | Develop and strengthen writing as needed by planning, revising, editing, rewriting, or trying a new approach | W5 pp. 116–121 |
| W.6 | Use technology to produce and publish writing, link to and cite sources; interact and collaborate with others | W6 pp. 122–127 |
| W.7 | Conduct short research projects to answer a question, drawing on several sources and additional related questions for further investigation | W7 pp. 128–133 |
| W.8 | Gather information from print and digital sources; assess the credibility of sources; quote or paraphrase while avoiding plagiarism and following a standard format for citation | W8 pp. 134–139 |
| W.9 | Draw evidence from literary or informational texts to support analysis, reflection, and research | W9 pp. 140–147 |
| W.10 | Write routinely over extended and shorter time frames for a range of tasks, purposes, and audiences | W10 pp. 148–153 |
| **Speaking and Listening** | | |
| SL.1 | Engage effectively in a range of collaborative discussions with diverse partners, building on others' ideas and expressing their own clearly | SL1 pp. 158–163 |
| SL.2 | Analyze the main ideas and supporting details presented in diverse media and formats and explain how the ideas clarify a topic, text, or issue under study | SL2 pp. 164–169 |
| SL.3 | Delineate a speaker's argument and specific claims evaluating the soundness of the reasoning and the relevance and sufficiency of the evidence | SL3 pp. 170–175 |
| SL.4 | Present claims and findings, emphasizing salient points in a focused coherent manner; use appropriate eye contact, adequate volume, and clear pronunciation | SL4 pp. 176–181 |
| SL.5 | Include multimedia components and visual displays in presentations to clarify claims and findings | SL5 pp. 182–187 |
| SL.6 | Adapt speech to a variety of contexts and tasks, demonstrating command of formal English when appropriate | SL6 pp. 188–193 |

| Mississippi Strand/Standard | Focus of Mississippi Standard | For More Information |
|---|---|---|
| **Language** | | |
| L.1 | Demonstrate command of the conventions of standard English grammar and usage when writing or speaking | L1 pp. 198–203 |
| L.2 | Demonstrate command of the conventions of standard English capitalization, punctuation, and spelling when writing | L2 pp. 204–209 |
| L.3 | Use knowledge of language and its conventions when writing, speaking, reading, or listening | L3 pp. 210–215 |
| L.4 | Determine or clarify the meaning of unknown and multiple-meaning words and phrases, choosing flexibly from an array of strategies | L4 pp. 216–221 |
| L.5 | Demonstrate understanding of figurative language, word relationships, and nuances in word meanings | L5 pp. 222–227 |
| L.6 | Acquire and use accurately general academic, and domain-specific words and phrases | L6 pp. 228–233 |
| **Reading History/Social Studies** | | |
| RH.1 | Cite textual evidence to support analysis of primary and secondary sources | R1 pp. 6–11 |
| RH.2 | Determine the central ideas or information of a primary or secondary source; provide an objective summary | R2 pp. 12–19 |
| RH.3 | Identify key steps in a text's description of a process related to history/social studies | R3 pp. 20–25 |
| RH.4 | Determine the meaning of words and phrases as they are used in a text, including vocabulary specific to history/social studies | R4 pp. 26–33 |
| RH.5 | Describe how a text presents information | R5 pp. 34–39 |
| RH.6 | Identify aspects of a text that reveal an author's point of view or purpose | R6 pp. 40–47 |
| RH.7 | Integrate visual information with other information in print and digital texts | R7 pp. 48–55 |
| RH.8 | Distinguish among fact, opinion, and reasoned judgment in a text | R8 pp. 56–63 |
| RH.9 | Analyze the relationship between a primary and secondary source on the same topic | R9 pp. 64–71 |
| RH.10 | Read and comprehend history/social studies texts of appropriate complexity independently with proficiency | R10 pp. 72–77 |
| **Reading Science/Technical Subjects** | | |
| RST.1 | Cite textual evidence to support analysis of science and technical texts | R1 pp. 6–11 |
| RST.2 | Determine the central ideas or conclusions of a text; provide an objective summary | R2 pp. 12–19 |
| RST.3 | Follow precisely a multistep procedure when carrying out experiments, taking measurements, or performing technical tasks | R3 pp. 20–25 |
| RST.4 | Determine the meaning of symbols, key terms, and other domain-specific words and phrases | R4 pp. 26–33 |
| RST.5 | Analyze the structure an author uses to organize a text, including how the major sections contribute to the whole | R5 pp. 34–39 |
| RST.6 | Analyze the author's purpose in providing an explanation, describing a procedure, or discussing an experiment | R6 pp. 40–47 |
| RST.7 | Integrate quantitative or technical information expressed in words with a version of the information expressed visually | R7 pp. 48–55 |
| RST.8 | Distinguish among facts, reasoned judgment based on research findings, and speculation in a text | R8 pp. 56–63 |
| RST.9 | Compare and contrast the information gained from experiments, simulations, video, or multimedia sources with that gained from reading a text on the same topic | R9 pp. 64–71 |
| RST.10 | Read and comprehend appropriately complex science/technical texts independently and proficiently | R10 pp. 72–77 |
| **Writing History/Social Studies and Science/Technical Subjects** | | |
| WHST.1 | Write arguments based on discipline-specific content | W1 pp. 82–89 |
| WHST.2 | Write informative/explanatory texts including the narration of historical events, scientific procedures/experiments, or technical processes | W2 pp. 90–99 |
| WHST.3 | NA | |
| WHST.4 | Produce writing in which the development, organization, and style are appropriate to the task, purpose, and audience | W4 pp. 110–115 |
| WHST.5 | Develop and strengthen writing as needed by planning, revising, editing, rewriting, or trying a new approach | W5 pp. 116–121 |

*(Continued)*

| Mississippi Strand/Standard | Focus of Mississippi Standard | For More Information |
|---|---|---|
| **Writing History/Social Studies and Science/Technical Subjects** | | |
| WHST.6 | Use technology to produce and publish writing as well as to interact with others; demonstrate keyboarding skills | W6 pp. 122–127 |
| WHST.7 | Conduct short research projects to answer a question, drawing on several sources and refocusing the inquiry when appropriate | W7 pp. 128–133 |
| WHST.8 | Gather information from print and digital sources; assess the credibility of sources; quote or paraphrase while avoiding plagiarism and providing basic bibliographic information | W8 pp. 134–139 |
| WHST.9 | Draw evidence from informational texts to support analysis, reflection, and research | W9 pp. 140–147 |
| WHST.10 | Write routinely over extended and shorter time frames for a range of tasks, purposes, and audiences | W10 pp. 148–153 |

# Mississippi, Grade 8

| Mississippi Strand/Standard | Focus of Mississippi Standard | For More Information |
|---|---|---|
| **Reading Literature** | | |
| RL.1 | Cite the textual evidence that most strongly supports an analysis of what the text says explicitly as well as inferences drawn from the text | R1 pp. 6–11 |
| RL.2 | Determine the theme or central idea of a text and analyze its development, including its relationship to the characters, setting, and plot; provide an objective summary of the text | R2 pp. 12–19 |
| RL.3 | Analyze how particular lines of dialogue or incidents in a story or drama propel the action, reveal aspects of a character, or provoke a decision | R3 pp. 20–25 |
| RL.4 | Determine the meaning of words and phrases as they are used in a text, including figurative and connotative meanings | R4 pp. 26–33 |
| RL.5 | Compare and contrast the structure of two or more texts and analyze how the differing structure of each contributes to its meaning and style | R5 pp. 34–39 |
| RL.6 | Analyze how differences in the points of view of the characters and the audience or reader create such effects as suspense or humor | R6 pp. 40–47 |
| RL.7 | Analyze the extent to which a filmed or live production of a story or drama stays faithful or departs from the text or script | R7 pp. 48–55 |
| RL.8 | NA | |
| RL.9 | Analyze how a modern work of fiction draws on themes, patterns of events, or character types from traditional stories, describing how the material is rendered new | R9 pp. 64–71 |
| RL.10 | Read and comprehend literature of appropriate complexity independently with proficiency | R10 pp. 72–77 |
| **Reading Informational Text** | | |
| RI.1 | Cite the textual evidence that most strongly supports an analysis of what the text says explicitly as well as inferences drawn from the text | R1 pp. 6–11 |
| RI.2 | Determine the central idea of a text and analyze its development, including its relationship to supporting ideas; provide an objective summary of the text | R2 pp. 12–19 |
| RI.3 | Analyze how a text makes connections among distinctions between individuals, ideas, or events | R3 pp. 20–25 |
| RI.4 | Determine the meaning of words and phrases as they are used in a text, including figurative, connotative, and technical meanings | R4 pp. 26–33 |
| RI.5 | Analyze the structure of a specific paragraph in a text, including the role of particular sentences in developing and refining a key concept | R5 pp. 34–39 |
| RI.6 | Determine an author's point of view or purpose in a text and analyze how the author acknowledges and responds to conflicting evidence or viewpoints | R6 pp. 40–47 |
| RI.7 | Evaluate the advantages and disadvantages of using different mediums to present a particular topic or idea | R7 pp. 48–55 |
| RI.8 | Delineate and evaluate the argument and specific claims in a text, assessing whether the reason is sound and the evidence is relevant and sufficient | R8 pp. 56–63 |
| RI.9 | Analyze a case in which two or more texts provide conflicting information on the same topic | R9 pp. 64–71 |
| RI.10 | Read and comprehend appropriately complex literary nonfiction, informational, and functional texts independently and proficiently | R10 pp. 72–77 |

| Mississippi Strand/Standard | Focus of Mississippi Standard | For More Information |
|---|---|---|
| **Writing** | | |
| W.1 | Write arguments to support claims with clear reasons and relevant evidence | W1 pp. 82–89 |
| W.2 | Write informative/explanatory texts to examine a topic and convey ideas, concepts, and information clearly | W2 pp. 90–99 |
| W.3 | Write narratives to develop real or imagined experiences or events using effective technique, descriptive details, and well-structured event sequences | W3 pp. 100–109 |
| W.4 | Produce writing in which the development, organization, and style are appropriate to the task, purpose, and audience | W4 pp. 110–115 |
| W.5 | Develop and strengthen writing as needed by planning, revising, editing, rewriting, or trying a new approach | W5 pp. 116–121 |
| W.6 | Use technology to produce and publish writing, link to and cite sources; interact and collaborate with others | W6 pp. 122–127 |
| W.7 | Conduct short research projects to answer a question, drawing on several sources and additional related questions for further investigation | W7 pp. 128–133 |
| W.8 | Gather information from print and digital sources; assess the credibility of sources; quote or paraphrase while avoiding plagiarism and following a standard format for citation | W8 pp. 134–139 |
| W.9 | Draw evidence from literary or informational texts to support analysis, reflection, and research | W9 pp. 140–147 |
| W.10 | Write routinely over extended and shorter time frames for a range of tasks, purposes, and audiences | W10 pp. 148–153 |
| **Speaking and Listening** | | |
| SL.1 | Engage effectively in a range of collaborative discussions with diverse partners, building on others' ideas and expressing their own clearly | SL1 pp. 158–163 |
| SL.2 | Analyze the purpose of information presented in diverse media and formats and evaluate the motives behind its presentation | SL2 pp. 164–169 |
| SL.3 | Delineate a speaker's argument and specific claims evaluating the soundness of the reasoning and the relevance and sufficiency of the evidence and identifying when irrelevant evidence is introduced | SL3 pp. 170–175 |
| SL.4 | Present claims and findings, emphasizing salient points in a focused coherent manner; use appropriate eye contact, adequate volume, and clear pronunciation | SL4 pp. 176–181 |
| SL.5 | Integrate multimedia components and visual displays into presentations to clarify information, strengthen claims and findings, and add interest | SL5 pp. 182–187 |
| SL.6 | Adapt speech to a variety of contexts and tasks, demonstrating command of formal English when appropriate | SL6 pp. 188–193 |
| **Language** | | |
| L.1 | Demonstrate command of the conventions of standard English grammar and usage when writing or speaking | L1 pp. 198–203 |
| L.2 | Demonstrate command of the conventions of standard English capitalization, punctuation, and spelling when writing | L2 pp. 204–209 |
| L.3 | Use knowledge of language and its conventions when writing, speaking, reading, or listening | L3 pp. 210–215 |
| L.4 | Determine or clarify the meaning of unknown and multiple-meaning words and phrases, choosing flexibly from an array of strategies | L4 pp. 216–221 |
| L.5 | Demonstrate understanding of figurative language, word relationships, and nuances in word meanings | L5 pp. 222–227 |
| L.6 | Acquire and use accurately general academic, and domain-specific words and phrases | L6 pp. 228–233 |
| **Reading History/Social Studies** | | |
| RH.1 | Cite textual evidence to support analysis of primary and secondary sources | R1 pp. 6–11 |
| RH.2 | Determine the central ideas or information of a primary or secondary source; provide an objective summary | R2 pp. 12–19 |
| RH.3 | Identify key steps in a text's description of a process related to history/social studies | R3 pp. 20–25 |
| RH.4 | Determine the meaning of words and phrases as they are used in a text, including vocabulary specific to history/social studies | R4 pp. 26–33 |
| RH.5 | Describe how a text presents information | R5 pp. 34–39 |

*(Continued)*

| Mississippi Strand/Standard | Focus of Mississippi Standard | For More Information |
|---|---|---|
| **Reading History/Social Studies** | | |
| RH.6 | Identify aspects of a text that reveal an author's point of view or purpose | R6 pp. 40–47 |
| RH.7 | Integrate visual information with other information in print and digital texts | R7 pp. 48–55 |
| RH.8 | Distinguish among fact, opinion, and reasoned judgment in a text | R8 pp. 56–63 |
| RH.9 | Analyze the relationship between a primary and secondary source on the same topic | R9 pp. 64–71 |
| RH.10 | Read and comprehend history/social studies texts of appropriate complexity independently with proficiency | R10 pp. 72–77 |
| **Reading Science/Technical Subjects** | | |
| RST.1 | Cite textual evidence to support analysis of science and technical texts | R1 pp. 6–11 |
| RST.2 | Determine the central ideas or conclusions of a text; provide an objective summary | R2 pp. 12–19 |
| RST.3 | Follow precisely a multistep procedure when carrying out experiments, taking measurements, or performing technical tasks | R3 pp. 20–25 |
| RST.4 | Determine the meaning of symbols, key terms, and other domain-specific words and phrases | R4 pp. 26–33 |
| RST.5 | Analyze the structure an author uses to organize a text, including how the major sections contribute to the whole | R5 pp. 34–39 |
| RST.6 | Analyze the author's purpose in providing an explanation, describing a procedure, or discussing an experiment | R6 pp. 40–47 |
| RST.7 | Integrate quantitative or technical information expressed in words with a version of the information expressed visually | R7 pp. 48–55 |
| RST.8 | Distinguish among facts, reasoned judgment based on research findings, and speculation in a text | R8 pp. 56–63 |
| RST.9 | Compare and contrast the information gained from experiments, simulations, video, or multimedia sources with that gained from reading a text on the same topic | R9 pp. 64–71 |
| RST.10 | Read and comprehend appropriately complex science/technical texts independently and proficiently | R10 pp. 72–77 |
| **Writing History/Social Studies and Science/Technical Subjects** | | |
| WHST.1 | Write arguments based on discipline-specific content | W1 pp. 82–89 |
| WHST.2 | Write informative/explanatory texts including the narration of historical events, scientific procedures/experiments, or technical processes | W2 pp. 90–99 |
| WHST.3 | NA | |
| WHST.4 | Produce writing in which the development, organization, and style are appropriate to the task, purpose, and audience | W4 pp. 110–115 |
| WHST.5 | Develop and strengthen writing as needed by planning, revising, editing, rewriting, or trying a new approach | W5 pp. 116–121 |
| WHST.6 | Use technology to produce and publish writing as well as to interact with others; demonstrate keyboarding skills | W6 pp. 122–127 |
| WHST.7 | Conduct short research projects to answer a question, drawing on several sources and refocusing the inquiry when appropriate | W7 pp. 128–133 |
| WHST.8 | Gather information from print and digital sources; assess the credibility of sources; quote or paraphrase while avoiding plagiarism and providing basic bibliographic information | W8 pp. 134–139 |
| WHST.9 | Draw evidence from informational texts to support analysis, reflection, and research | W9 pp. 140–147 |
| WHST.10 | Write routinely over extended and shorter time frames for a range of tasks, purposes, and audiences | W10 pp. 148–153 |

# Missouri, Grade 6

| Missouri Strand/Standard | Focus of Missouri Standard | For More Information |
|---|---|---|
| **Reading Literary Text** | | |
| RL.1 | Comprehend and Interpret Texts | |
| RL.1.A | Evidence/Inference: Draw conclusions, infer and analyze by citing textual evidence | R1 pp. 6–11 |

| Missouri Strand/Standard | Focus of Missouri Standard | For More Information |
|---|---|---|
| **Reading Literary Text** | | |
| RL.1.B | Word Meanings: Determine the meaning of words as they are used in the text | R4 pp. 28–33 |
| RL.1.C | Text Features: Interpret visual elements of text | R7 pp. 48–55 |
| RL.1.D | Summarize/Theme: Determine the theme and summarize the text | R2 pp. 12–19 |
| RL.2 | Analyze Craft and Structure | |
| RL.2.A | Structure: Analyze how a particular element contributes to meaning | R5 pp. 34–39 |
| RL.2.B | Point of View: Explain how the author develops the point of view of the narrator or speaker | R6 pp. 40–47 |
| RL.2.C | Craft and Meaning: Analyze how word choice contributes to meaning | R4 pp. 28–33 |
| RL.2.D | Interaction and Meaning: Describe how a plot unfolds and how the characters respond or change | R3 pp. 20–27 |
| RL.3 | Synthesize Ideas From Multiple Texts | |
| RL.3.A | Texts in Forms: Compare and contrast reading a text to listening to or viewing an audio, video, or live version of the same text | R7 pp. 48–55 |
| RL.3.B | Relationships in Texts: Compare and contrast texts in different genres that address similar topics | R9 pp. 64–71 |
| RL.3.C | Historical Context: Explain how the text reflects historical and/or cultural contexts | NA |
| RL.3.D | Comprehension: Read and comprehend texts read independently | R10 pp. 72–77 |
| **Reading Informational Text** | | |
| RI.1 | Comprehend and Interpret Texts | |
| RI.1.A | Evidence/Inference: Draw conclusions, infer and analyze by citing textual evidence | R1 pp. 6–11 |
| RI.1.B | Word Meanings: Determine the meaning of words as they are used in the text | R4 pp. 28–33 |
| RI.1.C | Text Features: Interpret visual elements of text | R7 pp. 48–55 |
| RI.1.D | Summarize/Claim: Explain the main idea and summarize the text | R2 pp. 12–19 |
| RI.2 | Analyze Craft and Structure | |
| RI.2.A | Structure: Analyze how a particular element contributes to meaning | R5 pp. 34–39 |
| RI.2.B | Point of View: Explain how an author's point of view is conveyed in a text | R6 pp. 40–47 |
| RI.2.C | Craft and Meaning: Analyze how word choice contributes to meaning | R4 pp. 28–33 |
| RI.2.D | Argument/Evidence: Identify an author's argument and distinguish between claims that are supported by evidence and those that are not | R8 pp. 56–63 |
| RI.3 | Synthesize Ideas From Multiple Texts | |
| RI.3.A | Texts/Forms: Compare and contrast reading a text to listening or viewing an audio or video version of the same text | R7 pp. 48–55 |
| RI.3.B | Relationships/Texts: Compare and contrast one author's presentation of events with another's | R9 pp. 64–71 |
| RI.3.C | Historical Context: Explain how the text reflects historical and/or cultural contexts | NA |
| RI.3.D | Comprehension: Read and comprehend informational texts read independently | R10 pp. 72–77 |
| **Writing and Researching** | | |
| W.1 | Approaching the Task as a Researcher | |
| W.1.A | Research: Conduct research to answer a question; gather relevant information; assess credibility of sources; quote or paraphrase data and conclusions while avoiding plagiarism | W7 pp. 128–133 W8 pp. 134–139 |
| W.2 | Approaching the Task as a Writer | |
| W.2.A | Development: Follow a writing process to produce clear and coherent narrative, expository, and argumentative writing appropriate to the task, purpose, and audience | W1 pp. 84–89 W2 pp. 90–99 W3 pp. 100–109 W4 pp. 110–115 |
| W.3 | Approaching the Task as a Reader | |
| W.3.A | Revise and Edit: Review, revise and edit writing (organization and content; word choice, syntax, style; conventions; transitions) with consideration for the task, purpose, and audience; use technology to produce and publish writing | W1 pp. 84–89 W2 pp. 90–99 W3 pp. 100–109 W5 pp. 116–121 W6 pp. 122–127 L1 pp. 198–203 L2 pp. 204–209 |

*(Continued)*

| Missouri Strand/Standard | Focus of Missouri Standard | For More Information |
|---|---|---|
| **Speaking and Listening** | | |
| SL.1 | Collaborating | |
| SL.1.A | Conversations: Follow rules for discussions and decision-making | SL1 pp. 158–163 |
| SL.1.B | Questioning: Delineate a speaker's argument and distinguish between supported and unsupported claims; make comments that contribute to the topic under discussion | SL1 pp. 158–163 SL3 pp. 170–175 |
| SL.1.C | Viewpoints of Others: Demonstrate understanding of multiple perspectives through reflection and paraphrasing | SL1 pp. 158–163 SL2 pp. 164–169 |
| SL.2 | Presenting | |
| SL.2.A | Verbal Delivery: Speak clearly, audibly, and to the point; use conventions of language appropriate to task, purpose, and audience | SL4 pp. 176–181 |
| SL.2.B | Nonverbal: Make eye contact with listeners | SL4 pp. 176–181 |
| SL.2.C | Multimedia: Include multimedia components to clarify claims, findings, and ideas | SL4 pp. 176–181 SL5 pp. 182–187 |

# Missouri, Grade 7

| Missouri Strand/Standard | Focus of Missouri Standard | For More Information |
|---|---|---|
| **Reading Literary Text** | | |
| RL.1 | Comprehend and Interpret Texts | |
| RL.1.A | Evidence/Inference: Draw conclusions, infer and analyze by citing textual evidence | R1 pp. 6–11 |
| RL.1.B | Word Meanings: Determine the meaning of words as they are used in the text | R4 pp. 28–33 |
| RL.1.C | Text Features: Interpret visual elements of text | R7 pp. 48–55 |
| RL.1.D | Summarize/Theme: Determine the theme and summarize the text | R2 pp. 12–19 |
| RL.2 | Analyze Craft and Structure | |
| RL.2.A | Structure: Analyze how a text's form or structure contributes to meaning | R5 pp. 34–39 |
| RL.2.B | Point of View: Explain how the author develops the points of view of the characters or narrators | R6 pp. 40–47 |
| RL.2.C | Craft and Meaning: Analyze how word choice contributes to meaning and tone | R4 pp. 28–33 |
| RL.2.D | Interaction and Meaning: Analyze how setting, characters, and plot affect each other and contribute to meaning | R3 pp. 20–27 |
| RL.3 | Synthesize Ideas From Multiple Texts | |
| RL.3.A | Texts in Forms: Compare and contrast reading a text to its audio, video, or live version, analyzing how each medium's techniques contribute to meaning | R7 pp. 48–55 |
| RL.3.B | Relationships in Texts: Compare and contrast a fictional portrayal with realistic accounts of the same subject | R9 pp. 64–71 |
| RL.3.C | Historical Context: Explain how the text reflects historical and/or cultural contexts | NA |
| RL.3.D | Comprehension: Read and comprehend texts read independently | R10 pp. 72–77 |
| **Reading Informational Text** | | |
| RI.1 | Comprehend and Interpret Texts | |
| RI.1.A | Evidence/Inference: Draw conclusions, infer and analyze by citing textual evidence | R1 pp. 6–11 |
| RI.1.B | Word Meanings: Determine the meaning of words as they are used in the text | R4 pp. 28–33 |
| RI.1.C | Text Features: Interpret visual elements of text | R7 pp. 48–55 |
| RI.1.D | Summarize/Claim: Explain the main idea, explain the relationship to supporting evidence, and summarize the text | R2 pp. 12–19 |

## Reading Informational Text

| Missouri Strand/Standard | Focus of Missouri Standard | For More Information |
|---|---|---|
| RI.2 | Analyze Craft and Structure | |
| RI.2.A | Structure: Analyze how a particular element contributes to meaning | R5 pp. 34–39 |
| RI.2.B | Point of View: Explain how an author develops and distinguished point of view | R6 pp. 40–47 |
| RI.2.C | Craft and Meaning: Analyze how word choice contributes to meaning and tone | R4 pp. 28–33 |
| RI.2.D | Argument/Evidence: Evaluate an author's argument and assess the reasoning and evidence | R8 pp. 56–63 |
| RI.3 | Synthesize Ideas From Multiple Texts | |
| RI.3.A | Texts/Forms: Compare and contrast information presented in different mediums | R7 pp. 48–55 |
| RI.3.B | Relationships/Texts: Compare and contrast how authors writing about the same topic make decisions about craft and structure | R9 pp. 64–71 |
| RI.3.C | Historical Context: Explain how the text reflects historical and/or cultural contexts | NA |
| RI.3.D | Comprehension: Read and comprehend informational texts read independently | R10 pp. 72–77 |

## Writing and Researching

| Missouri Strand/Standard | Focus of Missouri Standard | For More Information |
|---|---|---|
| W.1 | Approaching the Task as a Researcher | |
| W.1.A | Research: Conduct research to answer a question; gather relevant information from multiple resources; assess credibility of sources; quote or paraphrase data and conclusions while avoiding plagiarism | W7 pp. 128–133 W8 pp. 134–139 |
| W.2 | Approaching the Task as a Writer | |
| W.2.A | Development: Follow a writing process to produce clear and coherent narrative, expository, and argumentative writing appropriate to the task, purpose, and audience | W1 pp. 84–89 W2 pp. 90–99 W3 pp. 100–109 W4 pp. 110–115 |
| W.3 | Approaching the Task as a Reader | |
| W.3.A | Revise and Edit: Review, revise and edit writing (organization and content; word choice, syntax, style; conventions; transitions) with consideration for the task, purpose, and audience; use technology to produce and publish writing | W1 pp. 84–89 W2 pp. 90–99 W3 pp. 100–109 W5 pp. 116–121 W6 pp. 122–127 L1 pp. 198–203 L2 pp. 204–209 |

## Speaking and Listening

| Missouri Strand/Standard | Focus of Missouri Standard | For More Information |
|---|---|---|
| SL.1 | Collaborating | |
| SL.1.A | Conversations: Follow rules for discussions and decision-making | SL1 pp. 158–163 |
| SL.1.B | Questioning: Delineate a speaker's argument, evaluating reasoning and posing questions that elicit elaboration; respond to comments with ideas that bring the discussion back on topic | SL1 pp. 158–163 SL3 pp. 170–175 |
| SL.1.C | Viewpoints of Others: Acknowledge new information expressed by others and modify own views when warranted | SL1 pp. 158–163 SL2 pp. 164–169 |
| SL.2 | Presenting | |
| SL.2.A | Verbal Delivery: Speak clearly, audibly, and to the point; use conventions of language appropriate to task, purpose, and audience | SL4 pp. 176–181 SL6 pp. 188–193 |
| SL.2.B | Nonverbal: Make eye contact with listeners and use effective gestures to communicate | SL4 pp. 176–181 |
| SL.2.C | Multimedia: Include multimedia components to clarify claims and findings, and emphasize significant points | SL4 pp. 176–181 SL5 pp. 182–187 |

# Missouri, Grade 8

| Missouri Strand/Standard | Focus of Missouri Standard | For More Information |
|---|---|---|
| **Reading Literary Text** | | |
| RL.1 | Comprehend and Interpret Texts | |
| RL.1.A | Evidence/Inference: Draw conclusions, infer and analyze by citing textual evidence | R1 pp. 6–11 |
| RL.1.B | Word Meanings: Determine the meaning of words as they are used in the text | R4 pp. 28–33 |
| RL.1.C | Text Features: Interpret visual elements of text | R7 pp. 48–55 |
| RL.1.D | Summarize/Theme: Determine the theme, analyze its development, and summarize the text | R2 pp. 12–19 |
| RL.2 | Analyze Craft and Structure | |
| RL.2.A | Structure: Analyze how a text's form or structure contributes to meaning | R5 pp. 34–39 |
| RL.2.B | Point of View: Analyze how differences in the points of view of the character and the audience create dramatic irony | R6 pp. 40–47 |
| RL.2.C | Craft and Meaning: Analyze how word choice and sentence structure contribute to meaning and tone | R4 pp. 28–33 |
| RL.2.D | Interaction and Meaning: Analyze how literary devices are used to develop setting, reveal characters, advance plot, and contribute to meaning | R3 pp. 20–27 |
| RL.3 | Synthesize Ideas From Multiple Texts | |
| RL.3.A | Texts in Forms: Analyze and how a visual production of a text stays faithful to or departs from the original, and evaluate the choices made by the director or actors | R7 pp. 48–55 |
| RL.3.B | Relationships in Texts: Explain how contemporary texts make use of characters or themes from older or traditional texts | R9 pp. 64–71 |
| RL.3.C | Historical Context: Explain how the text reflects historical and/or cultural contexts | NA |
| RL.3.D | Comprehension: Read and comprehend texts read independently | R10 pp. 72–77 |
| **Reading Informational Text** | | |
| RI.1 | Comprehend and Interpret Texts | |
| RI.1.A | Evidence/Inference: Draw conclusions, infer and analyze by citing textual evidence | R1 pp. 6–11 |
| RI.1.B | Word Meanings: Determine the meaning of words as they are used in the text | R4 pp. 28–33 |
| RI.1.C | Text Features: Interpret visual elements of text | R7 pp. 48–55 |
| RI.1.D | Summarize/Claim: Explain the main idea, explain the relationship to supporting evidence, and summarize the text | R2 pp. 12–19 |
| RI.2 | Analyze Craft and Structure | |
| RI.2.A | Structure: Analyze how organization or overall structure contributes to meaning | R5 pp. 34–39 |
| RI.2.B | Point of View: Explain how an author responds to different points of view in a text | R6 pp. 40–47 |
| RI.2.C | Craft and Meaning: Analyze how word choice and sentence structure contribute to meaning and tone | R4 pp. 28–33 |

| Missouri Strand/Standard | Focus of Missouri Standard | For More Information |
|---|---|---|
| **Reading Informational Text** | | |
| RI.2.D | Argument/Evidence: Evaluate an author's argument and assess the reasoning and evidence; recognize irrelevant evidence | R8 pp. 56–63 |
| RI.3 | Synthesize Ideas From Multiple Texts | |
| RI.3.A | Texts/Forms: Compare and contrast information presented in different mediums | R7 pp. 48–55 |
| **Writing and Researching** | | |
| RI.3.B | Relationships/Texts: Analyze texts that provide conflicting information on the same topic and identify where the texts disagree | R9 pp. 64–71 |
| RI.3.C | Historical Context: Explain how the text reflects historical and/or cultural contexts | NA |
| RI.3.D | Comprehension: Read and comprehend informational texts read independently | R10 pp. 72–77 |
| W.1 | Approaching the Task as a Researcher | |
| W.1.A | Research: Conduct research to answer a question; gather relevant information from multiple resources; assess credibility of sources; quote or paraphrase data and conclusions while avoiding plagiarism | W7 pp. 128–133 W8 pp. 134–139 |
| W.2 | Approaching the Task as a Writer | |
| W.2.A | Development: Follow a writing process to produce clear and coherent narrative, expository, and argumentative writing appropriate to the task, purpose, and audience | W1 pp. 84–89 W2 pp. 90–99 W3 pp. 100–109 W4 pp. 110–115 |
| W.3 | Approaching the Task as a Reader | |
| W.3.A | Revise and Edit: Review, revise and edit writing (organization and content; word choice, syntax, style; conventions; transitions) with consideration for the task, purpose, and audience; use technology to produce and publish writing | W1 pp. 84–89 W2 pp. 90–99 W3 pp. 100–109 W5 pp. 116–121 W6 pp. 122–127 L1 pp. 198–203 L2 pp. 204–209 |
| **Speaking and Listening** | | |
| SL.1 | Collaborating | |
| SL.1.A | Conversations: Follow rules for discussions and decision-making | SL1 pp. 158–163 |
| SL.1.B | Questioning: Delineate a speaker's argument, evaluating reasoning and posing questions that connect the ideas of several speakers; respond to comments with relevant evidence, observations, and ideas | SL1 pp. 158–163 SL3 pp. 170–175 |
| SL.1.C | Viewpoints of Others: Acknowledge new information expressed by others and modify own views when warranted | SL1 pp. 158–163 SL2 pp. 164–169 |
| SL.2 | Presenting | |
| SL.2.A | Verbal Delivery: Speak clearly, audibly, and to the point; use conventions of language appropriate to task, purpose, and audience | SL4 pp. 176–181 SL6 pp. 188–193 |
| SL.2.B | Nonverbal: Make eye contact with listeners and use effective gestures to communicate and engage | SL4 pp. 176–181 |
| SL.2.C | Multimedia: Include multimedia components to clarifyw information, strengthen claims and evidence, and add interest | SL4 pp. 176–181 SL5 pp. 182–187 |

# Nebraska, Grade 6

| Nebraska Strand/Standard | Focus of Nebraska Standard | For More Information |
|---|---|---|
| **LA6.1** | **Reading**: Students will learn and apply reading skills and strategies to comprehend text. | |
| LA6.1.1 | Concepts of Print: Mastered in Grade 1 | NA |
| LA6.1.2 | Phonological Awareness: Mastered in Grade 1 | NA |
| LA6.1.3 | Word Analysis: Students will use phonetic analysis to read and write grade-level text | NA |
| LA6.1.4 | Fluency: Students will develop accuracy, appropriate pace, phrasing, and expression while reading a variety of grade-level texts to support comprehension | R10 pp. 72–77 |
| LA6.1.5 | Vocabulary: Students will build and use conversational, academic, and content-specific grade-level vocabulary | R4 pp. 26–33 L3 pp. 210–215 L4 pp. 216–221 L5 pp. 222–227 L6 pp. 228–233 |
| LA6.1.6 | Comprehension: Students will construct meaning by using prior knowledge and text information while reading grade-level literary and informational texts | R1 pp. 6–11 R2 pp. 12–19 R3 pp. 20–25 R5 pp. 34–39 R6 pp. 40–47 R7 pp. 48–55 R8 pp. 56–63 R9 pp. 64–71 |
| **LA6.2** | **Writing:** Students will learn and apply writing skills and strategies to communicate | |
| LA6.2.1 | Writing Process: Students will apply the writing process to plan, draft, revise, edit, and publish writing using correct spelling, grammar, punctuation, and other conventions of standard English appropriate for grade-level | W4 pp. 110–115 W5 pp. 116–121 W6 pp. 122–127 W9 pp. 140–147 L1 pp. 198–203 L2 pp. 204–209 |
| LA6.2.2 | Writing Modes: Students will write in multiple modes for a variety of purposes and audiences across disciplines | W1 pp. 82–89 W2 pp. 90–99 W3 pp. 100–109 W7 pp. 128–133 W10 pp. 148–153 |
| **LA6.3** | **Speaking and Listening:** Students will develop and apply speaking and listening skills and strategies to communicate for a variety of purposes | |
| LA6.3.1 | Speaking: Students will develop, refine, and apply speaking skills and strategies to communicate for a variety of situations | SL4 pp. 176–181 SL5 pp. 182–187 SL6 pp. 188–193 |
| LA6.3.2 | Listening: Students will develop and demonstrate active listening skills across a variety of situations | SL2 pp. 164–169 SL3 pp. 170–175 |
| LA6.3.3 | Reciprocal Communication: Students will develop, apply, and adapt reciprocal communication skills | SL1 pp. 158–163 SL2 pp. 164–169 SL3 pp. 170–175 |
| **LA6.4** | **Multiple Literacies:** Students will apply information fluency and practice digital citizenship | |
| LA6.4.1 | Information Fluency: Students will evaluate, create, and communicate information in a variety of media and formats | R7 pp. 48–55 R8 pp. 56–63 W6 pp. 122–127 W8 pp. 134–139 SL5 pp. 182–187 |
| LA6.4.2 | Digital Citizenship: Students will practice the norms of appropriate and responsible technology use | W6 pp. 122–127 |

# Nebraska, Grade 7

| Nebraska Strand/Standard | Focus of Nebraska Standard | For More Information |
|---|---|---|
| **LA7.1** | **Reading**: Students will learn and apply reading skills and strategies to comprehend text. | |
| LA7.1.1 | Concepts of Print: Mastered in Grade 1 | NA |
| LA7.1.2 | Phonological Awareness: Mastered in Grade 1 | NA |
| LA7.1.3 | Word Analysis: Students will use phonetic analysis to read and write grade-level text | NA |
| LA7.1.4 | Fluency: Students will develop accuracy, appropriate pace, phrasing, and expression while reading a variety of grade-level texts to support comprehension | R10 pp. 72–77 |
| LA7.1.5 | Vocabulary: Students will build and use conversational, academic, and content-specific grade-level vocabulary | R4 pp. 26–33<br>L3 pp. 210–215<br>L4 pp. 216–221<br>L5 pp. 222–227<br>L6 pp. 228–233 |
| LA7.1.6 | Comprehension: Students will construct meaning by using prior knowledge and text information while reading grade-level literary and informational texts | R1 pp. 6–11<br>R2 pp. 12–19<br>R3 pp. 20–25<br>R5 pp. 34–39<br>R6 pp. 40–47<br>R7 pp. 48–55<br>R8 pp. 56–63<br>R9 pp. 64–71 |
| **LA7.2** | **Writing:** Students will learn and apply writing skills and strategies to communicate | |
| LA7.2.1 | Writing Process: Students will apply the writing process to plan, draft, revise, edit, and publish writing using correct spelling, grammar, punctuation, and other conventions of standard English appropriate for grade-level | W4 pp. 110–115<br>W5 pp. 116–121<br>W6 pp. 122–127<br>W9 pp. 140–147<br>L1 pp. 198–203<br>L2 pp. 204–209 |
| LA7.2.2 | Writing Modes: Students will write in multiple modes for a variety of purposes and audiences across disciplines | W1 pp. 82–89<br>W2 pp. 90–99<br>W3 pp. 100–109<br>W7 pp. 128–133<br>W10 pp. 148–153 |
| **LA7.3** | **Speaking and Listening:** Students will develop and apply speaking and listening skills and strategies to communicate for a variety of purposes | |
| LA7.3.1 | Speaking: Students will develop, refine, and apply speaking skills and strategies to communicate for a variety of situations | SL4 pp. 176–181<br>SL5 pp. 182–187<br>SL6 pp. 188–193 |
| LA7.3.2 | Listening: Students will develop and demonstrate active listening skills across a variety of situations | SL2 pp. 164–169<br>SL3 pp. 170–175 |
| LA7.3.3 | Reciprocal Communication: Students will develop, apply, and adapt reciprocal communication skills | SL1 pp. 158–163<br>SL2 pp. 164–169<br>SL3 pp. 170–175 |
| **LA7.4** | **Multiple Literacies:** Students will apply information fluency and practice digital citizenship | |
| LA7.4.1 | Information Fluency: Students will evaluate, create, and communicate information in a variety of media and formats | R7 pp. 48–55<br>R8 pp. 56–63<br>W6 pp. 122–127<br>W8 pp. 134–139<br>SL5 pp. 182–187 |
| LA7.4.2 | Digital Citizenship: Students will practice the norms of appropriate and responsible technology use | W6 pp. 122–127 |

# Nebraska, Grade 8

| Nebraska Strand/Standard | Focus of Nebraska Standard | For More Information |
|---|---|---|
| **LA8.1** | **Reading**: Students will learn and apply reading skills and strategies to comprehend text. | |
| LA8.1.1 | Concepts of Print: Mastered in Grade 1 | NA |
| LA8.1.2 | Phonological Awareness: Mastered in Grade 1 | NA |
| LA8.1.3 | Word Analysis: Students will use phonetic analysis to read and write grade-level text | NA |
| LA8.1.4 | Fluency: Students will develop accuracy, appropriate pace, phrasing, and expression while reading a variety of grade-level texts to support comprehension | R10 pp. 72–77 |
| LA8.1.5 | Vocabulary: Students will build and use conversational, academic, and content-specific grade-level vocabulary | R4 pp. 26–33<br>L3 pp. 210–215<br>L4 pp. 216–221<br>L5 pp. 222–227<br>L6 pp. 228–233 |
| LA8.1.6 | Comprehension: Students will construct meaning by using prior knowledge and text information while reading grade-level literary and informational texts | R1 pp. 6–11<br>R2 pp. 12–19<br>R3 pp. 20–25<br>R5 pp. 34–39<br>R6 pp. 40–47<br>R7 pp. 48–55<br>R8 pp. 56–63<br>R9 pp. 64–71 |
| **LA8.2** | **Writing:** Students will learn and apply writing skills and strategies to communicate | |
| LA8.2.1 | Writing Process: Students will apply the writing process to plan, draft, revise, edit, and publish writing using correct spelling, grammar, punctuation, and other conventions of standard English appropriate for grade-level | W4 pp. 110–115<br>W5 pp. 116–121<br>W6 pp. 122–127<br>W9 pp. 140–147<br>L1 pp. 198–203<br>L2 pp. 204–209 |
| LA8.2.2 | Writing Modes: Students will write in multiple modes for a variety of purposes and audiences across disciplines | W1 pp. 82–89<br>W2 pp. 90–99<br>W3 pp. 100–109<br>W7 pp. 128–133<br>W10 pp. 148–153 |
| **LA8.3** | **Speaking and Listening:** Students will develop and apply speaking and listening skills and strategies to communicate for a variety of purposes | |
| LA8.3.1 | Speaking: Students will develop, refine, and apply speaking skills and strategies to communicate for a variety of situations | SL4 pp. 176–181<br>SL5 pp. 182–187<br>SL6 pp. 188–193 |
| LA8.3.2 | Listening: Students will develop and demonstrate active listening skills across a variety of situations | SL2 pp. 164–169<br>SL3 pp. 170–175 |
| LA8.3.3 | Reciprocal Communication: Students will develop, apply, and adapt reciprocal communication skills | SL1 pp. 158–163<br>SL2 pp. 164–169<br>SL3 pp. 170–175 |
| **LA8.4** | **Multiple Literacies:** Students will apply information fluency and practice digital citizenship | |
| LA8.4.1 | Information Fluency: Students will evaluate, create, and communicate information in a variety of media and formats | R7 pp. 48–55<br>R8 pp. 56–63<br>W6 pp. 122–127<br>W8 pp. 134–139<br>SL5 pp. 182–187 |
| LA8.4.2 | Digital Citizenship: Students will practice the norms of appropriate and responsible technology use | W6 pp. 122–127 |

# New Jersey, Grade 6

| New Jersey Strand/Standard | Focus of New Jersey Standard | For More Information |
|---|---|---|
| **Reading Literature** | | |
| RL.1 | Cite textual evidence to support analysis of what the text says explicitly as well as inferences drawn from the text | R1 pp. 6–11 |
| RL.2 | Determine the theme or central idea of a text and how it is conveyed through particular details; provide an objective summary | R2 pp. 12–19 |
| RL.3 | Describe how a particular plot unfolds in a series of episodes as well as how the characters respond or change | R3 pp. 20–25 |
| RL.4 | Determine the meaning of words and phrases as they are used in a text, including figurative and connotative meanings | R4 pp. 26–33 |
| RL.5 | Analyze how a particular sentence, chapter, scene, or stanza fits into the overall structure of a text and contributes to the development of the theme, setting, or plot | R5 pp. 34–39 |
| RL.6 | Explain how an author develops the point of view of the narrator or speaker in a text | R6 pp. 40–47 |
| RL.7 | Compare and contrast the experience of reading a story, drama, or poem to listening to or viewing an audio, video, or live version of the text | R7 pp. 48–55 |
| RL.8 | NA | |
| RL.9 | Compare and contrast texts in different forms or genres in terms of their approaches to similar themes and topics | R9 pp. 64–71 |
| RL.10 | Read and comprehend literature of appropriate complexity independently with proficiency | R10 pp. 72–77 |
| **Reading Informational Text** | | |
| RI.1 | Cite textual evidence to support analysis of what the text says explicitly as well as inferences drawn from the text | R1 pp. 6–11 |
| RI.2 | Determine a central idea of a text and how it is conveyed through particular details; provide an objective summary | R2 pp. 12–19 |
| RI.3 | Analyze in detail how a key individual, event, or idea is introduced, illustrated, and elaborated in a text | R3 pp. 20–25 |
| RI.4 | Determine the meaning of words and phrases as they are used in a text, including figurative, connotative, and technical meanings | R4 pp. 26–33 |
| RI.5 | Analyze how a particular sentence, chapter, scene, or section fits into the overall structure of a text and contributes to the development of the ideas | R5 pp. 34–39 |
| RI.6 | Determine an author's point of view or purpose in a text and explain how it is conveyed in the text | R6 pp. 40–47 |
| RI.7 | Integrate information presented in different media or formats as well as in words to develop a coherent understanding of a topic or issue | R7 pp. 48–55 |
| RI.8 | Trace and evaluate the argument and specific claims that are supported by reasons and evidence from claims that are not | R8 pp. 56–63 |
| RI.9 | Compare and contrast one author's presentation of events with that of another | R9 pp. 64–71 |
| RI.10 | Read and comprehend appropriately complex literary nonfiction, informational, and functional texts independently and proficiently | R10 pp. 72–77 |
| **Writing** | | |
| W.1 | Write arguments to support claims with clear reasons and relevant evidence | W1 pp. 82–89 |
| W.2 | Write informative/explanatory texts to examine a topic and convey ideas, concepts, and information clearly | W2 pp. 90–99 |
| W.3 | Write narratives to develop real or imagined experiences or events using effective technique, descriptive details, and well-structured event sequences | W3 pp. 100–109 |

*(Continued)*

| New Jersey Strand/Standard | Focus of New Jersey Standard | For More Information |
|---|---|---|
| **Writing** | | |
| W.4 | Produce writing in which the development, organization, and style are appropriate to the task, purpose, and audience | W4 pp. 110–115 |
| W.5 | Develop and strengthen writing as needed by planning, revising, editing, rewriting, or trying a new approach | W5 pp. 116–121 |
| W.6 | Use technology to produce and publish writing as well as to interact with others; demonstrate keyboarding skills | W6 pp. 122–127 |
| W.7 | Conduct short research projects to answer a question, drawing on several sources and refocusing the inquiry when appropriate | W7 pp. 128–133 |
| W.8 | Gather information from print and digital sources; assess the credibility of sources; quote or paraphrase while avoiding plagiarism and providing basic bibliographic information | W8 pp. 134–139 |
| W.9 | Draw evidence from literary or informational texts to support analysis, reflection, and research | W9 pp. 140–147 |
| W.10 | Write routinely over extended and shorter time frames for a range of tasks, purposes, and audiences | W10 pp. 148–153 |
| **Speaking and Listening** | | |
| SL.1 | Engage effectively in a range of collaborative discussions with diverse partners, building on others' ideas and expressing their own clearly | SL1 pp. 158–163 |
| SL.2 | Interpret information presented in diverse media and formats and explain how it contributes to a topic, text, or issue under study | SL2 pp. 164–169 |
| SL.3 | Delineate a speaker's argument and specific claims that are supported by reasons and evidence from claims that are not | SL3 pp. 170–175 |
| SL.4 | Present claims and findings, sequencing ideas logically and using descriptions, facts, or details to accentuate main ideas or themes; use appropriate eye contact, adequate volume, and clear pronunciation | SL4 pp. 176–181 |
| SL.5 | Include multimedia components and visual displays in presentations to clarify information | SL5 pp. 182–187 |
| SL.6 | Adapt speech to a variety of contexts and tasks, demonstrating command of formal English when appropriate | SL6 pp. 188–193 |
| **Language** | | |
| L.1 | Demonstrate command of the conventions of standard English grammar and usage when writing or speaking | L1 pp. 198–203 |
| L.2 | Demonstrate command of the conventions of standard English capitalization, punctuation, and spelling when writing | L2 pp. 204–209 |
| L.3 | Use knowledge of language and its conventions when writing, speaking, reading, or listening | L3 pp. 210–215 |
| L.4 | Determine or clarify the meaning of unknown and multiple-meaning words and phrases, choosing flexibly from an array of strategies | L4 pp. 216–221 |
| L.5 | Demonstrate understanding of figurative language, word relationships, and nuances in word meanings | L5 pp. 222–227 |
| L.6 | Acquire and use accurately general academic, and domain-specific words and phrases | L6 pp. 228–233 |
| **Reading History/Social Studies** | | |
| RH.1 | Cite textual evidence to support analysis of primary and secondary sources | R1 pp. 6–11 |
| RH.2 | Determine the central ideas or information of a primary or secondary source; provide an objective summary | R2 pp. 12–19 |
| RH.3 | Identify key steps in a text's description of a process related to history/social studies | R3 pp. 20–25 |
| RH.4 | Determine the meaning of words and phrases as they are used in a text, including vocabulary specific to history/social studies | R4 pp. 26–33 |

| New Jersey Strand/Standard | Focus of New Jersey Standard | For More Information |
|---|---|---|
| **Reading History/Social Studies** | | |
| RH.5 | Describe how a text presents information | R5 pp. 34–39 |
| RH.6 | Identify aspects of a text that reveal an author's point of view or purpose | R6 pp. 40–47 |
| RH.7 | Integrate visual information with other information in print and digital texts | R7 pp. 48–55 |
| RH.8 | Distinguish among fact, opinion, and reasoned judgment in a text | R8 pp. 56–63 |
| RH.9 | Analyze the relationship between a primary and secondary source on the same topic | R9 pp. 64–71 |
| RH.10 | Read and comprehend history/social studies texts of appropriate complexity independently with proficiency | R10 pp. 72–77 |
| **Reading Science/Technical Subjects** | | |
| RST.1 | Cite textual evidence to support analysis of science and technical texts | R1 pp. 6–11 |
| RST.2 | Determine the central ideas or conclusions of a text; provide an objective summary | R2 pp. 12–19 |
| RST.3 | Follow precisely a multistep procedure when carrying out experiments, taking measurements, or performing technical tasks | R3 pp. 20–25 |
| RST.4 | Determine the meaning of symbols, key terms, and other domain-specific words and phrases | R4 pp. 26–33 |
| RST.5 | Analyze the structure an author uses to organize a text, including how the major sections contribute to the whole | R5 pp. 34–39 |
| RST.6 | Analyze the author's purpose in providing an explanation, describing a procedure, or discussing an experiment | R6 pp. 40–47 |
| RST.7 | Integrate quantitative or technical information expressed in words with a version of the information expressed visually | R7 pp. 48–55 |
| RST.8 | Distinguish among facts, reasoned judgment based on research findings, and speculation in a text | R8 pp. 56–63 |
| RST.9 | Compare and contrast the information gained from experiments, simulations, video, or multimedia sources with that gained from reading a text on the same topic | R9 pp. 64–71 |
| RST.10 | Read and comprehend appropriately complex science/technical texts independently and proficiently | R10 pp. 72–77 |
| **Writing History/Social Studies and Science/Technical Subjects** | | |
| WHST.1 | Write arguments based on discipline-specific content | W1 pp. 82–89 |
| WHST.2 | Write informative/explanatory texts including the narration of historical events, scientific procedures/experiments, or technical processes | W2 pp. 90–99 |
| WHST.3 | NA | |
| WHST.4 | Produce writing in which the development, organization, and style are appropriate to the task, purpose, and audience | W4 pp. 110–115 |
| WHST.5 | Develop and strengthen writing as needed by planning, revising, editing, rewriting, or trying a new approach | W5 pp. 116–121 |
| WHST.6 | Use technology to produce and publish writing as well as to interact with others; demonstrate keyboarding skills | W6 pp. 122–127 |
| WHST.7 | Conduct short research projects to answer a question, drawing on several sources and refocusing the inquiry when appropriate | W7 pp. 128–133 |
| WHST.8 | Gather information from print and digital sources; assess the credibility of sources; quote or paraphrase while avoiding plagiarism and providing basic bibliographic information | W8 pp. 134–139 |
| WHST.9 | Draw evidence from informational texts to support analysis, reflection, and research | W9 pp. 140–147 |
| WHST.10 | Write routinely over extended and shorter time frames for a range of tasks, purposes, and audiences | W10 pp. 148–153 |

# New Jersey, Grade 7

| New Jersey Strand/Standard | Focus of New Jersey Standard | For More Information |
|---|---|---|
| **Reading Literature** | | |
| RL.1 | Cite several pieces of textual evidence to support analysis of what the text says explicitly as well as inferences drawn from the text | R1 pp. 6–11 |
| RL.2 | Determine the theme or central idea of a text and analyze its development; provide an objective summary of the text | R2 pp. 12–19 |
| RL.3 | Analyze how particular elements of a story or drama interact | R3 pp. 20–25 |
| RL.4 | Determine the meaning of words and phrases as they are used in a text, including figurative and connotative meanings | R4 pp. 26–33 |
| RL.5 | Analyze how a drama's or poem's form or structure contributes to its meaning | R5 pp. 34–39 |
| RL.6 | Analyze how an author develops and contrasts the points of view of different characters or narrators in a text | R6 pp. 40–47 |
| RL.7 | Compare and contrast a written story, drama, or poem to its audio, filmed, staged, or multimedia version | R7 pp. 48–55 |
| RL.8 | NA | |
| RL.9 | Compare and contrast a fictional portrayal of a time, place, or character and a historical account of the same period | R9 pp. 64–71 |
| RL.10 | Read and comprehend literature of appropriate complexity independently with proficiency | R10 pp. 72–77 |
| **Reading Informational Text** | | |
| RI.1 | Cite several pieces of textual evidence to support analysis of what the text says explicitly as well as inferences drawn from the text | R1 pp. 6–11 |
| RI.2 | Determine two or more central ideas in a text and analyze their developments; provide an objective summary of the text | R2 pp. 12–19 |
| RI.3 | Analyze the interactions between individuals, events, and ideas in a text | R3 pp. 20–25 |
| RI.4 | Determine the meaning of words and phrases as they are used in a text, including figurative, connotative, and technical meanings | R4 pp. 26–33 |
| RI.5 | Analyze the structure an author uses to organize a text, including how the major sections contribute to the whole | R5 pp. 34–39 |
| RI.6 | Determine an author's point of view or purpose in a text and analyze how the author distinguishes his or her position from that of others | R6 pp. 40–47 |
| RI.7 | Compare and contrast a text to an audio, video, or multimedia version of the text | R7 pp. 48–55 |
| RI.8 | Trace and evaluate the argument and specific claims in a text, assessing whether the reason is sound and the evidence is relevant and sufficient | R8 pp. 56–63 |
| RI.9 | Analyze how two or more authors writing about the same topic shape their presentations of key information | R9 pp. 64–71 |
| RI.10 | Read and comprehend appropriately complex literary nonfiction, informational, and functional texts independently and proficiently | R10 pp. 72–77 |
| **Writing** | | |
| W.1 | Write arguments to support claims with clear reasons and relevant evidence | W1 pp. 82–89 |
| W.2 | Write informative/explanatory texts to examine a topic and convey ideas, concepts, and information clearly | W2 pp. 90–99 |
| W.3 | Write narratives to develop real or imagined experiences or events using effective technique, descriptive details, and well-structured event sequences | W3 pp. 100–109 |

| New Jersey Strand/Standard | Focus of New Jersey Standard | For More Information |
|---|---|---|
| **Writing** | | |
| W.4 | Produce writing in which the development, organization, and style are appropriate to the task, purpose, and audience | W4 pp. 110–115 |
| W.5 | Develop and strengthen writing as needed by planning, revising, editing, rewriting, or trying a new approach | W5 pp. 116–121 |
| W.6 | Use technology to produce and publish writing, link to and cite sources; interact and collaborate with others | W6 pp. 122–127 |
| W.7 | Conduct short research projects to answer a question, drawing on several sources and additional related questions for further investigation | W7 pp. 128–133 |
| W.8 | Gather information from print and digital sources; assess the credibility of sources; quote or paraphrase while avoiding plagiarism and following a standard format for citation | W8 pp. 134–139 |
| W.9 | Draw evidence from literary or informational texts to support analysis, reflection, and research | W9 pp. 140–147 |
| W.10 | Write routinely over extended and shorter time frames for a range of tasks, purposes, and audiences | W10 pp. 148–153 |
| **Speaking and Listening** | | |
| SL.1 | Engage effectively in a range of collaborative discussions with diverse partners, building on others' ideas and expressing their own clearly | SL1 pp. 158–163 |
| SL.2 | Analyze the main ideas and supporting details presented in diverse media and formats and explain how the ideas clarify a topic, text, or issue under study | SL2 pp. 164–169 |
| SL.3 | Delineate a speaker's argument and specific claims evaluating the soundness of the reasoning and the relevance and sufficiency of the evidence | SL3 pp. 170–175 |
| SL.4 | Present claims and findings, emphasizing salient points in a focused coherent manner; use appropriate eye contact, adequate volume, and clear pronunciation | SL4 pp. 176–181 |
| SL.5 | Include multimedia components and visual displays in presentations to clarify claims and findings | SL5 pp. 182–187 |
| SL.6 | Adapt speech to a variety of contexts and tasks, demonstrating command of formal English when appropriate | SL6 pp. 188–193 |
| **Language** | | |
| L.1 | Demonstrate command of the conventions of standard English grammar and usage when writing or speaking | L1 pp. 198–203 |
| L.2 | Demonstrate command of the conventions of standard English capitalization, punctuation, and spelling when writing | L2 pp. 204–209 |
| L.3 | Use knowledge of language and its conventions when writing, speaking, reading, or listening | L3 pp. 210–215 |
| L.4 | Determine or clarify the meaning of unknown and multiple-meaning words and phrases, choosing flexibly from an array of strategies | L4 pp. 216–221 |
| L.5 | Demonstrate understanding of figurative language, word relationships, and nuances in word meanings | L5 pp. 222–227 |
| L.6 | Acquire and use accurately general academic, and domain-specific words and phrases | L6 pp. 228–233 |
| **Reading History/Social Studies** | | |
| RH.1 | Cite textual evidence to support analysis of primary and secondary sources | R1 pp. 6–11 |
| RH.2 | Determine the central ideas or information of a primary or secondary source; provide an objective summary | R2 pp. 12–19 |
| RH.3 | Identify key steps in a text's description of a process related to history/social studies | R3 pp. 20–25 |
| RH.4 | Determine the meaning of words and phrases as they are used in a text, including vocabulary specific to history/social studies | R4 pp. 26–33 |

*(Continued)*

| New Jersey Strand/Standard | Focus of New Jersey Standard | For More Information |
|---|---|---|
| **Reading History/Social Studies** | | |
| RH.5 | Describe how a text presents information | R5 pp. 34–39 |
| RH.6 | Identify aspects of a text that reveal an author's point of view or purpose | R6 pp. 40–47 |
| RH.7 | Integrate visual information with other information in print and digital texts | R7 pp. 48–55 |
| RH.8 | Distinguish among fact, opinion, and reasoned judgment in a text | R8 pp. 56–63 |
| RH.9 | Analyze the relationship between a primary and secondary source on the same topic | R9 pp. 64–71 |
| RH.10 | Read and comprehend history/social studies texts of appropriate complexity independently with proficiency | R10 pp. 72–77 |
| **Reading Science/Technical Subjects** | | |
| RST.1 | Cite textual evidence to support analysis of science and technical texts | R1 pp. 6–11 |
| RST.2 | Determine the central ideas or conclusions of a text; provide an objective summary | R2 pp. 12–19 |
| RST.3 | Follow precisely a multistep procedure when carrying out experiments, taking measurements, or performing technical tasks | R3 pp. 20–25 |
| RST.4 | Determine the meaning of symbols, key terms, and other domain-specific words and phrases | R4 pp. 26–33 |
| RST.5 | Analyze the structure an author uses to organize a text, including how the major sections contribute to the whole | R5 pp. 34–39 |
| RST.6 | Analyze the author's purpose in providing an explanation, describing a procedure, or discussing an experiment | R6 pp. 40–47 |
| RST.7 | Integrate quantitative or technical information expressed in words with a version of the information expressed visually | R7 pp. 48–55 |
| RST.8 | Distinguish among facts, reasoned judgment based on research findings, and speculation in a text | R8 pp. 56–63 |
| RST.9 | Compare and contrast the information gained from experiments, simulations, video, or multimedia sources with that gained from reading a text on the same topic | R9 pp. 64–71 |
| RST.10 | Read and comprehend appropriately complex science/technical texts independently and proficiently | R10 pp. 72–77 |
| **Writing History/Social Studies and Science/Technical Subjects** | | |
| WHST.1 | Write arguments based on discipline-specific content | W1 pp. 82–89 |
| WHST.2 | Write informative/explanatory texts including the narration of historical events, scientific procedures/experiments, or technical processes | W2 pp. 90–99 |
| WHST.3 | NA | |
| WHST.4 | Produce writing in which the development, organization, and style are appropriate to the task, purpose, and audience | W4 pp. 110–115 |
| WHST.5 | Develop and strengthen writing as needed by planning, revising, editing, rewriting, or trying a new approach | W5 pp. 116–121 |
| WHST.6 | Use technology to produce and publish writing as well as to interact with others; demonstrate keyboarding skills | W6 pp. 122–127 |
| WHST.7 | Conduct short research projects to answer a question, drawing on several sources and refocusing the inquiry when appropriate | W7 pp. 128–133 |
| WHST.8 | Gather information from print and digital sources; assess the credibility of sources; quote or paraphrase while avoiding plagiarism and providing basic bibliographic information | W8 pp. 134–139 |
| WHST.9 | Draw evidence from informational texts to support analysis, reflection, and research | W9 pp. 140–147 |
| WHST.10 | Write routinely over extended and shorter time frames for a range of tasks, purposes, and audiences | W10 pp. 148–153 |

# New Jersey, Grade 8

| New Jersey Strand/Standard | Focus of New Jersey Standard | For More Information |
|---|---|---|
| **Reading Literature** | | |
| RL.1 | Cite the textual evidence that most strongly supports an analysis of what the text says explicitly as well as inferences drawn from the text | R1 pp. 6–11 |
| RL.2 | Determine the theme or central idea of a text and analyze its development, including its relationship to the characters, setting, and plot; provide an objective summary of the text | R2 pp. 12–19 |
| RL.3 | Analyze how particular lines of dialogue or incidents in a story or drama propel the action, reveal aspects of a character, or provoke a decision | R3 pp. 20–25 |
| RL.4 | Determine the meaning of words and phrases as they are used in a text, including figurative and connotative meanings | R4 pp. 26–33 |
| RL.5 | Compare and contrast the structure of two or more texts and analyze how the differing structure of each contributes to its meaning and style | R5 pp. 34–39 |
| RL.6 | Analyze how differences in the points of view of the characters and the audience or reader create such effects as suspense or humor | R6 pp. 40–47 |
| RL.7 | Analyze the extent to which a filmed or live production of a story or drama stays faithful or departs from the text or script | R7 pp. 48–55 |
| RL.8 | NA | |
| RL.9 | Analyze how a modern work of fiction draws on themes, patterns of events, or character types from traditional stories, describing how the material is rendered new | R9 pp. 64–71 |
| RL.10 | Read and comprehend literature of appropriate complexity independently with proficiency | R10 pp. 72–77 |
| **Reading Informational Text** | | |
| RI.1 | Cite the textual evidence that most strongly supports an analysis of what the text says explicitly as well as inferences drawn from the text | R1 pp. 6–11 |
| RI.2 | Determine the central idea of a text and analyze its development, including its relationship to supporting ideas; provide an objective summary of the text | R2 pp. 12–19 |
| RI.3 | Analyze how a text makes connections among distinctions between individuals, ideas, or events | R3 pp. 20–25 |
| RI.4 | Determine the meaning of words and phrases as they are used in a text, including figurative, connotative, and technical meanings | R4 pp. 26–33 |
| RI.5 | Analyze the structure of a specific paragraph in a text, including the role of particular sentences in developing and refining a key concept | R5 pp. 34–39 |
| RI.6 | Determine an author's point of view or purpose in a text and analyze how the author acknowledges and responds to conflicting evidence or viewpoints | R6 pp. 40–47 |
| RI.7 | Evaluate the advantages and disadvantages of using different mediums to present a particular topic or idea | R7 pp. 48–55 |
| RI.8 | Delineate and evaluate the argument and specific claims in a text, assessing whether the reason is sound and the evidence is relevant and sufficient | R8 pp. 56–63 |
| RI.9 | Analyze a case in which two or more texts provide conflicting information on the same topic | R9 pp. 64–71 |
| RI.10 | Read and comprehend appropriately complex literary nonfiction, informational, and functional texts independently and proficiently | R10 pp. 72–77 |
| **Writing** | | |
| W.1 | Write arguments to support claims with clear reasons and relevant evidence | W1 pp. 82–89 |
| W.2 | Write informative/explanatory texts to examine a topic and convey ideas, concepts, and information clearly | W2 pp. 90–99 |
| W.3 | Write narratives to develop real or imagined experiences or events using effective technique, descriptive details, and well-structured event sequences | W3 pp. 100–109 |
| W.4 | Produce writing in which the development, organization, and style are appropriate to the task, purpose, and audience | W4 pp. 110–115 |

*(Continued)*

| New Jersey Strand/Standard | Focus of New Jersey Standard | For More Information |
|---|---|---|
| **Writing** | | |
| W.5 | Develop and strengthen writing as needed by planning, revising, editing, rewriting, or trying a new approach | W5 pp. 116–121 |
| W.6 | Use technology to produce and publish writing, link to and cite sources; interact and collaborate with others | W6 pp. 122–127 |
| W.7 | Conduct short research projects to answer a question, drawing on several sources and additional related questions for further investigation | W7 pp. 128–133 |
| W.8 | Gather information from print and digital sources; assess the credibility of sources; quote or paraphrase while avoiding plagiarism and following a standard format for citation | W8 pp. 134–139 |
| W.9 | Draw evidence from literary or informational texts to support analysis, reflection, and research | W9 pp. 140–147 |
| W.10 | Write routinely over extended and shorter time frames for a range of tasks, purposes, and audiences | W10 pp. 148–153 |
| **Speaking and Listening** | | |
| SL.1 | Engage effectively in a range of collaborative discussions with diverse partners, building on others' ideas and expressing their own clearly | SL1 pp. 158–163 |
| SL.2 | Analyze the purpose of information presented in diverse media and formats and evaluate the motives behind its presentation | SL2 pp. 164–169 |
| SL.3 | Delineate a speaker's argument and specific claims evaluating the soundness of the reasoning and the relevance and sufficiency of the evidence and identifying when irrelevant evidence is introduced | SL3 pp. 170–175 |
| SL.4 | Present claims and findings, emphasizing salient points in a focused coherent manner; use appropriate eye contact, adequate volume, and clear pronunciation | SL4 pp. 176–181 |
| SL.5 | Integrate multimedia components and visual displays into presentations to clarify information, strengthen claims and findings, and add interest | SL5 pp. 182–187 |
| SL.6 | Adapt speech to a variety of contexts and tasks, demonstrating command of formal English when appropriate | SL6 pp. 188–193 |
| **Language** | | |
| L.1 | Demonstrate command of the conventions of standard English grammar and usage when writing or speaking | L1 pp. 198–203 |
| L.2 | Demonstrate command of the conventions of standard English capitalization, punctuation, and spelling when writing | L2 pp. 204–209 |
| L.3 | Use knowledge of language and its conventions when writing, speaking, reading, or listening | L3 pp. 210–215 |
| L.4 | Determine or clarify the meaning of unknown and multiple-meaning words and phrases, choosing flexibly from an array of strategies | L4 pp. 216–221 |
| L.5 | Demonstrate understanding of figurative language, word relationships, and nuances in word meanings | L5 pp. 222–227 |
| L.6 | Acquire and use accurately general academic, and domain-specific words and phrases | L6 pp. 228–233 |
| **Reading History/Social Studies** | | |
| RH.1 | Cite textual evidence to support analysis of primary and secondary sources | R1 pp. 6–11 |
| RH.2 | Determine the central ideas or information of a primary or secondary source; provide an objective summary | R2 pp. 12–19 |
| RH.3 | Identify key steps in a text's description of a process related to history/social studies | R3 pp. 20–25 |
| RH.4 | Determine the meaning of words and phrases as they are used in a text, including vocabulary specific to history/social studies | R4 pp. 26–33 |

| New Jersey Strand/Standard | Focus of New Jersey Standard | For More Information |
|---|---|---|
| **Reading History/Social Studies** | | |
| RH.5 | Describe how a text presents information | R5 pp. 34–39 |
| RH.6 | Identify aspects of a text that reveal an author's point of view or purpose | R6 pp. 40–47 |
| RH.7 | Integrate visual information with other information in print and digital texts | R7 pp. 48–55 |
| RH.8 | Distinguish among fact, opinion, and reasoned judgment in a text | R8 pp. 56–63 |
| RH.9 | Analyze the relationship between a primary and secondary source on the same topic | R9 pp. 64–71 |
| RH.10 | Read and comprehend history/social studies texts of appropriate complexity independently with proficiency | R10 pp. 72–77 |
| **Reading Science/Technical Subjects** | | |
| RST.1 | Cite textual evidence to support analysis of science and technical texts | R1 pp. 6–11 |
| RST.2 | Determine the central ideas or conclusions of a text; provide an objective summary | R2 pp. 12–19 |
| RST.3 | Follow precisely a multistep procedure when carrying out experiments, taking measurements, or performing technical tasks | R3 pp. 20–25 |
| RST.4 | Determine the meaning of symbols, key terms, and other domain-specific words and phrases | R4 pp. 26–33 |
| RST.5 | Analyze the structure an author uses to organize a text, including how the major sections contribute to the whole | R5 pp. 34–39 |
| RST.6 | Analyze the author's purpose in providing an explanation, describing a procedure, or discussing an experiment | R6 pp. 40–47 |
| RST.7 | Integrate quantitative or technical information expressed in words with a version of the information expressed visually | R7 pp. 48–55 |
| RST.8 | Distinguish among facts, reasoned judgment based on research findings, and speculation in a text | R8 pp. 56–63 |
| RST.9 | Compare and contrast the information gained from experiments, simulations, video, or multimedia sources with that gained from reading a text on the same topic | R9 pp. 64–71 |
| RST.10 | Read and comprehend appropriately complex science/technical texts independently and proficiently | R10 pp. 72–77 |
| **Writing History/Social Studies and Science/Technical Subjects** | | |
| WHST.1 | Write arguments based on discipline-specific content | W1 pp. 82–89 |
| WHST.2 | Write informative/explanatory texts including the narration of historical events, scientific procedures/experiments, or technical processes | W2 pp. 90–99 |
| WHST.3 | NA | |
| WHST.4 | Produce writing in which the development, organization, and style are appropriate to the task, purpose, and audience | W4 pp. 110–115 |
| WHST.5 | Develop and strengthen writing as needed by planning, revising, editing, rewriting, or trying a new approach | W5 pp. 116–121 |
| WHST.6 | Use technology to produce and publish writing as well as to interact with others; demonstrate keyboarding skills | W6 pp. 122–127 |
| WHST.7 | Conduct short research projects to answer a question, drawing on several sources and refocusing the inquiry when appropriate | W7 pp. 128–133 |
| WHST.8 | Gather information from print and digital sources; assess the credibility of sources; quote or paraphrase while avoiding plagiarism and providing basic bibliographic information | W8 pp. 134–139 |
| WHST.9 | Draw evidence from informational texts to support analysis, reflection, and research | W9 pp. 140–147 |
| WHST.10 | Write routinely over extended and shorter time frames for a range of tasks, purposes, and audiences | W10 pp. 148–153 |

# Oklahoma, Grade 6

| Oklahoma Strand/Standard | Focus of Oklahoma Standard | For More Information |
|---|---|---|
| **Speaking and Listening** | | |
| 1.R.1 | Actively listen and speak clearly using appropriate discussion rules | SL1 pp. 158–163 |
| 1.R.2 | Actively listen and interpret a speaker's messages and ask questions to clarify the speaker's purpose and perspective | SL3 pp. 170–175 |
| 1.R.3 | Engage in collaborative discussions | SL1 pp. 158–163 |
| 1.W.1 | Give formal and informal presentations, organizing information and determining appropriate content and purpose for audience | SL4 pp. 176–181 |
| 1.W.2 | Work in groups effectively and respectfully, valuing contributions by group members | SL1 pp. 158–163 |
| **Reading and Writing Process** | | |
| 2.R.1 | Create an objective summary, including main idea and supporting details, while maintaining meaning and sequence of events | R2 pp. 12–19 |
| 2.R.2 | Analyze details in literary and informational texts to distinguish genres | R9 pp. 64–71 |
| 2.R.3 | Paraphrase main ideas with supporting details | R2 pp. 12–19 |
| 2.W.1 | Apply components of a recursive writing process to create a focused, organized, coherent piece of writing | W4 pp. 110–115 |
| 2.W.2–3 | Plan, prewrite, and develop drafts; choose organizational structure, building on ideas in multi-paragraph essays | W4 pp. 110–115 |
| 2.W.4 | Edit and revise multiple drafts for purpose, organization, and coherence | W5 pp. 116–121 |
| 2.W.5 | Use resources to find correct spellings | L2 pp. 204–209 |
| **Critical Reading and Writing** | | |
| 3.R.1 | Compare and contrast stated or implied purpose of authors writing on the same topic | R9 pp. 64–71 |
| 3.R.2 | Evaluate how the point of view and perspective affect the text | R6 pp. 40–47 |
| 3.R.3 | Analyze how key literary elements (setting, plot, characters, characterization, theme) contribute to the meaning of the work | R2 pp. 12–19 R3 pp. 20–25 |
| 3.R.4 | Evaluate literary devices (e.g., simile, metaphor) to support interpretations of text | R4 pp. 26–33 |
| 3.R.5 | Categorize facts included in an argument as for or against an issue | R8 pp. 56–63 |
| 3.R.6 | Analyze the structures of texts and content by making inferences and use textual evidence to support understanding | R1 pp. 6–11 R5 pp. 34–39 |
| 3.R.7 | Analyze texts and ideas within and between texts | R9 pp. 64–71 |
| 3.W.1 | Write narratives incorporating plot, setting, characters, point of view, and conflict | W3 pp. 100–109 |
| 3.W.2 | Compose essays and reports about topics, incorporating evidence and maintaining an organized structure | W2 pp. 90–99 |
| 3.W.3–4 | Clearly state an opinion supported with facts and details; show relationships among facts, opinions, and supporting details | W1 pp. 82–89 |
| **Vocabulary** | | |
| 4.R.1 | Increase knowledge of academic, domain-appropriate, grade-level vocabulary to infer meaning of text | L6 pp. 228–233 |
| 4.R.2 | Use word parts to define and determine meaning of new words | L4 pp. 216–221 |
| 4.R.3 | Use context clues to determine or clarify word meaning | L4 pp. 216–221 |
| 4.R.4 | Infer relationships among words with multiple meanings, including synonyms, antonyms, and multiple meaning words | L5 pp. 222–227 |
| 4.R.5 | Use a dictionary, glossary, or thesaurus to find words | L4 pp. 216–233 |
| 4.W.1 | Use domain-appropriate vocabulary to communicate ideas in writing clearly | L6 pp. 228–233 |
| 4.W.2 | Select appropriate language to create a specific effect in writing | L6 pp. 228–233 |

| Oklahoma Strand/Standard | Focus of Oklahoma Standard | For More Information |
|---|---|---|
| **Language** | | |
| 5.R.1–3 | Recognize simple and compound sentences, verb tense, and subject-verb agreement | L1 pp. 198–203 |
| 5.W.1–5 | Write using correct mechanics; compose simple, compound, and complex sentences; use intensive and reflexive pronouns; correct inappropriate shifts in pronouns number and person; recognize and correct vague pronouns | L1 pp. 198–203 L2 pp. 204–209 L3 pp. 210–215 |
| **Research** | | |
| 6.R.1–3 | Use own questions to find information on a specific topic; record and organize information from sources; determine relevance and reliability of information | R7 pp. 48–55 W7 pp. 128–133 |
| 6.W.1–3 | Write research papers; refine a viable research question; organize information found during research | W7 pp. 128–133 W8 pp. 134–139 W9 pp. 140–145 |
| 6.W.4 | Summarize and present information in a report | SL4 pp. 176–181 |
| **Multimodal Literacies** | | |
| 7.R.1 | Compare and contrast the effectiveness of a variety of texts to generate and answer questions to create new understandings | R7 pp. 48–55 |
| 7.R.2 | Analyze the impact of selected media and formats on meaning | R9 pp. 64–71 |
| 7.W.1 | Create multimodal content that communicates ideas | W6 pp. 122–127 |
| 7.W.2 | Create presentations that integrate visual displays and other multimedia | SL5 pp. 182–187 |
| **Independent Reading and Writing** | | |
| 8.R | Select and read independently level-appropriate texts for academic and personal purposes | R10 pp. 72–77 |
| 8.W | Write independently for extended and shorter periods of time | W10 pp. 148–153 |

# Oklahoma, Grade 7

| Oklahoma Strand/Standard | Focus of Oklahoma Standard | For More Information |
|---|---|---|
| **Speaking and Listening** | | |
| 1.R.1 | Actively listen and speak clearly using appropriate discussion rules | SL1 pp. 158–163 |
| 1.R.2 | Actively listen and interpret a speaker's messages and ask questions to clarify the speaker's purpose and perspective | SL3 pp. 170–175 |
| 1.R.3 | Engage in collaborative discussions | SL1 pp. 158–163 |
| 1.W.1 | Give formal and informal presentations, providing evidence to support a main idea | SL4 pp. 176–181 |
| 1.W.2 | Work in groups effectively and respectfully, valuing contributions by group members | SL1 pp. 158–163 |
| **Reading and Writing Process** | | |
| 2.R.1 | Create an objective summary, including main idea and supporting details, while maintaining meaning and sequence of events | R2 pp. 12–19 |
| 2.R.2 | Analyze details in literary and informational texts to distinguish genres | R9 pp. 64–71 |
| 2.R.3 | Paraphrase main ideas with supporting details | R2 pp. 12–19 |
| 2.W.1 | Apply components of a recursive writing process to create a focused, organized, coherent piece of writing | W4 pp. 110–115 |
| 2.W.2–3 | Plan, prewrite, and develop drafts; choose organizational structure, building on ideas in multi-paragraph essays | W4 pp. 110–115 |
| 2.W.4 | Edit and revise multiple drafts for purpose, organization, and coherence | W5 pp. 116–121 |
| 2.W.5 | Use resources to find correct spellings | L2 pp. 204–209 |

*(Continued)*

| Oklahoma Strand/Standard | Focus of Oklahoma Standard | For More Information |
|---|---|---|
| **Critical Reading and Writing** | | |
| 3.R.1 | Compare and contrast stated or implied purpose of authors writing on the same topic | R9 pp. 64–71 |
| 3.R.2 | Evaluate how the point of view and perspective affect the text | R6 pp. 40–47 |
| 3.R.3 | Analyze how key literary elements (setting, plot, characters, characterization, theme) contribute to the meaning of the work | R2 pp. 12–19 R3 pp. 20–25 |
| 3.R.4 | Evaluate literary devices (e.g., simile, metaphor) to support interpretations of text | R4 pp. 26–33 |
| 3.R.5 | Distinguish factual claims from opinions | R8 pp. 56–63 |
| 3.R.6 | Analyze the structures of texts and content by making inferences and use textual evidence to support understanding | R1 pp. 6–11 R5 pp. 34–39 |
| 3.R.7 | Make connections between and across multiple texts | R9 pp. 64–71 |
| 3.W.1 | Write narratives incorporating plot, setting, characters, point of view, and conflict | W3 pp. 100–109 |
| 3.W.2 | Compose essays and reports about topics, incorporating evidence and maintaining an organized structure | W2 pp. 90–99 |
| 3.W.3–4 | Clearly state an opinion supported with facts and details; show relationships among facts, opinions, and supporting details | W1 pp. 82–89 |
| **Vocabulary** | | |
| 4.R.1 | Increase knowledge of academic, domain-appropriate, grade-level vocabulary to infer meaning of text | L6 pp. 228–233 |
| 4.R.2 | Use word parts to define and determine meaning of new words | L4 pp. 216–221 |
| 4.R.3 | Use context clues to determine or clarify word meaning | L4 pp. 216–221 |
| 4.R.4 | Infer relationships among words with multiple meanings, including synonyms, antonyms, and multiple meaning words | L5 pp. 222–227 |
| 4.R.5 | Use a dictionary, glossary, or thesaurus to find words | L4 pp. 216–233 |
| 4.W.1 | Use domain-appropriate vocabulary to communicate ideas in writing clearly | L6 pp. 228–233 |
| 4.W.2 | Select appropriate language to create a specific effect in writing | L6 pp. 228–233 |
| **Language** | | |
| 5.R.1–4 | Recognize the correct use of prepositional phrases and dependent clauses, simple and compound sentences, misplaced and dangling modifiers, and subject-verb agreement | L1 pp. 198–203 |
| 5.W.1–3 | Write using correct mechanics; compose simple, compound, and complex sentences; use prepositional phrases and clauses | L1 pp. 198–203 L2 pp. 204–209 L3 pp. 210–215 |
| **Research** | | |
| 6.R.1–3 | Use own viable questions and thesis statements to find information on a specific topic; follow ethical and legal guidelines for finding and recording information; determine relevance, reliability, and validity of information | R7 pp. 48–55 W7 pp. 128–133 |
| 6.W.1–3 | Write research papers; refine a viable research question; organize information found during research; quote, summarize, and paraphrase information | W7 pp. 128–133 W8 pp. 134–139 W9 pp. 140–145 |
| 6.W.4 | Summarize and present information in a report | SL4 pp. 176–181 |
| **Multimodal Literacies** | | |
| 7.R.1 | Compare and contrast the effectiveness of techniques used in a variety of texts to generate and answer questions to create new understandings | R7 pp. 48–55 |
| 7.R.2 | Analyze the impact of selected media and formats on meaning | R9 pp. 64–71 |
| 7.W.1 | Create multimodal content to complement and extend meaning | W6 pp. 122–127 |
| 7.W.2 | Utilize multimedia to clarify information and strengthen claims and evidence | SL5 pp. 182–187 |
| **Independent Reading and Writing** | | |
| 8.R | Select and read independently level-appropriate texts for academic and personal purposes | R10 pp. 72–77 |
| 8.W | Write independently for extended and shorter periods of time | W10 pp. 148–153 |

# Oklahoma, Grade 8

| Oklahoma Strand/Standard | Focus of Oklahoma Standard | For More Information |
|---|---|---|
| **Speaking and Listening** | | |
| 1.R.1 | Actively listen and speak clearly using appropriate discussion rules | SL1 pp. 158–163 |
| 1.R.2 | Actively listen and interpret a speaker's messages and ask questions to clarify the speaker's purpose and perspective | SL3 pp. 170–175 |
| 1.R.3 | Engage in collaborative discussions | SL1 pp. 158–163 |
| 1.W.1 | Give formal and informal presentations, providing evidence to support a main idea | SL4 pp. 176–181 |
| 1.W.2 | Work in groups effectively and respectfully, valuing contributions by group members | SL1 pp. 158–163 |
| **Reading and Writing Process** | | |
| 2.R.1 | Summarize and paraphrase ideas, while maintaining meaning and sequence of events | R2 pp. 12–19 |
| 2.R.2 | Analyze details in literary and informational texts to evaluate patterns of genres | R9 pp. 64–71 |
| 2.R.3 | Generalize main ideas with supporting details | R2 pp. 12–19 |
| 2.W.1 | Apply components of a recursive writing process to create a focused, organized, coherent piece of writing | W4 pp. 110–115 |
| 2.W.2–3 | Plan, prewrite, and develop drafts; choose organizational structure, building on ideas in multi-paragraph essays | W4 pp. 110–115 |
| 2.W.4 | Edit and revise multiple drafts for purpose, organization, and coherence | W5 pp. 116–121 |
| 2.W.5 | Use resources to find correct spellings | L2 pp. 204–209 |
| **Critical Reading and Writing** | | |
| 3.R.1 | Analyze works written on the same topic and compare the methods the authors use to achieve similar or different purposes | R9 pp. 64–71 |
| 3.R.2 | Evaluate points of view and perspectives and describe how this affects literary and/or informational text | R6 pp. 40–47 |
| 3.R.3 | Analyze how key literary elements (setting, plot, characters, characterization, theme) contribute to the meaning of the work | R2 pp. 12–19 R3 pp. 20–25 |
| 3.R.4 | Evaluate literary devices (e.g., simile, metaphor) to support interpretations of text | R4 pp. 26–33 |
| 3.R.5 | Evaluate textual evidence to determine whether a claim is substantiated or unsubstantiated | R8 pp. 56–63 |
| 3.R.6 | Analyze the structures of texts and content by making inferences about texts to draw logical conclusions | R1 pp. 6–11 R5 pp. 34–39 |
| 3.R.7 | Make connections between and across multiple texts | R9 pp. 64–71 |
| 3.W.1 | Write narratives incorporating plot, setting, characters, point of view, and conflict | W3 pp. 100–109 |
| 3.W.2 | Compose essays and reports about topics, incorporating evidence and maintaining an organized structure | W2 pp. 90–99 |
| 3.W.3–4 | Clearly state an opinion supported with facts and details; show relationships among facts, opinions, and supporting details | W1 pp. 82–89 |

*(Continued)*

| Oklahoma Strand/Standard | Focus of Oklahoma Standard | For More Information |
|---|---|---|
| **Vocabulary** | | |
| 4.R.1 | Increase knowledge of academic, domain-appropriate, grade-level vocabulary to infer meaning of text | L6 pp. 228–233 |
| 4.R.2 | Use word parts to define and determine meaning of new words | L4 pp. 216–221 |
| 4.R.3 | Use context clues to determine or clarify word meaning | L4 pp. 216–221 |
| 4.R.4 | Infer relationships among words with multiple meanings, including synonyms, antonyms, and multiple meaning words | L5 pp. 222–227 |
| 4.R.5 | Use a dictionary, glossary, or thesaurus to find words | L4 pp. 216–233 |
| 4.W.1 | Use domain-appropriate vocabulary to communicate ideas in writing clearly | L6 pp. 228–233 |
| 4.W.2 | Select appropriate language to create a specific effect in writing | L6 pp. 228–233 |
| **Language** | | |
| 5.R.1–4 | Recognize the correct use of verbals and clauses, active and passive voice, inappropriate shifts in verb tense, and subject-verb agreement | L1 pp. 198–203 |
| 5.W.1–5 | Write using correct mechanics; compose simple, compound, and complex sentences; use verbals in writing; form and use active and passive voice; form and use verbs in the indicative, imperative, interrogative, conditional, and subjunctive mood | L1 pp. 198–203 L2 pp. 204–209 L3 pp. 210–215 |
| **Research** | | |
| 6.R.1–3 | Use own viable questions and thesis statements to find information on a specific topic; follow ethical and legal guidelines for finding and recording information; determine relevance, reliability, and validity of information | R7 pp. 48–55 W7 pp. 128–133 |
| 6.W.1–3 | Write research papers; refine a viable research question; organize information found during research; quote, summarize, and paraphrase information | W7 pp. 128–133 W8 pp. 134–139 W9 pp. 140–145 |
| 6.W.4 | Summarize and present information in a report | SL4 pp. 176–181 |
| **Multimodal Literacies** | | |
| 7.R.1 | Determine the intended purposes of techniques used for rhetorical effects in a variety of texts | R7 pp. 48–55 |
| 7.R.2 | Analyze the impact of selected media and formats on meaning | R9 pp. 64–71 |
| 7.W.1 | Select, organize, or create multimodal content that encompasses different points of view | W6 pp. 122–127 |
| 7.W.2 | Utilize multimedia to clarify information and emphasize salient points | SL5 pp. 182–187 |
| **Independent Reading and Writing** | | |
| 8.R | Select and read independently level-appropriate texts for academic and personal purposes | R10 pp. 72–77 |
| 8.W | Write independently for extended and shorter periods of time | W10 pp. 148–153 |

| Pennsylvania Strand/Standard | Focus of Pennsylvania Standard | For More Information |
|---|---|---|
| **Reading Informational Text** | | |
| CC.1.2.A | Determine a central idea of a text and how it is conveyed through particular details; provide an objective summary | R2 pp. 12–19 |
| CC.1.2.B | Cite textual evidence to support analysis of what the text says explicitly as well as inferences drawn from the text | R1 pp. 6–11 |
| CC.1.2.C | Analyze in detail how a key individual, event, or idea is introduced, illustrated, and elaborated in a text | R3 pp. 20–25 |
| CC1.2.D | Determine an author's point of view or purpose in a text and explain how it is conveyed in the text | R6 pp. 40–47 |
| CC1.2.E | Analyze the author's structure through the use of paragraphs, chapters, or sections | R5 pp. 34–39 |
| CC1.2.F | Determine the meaning of words and phrases as they are used in a text, including figurative, connotative, and technical meanings | R4 pp. 26–33 |
| CC1.2.G | Integrate information presented in different media or formats as well as in words to develop a coherent understanding of a topic or issue | R7 pp. 48–55 |
| CC1.2.H | Evaluate an author's argument by examining claims and determining if they are supported by evidence | R8 pp. 56–63 |
| CC1.2.I | Compare and contrast one author's presentation of events with that of another | R9 pp. 64–71 |
| CC1.2.J | Acquire and use accurately general academic and domain-specific words and phrases; demonstrate independence in gathering vocabulary knowledge | L6 pp. 228–233 |
| CC1.2.K | Determine or clarify the meaning of unknown and multiple-meaning words and phrases, choosing flexibly from an array of strategies | L4 pp. 216–221 |
| CC1.2.L | Read and comprehend appropriately complex literary nonfiction, informational, and functional texts independently and proficiently | R10 pp. 72–77 |
| **Reading Literature** | | |
| CC1.3.A | Determine the theme or central idea of a text and how it is conveyed through particular details; provide an objective summary | R2 pp. 12–19 |
| CC1.3.B | Cite textual evidence to support analysis of what the text says explicitly as well as inferences drawn from the text | R1 pp. 6–11 |
| CC1.3.C | Describe how a particular plot unfolds in a series of episodes as well as how the characters respond or change | R3 pp. 20–25 |
| CC1.3.D | Explain how an author develops the point of view of the narrator or speaker in a text | R6 pp. 40–47 |
| CC1.3.E | Analyze how a particular sentence, chapter, scene, or stanza fits into the overall structure of a text and contributes to the development of the theme, setting, or plot | R5 pp. 34–39 |
| CC1.3.F | Determine the meaning of words and phrases as they are used in a text, including figurative and connotative meanings | R4 pp. 26–33 |
| CC1.3.G | Compare and contrast the experience of reading a story, drama, or poem to listening to or viewing an audio, video, or live version of the text | R7 pp. 48–55 |
| CC1.3.H | Compare and contrast texts in different forms or genres in terms of their approaches to similar themes and topics | R9 pp. 64–71 |
| CC1.3.I | Determine or clarify the meaning of unknown and multiple-meaning words and phrases, choosing flexibly from an array of strategies | L4 pp. 216–221 |
| CC1.3.J | Acquire and use accurately general academic and domain-specific words and phrases; demonstrate independence in gathering vocabulary knowledge | L6 pp. 228–233 |
| CC1.3.K | Read and comprehend literature of appropriate complexity independently with proficiency | R10 pp. 72–77 |
| **Writing** | | |
| CC1.4.A-F | Write informative/explanatory texts to effectively examine and convey complex ideas, concepts, and information; demonstrate command of the conventions of standard English capitalization, punctuation, and spelling when writing | W2 pp. 90–99 W4 pp. 110–115 L2 pp. 204–209 |
| CC1.4.G-L | Write arguments to support claims, using valid reasoning and relevant and sufficient evidence; demonstrate command of the conventions of standard English capitalization, punctuation, and spelling when writing | W1 pp. 82–89 W4 pp. 110–115 L2 pp. 204–209 |

*(Continued)*

| Pennsylvania Strand/Standard | Focus of Pennsylvania Standard | For More Information |
|---|---|---|
| **Writing** | | |
| CC1.4.M-R | Write narratives to develop real or imagined experiences or events using effective technique, well-chosen details, and well-structured event sequences; demonstrate command of the conventions of standard English capitalization, punctuation, and spelling when writing | W3 pp. 100–109 W4 pp. 110–115 L2 pp. 204–209 |
| CC1.4.S | Draw evidence from texts to support analysis, reflection, and research | W9 pp. 140–147 |
| CC1.4.T | Develop and strengthen writing as needed by planning, revising, and editing, rewriting, or trying a new approach | W5 pp. 116–121 |
| CC1.4.U | Use technology to produce and publish writing as well as to interact with others; demonstrate keyboarding skills | W6 pp. 122–127 |
| CC1.4.V | Conduct short research projects to answer a question, drawing on several sources and refocusing the inquiry when appropriate | W7 pp. 128–133 |
| CC1.4.W | Gather information from print and digital sources; assess the credibility of sources; quote or paraphrase while avoiding plagiarism and providing basic bibliographic information | W8 pp. 134–139 |
| CC1.4.X | Write routinely over extended and shorter time frames for a range of tasks, purposes, and audiences | W10 pp. 148–153 |
| CC1.5.A | Engage effectively in a range of collaborative discussions with diverse partners, building on others' ideas and expressing their own clearly | SL1 pp. 158–163 |
| CC1.5.B | Delineate a speaker's argument and specific claims that are supported by reasons and evidence from claims that are not | SL3 pp. 170–175 |
| CC1.5.C | Interpret information presented in diverse media and formats and explain how it contributes to a topic, text, or issue under study | SL2 pp. 164–169 |
| CC1.5.D | Present claims and findings, sequencing ideas logically and using descriptions, facts, or details to accentuate main ideas or themes; use appropriate eye contact, adequate volume, and clear pronunciation | SL4 pp. 176–181 |
| CC1.5.E | Adapt speech to a variety of contexts and tasks | SL6 pp. 188–193 |
| CC1.5.F | Include multimedia components and visual displays in presentations to clarify information | SL5 pp. 182–187 |
| CC1.5.G | Demonstrate command of the conventions of standard English when speaking | L1 pp. 198–203 |

# Pennsylvania, Grade 7

| Pennsylvania Strand/Standard | Focus of Pennsylvania Standard | For More Information |
|---|---|---|
| **Reading Informational Text** | | |
| CC.1.2.A | Determine two or more central ideas in a text and analyze their developments; provide an objective summary of the text | R2 pp. 12–19 |
| CC.1.2.B | Cite several pieces of textual evidence to support analysis of what the text says explicitly as well as inferences drawn from the text | R1 pp. 6–11 |
| CC.1.2.C | Analyze the interactions between individuals, events, and ideas in a text | R3 pp. 20–25 |
| CC.1.2.D | Determine an author's point of view or purpose in a text and analyze how the author distinguishes his or her position from that of others | R6 pp. 40–47 |
| CC1.2.E | Analyze the structure of the text through evaluation of the authors use of graphics, charts, and the major sections of the text | R5 pp. 34–39 |
| CC1.2.F | Determine the meaning of words and phrases as they are used in a text, including figurative, connotative, and technical meanings | R4 pp. 26–33 |
| CC1.2.G | Compare and contrast a text to an audio, video, or multimedia version of the text | R7 pp. 48–55 |
| CC1.2.H | Evaluate an author's argument, reasoning, and specific claims for the soundness of the argument and the relevance of the evidence | R8 pp. 56–63 |
| CC1.2.I | Analyze how two or more authors present and interpret facts on the same topic | R9 pp. 64–71 |
| CC1.2.J | Acquire and use accurately general academic and domain-specific words and phrases; demonstrate independence in gathering vocabulary knowledge | L6 pp. 228–233 |

| Pennsylvania Strand/Standard | Focus of Pennsylvania Standard | For More Information |
|---|---|---|
| **Reading Informational Text** | | |
| CC1.2.K | Determine or clarify the meaning of unknown and multiple-meaning words and phrases, choosing flexibly from an array of strategies | L4 pp. 216–221 |
| CC1.2.L | Read and comprehend appropriately complex literary nonfiction, informational, and functional texts independently and proficiently | R10 pp. 72–77 |
| **Reading Literature** | | |
| CC1.3.A | Determine a theme or central idea of a text and analyze its development; provide an objective summary of the text | R2 pp. 12–19 |
| CC1.3.B | Cite several pieces of textual evidence to support analysis of what the text says explicitly as well as inferences drawn from the text | R1 pp. 6–11 |
| CC1.3.C | Analyze how particular elements of a story or drama interact | R3 pp. 20–25 |
| CC1.3.D | Analyze how an author develops and contrasts the points of view of different characters or narrators in a text | R6 pp. 40–47 |
| CC1.3.E | Analyze how the form or structure of a text contributes to its meaning | R5 pp. 34–39 |
| CC1.3.F | Determine the meaning of words and phrases as they are used in a text, including figurative and connotative meanings | R4 pp. 26–33 |
| CC1.3.G | Compare and contrast a written story, drama, or poem to its audio, filmed, staged, or multimedia version | R7 pp. 48–55 |
| CC1.3.H | Compare and contrast a fictional portrayal of a time, place, or character and a historical account of the same period | R9 pp. 64–71 |
| CC1.3.I | Determine or clarify the meaning of unknown and multiple-meaning words and phrases, choosing flexibly from an array of strategies | L4 pp. 216–221 |
| CC1.3.J | Acquire and use accurately general academic and domain-specific words and phrases; demonstrate independence in gathering vocabulary knowledge | L6 pp. 228–233 |
| CC1.3.K | Read and comprehend literature of appropriate complexity independently with proficiency | R10 pp. 72–77 |
| **Writing** | | |
| CC1.4.A-F | Write informative/explanatory texts to effectively examine and convey complex ideas, concepts, and information; demonstrate command of the conventions of standard English capitalization, punctuation, and spelling when writing | W2 pp. 90–99 W4 pp. 110–115 L2 pp. 204–209 |
| CC1.4.G-L | Write arguments to support claims, using valid reasoning and relevant and sufficient evidence; demonstrate command of the conventions of standard English capitalization, punctuation, and spelling when writing | W1 pp. 82–89 W4 pp. 110–115 L2 pp. 204–209 |
| CC1.4.M-R | Write narratives to develop real or imagined experiences or events using effective technique, well-chosen details, and well-structured event sequences; demonstrate command of the conventions of standard English capitalization, punctuation, and spelling when writing | W3 pp. 100–109 W4 pp. 110–115 L2 pp. 204–209 |
| CC1.4.S | Draw evidence from literary or informational texts to support analysis, reflection, and research | W9 pp. 140–147 |
| CC1.4.T | Develop and strengthen writing as needed by planning, revising, and editing, rewriting, or trying a new approach | W5 pp. 116–121 |
| CC1.4.U | Use technology to produce and publish writing, link to and cite sources; interact and collaborate with others | W6 pp. 122–127 |
| CC1.4.V | Conduct short research projects to answer a question, drawing on several sources and generating additional related questions for further investigation | W7 pp. 128–133 |
| CC1.4.W | Gather information from print and digital sources; assess the credibility of sources; quote or paraphrase while avoiding plagiarism and following a standard format for citation | W8 pp. 134–139 |
| CC1.4.X | Write routinely over extended and shorter time frames for a range of tasks, purposes, and audiences | W10 pp. 148–153 |
| CC1.5.A | Engage effectively in a range of collaborative discussions with diverse partners, building on others' ideas and expressing their own clearly | SL1 pp. 158–163 |
| CC1.5.B | Delineate a speaker's argument and specific claims evaluating the soundness of the reasoning and the relevance and sufficiency of the evidence | SL3 pp. 170–175 |
| CC1.5.C | Analyze the main ideas and supporting details presented in diverse media and formats and explain how the ideas clarify a topic, text, or issue under study | SL2 pp. 164–169 |

*(Continued)*

| Pennsylvania Strand/Standard | Focus of Pennsylvania Standard | For More Information |
|---|---|---|
| **Writing** | | |
| CC1.5.D | Present claims and findings, emphasizing salient points in a focused coherent manner; use appropriate eye contact, adequate volume, and clear pronunciation | SL4 pp. 176–181 |
| CC1.5.E | Adapt speech to a variety of contexts and tasks | SL6 pp. 188–193 |
| CC1.5.F | Include multimedia components and visual displays in presentations to clarify claims and findings | SL5 pp. 182–187 |
| CC1.5.G | Demonstrate command of the conventions of standard English when speaking | L1 pp. 198–203 |

# Pennsylvania, Grade 8

| Pennsylvania Strand/Standard | Focus of Pennsylvania Standard | For More Information |
|---|---|---|
| **Reading Informational Text** | | |
| CC.1.2.A | Determine the central idea of a text and analyze its development, including its relationship to supporting ideas; provide an objective summary of the text | R2 pp. 12–19 |
| CC.1.2.B | Cite the textual evidence that most strongly supports an analysis of what the text says explicitly as well as inferences drawn from the text | R1 pp. 6–11 |
| CC.1.2.C | Analyze how a text makes connections among distinctions between individuals, ideas, or events | R3 pp. 20–25 |
| CC1.2.D | Determine an author's point of view or purpose in a text and analyze how the author acknowledges and responds to conflicting evidence or viewpoints | R6 pp. 40–47 |
| CC1.2.E | Analyze the structure of the text through evaluation of the author's use of specific sentences and paragraphs to develop and refine a concept | R5 pp. 34–39 |
| CC1.2.F | Analyze the influence of words and phrases as they are used in a text, including figurative, connotative, and technical meanings | R4 pp. 26–33 |
| CC1.2.G | Evaluate the advantages and disadvantages of using different mediums to present a particular topic or idea | R7 pp. 48–55 |
| CC1.2.H | Evaluate an author's argument, reasoning, and specific claims for the soundness of the arguments and the relevance of the evidence | R8 pp. 56–63 |
| CC1.2.I | Analyze two or more texts that provide conflicting information on the same topic | R9 pp. 64–71 |
| CC1.2.J | Acquire and use accurately general academic and domain-specific words and phrases; demonstrate independence in gathering vocabulary knowledge | L6 pp. 228–233 |
| CC1.2.K | Determine or clarify the meaning of unknown and multiple-meaning words and phrases, choosing flexibly from an array of strategies | L4 pp. 216–221 |
| CC1.2.L | Read and comprehend appropriately complex literary nonfiction, informational, and functional texts independently and proficiently | R10 pp. 72–77 |
| **Reading Literature** | | |
| CC1.3.A | Determine a theme or central idea of a text and analyze its development, including its relationship to the characters, setting, and plot; provide an objective summary of the text | R2 pp. 12–19 |
| CC1.3.B | Cite the textual evidence that most strongly supports an analysis of what the text says explicitly as well as inferences drawn from the text | R1 pp. 6–11 |
| CC1.3.C | Analyze how particular lines of dialogue or incidents in a story or drama propel the action, reveal aspects of a character, or provoke a decision | R3 pp. 20–25 |
| CC1.3.D | Analyze how differences in the points of view of the characters and the audience or reader create such effects as suspense or humor | R6 pp. 40–47 |

| Pennsylvania Strand/Standard | Focus of Pennsylvania Standard | For More Information |
|---|---|---|
| **Reading Literature** | | |
| CC1.3.E | Compare and contrast the structure of two or more texts and analyze how the differing structure of each contributes to its meaning and style | R5 pp. 34–39 |
| CC1.3.F | Analyze the influence of words and phrases in a text, including figurative and connotative meanings | R4 pp. 26–33 |
| CC1.3.G | Analyze the extent to which a filmed or live production of a story or drama stays faithful or departs from the text or script | R7 pp. 48–55 |
| CC1.3.H | Analyze how a modern work of fiction draws on themes, patterns of events, or character types from traditional works, and how the material is rendered new | R9 pp. 64–71 |
| CC1.3.I | Determine or clarify the meaning of unknown and multiple-meaning words and phrases, choosing flexibly from an array of strategies | L4 pp. 216–221 |
| CC1.3.J | Acquire and use accurately general academic and domain-specific words and phrases; demonstrate independence in gathering vocabulary knowledge | L6 pp. 228–233 |
| CC1.3.K | Read and comprehend literature of appropriate complexity independently with proficiency | R10 pp. 72–77 |
| **Writing** | | |
| CC1.4.A-F | Write informative/explanatory texts to effectively examine and convey complex ideas, concepts, and information; demonstrate command of the conventions of standard English capitalization, punctuation, and spelling when writing | W2 pp. 90–99 W4 pp. 110–115 L2 pp. 204–209 |
| CC1.4.G-L | Write arguments to support claims, using valid reasoning and relevant and sufficient evidence; demonstrate command of the conventions of standard English capitalization, punctuation, and spelling when writing | W1 pp. 82–89 W4 pp. 110–115 L2 pp. 204–209 |
| CC1.4.M-R | Write narratives to develop real or imagined experiences or events using effective technique, well-chosen details, and well-structured event sequences; demonstrate command of the conventions of standard English capitalization, punctuation, and spelling when writing | W3 pp. 100–109 W4 pp. 110–115 L2 pp. 204–209 |
| CC1.4.S | Draw evidence from literary or informational texts to support analysis, reflection, and research | W9 pp. 140–147 |
| CC1.4.T | Develop and strengthen writing as needed by planning, revising, and editing, rewriting, or trying a new approach | W5 pp. 116–121 |
| CC1.4.U | Use technology to produce and publish writing and present the relationships between information and ideas efficiently; interact and collaborate with others | W6 pp. 122–127 |
| CC1.4.V | Conduct short research projects to answer a question, drawing on several sources and generating additional related questions for further investigation | W7 pp. 128–133 |
| CC1.4.W | Gather information from print and digital sources; assess the credibility of sources; quote or paraphrase while avoiding plagiarism and following a standard format for citation | W8 pp. 134–139 |
| CC1.4.X | Write routinely over extended and shorter time frames for a range of tasks, purposes, and audiences | W10 pp. 148–153 |
| CC1.5.A | Engage effectively in a range of collaborative discussions with diverse partners, building on others' ideas and expressing their own clearly | SL1 pp. 158–163 |
| CC1.5.B | Delineate a speaker's argument and specific claims evaluating the soundness of the reasoning and the relevance and sufficiency of the evidence and identifying when irrelevant evidence is introduced | SL3 pp. 170–175 |
| CC1.5.C | Analyze the purpose of information presented in diverse media and formats and evaluate the motives behind its presentation | SL2 pp. 164–169 |
| CC1.5.D | Present claims and findings, emphasizing salient points in a focused coherent manner; use appropriate eye contact, adequate volume, and clear pronunciation | SL4 pp. 176–181 |
| CC1.5.E | Adapt speech to a variety of contexts and tasks | SL6 pp. 188–193 |
| CC1.5.F | Integrate multimedia and visual displays into presentations to add interest, clarify information, and strengthen claims and findings | SL5 pp. 182–187 |
| CC1.5.G | Demonstrate command of the conventions of standard English when speaking | L1 pp. 198–203 |

# South Carolina, Grade 6

| South Carolina Strand/Standard | Focus of South Carolina Standard | For More Information |
|---|---|---|
| **Reading Literary Text** | | |
| 5.1 | Cite textual evidence to support analysis of what the text says explicitly as well as inferences drawn from the text | R1 pp. 6–11 |
| 6.1 | Determine a theme of a text and how it is conveyed through particular details; summarize the text | R2 pp. 12–19 |
| 7.1 | Compare and contrast a narrative, drama, or poem read to a live version of the same text | R7 pp. 48–55 |
| 7.2 | Compare and contrast texts in different forms or genres in terms of their approaches to similar topics | R9 pp. 64–71 |
| 8.1 | Describe how a plot in a narrative or drama unfolds in a series of episodes as well as how the characters respond or change | R3 pp. 20–25 |
| 9.1, 9.2 | Determine the meaning of words and phrases as they are used in a text, including figurative and connotative meanings; analyze the impact of word choice on meaning and tone | R4 pp. 26–33 |
| 10.1 | Use the overall meaning of a text or a word's position or function to determine the meaning of a word or phrase | L4 pp. 216–221 |
| 10.6 | Acquire and use accurately general academic, and domain-specific words and phrases | L6 pp. 228–233 |
| 11.1 | Explain how an author's development of the point of view of the narrator or speaker impacts content, meaning, and style | R6 pp. 40–47 |
| 12.1–12.2 | Analyze how a particular sentence, chapter, scene, or stanza fits into the overall structure of a text and contributes to the development of the theme, setting, or plot; compare and contrast how different text structures contribute to meaning | R5 pp. 34–39 |
| 13.1–13.3 | Read and respond to grade-level text independently, with proficiency, for variety of purposes | R10 pp. 72–77 |
| **Reading Informational Text** | | |
| 5.1 | Cite strong textual evidence to support analysis of what the text says explicitly and implicitly | R1 pp. 6–11 |
| 6.1 | Summarize a text with two or more central ideas; cite supporting details | R2 pp. 12–19 |
| 7.1 | Integrate information presented in different media or formats to develop a coherent understanding of a topic or issue | R7 pp. 48–55 |
| 8.1 | Determine the meaning of words and phrases in a text; analyze the impact of specific word choices | R4 pp. 26–33 |
| 8.2 | Identify text features and structures that support an author's claims or ideas | R5 pp. 34–39 |
| 9.1, 9.2 | Determine the meaning of a word or phrase using the overall meaning of a text or a word's position or function; determine or clarify the meaning of a word or phrase using knowledge of word patterns, origins, bases, and affixes | L4 pp. 216–221 |
| 10.1 | Analyze multiple accounts of the same event or topic | R6 pp. 40–47 R9 pp. 64–71 |
| 11.1 | Identify text features and structures that support an author's idea or claim | R5 pp. 34–39 |
| 11.2 | Trace and evaluate the argument and specific claims, distinguishing claims that are supported by reasons and evidence from claims that are not | R8 pp. 56–63 |
| 12.1–12.3 | Read, comprehend, and respond to grade-level informational texts independently and proficiently, for a variety of purposes | R10 pp. 72–77 |
| **Writing** | | |
| 1.1 | Write arguments to support claims, using valid reasoning and relevant and sufficient evidence; use an appropriate organizational structure; develop and strengthen writing as needed by planning, revising, and editing, rewriting; gather information from multiple sources; assess usefulness of sources; integrate information, avoiding plagiarism | W1 pp. 82–89 W4 pp. 110–115 W5 pp. 116–122 W8 pp. 134–139 W9 pp. 140–147 |
| 2.1 | Write informative/explanatory texts to effectively examine and convey complex ideas, concepts, and information; use appropriate transitions, precise language, and a concluding statement; develop and strengthen writing as needed by planning, revising, and editing, rewriting; gather information from multiple sources; assess usefulness of sources; integrate information, avoiding plagiarism | W2 pp. 90–99 W4 pp. 110–115 W5 pp. 116–122 W8 pp. 134–139 W9 pp. 140–147 |
| 3.1 | Write narratives to develop real or imagined experiences or events using effective technique, well-chosen details, and well-structured event sequences; develop and strengthen writing as needed by planning, revising, and editing, rewriting | W3 pp. 100–109 W4 pp. 110–115 W5 pp. 116–122 |

| South Carolina Strand/Standard | Focus of South Carolina Standard | For More Information |
|---|---|---|
| **Writing** | | |
| 4 | Demonstrate command of the conventions of standard English grammar and usage when writing or speaking | L1 pp. 198–203 |
| 5 | Demonstrate command of the conventions of standard English capitalization, punctuation, and spelling when writing | L2 pp. 204–209 |
| 6.1 | Write routinely over short and extended time frames for a range of audiences, tasks, and purposes | W10 pp. 148–153 |
| **Communication** | | |
| 1.1, 1.2 | Consider viewpoints of others by listening, reflecting and formulating questions; support others to reach common understandings; participate in discussions, ask and respond to probing questions to acquire and confirm information | SL1 pp. 158–163 |
| 1.3 | Apply effective communication techniques and the use of formal and informal voice based on audience and setting | SL6 pp. 188–193 |
| 1.4, 1.5 | Engage in focused conversations; build on the ideas of others; pose and respond to questions to clarify thinking and express new thoughts; review and reflect on the main ideas expressed to demonstrate understanding of diverse perspectives | SL1 pp. 158–163 |
| 2.1 | Gather information to articulate claims and findings; sequence ideas logically; express perspectives clearly | SL4 pp. 176–181 |
| 2.2 | Distinguish between credible and non-credible sources of information | SL3 pp. 170–175 |
| 2.3 | Quote or paraphrase others while avoiding plagiarism and providing basic bibliographic information | W8 pp. 134–139 |
| 2.4 | Adapt speech to a variety of contexts and tasks; demonstrate a command of formal English when appropriate | SL6 pp. 188–193 |
| 3.1 | Analyze the impact of selected media and formats on meaning | SL2 pp. 164–169 |
| 3.2 | Utilize multimedia to enrich presentations | SL5 pp. 182–187 |
| 4 | Critique how a speaker addresses content and uses stylistic and structural craft techniques to engage, inform, and impact audiences | SL2 pp. 164–169 SL3 pp. 170–175 |
| 5 | Incorporate craft techniques to engage and impact audience and convey messages | SL4 pp. 176–181 SL5 pp. 182–187 |

# South Carolina, Grade 7

| South Carolina Strand/Standard | Focus of South Carolina Standard | For More Information |
|---|---|---|
| **Reading Literary Text** | | |
| 5.1 | Cite multiple examples of textual evidence to support analysis of what the text says explicitly as well as inferences drawn from the text | R1 pp. 6–11 |
| 6.1 | Determine one or more themes of a text and analyze the development; summarize the text | R2 pp. 12–19 |
| 7.1 | Interpret how a literary text relates to diverse media | R7 pp. 48–55 |
| 7.2 | Compare and contrast a literary depiction of a time, place, or character to a historical account of the same period | R9 pp. 64–71 |
| 8.1 | Analyze how setting shapes the characters and/or plot and how particular elements of a narrative or drama interact | R3 pp. 20–25 |
| 9.1, 9.2 | Determine the meaning of words and phrases as they are used in a text, including figurative and connotative meanings; analyze the impact of word choice on meaning and tone | R4 pp. 26–33 |
| 10.1 | Use context clues to determine meaning of words and phrases | L4 pp. 216–221 |
| 10.6 | Acquire and use accurately general academic, and domain-specific words and phrases | L6 pp. 228–233 |
| 11.1 | Analyze how an author develops and contrasts points of view to impact content, meaning, and style | R6 pp. 40–47 |

*(Continued)*

| South Carolina Strand/Standard | Focus of South Carolina Standard | For More Information |
|---|---|---|
| **Reading Literary Text** | | |
| 12.1–12.2 | Analyze how complex text structures contribute to the development of the theme, setting, or plot; analyze the author's choice of structures and how they impact meaning | R5 pp. 34–39 |
| 13.1–13.3 | Read and respond to grade-level text independently, with proficiency, for variety of purposes | R10 pp. 72–77 |
| **Reading Informational Text** | | |
| 5.1 | Cite multiple examples of textual evidence to support analysis of what the text says explicitly and implicitly | R1 pp. 6–11 |
| 6.1 | Summarize a text with two or more central ideas; cite supporting details | R2 pp. 12–19 |
| 7.1 | Compare and contrast a text to an audio, video, or multimedia version of the text | R7 pp. 48–55 |
| 8.1 | Determine the meaning of words and phrases in a text; analyze the impact of specific word choices | R4 pp. 26–33 |
| 8.2 | Determine the impact of text features and structures on an author's claims or ideas | R5 pp. 34–39 |
| 9.1, 9.2 | Determine the meaning of a word or phrase using the overall meaning of a text or a word's position or function; determine or clarify the meaning of a word or phrase using knowledge of word patterns, origins, bases, and affixes | L4 pp. 216–221 |
| 10.1 | Determine an author's perspective or purpose and analyze how the author distinguishes his/her position from others | R6 pp. 40–47 R9 pp. 64–71 |
| 11.1 | Determine the impact of text features and structures on an author's ideas or claims | R5 pp. 34–39 |
| 11.2 | Trace and evaluate the argument and specific claims, assessing whether reasoning is sound and evidence is relevant and sufficient | R8 pp. 56–63 |
| 12.1–12.3 | Read, comprehend, and respond to grade-level informational texts independently and proficiently, for a variety of purposes | R10 pp. 72–77 |
| **Writing** | | |
| 1.1 | Write arguments to support claims, using valid reasoning and relevant and sufficient evidence; use an appropriate organizational structure; develop and strengthen writing as needed by planning, revising, editing, rewriting; gather information from multiple sources; assess usefulness of sources; integrate information, avoiding plagiarism | W1 pp. 82–89 W4 pp. 110–115 W5 pp. 116–122 W8 pp. 134–139 W9 pp. 140–147 |
| 2.1 | Write informative/explanatory texts to effectively examine and convey complex ideas, concepts, and information; use appropriate transitions, precise language, and a concluding statement; develop and strengthen writing as needed by planning, revising, editing, rewriting; gather information from multiple sources; assess usefulness of sources; integrate information, avoiding plagiarism | W2 pp. 90–99 W4 pp. 110–115 W5 pp. 116–122 W8 pp. 134–139 W9 pp. 140–147 |
| 3.1 | Write narratives to develop real or imagined experiences or events using effective technique, well-chosen details, and well-structured event sequences; develop and strengthen writing as needed by planning, revising, editing, rewriting | W3 pp. 100–109 W4 pp. 110–115 W5 pp. 116–122 |
| 4 | Demonstrate command of the conventions of standard English grammar and usage when writing or speaking | L1 pp. 198–203 |
| 5 | Demonstrate command of the conventions of standard English capitalization, punctuation, and spelling when writing | L2 pp. 204–209 |
| 6.1 | Write routinely over short and extended time frames for a range of audiences, tasks, and purposes | W10 pp. 148–153 |
| **Communication** | | |
| 1.1, 1.2 | Prepare for and engage in conversations to explore complex concepts, ideas, and texts, share ideas and consider alternate viewpoints; participate in discussions, ask probing questions and share evidence | SL1 pp. 158–163 |
| 1.3 | Apply effective communication techniques and the use of formal and informal voice based on audience and setting | SL6 pp. 188–193 |
| 1.4, 1.5 | Engage in a range of collaborative discussions; consider new ideas and diverse perspectives of others | SL1 pp. 158–163 |
| 2.1 | Gather information to articulate claims and findings; articulate claims and findings, emphasizing salient points in a focused coherent manner | SL4 pp. 176–181 |
| 2.2 | Analyze and evaluate the credibility of information and accuracy of findings | SL3 pp. 170–175 |
| 2.3 | Quote or paraphrase others while avoiding plagiarism and following a standard format for citation | W8 pp. 134–139 |
| 2.4 | Adapt speech to a variety of contexts and tasks; demonstrate a command of formal English when appropriate | SL6 pp. 188–193 |

| South Carolina Strand/Standard | Focus of South Carolina Standard | For More Information |
|---|---|---|
| **Communication** | | |
| 3.1 | Analyze the impact of selected media and formats on meaning | SL2 pp. 164–169 |
| 3.2 | Utilize multimedia to clarify and strengthen presentations | SL5 pp. 182–187 |
| 4 | Critique how a speaker addresses content and uses stylistic and structural craft techniques to engage, inform, and impact audiences | SL2 pp. 164–169 SL3 pp. 170–175 |
| 5 | Incorporate craft techniques to engage and impact audience and convey messages | SL4 pp. 176–181 SL5 pp. 182–187 |

# South Carolina, Grade 8

| South Carolina Strand/Standard | Focus of South Carolina Standard | For More Information |
|---|---|---|
| **Reading Literary Text** | | |
| 5.1 | Cite evidence that most strongly supports analysis of what the text says explicitly as well as inferences drawn from the text | R1 pp. 6–11 |
| 6.1 | Determine one or more themes of a text and analyze the development and relationship to character, setting, and plot; summarize the text | R2 pp. 12–19 |
| 7.1 | Interpret how a literary text relates to diverse media | R7 pp. 48–55 |
| 7.2 | Compare and contrast a literary depiction of a time, place, or character to a historical account of the same period | R9 pp. 64–71 |
| 8.1 | Analyze how setting shapes the characters and/or plot and how particular elements of a narrative or drama interact | R3 pp. 20–25 |
| 9.1, 9.2 | Determine the meaning of words and phrases as they are used in a text, including figurative and connotative meanings; analyze the impact of word choice on meaning and tone | R4 pp. 26–33 |
| 10.1 | Use context clues to determine meaning of words and phrases | L4 pp. 216–221 |
| 10.6 | Acquire and use accurately general academic, and domain-specific words and phrases | L6 pp. 228–233 |
| 11.1 | Analyze how the author's development of perspectives of the characters and the audience or reader create such effects as suspense or humor | R6 pp. 40–47 |
| 12.1–12.2 | Compare and contrast the structure of two or more texts with similar topics and analyze how the differing structure of each contributes to its meaning and style; analyze the author's choice of structures and how they impact meaning | R5 pp. 34–39 |
| 13.1–13.3 | Read and respond to grade-level text independently, with proficiency, for variety of purposes | R10 pp. 72–77 |
| **Reading Informational Text** | | |
| 5.1 | Cite the evidence that most strongly supports analysis of what the text says explicitly and implicitly | R1 pp. 6–11 |
| 6.1 | Summarize a text with two or more central ideas; cite supporting details | R2 pp. 12–19 |
| 7.1 | Evaluate the advantages and disadvantages of using different mediums to present a particular topic or idea | R7 pp. 48–55 |
| 8.1 | Determine the meaning of words and phrases in a text; analyze the impact of specific word choices | R4 pp. 26–33 |
| 8.2 | Analyze the impact of text features and structures on authors' similar claims or ideas about the same topic | R5 pp. 34–39 |
| 9.1, 9.2 | Determine the meaning of a word or phrase using the overall meaning of a text or a word's position or function; determine or clarify the meaning of a word or phrase using knowledge of word patterns, origins, bases, and affixes | L4 pp. 216–221 |

*(Continued)*

| South Carolina Strand/Standard | Focus of South Carolina Standard | For More Information |
|---|---|---|
| **Reading Informational Text** | | |
| 10.1 | Determine an author's perspective or purpose and analyze how the author distinguishes his/her position from others | R6 pp. 40–47 R9 pp. 64–71 |
| 11.1 | Determine the impact of text features and structures on an author's ideas or claims | R5 pp. 34–39 |
| 11.2 | Analyze and evaluate the argument and specific claims, assessing whether reasoning is sound and evidence is relevant and sufficient | R8 pp. 56–63 |
| 12.1–12.3 | Read, comprehend, and respond to grade-level informational texts independently and proficiently, for a variety of purposes | R10 pp. 72–77 |
| **Writing** | | |
| 1.1 | Write arguments to support claims, using valid reasoning and relevant and sufficient evidence; use an appropriate organizational structure; develop and strengthen writing as needed by planning, revising, editing, rewriting; gather information from multiple sources; assess usefulness of sources; integrate information, avoiding plagiarism | W1 pp. 82–89 W4 pp. 110–115 W5 pp. 116–122 W8 pp. 134–139 W9 pp. 140–147 |
| 2.1 | Write informative/explanatory texts to effectively examine and convey complex ideas, concepts, and information; use appropriate transitions, precise language, and a concluding statement; develop and strengthen writing as needed by planning, revising, editing, rewriting; gather information from multiple sources; assess usefulness of sources; integrate information, avoiding plagiarism | W2 pp. 90–99 W4 pp. 110–115 W5 pp. 116–122 W8 pp. 134–139 W9 pp. 140–147 |
| 3.1 | Write narratives to develop real or imagined experiences or events using effective technique, well-chosen details, and well-structured event sequences; develop and strengthen writing as needed by planning, revising, editing, rewriting | W3 pp. 100–109 W4 pp. 110–115 W5 pp. 116–122 |
| 4 | Demonstrate command of the conventions of standard English grammar and usage when writing or speaking | L1 pp. 198–203 |
| 5 | Demonstrate command of the conventions of standard English capitalization, punctuation, and spelling when writing | L2 pp. 204–209 |
| 6.1 | Write routinely over short and extended time frames for a range of audiences, tasks, and purposes | W10 pp. 148–153 |
| **Communication** | | |
| 1.1, 1.2 | Prepare for and engage in conversations to explore complex concepts, ideas, and texts, build coherent lines of thinking; participate in discussions, connect the ideas of several speakers and respond with relevant ideas | SL1 pp. 158–163 |
| 1.3 | Apply effective communication techniques based on a variety of contexts and tasks | SL6 pp. 188–193 |
| 1.4, 1.5 | Engage in a range of collaborative discussions; consider new ideas and diverse perspectives of others | SL1 pp. 158–163 |
| 2.1 | Gather information to develop ideas, claims, or perspectives, emphasizing salient points in a focused coherent manner | SL4 pp. 176–181 |
| 2.2 | Analyze and evaluate the credibility of information and accuracy of findings | SL3 pp. 170–175 |
| 2.3 | Quote and paraphrase data and conclusions while avoiding plagiarism and following a standard format for citation | W8 pp. 134–139 |
| 2.4 | Adapt speech to a variety of contexts and tasks; demonstrate a command of formal English when appropriate | SL6 pp. 188–193 |
| 3.1 | Analyze the impact of selected media and formats on meaning | SL2 pp. 164–169 |
| 3.2 | Utilize multimedia to clarify information and emphasize salient points | SL5 pp. 182–187 |
| 4 | Critique how a speaker addresses content and uses stylistic and structural craft techniques to engage, inform, and impact audiences | SL2 pp. 164–169 SL3 pp. 170–175 |
| 5 | Incorporate craft techniques to engage and impact audience and convey messages | SL4 pp. 176–181 SL5 pp. 182–187 |

# Tennessee, Grade 6

| Tennessee Strand/Standard | Focus of Tennessee Standard | For More Information |
|---|---|---|
| **Reading Literature** | | |
| RL.1 | Cite textual evidence to support analysis of what the text says explicitly as well as inferences drawn from the text | R1 pp. 6–11 |
| RL.2 | Determine the theme or central idea of a text and how it is conveyed through particular details; provide an objective summary | R2 pp. 12–19 |
| RL.3 | Describe how a particular plot unfolds in a series of episodes as well as how the characters respond or change | R3 pp. 20–25 |
| RL.4 | Determine the meaning of words and phrases as they are used in a text, including figurative and connotative meanings | R4 pp. 26–33 |
| RL.5 | Analyze how a particular sentence, chapter, scene, or stanza fits into the overall structure of a text and contributes to the development of the theme, setting, or plot | R5 pp. 34–39 |
| RL.6 | Explain how an author develops the point of view of the narrator or speaker in a text | R6 pp. 40–47 |
| RL.7 | Compare and contrast the experience of reading a story, drama, or poem to listening to or viewing an audio, video, or live version of the text | R7 pp. 48–55 |
| RL.8 | NA | |
| RL.9 | Compare and contrast texts in different forms or genres in terms of their approaches to similar themes and topics | R9 pp. 64–71 |
| RL.10 | Read and comprehend literature of appropriate complexity independently with proficiency | R10 pp. 72–77 |
| **Reading Informational Text** | | |
| RI.1 | Cite textual evidence to support analysis of what the text says explicitly as well as inferences drawn from the text | R1 pp. 6–11 |
| RI.2 | Determine a central idea of a text and how it is conveyed through particular details; provide an objective summary | R2 pp. 12–19 |
| RI.3 | Analyze in detail how a key individual, event, or idea is introduced, illustrated, and elaborated in a text | R3 pp. 20–25 |
| RI.4 | Determine the meaning of words and phrases as they are used in a text, including figurative, connotative, and technical meanings | R4 pp. 26–33 |
| RI.5 | Analyze how a particular sentence, chapter, scene, or section fits into the overall structure of a text and contributes to the development of the ideas | R5 pp. 34–39 |
| RI.6 | Determine an author's point of view or purpose in a text and explain how it is conveyed in the text | R6 pp. 40–47 |
| RI.7 | Integrate information presented in different media or formats as well as in words to develop a coherent understanding of a topic or issue | R7 pp. 48–55 |
| RI.8 | Trace and evaluate the argument and specific claims that are supported by reasons and evidence from claims that are not | R8 pp. 56–63 |
| RI.9 | Compare and contrast one author's presentation of events with that of another | R9 pp. 64–71 |
| RI.10 | Read and comprehend appropriately complex literary nonfiction, informational, and functional texts independently and proficiently | R10 pp. 72–77 |
| **Writing** | | |
| W.1 | Write arguments to support claims with clear reasons and relevant evidence | W1 pp. 82–89 |
| W.2 | Write informative/explanatory texts to examine a topic and convey ideas, concepts, and information clearly | W2 pp. 90–99 |
| W.3 | Write narratives to develop real or imagined experiences or events using effective technique, descriptive details, and well-structured event sequences | W3 pp. 100–109 |

*(Continued)*

| Tennessee Strand/Standard | Focus of Tennessee Standard | For More Information |
|---|---|---|
| **Writing** | | |
| W.4 | Produce writing in which the development, organization, and style are appropriate to the task, purpose, and audience | W4 pp. 110–115 |
| W.5 | Develop and strengthen writing as needed by planning, revising, editing, rewriting, or trying a new approach | W5 pp. 116–121 |
| W.6 | Use technology to produce and publish writing as well as to interact with others; demonstrate keyboarding skills | W6 pp. 122–127 |
| W.7 | Conduct short research projects to answer a question, drawing on several sources and refocusing the inquiry when appropriate | W7 pp. 128–133 |
| W.8 | Gather information from print and digital sources; assess the credibility of sources; quote or paraphrase while avoiding plagiarism and providing basic bibliographic information | W8 pp. 134–139 |
| W.9 | Draw evidence from literary or informational texts to support analysis, reflection, and research | W9 pp. 140–147 |
| W.10 | Write routinely over extended and shorter time frames for a range of tasks, purposes, and audiences | W10 pp. 148–153 |
| **Speaking and Listening** | | |
| SL.1 | Engage effectively in a range of collaborative discussions with diverse partners, building on others' ideas and expressing their own clearly | SL1 pp. 158–163 |
| SL.2 | Interpret information presented in diverse media and formats and explain how it contributes to a topic, text, or issue under study | SL2 pp. 164–169 |
| SL.3 | Delineate a speaker's argument and specific claims that are supported by reasons and evidence from claims that are not | SL3 pp. 170–175 |
| SL.4 | Present claims and findings, sequencing ideas logically and using descriptions, facts, or details to accentuate main ideas or themes; use appropriate eye contact, adequate volume, and clear pronunciation | SL4 pp. 176–181 |
| SL.5 | Include multimedia components and visual displays in presentations to clarify information | SL5 pp. 182–187 |
| SL.6 | Adapt speech to a variety of contexts and tasks, demonstrating command of formal English when appropriate | SL6 pp. 188–193 |
| **Language** | | |
| L.1 | Demonstrate command of the conventions of standard English grammar and usage when writing or speaking | L1 pp. 198–203 |
| L.2 | Demonstrate command of the conventions of standard English capitalization, punctuation, and spelling when writing | L2 pp. 204–209 |
| L.3 | Use knowledge of language and its conventions when writing, speaking, reading, or listening | L3 pp. 210–215 |
| L.4 | Determine or clarify the meaning of unknown and multiple-meaning words and phrases, choosing flexibly from an array of strategies | L4 pp. 216–221 |
| L.5 | Demonstrate understanding of figurative language, word relationships, and nuances in word meanings | L5 pp. 222–227 |
| L.6 | Acquire and use accurately general academic, and domain-specific words and phrases | L6 pp. 228–233 |
| **Reading History/Social Studies** | | |
| RH.1 | Cite textual evidence to support analysis of primary and secondary sources | R1 pp. 6–11 |
| RH.2 | Determine the central ideas or information of a primary or secondary source; provide an objective summary | R2 pp. 12–19 |
| RH.3 | Identify key steps in a text's description of a process related to history/social studies | R3 pp. 20–25 |
| RH.4 | Determine the meaning of words and phrases as they are used in a text, including vocabulary specific to history/social studies | R4 pp. 26–33 |

| Tennessee Strand/Standard | Focus of Tennessee Standard | For More Information |
|---|---|---|
| **Reading History/Social Studies** | | |
| RH.5 | Describe how a text presents information | R5 pp. 34–39 |
| RH.6 | Identify aspects of a text that reveal an author's point of view or purpose | R6 pp. 40–47 |
| RH.7 | Integrate visual information with other information in print and digital texts | R7 pp. 48–55 |
| RH.8 | Distinguish among fact, opinion, and reasoned judgment in a text | R8 pp. 56–63 |
| RH.9 | Analyze the relationship between a primary and secondary source on the same topic | R9 pp. 64–71 |
| RH.10 | Read and comprehend history/social studies texts of appropriate complexity independently with proficiency | R10 pp. 72–77 |
| **Reading Science/Technical Subjects** | | |
| RST.1 | Cite textual evidence to support analysis of science and technical texts | R1 pp. 6–11 |
| RST.2 | Determine the central ideas or conclusions of a text; provide an objective summary | R2 pp. 12–19 |
| RST.3 | Follow precisely a multistep procedure when carrying out experiments, taking measurements, or performing technical tasks | R3 pp. 20–25 |
| RST.4 | Determine the meaning of symbols, key terms, and other domain-specific words and phrases | R4 pp. 26–33 |
| RST.5 | Analyze the structure an author uses to organize a text, including how the major sections contribute to the whole | R5 pp. 34–39 |
| RST.6 | Analyze the author's purpose in providing an explanation, describing a procedure, or discussing an experiment | R6 pp. 40–47 |
| RST.7 | Integrate quantitative or technical information expressed in words with a version of the information expressed visually | R7 pp. 48–55 |
| RST.8 | Distinguish among facts, reasoned judgment based on research findings, and speculation in a text | R8 pp. 56–63 |
| RST.9 | Compare and contrast the information gained from experiments, simulations, video, or multimedia sources with that gained from reading a text on the same topic | R9 pp. 64–71 |
| RST.10 | Read and comprehend appropriately complex science/technical texts independently and proficiently | R10 pp. 72–77 |
| **Writing History/Social Studies and Science/Technical Subjects** | | |
| WHST.1 | Write arguments based on discipline-specific content | W1 pp. 82–89 |
| WHST.2 | Write informative/explanatory texts including the narration of historical events, scientific procedures/experiments, or technical processes | W2 pp. 90–99 |
| WHST.3 | NA | |
| WHST.4 | Produce writing in which the development, organization, and style are appropriate to the task, purpose, and audience | W4 pp. 110–115 |
| WHST.5 | Develop and strengthen writing as needed by planning, revising, editing, rewriting, or trying a new approach | W5 pp. 116–121 |
| WHST.6 | Use technology to produce and publish writing as well as to interact with others; demonstrate keyboarding skills | W6 pp. 122–127 |
| WHST.7 | Conduct short research projects to answer a question, drawing on several sources and refocusing the inquiry when appropriate | W7 pp. 128–133 |
| WHST.8 | Gather information from print and digital sources; assess the credibility of sources; quote or paraphrase while avoiding plagiarism and providing basic bibliographic information | W8 pp. 134–139 |
| WHST.9 | Draw evidence from informational texts to support analysis, reflection, and research | W9 pp. 140–147 |
| WHST.10 | Write routinely over extended and shorter time frames for a range of tasks, purposes, and audiences | W10 pp. 148–153 |

# Tennessee, Grade 7

| Tennessee Strand/Standard | Focus of Tennessee Standard | For More Information |
|---|---|---|
| **Reading Literature** | | |
| RL.1 | Cite several pieces of textual evidence to support analysis of what the text says explicitly as well as inferences drawn from the text | R1 pp. 6–11 |
| RL.2 | Determine the theme or central idea of a text and analyze its development; provide an objective summary of the text | R2 pp. 12–19 |
| RL.3 | Analyze how particular elements of a story or drama interact | R3 pp. 20–25 |
| RL.4 | Determine the meaning of words and phrases as they are used in a text, including figurative and connotative meanings | R4 pp. 26–33 |
| RL.5 | Analyze how a drama's or poem's form or structure contributes to its meaning | R5 pp. 34–39 |
| RL.6 | Analyze how an author develops and contrasts the points of view of different characters or narrators in a text | R6 pp. 40–47 |
| RL.7 | Compare and contrast a written story, drama, or poem to its audio, filmed, staged, or multimedia version | R7 pp. 48–55 |
| RL.8 | NA | |
| RL.9 | Compare and contrast a fictional portrayal of a time, place, or character and a historical account of the same period | R9 pp. 64–71 |
| RL.10 | Read and comprehend literature of appropriate complexity independently with proficiency | R10 pp. 72–77 |
| **Reading Informational Text** | | |
| RI.1 | Cite several pieces of textual evidence to support analysis of what the text says explicitly as well as inferences drawn from the text | R1 pp. 6–11 |
| RI.2 | Determine two or more central ideas in a text and analyze their developments; provide an objective summary of the text | R2 pp. 12–19 |
| RI.3 | Analyze the interactions between individuals, events, and ideas in a text | R3 pp. 20–25 |
| RI.4 | Determine the meaning of words and phrases as they are used in a text, including figurative, connotative, and technical meanings | R4 pp. 26–33 |
| RI.5 | Analyze the structure an author uses to organize a text, including how the major sections contribute to the whole | R5 pp. 34–39 |
| RI.6 | Determine an author's point of view or purpose in a text and analyze how the author distinguishes his or her position from that of others | R6 pp. 40–47 |
| RI.7 | Compare and contrast a text to an audio, video, or multimedia version of the text | R7 pp. 48–55 |
| RI.8 | Trace and evaluate the argument and specific claims in a text, assessing whether the reason is sound and the evidence is relevant and sufficient | R8 pp. 56–63 |
| RI.9 | Analyze how two or more authors writing about the same topic shape their presentations of key information | R9 pp. 64–71 |
| RI.10 | Read and comprehend appropriately complex literary nonfiction, informational, and functional texts independently and proficiently | R10 pp. 72–77 |
| **Writing** | | |
| W.1 | Write arguments to support claims with clear reasons and relevant evidence | W1 pp. 82–89 |
| W.2 | Write informative/explanatory texts to examine a topic and convey ideas, concepts, and information clearly | W2 pp. 90–99 |
| W.3 | Write narratives to develop real or imagined experiences or events using effective technique, descriptive details, and well-structured event sequences | W3 pp. 100–109 |

| Tennessee Strand/Standard | Focus of Tennessee Standard | For More Information |
|---|---|---|
| **Writing** | | |
| W.4 | Produce writing in which the development, organization, and style are appropriate to the task, purpose, and audience | W4 pp. 110–115 |
| W.5 | Develop and strengthen writing as needed by planning, revising, editing, rewriting, or trying a new approach | W5 pp. 116–121 |
| W.6 | Use technology to produce and publish writing, link to and cite sources; interact and collaborate with others | W6 pp. 122–127 |
| W.7 | Conduct short research projects to answer a question, drawing on several sources and additional related questions for further investigation | W7 pp. 128–133 |
| W.8 | Gather information from print and digital sources; assess the credibility of sources; quote or paraphrase while avoiding plagiarism and following a standard format for citation | W8 pp. 134–139 |
| W.9 | Draw evidence from literary or informational texts to support analysis, reflection, and research | W9 pp. 140–147 |
| W.10 | Write routinely over extended and shorter time frames for a range of tasks, purposes, and audiences | W10 pp. 148–153 |
| **Speaking and Listening** | | |
| SL.1 | Engage effectively in a range of collaborative discussions with diverse partners, building on others' ideas and expressing their own clearly | SL1 pp. 158–163 |
| SL.2 | Analyze the main ideas and supporting details presented in diverse media and formats and explain how the ideas clarify a topic, text, or issue under study | SL2 pp. 164–169 |
| SL.3 | Delineate a speaker's argument and specific claims evaluating the soundness of the reasoning and the relevance and sufficiency of the evidence | SL3 pp. 170–175 |
| SL.4 | Present claims and findings, emphasizing salient points in a focused coherent manner; use appropriate eye contact, adequate volume, and clear pronunciation | SL4 pp. 176–181 |
| SL.5 | Include multimedia components and visual displays in presentations to clarify claims and findings | SL5 pp. 182–187 |
| SL.6 | Adapt speech to a variety of contexts and tasks, demonstrating command of formal English when appropriate | SL6 pp. 188–193 |
| **Language** | | |
| L.1 | Demonstrate command of the conventions of standard English grammar and usage when writing or speaking | L1 pp. 198–203 |
| L.2 | Demonstrate command of the conventions of standard English capitalization, punctuation, and spelling when writing | L2 pp. 204–209 |
| L.3 | Use knowledge of language and its conventions when writing, speaking, reading, or listening | L3 pp. 210–215 |
| L.4 | Determine or clarify the meaning of unknown and multiple-meaning words and phrases, choosing flexibly from an array of strategies | L4 pp. 216–221 |
| L.5 | Demonstrate understanding of figurative language, word relationships, and nuances in word meanings | L5 pp. 222–227 |
| L.6 | Acquire and use accurately general academic, and domain-specific words and phrases | L6 pp. 228–233 |
| **Reading History/Social Studies** | | |
| RH.1 | Cite textual evidence to support analysis of primary and secondary sources | R1 pp. 6–11 |
| RH.2 | Determine the central ideas or information of a primary or secondary source; provide an objective summary | R2 pp. 12–19 |
| RH.3 | Identify key steps in a text's description of a process related to history/social studies | R3 pp. 20–25 |
| RH.4 | Determine the meaning of words and phrases as they are used in a text, including vocabulary specific to history/social studies | R4 pp. 26–33 |

*(Continued)*

| Tennessee Strand/Standard | Focus of Tennessee Standard | For More Information |
|---|---|---|
| **Reading History/Social Studies** | | |
| RH.5 | Describe how a text presents information | R5 pp. 34–39 |
| RH.6 | Identify aspects of a text that reveal an author's point of view or purpose | R6 pp. 40–47 |
| RH.7 | Integrate visual information with other information in print and digital texts | R7 pp. 48–55 |
| RH.8 | Distinguish among fact, opinion, and reasoned judgment in a text | R8 pp. 56–63 |
| RH.9 | Analyze the relationship between a primary and secondary source on the same topic | R9 pp. 64–71 |
| RH.10 | Read and comprehend history/social studies texts of appropriate complexity independently with proficiency | R10 pp. 72–77 |
| **Reading Science/Technical Subjects** | | |
| RST.1 | Cite textual evidence to support analysis of science and technical texts | R1 pp. 6–11 |
| RST.2 | Determine the central ideas or conclusions of a text; provide an objective summary | R2 pp. 12–19 |
| RST.3 | Follow precisely a multistep procedure when carrying out experiments, taking measurements, or performing technical tasks | R3 pp. 20–25 |
| RST.4 | Determine the meaning of symbols, key terms, and other domain-specific words and phrases | R4 pp. 26–33 |
| RST.5 | Analyze the structure an author uses to organize a text, including how the major sections contribute to the whole | R5 pp. 34–39 |
| RST.6 | Analyze the author's purpose in providing an explanation, describing a procedure, or discussing an experiment | R6 pp. 40–47 |
| RST.7 | Integrate quantitative or technical information expressed in words with a version of the information expressed visually | R7 pp. 48–55 |
| RST.8 | Distinguish among facts, reasoned judgment based on research findings, and speculation in a text | R8 pp. 56–63 |
| RST.9 | Compare and contrast the information gained from experiments, simulations, video, or multimedia sources with that gained from reading a text on the same topic | R9 pp. 64–71 |
| RST.10 | Read and comprehend appropriately complex science/technical texts independently and proficiently | R10 pp. 72–77 |
| **Writing History/Social Studies and Science/Technical Subjects** | | |
| WHST.1 | Write arguments based on discipline-specific content | W1 pp. 82–89 |
| WHST.2 | Write informative/explanatory texts including the narration of historical events, scientific procedures/experiments, or technical processes | W2 pp. 90–99 |
| WHST.3 | NA | |
| WHST.4 | Produce writing in which the development, organization, and style are appropriate to the task, purpose, and audience | W4 pp. 110–115 |
| WHST.5 | Develop and strengthen writing as needed by planning, revising, editing, rewriting, or trying a new approach | W5 pp. 116–121 |
| WHST.6 | Use technology to produce and publish writing as well as to interact with others; demonstrate keyboarding skills | W6 pp. 122–127 |
| WHST.7 | Conduct short research projects to answer a question, drawing on several sources and refocusing the inquiry when appropriate | W7 pp. 128–133 |
| WHST.8 | Gather information from print and digital sources; assess the credibility of sources; quote or paraphrase while avoiding plagiarism and providing basic bibliographic information | W8 pp. 134–139 |
| WHST.9 | Draw evidence from informational texts to support analysis, reflection, and research | W9 pp. 140–147 |
| WHST.10 | Write routinely over extended and shorter time frames for a range of tasks, purposes, and audiences | W10 pp. 148–153 |

# Tennessee, Grade 8

| Tennessee Strand/Standard | Focus of Tennessee Standard | For More Information |
|---|---|---|
| **Reading Literature** | | |
| RL.1 | Cite the textual evidence that most strongly supports an analysis of what the text says explicitly as well as inferences drawn from the text | R1 pp. 6–11 |
| RL.2 | Determine the theme or central idea of a text and analyze its development, including its relationship to the characters, setting, and plot; provide an objective summary of the text | R2 pp. 12–19 |
| RL.3 | Analyze how particular lines of dialogue or incidents in a story or drama propel the action, reveal aspects of a character, or provoke a decision | R3 pp. 20–25 |
| RL.4 | Determine the meaning of words and phrases as they are used in a text, including figurative and connotative meanings | R4 pp. 26–33 |
| RL.5 | Compare and contrast the structure of two or more texts and analyze how the differing structure of each contributes to its meaning and style | R5 pp. 34–39 |
| RL.6 | Analyze how differences in the points of view of the characters and the audience or reader create such effects as suspense or humor | R6 pp. 40–47 |
| RL.7 | Analyze the extent to which a filmed or live production of a story or drama stays faithful or departs from the text or script | R7 pp. 48–55 |
| RL.8 | NA | |
| RL.9 | Analyze how a modern work of fiction draws on themes, patterns of events, or character types from traditional stories, describing how the material is rendered new | R9 pp. 64–71 |
| RL.10 | Read and comprehend literature of appropriate complexity independently with proficiency | R10 pp. 72–77 |
| **Reading Informational Text** | | |
| RI.1 | Cite the textual evidence that most strongly supports an analysis of what the text says explicitly as well as inferences drawn from the text | R1 pp. 6–11 |
| RI.2 | Determine the central idea of a text and analyze its development, including its relationship to supporting ideas; provide an objective summary of the text | R2 pp. 12–19 |
| RI.3 | Analyze how a text makes connections among distinctions between individuals, ideas, or events | R3 pp. 20–25 |
| RI.4 | Determine the meaning of words and phrases as they are used in a text, including figurative, connotative, and technical meanings | R4 pp. 26–33 |
| RI.5 | Analyze the structure of a specific paragraph in a text, including the role of particular sentences in developing and refining a key concept | R5 pp. 34–39 |
| RI.6 | Determine an author's point of view or purpose in a text and analyze how the author acknowledges and responds to conflicting evidence or viewpoints | R6 pp. 40–47 |
| RI.7 | Evaluate the advantages and disadvantages of using different mediums to present a particular topic or idea | R7 pp. 48–55 |
| RI.8 | Delineate and evaluate the argument and specific claims in a text, assessing whether the reason is sound and the evidence is relevant and sufficient | R8 pp. 56–63 |
| RI.9 | Analyze a case in which two or more texts provide conflicting information on the same topic | R9 pp. 64–71 |
| RI.10 | Read and comprehend appropriately complex literary nonfiction, informational, and functional texts independently and proficiently | R10 pp. 72–77 |
| **Writing** | | |
| W.1 | Write arguments to support claims with clear reasons and relevant evidence | W1 pp. 82–89 |
| W.2 | Write informative/explanatory texts to examine a topic and convey ideas, concepts, and information clearly | W2 pp. 90–99 |

*(Continued)*

| Tennessee Strand/Standard | Focus of Tennessee Standard | For More Information |
|---|---|---|
| **Writing** | | |
| W.3 | Write narratives to develop real or imagined experiences or events using effective technique, descriptive details, and well-structured event sequences | W3 pp. 100–109 |
| W.4 | Produce writing in which the development, organization, and style are appropriate to the task, purpose, and audience | W4 pp. 110–115 |
| W.5 | Develop and strengthen writing as needed by planning, revising, editing, rewriting, or trying a new approach | W5 pp. 116–121 |
| W.6 | Use technology to produce and publish writing, link to and cite sources; interact and collaborate with others | W6 pp. 122–127 |
| W.7 | Conduct short research projects to answer a question, drawing on several sources and additional related questions for further investigation | W7 pp. 128–133 |
| W.8 | Gather information from print and digital sources; assess the credibility of sources; quote or paraphrase while avoiding plagiarism and following a standard format for citation | W8 pp. 134–139 |
| W.9 | Draw evidence from literary or informational texts to support analysis, reflection, and research | W9 pp. 140–147 |
| W.10 | Write routinely over extended and shorter time frames for a range of tasks, purposes, and audiences | W10 pp. 148–153 |
| **Speaking and Listening** | | |
| SL.1 | Engage effectively in a range of collaborative discussions with diverse partners, building on others' ideas and expressing their own clearly | SL1 pp. 158–163 |
| SL.2 | Analyze the purpose of information presented in diverse media and formats and evaluate the motives behind its presentation | SL2 pp. 164–169 |
| SL.3 | Delineate a speaker's argument and specific claims evaluating the soundness of the reasoning and the relevance and sufficiency of the evidence and identifying when irrelevant evidence is introduced | SL3 pp. 170–175 |
| SL.4 | Present claims and findings, emphasizing salient points in a focused coherent manner; use appropriate eye contact, adequate volume, and clear pronunciation | SL4 pp. 176–181 |
| SL.5 | Integrate multimedia components and visual displays into presentations to clarify information, strengthen claims and findings, and add interest | SL5 pp. 182–187 |
| SL.6 | Adapt speech to a variety of contexts and tasks, demonstrating command of formal English when appropriate | SL6 pp. 188–193 |
| **Language** | | |
| L.1 | Demonstrate command of the conventions of standard English grammar and usage when writing or speaking | L1 pp. 198–203 |
| L.2 | Demonstrate command of the conventions of standard English capitalization, punctuation, and spelling when writing | L2 pp. 204–209 |
| L.3 | Use knowledge of language and its conventions when writing, speaking, reading, or listening | L3 pp. 210–215 |
| L.4 | Determine or clarify the meaning of unknown and multiple-meaning words and phrases, choosing flexibly from an array of strategies | L4 pp. 216–221 |
| L.5 | Demonstrate understanding of figurative language, word relationships, and nuances in word meanings | L5 pp. 222–227 |
| L.6 | Acquire and use accurately general academic, and domain-specific words and phrases | L6 pp. 228–233 |
| **Reading History/Social Studies** | | |
| RH.1 | Cite textual evidence to support analysis of primary and secondary sources | R1 pp. 6–11 |
| RH.2 | Determine the central ideas or information of a primary or secondary source; provide an objective summary | R2 pp. 12–19 |
| RH.3 | Identify key steps in a text's description of a process related to history/social studies | R3 pp. 20–25 |

| Tennessee Strand/Standard | Focus of Tennessee Standard | For More Information |
|---|---|---|
| **Reading History/Social Studies** | | |
| RH.4 | Determine the meaning of words and phrases as they are used in a text, including vocabulary specific to history/social studies | R4 pp. 26–33 |
| RH.5 | Describe how a text presents information | R5 pp. 34–39 |
| RH.6 | Identify aspects of a text that reveal an author's point of view or purpose | R6 pp. 40–47 |
| RH.7 | Integrate visual information with other information in print and digital texts | R7 pp. 48–55 |
| RH.8 | Distinguish among fact, opinion, and reasoned judgment in a text | R8 pp. 56–63 |
| RH.9 | Analyze the relationship between a primary and secondary source on the same topic | R9 pp. 64–71 |
| RH.10 | Read and comprehend history/social studies texts of appropriate complexity independently with proficiency | R10 pp. 72–77 |
| **Reading Science/Technical Subjects** | | |
| RST.1 | Cite textual evidence to support analysis of science and technical texts | R1 pp. 6–11 |
| RST.2 | Determine the central ideas or conclusions of a text; provide an objective summary | R2 pp. 12–19 |
| RST.3 | Follow precisely a multistep procedure when carrying out experiments, taking measurements, or performing technical tasks | R3 pp. 20–25 |
| RST.4 | Determine the meaning of symbols, key terms, and other domain-specific words and phrases | R4 pp. 26–33 |
| RST.5 | Analyze the structure an author uses to organize a text, including how the major sections contribute to the whole | R5 pp. 34–39 |
| RST.6 | Analyze the author's purpose in providing an explanation, describing a procedure, or discussing an experiment | R6 pp. 40–47 |
| RST.7 | Integrate quantitative or technical information expressed in words with a version of the information expressed visually | R7 pp. 48–55 |
| RST.8 | Distinguish among facts, reasoned judgment based on research findings, and speculation in a text | R8 pp. 56–63 |
| RST.9 | Compare and contrast the information gained from experiments, simulations, video, or multimedia sources with that gained from reading a text on the same topic | R9 pp. 64–71 |
| RST.10 | Read and comprehend appropriately complex science/technical texts independently and proficiently | R10 pp. 72–77 |
| **Writing History/Social Studies and Science/Technical Subjects** | | |
| WHST.1 | Write arguments based on discipline-specific content | W1 pp. 82–89 |
| WHST.2 | Write informative/explanatory texts including the narration of historical events, scientific procedures/experiments, or technical processes | W2 pp. 90–99 |
| WHST.3 | NA | |
| WHST.4 | Produce writing in which the development, organization, and style are appropriate to the task, purpose, and audience | W4 pp. 110–115 |
| WHST.5 | Develop and strengthen writing as needed by planning, revising, editing, rewriting, or trying a new approach | W5 pp. 116–121 |
| WHST.6 | Use technology to produce and publish writing as well as to interact with others; demonstrate keyboarding skills | W6 pp. 122–127 |
| WHST.7 | Conduct short research projects to answer a question, drawing on several sources and refocusing the inquiry when appropriate | W7 pp. 128–133 |
| WHST.8 | Gather information from print and digital sources; assess the credibility of sources; quote or paraphrase while avoiding plagiarism and providing basic bibliographic information | W8 pp. 134–139 |
| WHST.9 | Draw evidence from informational texts to support analysis, reflection, and research | W9 pp. 140–147 |
| WHST.10 | Write routinely over extended and shorter time frames for a range of tasks, purposes, and audiences | W10 pp. 148–153 |

# Utah, Grade 6

| Utah Strand/Standard | Focus of Utah Standard | For More Information |
|---|---|---|
| **Reading Literature** | | |
| RL.1 | Cite textual evidence to support analysis of what the text says explicitly as well as inferences drawn from the text | R1 pp. 6–11 |
| RL.2 | Determine the theme or central idea of a text and how it is conveyed through particular details; provide an objective summary | R2 pp. 12–19 |
| RL.3 | Describe how a particular plot unfolds in a series of episodes as well as how the characters respond or change | R3 pp. 20–25 |
| RL.4 | Determine the meaning of words and phrases as they are used in a text, including figurative and connotative meanings | R4 pp. 26–33 |
| RL.5 | Analyze how a particular sentence, chapter, scene, or stanza fits into the overall structure of a text and contributes to the development of the theme, setting, or plot | R5 pp. 34–39 |
| RL.6 | Explain how an author develops the point of view of the narrator or speaker in a text | R6 pp. 40–47 |
| RL.7 | Compare and contrast the experience of reading a story, drama, or poem to listening to or viewing an audio, video, or live version of the text | R7 pp. 48–55 |
| RL.8 | NA | |
| RL.9 | Compare and contrast texts in different forms or genres in terms of their approaches to similar themes and topics | R9 pp. 64–71 |
| RL.10 | Read and comprehend literature of appropriate complexity independently with proficiency | R10 pp. 72–77 |
| **Reading Informational Text** | | |
| RI.1 | Cite textual evidence to support analysis of what the text says explicitly as well as inferences drawn from the text | R1 pp. 6–11 |
| RI.2 | Determine a central idea of a text and how it is conveyed through particular details; provide an objective summary | R2 pp. 12–19 |
| RI.3 | Analyze in detail how a key individual, event, or idea is introduced, illustrated, and elaborated in a text | R3 pp. 20–25 |
| RI.4 | Determine the meaning of words and phrases as they are used in a text, including figurative, connotative, and technical meanings | R4 pp. 26–33 |
| RI.5 | Analyze how a particular sentence, chapter, scene, or section fits into the overall structure of a text and contributes to the development of the ideas | R5 pp. 34–39 |
| RI.6 | Determine an author's point of view or purpose in a text and explain how it is conveyed in the text | R6 pp. 40–47 |
| RI.7 | Integrate information presented in different media or formats as well as in words to develop a coherent understanding of a topic or issue | R7 pp. 48–55 |
| RI.8 | Trace and evaluate the argument and specific claims that are supported by reasons and evidence from claims that are not | R8 pp. 56–63 |
| RI.9 | Compare and contrast one author's presentation of events with that of another | R9 pp. 64–71 |
| RI.10 | Read and comprehend appropriately complex literary nonfiction, informational, and functional texts independently and proficiently | R10 pp. 72–77 |
| **Writing** | | |
| W.1 | Write arguments to support claims with clear reasons and relevant evidence | W1 pp. 82–89 |
| W.2 | Write informative/explanatory texts to examine a topic and convey ideas, concepts, and information clearly | W2 pp. 90–99 |
| W.3 | Write narratives to develop real or imagined experiences or events using effective technique, descriptive details, and well-structured event sequences | W3 pp. 100–109 |

| Utah Strand/Standard | Focus of Utah Standard | For More Information |
|---|---|---|
| **Writing** | | |
| W.4 | Produce writing in which the development, organization, and style are appropriate to the task, purpose, and audience | W4 pp. 110–115 |
| W.5 | Develop and strengthen writing as needed by planning, revising, editing, rewriting, or trying a new approach | W5 pp. 116–121 |
| W.6 | Use technology to produce and publish writing as well as to interact with others; demonstrate keyboarding skills | W6 pp. 122–127 |
| W.7 | Conduct short research projects to answer a question, drawing on several sources and refocusing the inquiry when appropriate | W7 pp. 128–133 |
| W.8 | Gather information from print and digital sources; assess the credibility of sources; quote or paraphrase while avoiding plagiarism and providing basic bibliographic information | W8 pp. 134–139 |
| W.9 | Draw evidence from literary or informational texts to support analysis, reflection, and research | W9 pp. 140–147 |
| W.10 | Write routinely over extended and shorter time frames for a range of tasks, purposes, and audiences | W10 pp. 148–153 |
| **Speaking and Listening** | | |
| SL.1 | Engage effectively in a range of collaborative discussions with diverse partners, building on others' ideas and expressing their own clearly | SL1 pp. 158–163 |
| SL.2 | Interpret information presented in diverse media and formats and explain how it contributes to a topic, text, or issue under study | SL2 pp. 164–169 |
| SL.3 | Delineate a speaker's argument and specific claims that are supported by reasons and evidence from claims that are not | SL3 pp. 170–175 |
| SL.4 | Present claims and findings, sequencing ideas logically and using descriptions, facts, or details to accentuate main ideas or themes; use appropriate eye contact, adequate volume, and clear pronunciation | SL4 pp. 176–181 |
| SL.5 | Include multimedia components and visual displays in presentations to clarify information | SL5 pp. 182–187 |
| SL.6 | Adapt speech to a variety of contexts and tasks, demonstrating command of formal English when appropriate | SL6 pp. 188–193 |
| **Language** | | |
| L.1 | Demonstrate command of the conventions of standard English grammar and usage when writing or speaking | L1 pp. 198–203 |
| L.2 | Demonstrate command of the conventions of standard English capitalization, punctuation, and spelling when writing | L2 pp. 204–209 |
| L.3 | Use knowledge of language and its conventions when writing, speaking, reading, or listening | L3 pp. 210–215 |
| L.4 | Determine or clarify the meaning of unknown and multiple-meaning words and phrases, choosing flexibly from an array of strategies | L4 pp. 216–221 |
| L.5 | Demonstrate understanding of figurative language, word relationships, and nuances in word meanings | L5 pp. 222–227 |
| L.6 | Acquire and use accurately general academic, and domain-specific words and phrases | L6 pp. 228–233 |
| **Reading History/Social Studies** | | |
| RH.1 | Cite textual evidence to support analysis of primary and secondary sources | R1 pp. 6–11 |
| RH.2 | Determine the central ideas or information of a primary or secondary source; provide an objective summary | R2 pp. 12–19 |
| RH.3 | Identify key steps in a text's description of a process related to history/social studies | R3 pp. 20–25 |
| RH.4 | Determine the meaning of words and phrases as they are used in a text, including vocabulary specific to history/social studies | R4 pp. 26–33 |

*(Continued)*

| Utah Strand/Standard | Focus of Utah Standard | For More Information |
|---|---|---|

## Reading History/Social Studies

| Utah Strand/Standard | Focus of Utah Standard | For More Information |
|---|---|---|
| RH.5 | Describe how a text presents information | R5 pp. 34–39 |
| RH.6 | Identify aspects of a text that reveal an author's point of view or purpose | R6 pp. 40–47 |
| RH.7 | Integrate visual information with other information in print and digital texts | R7 pp. 48–55 |
| RH.8 | Distinguish among fact, opinion, and reasoned judgment in a text | R8 pp. 56–63 |
| RH.9 | Analyze the relationship between a primary and secondary source on the same topic | R9 pp. 64–71 |
| RH.10 | Read and comprehend history/social studies texts of appropriate complexity independently with proficiency | R10 pp. 72–77 |

## Reading Science/Technical Subjects

| Utah Strand/Standard | Focus of Utah Standard | For More Information |
|---|---|---|
| RST.1 | Cite textual evidence to support analysis of science and technical texts | R1 pp. 6–11 |
| RST.2 | Determine the central ideas or conclusions of a text; provide an objective summary | R2 pp. 12–19 |
| RST.3 | Follow precisely a multistep procedure when carrying out experiments, taking measurements, or performing technical tasks | R3 pp. 20–25 |
| RST.4 | Determine the meaning of symbols, key terms, and other domain-specific words and phrases | R4 pp. 26–33 |
| RST.5 | Analyze the structure an author uses to organize a text, including how the major sections contribute to the whole | R5 pp. 34–39 |
| RST.6 | Analyze the author's purpose in providing an explanation, describing a procedure, or discussing an experiment | R6 pp. 40–47 |
| RST.7 | Integrate quantitative or technical information expressed in words with a version of the information expressed visually | R7 pp. 48–55 |
| RST.8 | Distinguish among facts, reasoned judgment based on research findings, and speculation in a text | R8 pp. 56–63 |
| RST.9 | Compare and contrast the information gained from experiments, simulations, video, or multimedia sources with that gained from reading a text on the same topic | R9 pp. 64–71 |
| RST.10 | Read and comprehend appropriately complex science/technical texts independently and proficiently | R10 pp. 72–77 |

## Writing History/Social Studies and Science/Technical Subjects

| Utah Strand/Standard | Focus of Utah Standard | For More Information |
|---|---|---|
| WHST.1 | Write arguments based on discipline-specific content | W1 pp. 82–89 |
| WHST.2 | Write informative/explanatory texts including the narration of historical events, scientific procedures/experiments, or technical processes | W2 pp. 90–99 |
| WHST.3 | NA | |
| WHST.4 | Produce writing in which the development, organization, and style are appropriate to the task, purpose, and audience | W4 pp. 110–115 |
| WHST.5 | Develop and strengthen writing as needed by planning, revising, editing, rewriting, or trying a new approach | W5 pp. 116–121 |
| WHST.6 | Use technology to produce and publish writing as well as to interact with others; demonstrate keyboarding skills | W6 pp. 122–127 |
| WHST.7 | Conduct short research projects to answer a question, drawing on several sources and refocusing the inquiry when appropriate | W7 pp. 128–133 |
| WHST.8 | Gather information from print and digital sources; assess the credibility of sources; quote or paraphrase while avoiding plagiarism and providing basic bibliographic information | W8 pp. 134–139 |
| WHST.9 | Draw evidence from informational texts to support analysis, reflection, and research | W9 pp. 140–147 |
| WHST.10 | Write routinely over extended and shorter time frames for a range of tasks, purposes, and audiences | W10 pp. 148–153 |

# Utah, Grade 7

| Utah Strand/Standard | Focus of Utah Standard | For More Information |
|---|---|---|
| **Reading Literature** | | |
| RL.1 | Cite several pieces of textual evidence to support analysis of what the text says explicitly as well as inferences drawn from the text | R1 pp. 6–11 |
| RL.2 | Determine the theme or central idea of a text and analyze its development; provide an objective summary of the text | R2 pp. 12–19 |
| RL.3 | Analyze how particular elements of a story or drama interact | R3 pp. 20–25 |
| RL.4 | Determine the meaning of words and phrases as they are used in a text, including figurative and connotative meanings | R4 pp. 26–33 |
| RL.5 | Analyze how a drama's or poem's form or structure contributes to its meaning | R5 pp. 34–39 |
| RL.6 | Analyze how an author develops and contrasts the points of view of different characters or narrators in a text | R6 pp. 40–47 |
| RL.7 | Compare and contrast a written story, drama, or poem to its audio, filmed, staged, or multimedia version | R7 pp. 48–55 |
| RL.8 | NA | |
| RL.9 | Compare and contrast a fictional portrayal of a time, place, or character and a historical account of the same period | R9 pp. 64–71 |
| RL.10 | Read and comprehend literature of appropriate complexity independently with proficiency | R10 pp. 72–77 |
| **Reading Informational Text** | | |
| RI.1 | Cite several pieces of textual evidence to support analysis of what the text says explicitly as well as inferences drawn from the text | R1 pp. 6–11 |
| RI.2 | Determine two or more central ideas in a text and analyze their developments; provide an objective summary of the text | R2 pp. 12–19 |
| RI.3 | Analyze the interactions between individuals, events, and ideas in a text | R3 pp. 20–25 |
| RI.4 | Determine the meaning of words and phrases as they are used in a text, including figurative, connotative, and technical meanings | R4 pp. 26–33 |
| RI.5 | Analyze the structure an author uses to organize a text, including how the major sections contribute to the whole | R5 pp. 34–39 |
| RI.6 | Determine an author's point of view or purpose in a text and analyze how the author distinguishes his or her position from that of others | R6 pp. 40–47 |
| RI.7 | Compare and contrast a text to an audio, video, or multimedia version of the text | R7 pp. 48–55 |
| RI.8 | Trace and evaluate the argument and specific claims in a text, assessing whether the reason is sound and the evidence is relevant and sufficient | R8 pp. 56–63 |
| RI.9 | Analyze how two or more authors writing about the same topic shape their presentations of key information | R9 pp. 64–71 |
| RI.10 | Read and comprehend appropriately complex literary nonfiction, informational, and functional texts independently and proficiently | R10 pp. 72–77 |
| **Writing** | | |
| W.1 | Write arguments to support claims with clear reasons and relevant evidence | W1 pp. 82–89 |
| W.2 | Write informative/explanatory texts to examine a topic and convey ideas, concepts, and information clearly | W2 pp. 90–99 |
| W.3 | Write narratives to develop real or imagined experiences or events using effective technique, descriptive details, and well-structured event sequences | W3 pp. 100–109 |

*(Continued)*

| Utah Strand/Standard | Focus of Utah Standard | For More Information |
|---|---|---|
| **Writing** | | |
| W.4 | Produce writing in which the development, organization, and style are appropriate to the task, purpose, and audience | W4 pp. 110–115 |
| W.5 | Develop and strengthen writing as needed by planning, revising, editing, rewriting, or trying a new approach | W5 pp. 116–121 |
| W.6 | Use technology to produce and publish writing, link to and cite sources; interact and collaborate with others | W6 pp. 122–127 |
| W.7 | Conduct short research projects to answer a question, drawing on several sources and additional related questions for further investigation | W7 pp. 128–133 |
| W.8 | Gather information from print and digital sources; assess the credibility of sources; quote or paraphrase while avoiding plagiarism and following a standard format for citation | W8 pp. 134–139 |
| W.9 | Draw evidence from literary or informational texts to support analysis, reflection, and research | W9 pp. 140–147 |
| W.10 | Write routinely over extended and shorter time frames for a range of tasks, purposes, and audiences | W10 pp. 148–153 |
| **Speaking and Listening** | | |
| SL.1 | Engage effectively in a range of collaborative discussions with diverse partners, building on others' ideas and expressing their own clearly | SL1 pp. 158–163 |
| SL.2 | Analyze the main ideas and supporting details presented in diverse media and formats and explain how the ideas clarify a topic, text, or issue under study | SL2 pp. 164–169 |
| SL.3 | Delineate a speaker's argument and specific claims evaluating the soundness of the reasoning and the relevance and sufficiency of the evidence | SL3 pp. 170–175 |
| SL.4 | Present claims and findings, emphasizing salient points in a focused coherent manner; use appropriate eye contact, adequate volume, and clear pronunciation | SL4 pp. 176–181 |
| SL.5 | Include multimedia components and visual displays in presentations to clarify claims and findings | SL5 pp. 182–187 |
| SL.6 | Adapt speech to a variety of contexts and tasks, demonstrating command of formal English when appropriate | SL6 pp. 188–193 |
| **Language** | | |
| L.1 | Demonstrate command of the conventions of standard English grammar and usage when writing or speaking | L1 pp. 198–203 |
| L.2 | Demonstrate command of the conventions of standard English capitalization, punctuation, and spelling when writing | L2 pp. 204–209 |
| L.3 | Use knowledge of language and its conventions when writing, speaking, reading, or listening | L3 pp. 210–215 |
| L.4 | Determine or clarify the meaning of unknown and multiple-meaning words and phrases, choosing flexibly from an array of strategies | L4 pp. 216–221 |
| L.5 | Demonstrate understanding of figurative language, word relationships, and nuances in word meanings | L5 pp. 222–227 |
| L.6 | Acquire and use accurately general academic, and domain-specific words and phrases | L6 pp. 228–233 |
| **Reading History/Social Studies** | | |
| RH.1 | Cite textual evidence to support analysis of primary and secondary sources | R1 pp. 6–11 |
| RH.2 | Determine the central ideas or information of a primary or secondary source; provide an objective summary | R2 pp. 12–19 |
| RH.3 | Identify key steps in a text's description of a process related to history/social studies | R3 pp. 20–25 |
| RH.4 | Determine the meaning of words and phrases as they are used in a text, including vocabulary specific to history/social studies | R4 pp. 26–33 |
| RH.5 | Describe how a text presents information | R5 pp. 34–39 |

| Utah Strand/Standard | Focus of Utah Standard | For More Information |
|---|---|---|
| **Reading History/Social Studies** | | |
| RH.6 | Identify aspects of a text that reveal an author's point of view or purpose | R6 pp. 40–47 |
| RH.7 | Integrate visual information with other information in print and digital texts | R7 pp. 48–55 |
| RH.8 | Distinguish among fact, opinion, and reasoned judgment in a text | R8 pp. 56–63 |
| RH.9 | Analyze the relationship between a primary and secondary source on the same topic | R9 pp. 64–71 |
| RH.10 | Read and comprehend history/social studies texts of appropriate complexity independently with proficiency | R10 pp. 72–77 |
| **Reading Science/Technical Subjects** | | |
| RST.1 | Cite textual evidence to support analysis of science and technical texts | R1 pp. 6–11 |
| RST.2 | Determine the central ideas or conclusions of a text; provide an objective summary | R2 pp. 12–19 |
| RST.3 | Follow precisely a multistep procedure when carrying out experiments, taking measurements, or performing technical tasks | R3 pp. 20–25 |
| RST.4 | Determine the meaning of symbols, key terms, and other domain-specific words and phrases | R4 pp. 26–33 |
| RST.5 | Analyze the structure an author uses to organize a text, including how the major sections contribute to the whole | R5 pp. 34–39 |
| RST.6 | Analyze the author's purpose in providing an explanation, describing a procedure, or discussing an experiment | R6 pp. 40–47 |
| RST.7 | Integrate quantitative or technical information expressed in words with a version of the information expressed visually | R7 pp. 48–55 |
| RST.8 | Distinguish among facts, reasoned judgment based on research findings, and speculation in a text | R8 pp. 56–63 |
| RST.9 | Compare and contrast the information gained from experiments, simulations, video, or multimedia sources with that gained from reading a text on the same topic | R9 pp. 64–71 |
| RST.10 | Read and comprehend appropriately complex science/technical texts independently and proficiently | R10 pp. 72–77 |
| **Writing History/Social Studies and Science/Technical Subjects** | | |
| WHST.1 | Write arguments based on discipline-specific content | W1 pp. 82–89 |
| WHST.2 | Write informative/explanatory texts including the narration of historical events, scientific procedures/experiments, or technical processes | W2 pp. 90–99 |
| WHST.3 | NA | |
| WHST.4 | Produce writing in which the development, organization, and style are appropriate to the task, purpose, and audience | W4 pp. 110–115 |
| WHST.5 | Develop and strengthen writing as needed by planning, revising, editing, rewriting, or trying a new approach | W5 pp. 116–121 |
| WHST.6 | Use technology to produce and publish writing as well as to interact with others; demonstrate keyboarding skills | W6 pp. 122–127 |
| WHST.7 | Conduct short research projects to answer a question, drawing on several sources and refocusing the inquiry when appropriate | W7 pp. 128–133 |
| WHST.8 | Gather information from print and digital sources; assess the credibility of sources; quote or paraphrase while avoiding plagiarism and providing basic bibliographic information | W8 pp. 134–139 |
| WHST.9 | Draw evidence from informational texts to support analysis, reflection, and research | W9 pp. 140–147 |
| WHST.10 | Write routinely over extended and shorter time frames for a range of tasks, purposes, and audiences | W10 pp. 148–153 |

# Utah, Grade 8

| Utah Strand/Standard | Focus of Utah Standard | For More Information |
|---|---|---|
| **Reading Literature** | | |
| RL.1 | Cite the textual evidence that most strongly supports an analysis of what the text says explicitly as well as inferences drawn from the text | R1 pp. 6–11 |
| RL.2 | Determine the theme or central idea of a text and analyze its development, including its relationship to the characters, setting, and plot; provide an objective summary of the text | R2 pp. 12–19 |
| RL.3 | Analyze how particular lines of dialogue or incidents in a story or drama propel the action, reveal aspects of a character, or provoke a decision | R3 pp. 20–25 |
| RL.4 | Determine the meaning of words and phrases as they are used in a text, including figurative and connotative meanings | R4 pp. 26–33 |
| RL.5 | Compare and contrast the structure of two or more texts and analyze how the differing structure of each contributes to its meaning and style | R5 pp. 34–39 |
| RL.6 | Analyze how differences in the points of view of the characters and the audience or reader create such effects as suspense or humor | R6 pp. 40–47 |
| RL.7 | Analyze the extent to which a filmed or live production of a story or drama stays faithful or departs from the text or script | R7 pp. 48–55 |
| RL.8 | NA | |
| RL.9 | Analyze how a modern work of fiction draws on themes, patterns of events, or character types from traditional stories, describing how the material is rendered new | R9 pp. 64–71 |
| RL.10 | Read and comprehend literature of appropriate complexity independently with proficiency | R10 pp. 72–77 |
| **Reading Informational Text** | | |
| RI.1 | Cite the textual evidence that most strongly supports an analysis of what the text says explicitly as well as inferences drawn from the text | R1 pp. 6–11 |
| RI.2 | Determine the central idea of a text and analyze its development, including its relationship to supporting ideas; provide an objective summary of the text | R2 pp. 12–19 |
| RI.3 | Analyze how a text makes connections among distinctions between individuals, ideas, or events | R3 pp. 20–25 |
| RI.4 | Determine the meaning of words and phrases as they are used in a text, including figurative, connotative, and technical meanings | R4 pp. 26–33 |
| RI.5 | Analyze the structure of a specific paragraph in a text, including the role of particular sentences in developing and refining a key concept | R5 pp. 34–39 |
| RI.6 | Determine an author's point of view or purpose in a text and analyze how the author acknowledges and responds to conflicting evidence or viewpoints | R6 pp. 40–47 |
| RI.7 | Evaluate the advantages and disadvantages of using different mediums to present a particular topic or idea | R7 pp. 48–55 |
| RI.8 | Delineate and evaluate the argument and specific claims in a text, assessing whether the reason is sound and the evidence is relevant and sufficient | R8 pp. 56–63 |
| RI.9 | Analyze a case in which two or more texts provide conflicting information on the same topic | R9 pp. 64–71 |
| RI.10 | Read and comprehend appropriately complex literary nonfiction, informational, and functional texts independently and proficiently | R10 pp. 72–77 |
| **Writing** | | |
| W.1 | Write arguments to support claims with clear reasons and relevant evidence | W1 pp. 82–89 |
| W.2 | Write informative/explanatory texts to examine a topic and convey ideas, concepts, and information clearly | W2 pp. 90–99 |

| Utah Strand/Standard | Focus of Utah Standard | For More Information |
|---|---|---|
| **Writing** | | |
| W.3 | Write narratives to develop real or imagined experiences or events using effective technique, descriptive details, and well-structured event sequences | W3 pp. 100–109 |
| W.4 | Produce writing in which the development, organization, and style are appropriate to the task, purpose, and audience | W4 pp. 110–115 |
| W.5 | Develop and strengthen writing as needed by planning, revising, editing, rewriting, or trying a new approach | W5 pp. 116–121 |
| W.6 | Use technology to produce and publish writing, link to and cite sources; interact and collaborate with others | W6 pp. 122–127 |
| W.7 | Conduct short research projects to answer a question, drawing on several sources and additional related questions for further investigation | W7 pp. 128–133 |
| W.8 | Gather information from print and digital sources; assess the credibility of sources; quote or paraphrase while avoiding plagiarism and following a standard format for citation | W8 pp. 134–139 |
| W.9 | Draw evidence from literary or informational texts to support analysis, reflection, and research | W9 pp. 140–147 |
| W.10 | Write routinely over extended and shorter time frames for a range of tasks, purposes, and audiences | W10 pp. 148–153 |
| **Speaking and Listening** | | |
| SL.1 | Engage effectively in a range of collaborative discussions with diverse partners, building on others' ideas and expressing their own clearly | SL1 pp. 158–163 |
| SL.2 | Analyze the purpose of information presented in diverse media and formats and evaluate the motives behind its presentation | SL2 pp. 164–169 |
| SL.3 | Delineate a speaker's argument and specific claims evaluating the soundness of the reasoning and the relevance and sufficiency of the evidence and identifying when irrelevant evidence is introduced | SL3 pp. 170–175 |
| SL.4 | Present claims and findings, emphasizing salient points in a focused coherent manner; use appropriate eye contact, adequate volume, and clear pronunciation | SL4 pp. 176–181 |
| SL.5 | Integrate multimedia components and visual displays into presentations to clarify information, strengthen claims and findings, and add interest | SL5 pp. 182–187 |
| SL.6 | Adapt speech to a variety of contexts and tasks, demonstrating command of formal English when appropriate | SL6 pp. 188–193 |
| **Language** | | |
| L.1 | Demonstrate command of the conventions of standard English grammar and usage when writing or speaking | L1 pp. 198–203 |
| L.2 | Demonstrate command of the conventions of standard English capitalization, punctuation, and spelling when writing | L2 pp. 204–209 |
| L.3 | Use knowledge of language and its conventions when writing, speaking, reading, or listening | L3 pp. 210–215 |
| L.4 | Determine or clarify the meaning of unknown and multiple-meaning words and phrases, choosing flexibly from an array of strategies | L4 pp. 216–221 |
| L.5 | Demonstrate understanding of figurative language, word relationships, and nuances in word meanings | L5 pp. 222–227 |
| L.6 | Acquire and use accurately general academic, and domain-specific words and phrases | L6 pp. 228–233 |
| **Reading History/Social Studies** | | |
| RH.1 | Cite textual evidence to support analysis of primary and secondary sources | R1 pp. 6–11 |
| RH.2 | Determine the central ideas or information of a primary or secondary source; provide an objective summary | R2 pp. 12–19 |
| RH.3 | Identify key steps in a text's description of a process related to history/social studies | R3 pp. 20–25 |

*(Continued)*

| Utah Strand/Standard | Focus of Utah Standard | For More Information |
|---|---|---|
| **Reading History/Social Studies** | | |
| RH.4 | Determine the meaning of words and phrases as they are used in a text, including vocabulary specific to history/social studies | R4 pp. 26–33 |
| RH.5 | Describe how a text presents information | R5 pp. 34–39 |
| RH.6 | Identify aspects of a text that reveal an author's point of view or purpose | R6 pp. 40–47 |
| RH.7 | Integrate visual information with other information in print and digital texts | R7 pp. 48–55 |
| RH.8 | Distinguish among fact, opinion, and reasoned judgment in a text | R8 pp. 56–63 |
| RH.9 | Analyze the relationship between a primary and secondary source on the same topic | R9 pp. 64–71 |
| RH.10 | Read and comprehend history/social studies texts of appropriate complexity independently with proficiency | R10 pp. 72–77 |
| **Reading Science/Technical Subjects** | | |
| RST.1 | Cite textual evidence to support analysis of science and technical texts | R1 pp. 6–11 |
| RST.2 | Determine the central ideas or conclusions of a text; provide an objective summary | R2 pp. 12–19 |
| RST.3 | Follow precisely a multistep procedure when carrying out experiments, taking measurements, or performing technical tasks | R3 pp. 20–25 |
| RST.4 | Determine the meaning of symbols, key terms, and other domain-specific words and phrases | R4 pp. 26–33 |
| RST.5 | Analyze the structure an author uses to organize a text, including how the major sections contribute to the whole | R5 pp. 34–39 |
| RST.6 | Analyze the author's purpose in providing an explanation, describing a procedure, or discussing an experiment | R6 pp. 40–47 |
| RST.7 | Integrate quantitative or technical information expressed in words with a version of the information expressed visually | R7 pp. 48–55 |
| RST.8 | Distinguish among facts, reasoned judgment based on research findings, and speculation in a text | R8 pp. 56–63 |
| RST.9 | Compare and contrast the information gained from experiments, simulations, video, or multimedia sources with that gained from reading a text on the same topic | R9 pp. 64–71 |
| RST.10 | Read and comprehend appropriately complex science/technical texts independently and proficiently | R10 pp. 72–77 |
| **Writing History/Social Studies and Science/Technical Subjects** | | |
| WHST.1 | Write arguments based on discipline-specific content | W1 pp. 82–89 |
| WHST.2 | Write informative/explanatory texts including the narration of historical events, scientific procedures/experiments, or technical processes | W2 pp. 90–99 |
| WHST.3 | NA | |
| WHST.4 | Produce writing in which the development, organization, and style are appropriate to the task, purpose, and audience | W4 pp. 110–115 |
| WHST.5 | Develop and strengthen writing as needed by planning, revising, editing, rewriting, or trying a new approach | W5 pp. 116–121 |
| WHST.6 | Use technology to produce and publish writing as well as to interact with others; demonstrate keyboarding skills | W6 pp. 122–127 |
| WHST.7 | Conduct short research projects to answer a question, drawing on several sources and refocusing the inquiry when appropriate | W7 pp. 128–133 |
| WHST.8 | Gather information from print and digital sources; assess the credibility of sources; quote or paraphrase while avoiding plagiarism and providing basic bibliographic information | W8 pp. 134–139 |
| WHST.9 | Draw evidence from informational texts to support analysis, reflection, and research | W9 pp. 140–147 |
| WHST.10 | Write routinely over extended and shorter time frames for a range of tasks, purposes, and audiences | W10 pp. 148–153 |

# Virginia, Grade 6

| Virginia Strand/Standard | Focus of Virginia Standard | For More Information |
|---|---|---|
| **Speaking, Listening, Media Literacy** | | |
| 6.1 | Participate in and contribute to small-group activities | SL1 pp. 158–163 |
| 6.2 | Present, listen critically, and express opinions in oral presentations | SL4 pp. 176–181 SL5 pp. 158–163 SL6 pp. 164–169 |
| 6.3 | Understand the elements of medial literacy | SL2 pp. 164–169 SL3 pp. 176–181 |
| **Reading** | | |
| 6.4 | Read and learn meanings of unfamiliar words and phrases within authentic texts | R4 pp. 26–33 L4 pp. 216–221 L5 pp. 222–227 L6 pp. 228–231 |
| 6.5 | Read and demonstrate comprehension of fictional texts, narrative nonfiction, and poetry | |
| | • Identify the elements of narrative structure; explain how character and plot development are used | R3 pp. 20–25 |
| | • Make, confirm, and revise predictions; draw conclusions and make inferences | R1 pp. 6–11 |
| | • Identify main idea and supporting details | R2 pp. 12–19 |
| | • Analyze the author's use of figurative language; describe how word choice and imagery contribute to meaning | R4 pp. 26–33 |
| | • Identify transitional words and phrases that signal an organizational pattern | R5 pp. 34–39 |
| | • Use reading strategies throughout the reading process to monitor comprehension | R10 pp. 60–65 |
| | • Describe the impact of cause and effect relationships and their impact on plot | R3 pp. 20–25 |
| 6.6 | Read and demonstrate comprehension of nonfiction texts | |
| | • Use text structures such as type, headings, and graphics to predict and categorize information in texts | R7 pp. 42–47 |
| | • Identify the main idea and summarize supporting details | R2 pp. 12–19 |
| | • Identify questions to be asked; make revise, confirm predictions | R1 pp. 6–11 |
| | • Compare and contrast information about one topic which may be contained in different selections | R9 pp. 64–69 |
| | • Identify author's organizational patterns | R5 pp. 34–39 |
| | • Identify cause and effect relationships; differentiate between fact and opinion | R8 pp. 56–63 |
| | • Use reading strategies to monitor comprehension throughout the reading process | R10 pp. 60–65 |
| **Writing** | | |
| 6.7 | Write narration, description, exposition, and persuasion | W1 pp. 82–89 W2 pp. 90–99 W3 pp. 100–109 W4 pp. 110–115 W5 pp. 116–121 |
| 6.8 | Edit writing for correct grammar, capitalization, spelling, punctuation, sentence structure, and paragraphing | L1 pp. 198–203 L2 pp. 204–209 |
| **Research** | | |
| 6.9 | Find, evaluate, and select appropriate resources for a research project | W6 pp. 122–127 W7 pp. 128–133 W8 pp. 134–139 |

# Virginia, Grade 7

| Virginia Strand/Standard | Focus of Virginia Standard | For More Information |
|---|---|---|
| **Speaking, Listening, Media Literacy** | | |
| 7.1 | Participate in and contribute to conversations, group discussions, and oral presentations | SL1 pp. 158–163<br>SL4 pp. 176–181 |
| 7.2 | Identify and demonstrate the relationship between a speaker's verbal and nonverbal messages | SL2 pp. 164–169 |
| 7.3 | Understand the elements of medial literacy | SL2 pp. 164–169<br>SL3 pp. 176–181<br>SL5 pp. 182–187 |
| **Reading** | | |
| 7.4 | Read to determine the meanings and pronunciations of unfamiliar words and phrases within authentic texts | R4 pp. 26–33<br>L4 pp. 216–221<br>L5 pp. 222–227<br>L6 pp. 228–231 |
| 7.5 | Read and demonstrate comprehension of fictional texts, narrative nonfiction, and poetry | |
| | • Describe the elements of narrative structure | R3 pp. 20–25 |
| | • Make, confirm, and revise predictions; draw conclusions and make inferences | R1 pp. 6–11 |
| | • Identify main idea and supporting details | R2 pp. 12–19 |
| | • Describe the impact of word choice, imagery, and literary devices | R4 pp. 26–33 |
| | • Identify the author's organizational pattern | R5 pp. 34–39 |
| | • Use reading strategies throughout the reading process to monitor comprehension | R10 pp. 60–65 |
| | • Compare and contrast various forms and genres of fictional text | R7 pp. 48–55 |
| 7.6 | Read and demonstrate comprehension of nonfiction texts | |
| | • Use text structures to aid comprehension | R7 pp. 42–47 |
| | • Identify the main idea and summarize supporting details | R2 pp. 12–19 |
| | • Draw conclusions and make inferences | R1 pp. 6–11 |
| | • Identify the source, viewpoint, and purpose of texts | R6 pp. 40–47 |
| | • Identify author's organizational patterns | R5 pp. 34–39 |
| | • Identify cause and effect relationships; differentiate between fact and opinion | R8 pp. 56–63 |
| | • Use reading strategies to monitor comprehension throughout the reading process | R10 pp. 60–65 |
| **Writing** | | |
| 7.7 | Write narration, description, exposition, and persuasion | W1 pp. 82–89<br>W2 pp. 90–99<br>W3 pp. 100–109<br>W4 pp. 110–115<br>W5 pp. 116–121 |
| 7.8 | Edit writing for correct grammar, capitalization, spelling, punctuation, sentence structure, and paragraphing | L1 pp. 198–203<br>L2 pp. 204–209 |
| **Research** | | |
| 7.9 | Find, evaluate, and select appropriate resources for a research project | W6 pp. 122–127<br>W7 pp. 128–133<br>W8 pp. 134–139 |

# Virginia, Grade 8

| Virginia Strand/Standard | Focus of Virginia Standard | For More Information |
|---|---|---|
| **Speaking, Listening, Media Literacy** | | |
| 8.1 | Use interviewing techniques to gain information | SL1 pp. 158–163<br>SL3 pp. 176–181 |
| 8.2 | Develop and deliver oral presentations | SL4 pp. 176–181<br>SL5 pp. 182–187<br>SL6 pp. 188–193 |
| 8.3 | Analyze, develop, and produce creative or informational media messages | SL2 pp. 164–169<br>SL3 pp. 176–181<br>SL5 pp. 182–187 |
| **Reading** | | |
| 8.4 | Apply knowledge of word origins, analogies, and figurative language to extend vocabulary development | R4 pp. 26–33<br>L4 pp. 216–221<br>L5 pp. 222–227<br>L6 pp. 228–231 |
| 8.5 | Read and analyze a variety of fictional texts, narrative nonfiction, and poetry | |
| | • Explain how authors use characters, conflict, point of view, voice, and tone | R3 pp. 20–25 |
| | • Understand the author's use of conventional elements and characteristics within a variety of genres | R9 pp. 64–71 |
| | • Make inferences and draw conclusions, using evidence from the text as support | R1 pp. 6–11 |
| | • Identify main idea and summarize using supporting details | R2 pp. 12–19 |
| | • Identify and ask questions that clarify various viewpoints | R6 pp. 40–47 |
| | • Identify the author's organizational pattern | R5 pp. 34–39 |
| | • Use reading strategies throughout the reading process to monitor comprehension | R10 pp. 60–65 |
| | • Compare and contrast various forms and genres of fictional text | R7 pp. 48–55 |
| 8.6 | Read, comprehend, and analyze a variety of nonfiction texts | |
| | • Identify the main idea and summarize the text using supporting details | R2 pp. 12–19 |
| | • Draw conclusions and make inferences using evidence from the text as support | R1 pp. 6–11 |
| | • Analyze the author's qualifications, viewpoint, and impact | R6 pp. 40–47 |
| | • Analyze the author's use of text structures and word choice | R5 pp. 34–39 |
| | • Identify cause and effect relationships; differentiate between fact and opinion | R8 pp. 56–63 |
| | • Use reading strategies to monitor comprehension throughout the reading process | R10 pp. 60–65 |
| **Writing** | | |
| 8.7 | Write in a variety of forms, including narration, exposition, persuasion, and informational | W1 pp. 82–89<br>W2 pp. 90–99<br>W3 pp. 100–109<br>W4 pp. 110–115<br>W5 pp. 116–121 |
| 8.8 | Edit writing for correct grammar, capitalization, spelling, punctuation, sentence structure, and paragraphing | L1 pp. 198–203<br>L2 pp. 204–209 |
| **Research** | | |
| 8.9 | Apply knowledge of appropriate reference materials to produce a research product | W6 pp. 122–127<br>W7 pp. 128–133<br>W8 pp. 134–139 |

# West Virginia, Grade 6

| West Virginia Strand/Standard | Focus of West Virginia Standard | For More Information |
|---|---|---|
| **Reading Literature** | | |
| R.C1.1 | Cite textual evidence to support analysis of what the text says explicitly as well as inferences drawn from the text | R1 pp. 6–11 |
| R.C1.2 | Determine the theme or central idea of a text and how it is conveyed through particular details; provide an objective summary | R2 pp. 12–19 |
| R.C1.3 | Describe how a particular plot unfolds in a series of episodes as well as how the characters respond or change | R3 pp. 20–25 |
| R.C2.1 | Determine the meaning of words and phrases as they are used in a text, including figurative and connotative meanings | R4 pp. 26–33 |
| R.C2.2 | Analyze how a particular sentence, chapter, scene, or stanza fits into the overall structure of a text and contributes to the development of the theme, setting, or plot | R5 pp. 34–39 |
| R.C2.3 | Explain how an author develops the point of view of the narrator or speaker in a text | R6 pp. 40–47 |
| R.C3.1 | Compare and contrast the experience of reading a story, drama, or poem to listening to or viewing an audio, video, or live version of the text | R7 pp. 48–55 |
| R.C3.2 | Compare and contrast texts in different forms or genres in terms of their approaches to similar themes and topics | R9 pp. 64–71 |
| R.C4.1 | Read and comprehend literature of appropriate complexity independently with proficiency | R10 pp. 72–77 |
| **Reading Informational Text** | | |
| R.C1.4 | Cite textual evidence to support analysis of what the text says explicitly as well as inferences drawn from the text | R1 pp. 6–11 |
| R.C1.5 | Determine a central idea of a text and how it is conveyed through particular details; provide an objective summary | R2 pp. 12–19 |
| R.C1.6 | Analyze in detail how a key individual, event, or idea is introduced, illustrated, and elaborated in a text | R3 pp. 20–25 |
| R.C2.4 | Determine the meaning of words and phrases as they are used in a text, including figurative, connotative, and technical meanings | R4 pp. 26–33 |
| R.C2.5 | Analyze how a particular sentence, chapter, scene, or section fits into the overall structure of a text and contributes to the development of the ideas | R5 pp. 34–39 |
| R.C2.6 | Determine an author's point of view or purpose in a text and explain how it is conveyed in the text | R6 pp. 40–47 |
| R.C3.3 | Integrate information presented in different media or formats as well as in words to develop a coherent understanding of a topic or issue | R7 pp. 48–55 |
| R.C3.4 | Trace and evaluate the argument and specific claims, distinguishing claims that are supported by reasons and evidence from claims that are not | R8 pp. 56–63 |
| R.C3.5 | Compare and contrast one author's presentation of events with that of another | R9 pp. 64–71 |
| R.C4.2 | Read and comprehend appropriately complex literary nonfiction, informational, and functional texts independently and proficiently | R10 pp. 72–77 |
| **Writing** | | |
| W.C9.1 | Write arguments to support claims with clear reasons and relevant evidence | W1 pp. 82–89 |
| W.C9.2 | Write informative/explanatory texts to examine a topic and convey ideas, concepts, and information clearly | W2 pp. 90–99 |
| W.C9.3 | Write narratives to develop real or imagined experiences or events using effective technique, descriptive details, and well-structured event sequences | W3 pp. 100–109 |
| W.C10.1 | Produce writing in which the development, organization, and style are appropriate to the task, purpose, and audience | W4 pp. 110–115 |
| W.C10.2 | Develop and strengthen writing as needed by planning, revising, editing, rewriting, or trying a new approach | W5 pp. 116–121 |
| W.C10.3 | Use technology to produce and publish writing as well as to interact with others; demonstrate keyboarding skills | W6 pp. 122–127 |
| W.C11.1 | Conduct short research projects to answer a question, drawing on several sources and refocusing the inquiry when appropriate | W7 pp. 128–133 |

| West Virginia Strand/Standard | Focus of West Virginia Standard | For More Information |
|---|---|---|
| **Writing** | | |
| W.C11.2 | Gather information from print and digital sources; assess the credibility of sources; quote or paraphrase while avoiding plagiarism and providing basic bibliographic information | W8 pp. 134–139 |
| W.C11.3 | Draw evidence from literary or informational texts to support analysis, reflection, and research | W9 pp. 140–147 |
| W.C12.1 | Write routinely over extended and shorter time frames for a range of tasks, purposes, and audiences | W10 pp. 148–153 |
| **Speaking and Listening** | | |
| SL.C13.1 | Engage effectively in a range of collaborative discussions with diverse partners, building on others' ideas and expressing their own clearly | SL1 pp. 158–163 |
| SL.C13.2 | Interpret information presented in diverse media and formats and explain how it contributes to a topic, text, or issue under study | SL2 pp. 164–169 |
| SL.C13.3 | Delineate a speaker's argument and specific claims that are supported by reasons and evidence from claims that are not | SL3 pp. 170–175 |
| SL.C14.1 | Present claims and findings, sequencing ideas logically and using descriptions, facts, or details to accentuate main ideas or themes; use appropriate eye contact, adequate volume, and clear pronunciation | SL4 pp. 176–181 |
| SL.C14.2 | Include multimedia components and visual displays in presentations to clarify information | SL5 pp. 182–187 |
| SL.C14.3 | Adapt speech to a variety of contexts and tasks, demonstrating command of formal English when appropriate | SL6 pp. 188–193 |
| **Language** | | |
| L.C15.1 | Demonstrate command of the conventions of standard English grammar and usage when writing or speaking | L1 pp. 198–203 |
| L.C15.2 | Demonstrate command of the conventions of standard English capitalization, punctuation, and spelling when writing | L2 pp. 204–209 |
| L.C16.1 | Use knowledge of language and its conventions when writing, speaking, reading, or listening | L3 pp. 210–215 |
| L.C17.1 | Determine or clarify the meaning of unknown and multiple-meaning words and phrases, choosing flexibly from an array of strategies | L4 pp. 216–221 |
| L.C17.2 | Demonstrate understanding of figurative language, word relationships, and nuances in word meanings | L5 pp. 222–227 |
| L.C17.3 | Acquire and use accurately general academic, and domain-specific words and phrases | L6 pp. 228–233 |

# West Virginia, Grade 7

| West Virginia Strand/Standard | Focus of West Virginia Standard | For More Information |
|---|---|---|
| **Reading Literature** | | |
| R.C1.1 | Cite several pieces of textual evidence to support analysis of what the text says explicitly as well as inferences drawn from the text | R1 pp. 6–11 |
| R.C1.2 | Determine the theme or central idea of a text and analyze its development; provide an objective summary of the text | R2 pp. 12–19 |
| R.C1.3 | Analyze how particular elements of a story or drama interact | R3 pp. 20–25 |
| R.C2.1 | Determine the meaning of words and phrases as they are used in a text, including figurative and connotative meanings | R4 pp. 26–33 |
| R.C2.2 | Analyze how a drama's or poem's form or structure contributes to its meaning | R5 pp. 34–39 |
| R.C2.3 | Analyze how an author develops and contrasts the points of view of different characters or narrators in a text | R6 pp. 40–47 |
| R.C3.1 | Compare and contrast a written story, drama, or poem to its audio, filmed, staged, or multimedia version | R7 pp. 48–55 |

*(Continued)*

| West Virginia Strand/Standard | Focus of West Virginia Standard | For More Information |
|---|---|---|
| **Reading Literature** | | |
| R.C3.2 | Compare and contrast a fictional portrayal of a time, place, or character and a historical account of the same period | R9 pp. 64–71 |
| R.C4.1 | Read and comprehend literature of appropriate complexity independently with proficiency | R10 pp. 72–77 |
| **Reading Informational Text** | | |
| R.C1.4 | Cite several pieces of textual evidence to support analysis of what the text says explicitly as well as inferences drawn from the text | R1 pp. 6–11 |
| R.C1.5 | Determine two or more central ideas in a text and analyze their developments; provide an objective summary of the text | R2 pp. 12–19 |
| R.C1.6 | Analyze the interactions between individuals, events, and ideas in a text | R3 pp. 20–25 |
| R.C2.4 | Determine the meaning of words and phrases as they are used in a text, including figurative, connotative, and technical meanings | R4 pp. 26–33 |
| R.C2.5 | Analyze the structure an author uses to organize a text, including how the major sections contribute to the whole | R5 pp. 34–39 |
| R.C2.6 | Determine an author's point of view or purpose in a text and analyze how the author distinguishes his or her position from that of others | R6 pp. 40–47 |
| R.C3.3 | Compare and contrast a text to an audio, video, or multimedia version of the text | R7 pp. 48–55 |
| R.C3.4 | Trace and evaluate the argument and specific claims in a text, assessing whether the reason is sound and the evidence is relevant and sufficient | R8 pp. 56–63 |
| R.C3.5 | Analyze how two or more authors writing about the same topic shape their presentations of key information | R9 pp. 64–71 |
| R.C4.2 | Read and comprehend appropriately complex literary nonfiction, informational, and functional texts independently and proficiently | R10 pp. 72–77 |
| **Writing** | | |
| W.C9.1 | Write arguments to support claims with clear reasons and relevant evidence | W1 pp. 82–89 |
| W.C9.2 | Write informative/explanatory texts to examine a topic and convey ideas, concepts, and information clearly | W2 pp. 90–99 |
| W.C9.3 | Write narratives to develop real or imagined experiences or events using effective technique, descriptive details, and well-structured event sequences | W3 pp. 100–109 |
| W.C10.1 | Produce writing in which the development, organization, and style are appropriate to the task, purpose, and audience | W4 pp. 110–115 |
| W.C10.2 | Develop and strengthen writing as needed by planning, revising, editing, rewriting, or trying a new approach | W5 pp. 116–121 |
| W.C10.3 | Use technology to produce and publish writing, link to and cite sources; interact and collaborate with others | W6 pp. 122–127 |
| W.C11.1 | Conduct short research projects to answer a question, drawing on several sources and generating additional related questions for further investigation | W7 pp. 128–133 |
| W.C11.2 | Gather information from print and digital sources; assess the credibility of sources; quote or paraphrase while avoiding plagiarism and following a standard format for citation | W8 pp. 134–139 |
| W.C11.3 | Draw evidence from literary or informational texts to support analysis, reflection, and research | W9 pp. 140–147 |
| W.C12.1 | Write routinely over extended and shorter time frames for a range of tasks, purposes, and audiences | W10 pp. 148–153 |
| **Speaking and Listening** | | |
| SL.C13.1 | Engage effectively in a range of collaborative discussions with diverse partners, building on others' ideas and expressing their own clearly | SL1 pp. 158–163 |
| SL.C13.2 | Analyze the main ideas and supporting details presented in diverse media and formats and explain how the ideas clarify a topic, text, or issue under study | SL2 pp. 164–169 |
| SL.C13.3 | Delineate a speaker's argument and specific claims evaluating the soundness of the reasoning and the relevance and sufficiency of the evidence | SL3 pp. 170–175 |
| SL.C14.1 | Present claims and findings, emphasizing salient points in a focused coherent manner; use appropriate eye contact, adequate volume, and clear pronunciation | SL4 pp. 176–181 |
| SL.C14.2 | Include multimedia components and visual displays in presentations to clarify claims and findings | SL5 pp. 182–187 |
| SL.C14.3 | Adapt speech to a variety of contexts and tasks, demonstrating command of formal English when appropriate | SL6 pp. 188–193 |

| West Virginia Strand/Standard | Focus of West Virginia Standard | For More Information |
|---|---|---|
| **Language** | | |
| L.C15.1 | Demonstrate command of the conventions of standard English grammar and usage when writing or speaking | L1 pp. 198–203 |
| L.C15.2 | Demonstrate command of the conventions of standard English capitalization, punctuation, and spelling when writing | L2 pp. 204–209 |
| L.C16.1 | Use knowledge of language and its conventions when writing, speaking, reading, or listening | L3 pp. 210–215 |
| L.C17.1 | Determine or clarify the meaning of unknown and multiple-meaning words and phrases, choosing flexibly from an array of strategies | L4 pp. 216–221 |
| L.C17.2 | Demonstrate understanding of figurative language, word relationships, and nuances in word meanings | L5 pp. 222–227 |
| L.C17.3 | Acquire and use accurately general academic, and domain-specific words and phrases | L6 pp. 228–233 |

# West Virginia, Grade 8

| West Virginia Strand/Standard | Focus of West Virginia Standard | For More Information |
|---|---|---|
| **Reading Literature** | | |
| R.C1.1 | Cite the textual evidence that most strongly supports an analysis of what the text says explicitly as well as inferences drawn from the text | R1 pp. 6–11 |
| R.C1.2 | Determine the theme or central idea of a text and analyze its development, including its relationship to the characters, setting, and plot; provide an objective summary of the text | R2 pp. 12–19 |
| R.C1.3 | Analyze how particular lines of dialogue or incidents in a story or drama propel the action, reveal aspects of a character, or provoke a decision | R3 pp. 20–25 |
| R.C2.1 | Determine the meaning of words and phrases as they are used in a text, including figurative and connotative meanings | R4 pp. 26–33 |
| R.C2.2 | Compare and contrast the structure of two or more texts and analyze how the differing structure of each contributes to its meaning and style | R5 pp. 34–39 |
| R.C2.3 | Analyze how differences in the points of view of the characters and the audience or reader create such effects as suspense or humor | R6 pp. 40–47 |
| R.C3.1 | Analyze the extent to which a filmed or live production of a story or drama stays faithful or departs from the text or script | R7 pp. 48–55 |
| R.C3.2 | Analyze how a modern work of fiction draws on themes, patterns of events, or character types from traditional stories, describing how the material is rendered new | R9 pp. 64–71 |
| R.C4.1 | Read and comprehend literature of appropriate complexity independently with proficiency | R10 pp. 72–77 |
| **Reading Informational Text** | | |
| R.C1.4 | Cite the textual evidence that most strongly supports an analysis of what the text says explicitly as well as inferences drawn from the text | R1 pp. 6–11 |
| R.C1.5 | Determine the central idea of a text and analyze its development, including its relationship to supporting ideas; provide an objective summary of the text | R2 pp. 12–19 |
| R.C1.6 | Analyze how a text makes connections among distinctions between individuals, ideas, or events | R3 pp. 20–25 |
| R.C2.4 | Determine the meaning of words and phrases as they are used in a text, including figurative, connotative, and technical meanings | R4 pp. 26–33 |
| R.C2.5 | Analyze the structure of a specific paragraph in a text, including the role of particular sentences in developing and refining a key concept | R5 pp. 34–39 |
| R.C2.6 | Determine an author's point of view or purpose in a text and analyze how the author acknowledges and responds to conflicting evidence or viewpoints | R6 pp. 40–47 |
| R.C3.3 | Evaluate the advantages and disadvantages of using different mediums to present a particular topic or idea | R7 pp. 48–55 |

*(Continued)*

| West Virginia Strand/Standard | Focus of West Virginia Standard | For More Information |
|---|---|---|
| **Reading Informational Text** | | |
| R.C3.4 | Delineate and evaluate the argument and specific claims in a text, assessing whether the reason is sound and the evidence is relevant and sufficient | R8 pp. 56–63 |
| R.C3.5 | Analyze a case in which two or more texts provide conflicting information on the same topic | R9 pp. 64–71 |
| R.C4.2 | Read and comprehend appropriately complex literary nonfiction, informational, and functional texts independently and proficiently | R10 pp. 72–77 |
| **Writing** | | |
| W.C9.1 | Write arguments to support claims with clear reasons and relevant evidence | W1 pp. 82–89 |
| W.C9.2 | Write informative/explanatory texts to examine a topic and convey ideas, concepts, and information clearly | W2 pp. 90–99 |
| W.C9.3 | Write narratives to develop real or imagined experiences or events using effective technique, descriptive details, and well-structured event sequences | W3 pp. 100–109 |
| W.C10.1 | Produce writing in which the development, organization, and style are appropriate to the task, purpose, and audience | W4 pp. 110–115 |
| W.C10.2 | Develop and strengthen writing as needed by planning, revising, editing, rewriting, or trying a new approach | W5 pp. 116–121 |
| W.C10.3 | Use technology to produce and publish writing, link to and cite sources; interact and collaborate with others | W6 pp. 122–127 |
| W.C11.1 | Conduct short research projects to answer a question, drawing on several sources and generating additional related questions for further investigation | W7 pp. 128–133 |
| W.C11.2 | Gather information from print and digital sources; assess the credibility of sources; quote or paraphrase while avoiding plagiarism and following a standard format for citation | W8 pp. 134–139 |
| W.C11.3 | Draw evidence from literary or informational texts to support analysis, reflection, and research | W9 pp. 140–147 |
| W.C12.1 | Write routinely over extended and shorter time frames for a range of tasks, purposes, and audiences | W10 pp. 148–153 |
| **Speaking and Listening** | | |
| SL.C13.1 | Engage effectively in a range of collaborative discussions with diverse partners, building on others' ideas and expressing their own clearly | SL1 pp. 158–163 |
| SL.C13.2 | Analyze the purpose of information presented in diverse media and formats and evaluate the motives behind its presentation | SL2 pp. 164–169 |
| SL.C13.3 | Delineate a speaker's argument and specific claims evaluating the soundness of the reasoning and the relevance and sufficiency of the evidence and identifying when irrelevant evidence is introduced | SL3 pp. 170–175 |
| SL.C14.1 | Present claims and findings, emphasizing salient points in a focused coherent manner; use appropriate eye contact, adequate volume, and clear pronunciation | SL4 pp. 176–181 |
| SL.C14.2 | Integrate multimedia components and visual displays into presentations to clarify information, strengthen claims and findings, and add interest | SL5 pp. 182–187 |
| SL.C14.3 | Adapt speech to a variety of contexts and tasks, demonstrating command of formal English when appropriate | SL6 pp. 188–193 |
| **Language** | | |
| L.C15.1 | Demonstrate command of the conventions of standard English grammar and usage when writing or speaking | L1 pp. 198–203 |
| L.C15.2 | Demonstrate command of the conventions of standard English capitalization, punctuation, and spelling when writing | L2 pp. 204–209 |
| L.C16.1 | Use knowledge of language and its conventions when writing, speaking, reading, or listening | L3 pp. 210–215 |
| L.C17.1 | Determine or clarify the meaning of unknown and multiple-meaning words and phrases, choosing flexibly from an array of strategies | L4 pp. 216–221 |
| L.C17.2 | Demonstrate understanding of figurative language, word relationships, and nuances in word meanings | L5 pp. 222–227 |
| L.C17.3 | Acquire and use accurately general academic, and domain-specific words and phrases | L6 pp. 228–233 |

# The Complete Common Core State Standards: Decoded

# Part 1

# The Common Core State Standards

## Reading

# College and Career Readiness Anchor Standards for
# *Reading 6–8*

**Source: Common Core State Standards**

The grades 6–12 standards on the following pages define what students should understand and be able to do by the end of each grade. They correspond to the College and Career Readiness (CCR) anchor standards by number. The CCR and grade-specific standards are necessary complements—the former providing broad standards, the latter providing additional specificity—that together define the skills and understandings that all students must demonstrate.

## Key Ideas and Details

1. Read closely to determine what the text says explicitly and to make logical inferences from it; cite specific textual evidence when writing or speaking to support conclusions drawn from the text.
2. Determine central ideas or themes of a text and analyze their development; summarize the key supporting details and ideas.
3. Analyze how and why individuals, events, and ideas develop and interact over the course of a text.

## Craft and Structure

4. Interpret words and phrases as they are used in a text, including determining technical, connotative, and figurative meanings, and analyze how specific word choices shape meaning or tone.
5. Analyze the structure of texts, including how specific sentences, paragraphs, and larger portions of the text (e.g., a section, chapter, scene, or stanza) relate to one another and the whole.
6. Assess how point of view or purpose shapes the content and style of a text.

## Integration of Knowledge and Ideas

7. Integrate and evaluate content presented in diverse formats and media, including visually and quantitatively, as well as in words.*
8. Delineate and evaluate the argument and specific claims in a text, including the validity of the reasoning as well as the relevance and sufficiency of the evidence.
9. Analyze how two or more texts address similar themes or topics to build knowledge or to compare the approaches the authors take.

## Range of Reading and Level of Text Complexity

10. Read and comprehend complex literary and informational texts independently and proficiently.

## Note on Range and Content of Student Reading

To become college and career ready, students must grapple with works of exceptional craft and thought whose range extends across genres, cultures, and centuries. Such works offer profound insights into the human condition and serve as models for students' thinking and writing. Along with high-quality contemporary works, these texts should be chosen from among seminal U.S. documents, the classics of American literature, and the timeless dramas of Shakespeare. Through wide and deep reading of literature and literary nonfiction of steadily increasing sophistication, students gain a reservoir of literary and cultural knowledge, references, and images; the ability to evaluate intricate arguments; and the capacity to surmount the challenges posed by complex texts.

* Please consult the full Common Core State Standards document (and all updates and appendices) at http://www.corestandards.org/ELA-Literacy. See "Research to Build Knowledge" in the Writing section and "Comprehension and Collaboration" in the Speaking and Listening section for additional standards relevant to gathering, assessing, and applying information from print and digital sources.

# College and Career Readiness Anchor Standards for

## *Reading*

The College and Career Readiness (CCR) anchor standards are the same for all middle and high school students, regardless of subject area or grade level. What varies is the specific content at each grade level, most notably the level of complexity of the texts, skills, and knowledge at each subsequent grade level in each disciplinary domain. The guiding principle here is that the core reading skills should not change as students advance; rather, the level at which they learn and can perform those skills should increase in complexity as students move from one grade to the next.

## Key Ideas and Details

This first strand of reading standards emphasizes students' ability to identify key ideas and themes in a text, whether literary, informational, primary, or foundational and whether in print, graphic, quantitative, or mixed media formats. The focus of this first set of standards is on *reading to understand*, during which students focus on *what* the text says. The premise is that students cannot delve into the deeper (implicit) meaning of any text if they cannot first grasp the surface (explicit) meaning of that text. Beyond merely identifying these ideas, readers must learn to see how these ideas and themes, or the story's characters and events, develop and evolve over the course of a text. Such reading demands that students know how to identify, evaluate, assess, and analyze the elements of a text for their importance, function, and meaning within the text.

## Craft and Structure

The second set of standards builds on the first, focusing not on *what* the text says but *how* it says it, the emphasis here being on analyzing how texts are made to serve a function or achieve a purpose. These standards ask readers to examine the choices the author makes in words and sentence and paragraph structure and how these choices contribute to the meaning of the text and the author's larger purpose. Inherent in the study of craft and structure is how these elements interact with and influence the ideas and details outlined in the first three standards.

## Integration of Knowledge and Ideas

This third strand might be summed up as *reading to extend or deepen one's knowledge* of a subject by comparing what a range of sources have said about it over time and across different media. In addition, these standards emphasize the importance of being able to read the arguments; that is, they look at how to identify the claims the texts make and evaluate the evidence used to support those claims regardless of the media. Finally, these standards ask students to analyze the choice of means and medium the author chooses and the effect those choices have on ideas and details. Thus, if a writer integrates words, images, and video in a mixed media text, readers should be able to examine how and why the author did that for stylistic and rhetorical purposes.

## Range of Reading and Level of Text Complexity

The Common Core State Standards document itself offers the most useful explanation of what this last standard means in a footnote titled "Note on range and content of student reading," which accompanies the reading standards:

> To become college and career ready, students must grapple with works of exceptional craft and thought whose range extends across genres, cultures, and centuries. Such works offer profound insights into the human condition and serve as models for students' own thinking and writing. Along with high-quality contemporary works, these texts should be chosen from among seminal U.S. documents, the classics of American literature, and the timeless dramas of Shakespeare. Through wide and deep reading of literature and literary nonfiction of steadily increasing sophistication, students gain a reservoir of literary and cultural knowledge, references, and images; the ability to evaluate intricate arguments; and the capacity to surmount the challenges posed by complex texts. (CCSS 2010, p. 35)

**Reading 1:** Read closely to determine what the text says explicitly and to make logical inferences from it; cite specific textual evidence when writing or speaking to support conclusions drawn from the text.

## Literature

**6** Cite textual evidence to support analysis of what the text says explicitly as well as inferences drawn from the text.

**7** Cite **several pieces** of textual evidence to support analysis of what the text says explicitly as well as inferences drawn from the text.

**8** Cite the textual evidence **that most strongly** supports an analysis of what the text says explicitly as well as inferences drawn from the text.

## Informational Text

**6** Cite textual evidence to support analysis of what the text says explicitly as well as inferences drawn from the text.

**7** Cite **several pieces** of textual evidence to support analysis of what the text says explicitly as well as inferences drawn from the text.

**8** Cite the textual evidence **that most strongly** supports an analysis of what the text says explicitly as well as inferences drawn from the text.

## History/Social Studies

**6** Cite specific textual evidence to support analysis of primary and secondary sources.

**7** Cite specific textual evidence to support analysis of primary and secondary sources.

**8** Cite specific textual evidence to support analysis of primary and secondary sources.

## Science/Technical Subjects

**6** Cite specific textual evidence to support analysis of science and technical texts.

**7** Cite specific textual evidence to support analysis of science and technical texts.

**8** Cite specific textual evidence to support analysis of science and technical texts.

## What the **Student** Does

### Literature

**6** **Gist:** Say what happens or is said in the text, citing a piece of evidence from the text that supports your inference.

- What happens or is said in this text?
- What piece of evidence supports your inference as to the explicit meaning of the text?

**7** **Gist:** Say what happens or is said in the text, citing several pieces of evidence from the text that support your inferences.

- What happens or is said in this text?
- What pieces of evidence support your inference as to the explicit meaning of the text?

**8** **Gist:** Say what happens or is said in the text, citing the strongest, most compelling evidence from the text itself that supports your inferences.

- What happens or is said in this text?
- What pieces of evidence provide the strongest support for your inferences?

### History/Social Studies

**6** **Gist:** Say what the primary or secondary source says, citing evidence from the text that supports your analysis.

- Is this a primary or secondary source?
- What does the text say?
- What evidence can you cite to support your analysis of the text's meaning?

**7** **Gist:** Say what the primary or secondary source says, citing evidence from the text that supports your analysis.

- Is this a primary or secondary source?
- What does the text say?
- What evidence can you cite to support your analysis of the text's meaning?

**8** **Gist:** Say what the primary or secondary source says, citing evidence from the text that supports your analysis.

- Is this a primary or secondary source?
- What does the text say?
- What evidence can you cite to support your analysis of the text's meaning?

### Informational Text

**6** **Gist:** Say what happens or is said in the text, citing a piece of evidence from the text that supports your inference.

- What happens or is said in this text?
- What piece of evidence supports your inference as to the explicit meaning of the text?

**7** **Gist:** Say what happens or is said in the text, citing several pieces of evidence from the text itself to support your inferences.

- What happens or is said in this text?
- What pieces of evidence support your inference as to the explicit meaning of the text?

**8** **Gist:** Say what happens or is said in the text, citing several pieces of evidence from the text itself to support your inferences.

- What happens or is said in this text?
- What pieces of evidence provide the strongest support for your inferences?

### Science/Technical Subjects

**6** **Gist:** Say what the scientific or technical text says, citing evidence from the text that supports your analysis.

- Is this a primary or secondary source?
- What does the text say?
- What evidence can you cite to support your analysis of the text's meaning?

**7** **Gist:** Say what the scientific or technical text says, citing evidence from the text that supports your analysis.

- Is this a primary or secondary source?
- What does the text say?
- What evidence can you cite to support your analysis of the text's meaning?

**8** **Gist:** Say what the scientific or technical text says, citing evidence from the text that supports your analysis.

- Is this a primary or secondary source?
- What does the text say?
- What evidence can you cite to support your analysis of the text's meaning?

What the **Teacher** Does

**To teach students how to "read closely," do the following:**

- Provide students access to the text—via tablet or photocopy—so they can annotate it as directed.
- Model close reading for students by thinking aloud as you go through the text with them or displaying your annotations on a tablet via an LCD projector; show them how to examine a text by scrutinizing its words, sentence structures, or any other details needed to understand its explicit meaning.
- Display the text via tablet or computer as you direct students' attention—by highlighting, circling, or otherwise drawing their attention—to specific words, sentences, or paragraphs that are essential to the meaning of the text; as you do this, ask them to explain what a word means or how it is used in that sentence, or how a specific sentence contributes to the meaning of the larger text.
- Pose questions—about words, actions, or details—that require students to look closely at the text for answers.

**To get students to determine "what the text says explicitly," do the following:**

- Ask students to "say what it *says*"—not what it means, since the emphasis here is on its literal meaning.
- Offer students an example of what it means to read explicitly and support your inferences with evidence; then tell them what a passage explicitly says, and ask them to find evidence inside the text to support their statement about its meaning.
- Give students several pieces of evidence and ask them to determine what explicit idea in the text the evidence supports.

**To develop students' ability to "cite specific textual evidence," do the following:**

- Offer them a set of samples of evidence of different degrees of specificity and quality to evaluate, requiring them to choose the one that is best and provide a rationale for their choice.
- Show students how you would choose evidence from the text to support your inference; discuss with them the questions you would ask to arrive at that selection.

**To "make logical inferences," ask students to do the following:**

- Take what they *learn* (from the text about this subject) to what they already *know* (about that subject); then *confirm* that their reasoning is sound by finding evidence that supports their inferences.
- Think aloud (with your guidance) about the process and how they make such inferences, and then have students find and use evidence to support their inferences.

**To find the textual evidence "that most strongly supports _____," do the following:**

- Create with your students—through collaborative groups or class discussion—a list of different pieces of evidence they might cite; together, develop and apply criteria by which to evaluate the different pieces to identify those which would offer the strongest, most effective support; then ask them to apply these same criteria to new evidence they find themselves as they read the rest of this article or another.

**To help your English Language Learners, try this one strategy:**

- Repeat the process used to make such inferences, verbally labeling each step as you demonstrate it; then ask them to demonstrate their ability to do it on their own or with your prompting. Post the steps (e.g., "Inferences = What You Know + What You Learned") with an example on a poster or handout they can reference on their own as needed.

*Notes*

**Academic Vocabulary:** Key Words and Phrases

**Analysis of primary and secondary sources:** Primary sources are those accounts recorded from people who witnessed or participated in the event themselves; these sources include journals, letters, and oral history recordings; secondary sources are those written by others *based on* primary sources and the opinions of scholars past and present.

**Cite specific textual evidence:** All claims, assertions, or arguments about what a text means or says require evidence from within the text itself, not the reader's opinion or experience; students should be able to quote or refer to a specific passage from the text to support their idea.

**Conclusions drawn from the text:** Readers take a group of details (different findings, series of events, related examples) and draw from them an insight or understanding about their meaning or importance within the passage or the text as a whole.

**Evidence that most strongly supports an analysis:** Evidence in general includes facts, data, quotations, and any other sources of data that support the claims writers make; in this case, however, it refers to only that evidence that "most strongly supports an analysis." Such evidence would typically be more precise, specific, and effective in its ability to back up one's analysis.

**Explicitly:** This refers to anything clearly stated in great or precise detail; it may suggest factual information or literal meaning, though not necessarily the case.

**Informational text:** These include nonfiction texts from a range of sources and written for a variety of purposes, everything from essays to advertisements, historical documents to op/ed pieces. Informational texts include written arguments as well as infographics.

**Literature:** This refers to fiction, poetry, drama, and graphic stories but also artworks such as master paintings or works by preeminent photographers.

**Logical inferences [drawn from the text]:** To infer, readers add what they *learned* from the text to what they already *know* about the subject; however, for the inference to be "logical," it must be based on evidence *from the text*.

**Primary and secondary sources:** *Primary sources* are those documents—letters, journals, oral histories, and the like—recorded by those who participated in or observed the events firsthand; *secondary sources* are those articles that draw on such primary sources and others to examine or explain events authors did not witness themselves.

**Read closely (close reading):** This refers to reading that emphasizes not only surface details but the deeper meaning and larger connections between words, sentences, and the full text; it also demands scrutiny of craft, including arguments and style used by the author.

**Several pieces of textual evidence:** Evidence is described above; this phrase refers to the act of including evidence not from several *different* texts but different pieces of textual evidence—a number of quotations, some data, several specific examples, for example—from *one* text the student is reading.

**Support analysis:** This is related to "citing textual evidence." This phrase requires readers to back up their claims about what a text says with evidence, such as examples, details, or quotations.

**Text:** In its broadest meaning, a text is whatever one is trying to read: a poem, essay, or article; in its more modern sense, a text can also be an image, an artwork, speech, or multimedia format such as a website, film, or social media message, such as a Tweet.

**Textual evidence:** Not all evidence is created equal; students need to choose those examples or quotations that provide the best example of what they are saying or most compelling quotation to support their assertion.

*Notes*

**Reading 2:** Determine central ideas or themes of a text and analyze their development; summarize the key supporting details and ideas.

## Literature

**6** Determine a theme or central idea of a text and how it is conveyed through particular details; provide a summary of the text distinct from personal opinions or judgments.

**7** Determine a theme or central idea of a text and **analyze its development over the course of the text**; provide an **objective** summary of the text.

**8** Determine a theme or central idea of a text and analyze its development over the course of the text, **including its relationship to the characters, setting, and plot**; provide an objective summary of the text.

## Informational Text

**6** Determine a central idea of a text and how it is conveyed through particular details; provide a summary of the text distinct from personal opinions or judgments.

**7** Determine **two or more** central ideas in a text and **analyze their development over the course of the text**; provide an **objective** summary of the text.

**8** Determine a central idea of a text and analyze its development over the course of the text, **including its relationship to supporting ideas**; provide an objective summary of the text.

## What the **Student** Does

| Literature | Informational Text |
|---|---|

**Literature**

**6** **Gist:** Identify a main idea or theme, examining how the author introduces and develops this idea or theme through specific details, and summarizing the text without commenting on or evaluating it.

- What key idea and theme does the author introduce and develop?
- What specific details does the author use to convey this idea?
- What details and facts must a summary of the text include (that offer no opinion or judgment)?

**7** **Gist:** Identify a main idea or theme, examining how the author introduces and develops this idea or theme throughout the text, and summarizing the text with objectivity.

- What key idea and theme does the author introduce and develop throughout?
- What specific details does the author use to convey this idea?
- What details and facts must an objective summary of the text include?

**8** **Gist:** Identify a main idea or theme, examining how the author develops it throughout, focusing on the connection between the main idea and the characters, setting, and plot, then summarizing the text with objectivity.

- What key idea and theme does the author introduce and develop throughout?
- How does the author use characters, setting, and plot to develop this theme?
- What details and facts must an objective summary of the text include?

**Informational Text**

**6** **Gist:** Identify a main idea or theme, examining how the author introduces and develops this idea or theme through specific details, and summarizing the text without commenting on or evaluating it.

- What key idea and theme does the author introduce and develop?
- What specific details does the author use to convey this idea?
- What details and facts must a summary of the text include (that offer no opinion or judgment)?

**7** **Gist:** Identify two or more big ideas in the text, analyzing how the author introduces and develops them throughout the text, and summarizing the text with objectivity.

- What central ideas does the author introduce and develop throughout?
- How does the author develop this theme or central idea throughout the text?
- What details and facts must an objective summary of the text include?

**8** **Gist:** Identify a main idea or theme, examining how the author develops it throughout, focusing on the connection between the main idea and the supporting ideas, then summarizing the text with objectivity.

- What key idea and theme does the author introduce and develop throughout?
- How does the author use supporting ideas to develop the main idea or theme?
- What details and facts must an objective summary of the text include?

**Reading 2:** Determine central ideas or themes of a text and analyze their development; summarize the key supporting details and ideas.

## History/Social Studies

**6** Determine the central ideas or information of a primary or secondary source; provide an accurate summary of the source distinct from prior knowledge or opinions.

**7** Determine the central ideas or information of a primary or secondary source; provide an accurate summary of the source distinct from prior knowledge or opinions.

**8** Determine the central ideas or information of a primary or secondary source; provide an accurate summary of the source distinct from prior knowledge or opinions.

## Science/Technical Subjects

**6** Determine the central ideas or conclusions of a text; provide an accurate summary of the text distinct from prior knowledge or opinions.

**7** Determine the central ideas or conclusions of a text; provide an accurate summary of the text distinct from prior knowledge or opinions.

**8** Determine the central ideas or conclusions of a text; provide an accurate summary of the text distinct from prior knowledge or opinions.

## What the **Student** Does

### History/Social Studies

**6** **Gist:** Identify the main ideas or information in a primary or secondary source, summarizing the text accurately and without bias.

- What type of source is this: primary or secondary?
- What key ideas or information does the author introduce and develop throughout?
- What details and information must an objective summary of the text include?

**7** **Gist:** Identify the main ideas or information in a primary or secondary source, summarizing the text accurately and without bias.

- What type of source is this: primary or secondary?
- What key ideas or information does the author introduce and develop throughout?
- What details and information must an objective summary of the text include?

**8** **Gist:** Identify the main ideas or information in a primary or secondary source, summarizing the text accurately and without bias.

- What type of source is this: primary or secondary?
- What key ideas or information does the author introduce and develop throughout?
- What details and information must an objective summary of the text include?

### Science/Technical Subjects

**6** **Gist:** Identify the main ideas or findings in the text, summarizing the text accurately and without bias.

- What is the subject of this text?
- What key ideas or conclusions does the author discuss in this text?
- What details and information must a summary of the text include (that suggest no opinion or bias)?

**7** **Gist:** Identify the main ideas or findings in the text, summarizing the text accurately and without bias.

- What is the subject of this text?
- What key ideas or conclusions does the author discuss in this text?
- What details and information must a summary of the text include (that suggest no opinion or bias)?

**8** **Gist:** Identify the main ideas or findings in the text, summarizing the text accurately and without bias.

- What is the subject of this text?
- What key ideas or conclusions does the author discuss in this text?
- What details and information must a summary of the text include (that suggest no opinion or bias)?

## What the **Teacher** Does

**To have students "determine the central ideas and themes of a text," do the following:**

- Ask students to generate all possible ideas and themes after skimming and scanning the text; then determine which of them the text most fully develops.
- Tell students to figure out which words, phrases, or images recur throughout the text that might signal they are the central idea?
- Have students consider what hints the title, sub-headings, bold words, graphics, images, or captions offer to the central ideas.
- Complete a think-aloud with students when working with new or complex texts to model the questions you ask and mental moves you make as an experienced reader of this type of text to make sense of it.

**To have students "analyze the development" of central ideas or themes, do the following:**

- Direct students to underline, label, or somehow code all the words, images, or other details related to the central ideas or themes throughout the text; then examine how their use evolves over the course of the text.
- Provide students with sentence frames ("Early on the author says X about _____, then suggests Y, finally arguing Z about _____ by the end.") or graphic organizers that help them map an idea from the beginning to the end of the text to better see how it develops (through word choice, imagery, figurative speech).
- Ask how one set of images, allusions, or ideas builds on or is otherwise related to those that precede it.
- Use a graphic organizer (e.g., one with two or more columns) to jot down the details related to each key theme, looking for patterns across the columns as you go.
- Have students monitor the author's diction and tone as they are applied to the central idea(s) over the course of the text to note when, how, and why they change.

**To have students "provide an objective summary of the text," do the following:**

- Create for (or with) your students an objectivity continuum (i.e., that goes from objective at one end to subjective at the other end, with gradations and descriptors in between); then ask them to put a word, phrase, or idea on there to measure its objectivity, taking time to discuss how they might increase objectivity by rephrasing it.
- Develop with students a continuum of importance to help them learn to evaluate which details are most important to include in a summary.
- Clarify the difference between *objective* and *subjective* by giving examples of each about a different but similar text before they attempt to write an "objective summary" of other texts.
- Have students study models of effective (and ineffective) summaries.
- Provide sentence stems typical of those used to summarize this type of text (In _____, Author X argues that _____).

**To have students "determine two or more central ideas in a text," do the following:**

- Have students skim a text to get the gist and discover what ideas the text treats most seriously and thoroughly from beginning to end; then ask them to make a list of those ideas, determining by some criteria you provide or they develop those few ideas that merit scrutiny as a result of the author's treatment throughout the text.
- Show students how to use the search function of a web browser or an ebook reader to determine (by frequency of reference, repetition of the word) how central an idea is within a text.

**To have students determine main ideas in a primary or secondary source, do the following:**

- Have them first determine whether it is a primary or secondary source so they can figure out the type of questions they should ask.
- Guide them through the features and context of such a text to show them how to determine the ideas and information most important to the original context in which it was written.

**To help your English Language Learners, try this one thing:**

- Make a point of confirming that they know the key concepts—themes, analyze, summarize, and supporting details.

**Academic Vocabulary:** Key Words and Phrases

**Accurate summary:** This identifies the key ideas, details, or events in the text and reports them with an emphasis on who did what to whom and when; in other words, the emphasis is on retelling what happened or what the text says with utmost fidelity to the text itself, thus requiring students to check what they say against what the text says happened.

**Analyze their development over the course of the text:** This refers to the careful and close examination of the parts or elements from which something is made and how those parts affect or function within the whole to create meaning.

**Conclusions of a text:** In a scientific or technical text, these might be the key discoveries located at the end of the text under a heading such as "conclusions" if the article, chapter, or report follows the conventions of a scientific report or paper.

**Conveyed through particular details:** This refers to the way authors might explore an idea (e.g., the sense of isolation that often appears throughout dystopian novels) by referring to it directly or indirectly through details that evoke the idea of such isolation.

**Determine central ideas:** Some ideas are more important to a work than are others; these are the ideas you could not cut out without fundamentally changing the meaning or quality of the text. Think of the "central ideas" of a text as you would the beams in a building: They are the main elements that make up the text and that all the supporting details help to develop.

**Development:** Think of a grain of rice added to others one at a time to form a pile; this is how writers develop their ideas—by adding imagery, details, examples, and other information over the course of the text. Thus, when people "analyze [the] development" of an idea or theme, for example, they look at how the author does this and what effect such development has on the meaning of the text.

**Distinct from prior knowledge or opinions:** In the History/Social Studies standard, this phrase distinguishes objective summary (the facts of what the text says) from personal opinion (what students think, how they feel about the text, and what it says). It is an important difference given the Common Core's emphasis on analytical thinking versus personal response.

**Including its relationship to supporting ideas:** Central ideas rely on the "supporting ideas" to help explore and sustain an idea or theme throughout. The writer might take an idea or theme such as the resiliency of the human spirit, for example, and build on it through examples or anecdotes, all of which complement each other as a way of developing that idea over the course of the text.

**Key supporting details and ideas:** Important details and ideas support the larger ideas the text develops over time. These details and ideas appear as examples, quotations, or other information used to advance the author's claim(s). Not all details and ideas are equally important, however; so students must learn to identify those that matter the most in the context of the text.

**Objective summary:** This describes key ideas, details, or events in the text and reports them without adding any commentary or outside description; it is similar to an evening "recap" of the news that attempts to answer the essential reporter's question—who, what, where, when, why, and how—*without* commentary.

**Over the course of the text:** Whether a 14-line sonnet or a 500-page novel, all texts have ideas the writer explores at length and in depth. The idea of love first introduced in the opening chapter, act, or stanza becomes a plaything in the hands of the author who looks at it from different angles, in different contexts, showing how the idea—or our understanding of it—evolves over time in the text.

**Themes:** This refers to the ideas the text explains, develops, and explores; there can be more than one, but themes are what the text is actually *about*.

**Reading 3:** Analyze how and why individuals, events, and ideas develop and interact over the course of a text.

## Literature

**6**   Describe how a particular story's or drama's plot unfolds in a series of episodes as well as how the characters respond or change as the plot moves toward a resolution.

**7**   Analyze how particular elements of a story or drama interact (e.g., how setting shapes the characters or plot).

**8**   Analyze how particular lines of dialogue or incidents in a story or drama propel the action, reveal aspects of a character, or provoke a decision.

## Informational Text

**6**   Analyze in detail how a key individual, event, or idea is introduced, illustrated, and elaborated in a text (e.g., through examples or anecdotes).

**7**   Analyze **the interactions between** individuals, events, and ideas in a text (**e.g., how ideas influence individuals or events, or how individuals influence ideas or events**).

**8**   Analyze **how a text makes connections among and distinctions** between individuals, ideas, or events (**e.g., through comparisons, analogies, or categories**).

## History/Social Studies

**6**   Identify key steps in a text's description of a process related to history/social studies (e.g., how a bill becomes law, how interest rates are raised or lowered).

**7**   Identify key steps in a text's description of a process related to history/social studies (e.g., how a bill becomes law, how interest rates are raised or lowered).

**8**   Identify key steps in a text's description of a process related to history/social studies (e.g., how a bill becomes law, how interest rates are raised or lowered).

## Science/Technical Subjects

**6**   Follow precisely a multistep procedure when carrying out experiments, taking measurements, or performing technical tasks.

**7**   Follow precisely a multistep procedure when carrying out experiments, taking measurements, or performing technical tasks.

**8**   Follow precisely a multistep procedure when carrying out experiments, taking measurements, or performing technical tasks.

## What the **Student** Does

## Literature

**6 Gist:** Explain how the plot of a story or play progresses, noting how characters evolve as the plot develops and approaches resolution.

- What are the key moments in the story?
- How do the characters respond or change as the plot develops over time?
- How are the series of events in the story organized?

**7 Gist:** Examine the interplay between specific narrative elements (e.g., setting, plot, characters), noting how they affect each other and thus contribute to the story's meaning.

- Which story elements matter most?
- Which elements affect others most?
- How does each element affect the others?

**8 Gist:** Examine specific events or lines of dialogue to determine how they advance the plot, uncover character details, or force characters to act (e.g., make a decision).

- Which events or specific lines of dialogue most affect the story?
- How do these events or specific lines affect the story the most?
- What does this event or dialogue reveal about the character?

## History/Social Studies

**6 Gist:** Determine which steps matter most in a process studied in history/social studies (e.g., how a bill becomes a law, how interest rates are raised or lowered).

- What process are you studying?
- How is the process structured?
- Which step(s) in the process matter most?

**7 Gist:** Determine which steps matter most in a process studied in history/social studies (e.g., how a bill becomes a law, how interest rates are raised or lowered).

- What process are you studying?
- How is the process structured?
- Which step(s) in the process matter most?

**8 Gist:** Determine which steps matter most in a process studied in history/social studies (e.g., how a bill becomes a law, how interest rates are raised or lowered).

- What process are you studying?
- How is the process structured?
- Which step(s) in the process matter most?

## Informational Text

**6 Gist:** Explain in detail how the author introduces, illustrates, or develops a salient person, incident, or idea (e.g., by using examples or anecdotes).

- What are the key moments, characters, or ideas in the story?
- How does the author introduce or develop this idea, event, or person?
- How does this idea, event, or person evolve over the course of the text?

**7 Gist:** Explain how specific people, incidents, or ideas in a text interact with and influence each other (e.g., how an idea or event can influence a person).

- What are the key moments, characters, or ideas in the story?
- How do these different elements interact with and influence each other?
- What evidence or examples can you provide to support your claim(s)?

**8 Gist:** Explain the techniques (e.g., analogies, categories) used to connect and distinguish between people, ideas, and events.

- What is the subject, content, or focus of this text—people, events, or ideas?
- What connection is the author trying to make in this text?
- What techniques does the author use to make connections or distinctions between different elements?

## Science/Technical Subjects

**6 Gist:** Complete a multistep process with precision during an experiment (e.g., take measurements, perform technical tasks).

- What is the procedure?
- What are the precise steps in the procedure?
- What tools or other items do you need to complete the procedure?

**7 Gist:** Complete a multistep process with precision during an experiment (e.g., take measurements, perform technical tasks).

- What is the procedure?
- What are the precise steps in the procedure?
- What tools or other items do you need to complete the procedure?

**8 Gist:** Complete a multistep process with precision during an experiment (e.g., take measurements, perform technical tasks).

- What is the procedure?
- What are the precise steps in the procedure?
- What tools or other items do you need to complete the procedure?

## What the **Teacher** Does

**To have students analyze how complex characters develop and interact, do the following:**

- Have students generate a list of all the characters, and then determine, according to the criteria they create, which ones are complex and the nature of that complexity.
- Have students build a plot map—individually, in groups, or as a class—noting each time certain key characters interact; analyze who does or says what, in each situation, and its effect on the text.
- Have students identify the motivations of key characters and those points where their motivations conflict with other characters' motivations; then examine what those conflicts reveal about the characters and how they affect the text as a whole.

**To have students analyze how dialogue and events affect the story, do the following:**

- Ask students to locate specific passages or key moments in the text where complex characters do or say something that affects the plot or develops a theme; ask them to make a claim about how this element affects the text and provide textual evidence.
- Create a graphic chart or plot diagram with students and ask them to analyze the plot for moments when characters do something that affects the plot—increase tension, cause change—in a measurable, discernible way. This is sometimes called a "fever chart" to represent the rising and falling action of events in the story.

**To have students identify key steps in a text's description of a process, do the following:**

- Provide students with a set of scrambled steps in a process or procedure, asking them to sort them based on some principle; then consider, if time allows, having them write a paragraph with appropriate transitions for each step.
- Direct students' attention to the words or other indicators that signal steps or a sequence, especially in those texts that are not arranged as a numbered list (e.g., a paragraph with transition or other signal words).

**To have students analyze how an author makes connections and distinctions, do the following:**

- Ask students to use some sort of graphic organizer with columns for what the author connects and how (The author links A to B by doing C to show D). Do the same for distinctions, providing appropriate academic language to help students articulate these distinctions clearly (The author differentiates between A and B by pointing out C to emphasize D).

**To have students analyze in detail how authors introduce, illustrate, or elaborate, do the following:**

- Direct students' attention to that portion of the text that serves to *introduce* the idea, asking them to indicate the details of the introduction that serve this end.
- Use the highlighting or color-coding features of the application to emphasize the parts of the text—whether words, typography, phrases, or whole paragraphs—that help to introduce, illustrate, or elaborate. This might mean highlighting, for example, all the signal phrases, such as *for example*, that indicate the writer is about to illustrate a point just made in the text.

**To have students analyze how and why elements interact over the course of a text, do the following:**

- Have students create a timeline for the text—a list or a more graphic timeline—that shows all the events in sequence, evaluated or ranked by their importance or effect on later events.
- Have students highlight or use sticky notes to identify all references to an event so students can retrace the events after reading the document to evaluate how one led to or impacted another.
- Provide students a sample that shows the event, its explanations, and textual evidence, which students must learn to evaluate by identifying the most fitting explanations and evidence. Then have them find the next event, its explanation, and evidence so they show they can do this independently.

**To help your English Language Learners, try this:**

- Evaluate the language used in the text and any directions for the assignment, and when discussing the assignment in class, find ways you could make the assignment more accessible.

**Academic Vocabulary:** Key Words and Phrases

**Actions or events:** "Actions" refers to what happens, what people *do*; in English, it is the actions of characters we study; in history, it is the actions of people who *rebel, discover, or invent*; in science, it is the actions we must do in the context of a procedure. "Events" are those moments in a story or history or any other field when things change in ways that merit the time we spend studying them (war or social movements).

**Characters:** Characters can be simple (flat, static) or complex (round, dynamic); only characters who change, who have a rich inner life that interacts with people and their environment could be considered "complex." This is often represented as an arc—what they are like or where they are when the story begins and when it *ends*.

**Connections:** Often it is the unexpected connection the author makes between ideas, events, or characters that leads to the greatest insight for us when reading. We could not anticipate that two elements that seemed so separate could be so linked; this is the epiphany that comes from attention to detail.

**Develop and interact:** As stories unfold, events and characters change; these changes are the consequence of interactions that take place between people, events, and ideas within a story or an actual social event, such as "the Twitter Revolution" in Iran where events, people, and ideas all resulted in a variety of changes and developments because of multiple interactions between people, events, and ideas like social media. To "develop" is to otherwise change, increasing or decreasing in importance, growing more complex or evolving into something different altogether.

**Distinctions:** Just as compelling connections reveal important insights, so do distinctions that reveal differences between different people, texts, events, or ideas; often, it is these distinctions that come from close reading that distinguish the reader's performance, allowing them to show what others missed.

**Follow precisely a multistep procedure:** The key word here is *precisely*; for in this context, the word applies to experiments and measurements, both of which rely on accuracy and precision; the other important word is *multistep*, for any such procedure involves multiple steps that must, in most cases, be followed in some established or imposed order to arrive at the proper result.

**Introduced, illustrated, and elaborated:** To "introduce" is to provide some background information that establishes the subject, the reason, the meaning, the purpose, the context, or other information we need to know up front. To "illustrate" something is, in the context of reading, to provide examples that *show* whatever you are writing about; thus, one would provide an example to illustrate what they meant when they said that a social media revolution was "different" from a civil movement, such as the Montgomery bus boycott. To "elaborate" is to give more details, description, or evidence about what they meant when they said that a text was about how an event changed society.

**Key steps in the description of a process:** Whether in social studies or science, the idea here is that some steps or stages are more crucial in any series of steps or stages than others; students must be able to discern this so they can understand why they are so important and how they affect other people or events.

**Performing technical tasks attending to special cases:** In a science or technical subjects class, one performs "technical tasks" when they experiment in a lab or with models; those tasks attending to (i.e., dealing with or done as a result of) special cases would be the more complex tasks as a result of their unique conditions that invite exceptions or innovative approaches to solving the problem.

**Propel the action:** In the 6–8 standards, this is known as "advance the plot." Every event or detail should move the story ahead in some useful or meaningful way toward its ultimate purpose or resolution. It should make things *happen*.

**Reading 4:** Interpret words and phrases as they are used in a text, including determining technical, connotative, and figurative meanings, and analyze how specific word choices shape meaning or tone.

## Literature

**6** Determine the meaning of words and phrases as they are used in a text, including figurative and connotative meanings; analyze the impact of a specific word choice on meaning and tone.

**7** Determine the meaning of words and phrases as they are used in a text, including figurative and connotative meanings; analyze the impact **of rhymes and other repetitions of sounds (e.g., alliteration) on a specific verse or stanza of a poem or section of a story or drama.**

**8** Determine the meaning of words and phrases as they are used in a text, including figurative and connotative meanings; analyze the impact of **specific word choices on meaning and tone, including analogies or allusions to other texts.**

## Informational Text

**6** Determine the meaning of words and phrases as they are used in a text, including figurative, connotative, and technical meanings.

**7** Determine the meaning of words and phrases as they are used in a text, including figurative, connotative, and technical meanings; **analyze the impact of a specific word choice on meaning and tone.**

**8** Determine the meaning of words and phrases as they are used in a text, including figurative, connotative, and technical meanings; analyze the impact of specific word choices on meaning and tone, **including analogies or allusions to other texts.**

## What the **Student** Does

## Literature

**6** **Gist:** Figure out what words and phrases mean in context, taking into consideration both their figurative and connotative meanings, and how a specific word choice affects the meaning and tone of the text.

- Which words or phrases contribute the most to the meaning or tone of a text?
- Which words have different figurative or connotative meanings?
- How does the author's choice of words affect the meaning and tone of the text?

**7** **Gist:** Figure out what words and phrases mean in context, taking into consideration both their figurative and connotative meanings, and how rhyme and other repeated sounds (e.g., alliteration) affect a particular part (verse, stanza, or section) of a poem or story.

- Which words or phrases contribute the most to the meaning or tone of a text?
- Which words have different figurative or connotative meanings?
- How does the use of rhyme or other repeated sounds affect the poem or story?

**8** **Gist:** Figure out what words and phrases mean in context, taking into consideration both their figurative and connotative meanings, and how the author's use of specific words, analogies, or textual allusions affects the meaning or tone of the text.

- Which words or phrases contribute the most to the meaning or tone of a text?
- Which words have different figurative or connotative meanings?
- How does the author's use of specific words, analogies, or allusions to other texts contribute to the meaning and tone?

## Informational Text

**6** **Gist:** Figure out what words and phrases mean in context, taking into consideration both their figurative and connotative meanings, as well as their specialized or disciplinary meaning.

- Which words or phrases contribute the most to the meaning or tone of a text?
- Which words have different figurative or connotative meanings?
- Which words are used according to their technical meaning in this context?

**7** **Gist:** Figure out what words and phrases mean in context, taking into consideration their figurative, connotative, and technical meanings, and how specific word choices affect the meaning and tone.

- Which words or phrases contribute the most to the meaning or tone of a text?
- Which words have different figurative, connotative, and technical meanings?
- How does a specific word choice contribute to the meaning or tone?

**8** **Gist:** Figure out what words and phrases mean in context, taking into consideration their figurative, connotative, and technical meanings, and how the author's use of specific words, analogies, or allusions affects the meaning and tone of the text.

- Which words or phrases contribute the most to the meaning or tone of a text?
- Which words have different figurative, connotative, and technical meanings?
- How does a specific word choice contribute to the meaning or tone?

**Reading 4:** Interpret words and phrases as they are used in a text, including determining technical, connotative, and figurative meanings, and analyze how specific word choices shape meaning or tone.

## History/Social Studies

**6** Determine the meaning of words and phrases as they are used in a text, including vocabulary specific to domains related to history/social studies.

**7** Determine the meaning of words and phrases as they are used in a text, including vocabulary specific to domains related to history/social studies.

**8** Determine the meaning of words and phrases as they are used in a text, including vocabulary specific to domains related to history/social studies.

## Science/Technical Subjects

**6** Determine the meaning of symbols, key terms, and other domain-specific words and phrases as they are used in a specific scientific or technical context relevant to grades 6–8 texts and topics.

**7** Determine the meaning of symbols, key terms, and other domain-specific words and phrases as they are used in a specific scientific or technical context relevant to grades 6–8 texts and topics.

**8** Determine the meaning of symbols, key terms, and other domain-specific words and phrases as they are used in a specific scientific or technical context relevant to grades 6–8 texts and topics.

## What the **Student** Does

| History/Social Studies | Science/Technical Subjects |

### History/Social Studies

**6** **Gist:** Figure out what words and phrases mean in context, noting also any discipline-specific terms used in history or social studies texts.

- Which words or phrases contribute most to the meaning of a text?
- Which words are unique to the discipline you are studying?
- What does that word or phrase mean in the context of this text?

**7** **Gist:** Figure out what words and phrases mean in context, noting also any discipline-specific terms used in history or social studies texts.

- Which words or phrases contribute most to the meaning of a text?
- Which words are unique to the discipline you are studying?
- What does that word or phrase mean in the context of this text?

**8** **Gist:** Figure out what words and phrases mean in context, noting also any discipline-specific terms used in history or social studies texts.

- Which words or phrases contribute most to the meaning of a text?
- Which words are unique to the discipline you are studying?
- What does that word or phrase mean in the context of this text?

### Science/Technical Subjects

**6** **Gist:** Figure out the meaning of pivotal and discipline-specific words and phrases, and symbols used in grades 6–8 scientific or technical texts.

- Which key words or phrases must you understand to comprehend this text?
- Which symbols are essential to know when reading this type of text?
- What does this domain-specific word or phrase mean in this context?

**7** **Gist:** Figure out the meaning of pivotal and discipline-specific words and phrases, and symbols used in grades 6–8 scientific or technical texts.

- Which key words or phrases must you understand to comprehend this text?
- Which symbols are essential to know when reading this type of text?
- What does this domain-specific word or phrase mean in this context?

**8** **Gist:** Figure out the meaning of pivotal and discipline-specific words and phrases, and symbols used in grades 6–8 scientific or technical texts.

- Which key words or phrases must you understand to comprehend this text?
- Which symbols are essential to know when reading this type of text?
- What does this domain-specific word or phrase mean in this context?

What the **Teacher** Does

**To have students interpret words and phrases as they are used in a text, do the following:**

- Direct students' attention to the words, phrases, and other details (captions, diagrams, images) in a sentence and those around it. Point out the ways authors add details to clarify the meaning of words: definition clues such as explanations, synonyms, phrases, and clauses; restatement of the word or phrase (e.g., *In other words*); contrast or antonym clues that help define what a word means by using words that mean the exact opposite; other clues such as typography, proximity to images, and the author's general tone.
- Tell students that not all words can be understood through context clues; help them see where context clues can confuse.
- Complete a think-aloud while reading to the class to show how you puzzle out a word or phrase using syntactic, semantic, typographic, etymological, and other types of information to decipher words.

**To have students determine the figurative and connotative meaning of words, do the following:**

- Identify with students figurative language or words with other connotative meanings; then have them determine the literal or denotative meaning of those words; then ask them to determine, in light of how the words are used, the figurative or connotative meaning.
- Direct students' attention to words used figuratively (simile, metaphor, analogy, euphemism, and pun) and ask them to determine a word's meaning and explain how its use affects the meaning of other words around it or contributes to the meaning of the text.
- Have them assess whether a set or series of words used figuratively has a unifying theme (e.g., they are all related to gardens, sports, the law) and, if they do, what it is and how that set of thematic words adds meaning to the text.

**To have students analyze the impact of word choice on meaning and tone, do the following:**

- Complete a think-aloud as you read through a text, noting the author's use of certain words that combine with others (through sound, imagery, meaning, stylistic or rhetorical effect) to add meaning or serve some other purpose (e.g., to reinforce a theme).
- Direct students to highlight, code, or otherwise indicate (by alternately circling, underlining, putting dotted lines under words) those words or phrases that are connected; ask them then what conclusions they can draw from the patterns, connections, or general use of words about their meaning.
- Provide students a list of words or phrases with a common theme left unstated; ask them what the words have in common and how that relates to the text from which they come.

**To help students understand discipline-specific words, symbols, and terms, do the following:**

- Show students how to make use of any textual features—sidebars, captions, typography (is the word in **bold** and, thus, in the glossary), diagrams, footers, or glossaries in the chapter or in the appendix—available in the textbook.
- Teach students, when appropriate, the root words or etymology of certain subject-specific words (bio = life, ology = study of) as part of the study of any discipline.

**To have students analyze how authors use analogies and allusions, do the following:**

- Provide a focused lesson on analogies (perhaps extending it to distinguish between analogies, similes, and metaphors), illustrating with examples; then model for the class how to read for them in the assigned text; once they understand, have them apply the ideas on their own to the rest of the text.
- Read aloud for students the text that has some good examples of allusions in it, explaining to them how these function and how you determine that they are, in fact, functioning as allusions.

**To help your English Language Learners, try this:**

- Use these words as often as possible, speaking them aloud so students hear them used in context and pronounced correctly.

**Academic Vocabulary:** Key Words and Phrases

**Analogies and allusions:** Analogies are those words or phrases that compare two things, often based on similar structures or qualities, to explain or clarify some other point; allusions can include, in some cases, as little as a word but often a more developed reference to an image, a story, or some passage in the Bible, for example, that the writer uses to make a point by suggesting some point of similarity (e.g., that a place was an Eden).

**Connotative meanings:** Words have a primary or literal meaning; some also have a secondary or connotative meaning, which implies an additional idea or feeling related to the word or phrase.

**Domain-specific words and phrases:** Within each discipline or branch of that discipline, certain words (cell, division) have a domain-specific use in, for example, biology; other words, however, are unique to that discipline and are, thus, essential for students to know in order to read, discuss, and write about complex texts in that subject.

**Figurative meanings:** Figures of speech (or figurative language) are those often colorful ways we develop of saying something; they include euphemism, hyperbole, irony, understatement, metaphor, simile, and paradox, among others. Some of them are specific to an era, region, or social group and, thus, can confuse readers.

**Impact of rhymes and other repetitions of sounds:** Though we associate the role sound plays more with poetry, it often plays a key role also in drama and, depending on the author's style, in fiction. It can have a number of effects: emphasis, pleasure, association, mimicry of action, or reinforcing to imagery.

**Impact of specific word choice on meaning and tone:** Each word comes with its own denotative and connotative meaning which, in a piece of writing being read closely, will be in the author's mind and, thus, one of the many tools for creating meaning and evoking a certain tone. If, for example, a writer uses a word that is very formal, archaic, or otherwise outdated, it will create in the reader's mind a certain impression and tone that shapes how that student interprets what the author means. In short, the writer's choices shape meaning or tone: Certain words carry added, often implied meanings; we describe these as "loaded words," for they have the power to affect the meaning of the words around them or to influence the speaker's tone (e.g., turning it from sincere to ironic).

**Interpret:** This is best understood as a way of explaining what an author wrote using more accessible, familiar language for those who lack experience with or knowledge of the subject or this type of text.

**Key terms:** In highly technical or scientific subjects, certain terms represent the precision and accuracy that discipline demands. In some subjects, a certain term (e.g., *evolution, uncertainty,* or *entropy*) represents a specific idea or applies to a very precise process.

**Symbols:** In humanities classes, a symbol suggests some greater meaning when it is attached to an idea; thus, the bald eagle symbolizes the American spirit; in science and math, however, symbols represent operations, procedures, and concepts such as change ($\Delta$) or pi ($\pi$).

**Technical meanings:** These would be words with specialized meanings specific to the subject being investigated, explained, or argued about; one example might be the distinctions made between political philosophies, such as libertarian and republican.

**Tone:** When thinking of tone, think about tone *of voice*. The formal tone of the Constitution matches its importance and subject; the informal tone of a literary text signals the relationship between the individuals and reveals the character of the speaker.

**Words and phrases as they are used in a text:** Close reading seeks to understand what the text really says; to do this, students must scrutinize the words and phrases used by the author, as they are the key to determining what the author really means or what the text says; also, they are an essential source of evidence.

**Reading 5:** Analyze the structure of texts, including how specific sentences, paragraphs, and larger portions of the text (e.g., a section, chapter, scene, or stanza) relate to one another and the whole.

## Literature

**6** Analyze how a particular sentence, chapter, scene, or stanza fits into the overall structure of a text and contributes to the development of the theme, setting, or plot.

**7** Analyze how a **drama's or poem's form or structure (e.g., soliloquy, sonnet) contributes to its meaning.**

**8** Compare and contrast the structure of two or more texts and analyze how the differing structure of each text contributes to its meaning and style.

## Informational Text

**6** Analyze how a particular sentence, paragraph, chapter, or section fits into the overall structure of a text and contributes to the development of the ideas.

**7** Analyze the structure an author uses to organize a text, including how the major sections contribute **to the whole** and to the development of the ideas.

**8** Analyze in detail the structure of a specific paragraph in a text, including the role of particular sentences in developing and refining a key concept.

## History/Social Studies

**6** Describe how a text presents information (e.g., sequentially, comparatively, causally).

**7** Describe how a text presents information (e.g., sequentially, comparatively, causally).

**8** Describe how a text presents information (e.g., sequentially, comparatively, causally).

## Science/Technical Subjects

**6** Analyze the structure an author uses to organize a text, including how the major sections contribute to the whole and to an understanding of the topic.

**7** Analyze the structure an author uses to organize a text, including how the major sections contribute to the whole and to an understanding of the topic.

**8** Analyze the structure an author uses to organize a text, including how the major sections contribute to the whole and to an understanding of the topic.

## What the **Student** Does

### Literature

**6 Gist:** Break down the text's structure to see how *one* component—a sentence, chapter, scene, or stanza—helps develop the theme, setting, or plot.

- Which component—a sentence, chapter, scene, or stanza—contributes most to the development of the theme, setting, or plot?
- How does this specific component affect the development of the theme, setting, or plot of this text?

**7 Gist:** Break down the design of a poem or play to show how *one* component (e.g., a soliloquy, a sonnet) adds to the meaning of that text.

- Which form or structure (e.g., a soliloquy, a sonnet) does the author use in this play or poem?
- How does the author's use of this specific form or structure contribute to the meaning of the poem or play?

**8 Gist:** Examine the similarities and differences between the design of multiple texts, explaining how these different designs affect the meaning and style of each text.

- What are the key structural similarities and differences between these different texts?
- How do the different structures contribute to the meaning and style of each text?

### History/Social Studies

**6 Gist:** Discuss the structural approach the author uses to present information in this text (e.g., sequential, comparison/contrast, cause-effect).

- What information is the author examining in this text?
- How does the author organize the information presented in this text (e.g., by time, category, problem-solution)?

**7 Gist:** Discuss the structural approach the author uses to present information in this text (e.g., sequential, comparison/contrast, cause-effect).

- What information is the author examining in this text?
- How does the author organize the information presented in this text (e.g., by time, category, problem-solution)?

**8 Gist:** Discuss the structural approach the author uses to present information in this text (e.g., sequential, comparison/contrast, cause-effect).

- What information is the author examining in this text?
- How does the author organize the information presented in this text (e.g., by time, category, problem-solution)?

### Informational Text

**6 Gist:** Break down the text's structure to see how *one* component—a sentence, paragraph, chapter, or section—helps develop the ideas in that text.

- Which component—a sentence, paragraph, chapter, or section—contributes most to the development of ideas in the text?
- How does this specific component help to develop the author's ideas?

**7 Gist:** Break down a text's design, showing how the major sections (e.g., chapters, subsections) add to the text as a whole and develop its ideas.

- Which organizational approach (e.g., chapters, subsections) does the author use in this text?
- How does the author's use of this structure contribute to the text as a whole and the development of its ideas?

**8 Gist:** Break down the structure of a particular paragraph, examining in depth its design and how specific sentences enhance and clarify a main idea within that paragraph.

- What are the key structural elements in this paragraph that develop its ideas?
- Which sentence in this paragraph does most to develop and refine a key idea—and how does it do that?

### Science/Technical Subjects

**6 Gist:** Break down the organizational approach to the text, examining how the main sections add to the meaning of the text as a whole and help the reader understand the subject discussed in the text.

- What organizational techniques or patterns does the author use in this text?
- How do this organizational approach and the main sections improve the text and the reader's understanding of it?

**7 Gist:** Break down the organizational approach to the text, examining how the main sections add to the meaning of the text as a whole and help the reader understand the subject discussed in the text.

- What organizational techniques or patterns does the author use in this text?
- How do this organizational approach and the main sections improve the text and the reader's understanding of it?

**8 Gist:** Break down the organizational approach to the text, examining how the main sections add to the meaning of the text as a whole and help the reader understand the subject discussed in the text.

- What organizational techniques or patterns does the author use in this text?
- How do this organizational approach and the main sections improve the text and the reader's understanding of it?

What the **Teacher** Does

**To have students analyze the structure of texts, do the following:**

- Have students determine the author's purpose, audience, and occasion for a text; then ask them to identify how these factors influence the choices the author made about the text's structure.
- Identify the organizational pattern or rhetorical mode of this text—compare–contrast, problem–solution, cause–effect, chronological, and so on—and then examine what additional choices the author makes and how these choices shape the meaning.
- Model for students how you determine the structure of a complex text and use that knowledge to better understand and analyze the text through close reading.
- Locate all structural elements—transitions, subheadings, parallel plots, shifts in time—and analyze how they affect the reader's response and the text's meaning.

**To have students analyze how a poem or drama's structure or form contributes, do the following:**

- Explain to students or have them identify the form (e.g., sonnet, sestina, monologue) the writer is using; then point out or direct them to locate those organizational devices the writer uses to add meaning or create a style appropriate to their purpose.
- Have students rewrite the passage or text in a different genre (e.g., if it is a sonnet, have them write a paragraph; if a soliloquy, have them write a third-person narrative or reflective essay) to better understand what is unique to the structure or form the author chose.

**To have students compare and contrast the structure of two or more texts, do the following:**

- Consider having students parse the text out into some sort of outline form that reveals, through a more spatial arrangement, how the two texts are structured; this is easily done on the computer where the return and tab keys allow students to manipulate the text quickly and easily in helpful ways.
- Using color coding on the display screen, think aloud for students as you move through the parallel texts, showing them how to read *across* the texts to compare and contrast them, focusing in this case on the nature and meaning of their differences.

**To have students analyze the structure of a specific paragraph in a text, do the following:**

- Develop a numerical system (or use Frances Christensen's model) that allows students to analyze and represent the different levels or relationships between sentences within a specific paragraph, assigning the main or controlling idea the number 1.

**To have students analyze the author's choices about structure and order within, do the following:**

- Help students determine the organizational pattern of the text (e.g., sequential, chronological) and its rhetorical mode (to define, compare, explain); then, first together, and then have students on their own, assess how each sentence and other elements within the text create order and meaning while also helping the author achieve the purpose.

**To have students analyze sentences, paragraphs, and larger sections, do the following:**

- Have students create what some call a "backward outline" of the text (to analyze instead of compose such a text) to show how it is organized around a main idea or claim and the relationship of each section to the larger structure of the text.
- Ask students to annotate a text specifically to identify those sentences that create structure or cause significant moments within the text at the paragraph level. These might be sentences that shift the focus of the text to new topics or to other perspectives on the same subject; they might be sentences that emphasize a certain key idea, event, or other aspect of the text.

**To help your English Language Learners, try this:**

- Use an LCD projector to display different versions of the same text that show it unchanged, formatted to reveal, for example, all the transitions (in one highlighted color) in another version, and, in a different slide, certain key sentences within the paragraph or text that are particularly important (highlighted in a different version) to help these students better grasp the abstract and, for some, foreign concept of structure and its effect on the larger text.

**Academic Vocabulary:** Key Words and Phrases

**A drama's or poem's form or structure (e.g., soliloquy, sonnet):** Some of these forms and structures come with their own established conventions, such as the Shakespearean or Petrarchan sonnet and their prescribed patterns and structures; others, such as some dramatic forms, may have structures more specific to that context or norms the author has established for a play.

**Advance an explanation or analysis:** Authors use devices such as transitions, organizational patterns (compare–contrast, cause–effect), and strategies (chronological order, order of importance) that allow them to emphasize certain ideas to advance their analysis or explanation of these ideas.

**Analyze the structure of a specific paragraph or group of sentences:** This involves considering how information in general and sentences in particular are arranged within a paragraph, particularly as it relates to the author's purpose; also crucial is the sequence or arrangement of the sentences within that paragraph, especially as they express cause or otherwise serve to develop an idea.

**Compare and contrast the differing structure of each text:** This asks students to identify and analyze what is similar (compare) and different (contrast), focusing on the *differences* between the two structures and how those affect the meaning of the text.

**Contributes to the development of the theme, setting, or plot:** This standard focuses on how *one* sentence, chapter, scene, or stanza can help to evoke, establish, or reinforce—that is, "develop"—the theme, setting, or plot by adding specific details, making a vital connection, or adding imagery to the story or poem.

**Developing and refining a key concept:** Such a concept is similar to a central idea in the full text, some idea that the text is examining at length or in depth;

thus, all the other structural elements discussed in this standard serve simultaneously to elaborate on and refine that idea to its fullest and finest details.

**How a particular sentence fits into the overall structure:** It might help to think of such a sentence or other single component as a *keystone* or *cornerstone* that bears the weight of an arch or wall; in other words, these elements "fit" into the overall structure in ways that add real substance to the text in which they are used. One might look for them as points of emphasis or transition.

**Relate to each other and the whole:** Throughout this standard, students are being asked to consider the part in its relation to the whole; this then refers to how the sentence relates to the paragraph of which it is a part, or the paragraph in relation to the whole, the scene in relation to the act—or the whole play. These smaller parts might be compared to cells in a larger organism of the text or the studs that hold up the walls in a larger structure.

**Specific sentences, paragraphs, or larger portions of a text:** This refers to the levels at which authors treat and develop ideas throughout the text; some authors work at the micro level (sentence) and others emphasize the macro level (section/chapter).

**Structure of texts:** This refers to how authors organize their ideas and the text as a whole. Through structural patterns—at the sentence-, the paragraph-, and the whole-text level—authors emphasize certain ideas and create such effects as tension, mystery, and humor.

**The major sections:** While these could refer to any number of components, they are best understood as large chunks of a text—sections that follow subheadings, chapters, extended passages, or whole scenes or even acts in a play. They are, in the language of construction, "load-bearing walls" without which the full text could not be expected to stand on its own.

*Notes*

**Reading 6:** Assess how point of view or purpose shapes the content and style of a text.

## Literature

**6** Explain how an author develops the point of view of the narrator or speaker in a text.

**7** **Analyze** how an author develops **and contrasts** the points of view of **different characters** or narrators in a text.

**8** Analyze how **differences in the points of view of the characters and the audience or reader** (e.g., created through the use of dramatic irony) create such effects as suspense or humor.

## Informational Text

**6** Determine an author's point of view or purpose in a text and explain how it is conveyed in the text.

**7** Determine an author's point of view or purpose in a text **and analyze how the author distinguishes his or her position from that of others.**

**8** Determine an author's point of view or purpose in a text and analyze how the author **acknowledges and responds to conflicting evidence or viewpoints.**

## What the **Student** Does

### Literature

**6** **Gist:** Describe the techniques the author uses to establish and elaborate on the narrator's or speaker's point of view in the poem, play, or story.

- Who is telling the story or speaking in this poem—and from what point of view?
- Why does the author tell the story from this point of view?
- What techniques or devices does the author use to develop the point of view of the speaker or narrator?

**7** **Gist:** Identify and discuss any techniques the author uses to establish various characters' or narrators' points of view, taking time also to analyze how the author conveys the differences between these points of view in the text.

- Who is telling the story or speaking in this poem, play, or story?
- Why does the author tell the story from these different characters' perspectives?
- What techniques does the author use to develop and distinguish between the different characters' or narrators' points of view?

**8** **Gist:** Identify different viewpoints between characters and the audience or reader, examining how the author uses techniques such as dramatic irony to create a mood of suspense or humor at that point in the text.

- How are the reader's or audience's points of view different from the characters' in a play or story?
- What techniques does the author use (e.g., dramatic irony) to create such effects as suspense, mystery, or humor?
- How does the author use these techniques to create such a mood or effect in the reader or audience?

### Informational Text

**6** **Gist:** Infer the author's point of view or objective, describing the techniques used to express his or her perspective and purpose in this text.

- What is the subject of this text?
- What is the author's point of view or purpose regarding this subject?
- What techniques or devices does the author use to develop the point of view or achieve this purpose?

**7** **Gist:** Infer the author's point of view or objective, explaining those techniques the author uses to distinguish his or her view or stance from others'.

- What is the subject of this text?
- What is the author's point of view or purpose regarding this subject?
- What techniques or devices does the author use to distinguish his or her position from others' on this subject?

**8** **Gist:** Infer the author's point of view or objective, explaining those techniques used to acknowledge and respond to evidence or points of view that conflict with the author's own.

- What is the subject of this text?
- What is the author's point of view or purpose regarding this subject?
- Where and how does the author acknowledge and respond to evidence or viewpoints that conflict with their own?

**Reading 6:**  Assess how point of view or purpose shapes the content and style of a text.

## History/Social Studies

**6**  Identify aspects of a text that reveal an author's point of view or purpose (e.g., loaded language, inclusion or avoidance of particular facts).

**7**  Identify aspects of a text that reveal an author's point of view or purpose (e.g., loaded language, inclusion or avoidance of particular facts).

**8**  Identify aspects of a text that reveal an author's point of view or purpose (e.g., loaded language, inclusion or avoidance of particular facts).

## Science/Technical Subjects

**6**  Analyze the author's purpose in providing an explanation, describing a procedure, or discussing an experiment in a text.

**7**  Analyze the author's purpose in providing an explanation, describing a procedure, or discussing an experiment in a text.

**8**  Analyze the author's purpose in providing an explanation, describing a procedure, or discussing an experiment in a text.

## What the **Student** Does

| History/Social Studies | Science/Technical Subjects |

### History/Social Studies

**6** **Gist:** Determine which elements of a text reveal the author's perspective or objective, noting, for example, any use of loaded language or the inclusion or omission of key facts or details.

- What is the subject of this text?
- What is the author's attitude toward or purpose regarding this subject?
- How do the aspects of this text—the use of language, treatment of facts, or other key details—reveal the author's point of view or purpose?

**7** **Gist:** Determine which elements of a text reveal the author's perspective or objective, noting, for example, any use of loaded language or the inclusion or omission of key facts or details.

- What is the subject of this text?
- What is the author's attitude toward or purpose regarding this subject?
- How do the aspects of this text—the use of language, treatment of facts, or other key details—reveal the author's point of view or purpose?

**8** **Gist:** Determine which elements of a text reveal the author's perspective or objective, noting, for example, any use of loaded language or the inclusion or omission of key facts or details.

- What is the subject of this text?
- What is the author's attitude toward or purpose regarding this subject?
- How do the aspects of this text—the use of language, treatment of facts, or other key details—reveal the author's point of view or purpose?

### Science/Technical Subjects

**6** **Gist:** Examine why the author explains or describes a procedure, or takes time to mention an experiment, connecting the author's motive in doing so with his or her overarching purpose in the text.

- What does the author explain—and why?
- What procedure does the author describe—and why?
- Why does the author take time to discuss this particular experiment in the context of the writing?

**7** **Gist:** Examine why the author explains or describes a procedure, or takes time to mention an experiment, connecting the author's motive in doing so with his or her overarching purpose in the text.

- What does the author explain—and why?
- What procedure does the author describe—and why?
- Why does the author take time to discuss this particular experiment in the context of the writing?

**8** **Gist:** Examine why the author explains or describes a procedure, or takes time to mention an experiment, connecting the author's motive in doing so with his or her overarching purpose in the text.

- What does the author explain—and why?
- What procedure does the author describe—and why?
- Why does the author take time to discuss this particular experiment in the context of the writing?

What the **Teacher** Does

**To have students assess how point of view or purpose shapes content and style, do the following:**

- Define and discuss with students just what point of view (POV) means and entails, providing not just written and spoken definitions but also visual illustrations with drawings, images, artworks, or film clips.
- Extend the lesson to include the different types of POV—omniscient, unreliable, first, second, third person—and how this notion of point of view relates to the narrator, especially when that narrator is an unreliable narrator. To clarify these elements of POV, students could apply the ideas to previously read stories to show what they know before moving into new ones.
- Have students first determine what the POV in the text is; then ask students to determine why the author chose *that* POV as a means to achieve the purpose.
- Direct students to generate words that characterize the style of the writing; then ask them to explain how these words are shaped by the POV (i.e., how the point of view guided the writer to make certain choices about diction, tone, or setting).

**To have students acknowledge and respond to conflicting evidence or views, do the following:**

- Label for students the claim or point of view being made, and then the corresponding counterclaim or conflicting evidence, pointing out to them the basis of the challenge; ask them to evaluate, through discussion, the quality of the conflicting evidence and to generate a fitting response, explaining why it is a sound, logical, and effective response.
- Post a claim that relates to your subject, and ask the class to generate viable objections and the reasoning behind them; then debrief as a class, examining what makes for a good response to conflicting evidence or view.

**To have students identify aspects that reveal an author's POV or purpose, do the following:**

- Put a list of words, sentences, or an extended passage on the display, asking students to find those words, structures, figures of speech, or other elements that imply a certain perspective or indicate the author's purpose; as an alternative, give students the same examples or an extended passage on a handout and ask them to annotate all words that reveal POV or purpose, and then explain in the margins how they do this.

**To have students compare the POV of two or more authors, do the following:**

- Begin by modeling for students what it looks like to compare two authors in this way, discussing aloud with the class what you are doing and why, and how you would, for example, use these details in your written analysis of the two sources.
- Create a three-column organizer with key topics common to both listed in the middle column; as students go through the text, have them gather examples and observations about the two authors' treatment of the topic, listing these under the respective titles for later use.
- Repeat the same process when students are examining different POVs on historical events (e.g., Korean War) by listing the claims, reasons, and evidence for those acts or events under the appropriate columns.

**To have students analyze an author's explanation, description, or discussion, do the following:**

- Generate different reasons *why* an author would explain, describe, or discuss scientific procedures and how such explanations relate to questions the author tries to answer.

**To help your English Language Learners, try this:**

- Make connections to students' cultures or experiences to help explain their different POV about some subjects so they get a more personal, concrete grasp of subject.

**Academic Vocabulary:** Key Words and Phrases

**Acknowledge and respond:** In the language of academic argument, this means conceding that there are other perspectives, other interpretations than the one you offer; by way of clarifying and advancing your ideas, it is best to acknowledge these other, conflicting perspectives and respond to them by explaining how your ideas address their questions or criticisms.

**Aspects of a text that reveal an author's POV or purpose:** This phrase appears in the history/social studies standard where it draws students' attention to the ways people, organizations, and governments have "revealed" their perspectives and purposes through the words and facts they use—and omit—in the foundational and seminal documents.

**Assess:** In this instance, *assess* means not to test but to determine what the point of view is and how it shapes the story.

**Conflicting evidence or viewpoints:** Evidence is "conflicting" when it contradicts what the writers have offered as their claim; thus, the writer must address and resolve that conflict or opposing viewpoint on the way to advancing and clarifying their own.

**Content and style of a text:** The perspective from which you tell a story limits what content you can include and the style you use when you write about it. Point of view determines what the narrator sees, knows, hears, and can say—and how he can say it.

**Develops the point of view:** This applies to those efforts the author makes to fully realize or bring to life a fictional character or speaker in a poem by establishing and "developing" a narrator's point of view.

**Irony:** This is a tone or device that adds subtle humor, typically at a character's expense, as a result of a meaningful difference between what is said and what is really meant (verbal irony), what a character/narrator thinks is true and what actually is (situational irony), or when the audience knows things the character does not about a person or situation (dramatic irony).

**Evidence:** This includes, when taken from reliable sources, facts, examples, data in the form of statistics, findings, or results (from surveys, observations, experiments), expert opinions, interviews (of experts or firsthand witnesses), and quotations from the text.

**Inclusion or avoidance of particular facts:** This technique includes or ignores certain inconvenient facts that some avoid, ignore, or deliberately omit (i.e., "cherry picking") to convey a certain perspective or achieve a dubious objective.

**Loaded language:** Whether words, phrases, or whole sentences, these are used in ways that carry additional, often coercive, connotations, in an attempt to influence an audience or reader through emotional appeals or such questions as, "You're not a *Communist*, are you?"

**Narrator or speaker:** A narrator is traditionally one telling the story in a novel or work of short fiction; think of a voice-over in a film as a variation; a speaker, on the other hand, is what one generally calls the voice of a poem, which one should *not* assume is the poet.

**Point of view (POV):** This is the place, vantage point, or consciousness through which we hear or see someone describe a situation, tell a story, or make an argument. Different POVs are distinguished by how much the narrator or reporter knows: first-person (I/me) or third-person (she/they); an *omniscient* POV knows what everyone thinks and feels; a *limited* POV knows only so much about a character or knows only what one character (out of many) thinks; an *unreliable* narrator is not trustworthy. In some cases, multiple POVs can be used or represented within one text.

**Purpose:** People want to accomplish one of four purposes when they write or speak: persuade, inform, express, or entertain. One could add others—to explain or inspire, for example—but these four account for most situations.

**Reading 7:** Integrate and evaluate content presented in diverse formats and media, including visually and quantitatively, as well as in words.*

## Literature

**6** Compare and contrast the experience of reading a story, drama, or poem to listening to or viewing an audio, video, or live version of the text, including contrasting what they "see" and "hear" when reading the text to what they perceive when they listen or watch.

**7** Compare and contrast a **written** story, drama, or poem **to its audio, filmed, staged, or multimedia version, analyzing the effects of techniques unique to each medium (e.g., lighting, sound, color, or camera focus and angles in a film).**

**8** Analyze the extent to which a filmed or live production of a story or drama stays faithful to or departs from the text or script, evaluating the choices made by the director or actors.

## Informational Text

**6** Integrate information presented in different media or formats (e.g., visually, quantitatively) as well as in words to develop a coherent understanding of a topic or issue.

**7** Compare and contrast a text to an audio, video, or multimedia version of the text, analyzing each medium's portrayal of the subject (e.g., how the delivery of a speech affects the impact of the words).

**8** Evaluate the advantages and disadvantages of using different mediums (e.g., print or digital text, video, multimedia) to present a particular topic or idea.

* Please consult the full Common Core State Standards document (and all updates and appendices) at http://www.corestandards.org/ELA-Literacy. See "Research to Build Knowledge" in the Writing section and "Comprehension and Collaboration" in Speaking and Listening section for additional standards relevant to gathering, assessing, and applying information from print and digital sources.

*Source:* Copyright © 2010. National Governors Association Center for Best Practices and Council of Chief State School Officers. All rights reserved.

## What the **Student** Does

| Literature | Informational Text |
|---|---|

### Literature

**6** **Gist:** Examine the similarities and differences between reading a text and experiencing a recorded or live performance of it, noting how reading the text (i.e., making a movie of the text in one's head) differs from experiencing it live (i.e., letting others interpret what the text means or the characters are like).

- How is reading a play, poem, or story similar to and different from the experience of listening to or watching a recorded or live performance of it?
- How does the medium or format in which you experience the text affect your understanding or experience of it?

**7** **Gist:** Examine the differences and similarities between reading a story, drama, or poem and listening to or watching the same text recorded or performed live, comparing these different versions in various media formats and analyzing how various camera angles, lighting, sound, and other effects unique to each medium impact the message.

- How does the written story differ from the performed/produced version?
- How do the different techniques in various media affect the meaning and experience of the story, drama, or poem?

**8** **Gist:** Examine the performance or production of a story or drama, noting where each version—written and filmed/performed—aligns with and diverges from the original text or script, and then determine whether the choices made in performing those two enhanced or diminished its impact.

- Where does the film depart from and adhere to the original (written) text—and to what effect?
- What of the actors' and director's choices contributed most significantly to the film or live version of the text?

### Informational Text

**6** **Gist:** Gather and use information expressed in writing and various media or visual formats (table, image, graph, diagram, flowchart) to draw conclusions about the meaning of a subject or issue.

- What is the subject of the written text—and what does that text say about it?
- What key ideas and information can you draw from the media, quantitative, or visual formats used to convey other aspects of this subject or issue?

**7** **Gist:** Examine the similarities and differences between an original (written) and produced version (filmed, audio, or mixed media), focusing on how words delivered in performance instead of on the page impact the meaning or effect of those words.

- How is this adaptation of the original similar to or different from the original?
- How does the medium used impact the effect of the words when read versus produced as a multimedia text?

**8** **Gist:** Assess the advantages and disadvantages of one medium over another (e.g., print or digital, video or audio) prior to giving a presentation.

- What are the available media formats (print or digital, video or multimedia) to choose from for this presentation?
- What are the advantages and disadvantages of each medium for this particular presentation?

**Reading 7:** Integrate and evaluate content presented in diverse formats and media, including visually and quantitatively, as well as in words.*

## History/Social Studies

**6** Integrate visual information (e.g., in charts, graphs, photographs, videos, or maps) with other information in print and digital texts.

**7** Integrate visual information (e.g., in charts, graphs, photographs, videos, or maps) with other information in print and digital texts.

**8** Integrate visual information (e.g., in charts, graphs, photographs, videos, or maps) with other information in print and digital texts.

## Science/Technical Subjects

**6** Integrate quantitative or technical information expressed in words in a text with a version of that information expressed visually (e.g., in a flowchart, diagram, model, graph, or table).

**7** Integrate quantitative or technical information expressed in words in a text with a version of that information expressed visually (e.g., in a flowchart, diagram, model, graph, or table).

**8** Integrate quantitative or technical information expressed in words in a text with a version of that information expressed visually (e.g., in a flowchart, diagram, model, graph, or table).

* Please consult the full Common Core State Standards document (and all updates and appendices) at http://www.corestandards.org/ELA-Literacy. See "Research to Build Knowledge" in the Writing section and "Comprehension and Collaboration" in the Speaking and Listening section for additional standards relevant to gathering, assessing, and applying information from print and digital sources.

## What the **Student** Does

| History/Social Studies | Science/Technical Subjects |
|---|---|

### History/Social Studies

**6** **Gist:** Combine visual information, such as charts, graphs, images, or maps, with print or digital texts, drawing conclusions about the topic they are discussing.

- What is the topic you are investigating?
- What do these different media and formats (charts, graphs, photographs, videos, or maps) say about this subject?

**7** **Gist:** Combine visual information, such as charts, graphs, images, or maps, with print or digital texts, drawing conclusions about the topic they are discussing.

- What is the topic you are investigating?
- What do these different media and formats (charts, graphs, photographs, videos, or maps) say about this subject?

**8** **Gist:** Combine visual information, such as charts, graphs, images, or maps, with print or digital texts, drawing conclusions about the topic they are discussing.

- What is the topic you are investigating?
- What do these different media and formats (charts, graphs, photographs, videos, or maps) say about this subject?

### Science/Technical Subjects

**6** **Gist:** Combine quantitative or technical information into a written and visual explanation (table, image, graph, diagram, or flowchart) that conveys the ideas and information in the different texts.

- What is the subject of the written text—and what does that text say about it?
- Which visual format(s) would best join with the written version to express the original information or ideas?

**7** **Gist:** Combine quantitative or technical information into a written and visual explanation (table, image, graph, diagram, or flowchart) that conveys the ideas and information in the different texts.

- What is the subject of the written text—and what does that text say about it?
- Which visual format(s) would best join with the written version to express the original information or ideas?

**8** **Gist:** Combine quantitative or technical information into a written and visual explanation (table, image, graph, diagram, or flowchart) that conveys the ideas and information in the different texts.

- What is the subject of the written text—and what does that text say about it?
- Which visual format(s) would best join with the written version to express the original information or ideas?

What the **Teacher** Does

**To integrate and evaluate content in diverse formats and media, do the following:**

- Have students start with what the different sources—regardless of format or media—are saying about the subject and how it differs from what other sources are saying about the same subject.
- Have students create or locate the criteria by which the content in these different formats and media will be evaluated and then apply those criteria to these sources.
- Generate questions students should use to guide their reading of different texts across formats and media, including visual and quantitative documents on their own or embedded into a larger written document.

**To have students analyze a subject in two different artistic mediums, do the following:**

- Demonstrate for students how you read such artistic texts, thinking aloud about the questions you ask, what you ask them about, and how you use them to understand and note what is emphasized in artworks, including paintings and photographs, such as those by Dorothea Lange that achieve a level of artistic and thematic complexity.
- Ask students to first list, then use, the questions they generate or learn to ask when analyzing artworks.
- View with students the artistic works online through, for example, Google Art Project, in pairs in the lab where they view and discuss the works in depth and take notes for use in subsequent papers.
- Have students study examples of established art critics evaluating the same or similar works through sources such as the *Wall Street Journal* column "A Masterpiece," in which a critic shows not only how to read such artworks but also how to write about them.

**To integrate and evaluate multiple sources of information, do the following:**

- Develop a focus question students then seek to answer with evidence or examples from different

sources, including quantitative, visual, or multimedia sources.

- Model for the class how you integrate ideas from these different sources and formats into one coherent view about a subject; then use examples, details, or quotations from those sources when writing or speaking about them to support your claims about what they mean or why they are important.

**To have students analyze multiple interpretations of a literary text, do the following:**

- Set up some sort of note-taking format—several columns, one for each version of the work you are studying—and have students identify key points of emphasis across the interpretations worth comparing (e.g., how each version of *Hamlet* interprets Claudius's opening address to the assembled guests).
- Have students gather different artists' renderings of a character, story, or scene from a literary work, and then compare them with the source text (e.g., view different paintings of Ophelia and compare these with the lines from *Hamlet* that describe her).

**To have students integrate quantitative or technical with qualitative analysis, do the following:**

- Think aloud as you model this for students, describing what you do, how you do it, and why; use the appropriate terms for the types of charts or data you refer to, and discuss the questions you use to evaluate these different analytical forms to answer a question or solve a problem.

**To help your English Language Learners, try this:**

- Prepare these students with information about each format (charts, graphs) or type of media needed to understand what they hear, see, or read since these may be new forms or concepts to some.

**Academic Vocabulary:** Key Words and Phrases

**Analysis (technical vs. quantitative):** To analyze, one breaks something into its components, the parts from which it is made, thereby, attempting to understand how it works or what effect it has. Here, the author analyzes something either by technical/quantitative means (charts, diagrams, numerical or statistical representations) or qualitative methods (written narrative).

**Artistic mediums:** *Medium* refers to the form one uses to express an idea; options include words, images, and sounds; It can also mean a painting, movie, photograph, mixed media work, or printed page.

**Digital text:** Any document of any sort created or reformatted to be read, viewed, or experienced on a computer, tablet, smartphone, or other digital technology that is interactive, multiple-media, or web-enabled, or otherwise incorporates digital technology.

**Diverse formats:** Consider the same information presented in numbers, narrative, and images; graphic, written, mixed media, or spoken formats not only allow the reader to consider a subject from multiple perspectives but also to see how and why others communicate this information differently through these diverse formats.

**Information expressed visually or mathematically:** See "Analysis." The emphasis here is on how the same ideas are expressed in different ways or to different effects in one form or another.

**Integrate:** Readers must combine different perspectives from various media into a coherent understanding or position about the subject.

**Representation of a subject or key scene:** As it is used here, this refers to a subject or key scene that appears in different mediums; so one would examine, for example, the moment Cain killed Abel as it was interpreted by authors, poets, painters, filmmakers, and so on to see what insights one medium offers that another cannot.

**Version:** One could compare Coppola's treatment of Conrad's *Heart of Darkness* in his movie *Apocalypse Now*; or one could contrast different films of *Hamlet* available, from the most modern adaptation to the more classical performances.

**Visual form/visually:** Visual explanations, often called "infographics," may include the traditional pie chart or bar graph but may also incorporate many other features that make these visual or graphic forms much more complex than the previous generation of such texts. Thus, to read these visuals, students must be able to read them as arguments, explanations, or even narratives expressed through numbers and signs, patterns and shapes; they must learn to restate them in words.

*Notes*

**Reading 8:** Delineate and evaluate the argument and specific claims in a text, including the validity of the reasoning as well as the relevance and sufficiency of the evidence.

## Literature

**6** (Not applicable to literature)

**7** (Not applicable to literature)

**8** (Not applicable to literature)

## Informational Text

**6** Trace and evaluate the argument and specific claims in a text, distinguishing claims that are supported by reasons and evidence from claims that are not.

**7** Trace and evaluate the argument and specific claims in a text, **assessing whether the reasoning is sound and the evidence is relevant and sufficient to support the claims.**

**8** **Delineate and** evaluate the argument and specific claims in a text, assessing whether the reasoning is sound and the evidence is relevant and sufficient; **recognize when irrelevant evidence is introduced.**

## What the **Student** Does

| Literature | Informational Text |
| --- | --- |

**6** **Gist:** The 6–8 Common Core State Standards claim this standard is "not applicable to literature."

**6** **Gist:** Follow an argument to examine how the author develops it throughout the text, assessing specific claims to determine their quality and the degree to which they are (or are not) supported by reasons and evidence.

- What argument and claims does this text make—and how do these evolve as you trace them from beginning to end?
- Which claims are supported by reasons and evidence—and which are not?
- What criteria should you apply when evaluating the argument and claims?

**7** **Gist:** The 6–8 Common Core State Standards claim this standard is "not applicable to literature."

**7** **Gist:** Follow an argument to examine how the author develops it throughout the text, assessing specific claims and the extent to which they are supported by sound reasoning and evidence that is both relevant and sufficient.

- What argument or claims does this text make—and how do these evolve as you trace them from beginning to end?
- How sound is the reasoning behind the argument and claims?
- How can you determine whether the evidence is relevant and sufficient?

**8** **Gist:** The 6–8 Common Core State Standards claim this standard is "not applicable to literature."

**8** **Gist:** Follow the details of an argument while examining its development throughout the text, assessing specific claims and the extent to which they are supported by sound reasoning and evidence that is both relevant and sufficient (noting any efforts to include evidence that is irrelevant).

- What argument or claims does this text make—and how do these evolve as you trace them from beginning to end?
- How sound is the reasoning behind the argument and claims?
- How can you determine whether the evidence is relevant and sufficient?

**Reading 8:** Delineate and evaluate the argument and specific claims in a text, including the validity of the reasoning as well as the relevance and sufficiency of the evidence.

## History/Social Studies

**6** Distinguish among fact, opinion, and reasoned judgment in a text.

**7** Distinguish among fact, opinion, and reasoned judgment in a text.

**8** Distinguish among fact, opinion, and reasoned judgment in a text.

## Science/Technical Subjects

**6** Distinguish among facts, reasoned judgment based on research findings, and speculation in a text.

**7** Distinguish among facts, reasoned judgment based on research findings, and speculation in a text.

**8** Distinguish among facts, reasoned judgment based on research findings, and speculation in a text.

## What the **Student** Does

### History/Social Studies

**6** **Gist:** Determine which elements are facts, opinions, or reasoned judgments, which are based on our own considered opinion when we lack complete information but are able to make informed decisions.

- Which elements here are facts and which are opinions?
- What are your reasoned judgments based on in this situation?
- What evidence can you provide to support your reasoned judgment?

**7** **Gist:** Determine which elements are facts, opinions, or reasoned judgments, which are based on our own considered opinion when we lack complete information but are able to make informed decisions.

- Which elements here are facts and which are opinions?
- What are your reasoned judgments based on in this situation?
- What evidence can you provide to support your reasoned judgment?

**8** **Gist:** Determine which elements are facts, opinions, or reasoned judgments, which are based on our own considered opinion when we lack complete information but are able to make informed decisions.

- Which elements here are facts and which are opinions?
- What are your reasoned judgments based on in this situation?
- What evidence can you provide to support your reasoned judgment?

### Science/Technical Subjects

**6** **Gist:** Determine what is a fact, a reasoned judgment supported by research, and mere conjecture that lacks any evidence (i.e., a guess).

- Which elements here are facts?
- What research findings are your reasoned judgments based on?
- Why do you think a certain piece of information is conjecture?

**7** **Gist:** Determine what is a fact, a reasoned judgment supported by research, and mere conjecture that lacks any evidence (i.e., a guess).

- Which elements here are facts?
- What research findings are your reasoned judgments based on?
- Why do you think a certain piece of information is conjecture?

**8** **Gist:** Determine what is a fact, a reasoned judgment supported by research, and mere conjecture that lacks any evidence (i.e., a guess).

- Which elements here are facts?
- What research findings are your reasoned judgments based on?
- Why do you think a certain piece of information is conjecture?

What the **Teacher** Does

### To have students delineate the argument, do the following:

- Tell students first how to identify what the argument *is* and how you figured that out so they know where to direct their critical attention.
- Ask students to label, list, or otherwise identify the following elements related to the argument: the claims made in the text, the reasons stated or implied for those claims, any evidence cited, and how that evidence relates to and supports the claims.
- List on the board three primary goals of argument in academic writing: *to explain ideas or positions* to others, *to persuade people* to change what they think, or *to mediate or reconcile conflicts* between parties about the truth, meaning, or importance of something. Provide students examples, when first introducing them to reading arguments, of different types of arguments, asking them to sort them into the appropriate categories listed above.
- Assign the class arguments written about topics similar to those they are studying, which they must then examine closely to determine the type of argument and the claims made about it.

### To have students evaluate the specific claims made in these different texts, do the following:

- Have students first determine what type of claims they encounter: claims of fact (X is—or is *not*—true), claims of value (X is valid or not, right or wrong, important or not), and claims of policy (X must—or must *not*—be changed).
- Have students go through a complex text that makes such claims and identify the precise claim and its type.

### To have students distinguish claims with and without support from reasons or evidence, do the following:

- Provide several models that, taken as a whole, create some sort of continuum of support for claims; these would constitute a range of quality. Have them examine and create descriptors for the different claims—think of it as something akin to rubric language—which they can then apply to subsequent claims they read.
- Give students a set of criteria for claims with and without support; after clarifying these terms and concepts, have them sort a collection of different claims into one column or the other, providing a rationale for their decision.

### To have students assess if the reasoning is sound and the evidence relevant and sufficient, do the following:

- Introduce to students the idea of fallacies and the qualities of sound reasoning; have them then apply these qualities and use the key fallacies to assess the soundness of the reasoning.
- Clarify the ideas of *relevant* and *sufficient* for the class, offering examples that illustrate that boundary between relevant and irrelevant, sufficient and insufficient; think aloud about why one is or is not sufficient, pointing out specific details.

### To have students distinguish among fact, opinion, and reasoned judgment, do the following:

- Teach students which questions to ask to determine if the evidence is relevant, accurate, and sufficient to support their claim.
- Provide students with a range of models for them to practice evaluating, each one positioned to be just a little more complex than the previous one to help them refine their application of criteria for an effective claim or piece of evidence.

### To have students distinguish among facts, reasoned judgments, and speculation, do the following:

- Define and offer students examples of each of these; then ask them to sort a scrambled set of them into the proper categories or label them if scrambled on a page; finally, have them write academic sentences (X is a fact given that _____, but Y is mere speculation) about these as they apply to the texts students are reading.

### To help your English Language Learners, try this:

- Try using different colored highlighters or an LCD projector to allow you to better identify and represent the role of the different elements of argument. Remember also that argument may raise cultural issues with those from cultures where it is disrespectful to argue.

**Academic Vocabulary:** Key Words and Phrases

**Argument:** The writer or speaker adopts a position about which he or she attempts to persuade others to think or feel differently about an issue, to change how they act, or to resolve disagreements between themselves and other parties about an issue. Writers and speakers accomplish these ends by presenting claims supported with reasons, evidence, and appeals. Arguments are related to but different from claims, propositions, thesis statements, or assertions.

**Assess:** Assessment in this context is all about the logic of one's claims. Such assessment asks one to examine the reliability, credibility, and timeliness of all sources used to support one's claims.

**Based on research findings:** This applies specifically to reasoned judgments which, in this case, would be based not on considered opinions or even facts but on research.

**Claims:** A specific assertion that authors want readers to accept as true and act on; the author's thesis is the *primary* claim he or she will make, develop, and support with evidence throughout the paper. Because a claim is debatable, it requires supporting evidence to counter inevitable challenges the critical readers will make as they assess the validity of the claims, logic, and evidence.

**Delineate:** The reader must be able to describe or represent in precise detail the author's argument, as well as claims, reasoning, and evidence; to delineate is to draw a line between what is and is *not* the exact argument, claim, reasoning, or evidence.

**Distinguish among fact, opinion, and speculation:** This calls for the reader to identify those different qualities or features that separate fact (indisputable evidence), opinion (view of judgment not based on fact), and speculation (conjecture without evidence).

**Evidence (relevance and sufficiency of):** It is the reader's job to determine if the evidence is, in fact, related to the claim and does, indeed, provide adequate support. If the evidence is from an unreliable source (personal experience) or is limited to a few details, the reader should consider the evidence irrelevant and insufficient.

**Reasoned judgment:** This involves more than facts or opinions; it is sometimes referred to as a "considered opinion" based on well-reasoned judgments about the proper course of action; the commonly used example is the judge who, we assume, engages in reasoned judgment when handing down a judgment based on evidence that is sound, relevant, and valid.

**Reasoning:** Readers are looking to determine if the student's logic is based on valid, reliable evidence from current and credible sources or on one or more fallacies that are false or misleading, connected as they are by dubious links between the claim and evidence.

**Sound:** When applied to reasoning or judgment, it means that the decision is based on reason and sense; it means that the argument or claims are strong, sturdy, and able to do the job.

**Trace the argument:** One follows the argument as the text unfolds over the course of the text, noting how authors develop it and use evidence to support their claims as they go.

**Validity of the reasoning:** This refers to the quality of one's thinking being logically or factually sound, cogent.

*Notes*

**Reading 9:** Analyze how two or more texts address similar themes or topics to build knowledge or to compare the approaches the authors take.

## Literature

**6** Compare and contrast texts in different forms or genres (e.g., stories and poems; historical novels and fantasy stories) in terms of their approaches to similar themes and topics.

**7** Compare and contrast a fictional portrayal of a time, place, or character and a historical account of the same period as a means of understanding how authors of fiction use or alter history.

**8** Analyze how a modern work of fiction draws on themes, patterns of events, or character types from myths, traditional stories, or religious works such as the Bible, including describing how the material is rendered new.

## Informational Text

**6** Compare and contrast one author's presentation of events with that of another (e.g., a memoir written by and a biography on the same person).

**7** Analyze how two or more authors writing about the same topic shape their presentations of key information by emphasizing different evidence or advancing different interpretations of facts.

**8** Analyze a case in which two or more texts provide conflicting information on the same topic and identify where the texts disagree on matters of fact or interpretation.

## What the **Student** Does

### Literature

**6** **Gist:** Examine how various forms and genres (e.g., stories and poems, historical and fantasy stories) treat similar themes and topics, noting the similarities and differences in their respective approaches.

- What type of text is this?
- How is this text similar to and different in its treatment of specific themes and topics from some other type of text?

**7** **Gist:** Examine the similarities and differences between two accounts of a time, place, or character in history, one fictional and the other a firsthand report, focusing on how authors treat historical events through fiction differently from the original account.

- What historical time, place, or character does this fiction or firsthand account cover?
- How is the fictional treatment similar to and different from the nonfiction treatment?

**8** **Gist:** Examine how contemporary authors recast traditional myths, stories, or religious texts such as the Bible into modern stories that adopt or adapt similar themes, story structures, or character types, discussing how they make the old and foreign seem new and familiar.

- What themes, structures, or character types does this modern story borrow from older, traditional texts?
- How does the author's use of these old stories make them seem new?

### Informational Text

**6** **Gist:** Examine how two authors treat the same events, noting how a memoir by a historical figure is similar to and different from, for example, a historian's book about that same event.

- What subject do these two texts explore?
- How does the treatment of the subject differ in the two different accounts?

**7** **Gist:** Discuss the treatment of the same topic by two or more authors, noting how each one emphasizes certain pieces of evidence over others or advances an alternative explanation of events based on different evidence or interpretation of the facts.

- Which details, facts, or evidence do the authors emphasize?
- Where and when do the authors' examples and evidence or explanations and interpretations differ and agree?

**8** **Gist:** Examine the treatment of a topic in two or more texts that offer conflicting accounts, determining where those texts contradict or disagree with each other about the facts.

- What subject do these different texts explore?
- Where, how, and why do these different texts disagree about the meaning or accuracy of any interpretations?

**Reading 9:** Analyze how two or more texts address similar themes or topics to build knowledge or to compare the approaches the authors take.

## History/Social Studies

**6** Analyze the relationship between a primary and secondary source on the same topic.

**7** Analyze the relationship between a primary and secondary source on the same topic.

**8** Analyze the relationship between a primary and secondary source on the same topic.

## Science/Technical Subjects

**6** Compare and contrast the information gained from experiments, simulations, video, or multimedia sources with that gained from reading a text on the same topic.

**7** Compare and contrast the information gained from experiments, simulations, video, or multimedia sources with that gained from reading a text on the same topic.

**8** Compare and contrast the information gained from experiments, simulations, video, or multimedia sources with that gained from reading a text on the same topic.

What the **Student** Does

## History/Social Studies

**6** **Gist:** Examine how a primary and secondary source each treat the same topic, focusing on the nature of the relationship between these two sources.

- How does the primary source compare with the secondary source in its treatment of the same topic?
- How would you describe the relationship between these two sources in terms of their respective treatment of this topic?

**7** **Gist:** Examine how a primary and secondary source each treat the same topic, focusing on the nature of the relationship between these two sources.

- How does the primary source compare with the secondary source in its treatment of the same topic?
- How would you describe the relationship between these two sources in terms of their respective treatment of this topic?

**8** **Gist:** Examine how a primary and secondary source each treat the same topic, focusing on the nature of the relationship between these two sources.

- How does the primary source compare with the secondary source in its treatment of the same topic?
- How would you describe the relationship between these two sources in terms of their respective treatment of this topic?

## Science/Technical Subjects

**6** **Gist:** Examine the information gathered from various sources (e.g., experiments, simulations, multimedia), comparing and contrasting content from those sources with information obtained from reading a text about the same subject.

- What is the subject you are examining across all these different types of text?
- How does information about this subject gleaned from a printed text compare with that gathered from other sources (e.g., experiments and simulations)?

**7** **Gist:** Examine the information gathered from various sources (e.g., experiments, simulations, multimedia), comparing and contrasting content from those sources with information obtained from reading a text about the same subject.

- What is the subject you are examining across all these different types of text?
- How does information about this subject gleaned from a printed text compare with that gathered from other sources (e.g., experiments and simulations)?

**8** **Gist:** Examine the information gathered from various sources (e.g., experiments, simulations, multimedia), comparing and contrasting content from those sources with information obtained from reading a text about the same subject.

- What is the subject you are examining across all these different types of text?
- How does information about this subject gleaned from a printed text compare with that gathered from other sources (e.g., experiments and simulations)?

What the **Teacher** Does

**To have students analyze how two or more texts address similar themes or topics, do the following:**

- Use colors (as you display the text or a passage via LCD projector) to code the two themes or topics as they appear or develop and refer to each other; narrate your thinking aloud as you do this, so students see what you do and understand how the colors that represent each theme or topic connect with the others throughout the text.

- Have students use highlighters or digital color tools (if they are working on-screen) to examine the development of ideas into a larger fabric of knowledge about an idea over time or examine how each author approaches the treatment of these ideas in their texts compared with the others being studied. Let students' reading be guided by the question, What patterns emerge over the course of the text as these different authors explore this theme?

**To have students analyze how an author draws on and transforms source material, do the following:**

- Assign students the original source text (e.g., an Aesop fable) on which the literary text is based, having them then identify all the corresponding elements of that story, fable, or pattern in the modern version they are reading, discussing or writing about what these older sources add to the new story.

- Have students read multiple versions of a source text (e.g., different versions of a folktale from different cultures or traditions) in conjunction with the poem or story that borrows from it, having them identify the common elements between each (e.g., a trickster character); an alternative is to give them a list of such characters or patterns with descriptions and then direct them to find examples of them in the story.

**To have students compare and contrast information from experiments, do the following:**

- Provide students with graphic organizers for taking structured notes (e.g., two columns, with similarities and differences at the head of each) to gather and organize such information from experiments or other sources in a way that reveals those patterns.

- Display on the projector (using an iPad or computer) the way you would evaluate and sort such information during and/or after an experiment, modeling for them how you would set it up before you began the experiment, simulation, or video they watched.

**To have students examine the treatment or use of primary and secondary sources, do the following:**

- Offer students several clear examples of primary and secondary sources first so they know what these terms mean and how they differ so they will know them when they see or read them.

- Have students use a graphic organizer with multiple columns for each source; have students jot down key ideas or quotations that represent how each source treats that idea, drawing conclusions about how they compare when you are finished and citing examples to support and illustrate your claims.

**To have students analyze a case in which two texts provide conflicting information, do the following:**

- Format a document to create parallel (side-by-side) texts so students can read across texts, noting where the two texts differ in a discernible way from each other, and then draw conclusions about the meaning of those discrepancies.

**To help your English Language Learners, try this:**

- Read aloud from these texts as you display them or as students follow along on copies of their own so they see and hear the more antiquated language of these often older or more complex texts. If available, you might also consider bringing in versions of some of these archetypal stories or tales (or their modern adaptations into literature) from their original countries by way of not just celebrating those students' cultures but further illustrating how universal those stories, themes, and patterns actually are.

**Academic Vocabulary:** Key Words and Phrases

**Analyze the relationship between a primary and secondary source:** Secondary sources are books and articles written by someone who was not present at the event they discuss; such writers rely on extensive primary sources to write these secondary sources. In analyzing the relationship between them, one might consider why or how a writer is using a given primary source in relation to their purpose and the topic.

**Approaches to similar themes and topics:** As it applies to several of the standards here, this phrase refers to the act of comparing and contrasting the "approaches" of different texts, authors, or types of text when reading different texts on a topic.

**Approaches:** *The approaches the authors take* could refer to the choices the author makes about stylistic elements such as voice, imagery, or format; it could also refer to the author's choice to approach the subject through a particular point of view or genre.

**Build knowledge:** This stresses the author's efforts to build the reader's knowledge about the subject of the text; given the reference to several foundational or canonical texts, this would mean looking at how the author draws on and provides for the reader the necessary information to read and understand those stories alluded to or embedded within the story.

**Compare and contrast two authors' presentations of events:** Look at the similarities (*compare*) and differences (*contrast*) when examining how the authors of two (or more) different books "present" their subject (e.g., an event, a person, or an action).

**Draws on themes, patterns of events, or character types:** Another word for these is *archetypes*; the idea is that these themes, patterns, and types are found across cultures and eras going back to our very beginnings and, thus, represent enduring ideas or patterns we can use today to express those ideas. Authors adapt these stories for our modern tastes, transforming them in the process so they seem new but add depth to the text through the resonant echoes of older, familiar stories.

**Fictional portrayal of a time, place, or character:** This is another way of saying *historical fiction*.

**Findings:** This refers to the results from a scientific study: That is, it refers to what the scientist *found* as a result of an experiment. The reader's job is to evaluate how credible these findings are in light of what we know to be true and the evidence the writer provides.

**Historical account of the same period:** This refers to nonfiction, historical texts that are written about a given person or period; examples include personal histories set in a specific time such as Douglass's *Narrative of a Slave* or nonfiction books about a historical event such as Kearns Goodwin's *Team of Rivals*.

**How authors of fiction use or alter history:** Some writers of historical fiction take greater liberties with the facts than others; thus, some "use" history as a guide, following its general outlines when writing fiction; others see facts as sometimes standing in the way of the "truth" and rearrange or even ignore them, creating instead a narrative they think offers more insight.

**Texts provide conflicting information on the same topic:** On occasion, a text may base its claims or premises on information that contradicts the sources used by others writing about the same topic; when this happens, writers must sort out the truth, perhaps consulting other, more reliable sources.

*Notes*

**Reading 10:** Read and comprehend complex literary and informational texts independently and proficiently.

## Literature

**6** By the end of the year, read and comprehend literature, including stories, dramas, and poems, in the grades 6–8 text complexity band proficiently, with scaffolding as needed at the high end of the range.

**7** By the end of the year, read and comprehend literature, including stories, dramas, and poems, in the grades 6–8 text complexity band proficiently, with scaffolding as needed at the high end of the range.

**8** By the end of the year, read and comprehend literature, including stories, dramas, and poems, at the high end of the grades 6–8 text complexity band **independently and proficiently.**

## Informational Text

**6** By the end of the year, read and comprehend literary nonfiction in the grades 6–8 text complexity band proficiently, with scaffolding as needed at the high end of the range.

**7** By the end of the year, read and comprehend literary nonfiction in the grades 6–8 text complexity band proficiently, with scaffolding as needed at the high end of the range.

**8** By the end of the year, read and comprehend literary nonfiction at the high end of the grades 6–8 text complexity band **independently and proficiently.**

## History/Social Studies

**6** By the end of grade 8, read and comprehend history/social studies texts in the grades 6–8 text complexity band independently and proficiently.

**7** By the end of grade 8, read and comprehend history/social studies texts in the grades 6–8 text complexity band independently and proficiently.

**8** By the end of grade 8, read and comprehend history/social studies texts in the grades 6–8 text complexity band independently and proficiently.

## Science/Technical Subjects

**6** By the end of grade 8, read and comprehend science/technical texts in the grades 6–8 text complexity band independently and proficiently.

**7** By the end of grade 8, read and comprehend science/technical texts in the grades 6–8 text complexity band independently and proficiently.

**8** By the end of grade 8, read and comprehend science/technical texts in the grades 6–8 text complexity band independently and proficiently.

# Common Core Reading Standard 10

## What the **Student** Does

### Literature

**6** **Gist:** Read a range of literary texts—fiction, poetry, and drama—within the grades 6–8 text complexity band, receiving help only when needed as they reach the high end of the 6–8 complexity band.

- How complex is this text?
- How much more complex is this text?
- What sort of support, if any, would help?

**7** **Gist:** Read a range of literary texts—fiction, poetry, and drama—within the grades 6–8 text complexity band, receiving help only when needed as they reach the high end of the 6–8 complexity band.

- How complex is this text?
- How much more complex is this text?
- What sort of support, if any, would help?

**8** **Gist:** Read a range of literary texts—fiction, poetry, and drama—within the grades 6–8 text complexity band, receiving help only when needed as they reach the high end of the 6–8 complexity band.

- How complex is this text?
- How much more complex is this text?
- What sort of support, if any, would help?

### History/Social Studies

**6** **Gist:** Read a range of history and social studies texts appropriate for grades 6–8 text complexity, able to resolve any problems on their own and apply those techniques that will allow them to read all types of texts at each grade level with competence.

- How complex is this text?
- How much more complex is this text?
- Which strategies or techniques should I use to solve any comprehension problems in this text?

**7** **Gist:** Read a range of history and social studies texts appropriate for grades 6–8 text complexity, able to resolve any problems on their own and apply those techniques that will allow them to read all types of texts at each grade level with competence.

- How complex is this text?
- How much more complex is this text?
- Which strategies or techniques should I use to solve any comprehension problems in this text.

**8** **Gist:** Read a range of history and social studies texts appropriate for grades 6–8 text complexity, able to resolve any problems on their own and apply those techniques that will allow them to read all types of texts at each grade level with competence.

- How complex is this text?
- How much more complex is this text?
- Which strategies or techniques should I use to solve any comprehension problems in this text.

### Informational Text

**6** **Gist:** Read a range of literary nonfiction appropriate for the grades 6–8 text complexity band, receiving help only when needed as they reach the high end of the 6–8 complexity band.

- How complex is this text?
- How much more complex is this text?
- What sort of support, if any, is needed?

**7** **Gist:** Read a range of literary nonfiction appropriate for the grades 6–8 text complexity band, receiving help only when needed as they reach the high end of the 6–8 complexity band.

- How complex is this text?
- How much more complex is this text?
- What sort of support, if any, is needed?

**8** **Gist:** Read a range of literary nonfiction appropriate for the grades 6–8 text complexity band, receiving help only when needed as they reach the high end of the 6–8 complexity band.

- How complex is this text?
- How much more complex is this text?
- What sort of support, if any, is needed?

### Science/Technical Subjects

**6** **Gist:** Read an array of texts appropriate for science and technical subjects in the grades 6–8 text complexity band, able to resolve any problems on their own and apply those techniques that will allow them to read all types of texts at each grade level with competence.

- How complex is this text?
- How much more complex is this text?
- Which strategies or techniques should I use to solve any comprehension problems in this text?

**7** **Gist:** Read an array of texts appropriate for science and technical subjects in the grades 6–8 text complexity band, able to resolve any problems on their own and apply those techniques that will allow them to read all types of texts at each grade level with competence.

- How complex is this text?
- How much more complex is this text?
- Which strategies or techniques should I use to solve any comprehension problems in this text?

**8** **Gist:** Read an array of texts appropriate for science and technical subjects in the grades 6–8 text complexity band, able to resolve any problems on their own and apply those techniques that will allow them to read all types of texts at each grade level with competence.

- How complex is this text?
- How much more complex is this text?
- Which strategies or techniques should I use to solve any comprehension problems in this text?

**To help students comprehend complex texts independently and proficiently, do the following:**

- Assign an array of literary (novels, plays, and poems) and informational texts (literary nonfiction, essays, biographies, and historical accounts) to be read in class and outside, so students can build their stamina, speed, and confidence with longer and more complex texts.
- Organize students into groups (inquiry circles, literature circles, book clubs); each group reads a different book or the same as the others, using the discussion within the group to help them work through the challenges the book presents and engage in more independent discussions about the book.
- Engage in a full-class close reading on occasion, modeling what such close reading looks like and discussing how you do it as you go; then let students take on more of the responsibility for reading and discussing, which teachers first facilitate, then relinquish.
- Teach students a range of questions to ask when they read different types of texts and techniques they can use throughout their reading process as needed with different types of texts before, during, and after they read each text.
- Assign a series of readings, both informational and literary, about the same subject (e.g., survival, transformation, the environment) to understand it in depth from different perspectives.
- Evaluate the texts you assign using the Common Core complexity criteria and arrange them, when possible, in order of complexity so students are consistently reading texts that challenge them (not merely with their length but also in their complexity) more than those they previously read.

**To have students provide scaffolding as needed at the high end of the range, do the following:**

- Provide targeted questions or directions students can use to guide them when engaging in close reading of any type of text; such questions might direct their attention to stylistic elements or rhetorical features, nuances of plot or character, or how these elements interact with each other and the setting in the story.
- Encourage students to consult annotated versions of the texts they are studying in their textbooks or that you provide (or find available online) as students develop their capacity to read closely, gradually phasing out such support as they develop independence.

**To have students develop their ability to read complex history and science texts, do the following:**

- Expose students to an array of texts written by experts in the fields in popular journals (e.g., *Discovery*, *Scientific American*) and other sources (blogs, reports, news articles) where the quality of the writing will challenge them, and because of the often shorter nature of the articles, require students to consider the subject from a range of perspectives, sources, or fields.
- Include in the history, social science, science, or technical subjects longer texts, including books or long-form journalism about scientific, technical, economic, or historical events and processes written by leading authors and journalists in those fields. Students might read these longer works as part of an ongoing inquiry into the environment, historical events, or cultures, giving a presentation or writing a report when they finish.

**To help your English Language Learners, try this:**

- Help them find books and other texts appropriate to their current reading level but that challenge them with ideas, language, and other elements that are new or more complex than previous texts they have read.

**Academic Vocabulary:** Key Words and Phrases

**Complex literary and informational texts:** *Complex* is not the same as *difficult*; literary and informational texts are complex for different reasons as they are written for mostly different purposes. In the context of the standards, complexity is one measure of a work's quality but is at the heart of the CCSS when it comes to reading.

**High end of the range:** For middle school, this means the high end of the 8th grade in text complexity; students reading at this level at the end of a year should be able to read independently, with little, less, or no teachers' guidance.

**History/social studies texts:** Those texts commonly studied in history and social studies classes, including graphs, maps, primary source documents, foundational and seminal documents, and a range of informational texts that explain the importance of key individuals and the cause and effect of various historical events and eras.

**Independently:** One is able to read whatever texts are assigned without the aid of the teacher or, when challenged by the teacher with a complex text, is able to do the work as assigned without the aid of scaffolding or guided instruction.

**Informational:** Texts designed to inform, though this can include argument, a range of expository texts, and also a range of media and formats, including infographics and videos.

**Literary nonfiction:** Informational texts, often books or essays, that use novelistic and other literary techniques to engage readers, and then use the story to convey the information. Examples would include *Freedom Walkers* and *This Land Was Made for You and Me*.

**Proficiently:** This describes the way and the level at which the individual student is able to read complex texts; proficiency is equated with skill, though not mastery.

**Scaffolding:** This is support from teachers, aides, or other students who help a student read a text or complete a task; examples include providing background knowledge, reading aloud, or any other strategy designed to help students become independent readers or writers.

**Science/technical texts:** These texts include many types and formats, all of which fall into the informational text category, but which may include infographic or quantitative texts, as well as narratives of lab procedures that explain how they arrived at a result. Such highly technical texts stress clarity through objective, structured prose.

**Text complexity band:** The individual text complexity bands correspond with associated grade levels (6–8). The levels themselves are determined by the three-part model of text complexity discussed in Appendix A of the complete CCSS document. The three factors in text complexity are *qualitative dimensions* (levels of meaning, language complexity as determined by an attentive reader), *quantitative dimensions* (word length and frequency, sentence length and cohesion), and *reader and task considerations* (factors related to a specific reader such as motivation, background knowledge, or persistence; others associated with the task itself such as the purpose or demands of the task itself).

*Notes*

# Part 2

# The Common Core State Standards

## Writing

# College and Career Readiness Anchor Standards for
# *Writing 6–8*

**Source:
Common Core
State Standards**

The grades 6–12 standards on the following pages define what students should understand and be able to do by the end of each grade. They correspond to the CCR anchor standards by number. The CCR and grade-specific standards are necessary complements—the former providing broad standards, the latter providing additional specificity—that together define the skills and understandings that all students must demonstrate.

## Text Types and Purposes*

1. Write arguments to support claims in an analysis of substantive topics or texts, using valid reasoning and relevant and sufficient evidence.
2. Write informative/explanatory texts to examine and convey complex ideas and information clearly and accurately through the elective selection, organization, and analysis of content.
3. Write narratives to develop real or imagined experiences or events using elective technique, well-chosen details, and well-structured event sequences.

## Production and Distribution of Writing

4. Produce clear and coherent writing in which the development, organization, and style are appropriate to task, purpose, and audience.
5. Develop and strengthen writing as needed by planning, revising, editing, rewriting, or trying a new approach.
6. Use technology, including the Internet, to produce and publish writing and to interact and collaborate with others.

## Research to Build and Present Knowledge

7. Conduct short as well as more sustained research projects based on focused questions, demonstrating understanding of the subject under investigation.
8. Gather relevant information from multiple print and digital sources, assess the credibility and accuracy of each source, and integrate the information while avoiding plagiarism.
9. Draw evidence from literary or informational texts to support analysis, reflection, and research.

## Range of Writing

10. Write routinely over extended times (time for research, reflection, and revision) and shorter times (a single sitting or a day or two) for a range of tasks, purposes, and audiences.

## Note on Range and Content of Student Writing

For students, writing is a key means of asserting and defending claims, showing what they know about a subject, and conveying what they have experienced, imagined, thought, and felt. To be CCR writers, students must take task, purpose, and audience into careful consideration, choosing words, information, structures, and formats deliberately. They need to know how to combine elements of different kinds of writing—for example, to use narrative strategies within argument and explanation within narrative—to produce complex and nuanced writing. They need to be able to use technology strategically when creating, refining, and collaborating on writing. They have to become adept at gathering information, evaluating sources, and citing material accurately and reporting findings from their research and analysis of sources in a clear and cogent manner. They must have the flexibility, concentration, and fluency to produce high-quality, first-draft text under a tight deadline as well as the capacity to revisit and make improvements to a piece of writing over multiple drafts when circumstances encourage or require it.

* These broad types of writing include many subgenres. See Appendix A for definitions of key writing types.

# College and Career Readiness Anchor Standards for

# Writing

The College and Career Readiness (CCR) anchor standards are the same for all middle and high school students, regardless of subject area or grade level. What varies is the sophistication of the writing of the three types—argument, informative/explanatory, and narrative—stressed at each subsequent grade level in each disciplinary domain. The core writing skills should not change as students advance; rather, the level at which they learn and can perform those skills should increase in complexity as students move from one grade to the next.

## Text Types and Purposes*

Argument appears first as it is essential to success in college and develops the critical faculties needed in the adult world. Crafting arguments requires students to analyze texts or topics and determine which evidence best supports their arguments. Informational/explanatory writing conveys ideas, events, and findings by choosing and explaining the behavior, meaning, or importance of key details.

Students draw from a range of sources, including primary and secondary sources. Narrative writing includes not just stories but accounts of historical events and lab procedures. Students write to change minds, hearts, and actions (argument); to extend readers' knowledge or acceptance of ideas and procedures (informational/explanatory); and to inform, inspire, persuade, or entertain (narrative).

## Production and Distribution of Writing

This set of anchor standards involves the stages of the writing process. These standards also highlight the importance of knowing who the audience is and the style and format the writer should use to achieve a purpose. Students also learn the skills needed throughout the writing process:

generating ideas and trying other styles, structures, perspectives, or processes as they bring their ideas into focus and some final form. Finally, these standards call for writers to use technology not only to publish but to collaborate throughout the writing process with others.

## Research to Build and Present Knowledge

These standards focus on inquiry processes of varying lengths, all of which should develop students' knowledge of the subject they are investigating and the skills needed to conduct that investigation. Students acquire and refine the ability to find, evaluate, and use a range of sources

during these research projects, which can take as long as a period to as much as a month. Such inquiries demand students correctly cite the source of all information to ensure they learn what plagiarism is and how to avoid it.

## Range of Writing

This standard emphasizes not only what students write but how often and for what purposes they write over the course of the school year. Writing, as this standard makes clear, is something students should be doing constantly and for

substantial lengths of time. Also, they should write for an array of reasons and audiences and in response to a mix of topics and tasks.

---

* These broad types of writing include many subgenres. See Appendix A for definitions of key writing types.

**Writing 1:** Write arguments to support claims in an analysis of substantive topics or texts, using valid reasoning and relevant and sufficient evidence.

## English Language Arts

**6** Write arguments to support claims with clear reasons and relevant evidence.

   a. Introduce claim(s) and organize the reasons and evidence clearly.

   b. Support claim(s) with clear reasons and relevant evidence, using credible sources and demonstrating an understanding of the topic or text.

   c. Use words, phrases, and clauses to clarify the relationships among claim(s) and reasons.

   d. Establish and maintain a formal style.

   e. Provide a concluding statement or section that follows from the argument presented.

**7** Write arguments to support claims with clear reasons and relevant evidence.

   a. Introduce claim(s), **acknowledge alternate or opposing claims, and** organize the reasons and evidence **logically**.

   b. Support claim(s) with **logical reasoning** and relevant evidence, using **accurate**, credible sources and demonstrating an understanding of the topic or text.

   c. Use words, phrases, and clauses to **create cohesion** and clarify the relationships among claim(s), reasons, **and evidence**.

   d. Establish and maintain a formal style.

   e. Provide a concluding statement or section that follows from **and supports** the argument presented.

## History/Social Studies, Science, and Technical Studies

**6** Write arguments focused on discipline-specific content.

   a. Introduce claim(s) about a topic or issue, acknowledge and distinguish the claim(s) from alternate or opposing claims, and organize the reasons and evidence logically.

   b. Support claim(s) with logical reasoning and relevant, accurate data and evidence that demonstrate an understanding of the topic or text, using credible sources.

   c. Use words, phrases, and clauses to create cohesion and clarify the relationships among claim(s), counterclaims, reasons, and evidence.

   d. Establish and maintain a formal style.

   e. Provide a concluding statement or section that follows from and supports the argument presented.

**7** Write arguments focused on discipline-specific content.

   a. Introduce claim(s) about a topic or issue, acknowledge and distinguish the claim(s) from alternate or opposing claims, and organize the reasons and evidence logically.

   b. Support claim(s) with logical reasoning and relevant, accurate data and evidence that demonstrate an understanding of the topic or text, using credible sources.

   c. Use words, phrases, and clauses to create cohesion and clarify the relationships among claim(s), counterclaims, reasons, and evidence.

   d. Establish and maintain a formal style.

   e. Provide a concluding statement or section that follows from and supports the argument presented.

\* These broad types of writing include many subgenres. See Appendix A for definitions of key writing types.

## What the **Student** Does

### English Language Arts

**6** **Gist:** Construct arguments to defend claims which, when introduced, say *what* you claim and *why*, providing strong reasons and evidence from credible sources that show students understand the text or topic. Students clarify these different relationships among claim(s) and reasons by choosing language (words, phrases, clauses) and adopting a formal style that suits and maintain their argument until the conclusion, where they connect all ideas, claims, and reasons in a logical way that proceeds from and supports their argument.

- What do you claim—and *why*?
- What evidence, from *reliable* sources, do you offer to support your claim(s)?
- How does your conclusion follow from all that precedes it?

**7** **Gist:** Construct arguments to defend claims which, when introduced, say *what* you claim and *why*, providing logical reasons and evidence from responsible and reliable sources that show students understand the text or topic. Here, students also identify and make concessions to conflicting or differing claims, which are arranged logically. Students clarify these different relationships among claim(s) and reasons by choosing language (words, phrases, clauses) and adopting a formal style that adds cohesion and clarity up through the conclusion, where they connect all ideas, claims, and reasons in a logical way that proceeds from and supports their argument.

- What do you claim—and *why*?
- What are the other perspectives—alternative, conflicting—you should be considering?
- How does your conclusion follow from all that precedes it?

### History/Social Studies, Science, and Technical Studies

**6** **Gist:** Construct arguments about disciplinary ideas or content, introducing *what* you claim and *why*, providing logical reasons, evidence, and data from responsible and reliable sources that show students understand the text or topic, even as you concede that there are other perspectives and counterclaims. Here, students also identify and explain how their claims are different from the conflicting or differing claims. Students clarify these different relationships among claim(s), counterclaims, reasons, and evidence by choosing language (words, phrases, clauses) and adopting a formal style that adds cohesion and clarity up through the conclusion, where they connect all the ideas, claims, and reasons in a logical way that proceeds from and supports their argument.

- What do you claim, why, and how is your claim distinct from all others about this subject?
- What other perspectives—alternative, conflicting—should you be considering?
- How does your conclusion follow from all that precedes it?

**7** **Gist:** Construct arguments about disciplinary ideas or content, introducing *what* you claim and *why*, providing logical reasons, evidence, and data from responsible and reliable sources that show students understand the text or topic, even as you concede that there are other perspectives and counterclaims. Here, students also identify and explain how their claims are different from the conflicting or differing claims. Students clarify these different relationships among claim(s), counterclaims, reasons, and evidence by choosing language (words, phrases, clauses) and adopting a formal style that adds cohesion and clarity up through the conclusion, where they connect all the ideas, claims, and reasons in a logical way that proceeds from and supports their argument.

- What do you claim, why, and how is your claim distinct from all others about this subject?
- What other perspectives—alternative, conflicting—should you be considering?
- How does your conclusion follow from all that precedes it?

**Writing 1:** Write arguments to support claims in an analysis of substantive topics or texts, using valid reasoning and relevant and sufficient evidence.

## English Language Arts

**8** Write arguments to support claims with clear reasons and relevant evidence.

a. Introduce claim(s), acknowledge and **distinguish the claim(s)** from alternate or opposing claims, and organize the reasons and evidence logically.
b. Support claim(s) with logical reasoning and relevant evidence, using accurate, credible sources and demonstrating an understanding of the topic or text.
c. Use words, phrases, and clauses to create cohesion and clarify the relationships among claim(s), **counterclaims**, reasons, and evidence.
d. Establish and maintain a formal style.
e. Provide a concluding statement or section that follows from and supports the argument presented.

## History/Social Studies, Science, and Technical Studies

**8** Write arguments focused on discipline specific content.

a. Introduce claim(s) about a topic or issue, acknowledge and distinguish the claim(s) from alternate or opposing claims, and organize the reasons and evidence logically.
b. Support claim(s) with logical reasoning and relevant, accurate data and evidence that demonstrate an understanding of the topic or text, using credible sources.
c. Use words, phrases, and clauses to create cohesion and clarify the relationships among claim(s), counterclaims, reasons, and evidence.
d. Establish and maintain a formal style.
e. Provide a concluding statement or section that follows from and supports the argument presented.

* These broad types of writing include many subgenres. See Appendix A for definitions of key writing types.

## What the **Student** Does

### English Language Arts

**8** **Gist:** Construct arguments to defend claims which, when introduced, say *what* you claim and *why*, providing logical reasons and evidence from responsible and reliable sources that show students understand the text or topic. Here, students also identify and explain how their claims are different from the conflicting or differing claims. Students clarify these different relationships among claim(s), counterclaims, reasons, and evidence by choosing language (words, phrases, clauses) and adopting a formal style that adds cohesion and clarity up through the conclusion, where they connect all the ideas, claims, and reasons in a logical way that proceeds from and supports their argument.

- What do you claim, why, and how is your claim distinct from all others about this subject?
- What other perspectives—alternative, conflicting— should you be considering?
- How does your conclusion follow from all that precedes it?

### History/Social Studies, Science, and Technical Studies

**8** **Gist:** Construct arguments about disciplinary ideas or content, introducing *what* you claim and *why*, providing logical reasons, evidence, and data from responsible and reliable sources that show students understand the text or topic, even as you concede that there are other perspectives and counterclaims. Here, students also identify and explain how their claims are different from the conflicting or differing claims. Students clarify these different relationships among claim(s), counterclaims, reasons, and evidence by choosing language (words, phrases, clauses) and adopting a formal style that adds cohesion and clarity up through the conclusion, where they connect all the ideas, claims, and reasons in a logical way that proceeds from and supports their argument.

- What do you claim, why, and how is your claim distinct from all others about this subject?
- What other perspectives—alternative, conflicting— should you be considering?
- How does your conclusion follow from all that precedes it?

What the **Teacher** Does

**To help students understand and learn to write arguments, do the following:**

- Provide students with a range of sample arguments so they learn to distinguish between effective and ineffective arguments.
- Have students read whole papers to see how writers use claims and evidence over the course of the whole text.
- Keep and use both professional and student models for subsequent study of what to do—and what *not* to do.
- Require students to label the elements of their argument (e.g., claim, evidence, reason), and evaluate the quality of each in light of whatever criteria are most appropriate on that occasion.
- Help students establish and apply criteria for determining the quality of topics and texts, claims and counterclaims, evidence and reasons.
- Use structured note-taking formats (e.g., columns with headers such as claim, reason, evidence) in the early stages to help students understand the elements and see how they work together to support the argument.

**To evaluate others' and make their own claims, do the following:**

- Give students sets of claims with varying degrees of specificity and insight; ask them to evaluate each by some criteria or arrange them all on a continuum of quality.
- Ask students to provide a list of possible counterclaims, alternative positions, values, or biases to consider when writing their claims or evaluating/responding to those of others.
- Generate questions to help students analyze texts and topics, evidence and reasoning, and claims and counterclaims when developing or supporting their claims.

**To use words, phrases, and clauses to clarify the relationships, do the following:**

- Distribute highlighters or crayons, and then ask students to indicate those words that create cohesion by linking or serving as transitions between claims and reasons, reasons and evidence, and claims and counterclaims.
- Together, examine sentences for a variety of style and syntax, especially as these help clarify and emphasize the relationships and general cohesion between the different elements.
- Generate words that are appropriate to the tone, topic, and type of argument, as well as the audience, occasion, and purpose; this can be done as a class, in groups, or independently.
- Invite students to use such techniques as backward outlining to assess the logic of their arguments within a paragraph or the whole text.

**To teach students how to generate, evaluate, and use evidence, do the following:**

- Have students investigate how they might use data—statistics, surveys, or other quantitative information—to support their claims; include in this discussion why they should or should not do so.
- Show students how to gather and evaluate evidence when preparing to write (e.g., during the research/prewriting phase).

**To introduce or extend knowledge of other aspects of argument, do the following:**

- Discuss with students the formats and styles used by different disciplines or on special occasions.
- Develop a guide or scoring rubric based on the Common Core writing standard description for argument.
- Think aloud about an effective and ineffective model, or some portion (e.g., introducing the claims) of the paper; you might display it on a big screen as you walk through it and point out what is and is not effective and why that is.
- Bring in other forms of argument—visual, infographic, multimedia—to deepen their understanding of argument.
- Avoid separating writing arguments from the equally important study of argument in reading and speaking.

**To help your English Language Learners, try this:**

- Discuss the *idea* of argument, as it may be a foreign and even troubling concept for many students, given their culture's emphasis on respect for authorities and elders.

**Academic Vocabulary:** Key Words and Phrases

**Analysis:** This refers to dividing ideas, content, or processes into separate elements to examine what it is, how it works, and what it is made from.

**Argument:** Arguments have three objectives: to explain, to persuade, and to mediate conflicts between positions, readers, or ideas. Writers make logical claims—supported with reasons, evidence, and different appeals—to advance their argument(s).

**Claim:** This is a word with many apparent, sometimes confusing iterations: *proposition, assertion, thesis*; it is sometimes mistaken for *argument*. Not the same as the subject or topic: A claim must be able to be argued and must require defense through evidence. Alternate or opposing claims suggest other, sometimes contradictory claims one should consider. Effective claims are precise, clear, properly qualified, and affirmative. A thesis statement is the writer's main claim.

**Clarify the relationships between claim(s) and reasons:** Writers should have a reason for the claim(s) they make. They think X *(the claim) is true because of Y (a reason).* This relationship between claims and reasons should be based on evidence, not opinions or preferences.

**Cohesion:** One idea or sentence connects to another to create a sense of flow; reasons, claims, evidence, and ideas all work together.

**Concluding statement or section:** Writers provide some statement or section that connects all the claims and evidence, and then show how they support the argument presented in the paper or speech.

**Distinguish:** This means to perceive something as, to explain how something is, or to argue that it is different or distinct from others that seem, on the surface, similar.

**Establish the significance of the claim:** *Significance* is also sometimes replaced with *substantive*; however, both mean the claim should be important, based on real and thorough knowledge about the subject.

**Evidence:** Each discipline has its own standards for evidence, but most lists would include quotations, observations, interviews, examples, facts, data, results from surveys and experiments, and, when appropriate, personal experience.

**Formal style:** The writer uses words and tone appropriate for occasion and audience; This includes a more objective tone to suggest some critical distance from the subject or claim.

**Reasons/reasoning:** Writers must base their claims and ideas on more than personal preferences or opinions when constructing arguments; reasons demand evidence, information, and logic.

**Substantive topics or texts:** Writers are expected to be writing about compelling, important ideas or texts that examine big questions meant to challenge the reader.

*Notes*

**Writing 2:** Write informative/explanatory texts to examine and convey complex ideas and information clearly and accurately through the effective selection, organization, and analysis of content.

## English Language Arts

6  Write informative/explanatory texts to examine a topic and convey ideas, concepts, and information through the selection, organization, and analysis of relevant content.

  a. Introduce a topic; organize ideas, concepts, and information, using strategies such as definition, classification, comparison/contrast, and cause/effect; include formatting (e.g., headings), graphics (e.g., charts, tables), and multimedia when useful to aiding comprehension.
  b. Develop the topic with relevant facts, definitions, concrete details, quotations, or other information and examples.
  c. Use appropriate transitions to clarify the relationships among ideas and concepts.
  d. Use precise language and domain-specific vocabulary to inform about or explain the topic.
  e. Establish and maintain a formal style.
  f. Provide a concluding statement or section that follows from the information or explanation presented.

## History/Social Studies, Science, and Technical Studies

6  Write informative/explanatory texts, including the narration of historical events, scientific procedures/experiments, or technical processes.

  a. Introduce a topic clearly, previewing what is to follow; organize ideas, concepts, and information into broader categories as appropriate to achieving purpose; include formatting (e.g., headings), graphics (e.g., charts, tables), and multimedia when useful to aiding comprehension.
  b. Develop the topic with relevant, well-chosen facts, definitions, concrete details, quotations, or other information and examples.
  c. Use appropriate and varied transitions to create cohesion and clarify the relationships among ideas and concepts.
  d. Use precise language and domain-specific vocabulary to inform about or explain the topic.
  e. Establish and maintain a formal style and objective tone.
  f. Provide a concluding statement or section that follows from and supports the information or explanation presented.

* These broad types of writing include many subgenres. See Appendix A for definitions of key writing types.

## What the **Student** Does

### English Language Arts

**6** **Gist:** Explain or provide information about a subject or idea(s), choosing only the details and information related to the topic, which are then introduced, organized (e.g., by classification, cause and effect, definition) and elaborated upon through the use of graphics (e.g., tables and charts) and document design (e.g., subheaders). Students further build on these ideas by including facts, examples, concrete details, and evidence, usually in the form of quotations. Students help all these details flow and reveal the links between these ideas by making careful use of transitions which, along with precise vocabulary, aid the writer trying to explain the topic. Finally, after establishing and maintaining a formal style appropriate to the audience and purpose, students bring their paper to an end, drawing what conclusions there are about this subject and conveying them in a way that makes for a coherent and useful ending that logically connects to all that preceded it.

- What is the topic—and your purpose?
- What information and details should you include?
- How should you organize the contents so they convey the full sense of this topic?

### History/Social Studies, Science, and Technical Studies

**6** **Gist:** Explain or provide idea(s), historical events, scientific procedures/experiments, or technical processes, choosing only the details and information related to the topic, which are then introduced in a way that both is clear and allows readers to anticipate what will come after, organized into more general categories and elaborated upon through the use of graphics (e.g., tables and charts) and document design (e.g., subheaders). Students further build on these ideas by including compelling, insightful facts, examples, concrete details, and evidence, usually in the form of quotations. Students help these details flow and reveal the links between these ideas by making careful use of transitions, which improve cohesion, and precise vocabulary, which aids the writer trying to explain the topic. Finally, after establishing and maintaining a formal style appropriate to the audience and purpose, students bring their paper to an end, drawing what conclusions there are about this subject and conveying them in a way that makes for a coherent and useful ending that logically connects to all that preceded it and provides the necessary support for those ideas explained or presented.

- What is the topic—and your purpose?
- How do you use transitions to create greater cohesion and show the relationships among ideas here?
- How should you organize the contents so they convey the full sense of this topic?

**Writing 2:** Write informative/explanatory texts to examine and convey complex ideas and information clearly and accurately through the effective selection, organization, and analysis of content.

## English Language Arts

**7** Write informative/explanatory texts to examine a topic and convey ideas, concepts, and information through the selection, organization, and analysis of relevant content.

a. Introduce a topic **clearly, previewing what is to follow**; organize ideas, concepts, and information, using strategies such as definition, classification, comparison/contrast, and cause/effect; include formatting (e.g., headings), graphics (e.g., charts, tables), and multimedia when useful to aiding comprehension

b. Develop the topic with relevant facts, definitions, concrete details, quotations, or other information and examples.

c. Use appropriate transitions to **create cohesion and** clarify the relationships among ideas and concepts.

d. Use precise language and domain-specific vocabulary to inform about or explain the topic.

e. Establish and maintain a formal style.

f. Provide a concluding statement or section that follows from **and supports** the information or explanation presented.

## History/Social Studies, Science, and Technical Studies

**7** Write informative/explanatory texts, including the narration of historical events, scientific procedures/experiments, or technical processes.

a. Introduce a topic clearly, previewing what is to follow; organize ideas, concepts, and information into broader categories as appropriate to achieving purpose; include formatting (e.g., headings), graphics (e.g., charts, tables), and multimedia when useful to aiding comprehension.

b. Develop the topic with relevant, well-chosen facts, definitions, concrete details, quotations, or other information and examples.

c. Use appropriate and varied transitions to create cohesion and clarify the relationships among ideas and concepts.

d. Use precise language and domain-specific vocabulary to inform about or explain the topic.

e. Establish and maintain a formal style and objective tone.

f. Provide a concluding statement or section that follows from and supports the information or explanation presented.

---

\* These broad types of writing include many subgenres. See Appendix A for definitions of key writing types.

*Source:* Copyright © 2010. National Governors Association Center for Best Practices and Council of Chief State School Officers. All rights reserved.

## What the **Student** Does

### English Language Arts

**7** **Gist:** Explain or provide information about a subject or idea(s), choosing only the details and information related to the topic, which are then introduced in a way that both is clear and allows readers to anticipate what will come after, organized (e.g., by classification, cause and effect, definition) and elaborated upon through the use of graphics (e.g., tables and charts) and document design (e.g., subheaders). Students further build on these ideas by including facts, examples, concrete details, and evidence, usually in the form of quotations. Students help these details flow and reveal the links between these ideas by making careful use of transitions, which improve cohesion, and precise vocabulary, which aids the writer trying to explain the topic. Finally, after establishing and maintaining a formal style appropriate to the audience and purpose, students bring their paper to an end, drawing what conclusions there are about this subject and conveying them in a way that makes for a coherent and useful ending that logically connects to all that preceded it and provides the necessary support for those ideas explained or presented.

- What is the topic—and your purpose?
- How do you use transitions to create greater cohesion and show the relationships among ideas here?
- How should you organize the contents so they convey the full sense of this topic?

### History/Social Studies, Science, and Technical Studies

**7** **Gist:** Explain or provide idea(s), historical events, scientific procedures/experiments, or technical processes, choosing only the details and information related to the topic, which are then introduced in a way that both is clear and allows readers to anticipate what will come after, organized into more general categories and elaborated upon through the use of graphics (e.g., tables and charts) and document design (e.g., subheaders). Students further build on these ideas by including compelling, insightful facts, examples, concrete details, and evidence, usually in the form of quotations. Students help these details flow and reveal the links between these ideas by making careful use of transitions, which improve cohesion, and precise vocabulary, which aids the writer trying to explain the topic. Finally, after establishing and maintaining a formal style appropriate to the audience and purpose, students bring their paper to an end, drawing what conclusions there are about this subject and conveying them in a way that makes for a coherent and useful ending that logically connects to all that preceded it and provides the necessary support for those ideas explained or presented.

- What is the topic—and your purpose?
- How do you use transitions to create greater cohesion and show the relationships among ideas here?
- How should you organize the contents so they convey the full sense of this topic?

**Writing 2:** Write informative/explanatory texts to examine and convey complex ideas and information clearly and accurately through the effective selection, organization, and analysis of content.

## English Language Arts

**8** Write informative/explanatory texts to examine a topic and convey ideas, concepts, and information through the selection, organization, and analysis of relevant content.

a. Introduce a topic clearly, previewing what is to follow; organize ideas, concepts, and information **into broader categories**; include formatting (e.g., headings), graphics (e.g., charts, tables), and multimedia when useful to aiding comprehension.
b. Develop the topic with relevant, **well-chosen facts**, definitions, concrete details, quotations, or other information and examples.
c. Use appropriate and varied transitions to create cohesion and clarify the relationships among ideas and concepts.
d. Use precise language and domain-specific vocabulary to inform about or explain the topic.
e. Establish and maintain a formal style.
f. Provide a concluding statement or section that follows from and supports the information or explanation presented.

## History/Social Studies, Science, and Technical Studies

**8** Write informative/explanatory texts, including the narration of historical events, scientific procedures/experiments, or technical processes.

a. Introduce a topic clearly, previewing what is to follow; organize ideas, concepts, and information into broader categories as appropriate to achieving purpose; include formatting (e.g., headings), graphics (e.g., charts, tables), and multimedia when useful to aiding comprehension.
b. Develop the topic with relevant, well-chosen facts, definitions, concrete details, quotations, or other information and examples.
c. Use appropriate and varied transitions to create cohesion and clarify the relationships among ideas and concepts.
d. Use precise language and domain-specific vocabulary to inform about or explain the topic.
e. Establish and maintain a formal style and objective tone.
f. Provide a concluding statement or section that follows from and supports the information or explanation presented.

---

\* These broad types of writing include many subgenres. See Appendix A for definitions of key writing types.

## What the **Student** Does

### English Language Arts

**8** **Gist:** Explain or provide information about a subject or idea(s), choosing only the details and information related to the topic, which are then introduced in a way that both is clear and allows readers to anticipate what will come after, organized into more general categories and elaborated upon through the use of graphics (e.g., tables and charts) and document design (e.g., subheaders). Students further build on these ideas by including compelling, insightful facts, examples, concrete details, and evidence, usually in the form of quotations. Students help these details flow and reveal the links between these ideas by making careful use of transitions, which improve cohesion, and precise vocabulary, which aids the writer trying to explain the topic. Finally, after establishing and maintaining a formal style appropriate to the audience and purpose, students bring their paper to an end, drawing what conclusions there are about this subject and conveying them in a way that makes for a coherent and useful ending that logically connects to all that preceded it and provides the necessary support for those ideas explained or presented.

- What is the topic—and your purpose?
- How do you use transitions to create greater cohesion and show the relationships among ideas here?
- How should you organize the contents so they convey the full sense of this topic?

### History/Social Studies, Science, and Technical Studies

**8** **Gist:** Explain or provide idea(s), historical events, scientific procedures/experiments, or technical processes, choosing only the details and information related to the topic, which are then introduced in a way that both is clear and allows readers to anticipate what will come after, organized into more general categories and elaborated upon through the use of graphics (e.g., tables and charts) and document design (e.g., subheaders). Students further build on these ideas by including compelling, insightful facts, examples, concrete details, and evidence, usually in the form of quotations. Students help these details flow and reveal the links between these ideas by making careful use of transitions, which improve cohesion, and precise vocabulary, which aids the writer trying to explain the topic. Finally, after establishing and maintaining a formal style appropriate to the audience and purpose, students bring their paper to an end, drawing what conclusions there are about this subject and conveying them in a way that makes for a coherent and useful ending that logically connects to all that preceded it and provides the necessary support for those ideas explained or presented.

- What is the topic—and your purpose?
- How do you use transitions to create greater cohesion and show the relationships among ideas here?
- How should you organize the contents so they convey the full sense of this topic?

## What the **Teacher** Does

**To introduce students to informative/ explanatory texts, do the following:**

- Show them a range of examples—from students, professional writers, or even yourself—so they see what it is that you want them to do and get a sense of what they should include.
- Discuss the contents, conventions, and other elements of the type of informational/explanatory text you want them to write.
- Give students a copy of a sample text and, if possible, display it on a screen so you can annotate portions of it while discussing the writer's decisions and the text's relevant features.

**To format and integrate graphics and multimedia into the text, have students do the following:**

- Offer direct instruction to the whole class or a smaller group of students who need to learn how to use those features of the word processor or other software applications.
- Give students step-by-step directions or create a link to a web tutorial they can watch if they do not know how.
- Give them samples that show them different types of graphs, tables, and other options they might consider when incorporating information or data into their papers.

**To develop their topic with details, examples, and information, have students do the following:**

- Work directly with them to generate ideas and gather evidence, data, examples, or other content; then develop with them criteria for how to evaluate and choose the best of the bunch to work into their writing.
- Use sentence stems or templates from a book like *They Say/I Say* (by Graff and Birkenstein) to teach students how to introduce or frame the quotation and then comment on the meaning or importance of that quotation.

**To have students use varied transitions to link ideas and create cohesion, do the following:**

- Generate with students or provide them a list of transition words and phrases specific to the type of writing they are doing (e.g., cause–effect, compare–contrast).

- Have students go through their papers once they have a complete draft and highlight the first six words of each sentence; then they can evaluate existing transitions and add others where they would improve clarity and cohesion.

**To help students use precise language and academic vocabulary, do the following:**

- Direct them to circle any words in their papers that are abstract, too general, or otherwise ineffective; then have them generate words that could replace weaker words or phrases.
- Generate with the class words they might or should use when writing about a specific subject, procedure, event, or person; this might include specific verbs, nouns, and adjectives for use when, for example, explaining a process or procedure.
- Provide examples of or demonstrate for them how to use other techniques such as metaphors, similes, and analogies.

**To establish and maintain the conventions for a discipline, have students do the following:**

- Establish for the class the proper tone, format, and other genre conventions for the type of discipline-specific writing assigned.
- Give students a checklist or annotated sample that illustrates all the discipline-specific conventions they must include.

**To prepare them to write about historical events, procedures, processes, or complex ideas, have students do the following:**

- Discuss the ideas, details, or other contents that they should include to help them generate new ideas about what to say and how to organize it when they begin to write.

**To help your English Language Learners, try this one thing:**

- Break the process into stages, providing students with examples and instruction at each stage before moving on to the next to ensure they understand and are doing the work correctly.

**Academic Vocabulary:** Key Words and Phrases

**Audience's knowledge of the topic:** This phrase emphasizes clarity in writing; thus, if writers ignore the audience's lack or excess of knowledge about a topic, he or she risks confusing or insulting them.

**Cohesion:** This refers to how well things stick together to create a clear flow from one idea to the next. Generally, the beginning of a sentence should clearly connect to the words at the end of the previous sentence as the writing unfolds.

**Complex ideas:** Since students will be writing about an idea from multiple perspectives or drawing evidence from multiple sources to support their claims about a text or subject, writing about such complex ideas, which are often abstract, poses unique challenges.

**Concrete details:** This refers to specific details that refer to actual objects or places; it is the difference between Thomas Jefferson declaring the British guilty of "repeated injuries and usurpations" and listing the crimes committed by the British under its "absolute Tyranny" against the American colonies in the Declaration of Independence.

**Domain-specific vocabulary:** When writing about any topic or text in a specific subject, writers must explain or describe it using the language of that discipline if they are to be accurate and precise.

**Explanatory texts:** Such texts are defined by their objective: to explain to or to inform the audience about a topic using facts and an objective tone; the writer's role here is to report what he or she sees.

**Formatting:** Today's technology allows writers to emphasize ideas, connections, or other details through headers, fonts (style, size, or typeface), color, graphics, and spatial arrangement on the page.

**Graphics:** This includes tables and graphs, charts and images, and infographics, which incorporate many graphic elements to represent the complexity of a process, idea, or event.

**Narration of historical events, scientific procedures or experiments, or technical processes:** Don't mistake the word *narration* in this case to refer to a work of literature; rather, it applies here to giving a detailed account, providing an explanation or information about what people did, what they observed, and, by the conclusion, what it all meant during a procedure, a process, or an event.

**Objective tone:** The purpose of informational writing is to inform or explain but not persuade. An objective tone maintains a distance from its subject, interjecting no emotions about the subject.

**Organize ideas and information into broader categories:** Note that this addition to the standard appears in the grade 8 standard, thus, signaling that it is a more complex move for writers and thinkers; specifically, it means zooming out from a subject and viewing it within some larger scheme and set of categories (e.g., moving from details about an artist's process or a specific creature's habitat to details about the artist's work within a larger artistic movement or the creature's details viewed within the much larger ecosystem to which it belongs).

**Selection, organization, and analysis of content:** Writers choose the most important facts and details about the subject, organizing them to achieve a clear objective, and then analyzing how those elements relate to each other and the larger idea of the paper in general, while also analyzing what each detail contributes to the meaning of that text.

**Transitions:** They connect one sentence or idea to another, allowing writers to express the nature or importance of the relationship between those two ideas.

*Notes*

**Writing 3:** Write narratives to develop real or imagined experiences or events using effective technique, well-chosen details, and well-structured event sequences.

### English Language Arts

**6** Write narratives to develop real or imagined experiences or events using effective technique, relevant descriptive details, and well-structured event sequences.

  a. Engage and orient the reader by establishing a context and introducing a narrator and/or characters; organize an event sequence that unfolds naturally and logically.

  b. Use narrative techniques, such as dialogue, pacing, and description, to develop experiences, events, and/or characters.

  c. Use a variety of transition words, phrases, and clauses to convey sequence and signal shifts from one time frame or setting to another.

  d. Use precise words and phrases, relevant descriptive details, and sensory language to convey experiences and events.

  e. Provide a conclusion that follows from the narrated experiences or events.

### History/Social Studies, Science, and Technical Studies

**6** (See note; not applicable as a separate requirement.)

\* These broad types of writing include many subgenres. See Appendix A for definitions of key writing types.

*Note:* Students' narrative skills continue to grow in these grades. The Standards require that students be able to incorporate narrative elements effectively into arguments and informative/explanatory texts. In history/social studies, students must be able to incorporate narrative accounts into their analyses of individuals or events of historical import. In science and technical subjects, students must be able to write precise enough descriptions of the step-by-step procedures they use in their investigations or technical work that others can replicate them and (possibly) reach the same results.

*Source:* Copyright © 2010. National Governors Association Center for Best Practices and Council of Chief State School Officers. All rights reserved.

## What the **Student** Does

### English Language Arts

**6** **Gist:** Convey real or imagined experiences and events through narratives that employ appropriate methods, sensory details, and story structures which all draw the reader in and clarify what is happening and who is involved. Students arrange events into authentic sequences that are believable, adding dialogue, pacing, and description to bring the story and its characters alive. Students also ensure the narrative moves along by inserting various transitional words that orient readers when the story shifts in time or setting. In addition, students choose words with care, evoking through these words and phrases the full range of sensory details and emotions needed to convey the experiences or events being described. Finally, students give the story an ending that makes sense in light of all that came before it and provides the narrative a satisfying conclusion.

- What are you telling here: a real or imagined event?
- What happened—and why are you telling this story about it?
- What details must you include if you are to achieve your purpose by the end?

### History/Social Studies, Science, and Technical Studies

**6** The Common Core State Standards note that "writ[ing] narratives to develop real or imagined experiences or events" is "not applicable as a separate requirement." See the note at the bottom of the previous page for additional explanation.

**Writing 3:** Write narratives to develop real or imagined experiences or events using effective technique, well-chosen details, and well-structured event sequences.

## English Language Arts

**7** Write narratives to develop real or imagined experiences or events using effective technique, relevant descriptive details, and well-structured event sequences.

   a. Engage and orient the reader by establishing a context and **point of view** and introducing a narrator and/or characters; organize an event sequence that unfolds naturally and logically.
   b. Use narrative techniques, such as dialogue, pacing, and description, to develop experiences, events, and/or characters.
   c. Use a variety of transition words, phrases, and clauses to convey sequence and signal shifts from one time frame or setting to another.
   d. Use precise words and phrases, relevant descriptive details, and sensory language to **capture the action** and convey experiences and events.
   e. Provide a conclusion that follows from and reflects on the narrated experiences or events.

## History/Social Studies, Science, and Technical Studies

**7** (See note; not applicable as a separate requirement.)

---

\* These broad types of writing include many subgenres. See Appendix A for definitions of key writing types.

*Note:* Students' narrative skills continue to grow in these grades. The Standards require that students be able to incorporate narrative elements effectively into arguments and informative/explanatory texts. In history/social studies, students must be able to incorporate narrative accounts into their analyses of individuals or events of historical import. In science and technical subjects, students must be able to write precise enough descriptions of the step-by-step procedures they use in their investigations or technical work that others can replicate them and (possibly) reach the same results.

*Source:* Copyright © 2010. National Governors Association Center for Best Practices and Council of Chief State School Officers. All rights reserved.

## What the **Student** Does

### English Language Arts

**7** **Gist:** Convey real or imagined experiences and events through narratives that employ appropriate methods, sensory details, and story structures which all draw the reader in and clarify what is happening, who is involved, and the point of view from which we are experiencing this story. Students arrange events into authentic sequences that are believable, adding dialogue, pacing, and description to bring the story and its characters alive. Students also ensure the narrative moves along by inserting various transitional words that orient readers when the story shifts in time or setting. In addition, students choose words with care, evoking through these words and phrases the full range of sensory details and emotions needed to convey the action, experiences, or events being described. Finally, students give the story an ending that makes sense in light of all that came before it and provides the narrative a satisfying conclusion.

- What are you telling here—a real or imagined event—and from whose point of view?
- What happened—and why are you telling this story about it?
- How have you used language to better capture the action and convey the experiences or events described?

### History/Social Studies, Science, and Technical Studies

**7** The Common Core State Standards note that "writ[ing] narratives to develop real or imagined experiences or events" is "not applicable as a separate requirement." See the note at the bottom of the previous page for additional explanation.

**Writing 3:** Write narratives to develop real or imagined experiences or events using effective technique, well-chosen details, and well-structured event sequences.

## English Language Arts

**8** Write narratives to develop real or imagined experiences or events using effective technique, relevant descriptive details, and well-structured event sequences.

a. Engage and orient the reader by establishing a context and point of view and introducing a narrator and/or characters; organize an event sequence that unfolds naturally and logically.

b. Use narrative techniques, such as dialogue, pacing, description, **and reflection**, to develop experiences, events, and/or characters.

c. Use a variety of transition words, phrases, and clauses to convey sequence, signal shifts from one time frame or setting to another, **and show the relationships among experiences and events.**

d. Use precise words and phrases, relevant descriptive details, and sensory language to capture the action and convey experiences and events.

e. Provide a conclusion that follows from and reflects on the narrated experiences or events.

## History/Social Studies, Science, and Technical Studies

**8** (See note; not applicable as a separate requirement.)

---

\* These broad types of writing include many subgenres. See Appendix A for definitions of key writing types.

*Note:* Students' narrative skills continue to grow in these grades. The Standards require that students be able to incorporate narrative elements effectively into arguments and informative/explanatory texts. In history/social studies, students must be able to incorporate narrative accounts into their analyses of individuals or events of historical import. In science and technical subjects, students must be able to write precise enough descriptions of the step-by-step procedures they use in their investigations or technical work that others can replicate them and (possibly) reach the same results.

*Source:* Copyright © 2010. National Governors Association Center for Best Practices and Council of Chief State School Officers. All rights reserved.

## What the **Student** Does

### English Language Arts

**8** **Gist:** Convey real or imagined experiences and events through narratives that employ appropriate methods, sensory details, and story structures which all draw the reader in and clarify what is happening, who is involved, and the point of view from which we are experiencing this story. Students arrange events into authentic sequences that are believable, adding dialogue, pacing, reflection, and description to bring the story and its characters alive. Students also ensure the narrative moves along by inserting various transitional words that orient readers when the story shifts in time or setting and how events and experiences are related to each other. In addition, students choose words with care, evoking through these words and phrases the full range of sensory details and emotions needed to convey the action, experiences, or events being described. Finally, students give the story an ending that makes sense in light of all that came before it and provides the narrative a satisfying conclusion.

- What are you telling here—a real or imagined event— and from whose point of view?
- What happened—and why are you telling this story about it?
- How are the events and experiences throughout your narrative related to each other?

### History/Social Studies, Science, and Technical Studies

**8** The Common Core State Standards note that "writ[ing] narratives to develop real or imagined experiences or events" is "not applicable as a separate requirement." See the note at the bottom of the previous page for additional explanation.

What the **Teacher** Does

**To have students write narratives about real or imagined experiences, do the following:**

• Read a diverse sampling of narratives similar to and slightly different from the sort you want them to write.
• Guide students through the process of creating a story map, storyboard, or other graphic form that allows them to identify, discuss, and arrange the different events or scenes in the story.
• Generate with students or provide a list of the elements of an effective narrative of the story you are assigning.
• Consider allowing students to incorporate images in their narrative if they are appropriate and complement the narrative.

**To have students set out a problem or create a situation in a narrative, do the following:**

• Establish a problem up front that the story will examine and the protagonist will solve after a series of scenarios richly imagined.
• Ask students to imagine a situation in rich detail (perhaps one inspired by another book they have read or a subject or era they studied) and then describe how characters (or they, if it is a personal narrative) responded and changed over the course of the story.
• Lead students through the creation of a detailed observation about an event, process, or experience, guiding them by examples and questions that prompt them to add sensory details; then generate with them questions they should ask and apply to their narrative as they write the second part, which comments on the meaning or importance of what they observed.
• Have students describe the same event or experience from multiple perspectives to explore how point of view affects one's perception of an idea, event, or era or the people involved.

**To have students introduce or develop a narrator or characters in a narrative, do the following:**

• Help students develop questions that not only portray the character's physical persona but also reveal the character's personality and motivations within the context of the story.

• Provide students with a list of archetypal characters as a starting place to help them imagine their own.
• Ask students, when writing personal narratives that involve people they know, to fill in a graphic organizer with boxes describing what the person says, does, thinks, and feels prior to writing.

**To have students use a range of narrative techniques to engage the reader, do the following:**

• Introduce students to different plot lines and story structures, including the traditional linear format (exposition, rising action, conflict, falling action, and resolution) as well as more episodic or lyric narrative formats that string a series of impressions together as a way of telling a story about a person, an event, or an experience.
• Have students analyze the dialogue and other techniques used in the stories they study for ideas they can use in their own.

**To have students sequence events in a coherent way throughout a narrative, do the following:**

• Have students write on sticky notes or index cards key events or scenes in the narrative they are creating; then ask them to arrange them in different ways, stopping to explain to others what they are thinking, until they find the sequence that best works with the story they are trying to tell.
• Use a presentation software program to create the story as a series of slides, with notes and images on the slides so they can manipulate and better understand the elements of their story.

**To help your English Language Learners, try this one thing:**

• Give students the opportunity to draw out the story first as a cartoon strip with notes and captions and dialogue, in their own language if they prefer, before asking them to write the story; if possible, give them the chance to tell their story before writing it.

**Academic Vocabulary:** Key Words and Phrases

**Capture the action:** The choice of words is crucial in narrative writing when it comes to *showing* what is going on: sentence structures, word choice, and length of sentences—these all contribute to creating the mood, pacing, and feel of the story.

**Conclusion:** One always looks for some *point* or ideas that can be drawn from a story; otherwise, why tell it? Conclusions in narrative tales are often more subtle than other forms, whose structure dictates where and how to conclude the story.

**Description:** Stories rely on precise, detailed descriptions of people, places, and events to bring them alive in vivid ways that convey the emotions and capture the reader's imagination.

**Develop (experiences, events, or characters):** When one "develops," for example, characters in a story, one describes them in detail, adding specific details that bring the character alive; such development must also reflect the person, place, or events moving through time and, as a result, changing if they are to seem real.

**Engage the reader by establishing a context:** This is best understood, perhaps, by something Stephen King said somewhere about putting characters in a situation and the story (plot) being about how they behave once they are turned loose in that situation. This works just as well for fiction as nonfiction.

**Event sequences:** How the writer arranges the events directly affects how the story affects us; some events create tension, mystery, and surprise; others create humor, nostalgia, and wonder.

**Narrative:** This is a story one tells, whether in prose or verse, a novel or a play, or even a poem. A narrative can be fictional or grounded in facts, such as an autobiographical or historical narrative.

**Organize an event sequence:** This is what Madison Smartt Bell has referred to as "narrative design," meaning the arrangement of the events of a story—whether real or imagined—to achieve some effect; again, it applies equally to fiction and nonfiction.

**Pacing:** This is the speed at which the action unfolds or the story is told; pacing affects the tone, mood, and atmosphere, instilling in readers a feeling of anxiety, nostalgia, despair, or excitement.

**Points of view:** From whose perspective do we experience the story? Do we get the first-person point of view (I, me, my), second-person point of view (you, your), or third-person (he, his, them) point of view? How does the point of view affect our response to or the meaning of the story?

**Real or imagined experience:** Narratives that are imagined are fictional (novels, plays, poems, fairy tales); those that are real are based on personal or historical records (memoirs, autobiographies).

**Reflection:** This refers to the character—or, in the case of nonfiction, person—taking time to step back, gain some critical distance, and think about the meaning or importance of events and experiences.

**Resolution:** Also known as the falling action or dénouement, the resolution falls near the end of the story and involves all the conflicts and problems explored throughout the story. Complex literary narratives involve multiple conflicts or plot lines that culminate in often surprising, unpredictable resolutions.

**Sensory language:** This evokes a place, person, or situation through its use of smells, sounds, textures, and other such rich details.

**Signal Shifts:** Certain words and phrases function as signal words to indicate that the narrative is shifting to a different setting, narrator, point in the story, or point in time.

**Technique:** Literary narratives are carefully crafted to create certain emotional impacts on the reader; to study the technique is to study how the work affects the reader.

**Writing 4:** Produce clear and coherent writing in which the development, organization, and style are appropriate to task, purpose, and audience.

## English Language Arts

**6** Produce clear and coherent writing in which the development, organization, and style are appropriate to task, purpose, and audience.

> (Grade-specific expectations for writing types are defined in standards 1–3 above.)

**7** Produce clear and coherent writing in which the development, organization, and style are appropriate to task, purpose, and audience.

> (Grade-specific expectations for writing types are defined in standards 1–3 above.)

**8** Produce clear and coherent writing in which the development, organization, and style are appropriate to task, purpose, and audience.

> (Grade-specific expectations for writing types are defined in standards 1–3 above.)

## History/Social Studies, Science, and Technical Studies

**6** Produce clear and coherent writing in which the development, organization, and style are appropriate to task, purpose, and audience.

**7** Produce clear and coherent writing in which the development, organization, and style are appropriate to task, purpose, and audience.

**8** Produce clear and coherent writing in which the development, organization, and style are appropriate to task, purpose, and audience.

### What the **Student** Does

## English Language Arts

**6** **Gist:** Write with clarity and coherence, developing and organizing your ideas and creating a style that is appropriate to your audience, purpose, and occasion when composing those types outlined in writing standards 1–3.

- What is your topic and task for writing?
- What is your purpose: to inform, explain, argue, or entertain?
- What language, organization, and style is most appropriate for your writing task, purpose, and audience?

**7** **Gist:** Write with clarity and coherence, developing and organizing your ideas and creating a style that is appropriate to your audience, purpose, and occasion when composing those types outlined in writing standards 1–3.

- What is your topic and task for writing?
- What is your purpose: to inform, explain, argue, or entertain?
- What language, organization, and style is most appropriate for your writing task, purpose, and audience?

**8** **Gist:** Write with clarity and coherence, developing and organizing your ideas and creating a style that is appropriate to your audience, purpose, and occasion when composing those types outlined in writing standards 1–3.

- What is your topic and task for writing?
- What is your purpose: to inform, explain, argue, or entertain?
- What language, organization, and style is most appropriate for your writing task, purpose, and audience?

## History/Social Studies, Science, and Technical Studies

**6** **Gist:** Write with clarity and coherence, developing and organizing your ideas and creating a style that is appropriate to your audience, purpose, and occasion when composing those types outlined in writing standards 1–3.

- What is your topic and task for writing?
- What is your purpose: to inform, explain, argue, or entertain?
- What language, organization, and style is most appropriate for your writing task, purpose, and audience?

**7** **Gist:** Write with clarity and coherence, developing and organizing your ideas and creating a style that is appropriate to your audience, purpose, and occasion when composing those types outlined in writing standards 1–3.

- What is your topic and task for writing?
- What is your purpose: to inform, explain, argue, or entertain?
- What language, organization, and style is most appropriate for your writing task, purpose, and audience?

**8** **Gist:** Write with clarity and coherence, developing and organizing your ideas and creating a style that is appropriate to your audience, purpose, and occasion when composing those types outlined in writing standards 1–3.

- What is your topic and task for writing?
- What is your purpose: to inform, explain, argue, or entertain?
- What language, organization, and style is most appropriate for your writing task, purpose, and audience?

## What the **Teacher** Does

**To have students produce writing that is clear and coherent, do the following:**

- Establish for them first what these terms mean and why they are important to good writing by showing them models from different writers.
- Direct students to highlight or underline the subject of each sentence in their text; once they have done this, ask them to find all abstract subjects or long compound subjects and replace these with concrete subjects appropriate to the subject.
- Teach students how to determine the extent to which all the sentences in a paragraph and the larger piece itself work together to make one coherent whole; think of each sentence as a piece in a larger puzzle that should, when assembled, show us the big picture.
- Have students determine who the audience for the piece of writing will be, including their biases, current knowledge, expectations, and assumptions so you can anticipate and respond appropriately to their concerns and questions about your topic.
- Evaluate the task and all related directions to be sure students know what they must do, include, or avoid when writing.
- Establish a purpose for assignments—to convey ideas, events, or findings—by choosing and explaining the behavior, meaning, or importance of key details. Students might draw from sources, including primary and secondary sources; they also write to extend readers' knowledge or acceptance of ideas and procedures.

**To have students ensure that their writing is effectively organized, do the following:**

- Make clear—or have students determine—the task, purpose, and occasion for this writing; then have students determine the best way to organize, present, and develop the topic in the paper.
- Provide students with a variety of organizational structures to choose from, helping them to evaluate each in light of their purpose, the task, the audience, and the occasion.

- Have students create some sort of map, outline, or plan before writing to improve the organization of the writing; if students already have a draft, ask them to create a "reverse outline" that is based on the draft of the text they already wrote.

**To develop students' ideas to the fullest effect, have students do the following:**

- Gather and incorporate into the writing examples, details, data, information, or quotations that illustrate or support your ideas.
- Explain what the examples, details, data, information, or quotations mean and why they are important in relation to the main idea or claim you are developing.
- Consider integrating graphs, tables, charts, images, or infographics of some other sort to illustrate and reinforce some point students are trying to make.

**To have students determine what style is most appropriate to the occasion, do the following:**

- Show students samples from different authors or agencies so they see what real language and formats look like in this discipline for this type of text, purpose, and audience.
- Remind students to begin with the end in mind—the impression you hope to make or end you hope to achieve—and ask what choices they need to make about style and organization in light of their purpose.
- Ask them to consider the needs, expectations, or assumptions about their audience on this occasion and how you should write in light of that information to achieve your intended purpose.

**To help your English Language Learners, try this one thing:**

- Meet individually with your ELL students to ensure they have time and opportunity to talk about the assignment and their needs as they try to write it.

**Academic Vocabulary:** Key Words and Phrases

**Audience:** This is considered an essential part of the "rhetorical situation" when writing. Key considerations include who the audience is, what they already know or need to learn to understand the writer's message, and how the audience is likely to respond to what you write. What biases do they have that you must anticipate and address if you are to effectively advance your argument?

**Clear:** Clarity is a fundamental quality of good writing. Writers achieve such clarity by choosing precise words and joining them in logical ways through grammar that further enhances the clarity of the ideas expressed. They achieve this clarity by using concrete or specific nouns or subjects instead of abstractions; also, they include verbs that express actions and avoid unnecessary use of passive voice, which often undermines clarity in writing.

**Coherent:** Think of your words and sentences as building blocks in a larger structure, such as a wall; all work together to form a strong, stable structure that serves a purpose; so it is with coherent writing where each word and sentence adds to the larger whole of the text and, thereby, creates a sense of clarity.

**Development:** This includes everything from examples and quotations to details and other forms of evidence used to support and illustrate whatever the writer is saying about the subject. All such forms of development should extend, clarify, or otherwise enhance the writer's claims. Development can also come in the form of figures, tables, or images that add more information or further illustration.

**Organization:** No one approach or strategy is appropriate for organizing ideas in academic writing; what matters is that there is a clear, appropriate, logical, and effective structure to the ideas. One can arrange information from new to old, least to most important, areas of agreement to areas of disagreement, or more traditional forms such as spatial, sequential, and problem-solution, among others. Also important are the transitional phrases or words used to signal organizational shifts.

**Purpose:** Writers simply have *something* they are trying to accomplish through this piece; the writer's purpose also intersects with and is shaped by the rhetorical situation (occasion, topic, and audience). The most common purposes are to persuade, to inform/explain, to entertain, or to inspire.

**Style:** To speak of style is to discuss how the writing sounds, how it moves, and how it feels when one reads or hears it read; it involves the words and how those words are joined to others to form patterns of sound and meaning in the service of some larger idea or purpose so that the style complements and helps achieve the purpose.

**Task:** Whatever the directions tell the writer to do is the "task." Directions might ask the student to read one or more texts, drawing from them the details and examples necessary to support their argument about a subject, or the task might ask students to write a letter to the editor in which they take a position for or against a certain controversial subject, such as banning sodas in school or changing the age at which one can apply for a driver's license.

*Notes*

**Writing 5:** Develop and strengthen writing as needed by planning, revising, editing, rewriting, or trying a new approach.

## English Language Arts

**6** With some guidance and support from peers and adults, develop and strengthen writing as needed by planning, revising, editing, rewriting, or trying a new approach.

> (Editing for conventions should demonstrate command of Language standards 1–3 up to and including grade 6.)

**7** With some guidance and support from peers and adults, develop and strengthen writing as needed by planning, revising, editing, rewriting, or trying a new approach, **focusing on how well purpose and audience have been addressed.**

> (Editing for conventions should demonstrate command of Language standards 1–3 up to and including **grade 7.**)

**8** With some guidance and support from peers and adults, develop and strengthen writing as needed by planning, revising, editing, rewriting, or trying a new approach, focusing on how well purpose and audience have been addressed.

> (Editing for conventions should demonstrate command of Language standards 1–3 up to and including **grade 8.**)

## History/Social Studies, Science, and Technical Studies

**6** With some guidance and support from peers and adults, develop and strengthen writing as needed by planning, revising, editing, rewriting, or trying a new approach, focusing on how well purpose and audience have been addressed.

**7** With some guidance and support from peers and adults, develop and strengthen writing as needed by planning, revising, editing, rewriting, or trying a new approach, focusing on how well purpose and audience have been addressed.

**8** With some guidance and support from peers and adults, develop and strengthen writing as needed by planning, revising, editing, rewriting, or trying a new approach, focusing on how well purpose and audience have been addressed.

What the **Student** Does

## English Language Arts

**6** **Gist:** Generate and gather ideas about the topic with help from classmates and teachers, making a plan for how to write about and use those ideas, not only drafting what to say but deciding how best to say or organize it by choosing different formats, mixing media, or blending genres. Students then improve the writing by revising, editing, rewriting, or starting all over with a new idea.

- What sort of guidance or support do students need—and can who best provide it?
- How would it improve your paper to choose a different structure, format, or medium—or shift the emphasis to a different aspect of your topic?
- What other editing strategies should you consider besides using the spell- and grammar-check in your word processor?

**7** **Gist:** Generate and gather ideas about the topic with help from classmates and teachers, making a plan for how to write about and use those ideas, not only drafting what to say but deciding how best to say or organize it by choosing different formats, mixing media, or blending genres. Students then improve the writing by revising, editing, rewriting, or starting all over with a new idea, evaluating as they go the degree to which their purpose and audience have been attended to.

- What sort of guidance or support do students need—and can who best provide it?
- How would it improve your paper to choose a different structure, format, or medium—or shift the emphasis to a different aspect of your topic?
- How well have the writer's purpose and audience's needs been addressed?

**8** **Gist:** Generate and gather ideas about the topic with help from classmates and teachers, making a plan for how to write about and use those ideas, not only drafting what to say but deciding how best to say or organize it by choosing different formats, mixing media, or blending genres. Students then improve the writing by revising, editing, rewriting, or starting all over with a new idea, evaluating as they go the degree to which their purpose and audience have been attended to.

- What sort of guidance or support do students need—and who can best provide it?
- How would it improve your paper to choose a different structure, format, or medium—or shift the emphasis to a different aspect of your topic?
- How well have the writer's purpose and audience's needs been addressed?

## History/Social Studies, Science, and Technical Studies

**6** **Gist:** Generate and gather ideas about the topic with help from classmates and teachers, making a plan for how to write about and use those ideas, not only drafting what to say but deciding how best to say or organize it by choosing different formats, mixing media, or blending genres. Students then improve the writing by revising, editing, rewriting, or starting all over with a new idea, evaluating as they go the degree to which their purpose and audience have been attended to.

- What sort of guidance or support do students need—and who can best provide it?
- How would it improve your paper to choose a different structure, format, or medium—or shift the emphasis to a different aspect of your topic?
- How well have the writer's purpose and audience's needs been addressed?

**7** **Gist:** Generate and gather ideas about the topic with help from classmates and teachers, making a plan for how to write about and use those ideas, not only drafting what to say but deciding how best to say or organize it by choosing different formats, mixing media, or blending genres. Students then improve the writing by revising, editing, rewriting, or starting all over with a new idea, evaluating as they go the degree to which their purpose and audience have been attended to.

- What sort of guidance or support do students need—and who can best provide it?
- How would it improve your paper to choose a different structure, format, or medium—or shift the emphasis to a different aspect of your topic?
- How well have the writer's purpose and audience's needs been addressed?

**8** **Gist:** Generate and gather ideas about the topic with help from classmates and teachers, making a plan for how to write about and use those ideas, not only drafting what to say but deciding how best to say or organize it by choosing different formats, mixing media, or blending genres. Students then improve the writing by revising, editing, rewriting, or starting all over with a new idea, evaluating as they go the degree to which their purpose and audience have been attended to.

- What sort of guidance or support do students need—and who can best provide it?
- How would it improve your paper to choose a different structure, format, or medium—or shift the emphasis to a different aspect of your topic?
- How well have the writer's purpose and audience's needs been addressed?

What the **Teacher** Does

**To improve students' ability to plan prior to beginning to write, do the following:**

- Provide opportunities for generative conversations about the text, topic, or task *before* they begin to write about it; if possible, have them capture all ideas on posters, whiteboards, sticky notes, or other means, and then post them to an online site they can access later for further reference or even addition.
- Show students how you or professional writers prepare to write by either demonstrating live in front of them or providing examples of such notes and plans by major writers, many of which are available through the *Paris Review*.
- Expose them to a range of planning strategies—mapping, outlining, sticky notes or index cards, apps, or features of Microsoft Word you use—and then let them choose the one or ones that suit their ways of working best.

**To improve students' capacity to revise, edit, or rewrite, do the following:**

- Require them to focus on one specific aspect of the writing that would lead to improved clarity and comprehension by the audience; for example, students could revise the structure of the paper to improve the reader's ability to navigate and understand your complex ideas that are now brought into greater focus through the use of subheads.
- Teach students specific goals of editing—concision, for example—and then, after modeling for students (try using a portion of a student's paper), ask them to apply the techniques by cutting 50, 100, or many more words (depending on the length).
- Ask them to read their paper, and after each sentence, ask of that sentence (and their ideas), "So what?" If the next sentence does not answer that question, look for ways to rewrite the sentence or paragraph so that it does explain why any idea, quotation, or claim matters or what it means.
- After modeling for the class, have students read each other's papers, stopping at any point to jot a question in the margin about some aspect of the writing that they do not understand (e.g., "How does this relate to the previous sentence?").

**To help students develop and try new approaches to writing, do the following:**

- Show them what it means to rewrite the same story, event, or process by either modeling it for them live, bringing in several different versions of a paper about the same topic, or sharing samples from writers who tried the same method.
- Provide students with, for example, a list of different approaches to writing an introduction; then direct them to choose two or three of these techniques and write as many different introductions, each one in a style very different from the others; they can then seek feedback from peers about which version is most effective.

**To develop students' ability to focus on what is most significant, do the following:**

- Give them a graphic organizer of some sort (e.g., one shaped like a target) that is designed to establish a focus to which parts of the essay should connect in some substantial way.
- Have students write a reverse outline based on the essay's current content and organization.
- Ask students to determine what question their essay seeks to answer; then go through their drafts and ask what question each paragraph attempts to answer and how that question relates to the overarching question they are trying to answer in the paper.

**To help your English Language Learners, try this one thing:**

- Have students turn their entire paper into a sentence outline in the word processing program to examine the relationship between each sentence or paragraph and those that precede them, revising as necessary to improve the focus and flow of the paper.

**Academic Vocabulary:** Key Words and Phrases

**Audience:** Whether the audience is known (the teacher, the class, the school, or the local community) or unknown (a prospective employer, anyone who visits the class blog, or a wiki), students must consider who the audience is and what they do and do not know before writing.

**Conventions:** The rules that apply to and govern the genre, format, grammar, and other aspects of writing this paper, including spelling.

**Develop:** This refers to the process one follows to improve a piece of writing before one even sets words down on paper; that is, such steps as gathering and generating ideas for the writing, taking time to outline, brainstorm, or map one's ideas. Once those ideas are down in a rough draft, development means seeking for better words, editing unnecessary words, or improving clarity and cohesion by tightening the sentences.

**Editing:** When students rewrite the paper to make it more concise, coherent, or cohesive, they are editing; when one looks for and fixes spelling and mechanics, they are proofreading. Editing can and, with more fluent writers, does take place throughout the composing process, not just at the end, as with proofreading.

**New approach:** At some point, the writer may feel the current approach—the voice, the style, the perspective, or the stance—is not effective, at which point it makes sense to write the whole piece over in some new style, different format, or alternate perspective to better convey one's ideas to the audience on this occasion.

**Planning:** Students can do many things to plan: outline ideas, gather and generate ideas, or block off the main ideas before refining them into an outline; making concept maps, mind maps, or brainstorming to generate and make connections between ideas. Some make lists of what they need to do, read, or include; all

should review the assignment requirements repeatedly throughout the planning process to make sure they include all they should.

**Purpose:** We always have some purpose when we write, whether it is to persuade, inform, entertain, or inspire. It is essential that they know what it is they are trying to achieve (and for whom and under what circumstances) before they even begin to write as their purpose influences everything from the words and structures they choose to the media and formats they use. Even when the writing task is assigned or outlined on a timed writing exam, it is crucial that students learn to identify the purpose and approach the writing with that in mind as they plan, draft, edit, and revise their papers.

**Revising:** This does not mean, as some think, merely correcting or proofreading a paper. To *revise* is to *re-see*, to consider the paper or idea from a whole new angle or hear a different way to express an idea or emotion. Revising the paper should improve not just the clarity and cohesion but also the content as the writer strives to strengthen the arguments, the logic, and the style.

**Rewriting:** Student writers sometimes need to take a whole paper or some portion of it and rewrite it in light of what they learn after getting that first draft down. Sometimes used interchangeably with *revising*, this phase of the writing process involves not tweaking or polishing up what is there but replacing it with new ideas or language better suited to the audience, the purpose, or the occasion.

**Strengthen:** This is what revising for concision, clarity, and coherence does to the writing: It strengthens it by tightening the wording, refining the argument, and removing what is unnecessary so you can emphasize key ideas, reasoning, or evidence.

*Notes* :

**Writing 6:** Use technology, including the Internet, to produce and publish writing and to interact and collaborate with others.

## English Language Arts

**6** Use technology, including the Internet, to produce and publish writing as well as to interact and collaborate with others; demonstrate sufficient command of keyboarding skills to type a minimum of three pages in a single sitting.

**7** Use technology, including the Internet, to produce and publish writing **and link to and cite sources** as well as to interact and collaborate with others, **including linking to and citing sources.**

**8** Use technology, including the Internet, to produce and publish writing **and present the relationships between information and ideas efficiently** as well as to interact and collaborate with others.

## History/Social Studies, Science, and Technical Studies

**6** Use technology, including the Internet, to produce and publish writing and present the relationships between information and ideas clearly and efficiently.

**7** Use technology, including the Internet, to produce and publish writing and present the relationships between information and ideas clearly and efficiently.

**8** Use technology, including the Internet, to produce and publish writing and present the relationships between information and ideas clearly and efficiently.

* These broad types of writing include many subgenres. See Appendix A for definitions of key writing types.

## What the **Student** Does

## English Language Arts

**6** **Gist:** Compose texts using digital devices, software, websites, and other digital tools and collaborate with others (via Google Docs, chat, and other social media applications) on written and multimedia productions, using these tools to publish, distribute, and display work for different purposes and audiences. Students master the keyboard well enough to type at least three pages in a single sitting.

- What tools or technologies offer the greatest means of creating and working with others on this writing project?
- What opportunities should we consider for publishing writing to a larger audience?
- How well and how fast can you type?

**7** **Gist:** Compose texts using digital devices, software, websites, and other digital tools and collaborate with others on written and multi-media productions, using these tools to publish, distribute, and display work, which includes links to and citations of those sources.

- What tools or technologies offer the greatest means of creating and working with others on this writing project?
- What opportunities should we consider for publishing writing to a larger audience?
- What sources should include links and be cited?

**8** **Gist:** Compose texts using digital devices, software, websites, and other digital tools and collaborate with others on written and multimedia productions, using these tools to publish, distribute, and display work that shows the relationships between information and ideas in an effective way.

- What tools or technologies offer the greatest means of creating and working with others on this writing project?
- What opportunities should we consider for publishing writing to a larger audience?
- How would you describe (and present) the relationship between information and ideas efficiently?

## History/Social Studies, Science, and Technical Studies

**6** **Gist:** Compose texts using digital devices, software, websites, and other digital tools and publish, distribute, and display work that shows the relationships between information and ideas in an effective way.

- What tools or technologies offer the greatest benefit to students when writing such a paper?
- What opportunities should we consider for publishing writing to a larger audience?
- How would you describe (and present) the relationship between information and ideas efficiently?

**7** **Gist:** Compose texts using digital devices, software, websites, and other digital tools and publish, distribute, and display work that shows the relationships between information and ideas in an effective way.

- What tools or technologies offer the greatest benefit to students when writing such a paper?
- What opportunities should we consider for publishing writing to a larger audience?
- How would you describe (and present) the relationship between information and ideas efficiently?

**8** **Gist:** Compose texts using digital devices, software, websites, and other digital tools and publish, distribute, and display work that shows the relationships between information and ideas in an effective way.

- What tools or technologies offer the greatest benefit to students when writing such a paper?
- What opportunities should we consider for publishing writing to a larger audience?
- How would you describe (and present) the relationship between information and ideas efficiently?

What the **Teacher** Does

**To have students use technology to produce, publish, and collaborate, do the following:**

- Provide direct instruction as needed in the use of any devices, platforms, applications, or software for a given assignment.
- Ensure that students can access and use the technology as you intend or expect (e.g., if you say they must collaborate through an online discussion group, do all have access and know-how?).
- Display, when possible, the contents of your screen via a projector so they can follow along or check their work against yours if you are guiding them through a sequence of steps.
- Prepare ahead of time as needed (e.g., checking to see that the lab printer is working and loaded with paper) so that you will not lose instructional time.

**To have students use the Internet to produce writing, do the following:**

- Explore different online applications designed to help students generate, organize, and develop their ideas.
- Create links to specific resources you want students to visit for content to incorporate into their paper; such content might include primary source documents, images, or applications students can use to create infographics for their papers.
- Instruct students in the use of free programs such as Google Docs or various graphics applications that they can use to produce their texts or develop content to embed in those texts.

**To have students use technology to produce writing, do the following:**

- Look for ways to use technology—computers, tablets, displays, interactive whiteboards, document cameras—that are efficient, effective, and appropriate to the writing task.
- Evaluate the writing assignment for small but worthwhile opportunities that allow you to teach students additional features of word processing

(e.g., how to embed images, how to design the page so text flows around images, or how to insert headers), graphic design (e.g., infographics, images, or layout), multimedia formatting (e.g., how to embed a slide show or a video clip in a written document), or even just improved typing skills.

**To have students use the Internet to publish writing, do the following:**

- Consider carefully the options and implications of publishing student work (especially if it contains images or any copyrighted material) online.
- Try setting up a class blog to which all can contribute in one place so it is easier to maintain, monitor, and model how to use.
- Take those extra steps, when publishing for the entire world to see, that ensure that the writing is correct, appropriate, and formatted according to the platform they are using.

**To have students use technology to interact or collaborate, do the following:**

- Set up a group or collaborative space online (via Google Docs, a wiki site, or any other platform that allows users to create a password-protected space) where they can meet to discuss and respond to each other's ideas and writing in or outside of class.
- Gather useful links—to applications, primary source sites, exhibits, or other rich resources related to a paper they are writing—that they explore together in class or at home during the process of gathering and generating ideas for writing.

**To help your English Language Learners, try this one thing:**

- Make sure they have access to and know how to use the platform, application, software, computer, or tablet you are assuming all students have at home and know how to use in the ways you have assigned.

**Academic Vocabulary:** Key Words and Phrases

**Collaborate:** Students work together to come up with ideas for their writing or respond to each other's papers using features such as Comments (Google Docs) or Track Changes (Microsoft Word). This might include comments from the teacher or classmates about writing provided through recorded voice memos, features such as Microsoft Word Track Changes, or annotations of any sort offered through tablet applications that allow the reader to offer feedback via voice, digital highlighters, digital sticky notes, or annotations written on the digital document itself. Such feedback comes *throughout the entire composing process*. Students receive—from one or more sources—ideas about how they can improve some aspect of whatever they are writing.

**Display information flexibly and dynamically:** Information written for digital displays—computers, smartphones, tablets, computers, and televisions— affords the writer an array of formats and features. "Flexibly and dynamically" suggest that writers embed images and graphics as alternatives or supplements to words, and incorporate more dynamic forms such as embedded video, slide shows, or other interactive visuals available to those writing on and for computers.

**Interact:** Students collaborate in a written dialogue online through chat groups, social media, email, and other such interactive platforms to generate ideas about a text they are analyzing, a paper they are writing, or a topic they are exploring (prior to writing). Thus, they are using technology to facilitate and extend discussions, generate ideas, provide feedback to peers' papers, or write and share their writing with others for feedback or publication.

**Produce:** This refers to using a range of technology tools—computers, applications, digital cameras to capture images or make videos, instruments for scientific data gathering, software and advanced calculators for mathematics—to generate the content and help students write.

**Publish:** This means to use computers to publish and distribute quality materials around school, the community, or online.

**Technology:** This refers to using computers to compose, revise, and correct any papers; also, it implies using applications to gather or generate data, evidence, or content (in the form of quantitative information, examples, graphic displays, or still and video images) to incorporate into the paper itself. Technology is also an essential research tool for writers: the Internet in general, as well as specialized databases and other online resources. Using "technology" also means writing with and for a range of forms, formats, and features: essays, blogs, wikis, websites, multimedia presentations, or digital essays using the full spectrum of available digital features (color, size, hotlinks, or embedded media) to communicate or publish the work for audiences to read on smartphones, tablets, computers, presentation screens, and, of course, paper.

**Writing products:** Given the emphasis here on the use of technology, such products would include not only the traditional papers students write but also such new and emerging forms as blogs, wikis, websites, Tweets, presentations, and multimedia or hybrid texts.

*Notes*

**Writing 7:** Conduct short as well as more sustained research projects to answer a question (including a self-generated question) or solve a problem; narrow or broaden the inquiry when appropriate; synthesize multiple sources on the subject, demonstrating understanding of the subject under investigation.

## English Language Arts

**6** Conduct short research projects to answer a question, drawing on several sources and refocusing the inquiry when appropriate.

**7** Conduct short research projects to answer a question, drawing on several sources and **generating additional related, focused questions for further research and investigation.**

**8** Conduct short research projects to answer a question (**including a self-generated question**), drawing on several sources and generating additional related, focused questions **that allow for multiple avenues of exploration.**

## History/Social Studies, Science, and Technical Studies

**6** Conduct short research projects to answer a question (including a self-generated question), drawing on several sources and generating additional related, focused questions that allow for multiple avenues of exploration.

**7** Conduct short research projects to answer a question (including a self-generated question), drawing on several sources and generating additional related, focused questions that allow for multiple avenues of exploration.

**8** Conduct short research projects to answer a question (including a self-generated question), drawing on several sources and generating additional related, focused questions that allow for multiple avenues of exploration.

## What the **Student** Does

### English Language Arts

**6** **Gist:** Answer a research question through a brief investigation, using multiple sources and adjusting the focus of that inquiry when necessary.

- What is the subject of your inquiry—and the question you are attempting to answer about it?
- What questions should you ask when researching this topic?
- What are some different sources you should consult for this topic?

**7** **Gist:** Answer a research question through a brief investigation, using multiple sources and developing relevant follow-up questions to help focus and extend the inquiry into the topic.

- What is the subject of your inquiry—and the question you are attempting to answer about it?
- What sources should you consult for this topic?
- What other questions could you ask to refine or extend your inquiry into this subject?

**8** **Gist:** Answer a research question through a brief investigation (self-generated questions are permissible), using multiple sources and developing relevant follow-up questions that invite a range of possible investigations.

- What is the subject of your inquiry—and the question you are attempting to answer about it?
- What sources should you consult for this topic?
- What questions might you ask about this subject that would create opportunities to further explore this topic from different angles?

### History/Social Studies, Science, and Technical Studies

**6** **Gist:** Answer a research question through a brief investigation (self-generated questions are permissible), using multiple sources and developing relevant follow-up questions that invite a range of possible investigations.

- What is the subject of your inquiry—and the question you are attempting to answer about it?
- What sources should you consult for this topic?
- What questions might you ask about this subject that would create opportunities to further explore this topic from different angles?

**7** **Gist:** Answer a research question through a brief investigation (self-generated questions are permissible), using multiple sources and developing relevant follow-up questions that invite a range of possible investigations.

- What is the subject of your inquiry—and the question you are attempting to answer about it?
- What sources should you consult for this topic?
- What questions might you ask about this subject that would create opportunities to further explore this topic from different angles?

**8** **Gist:** Answer a research question through a brief investigation (self-generated questions are permissible), using multiple sources and developing relevant follow-up questions that invite a range of possible investigations.

- What is the subject of your inquiry—and the question you are attempting to answer about it?
- What sources should you consult for this topic?
- What questions might you ask about this subject that would create opportunities to further explore this topic from different angles?

What the **Teacher** Does

**To have students conduct short as well as more sustained research projects, do the following:**

- Organize units of study around a big idea, an essential question, or a cultural conflict; these might be framed as inquiries into long-standing arguments that provide students opportunities to formulate a response to or take a stand on the subject, which they then gather evidence to support.

- Identify key questions or problems students can investigate in some depth within the constraints of a class period, using their findings when writing, speaking, or interviewing someone about that subject. Students might, for example, investigate a specific aspect of the Holocaust to generate questions; they might also research a controversial topic such as cloning as part of a unit in both science and Language Arts where they are reading a science fiction story about that idea.

**To have students answer questions (including self-generated questions) or solve problems, do the following:**

- Discuss with students the process you or respected writers, scientists, historians, economists, and others go through to discover a subject, and then ask questions or identify problems.

- Pass out sticky notes to all in the class; then ask them to list a subject on the top of the note that relates to the text or topic the class is studying; then tell them to write a question about that text or topic that could be developed into a compelling paper. Finally, have them stick all the notes on the front board and let the whole class examine them as part of the process of learning to ask questions and solve problems in the papers they write.

**To have students narrow or broaden an inquiry into a subject, have students do the following:**

- Begin by restating their topic, task, inquiry, or problem as a question, making it as specific as they can

(i.e., what is the question your paper is trying to answer?).

- Narrow their inquiry by adding words and phrases that specifically relate to actions and relationships: *contribution, definition, cause, conflict, evolution,* or *interaction.*

- Extend or broaden their inquiry by investigating what others have found in the past and how that changed the understanding of that subject in the field; ask questions about the internal history of the subject (e.g., how has our perception or attitude toward _____ changed over the last decade—and why?) to connect it up to the larger questions within the field.

- Broaden or narrow their topic or problem by making room in students' inquiry for alternative or opposing perspectives on your topic or text; some might call this exploring the dialectic nature of any topic or text students might study.

**To have students synthesize multiple sources on a subject, do the following:**

- Ask students to identify key ideas, terms, perspectives, or arguments across sources; then guide them through the process, providing models as needed, of analyzing these connections to find some idea, question, or problem that links them all and is worth investigating.

- Give students a set of quotations or specific examples about an idea or problem that is examined by all these texts; then draw from those quotations some conclusion about the "real problem" or the "question no one is asking" about this subject.

**To help your English Language Learners, try this one thing:**

- Clarify what *synthesis* means and how to do it; but also take time to make sure they first comprehend the texts because students cannot synthesize different texts if they do not first understand them.

**Academic Vocabulary:** Key Words and Phrases

**Demonstrating understanding of the subject:** Students show the depth of their knowledge and their research skills by gathering a range of quality information, data, evidence, and examples related to the problem, question, or topic they are investigating; they then demonstrate what they have learned by choosing the most salient details and examples and using those to support their claims in a coherent, logical manner throughout the paper.

**Narrow or broaden the inquiry:** As students begin to investigate a question, problem, or topic, they often encounter information that suggests they open the inquiry a bit to allow for more perspectives or possible ideas to explore; at other times, they feel overwhelmed by all the information they find on a topic and would be better served by narrowing an inquiry to a more refined or specific question or topic about which they can make a reasonable claim.

**Questions (includes self-generated questions):** Researchers generate their own or investigate others' questions about a topic of substance; such questions are often the driving purpose of the research: *We are investigating* X *to determine how* X *leads to* Y.

**Research (short and more sustained):** Students and teachers are engaged in research any time they seek information about a question or subject, or ask themselves or others questions about causes, types, effects, meaning, and importance of anything they find themselves studying for class or their interests. Short or brief inquiries might involve getting some background knowledge on an author, a book, or a time period; in science, search for and consider previous findings for certain experiments; in social studies, dig up primary sources to see how people thought about an event at that time or opinion pieces in different newspapers to measure the response to an event (e.g., dropping of the atomic bomb) from different parts of the country or world. Longer, more sustained research projects demand far more depth and many more sources from different perspectives. It is a fundamental skill for success in college, one's career, and at home as a consumer who must increasingly take responsibility for researching the best health care program, insurance policy, or cell phone provider.

**Solve a problem:** Fundamental to the research task or process to answering some question—as a scientist, a historian, an economist, a consumer, or just a curious person. Embedded within this process are such skills as generating questions (to help frame or refine the problem), gathering data and possible solutions, and evaluating and choosing those solutions for which one finds the greatest support and evidence during one's research.

**Subject under investigation:** This refers to the topic, the research question, or the problem the student seeks to understand and develop an argument about after completing the research. This subject can come from students themselves or from a teacher or institution (e.g., college board or the students' state or district) that requires students to study in depth a sustained or brief a research project.

**Synthesize multiple sources:** Any genuine research project of any substance must consider the subject from different and competing angles if it is to arrive at any meaningful or significant insight. Also, one must consider multiple sources, some of which offer counterarguments or alternative perspectives if their claims and arguments are to be considered reliable, valid, and substantial. Of course these sources must all come from established, trustworthy sources if they are to be cited or used to support one's claims.

*Notes*

**Writing 8:** Gather relevant information from multiple print and digital sources, assess the credibility and accuracy of each source, and integrate the information while avoiding plagiarism.

## English Language Arts

**6** Gather relevant information from multiple print and digital sources; assess the credibility of each source; and quote or paraphrase the data and conclusions of others while avoiding plagiarism and providing basic bibliographic information for sources.

**7** Gather relevant information from multiple print and digital sources, **using search terms effectively**; assess the credibility **and accuracy** of each source; and quote or paraphrase the data and conclusions of others while avoiding plagiarism **and following a standard format for citation.**

**8** Gather relevant information from multiple print and digital sources, using search terms effectively; assess the credibility and accuracy of each source; and quote or paraphrase the data and conclusions of others while avoiding plagiarism and following a standard format for citation.

## History/Social Studies, Science, and Technical Studies

**6** Gather relevant information from multiple print and digital sources, using search terms effectively; assess the credibility and accuracy of each source; and quote or paraphrase the data and conclusions of others while avoiding plagiarism and following a standard format for citation.

**7** Gather relevant information from multiple print and digital sources, using search terms effectively; assess the credibility and accuracy of each source; and quote or paraphrase the data and conclusions of others while avoiding plagiarism and following a standard format for citation.

**8** Gather relevant information from multiple print and digital sources, using search terms effectively; assess the credibility and accuracy of each source; and quote or paraphrase the data and conclusions of others while avoiding plagiarism and following a standard format for citation.

## What the **Student** Does

### English Language Arts

**6** **Gist:** Search for and collect useful information—data, examples, quotations, even digital media—from a range of sources, both print and digital, determining the quality of these sources (i.e., credibility and accuracy) and quoting or paraphrasing others' ideas, taking care not to plagiarize and including some citation details about each source.

- What is the research question or the problem you will investigate—and which sources should you consider for that investigation?
- What questions should you ask to assess the credibility and relevancy of your different sources?
- Which details are so important you should quote or paraphrase them (as well as cite them)?

**7** **Gist:** Use search terms strategically to find and collect valuable information—data, examples, quotations, even digital media—from a range of sources, both print and digital, determining the quality of these sources (i.e., credibility and accuracy) and quoting or paraphrasing others' ideas, taking care not to plagiarize and citing each source according to the specified format.

- What is the research question or the problem you will investigate—and which sources should you consider for that investigation?
- What questions should you ask to assess the credibility and relevancy of your different sources?
- Which details are so important you should quote or paraphrase them (as well as cite them)?

**8** **Gist:** Use search terms strategically to find and collect valuable information—data, examples, quotations, even digital media—from a range of sources, both print and digital, determining the quality of these sources (i.e., credibility and accuracy) and quoting or paraphrasing others' ideas, taking care not to plagiarize and citing each source according to the specified format.

- What is the research question or the problem you will investigate—and which sources should you consider for that investigation?
- What questions should you ask to assess the credibility and relevancy of your different sources?
- Which details are so important you should quote or paraphrase them (as well as cite them)?

### History/Social Studies, Science, and Technical Studies

**6** **Gist:** Use search terms strategically to find and collect valuable information—data, examples, quotations, even digital media—from a range of sources, both print and digital, determining the quality of these sources (i.e., credibility and accuracy) and quoting or paraphrasing others' ideas, taking care not to plagiarize and citing each source according to the specified format.

- What is the research question or the problem you will investigate—and which sources should you consider for that investigation?
- What questions should you ask to assess the credibility and relevancy of your different sources?
- Which details are so important you should quote or paraphrase them (as well as cite them)?

**7** **Gist:** Use search terms strategically to find and collect valuable information—data, examples, quotations, even digital media—from a range of sources, both print and digital, determining the quality of these sources (i.e., credibility and accuracy) and quoting or paraphrasing others' ideas, taking care not to plagiarize and citing each source according to the specified format.

- What is the research question or the problem you will investigate—and which sources should you consider for that investigation?
- What questions should you ask to assess the credibility and relevancy of your different sources?
- Which details are so important you should quote or paraphrase them (as well as cite them)?

**8** **Gist:** Use search terms strategically to find and collect valuable information—data, examples, quotations, even digital media—from a range of sources, both print and digital, determining the quality of these sources (i.e., credibility and accuracy) and quoting or paraphrasing others' ideas, taking care not to plagiarize and citing each source according to the specified format.

- What is the research question or the problem you will investigate—and which sources should you consider for that investigation?
- What questions should you ask to assess the credibility and relevancy of your different sources?
- Which details are so important you should quote or paraphrase them (as well as cite them)?

## What the **Teacher** Does

**To have students gather relevant information, do the following:**

- Begin by first asking students to define the problem they are trying to solve or the question they are investigating.
- Present students with criteria you develop for—or with—them, or which are provided by other audiences for this assignment.
- Give or create with your students an effective means of collecting information, details, examples, data, and all other content for subsequent integration into their paper.

**To have students find relevant evidence from multiple print and digital sources, do the following:**

- Expose students to all the available sources—both print and multimedia—they can or must use for this paper, presentation, or project; then explain to them which one they should use for different purposes or content related to their inquiry.
- Collaborate with your school librarian to visit the library for an orientation session focusing on what print and digital resources are available for a specific project; such content might include primary source documents, images, or databases.
- Provide students with a print edition of an article, and then set them up to trace the same story across media to see how each treats it differently, taking time throughout that process to teach them how to read and synthesize the meaning from these different sources and integrate that content into their papers.

**To have students assess the credibility and accuracy of each source, do the following:**

- Instruct students in the questions they should ask to determine the credibility of any content but especially online sources.
- Create a structured note-taking handout students can use to determine the credibility of any sources they are evaluating; this note-taking sheet could double as a way of gathering citation information for future works cited on the paper.

**To have students integrate information without impeding the flow of the writing, do the following:**

- Demonstrate for students how to take only the relevant portion of any quotation and incorporate it into their sentences as evidence to support their ideas.
- Teach students to distinguish between direct and indirect quotes so they can choose the one that interferes least with the flow of the writing.
- Provide students with a range of samples illustrating the different ways one can integrate quotations of different lengths using punctuation (e.g., ellipses and brackets), formatting (e.g., block quotations), and paraphrase or indirect quotation.

**To have students avoid plagiarism when choosing and integrating sources, do the following:**

- Illustrate for your students the difference between the proper integration and citation of sources in a paper and the improper use (i.e., plagiarism) of such sources.
- Direct students, once they have a complete final draft, to highlight *all* content, in whatever form or from whatever source, that comes from a source other than themselves; then guide them through the process of determining whether it is properly cited to avoid any allegations of plagiarism.
- Encourage students to submit papers to such services as turnitin.com *before* submitting their final papers for further screening to be sure they identify all sources they should cite.

**To help your English Language Learners, try this one thing:**

- Talk with them about and take extra pains to ensure they understand the concept of plagiarism and its consequences as some English Language Learners come from countries where it is not considered plagiarism (or an offense) to use the words of others, often well-known writers and scholars, as their own.

**Academic Vocabulary:** Key Words and Phrases

**Accuracy:** The information is true, current, and precise whenever it is used as evidence for a claim or support for a hypothesis; the measurements use the appropriate terms for that subject or discipline to ensure maximum clarity and accuracy of reference.

**Assess:** Of all the information your search yields or all the quotations and evidence you *could* include in your paper, which should you use based on your criteria or research question?

**Citation:** These come in two formats and locations within the paper: in-text parenthetical citations (where the student quotes another's work) and at the end of the paper, in the works cited section that lists all works referred to in the paper. Which format you use (e.g., APA or MLA) depends on the field and the teacher's preferences.

**Credibility:** This is a measure of the believability of the writer or source of information, based on how current, established, and relevant the source is, as well as the *ethos* of the writer and any source cited. A related idea is that of authoritative sources: established sources affiliated with recognized publishers, reputable universities, or respected authors.

**Gather relevant information:** Information is only relevant to the degree that it answers the research question or supports an argument the writer makes; all else should be left out or dismissed as irrelevant. This is why it is so important to have a carefully conceived, clear, and narrow research question or problem one is reading to answer or solve: Then you know which information is most useful or relevant.

**Integrate information into the text selectively:** To weave the quotations, examples, details, or evidence into the paper through paraphrase or indirect or direct quotation, students need not include every word of a source when quoting it directly; instead, they embed it in their sentence in a way (by using ellipses to indicate omissions and brackets to signal additions) that maintains or enhances the flow of the text and ideas.

**Multiple print and digital sources:** Legitimate researchers consider an array of sources from different perspectives and media to be as thorough as possible in their analysis.

**Plagiarism:** This means including another's words as your own (without using quotation marks); those words can be copied from a famous writer, any website, or a fellow student. It is not plagiarism to use an author's words so long as you cite them and put quotation marks around those words being quoted.

**Standard format for citation:** This means MLA style for humanities citations and APA format for others, as well as various specialized formats for specific scientific papers and disciplines.

**Source:** Be mindful of the strengths and limitations of each source: Some sources may have particularly good data about one issue but not another; when assessing or quoting sources, it is vital to be aware of the quality and reputation of that source on this subject. A source may, for example, offer quality data about technology and teens but be weak when it comes to looking at technology and different cultural groups. Avoid overusing or relying exclusively on any one source: When researching a subject, students cannot rely on a few select sources that conveniently offer them a wealth of quotations or evidence. They need to reference (and make use of) a variety of sources that represent different perspectives and stances on the issue or question they are researching if their observations, conclusions, and arguments are to be credible.

*Notes*

**Writing 9:** Draw evidence from literary or informational texts to support analysis, reflection, and research.

## English Language Arts

**6** Draw evidence from literary or informational texts to support analysis, reflection, and research.

  a. Apply grade 6 Reading standards to literature (e.g., "Compare and contrast texts in different forms or genres [e.g., stories and poems; historical novels and fantasy stories] in terms of their approaches to similar themes and topics.").

  b. Apply grade 6 Reading standards to literary nonfiction (e.g., "Trace and evaluate the argument and specific claims in a text, distinguishing claims that are supported by reasons and evidence from claims that are not.").

**7** Draw evidence from literary or informational texts to support analysis, reflection, and research.

  a. Apply **grade 7 Reading standards** to literature (e.g., "**Compare and contrast a fictional portrayal of a time, place, or character and a historical account of the same period as a means of understanding how authors of fiction use or alter history.**").

  b. Apply **grade 7 Reading standards** to literary nonfiction (e.g. "Trace and evaluate the argument and specific claims in a text, **assessing whether the reasoning is sound and the evidence is relevant and sufficient to support the claims.**").

## History/Social Studies, Science, and Technical Studies

**6** Draw evidence from informational texts to support analysis, reflection, and research.

**7** Draw evidence from informational texts to support analysis, reflection, and research.

## What the **Student** Does

### English Language Arts

### History/Social Studies, Science, and Technical Studies

**6** **Gist:** Support their interpretations, analyses, reflections, or findings with evidence found in literary or informational texts, applying grade 6 standards for reading literature and informational texts. See the "Reading Standards" section for the full standards.

- What is the topic or text you are writing about—and what is your claim?
- What evidence can you find in the literary or informational text(s) to support your claim(s)?
- How does this evidence support your analysis, reflection, or findings?

**6** **Gist:** Students support their analyses, reflections, or research findings with evidence—examples, quotations, information, data—taken from informational texts.

- What is the topic or question you are writing about—and what's your claim?
- What evidence in the informational text(s), data set, or experiment supports your claim?
- How does this evidence support your analysis, reflection, or findings?

**7** **Gist:** Support their interpretations, analyses, reflections, or findings with evidence found in literary or informational texts, applying grade 7 standards for reading literature and informational texts. See the "Reading Standards" section for the full standards.

- What is the topic or text you are writing about—and what is your claim?
- What evidence can you find in the literary or informational text(s) to support your claim(s)?
- How does this evidence support your analysis, reflection, or findings?

**7** **Gist:** Students support their analyses, reflections, or research findings with evidence—examples, quotations, information, data—taken from informational texts.

- What is the topic or question you are writing about—and what's your claim?
- What evidence in the informational text(s), data set, or experiment supports your claim?
- How does this evidence support your analysis, reflection, or findings?

**Writing 9:** Draw evidence from literary or informational texts to support analysis, reflection, and research

### English Language Arts

**8** Draw evidence from literary or informational texts to support analysis, reflection, and research.

   a. Apply **grade 8 Reading standards** to literature (e.g., "**Analyze how a modern work of fiction draws on themes, patterns of events, or character types from myths, traditional stories, or religious works such as the Bible, including describing how the material is rendered new.**").

   b. Apply **grade 8 Reading standards** to literary nonfiction (e.g., "Delineate and evaluate the argument and specific claims in a text, assessing whether the reasoning is sound and the evidence is relevant and sufficient; **recognize when irrelevant evidence is introduced.**").

### History/Social Studies, Science, and Technical Studies

**8** Draw evidence from informational texts to support analysis, reflection, and research.

## What the **Student** Does

### English Language Arts

**8** **Gist:** Support their interpretations, analyses, reflections, or findings with evidence found in literary or informational texts, applying grade 8 standards for reading literature and informational texts. See the "Reading Standards" section for the full standards.

- What is the topic or text you are writing about—and what is your claim?
- What evidence can you find in the literary or informational text(s) to support your claim(s)?
- How does this evidence support your analysis, reflection, or findings?

### History/Social Studies, Science, and Technical Studies

**8** **Gist:** Students support their analyses, reflections, or research findings with evidence—examples, quotations, information, data—taken from informational texts.

- What is the topic or question you are writing about—and what's your claim?
- What evidence in the informational text(s), data set, or experiment supports your claim?
- How does this evidence support your analysis, reflection, or findings?

What the **Teacher** Does

**To have students draw evidence from literary or informational texts, do the following:**

- Require students to develop a working thesis or guiding question that gives them some means of evaluating the content of any text they read for useful evidence; without any such question or claim to guide them, readers will have no basis on which to evaluate the examples, findings, data, or quotations for possible use.
- Define and illustrate for students what *counts* as "evidence" so they know what it looks like and, thus, what to search for; this is particularly important for students learning to assess primary sources and other text types such as multimedia and infographics.
- Require students to annotate or code the texts they read with an eye toward using different elements as evidence in a subsequent paper; thus, for example, the teacher might show them how to put a Q in the margin to indicate, upon rereading later, the location of a possible quotation worth using; those using tablets can teach students how to use digital tools to annotate, search texts for specific words, and capture images for future use.

**To have students draw evidence from literary texts to support analysis and more, do the following:**

- Help students first learn what and how much of a passage to quote by illustrating the difference between using a full quotation (too long) and one that only uses the relevant portion (just right) and is written in the literary present tense.
- Clarify and illustrate for your students when, how, and why to use direct, indirect, and block quotations to support their thesis.
- Teach students how to use ellipses and brackets to edit quotations for concision and grammatical consistency; also, show them how to punctuate the quotation so that it blends in with the rest of the sentence without undermining their voice or style.
- Show students an exemplary sentence of literary analysis; then give students a claim and quotation from the text, asking them to write their analysis of how the evidence supports their claim; then direct them to make their own claim and find their own evidence from the text they are analyzing, bringing it all together in one sentence.

**To have students draw evidence from informational texts for analysis and more, do the following:**

- Introduce them to a wide range of sources of evidence, including examples, statistics, expert opinions, interviews, surveys, observations, experiments, primary source documents, and quotations.
- Establish with students—or apply from another source—specific criteria for selecting evidence, demonstrating how to assess the degree to which all evidence is valid, reliable, relevant, and sufficient.
- Permit and show students how to find and use evidence in different forms—graphs, images, charts, tables, even videos—and then integrate and comment on it to support their claims.

**To have students use evidence to support analysis, reflection, and research, do the following:**

- Display (on a projection screen and/or a handout) contrasting examples of evidence used to support the writer's ideas, ensuring a continuum of quality; have students evaluate, rank, and discuss.
- Together, analyze representative examples of how writers on the opinion page of major newspapers use evidence to support their analysis.

**To help your English Language Learners, try this one thing:**

- Ensure that these students know and can use the different technical terms related to evidence; then use a color-coding system on the computer to display your own, a student's, or a professional writer's sample so your ELL students can see the relationship between the writer's claims, evidence, and reasoning.

**Academic Vocabulary:** Key Words and Phrases

**Analysis:** This refers to the breaking down of the subject, text, event, or process into its component parts to understand what it means or how it works.

**Delineate and evaluate the reasoning:** This means to separate the different reasons and associated evidence behind any claims and to evaluate each claim apart from the others so you can determine, when writing about others' ideas, just how sound they are.

**Draw evidence:** The word *draw* here means to extract, as in d*raw water from a well*; thus, people draw out from all that they read, view, hear, or see about a subject the evidence that best supports their claims.

**Evidence:** Evidence comes in a variety of forms: quantitative data, observation, quotation, example, and findings from surveys and such queries. The reasoning behind your arguments must be based on sound premises; the connection between the claim and evidence used to support that claim should match or agree; otherwise, you offer fallacies such as the *hasty generalization*.

**Evidence is relevant and sufficient:** The data or examples you draw from the sources must be appropriate and useful for the claim you are making; it

must also be adequate (e.g., high quality, complete, or thorough) if it is to be effective, reliable, and credible.

**Reasoning:** This is the logic behind why you think something; it should be based on some credible logic if the reasoning is to be considered sound.

**Literary and informational texts:** Literary text includes fiction, drama, poetry, literary nonfiction, art, and graphic novels; informational texts include essays, articles, infographics, mixed media texts, primary source documents, and seminal and foundational documents.

**Literary nonfiction (creative nonfiction):** This includes essays, books, or other nonfiction texts such as biographies, memoirs, histories, or narrative accounts of events that use literary or novelistic techniques such as plot, characterization, and point of view in ways that bring the story, its events, and its characters alive.

**Support analysis, reflection, and research:** In short, it is urging you to provide evidence or examples to support and illustrate whatever analysis you offer, statement you make while reflecting, or finding you make from your research. The key habit of mind for this standard is to support what you say with sound and relevant evidence.

*Notes*

**Writing 10:** Write routinely over extended times (time for research, reflection, and revision) and shorter time (a single sitting or a day or two) for a range of tasks, purposes, and audiences.

## English Language Arts

**6** Write routinely over extended time frames (time for reflection and revision) and shorter time frames (a single sitting or a day or two) for a range of discipline-specific tasks, purposes, and audiences.

**7** Write routinely over extended time frames (time for reflection and revision) and shorter time frames (a single sitting or a day or two) for a range of discipline-specific tasks, purposes, and audiences.

**8** Write routinely over extended time frames (time for reflection and revision) and shorter time frames (a single sitting or a day or two) for a range of discipline-specific tasks, purposes, and audiences.

## History/Social Studies, Science, and Technical Studies

**6** Write routinely over extended time frames (time for reflection and revision) and shorter time frames (a single sitting or a day or two) for a range of discipline-specific tasks, purposes, and audiences.

**7** Write routinely over extended time frames (time for reflection and revision) and shorter time frames (a single sitting or a day or two) for a range of discipline-specific tasks, purposes, and audiences.

**8** Write routinely over extended time frames (time for reflection and revision) and shorter time frames (a single sitting or a day or two) for a range of discipline-specific tasks, purposes, and audiences.

## What the **Student** Does

### English Language Arts

**6** **Gist:** Write regularly for a range of reasons (e.g., to reflect, research, and revise) in different contexts and modes (timed, in-class, and extended tasks), for a variety of audiences.

- What is the subject, purpose, occasion, and audience for your writing?
- What questions should you ask or techniques should you use when writing this type of text or about this topic?
- What conventions or other ideas should you keep in mind when writing this sort of discipline-specific task?

**7** **Gist:** Write regularly for a range of reasons (e.g., to reflect, research, and revise) in different contexts and modes (timed, in-class, and extended tasks), for a variety of audiences.

- What is the subject, purpose, occasion, and audience for your writing?
- What questions should you ask or techniques should you use when writing this type of text or about this topic?
- What conventions or other ideas should you keep in mind when writing this sort of discipline-specific task?

**8** **Gist:** Write regularly for a range of reasons (e.g., to reflect, research, and revise) in different contexts and modes (timed, in-class, and extended tasks), for a variety of audiences.

- What is the subject, purpose, occasion, and audience for your writing?
- What questions should you ask or techniques should you use when writing this type of text or about this topic?
- What conventions or other ideas should you keep in mind when writing this sort of discipline-specific task?

### History/Social Studies, Science, and Technical Studies

**6** **Gist:** Write regularly for a range of reasons (e.g., to reflect, research, and revise) in different contexts and modes (timed, in-class, and extended tasks), for a variety of audiences.

- What is the subject, purpose, occasion, and audience for your writing?
- What questions should you ask or techniques should you use when writing this type of text or about this topic?
- What conventions or other ideas should you keep in mind when writing this sort of discipline-specific task?

**7** **Gist:** Write regularly for a range of reasons (e.g., to reflect, research, and revise) in different contexts and modes (timed, in-class, and extended tasks), for a variety of audiences.

- What is the subject, purpose, occasion, and audience for your writing?
- What questions should you ask or techniques should you use when writing this type of text or about this topic?
- What conventions or other ideas should you keep in mind when writing this sort of discipline-specific task?

**8** **Gist:** Write regularly for a range of reasons (e.g., to reflect, research, and revise) in different contexts and modes (timed, in-class, and extended tasks), for a variety of audiences.

- What is the subject, purpose, occasion, and audience for your writing?
- What questions should you ask or techniques should you use when writing this type of text or about this topic?
- What conventions or other ideas should you keep in mind when writing this sort of discipline-specific task?

What the **Teacher** Does

**To help students write routinely over extended time frames, do the following:**

- Provide regular opportunities for your students to research and then write about the big ideas, questions, and problems that are central to your class and subject area; such investigations might be major research papers or shorter inquiries into a specific topic related to a unit, a book, or a subject they are studying in class.
- Ask students to reflect on what they learn from a process or experience, how they learn it, and why it matters, or have them reflect on their evolving understanding of ideas, drawing examples and connections from the different units or texts they have studied over the semester.
- Make room in the composing process for time to revise, thereby fostering a culture of revision, a class where students feel they can try ideas and approaches, knowing they can revise.

**To have students write routinely over shorter time frames, do the following:**

- Have students write for a single sitting; such writing includes beginning the period by analyzing a text or writing about a topic the class will examine during that period; pause *during* class to write about or respond to a text, topic, or procedure the class has been studying for the period up to that point; wrap up the period by having students write a summary, synthesis, or response to what they have learned about a topic that day.
- Create opportunities for students to write as a way of building on what they read, viewed, or learned that day in class or the previous night for homework; thus, they might come in having read several chapters or short pieces about a topic, which they then synthesize in a paragraph that draws on the previous night's texts for evidence.
- Allow writing opportunities to extend over several days, each day, for example, culminating in a paragraph of

a larger paper the students write over the course of the week, and then spend the following week revising.

**To have students write for various discipline-specific tasks, do the following:**

- Create opportunities for students to produce those forms of writing common to the discipline you teach—reviews in an art class; opinion pieces in a government class; Supreme Court briefs in a history class; and poems, essays, and speeches in English classes—in the context of studying those forms.
- Incorporate the sort of writing practiced by people in your discipline as a way of thinking within the discipline; examples would include having students keep field notes like Lewis and Clark, lab notes such as all scientists use to record their thoughts and procedures, or jots, scribbles, and sketches by everyone from writers and scientists to designers and programmers.

**To have students write for various purposes, do the following:**

- Require students to write regularly to argue, inform/ explain, inspire, and entertain—to deepen and extend their own learning, to reflect on their processes or progress, to make connections across texts or ideas the class has studied lately.

**To help your English Language Learners, try this one thing:**

- Reinforce lessons and techniques from your class by giving all students—but especially your ELL students—the chance to keep practicing the different types of writing you teach them so the forms and features of these different types can become familiar and these students become fluent, confident academic writers.

**Academic Vocabulary:** Key Words and Phrases

**Audiences:** Students need to write for more than just their teachers; other audiences include classmates, other classes, parents, and local businesses and organizations, as well as those found online through blogs, wikis, social media, and other venues appropriate to students.

**Discipline-specific tasks, purposes, and audiences:** Each subject area has its own traditional forms as well as those types of writing specific to the academic work of those subjects (e.g., timed essays, summaries, analyses, and more). The emphasis here is on the idea that not all writing in all disciplines is written in the same way for the same reasons. The word *tasks* alludes not only the types of writing but also the ways of thinking when one writes; these are best understood through the verbs *summarize, synthesize, analyze, narrate, compare, contrast, evaluate, describe,* and so on.

**Extended time frames:** These are process papers or otherwise long-term assignments that might take anywhere from one week to more than a month in the event that students are writing major research projects over such an extended period as research papers that draw from a wide array of sources, some of which might be book length and, thus, require such longer periods. The reference to "research, reflection, and revision" suggests that students should have time to research a topic, reflect on their process, and revise their work, all of which demand substantial time and instruction.

**Purposes:** Authors' purposes are to inform, explain, persuade, entertain, and inspire.

**Range of tasks, purposes, and audiences:** See Discipline-specific entry above.

**Reflection:** Writing that looks back on events or experiences as well as within one's mind to consider what something means, what one learned, how things changed, or why something is important.

**Research:** This refers to a question one seeks to answer or a problem one aspires to solve because of investigating a subject in depth from a range of perspectives using different media.

**Revision:** This refers to changes made to a piece of writing not so much for correction or clarity, but to improve the content and ideas, which may evolve as the student learns more through additional research and reflection.

**Routinely:** This means to literally write as part of a routine in the class, for many reasons, not all of which are graded or even collected; writing is a dominant mode of the class as a performance in itself and as a means of preparing to write about a text or topic.

**Shorter time frames:** This might begin in class, finish for homework, and then get collected the next day; or it might be a timed, in-class assignments used to assess or extend learning. It is not the same as in-class writing; writing of this sort can also be done at home.

**Single sitting or a day or two:** This is writing that takes place in class, possibly but not necessarily under timed conditions.

**Tasks:** These are the things students are asked to write or do when they write; examples might include asking students to *read* and *summarize* a text, or asking students to *read* a collection of texts about a topic, and then *draw conclusions* about what the authors say about it; or they might be directed to *contrast* these competing views on the subject, and then *construct* an argument that *cites* evidence from those texts.

*Notes*

# Part 3

# The Common Core State Standards

## Speaking and Listening

# College and Career Readiness Anchor Standards for

# *Speaking and Listening 6–8*

**Source: Common Core State Standards**

The grades 6–12 standards on the following pages define what students should understand and be able to do by the end of each grade. They correspond to the CCR anchor standards by number. The CCR and grade-specific standards are necessary complements—the former providing broad standards, the latter providing additional specificity—that together define the skills and understandings that all students must demonstrate.

## Comprehension and Collaboration

1. Prepare for and participate effectively in a range of conversations and collaborations with diverse partners, building on others' ideas and expressing their own clearly and persuasively.

2. Integrate and evaluate information presented in diverse media and formats, including visually, quantitatively, and orally.

3. Evaluate a speaker's point of view, reasoning, and use of evidence and rhetoric.

## Presentation of Knowledge and Ideas

4. Present information, findings, and supporting evidence such that listeners can follow the line of reasoning and the organization, development, and style are appropriate to task, purpose, and audience.

5. Make strategic use of digital media and visual displays of data to express information and enhance understanding of presentations.

6. Adapt speech to a variety of contexts and communicative tasks, demonstrating command of formal English when indicated or appropriate.

## Note on Range and Content of Student Speaking and Listening

To become college and career ready, students must have ample opportunities to take part in a variety of rich, structured conversations—as part of a whole class, in small groups, and with a partner—built around important content in various domains. They must be able to contribute appropriately to these conversations, to make comparisons and contrasts, and to analyze and synthesize a multitude of ideas in accordance with the standards of evidence appropriate to a particular discipline. Whatever their intended major or profession, high school graduates will depend heavily on their ability to listen attentively to others so that they are able to build on others' meritorious ideas while expressing their own clearly and persuasively. New technologies have broadened and expanded the role that speaking and listening play in acquiring and sharing knowledge and have tightened their link to other forms of communication. The Internet has accelerated the speed at which connections between speaking, listening, reading, and writing can be made, requiring that students be ready to use these modalities nearly simultaneously. Technology itself is changing quickly, creating a new urgency for students to be adaptable in response to change.

# College and Career Readiness Anchor Standards for

## *Speaking and Listening*

The College and Career Readiness (CCR) anchor standards are the same for all middle and high school students, regardless of subject area or grade level. What varies is the sophistication of the speaking and listening they must do at subsequent grade levels in each disciplinary domain. The fundamental speaking skills should not change as students advance; rather, the level at which they learn and can perform those skills should increase in complexity as students move from one grade to the next.

## Comprehension and Collaboration

Discussion in one form or another is a vital, integral part of learning and classroom culture. To ensure students contribute substance, they are expected to read, write, or investigate as directed so they come to class ready to engage in the discussion of that topic or text with peers or the whole class. During these discussions, they learn to acknowledge and respond to others' ideas and incorporate those ideas, as well as others they discover through their research, as evidence to support their conclusions or claims. Details and evidence in various forms and from different sources is first evaluated, then selected as needed by the students to use in their presentations. When listening to others speak, students learn to listen for key details and qualities to evaluate the perspective, logic, evidence, and use of rhetoric in their presentation or speech.

## Presentation of Knowledge and Ideas

When giving a presentation, students carefully select which details and evidence to use when supporting their ideas or findings, organizing this information in a clear, concise manner that ensures the audience understands. To that end, students focus on how to best organize and develop their ideas and supporting evidence according to their purpose, audience, occasion, and appointed task. When appropriate, they use digital media to enhance, amplify, or otherwise improve their presentation, adapting their language and delivery as needed to the different contexts, tasks, or audiences.

**Speaking and Listening 1:** Prepare for and participate effectively in a range of conversations and collaborations with diverse partners, building on others' ideas and expressing their own clearly and persuasively.

## English Language Arts/History, Social Studies, Science and Technical Subjects

**6** Engage effectively in a range of collaborative discussions (one-on-one, in groups, and teacher led) with diverse partners on grade 6 topics, texts, and issues, building on others' ideas and expressing their own clearly.

  a. Come to discussions prepared, having read or studied required material; explicitly draw on that preparation by referring to evidence on the topic, text, or issue to probe and reflect on ideas under discussion.
  b. Follow rules for collegial discussions, set specific goals and deadlines, and define individual roles as needed.
  c. Pose and respond to specific questions with elaboration and detail by making comments that contribute to the topic, text, or issue under discussion.
  d. Review the key ideas expressed and demonstrate understanding of multiple perspectives through reflection and paraphrasing.

**7** Engage effectively in a range of collaborative discussions (one-on-one, in groups, and teacher led) with diverse partners on **grade 7** topics, texts, and issues, building on others' ideas and expressing their own clearly.

  a. Come to discussions prepared, having read or **researched material under study**; explicitly draw on that preparation by referring to evidence on the topic, text, or issue to probe and reflect on ideas under discussion.
  b. Follow rules for collegial discussions, **track progress toward** specific goals and deadlines, and define individual roles as needed.
  c. **Pose questions that elicit elaboration and respond to others' questions and comments with relevant observations and ideas that bring the discussion back on topic as needed.**
  d. **Acknowledge new information expressed by others and, when warranted, modify their own views.**

**8** Engage effectively in a range of collaborative discussions (one-on-one, in groups, and teacher led) with diverse partners on **grade 8** topics, texts, and issues, building on others' ideas and expressing their own clearly.

  a. Come to discussions prepared, having read or researched material under study; explicitly draw on that preparation by referring to evidence on the topic, text, or issue to probe and reflect on ideas under discussion.
  b. Follow rules for collegial discussions **and decision-making**, track progress toward specific goals and deadlines, and define individual roles as needed.
  c. Pose questions that **connect the ideas of several speakers** and respond to others' questions and comments with relevant **evidence, observations, and ideas.**
  d. Acknowledge new information expressed by others, and, when warranted, **qualify or justify their own views in light of the evidence presented.**

*Note:* Note that no distinction is made between the speaking and listening standards for English Language Arts, Social Studies, History, Science, and other technical subjects.

*Source:* Copyright © 2010. National Governors Association Center for Best Practices and Council of Chief State School Officers. All rights reserved.

## What the **Student** Does

## English Language Arts/History, Social Studies, Science and Technical Subjects

**6** **Gist:** Participate in different discussions (pairs, groups, full-class) with a range of peers about grade 6 topics, texts, and issues, adding to others' ideas while contributing their own. Arriving at these discussions prepared to discuss what they read or studied, students draw from what they learned, citing evidence in those texts during the discussion. As they participate and collaborate, students make goals, meet deadlines, and follow all guidelines for such academic discussions and their role in them. Also, when discussing or collaborating with others, students ask and answer questions, elaborating in some detail about how their remarks relate to the topic, text, or issue the class is studying. Finally, students restate and show they understand the different points of view raised by reflecting on and paraphrasing the most important ideas discussed.

- What topic, text, or issue is being discussed and what questions can you contribute?
- How can you best prepare to discuss this text, topic, or issue?
- What are the rules and roles for this discussion or collaboration?

**7** **Gist:** Participate in different discussions (pairs, groups, full-class) with a range of peers about grade 7 topics, texts, and issues, adding to others' ideas while contributing their own. Arriving at these discussions prepared to discuss what they read or researched, students draw from what they learned, citing evidence in those texts during the discussion. As they participate and collaborate, students monitor progress on goals and deadlines, following all guidelines for such academic discussions and their role in them. Also, when discussing or collaborating with others, students ask and respond to others' remarks by making cogent observations that help the discussion regain its focus. Finally, students recognize and respond to new ideas presented by others, adjusting their own views as needed.

- What topic, text, or issue is being discussed and what questions can you contribute?
- What rules and roles are central to this discussion or collaboration?
- What do you learn, and how does it require you to change your position or perspective?

**8** **Gist:** Participate in different discussions (pairs, groups, full-class) with a range of peers about grade 8 topics, texts, and issues, adding to others' ideas while contributing their own. Arriving at these discussions prepared to discuss what they have read or studied, students draw from what they learned, citing evidence in those texts during the discussion. As they participate and collaborate, students make goals, meet deadlines, and follow all guidelines for such academic discussions and their role in them. Also, when discussing or collaborating with others, students ask and answer questions that connect different speakers' ideas, bringing in relevant evidence, insights, and ideas in response to others' observations and claims. Finally, students restate and show they understand the different points of view by defending or clarifying their own views in response to the evidence provided.

- What topic, text, or issue is being discussed and what questions can you contribute?
- What rules and roles apply to this discussion, collaboration, or decision?
- What evidence, observations, or ideas are most important to consider in the discussion?

What the **Teacher** Does

**To prepare and help students to participate in conversations, do the following:**

- Send them home with specific questions to investigate—through research, reading, or just reflection—prior to a subsequent discussion the following day about that text or topic.
- Model for the students how to participate in the specific conversation for which you want to prepare them; this may involve sitting with one or more students and demonstrating how, for example, to discuss or respond to classmates' writing.
- Take them to the library or the lab to investigate online resources prior to a guest speaker; the goal of such inquiry should be specific questions they can pose to the guest the next day.
- Provide students with sentence templates that provide them with the language needed to enter the discussion (e.g., *I agree with what Maria said about ___, but disagree that___*), or generate with them the sorts of questions they should ask when discussing a particular text or topic.
- Review the conventions, rules, roles, or responsibilities that apply to a specialized discussion strategy (e.g., literature circles, Socratic dialogue, or great books discussion).
- Track participation by keeping a record of the exchange using visual codes that indicate who initiates, responds, or extends; use this to assess and provide feedback for students.

**To have students participate in a range of collaborations with diverse partners, do the following:**

- Create the culture of respect for other views and ideas within the class that is necessary for students to collaborate with others, articulating for the class (verbally, on handouts, and on posters) the norms when working with or responding to others.
- Investigate alternative venues such as video conferencing or chat for such collaboration with classmates, community members, or people from other countries.
- Use various strategies that require students to work with different people in various contexts and configurations

to solve problems, develop ideas, or improve each other's work.

**To have students build on others' ideas and effectively express their own, do the following:**

- Try, when establishing norms for class discussion early on, requiring students first to respond to other students' comments before they can offer a new one of their own.
- Direct students to synthesize the different perspectives so far by first writing and then sharing these synthesis statements about what everyone is actually saying.
- Post a list of follow-up questions they can use when asking classmates (or the teacher) to say more about an idea or comment they made in the course of the discussion; as the year passes, these can become more specific, such as challenging another speaker's reasoning or the validity of the evidence.

**To have students pose questions that elicit elaboration and connect others' ideas, do the following:**

- Introduce the idea of "follow-up" or "clarification" questions as ways to include or respond to other people's ideas, providing models that show what they are; explain how, when, and why to use them in small or full class discussions.
- List on the board or screen the ideas or comments made by different students during the discussion of a topic; emphasize the importance of listening to the class, asking them to hear in these different comments key connections they can frame in a question that shows they listened and heard the "idea behind the ideas" that they think is the real heart of the conversation about a text or topic.

**To help your English Language Learners, try this one thing:**

- Have the full class first write about a text or topic they will subsequently discuss together or in small groups; allow students to read what they wrote if they are not comfortable speaking extemporaneously in class or small groups.

**Academic Vocabulary:** Key Words and Phrases

**Acknowledge new information expressed by others:** During academic discussions, which are intended to generate new ideas and understandings about a topic or a text, students will inevitably encounter other views or new information that conflicts with their understanding, interpretation, or position.

**Building on others' ideas:** When one student makes a comment or observation, students "build on" it by adding connections and other insights that often begin with phrases such as "Picking up on what Martha just said, I noticed . . ." or "Marco made a good point about . . ."

**Clearly:** This means using the language appropriate to the discipline, topic, or text in ways that ensure precision, clarity, and accuracy.

**Collegial discussions:** This refers to discussing ideas, some of them contentious, with mutual respect for your colleagues even if you do not agree.

**Diverse partners (and perspectives):** This refers to people and ideas from different backgrounds, cultures, and perspectives than students' own; the idea is that one must know how and be able to converse with all people.

**Explicitly draw on that preparation:** This means to make use of the notes, ideas, and any materials the student prepared specifically for the discussion; this shows how thoroughly the student prepared and how well they anticipated the demands and directions of the discussion.

**Expressing:** This refers to articulating or conveying students' ideas instead of merely parroting back classmates' or the author's ideas.

**Ideas that bring the discussion back on topic:** Discussions inevitably raise new questions or connections that can easily lead the group away from the appointed topic or task; the group in general and those with such roles are responsible for finding ideas or questions that can be used to steer the conversation back on track.

**Individual roles:** This refers to the specific role students play or cultivate for themselves in academic discussions.

**Pose questions:** To "pose" is to ask; students ask each other or the teacher questions about the text, task, or topic during a discussion.

**Qualify or justify their views in light of the evidence:** When one encounters views or information that conflict with one's own, that person has to explain why they think as they do about a subject or text and, when necessary, justify their view or interpretation with evidence from the text or some other reliable source.

**Questions that elicit elaboration and respond to others' ideas:** During a legitimate, healthy conversation, all are responsible for including other views and making all in the group feel involved; sometimes a member is reluctant to join in, at which point the group or an appointed discussion leader should pose questions that help such people to join in and share or otherwise expand on their ideas.

**Relevant observations:** Any comments or questions that distract the group from the task or topic run the risk of undermining the discussion; though observations and ideas may seem off-topic, they are worth including so long as they are relevant and advance the discussion.

**Warranted:** This means when needed, appropriate, or otherwise called for; it is different from *warrant*, which is a rhetorical term that alerts readers to your assumptions.

*Notes*

**Speaking and Listening 2:**  Integrate and evaluate information presented in diverse media and formats, including visually, quantitatively, and orally.

## English Language Arts/History, Social Studies, Science and Technical Subjects

**6** Interpret information presented in diverse media and formats (e.g., visually, quantitatively, orally) and explain how it contributes to a topic, text, or issue under study.

**7** **Analyze the main ideas and supporting details** presented in diverse media and formats (e.g., visually, quantitatively, orally) and explain how **the ideas clarify** a topic, text, or issue under study.

**8** **Analyze the purpose of information** presented in diverse media and formats (e.g., visually, quantitatively, orally) and **evaluate the motives (e.g., social, commercial, political) behind its presentation.**

*Note:* Note that no distinction is made between the speaking and listening standards for English Language Arts, Social Studies, History, Science, and other technical subjects.

*Source:* Copyright © 2010. National Governors Association Center for Best Practices and Council of Chief State School Officers. All rights reserved.

## What the **Student** Does

## English Language Arts/History, Social Studies, Science and Technical Subjects

**6** **Gist:** Incorporate and assess the quality of information conveyed in different media and formats (e.g., visual, audio, oral, quantitative, and mixed media), describing how this information, regardless of its media or format, supports and adds to our understanding of the text, topic, or issue being studied.

- What is the topic of the presentation?
- What different media or formats are appropriate to this text, task, topic, or purpose?
- What questions should you ask to interpret or explain the meaning and importance of this content?

**7** **Gist:** Break down the main ideas and their supporting details to reveal their relationship as presented in different media and formats (e.g., visual, oral, quantitative), describing how these ideas improve others' understanding of a topic, text, or issue being studied.

- What are the topic, main ideas, and supporting details of the presentation?
- What is the relationship between and contribution of these main ideas and supporting details?
- How do the ideas included in the presentation clarify the topic, text, or idea?

**8** **Gist:** Determine and examine the objective of all information delivered in different media and formats (e.g., visual, oral, and quantitative), examining the motivations (e.g., social, commercial, political) that inform the presentation.

- What is the topic and purpose of the presentation?
- What different media or formats are appropriate to this text, task, topic, or purpose?
- What is the speaker or presenter's motivation and how is he or she going about achieving it?

**To have students integrate information presented in diverse formats and media, do the following:**

- Train students to look and listen for information presented through discussions, formal presentations, and online forums such as TED Talks; instruct students in how to best capture—by recording, taking notes, or deciding they would be better off just listening—the key information from a presentation.

- Play a recorded presentation (e.g., a commencement address, RSA Animate Talk, or @Google Talk) twice, the first time to get the gist and the second time, now that they know what to look and listen for, to take notes as they watch.

**To have students analyze the purpose of presentations in diverse formats and media, do the following:**

- Introduce students to the different purposes common to presenters of the sort you are having them watch or create: to persuade, to entertain, or to inform.

- Have students list any elements, features, or other aspects of the media or format they want to argue are used to achieve the presenter's purpose; on a more general level, students can list the different media and formats themselves that the presenter uses to achieve the purpose, and then further their analysis by explaining why the presenter chose that media or format for this purpose.

**To have students interpret information presented in diverse media and formats, do the following:**

- Begin by clarifying for students what it means to interpret another's text in whatever form or media; this means explaining to them such ideas as denotative and connotative meaning since one can interpret ideas or information at the denotative or literal level and miss entirely the deeper, connotative level of the text.

- Have students paraphrase the different texts they hear, view, or read, working in groups to discuss what others think these texts say and resolving discrepancies as they arise through discussion.

**To have students analyze the main ideas and supporting details, do the following:**

- Provide students with a graphic organizer that asks them to identify the main idea and explain why they think that is the main idea; then sort those supporting details into appropriate categories relative to the main ideas.

- Outline some portion of a text to show how ideas relate to each other; this is often called a "backward outline" since it is being created to analyze the relationship between main and supporting ideas instead of to create such a presentation.

**To have students explain how the ideas presented clarify a topic, text, or issue, do the following:**

- Model for students by thinking aloud as you view, listen to, or read a text; this means pausing the video, audio, or reading to indicate to students what you notice—a term, some feature, a phrase—and how it works to clarify the topic, text, or issue you are examining.

- Get ahold of a printed version of the presentation text so students can manipulate it, ideally on a computer; once you are all set up, have students rearrange the elements of the text spatially (called *parsing*) to represent and reveal the relationship between ideas and how they function to clarify.

**To help your English Language Learners, try this one thing:**

- Play any audio, video, or mixed media texts multiple times, discussing out loud for these students and the whole class your observations about how different formats and media are being used; then ask them to apply these ideas about analyzing the text to some other text they are studying. For ELLs, offer the online link to the audio and video versions of the text so they can replay it multiple times, thereby, improving their auditory comprehension.

**Academic Vocabulary:** Key Words and Phrases

**Analyze the main ideas and supporting details:** It is asking students to break down the different elements to reveal the main ideas and their relationship to the supporting details; this might include examining how structures, grammar, syntax, or more media-based features serve to emphasize the main or supporting ideas in the text you are studying.

**Evaluate the motives behind the presentation:** Anyone presenting to us has some motivation, be it to persuade, explain, or entertain; at times, such motives can be masked, the evaluator mistaking an attempt to explain for an effort to persuade, thus making it crucial to view the motives in context.

**Evaluate:** This means to determine the quality, value, use, or importance of data, details, or other forms of information one might include in one's presentation as evidence to support a position.

**Explain how it contributes to a topic:** This refers specifically to the way presenters and others can use diverse media and other formats when presenting information; in choosing to use other formats, such as a visual explanation, one necessarily contributes more (e.g., more clarity, structure, aesthetic impact, persuasion, or emotion).

**Format:** This is included as part of a speech or presentation charts, slides, graphics, or images, as well as multiple media, all of which allow the speaker to represent their ideas more fully and effectively.

**Information presented in diverse media and formats:** The content of presentations and speeches these days comes in many different modes, including still and video images, colors, and shapes, as well as more quantitative techniques such as charts, tables, and graphs.

**Integrate:** This means to join the different sources or data from them into one cohesive body of evidence used to support one's claims about what a speaker or author said or meant about a topic.

**Interpret:** Though related, to *interpret* is not the same thing as to *translate*, which calls for one to move something in one language or sign system into another; instead, to interpret means to make sense of what something is, does, or means. It is necessarily subjective, though more reliable interpretations will be based on reasonable judgments and informed opinions.

**Media:** This includes all the different forms your ideas and information, evidence, and data come in: print, audio, video, photograph; but also, mixed media, such as websites or presentation slides with embedded digital imagery (still photographs, videos, and animations) and audio.

**The motives (e.g., social, commercial, or political):** A *social* motive would mean to do something for the good of the society or community of which one is a part; a *commercial* motive, however, would mean one was driven to sell, to earn, or to promote a service, product, or business.

**Visually, quantitatively, orally:** This refers to images, video, art, or graphics of any other sort intended to convey the ideas the speaker wants to communicate; measureable means numerical, quantifiable data that is displayed or formatted so as to suit the speaker's purpose; spoken means whether in front of a live audience or for an anonymous listener viewing a slide show online with a voice-over instead.

*Notes*

**Speaking and Listening 3:** Evaluate a speaker's point of view, reasoning, and use of evidence and rhetoric.

### English Language Arts/History, Social Studies, Science and Technical Subjects

**6** Delineate a speaker's argument and specific claims, distinguishing claims that are supported by reasons and evidence from claims that are not.

**7** Delineate a speaker's argument and specific claims, **evaluating the soundness of the reasoning and the relevance and sufficiency of the evidence.**

**8** Delineate a speaker's argument and specific claims, evaluating the soundness of the reasoning and relevance and sufficiency of the evidence **and identifying when irrelevant evidence is introduced.**

*Note*: Note that no distinction is made between the speaking and listening standards for English Language Arts, Social Studies, History, Science, and other technical subjects.

*Source*: Copyright © 2010. National Governors Association Center for Best Practices and Council of Chief State School Officers. All rights reserved.

## What the **Student** Does

## English Language Arts/History, Social Studies, Science and Technical Subjects

**6** **Gist:** Separate out a speaker's argument from his or her specific claims, determining which claims are supported by reasons and evidence and which claims are not defended in this way.

- How would you characterize the relationship between the speaker's argument and specific claims?
- What criteria can you use to determine whether claims are supported or not?
- Which claims are (and are not) supported by reasons and evidence?

**7** **Gist:** After listening to a speaker, students report back in great detail the arguments of that speaker as well as the specific claims made. In recounting this speech, students then determine how strong and logical the reasoning of those claims was and whether the speaker offered sufficient evidence in support of the claims that were also relevant to the purpose.

- How would you characterize the relationship between the speaker's argument and specific claims?
- How would you judge the soundness of the speaker's reasoning?
- What evidence did the speaker offer in support of the claims—and was it both sufficient and relevant in light of the topic and purpose?

**8** **Gist:** After listening to a speaker, students report back in great detail the arguments of that speaker as well as the specific claims made. In recounting this speech, students then determine how strong and logical the reasoning of those claims was and the extent to which the evidence was relevant and sufficient, or, at times, irrelevant, thereby weakening the speaker's argument.

- How would you characterize the relationship between the speaker's argument and specific claims?
- How sound is the speaker's reasoning?
- What evidence would you describe as irrelevant—and by what criteria?

**To have students evaluate a speaker's point of view (POV), do the following:**

- Teach or extend students' existing knowledge of the concept of point of view as it relates to evaluating a speaker.
- Develop the habit in students of asking fundamental questions when examining their point of view when speaking; this is most easily remembered by teaching them to evaluate the speaker's POV using the acronym SOAPS: subject, occasion, audience, purpose, and speaker.
- Have students generate additional questions they can use to evaluate a speaker's point of view, including questions related to ethics, commitment, motive, originality, implications, and credibility.

**To have students evaluate a speaker's reasoning and use of evidence and rhetoric, do the following:**

- Clarify first what "reasoning" means and how it applies by providing examples of sound and unsound reasoning.
- Show students how to identify commonly used propaganda techniques: bandwagon, name-calling, transfer (making an illogical link between two unrelated things), emotional appeals, loaded words, stereotypes, and either/or thinking; when teaching these elements, seek online resources for examples from history and the current era, making additional connections between the spoken forms and print propaganda during, for example, World War II or in some of the novels they read.
- Provide and ask students to generate questions to use when evaluating the rhetoric of a speaker; these questions would focus on SOAPS as well as the three main rhetorical appeals speakers use to persuade their audience: ethos, logos, and pathos.

**To have students delineate a speaker's argument and specific claims, do the following:**

- Find or create a graphic organizer with spaces for students to list the different elements of a speaker's argument in some detail; this would include not only the speaker's argument, but also any evidence, reasoning, acknowledgment of other views, and a response to those other views. You might consider walking students through this process while projecting the organizer.
- Give students a printed copy of the speaker's text if possible, asking them to underline and label the speaker's argument and claims, as well as evidence and reasons.

**To have students evaluate how sound the reasoning in the speaker's argument is, do the following:**

- Have students code the speaker's argument—whether they are listening to or reading it—by creating some system that identifies what works and what does not and what is effective and what is not; this might mean creating a rating system or a set of codes such as + for strong.
- Set up sentence templates (e.g., X *strengthens the argument by noting that . . .* ) to help students evaluate the speaker's reasoning in a more analytical way that simultaneously improves their academic writing skills.

**To have students identify when the speaker introduces irrelevant evidence, do the following:**

- Generate or provide students with a succinct list of criteria for effective evidence, taking time to be sure they know these different terms and what they look like through examples; have them then apply these criteria to the evidence used by the speaker to support the claims. You could fit in an analytical sentence template here that would help students learn to articulate their critique of evidence (e.g., *While X offers evidence to support the position, this evidence is irrelevant as it focuses on . . .* ).

**To help your English Language Learners, try this one thing:**

- Use a speech that students can read (in print), hear (in audio), and watch (as a video). Use these versions in stages to help students evaluate different aspects of the speech. Presidential inaugurations and State of the Union speeches are most easily accessed for this purpose, but others are available.

**Academic Vocabulary:** Key Words and Phrases

**Delineate:** This means to report in detail and with great precision what someone wrote, said, or did; it originates from the notion of outlining something in detail.

**Distinguishing claims that are supported from those . . . :** This asks readers to identify those claims that the writer supports with reasons and evidence from those they do not support; to this we might add the distinction between those supported with relevant and sufficient evidence versus evidence that is irrelevant or flawed for one reason or another.

**Evidence:** This refers to the data, details, quotations, or examples the speaker uses in the presentation or speech and how credible, accurate, and valid it is; in addition, one would evaluate the ways the speaker *uses* this evidence to persuade or otherwise influence the audience.

**Irrelevant evidence:** This is evidence that has no substantial or relevant connection to the claim it is intended to support; it may also be irrelevant because it is no longer current and correct.

**Point of view:** Where does the speaker stand in relation to the subject and audience on this occasion? Is the speaker representing their own ideas or those of another person or agency? Point of view is vital in terms of any bias the speaker may reveal about the subject; point of view, when inappropriate to the occasion or audience, can dramatically undermine the speaker's credibility or reception.

**Reasoning:** This refers to the logic of the speakers as it relates to their ideas; it also refers to how well and to what end the speaker's ideas and the reasoning behind them connect with and complement each other to improve the coherence of the speech.

**Relevant and sufficient evidence:** This has to do with whether the evidence directly relates to and is adequate in quality and quantity to the claims it is meant to support.

**Rhetoric:** This refers to the speaker's use of any devices, techniques, or strategies to persuade or otherwise influence how the listener or audience thinks, acts, or feels about the topic being addressed.

**Soundness of the reasoning:** Think of a boat and whether it is "sound," which is to say strong and able to bear what is placed in it; so it is with reasoning in this instance: Are the reasons offered in support of the claims and evidence strong, logical, and effective in the context in which they are used?

*Notes*

**Speaking and Listening 4:** Present information, findings, and supporting evidence so listeners can follow the line of reasoning and the organization, development, and style are appropriate to task, purpose, and audience.

## English Language Arts/History, Social Studies, Science and Technical Subjects

6   Present claims and findings, sequencing ideas logically and using pertinent descriptions, facts, and details to accentuate main ideas or themes; use appropriate eye contact, adequate volume, and clear pronunciation.

7   Present claims and findings, **emphasizing salient points in a focused, coherent manner with** pertinent descriptions, facts, details, **and examples**; use appropriate eye contact, adequate volume, and clear pronunciation.

8   Present claims and findings, emphasizing salient points in a focused, coherent manner with **relevant evidence, sound valid reasoning, and well-chosen details**; use appropriate eye contact, adequate volume, and clear pronunciation.

*Note:* Note that no distinction is made between the speaking and listening standards for English Language Arts, Social Studies, History, Science, and other technical subjects.

## What the **Student** Does

## English Language Arts/History, Social Studies, Science and Technical Subjects

**6** **Gist:** Present claims and conclusions, organizing the content in a cogent, logical order, adding related information, key facts, and specific details to emphasize the main ideas and themes, while also using appropriate eye contact, volume, and pronunciation.

- What claims and findings are you presenting—and how should you arrange them?
- Which details, facts, or descriptions should you use to emphasize your main ideas and themes?
- How can you get feedback on your eye contact, volume, and pronunciation?

**7** **Gist:** Present claims and conclusions, focusing on the major ideas in a way that improves coherence, adding relevant descriptions, details, facts, and examples, while using appropriate eye contact, volume, and pronunciation.

- What claims and findings are you presenting—and how should you arrange them?
- What details or ideas would you consider "salient points" to emphasize?
- What examples should you provide to help emphasize the salient points?

**8** **Gist:** Present claims and conclusions, focusing on the major ideas in a way that improves coherence and uses evidence, sound reasoning, and details carefully selected, all the while speaking with appropriate eye contact, volume, and pronunciation.

- What claims and findings are you presenting—and how should you arrange them?
- Which details, facts, or descriptions should you use to emphasize your main ideas and themes?
- What criteria should you use to determine if your evidence is relevant, your reasoning sound and valid, and your details well-chosen?

## What the **Teacher** Does

**To have students present information and findings so that listeners can follow, do the following:**

- Identify for students the key elements that they should include, address, or accomplish in the speech they will give.
- Give students a tool, such as a storyboard organizer, or a technique, such as outlining, they can use to plan their speech in a way that listeners will follow; they should only use this technique, however, after they have generated many possible ideas about what they might say about their findings on this topic.
- Introduce students to the range of ways to make findings and information easier to grasp, including organizing patterns such as cause–effect, compare–contrast, problem–solution, chronological, and narrative; see Common Core Speaking and Listening Standard 5 for more detail about one of the best approaches: using more graphic formats, including tables, charts, and graphs.

**To have students present evidence in ways that listeners can follow, do the following:**

- Ask students to determine first what evidence they have or need to obtain to best support the claim they wish to make; or, if they have evidence but no claim yet, ask them then to draw whatever conclusions the evidence supports as a first step.
- Suggest that students identify a question their speech will attempt to answer and gather the evidence needed to support their answer to that question.
- Show students a range of ways to organize information and evidence (e.g., order of importance, classification); have them apply several of these different approaches to their information.
- Model for students how to map a speech for its logic using "chunking," a technique that is less structured and formal than outlining, allowing students to focus more on the structure and logic of the information and evidence they provide.
- Assess and provide feedback on the logic and quality of their evidence; another option would be to create a rubric students can use to evaluate their use of evidence in their speech.

**To have students help listeners follow the reasoning and organization, do the following:**

- Evaluate students' use of signal words or phrases that provide transitions from one idea to another, specifically those that clarify and reinforce reasoning and organization.
- Explain the idea of points of emphasis in a speech and how the speakers can organize the content and use their voice to reinforce certain information, ideas, or perspectives on the topic.
- Require students in the upper-grade levels to include in their speech competing interpretations or alternative points of view as a way to help listeners better understand the speaker's claim through contrast with others.

**To ensure students' organization, development, and style are appropriate, do the following:**

- Ask students to analyze their speech in light of organization and development (i.e., details, examples, evidence, and the subsequent discussion of the meaning and importance of these), explaining why they organize their content as they do and why they think it is the most effective approach for their speech.
- Give students a printed text of a speech they can annotate and view in class, as well; after guiding students through an analysis of the speaker's style (e.g., figurative language, diction, syntax, imagery, and tone), have them conduct a similar analysis to their speech once they show an acceptable mastery of the ideas.

**To help your English Language Learners, try this one thing:**

- Encourage (or even require if it seems best) your students to create an outline of the speech, doing this in stages so you can assess the structure, development, and content of the speech as they build it throughout this early stage of the process.

**Academic Vocabulary:** Key Words and Phrases

**Appropriate to the task, purpose, and audience:** How one organizes, develops, or speaks varies depending on the objective, their actual purpose, and the audience to whom they are speaking.

**Emphasizing salient points:** These are the more distinctive, compelling, or important points you hope to emphasize when writing or presenting.

**Findings:** This refers to conclusions drawn from observations, investigations, experiments, or inquiries about questions or problems.

**Focused, coherent manner:** This builds on the idea, mentioned earlier, that certain "salient points" should be emphasized but the writer must achieve this in a way that is focused and coherent if the ideas are to be adequately addressed.

**Line of reasoning:** Speakers link a series of ideas in some meaningful and clear way as they speak; it is sort of a connect-the-dots approach that links all the connections to show why one thinks as they do and/or how they arrived at a conclusion or argument.

**Logically:** When presenting information or findings and the evidence that supports them, as well as any subsequent discussion of the meaning of those findings, speakers must ensure that the ideas connect to each other in ways that enhance clarity and further the speaker's claims or explanations.

**Organization:** An appropriate and effective structure is vital to the speaker's success; whether organized to show cause–effect or problem–solution, from least to most important, or from past to present, the ideas put forth by the speaker require a clear organizing structure so listeners can hear and process the ideas presented.

**Pertinent descriptions:** Such descriptions include only those details most relevant or specific to the subject being described.

**Present:** When people are merely *speaking*, they can be standing at a podium telling a story, explaining what a text means, or discussing what they learned from an experience. When people *present*, they have a more specific purpose such as to persuade the audience to think or act in a certain way. To achieve this outcome, the presenter often uses evidence from a range of established sources, different media, or presentation software such as Keynote or PowerPoint.

**Supporting evidence:** This is data, information, quotations, examples, or other information that the speaker uses to back up whatever they are saying or presenting.

**Using pertinent descriptions ... to accentuate main ideas:** As mentioned earlier, *pertinent descriptions* are those details most relevant to a subject you are describing; in this case, however, the purpose of those details is to bring the main ideas into relief and, in doing so, accentuate or emphasize them.

*Notes*

**Speaking and Listening 5:** Make strategic use of digital media and visual displays of data to express information and enhance understanding of presentations.

### English Language Arts/History, Social Studies, Science and Technical Subjects

6 Include multimedia components (e.g., graphics, images, music, sound) and visual displays in presentations to clarify information.

7 Include multimedia components and visual displays in presentations to clarify **claims and findings and emphasize salient points.**

8 Integrate multimedia and visual displays into presentations to clarify **information, strengthen claims and evidence, and add interest.**

*Note:* Note that no distinction is made between the speaking and listening standards for English Language Arts, Social Studies, History, Science, and other technical subjects.

*Source:* Copyright © 2010. National Governors Association Center for Best Practices and Council of Chief State School Officers. All rights reserved.

## What the **Student** Does

## English Language Arts/History, Social Studies, Science and Technical Subjects

**6** **Gist:** Design and deliver presentations that incorporate multimedia components (e.g., audio, graphics, images, music, or sound) and visual displays of information (e.g., charts, graphs, or infographics) to explain the information presented.

- What is the subject and purpose of your presentation?
- Which elements and information are most important?
- What multimedia components (e.g., graphics, images, music, or sound) would clarify your ideas?
- What ideas will benefit most from the visual display of those details?

**7** **Gist:** Design and deliver presentations that incorporate multimedia components (e.g., audio, graphics, images, music, or sound) and visual displays of information (e.g., charts, graphs, or infographics) to explain claims and findings, while also stressing essential ideas.

- What is the subject and purpose of your presentation?
- Which elements and information are most important?
- What multimedia components (e.g., graphics, images, music, or sound) would clarify your ideas?
- Which claims, findings, or salient points should you use multimedia components to clarify or emphasize?

**8** **Gist:** Design and deliver presentations that incorporate multimedia components (e.g., audio, graphics, images, music, or sound) and visual displays of information (e.g., charts, graphs, or infographics) to explain information, enhance claims and evidence, and make the presentation more engaging.

- What is the subject and purpose of your presentation?
- Which elements and information are most important?
- What multimedia components (e.g., graphics, images, music, or sound) would clarify your ideas?
- What claims, information, evidence, or qualities (e.g,. how interesting it is) can you enhance?

What the **Teacher** Does

**To have students make strategic use of digital media and visual displays of data, do the following:**

- Outline and illustrate for students the four principles most commonly emphasized in all books about digital and visual design: contrast, repetition, alignment, and proximity; have them then apply these notions to their digital designs.
- Create and require students to follow a set of principles or guidelines for all presentation slides and visual displays (e.g., graphs, charts, infographics, or diagrams) they incorporate into their slides; provide a range of samples you assemble in a presentation of your own that embodies the principles of effective presentation design.
- Provide contrasting examples of different presentation slide designs with the same content to illustrate the effect of different fonts, layouts, colors, and content on presentations.
- Direct students to sites such as Duarte's (duarteshop .com) and Abela's (extremepresentation.com) for examples and guidelines for effective use and creation of visual displays of information.
- Do not allow students to incorporate distracting animations, wacky fonts, extended video clips, degraded or otherwise lower-grade images, useless sound effects, or any other elements that will detract from the effective presentation of the information; this is an important opportunity to *teach* design, which is an ever-increasing part of effective communication and composition now.

**To have students express information and enhance understanding of their ideas, do the following:**

- Emphasize to students the role and uses of story in any presentation and how they can use different elements—images, numbers, data, their voice, gestures, and storytelling itself—to convey their ideas with clarity and emphasis to make a more emotional impact on the audience while also enhancing understanding.

- Stress the importance of reducing any content that competes with or otherwise distracts from the content or point you are trying to make in your presentation.
- Encourage students to play around with visual explanations (graphs, charts, or diagrams) and visual narratives (images, video, diagrams, or cartoons) as well as color, font, and composition to convey the relationships between different parts of their subject more clearly and effectively—without adding distraction and confusion through extraneous elements.

**To have students make strategic use of digital media to add interest and impact, do the following:**

- Take time to teach students more about the principles of effective design so they can take time planning and designing their presentations with the greatest impact.
- Walk students through the process of finding, choosing, formatting, editing, and embedding digital content—images, video, or audio—into their presentations, giving them feedback as they work through the design and delivery process.
- Give students a tour of the different presentation applications—PowerPoint, Keynote, Google Presentation, Prezi, and any others that come along—and then let them choose the one they want to use for their presentation.
- Allow students the option of creating a stand-alone digital presentation (i.e., one that has a voice-over and can be uploaded and viewed online) instead of presenting to the class; a variation of this idea would be to require students to create digital media-based presentations that you and the class can view on tablets if that is an option in your classroom.

**To help your English Language Learners, try this one thing:**

- Take time to be sure they know how to use all these digital tools and have access to them to do what you are assigning; if they do not, make time in class for all to work on this assignment.

**Academic Vocabulary:** Key Words and Phrases

**Add interest:** One can "add interest" through content itself or certain effects that create a wow factor in the audience. Selective use of images, video, audio, or mixed media adds power, entertainment, and the possibility of emotional impact. One needs to be sure that any material included to "add interest" also complements the content; otherwise, it is mere fluff that adds to the length of the presentation and either distracts or frustrates the audience.

**Audio elements:** This refers to recorded content embedded in the presentation such as voice-over or featured content as in an interview (e.g., image of the person interviewed shown while audio interview plays). Music and sound effects (that serve a real purpose and enhance content) can be effective if used sparingly and in the right way. Other audio content can be made available through hotlinks to primary source recordings of, for example, presidential addresses.

**Data:** This is quantitative, measurable information that has been or could be analyzed and used as evidence to support a claim or to illustrate a point the speaker is trying to make in the presentation.

**Digital media:** This includes presentation software applications such as PowerPoint, Keynote, Google Presentation, and Prezi; also, it refers to digital images, screen captures of online material, stand-alone or embedded video, and audio and mixed media formats.

**Enhance understanding:** This refers to using all available media and methods—images, audio, multimedia, words, and graphs—in ways that make the abstract more concrete, more visual, more comprehensible. Through charts, images, graphs, or video, the speakers illustrate the processes, concepts, or procedures they are discussing, using these as tools to help the audience *see* what they are saying.

**Express information:** This means to put forth, to convey, or to relate data, ideas, details, and content to the audience in the clearest way possible.

**Graphical elements:** This means the use of such elements as diagrams, graphs, tables, and any other graphic elements that help the audience understand more easily and fully certain procedures or abstract ideas the speaker is discussing.

**Interactive elements:** Such elements would include handheld devices used to "vote" or otherwise interact with content the speaker displays to the audience; additional interactive features would include hotlinks that connect to content on other sites, video, images, or audio. If the presentation is being made through a tablet or a computer, the prerecorded presentation might have buttons, links, or other options to allow the viewer to interact with the content by choosing different paths or content.

**Salient points:** These are points that are most distinct or remarkable, the ones worth mentioning in the discussion, especially if the presentation is brief.

**Strategic use of digital media and visual displays:** The key term here is *strategic*, for the point the standard emphasizes is that any media in whatever form should be used to *enhance* content and *engage* viewers, not just make it look nice or try to make it "fun." Thus, *strategic* in this context means that all such "digital media and visual displays" are carefully chosen with a purpose in mind and used in specific ways to achieve that purpose or effect in the audience.

**Visual displays to clarify information:** This refers to tables, charts, graphs, or other infographics used to visually explain or otherwise convey an idea, especially one that is complicated or abstract.

**Visual elements:** This refers to color, shape, size, format, arrangement, and other elements that visually illustrate how data, ideas, and information are connected on slides, screens, or other formats used by the presenter.

**Speaking and Listening 6:** Adapt speech to a variety of contexts and communicative tasks, demonstrating command of formal English when indicated or appropriate.

## English Language Arts/History, Social Studies, Science and Technical Subjects

**6** Adapt speech to a variety of contexts and tasks, demonstrating command of formal English when indicated or appropriate.

   (See grade 6 Language standards 1 and 3 for specific expectations.)

**7** Adapt speech to a variety of contexts and tasks, demonstrating command of formal English when indicated or appropriate.

   (See **grade** 7 Language standards 1 and 3 for specific expectations.)

**8** Adapt speech to a variety of contexts and tasks, demonstrating command of formal English when indicated or appropriate.

   (See **grade** 8 Language standards 1 and 3 for specific expectations.)

*Note:* Note that no distinction is made between the speaking and listening standards for English Language Arts, Social Studies, History, Science, and other technical subjects.

*Source:* Copyright © 2010. National Governors Association Center for Best Practices and Council of Chief State School Officers. All rights reserved.

## What the **Student** Does

## English Language Arts/History, Social Studies, Science and Technical Subjects

**6** **Gist:** Decide what to say and how to say it, adjusting their voice and style to suit the occasion, purpose, and audience, while always modeling their command of formal English when it is appropriate.

- Who are you addressing on this occasion?
- What is the occasion on which you are speaking?
- How should you adapt your speech in light of the audience, purpose, and occasion of your talk?

**7** **Gist:** Decide what to say and how to say it, adjusting their voice and style to suit the occasion, purpose, and audience, while always modeling their command of formal English when it is appropriate.

- Who are you addressing on this occasion?
- What is the occasion on which you are speaking?
- How should you adapt your speech in light of the audience, purpose, and occasion of your talk?

**8** **Gist:** Decide what to say and how to say it, adjusting their voice and style to suit the occasion, purpose, and audience, while always modeling their command of formal English when it is appropriate.

- Who are you addressing on this occasion?
- What is the occasion on which you are speaking?
- How should you adapt your speech in light of the audience, purpose, and occasion of your talk?

What the **Teacher** Does

**To have students adapt a speech to a variety of contexts and tasks, do the following:**

- Discuss with and warn students about those problems or errors most common to language when spoken on formal or otherwise important occasions (e.g., job interviews). These problems include using slang, euphemisms, stereotypes, clichés, and incorrect grammar, usage, or vocabulary.
- Identify and instruct students to also be wary of using any of the following when speaking at a formal occasion: culturally insensitive language or remarks, jokes, sarcasm, irony, and jargon (unless the audience you are addressing would be fluent in such jargon, in which case it is acceptable).
- Remind students that appropriate anecdotes and figurative language can be effective ways to improve their speech and demonstrate their command of the language and make it more clear to the audience; such figurative language includes using analogies, similes, metaphors, hyperbole, and understatement.

**To have students demonstrate their command of formal English when appropriate, do the following:**

- Have students identify *before* they speak any words, phrases, or parts of the speech that cause them trouble when they speak; once identified, these portions might be replaced with words that are more familiar but no less appropriate for the occasion or audience.

- Have students deliver their own speeches, even if they are created on the spot, in different styles, having fun with it but not being in any way disrespectful to their proposed audience. Follow up with a chance to discuss the differences between the styles and which one is likely to be more effective and why.
- Make time to confer with students to discuss their speeches, making a special effort to identify any flaws that would undermine correctness and, thus, their credibility as a speaker in any situation that required a mastery of formal English.
- Allow time for the discussion with them individually or as a class (if it is a classwide issue) to discuss why this matters to colleges, the community at large, and especially employers.

**To help your English Language Learners, try this one thing:**

- Meet individually with them or, if appropriate, as a small group to walk through their speech, first editing for content, then for correctness; then have them do a read-through with you so they can get feedback about words, phrases, or sections of the speech that need to be changed. During this session, you might also model for them how to say or emphasize certain words while speaking. This sort of task, giving a speech in front of a group, is near the top of most people's list of anxieties, all the more so if you must give a speech in a language you are still learning, so it is important to do all you can to address the emotional aspect of such an assignment.

*Notes*

**Academic Vocabulary:** Key Words and Phrases

**Adapt speech:** This means to change the language, style of delivery, tone, or format of the presentation or speech as needed to suit the audience, purpose, and occasion. This could mean not using any digital media or presentation software that might interfere with the more intimate setting of the small group to which one is presenting; it might also mean using less formal but still grammatically correct language when presenting to a group the speaker knows or with whom the speaker wants to create a more familiar atmosphere as they speak.

**Appropriate:** Each presentation or talk has its own unique audience each time one speaks, so one must know how to speak—which words, tone, and style of address one should use when speaking on each occasion. What is appropriate on one occasion—informal, colloquial speech to a group of people you know—is inappropriate, even offensive the next time when the occasion is formal and the audience has completely different expectations. Certain things are *never* appropriate: spelling and formatting mistakes on handouts, slides, or other visual aids and slang, foul language, or otherwise rude terms or comments that undermine the speaker's credibility.

**Command of formal English:** The standards place a clear and consistent emphasis on a command of formal English—grammatically correct, clearly enunciated words delivered with good eye contact—as an essential ingredient in college or career success.

This means speaking in ways that would be appropriate when addressing customers, colleagues, classmates, or professors in college.

**Communicative tasks:** These "tasks" would include contributing to a discussion group in class, interviewing with a local business or organization for an internship, delivering a formal speech, debating a controversial issue with others, or presenting a formal topic or argument to a group with the idea of persuading them to act, think, or believe a certain way. Increasingly, these tasks and their related contexts will include, for example, conferring with people through online audio and video (or chat) platforms to collaborate, confer, or communicate.

**Contexts:** This refers to the place as much as the purpose of any speaking; examples include speaking in class, online, in small and larger groups, to the full class or larger groups, in the community at large, at work with customers and colleagues, or for interviews with bosses or organizations.

**Indicated:** One is sometimes asked to talk in a specific way to a group on a topic or occasion; thus, one looks to the prompt, directions, adviser, teacher, or other source for indications about how to speak on a given occasion to a particular audience about a particular topic. In the event that it is not indicated, the speaker must learn to determine themselves what is the most appropriate way to speak in a given situation.

*Notes*

# Part 4

# The Common Core State Standards

## *Language*

# College and Career Readiness Anchor Standards for

# *Language 6–8*

Source: Common Core State Standards

The grades 6–12 standards on the following pages define what students should understand and be able to do by the end of each grade. They correspond to the CCR anchor standards by number. The CCR and grade-specific standards are necessary complements—the former providing broad standards, the latter providing additional specificity—that together define the skills and understandings that all students must demonstrate.

## Conventions of Standard English

1. Demonstrate command of the conventions of standard English grammar and usage when writing or speaking.
2. Demonstrate command of the conventions of standard English capitalization, punctuation, and spelling when writing.

## Knowledge of Language

3. Apply knowledge of language to understand how language functions in different contexts, to make effective choices for meaning or style, and to comprehend more fully when reading or listening.

## Vocabulary Acquisition and Use

4. Determine or clarify the meaning of unknown and multiple-meaning words and phrases by using context clues, analyzing meaningful word parts, and consulting general and specialized reference materials, as appropriate.
5. Demonstrate understanding of figurative language, word relationships, and nuances in word meanings.
6. Acquire and use accurately a range of general academic and domain-specific words and phrases sufficient for reading, writing, speaking, and listening at the college and career readiness level; demonstrate independence in gathering vocabulary knowledge when considering a word or phrase important to comprehension or expression.

## Note on Range and Content of Student Language Use

To be college and career ready in language, students must have firm control over the conventions of standard English. At the same time, they must come to appreciate that language is at least as much a matter of craft as of rules and be able to choose words, syntax, and punctuation to express themselves and achieve particular functions and rhetorical effects. They must also have extensive vocabularies, built through reading and study, enabling them to comprehend complex texts and engage in purposeful writing about and conversations around content. They need to become skilled in determining or clarifying the meaning of words and phrases they encounter, choosing flexibly from an array of strategies to aid them. They must learn to see an individual word as part of a network of other words—words, for example, that have similar denotations but different connotations. The inclusion of language standards in their strand should not be taken as an indication that skills related to conventions, effective language use, and vocabulary are unimportant to reading, writing, speaking, and listening; indeed, they are inseparable from such contexts.

# College and Career Readiness Anchor Standards for

# *Language*

The College and Career Readiness (CCR) anchor standards are the same for all middle and high school students, regardless of subject area or grade level. What varies is the sophistication of the language—grammar, vocabulary, and figurative language—at subsequent grade levels in each disciplinary domain. The fundamental language skills should not change as students advance; rather, the level at which they learn and can perform those skills should increase in complexity as students move from one grade to the next.

## Conventions of Standard English

Simply put, students should know and use the proper forms of English—spelling, grammar, usage, and conventions—when speaking or writing for public purposes or audiences such as at work or school. The emphasis here is on the crucial role that such attention to correctness plays in college and the workplace, where first impressions matter and the smallest error can cost customers or money. This becomes all the more important in light of social media trends where businesses communicate more and more online, through social media, chat, and text messages.

## Knowledge of Language

This standard not only recognizes the range of functions language plays in creating style, voice, and meaning, but also, it emphasizes the importance of diction, syntax, and other factors as they relate to the writer's or speaker's ethos and general effect on the audience in a given context. One must, in other words, give serious thought to which words, which order, for which audience, and which purpose if one is to convey the meaning with maximum effect.

## Vocabulary Acquisition and Use

Vocabulary, so instrumental in reading, writing, and speaking/listening, is divided into several domains in these standards. First are those words that are unknown or have many possible meanings, the proper one(s) determined by the occasion or context in which they are used. An essential part of this standard involves using general and specialized reference materials in print or online to determine the etymology of words and learn more about their different meanings and usages. In addition to these words, students add to their word bank the way language is used figuratively, as well as through word relationships that suggest some association, connotation, or nuance depending on how it is used. Finally, students should pay most of their attention to those words that will help them understand or complete their assignments for school; this means learning those domain-specific words and phrases unique to each discipline that students routinely encounter when they read, write, speak, or listen. Over time, students should actively gather and work to grow their knowledge of and ability to use the words and phrases in each subject area to accommodate the increasing complexity of the texts and tasks they face at each subsequent grade level.

**Language 1:** Demonstrate command of the conventions of standard English grammar and usage when writing or speaking.

## English Language Arts/History, Social Studies, Science and Technical Subjects

**6** Demonstrate command of the conventions of standard English grammar and usage when writing or speaking.

    a. Ensure that pronouns are in the proper case (subjective, objective, possessive).
    b. Use intensive pronouns (e.g., *myself, ourselves*).
    c. Recognize and correct inappropriate shifts in pronoun number and person.*
    d. Recognize and correct vague pronouns (i.e., ones with unclear or ambiguous antecedents).*
    e. Recognize variations from standard English in their own and others' writing and speaking, and identify and use strategies to improve expression in conventional language.*

**7** Demonstrate command of the conventions of standard English grammar and usage when writing or speaking.

    a. **Explain the function of phrases and clauses in general and their function in specific sentences.**
    b. **Choose among simple, compound, complex, and compound-complex sentences to signal differing relationships among ideas.**
    c. **Place phrases and clauses within a sentence, recognizing and correcting misplaced and dangling modifiers.***

**8** Demonstrate command of the conventions of standard English grammar and usage when writing or speaking.

    a. Explain the function of **verbals (gerunds, participles, infinitives)** in general and their function in particular sentences.
    b. **Form and use verbs in the active and passive voice.**
    c. **Form and use verbs in the indicative, imperative, interrogative, conditional, and subjunctive mood.**
    d. **Recognize and correct inappropriate shifts in verb voice and mood.***

* *Note:* Beginning in grade 3, skills and understandings that are particularly likely to require continued attention in higher grades as they are applied to increasingly sophisticated writing and speaking are marked with an asterisk (*).

*Source:* Copyright © 2010. National Governors Association Center for Best Practices and Council of Chief State School Officers. All rights reserved.

## What the *Student* Does

## English Language Arts/History, Social Studies, Science and Technical Subjects

**6** **Gist:** Know the conventions of standard English grammar and usage, applying them whenever speaking or writing. Also, students check that they correctly use or, as needed, repair their pronouns in each of the following cases:

a. Pronouns in the proper case: subjective (I), objective (me), possessive (mine)
b. Intensive pronouns (e.g., *myself, ourselves*)
c. Inappropriate shifts in pronoun number and person (e.g., use *he* when it should be *she* or first-person [I] when it should be third-person [him])
d. Vague pronouns with an unclear or ambiguous antecedent (e.g., we do not know what *he, they, it,* or some other pronoun refers to)

In addition to using pronouns correctly, students also develop and demonstrate their ability to recognize and repair any incorrect or non-standard English (i.e., slang, dialects, idioms, or other variations) when writing, speaking, or reading their work or the work of others.

- What does each pronoun refer to—and do you offer clear antecedents to help readers?
- When you use a singular or plural pronoun, is it clear, correct, and consistent in its usage?
- Which words, phrases, or sentences are incorrect or nonstandard English—and how can you repair or restate them to make them correct?

**7** **Gist:** Know the conventions of standard English grammar and usage, applying them whenever speaking or writing, and doing the following with phrases, clauses, and sentences:

a. Know what phrases and clauses are and how they function in general and in specific sentences.
b. Know and select the type of sentence (simple, compound, complex, or compound-complex) that most effectively expresses the relationships between ideas.
c. Know and position phrases and clauses correctly and effectively within sentences and find and fix misplaced and dangling modifiers when necessary.

- How does this specific phrase or clause function in this sentence (i.e., how does it affect the meaning of the sentence)?
- Which of the different types of sentences (simple, compound, complex, or compound-complex) would best indicate or express the idea(s) you are trying to communicate?
- Where in this sentence can you position this specific phrase or clause so it will have the intended effect but not result in a misplaced or dangling modifier?

**8** **Gist:** Know the conventions of standard English grammar and usage, applying them whenever speaking or writing, and doing the following with verbs in their various forms when reading, writing, or speaking:

a. Know what verbals are (gerunds, participles, and infinitives) in general and how they function in a specific sentence.
b. Know the difference between active and passive voice, forming and using verbs to create the desired voice and effect.
c. Know the different moods of verbs (indicative, imperative, interrogative, conditional, and subjunctive mood); use them to create your intended effect.
d. Know how to find and fix any shifts in verb voice and mood that are incorrect, cause confusion, or undermine clarity.

- How do the verbals (or one specific type) in this text or a specific sentence affect the meaning or otherwise serve your (or the author's) purpose?
- Where do you or the author use the passive voice—and is it consistently used to achieve some proper effect or in a way that causes confusion?
- What is the proper voice and mood for this text—and does anything undermine these elements or others, such as coherence or clarity?

*Note:* The Common Core State Standards emphasize the notion of growing complexity or increasing ability within the anchor standards, treating each anchor standard in grades 6–8 as something akin to a continuum along which students progress over time; thus, this note for the Language Standards reiterates this emphasis, stressing that from grades 3–12, in this area of language study, certain aspects of language (e.g., unclear or ambiguous antecedents, for example, which the Stanford Study of Writing and its director, Andrea Lunsford, continue to identify as one of the "Top Twenty" most frequent errors in college freshman writers) are enduring challenges, not something students learn in third grade and never worry about again. As the note on the facing page says, these are problems that are "likely to require continued attention in higher grades."

**To have students show a command of standard English grammar and usage, do the following:**

- Teach students the various conventions appropriate to whatever type of writing they are doing, studying, or reading, providing a rich and varied array of examples of how these conventions are used in the world and by real writers.
- Cultivate an environment of respect and wonder relative to language in general and specific aspects of it in particular, one that invites students into language instead of inspiring fear of it; this can be done by bringing in real-world writing (or articles about such writing) that captures the power of language to shape our thinking and convey ideas.
- Invest in and continually add to your knowledge about language, grammar, and usage as these relate to the subjects you teach; share this learning with your students to establish and reinforce your authority when working with language.
- Try *always* to model the virtue of correctness when writing and speaking to your students; this means seeing every handout, every email to the class, and every homework assignment posted online for your students as an occasion to reinforce the importance of communicating clearly and correctly at all times.
- Use this three-step process to teach conventions: (1) Provide direct, separate instruction in the concept, what it is, how it works, and why they should know and use it. (2) Create opportunities to practice and refine their knowledge of the concept through simulations and feedback. (3) Apply the knowledge and use the learning in an actual piece of writing to demonstrate a full understanding of the concept, refining their use as needed through your feedback and opportunities to apply the learning in more sophisticated ways.
- Require that students *use* these conventions and constructions in their writing both to reinforce and to further develop their knowledge of these conventions

in their writing; a necessary adjunct to this requirement to use what they learn would be that you provide targeted, constructive feedback on their use, with the opportunity to revise in light of your comments, so they might refine their knowledge and use of these conventions until such actions are habits and the rules internalized.

- Find the latest version of Andrea Lunsford's "The 20 Most Common Errors in Undergraduate Writing," an ongoing study of college writing that lists the most frequent errors and provides information about their causes and remedies; it serves as a useful guide to your study of language conventions by narrowing your focus. See also books by Jeff Andersen and Michael W. Smith and Jeff Wilhelm.
- Provide mentoring texts that show how students should write certain constructions; however, make a point of finding or creating texts that are similar to the type of writing you want your students to do (e.g., sentences that show a variety of phrases and clauses used to modify and improve writing).
- Use these four sentence-composing techniques to improve students' confidence, fluency, and correctness when teaching different types of sentences and their related conventions: unscramble sentences dissembled for the purpose of studying their construction; imitate specific forms and conventions of writing your students are studying; combine multiple sentences into one as a way to learn a specific convention or construction; expand on sentences, beginning with a base or stem sentence and then adding to it those forms you are studying.

**To help your English Language Learners, try this one thing:**

- Provide many models and opportunities to practice when teaching these more advanced constructions and conventions.

**Academic Vocabulary:** Key Words and Phrases

**Active and passive voice:** The voice is said to be "active" when the subject is *acting* (Bob <u>gave</u> them money) and "passive" when being *acted upon* (Money <u>was given</u> to Bob). There are reasons both to use and to avoid using the passive; it is a valid construction, though if used ineffectively it undermines clarity.

**Clause:** This refers to a group of words with a subject *and* a predicate; there are two types: dependent (cannot stand alone) and independent (functions as a complete sentence). **Dependent:** <u>After they passed the laws</u>, many businesses struggled. **Independent:** After they passed the laws, <u>the economy recovered</u>.

**Types of sentences:** Sentences can be described by their grammatical structure or their function. The following sentence types focus on the former:

**Simple:** One independent clause and *no* dependent clause (e.g., The story is set in the future.)

**Complex:** One independent clause and *at least* one dependent clause (e.g., The story, <u>which takes place on Mars</u>, is set in the future.)

**Compound:** Two *or more* independent clauses and *no* dependent clause; the independent clauses can be joined by a conjunction (for, and, nor, but, or, yet, so), comma, or semicolon (e.g., <u>The story takes place on Mars</u>; <u>it is set in the future</u>.)

**Compound-complex:** Two *or more* independent clauses and *at least* one dependent clause (e.g., *Because the story takes place in the future*<sup>DEP CLAUSE</sup>, <u>the author set it on Mars</u><sup>INDEP CLAUSE</sup> and <u>made it possible for people to live wherever they chose</u><sup>INDEP CLAUSE</sup>.)

**Conventions:** This is a way of doing or using something—in this case, words, punctuation, grammar—as established and endorsed by a group that has agreed to observe certain practices or rules.

**Misplaced or dangling modifier:** This refers to modifying phrases that, due to incorrect placement, cause confusion (and, sometimes, laughter) by modifying the wrong thing. For example, <u>Waving and smiling at the crowd</u>, the politician's smile amazed them all. (Did his smile *really* "wave and smile at the crowd"?)

**Grammar:** This refers to the study of words and their component parts and how they combine to form sentences; it also means the structural relationships in language that contribute to their meaning.

**Mood:** This refers to the writer's attitude, which can be expressed as commands or directions (imperative mood), as a statement or declaration from the writer about what is a fact or opinion (indicative mood), as a question (interrogative mood), as a means of thinking about what is true beginning with the word *if* or some equivalent (conditional mood), or as an *if*-statement about a wish or a condition that something were true contrary to the facts (subjunctive mood).

**Phrase:** This refers to a group of words that functions as one unit but lacks a subject, verb, or both. **Example:** <u>The conclusion we reached</u> suggested the need for further research.

**Usage:** This refers to how one uses language—and if it is permitted or approved.

**Verb:** This refers to a word that names an action or state of being; verbs change form to indicate tense, number, voice, or mood.

**Verbals:** The three *verb forms*—gerunds, participles, and infinitives—function not as verbs but as nouns, adjectives, or adverbs; they consist of a verbal and any modifiers, objects, or complements. **Participial phrases** function as adjectives and include a present participle (the <u>falling</u> market) or past participle (the <u>broken</u> machine). **Gerunds** end in *–ing* and function as nouns (e.g., <u>Running</u> was his favorite sport.) **Infinitives** can function as nouns, adjectives, or adverbs (e.g., He hoped <u>to go</u> into teaching.)

**Language 2:** Demonstrate command of the conventions of standard English capitalization, punctuation, and spelling when writing.

## English Language Arts/History, Social Studies, Science and Technical Subjects

**6** Demonstrate command of the conventions of standard English capitalization, punctuation, and spelling when writing.

 a. Use punctuation (commas, parentheses, dashes) to set off nonrestrictive/parenthetical elements.*
 b. Spell correctly.

**7** Demonstrate command of the conventions of standard English capitalization, punctuation, and spelling when writing.

 a. **Use a comma to separate coordinate adjectives (e.g., *It was a fascinating, enjoyable movie* but not *He wore an old [,] green shirt*).**
 b. Spell correctly.

**8** Demonstrate command of the conventions of standard English capitalization, punctuation, and spelling when writing.

 a. Use **punctuation (comma, ellipsis, dash) to indicate a pause or break.**
 b. **Use an ellipsis to indicate an omission.**
 c. Spell correctly.

* *Note:* Beginning in grade 3, skills and understandings that are particularly likely to require continued attention in higher grades as they are applied to increasingly sophisticated writing and speaking are marked with an asterisk (*).

*Source:* Copyright © 2010. National Governors Association Center for Best Practices and Council of Chief State School Officers. All rights reserved.

## What the **Student** Does

## English Language Arts/History, Social Studies, Science, and Technical Subjects

**6** **Gist:** Show their knowledge of and ability to follow the conventions of capitalization, punctuation, and spelling when writing by spelling correctly and using punctuation to set off nonrestrictive and parenthetical elements as follows:

a. **Commas**: They enclose such elements *quietly*, giving little extra emphasis but clarifying the relationship between elements.

   o Example: The pitcher, <u>who had a strange wind-up</u>, won the Cy Young Award that year.

b. **Parentheses**: They enclose elements *clearly* but such elements are sometimes of secondary or limited importance and would often be better cut out in the first place.

   o Example: The pitcher had a strange new style (he developed it in secret during the off-season) that coaches said explained his new success.

c. **Dashes**: They enclose the elements but more *emphatically* than either commas or parentheses.

   o Example: The pitcher had many pitches—the "Moonball," the "Hot Potato," and one he called the "Screwball"—that no one had ever heard of until he joined the team.

- What words should—and should *not*—be capitalized?
- What words do you most often misspell, especially those the spellcheck is not likely to detect (e.g., *their, they're, there*)—and how can you check that you spelled those correctly throughout?
- Which of the three punctuation marks (commas, parentheses, and dashes) would be best to use in this situation given the effect you want to achieve?

**7** **Gist:** Show their knowledge of and ability to follow the conventions of capitalization, punctuation, and spelling, by spelling correctly and using a comma to separate coordinate adjectives.

   o Example: *It was a fascinating, enjoyable movie* would be correct. *He wore an old, green shirt* would be incorrect.

- What words should—and should *not*—be capitalized (and what is the rule on which your judgment is based)?
- What are the words you most commonly misspell, especially those the spellcheck is not likely to detect (e.g., *your, you're*)—and how can you check that you spelled those correctly throughout? (Tip: Use the search function, not the spellcheck!)
- What is the relationship between the adjectives and the noun they modify? (Tip: If you can put *and* between the two words, they are coordinate adjectives and should be separated by commas.)

**8** **Gist:** Show their knowledge of and ability to follow the conventions of capitalization, punctuation, and spelling by spelling correctly and using punctuation to indicate a pause, break, or omission as follows:

a. **Commas**: They set off things such as contrasting elements, interjections, direct address, and tag questions.

   o It is X, not Y, that led to Z.
   o It was, he insisted, over.

b. **Ellipsis**: Also called *ellipses*, these three equally spaced dots indicate words have been cut (omitted) or signal a pause or break in thought or speech. When used at the end, a fourth dot is added to serve as a period.

   o "Life . . . and happiness," these were the core of the Declaration of Independence.
   o When we are young . . . we think . . . well, we will always be young . . . but then we realize. . . .

c. **Dash**: Used alone—or in pairs—dashes create more emphasis or a more distinct break than ellipses or commas.

   o They were a remarkable band—one for the history books.
   o It was early in their career—before they had become The Beatles—that they developed the sound all would recognize as theirs alone.

- What words should—and should *not*—be capitalized (and *why*)?
- What are the words you most commonly misspell, especially those the spellcheck is not likely to detect (e.g., *believe, belief*)—and how can you check that you spelled those correctly throughout? (Tip: Use the search function, not the spellcheck!)
- Which of the three punctuation marks (commas, ellipses, and dashes) would be best to use in a situation given the effect you want to achieve?

What the **Teacher** Does

**To develop students' command of the conventions of standard English, do the following:**

- Emphasize, reinforce, and teach students how to capitalize, punctuate, and spell as needed within the context of your larger writing curriculum; for example, when teaching them how to create and use modifiers such as parenthetical or nonrestrictive elements, teach students how to punctuate them in context.

- Indicate how the writers you study apply these conventions to achieve clarity and convey relationships by using punctuation, such as the dash or ellipses to indicate a pause or break.

- Use multiple and contrasting models to show proper and incorrect use of conventions such as dash and comma, using such models to show when, how, where, and why to use the dash over the hyphen and the comma over the parentheses or dash.

- Honor at all times, when writing or speaking to students, the value of correctness; treat every assignment, email to students, and homework directions posted online as an opportunity to demonstrate and reiterate the importance of correctness.

- Teach conventions using this three-step approach: (1) Provide direct instruction in the concept, explaining what it is, how it works, and why they should know and use it. (2) Create opportunities to practice and refine the lesson through simulations and feedback. (3) Demonstrate what they learned in an actual piece of writing that shows they understand the concept.

- Provide targeted, constructive feedback about students' use of those conventions that have been the focus of recent instruction and the opportunity to revise in light of your comments.

- Require students to keep their own lists of conventions they need to learn or improve their use of; to these, they might add samples of correct—or incorrect—usage; they might consider extending their learning online by using sites like noredink.com to practice and improve their grammar skills.

- Use mentor texts similar to the type of writing you want your students to do (i.e., sentences that show how writers use punctuation in general and specific forms such as the dash, parentheses, and ellipses in particular).

- Limit the number of grammatical terms you actively teach so the focus remains how to write better instead of what to remember; you can reinforce the terms by routinely using them when discussing them.

- Generate with students a range of possible punctuation marks (e.g., a dash, parentheses, or comma) they might use in certain cases (e.g., to indicate a pause or break), and then try them out, discussing the effect of each as you display them on a screen; generate different punctuation strategies to create a particular effect (e.g., emphasis, setting off elements, or indicating an omission).

- Use these four sentence-composing techniques to improve students' confidence, fluency, and correctness when teaching different types of sentences and their related conventions: (1) unscramble sentences dissembled for the purpose of studying their construction, (2) imitate specific forms and conventions of writing your students are studying, (3) combine multiple sentences into one as a way to learn a specific convention or construction, and (4) expand on sentences, beginning with a base sentence and then adding to it those forms you are studying.

**To help your English Language Learners, try this one thing:**

- Try to limit the number of new conventions you introduce at any one time to avoid overwhelming your ELL students, and when you do introduce them, arrange your examples in a progression over time, starting with the most basic, easy-to-grasp examples you can find or create to convey the idea you are teaching.

**Academic Vocabulary:** Key Words and Phrases

**Capitalization:** Use uppercase letters not only to signal where sentences begin, but also to indicate that a word is a title, a person's name, a product or brand name, or some other form of proper noun. This is especially important in light of trends to ignore capitalization when texting that carry over into the workplace or classroom when writing more formal documents.

**Conventions:** This refers to those rules about which punctuation marks to use: how, when, why, and where to use them when writing different types of documents in various media.

**Coordinate adjectives:** These are a series of adjectives that all refer to and modify the same noun equally and should be punctuated by a comma that separates each of the coordinate adjectives.

**Dash:** Dashes emphasize what falls on the other side of or rests between them; they are more emphatic in their effect than parentheses or commas, though they can, at times, have the same emphatic break as a colon when used at the end of the sentence. Sometimes a dash is mistakenly replaced with a hyphen. Occasionally it is used to indicate dialogue (instead of quotation marks) by some fiction writers.

**Ellipsis (ellipses):** These are three equally spaced dots, often found in quotations or at the end of a sentence to indicate, in the case of the former, that words were omitted, and in the latter, a pause or break in thought. A fourth dot is added to serve as a period if the ellipses appear at the end of the sentence.

**Indicate a pause or break:** Some punctuation marks—notably the comma, dash, and ellipsis—allow the writer to create a sense of pausing or emphatic break in a text.

**Indicate an omission:** See the entry for *ellipsis*. When one takes words out of a direct quotation for any reason, one must indicate this omission using ellipses when directly quoting a text or person; it is not necessary or correct to do so with indirect quotations.

**Nonrestrictive/parenthetical elements:** Though these are separate, they are treated here in the standard as somewhat of a piece; in this sense, they both function to create some sort of interruption (marked by enclosing commas, dashes, or parentheses) that allows for additional information to be inserted, some idea to be emphasized, or an aside to be made midsentence.

**Punctuation:** This refers to all the marks—period, comma, colon, semicolon, dash, hyphen, quotation and question marks, parentheses, exclamation points, and others—that writers use to be clear, to make connections, and to create a style that suggests how the text should be read. It is, as some say, what makes the music of the writing happen in ways similar to musical notations that signal where, when, and how long to stop or speed up; where to pause; and what to emphasize.

**Standard English:** This refers to English as it should be written and spoken in the mainstream workplace or college classroom.

*Notes*

**Language 3:** Apply knowledge of language to understand how language functions in different contexts, to make effective choices for meaning or style, and to comprehend more fully when reading or listening.

## English Language Arts/History, Social Studies, Science and Technical Subjects

**6** Use knowledge of language and its conventions when writing, speaking, reading, or listening.

    a. Vary sentence patterns for meaning, reader/listener interest, and style.*
    b. Maintain consistency in style and tone.*

**7** Use knowledge of language and its conventions when writing, speaking, reading, or listening.

    a. **Choose language that expresses ideas precisely and concisely, recognizing and eliminating wordiness and redundancy.***

**8** Use knowledge of language and its conventions when writing, speaking, reading, or listening.

    a. **Use verbs in the active and passive voice and in the conditional and subjunctive mood to achieve particular effects (e.g., emphasizing the actor or the action; expressing uncertainty or describing a state contrary to fact).**

* Note: Beginning in grade 3, skills and understandings that are particularly likely to require continued attention in higher grades as they are applied to increasingly sophisticated writing and speaking are marked with an asterisk (*).

What the **Student** Does

# English Language Arts/History, Social Studies, Science and Technical Subjects

**6** **Gist:** Know about and use language in ways that add meaning and engage readers, but maintain a consistent style and tone when writing, reading, speaking or listening, using a variety of sentence lengths, patterns, and styles in order to enhance or affect meaning and engage readers or listeners, remaining consistent throughout.

- What is the average length of the sentences in your text?
- How do your sentences tend to begin—all the same way, or using a range of transitions and openings?
- What words would you use to describe the style and tone of this text—and to what extent is it consistent throughout?

**7** **Gist:** Know about and use language to express ideas with precision and concision when writing, reading, speaking, or listening, selecting only those words or sentences that contribute to the meaning or purpose of the text. Precision and concision are best achieved by realizing when one is using too many words or the same words repeatedly and then cutting all such unnecessary or redundant words.

- Which words in your text could be expressed with greater precision?
- Which words do you repeat or should you replace with other, more precise and engaging words?
- Which sentences have too many prepositions, a primary cause of wordiness?

**8** **Gist:** Know and use verbs to achieve specific effects such as emphasis, applying these conventions when students write, read, speak, or listen, using the active or passage voice as appropriate to emphasize who or what is doing what to whom, and using the conditional or subjunctive mood to express a specific mood or indicate their attitude.

- What effect are you—or the writer of the text you are reading—trying to achieve?
- What mood are you—or the writer of the text you are reading—trying to achieve?
- What are the specific reasons you are using the passive voice—and are they appropriate and effective?

What the **Teacher** Does

**To have students understand how language functions in different contexts, do the following:**

- Direct students to read the assigned texts closely, focusing their attention on the ways the author uses language—specifically through the mood, tone, patterns, and grammar—to create meaning or a style that contributes substance to the text; this might lead to such strategies as parsing the sentences to help students see the spatial relationship between parts of the sentences, or using color-coding functions on the computer when displaying the passages being analyzed.

- Use a range of contrasting models that clarify and extend students' understanding of how language can function within a text; this might mean showing them examples of the same passage modified to show the effect of it written as a series of simple sentences versus more sophisticated sentences in light of the topic or their purpose.

- Expose students to a wide variety of texts and authors, styles and genres, forms and formats so they not only learn from these practitioners the full range of choices they can make as writers, but also so they can learn how to read for these same elements.

**To help students make effective choices for meaning or style, do the following:**

- Provide feedback on their drafts throughout the process, offering them suggestions about the different choices they can make to emphasize or show the connection between certain ideas, events, or other details in the text.

- Create a slide show or handout that shows different iterations of the same idea or subject in various sentence formats, each one written to emphasize some different element or achieve a slightly different effect on the reader; have students evaluate these—on their own or by conferring with classmates—and agree on the one they think is best—and *why*.

**To enable students to write and edit for a specific discipline, do the following:**

- Introduce them to the established conventions specific to the writing of that discipline or genre as defined by the *MLA Handbook* or whatever other style guide sets the standards for that discipline or genre.

**To have students use language with precision and concision, do the following:**

- Ask them to highlight or circle all the prepositions in their paper; then, using Lanham's Paramedic Method (easily located online), have students edit for concision by requiring them to cut some specified number of words from the whole paper.

- Put a sample paper up (or create one) for display, and then show them how to locate and edit for precision those words that are generic or otherwise lack the appropriate precision.

**To improve students' knowledge of and ability to vary sentence patterns, do the following:**

- Give them a rubric with different traits on it related to syntax and style they can use to assess their own or another's writing.

- Direct students to count the average length of each sentence in their paper (or, given the limits of class time, the first page in a longer paper); ask them to jot down what they notice about length, sentence patterns (do they all sound the same), and the beginnings of their sentences; revise accordingly for greater variation, cohesion, and concision.

**To help your English Language Learners, try this one thing:**

- Provide them with a set of examples—of whatever aspect of style you are teaching—that show, through small incremental steps, the different changes; then ask them to explain the difference between each, to discuss what they notice and how the changes seem to affect the meaning or experience of the text.

**Academic Vocabulary:** Key Words and Phrases

**Active voice:** This emphasizes, through active verbs, what the subject is *doing* (John is stealing money.); it is favored by most writers for its ability to add more force to the writing.

**Concisely/concision:** This is related to but not the same as the *wordiness* entry; concision is the idea of trimming out words as needed till there is nothing extraneous to the writer's purpose; concision is the guiding principle and greatest challenge of this book that is in your hands.

**Conditional mood:** These sentences focus on questions of truth and are introduced by the word *if* or its equivalent.

**Effective choices for meaning or style:** Drawing on such elements as syntax, rhetoric, and diction, among others, writers choose words and other elements such as punctuation and then arrange those to some purpose (meaning) or effect (style).

**How language functions in different contexts:** We are always writing a specific type of text for an audience, on some occasion, for some purpose. How we write, what features or format we choose, which words or sentence types we include, what tone or style we adopt, these all relate to the context in which that document is written and so must be considered whether we are the writer, the speaker, the reader, or the listener.

**Knowledge of language:** This refers to language in all its forms and functions, including vocabulary, grammar, usage, syntax, rhetoric, diction, and style.

**Maintain consistency in style and tone:** This emphasizes the importance of being consistent in what one says and how they say it.

**Passive voice:** It emphasizes, through passive verbs, what was done but not who did it (Money was stolen.); it is favored by people who want to use language to cover up what they did.

**Precisely/precision:** This is best defined by Mark Twain as the difference between the word *fire* and *fire extinguisher*; one must use the correct, precise word if one is to convey an idea as clearly as possible or achieve the desired effect.

**Redundancy/redundant:** This refers to using the same words or language structures over and over until the reader grows bored or loses the ability to be surprised once the text has become predictable.

**Subjunctive:** More formal in tone, the subjunctive, which relies on dependent clauses that begin with *that* or *if*, states a wish or a contingency that is at odds with the known facts.

**Vary sentence patterns for meaning, reader interest, style:** Effective writers use a range of sentence patterns for different reasons, all of them listed here; think of music: if you heard the same musical phrase or three notes over and over you would turn it off. Varying sentence patterns includes using not only different patterns or types of sentences but also writing sentences of differing lengths in light of one's purpose, audience, occasion, and, in some cases, media or format.

**Wordiness:** Why use five words when one will do? Wordiness comes from many sources, but it is always something to avoid as too many words get in the way of the message you are trying to convey.

*Notes*

**Language 4:** Determine or clarify the meaning of unknown and multiple-meaning words and phrases by using context clues, analyzing meaningful word parts, and consulting general and specialized reference materials, as appropriate.

## English Language Arts/History, Social Studies, Science and Technical Subjects

**6** Determine or clarify the meaning of unknown and multiple-meaning words and phrases based on **grade 6 reading and content**, choosing flexibly from a range of strategies.

    a. Use context (e.g., the overall meaning of a sentence or paragraph; a word's position or function in a sentence) as a clue to the meaning of a word or phrase.

    b. Use common, grade-appropriate Greek or Latin affixes and roots as clues to the meaning of a word (e.g., *audience, auditory, audible*).

    c. Consult reference materials (e.g., dictionaries, glossaries, thesauruses), both print and digital, to find the pronunciation of a word or determine or clarify its precise meaning or its part of speech.

    d. Verify the preliminary determination of the meaning of a word or phrase (e.g., by checking the inferred meaning in context or in a dictionary).

**7** Determine or clarify the meaning of unknown and multiple-meaning words and phrases based on **grade 7 reading and content**, choosing flexibly from a range of strategies.

    a. Use context (e.g., the overall meaning of a sentence or paragraph; a word's position or function in a sentence) as a clue to the meaning of a word or phrase.

    b. Use common, grade-appropriate Greek or Latin affixes and roots as clues to the meaning of a word (e.g., *belligerent, bellicose, rebel*).

    c. Consult **general and specialized** reference materials (e.g., dictionaries, glossaries, thesauruses), both print and digital, to find the pronunciation of a word or determine or clarify its precise meaning or its part of speech.

    d. Verify the preliminary determination of the meaning of a word or phrase (e.g., by checking the inferred meaning in context or in a dictionary).

**8** Determine or clarify the meaning of unknown and multiple-meaning words or phrases based on **grade 8 reading and content**, choosing flexibly from a range of strategies.

    a. Use context (e.g., the overall meaning of a sentence or paragraph; a word's position or function in a sentence) as a clue to the meaning of a word or phrase.

    b. Use common, grade-appropriate Greek or Latin affixes and roots as clues to the meaning of a word (e.g., *precede, recede, secede*).

    c. Consult general and specialized reference materials (e.g., dictionaries, glossaries, thesauruses), both print and digital, to find the pronunciation of a word or determine or clarify its precise meaning or its part of speech.

    d. Verify the preliminary determination of the meaning of a word or phrase (e.g., by checking the inferred meaning in context or in a dictionary).

## What the **Student** Does

## English Language Arts/History, Social Studies, Science and Technical Subjects

**6** **Gist:** Choose a strategy that helps students understand or clarify the meaning of new or polysemous words (words with multiple meanings) they encounter when reading and listening to grade 6 reading and content. Specifically, these strategies include the following:

a. **Context Clues:** Readers use the general meaning of a sentence or paragraph, the location of a word or its function in a sentence (e.g., as a verb) to develop a sense of what the word or phrase means.
b. **Affixes and Roots:** Readers derive some idea about the meaning of a word by considering those Greek and Latin affixes and roots appropriate to grade 6 reading and content.
c. **Reference Materials:** Readers turn to a range of general print and digital reference works to learn how to pronounce a word and to understand what it means as it is used in this context; such works also clarify a word's meaning and its part of speech.
d. **Preliminary Determination:** Readers confirm their initial conception of what a word or phrase means by consulting a dictionary or seeing if the context supports their interpretation of the word or phrase.

- Which words or phrases in a sentence do you not understand—or prevent you from understanding other portions of the text?
- Which words have many different meanings or connotations—and seem most fitting in the context used in this text?
- What can you glean of the word's meaning from its context—its place in the sentence, its part of speech, and the way it is used or spoken?

**7** **Gist:** Choose a strategy that helps students understand or clarify the meaning of new or polysemous words (words with multiple meanings) they encounter when reading and listening to grade 6 reading and content. Specifically, these strategies include the following:

a. **Context Clues:** Readers use the general meaning of a sentence or paragraph, the location of a word or its function in a sentence (e.g., as a verb) to develop a sense of what the word or phrase means.
b. **Affixes and Roots:** Readers derive some idea about the meaning of a word by considering those Greek and Latin affixes and roots appropriate to grade 7 reading and content.
c. **Reference Materials:** Readers turn to a range of general and specialized print and digital reference works to learn how to pronounce a word and to understand what it means as it is used in this context; such works also clarify a word's meaning and its part of speech.
d. **Preliminary Determination:** Readers confirm their initial conception of what a word or phrase means by consulting a dictionary or seeing if the context supports their interpretation of the word or phrase.

- Which words or phrases in a sentence do you not understand—or prevent you from understanding other portions of the text?
- Which words have many different meanings or connotations—and seem most fitting in the context used in this text?
- What can you glean of the word's meaning from its context—its place in the sentence, its part of speech, and the way it is used or spoken?

**8** **Gist:** Choose a strategy that helps students understand or clarify the meaning of new or polysemous words (words with multiple meanings) they encounter when reading and listening to grade 6 reading and content. Specifically, these strategies include the following:

a. **Context Clues:** Readers use the general meaning of a sentence or paragraph, the location of a word or its function in a sentence (e.g., as a verb) to develop a sense of what the word or phrase means.
b. **Affixes and Roots:** Readers derive some idea about the meaning of a word by considering those Greek and Latin affixes and roots appropriate to grade 8 reading and content.
c. **Reference Materials:** Readers turn to a range of general and specialized print and digital reference works to learn how to pronounce a word and to understand what it means as it is used in this context; such works also clarify a word's meaning and its part of speech.
d. **Preliminary Determination:** Readers confirm their initial conception of what a word or phrase means by consulting a dictionary or seeing if the context supports their interpretation of the word or phrase.

- Which words or phrases in a sentence do you not understand—or prevent you from understanding other portions of the text?
- Which words have many different meanings or connotations—and seem most fitting in the context used in this text?
- What can you glean of the word's meaning from its context—its place in the sentence, its part of speech, and the way it is used or spoken?

What the **Teacher** Does

**To have students determine the meaning of unknown words and phrases, do the following:**

- Teach students a range of strategies to choose from, including using context clues, word parts, reference works, and available resources such as indexes, glossaries, sidebars, footnotes, and other texts you may be using as part of the unit.
- Model for students by thinking aloud how you handle unknown words when reading, noting that you first acknowledge that you do not know a word and wonder if you need to know it to understand the text; having decided you do, you would then try one of the strategies listed previously in an effort to infer its meaning; in the event that you cannot, you would actually turn to a dictionary to show them how you use it to decide which, of the many different definitions, is the one that best fits.
- Use this procedure developed by Robert Marzano in *Building Background Knowledge for Academic Achievement* to teach words you want students to know or that they have determined they do not understand but must learn to comprehend a text: (1) You describe, explain, or provide an example of the new term in association with the specific word you want them to learn. (2) Students then explain the new term, paraphrasing your description in their own words. (3) Students next represent the term in some graphic way that helps them understand and remember the word. (4) Students revisit the term over time, encountering it through various activities and contexts designed to deepen their fluency with that word. (5) You ask students to return to and discuss these target words with each other periodically. (6) You engage students in activities or games that invite them to interact with these terms to reinforce and deepen their understanding and fluency.

**To have students determine or clarify word meanings by analyzing word parts, do the following:**

- Work with students to identify the suffixes, prefixes, and roots that make up a particular word; sometimes it is best to ask them if the root calls to mind other, more familiar, words that can help them access the word's meaning.
- Model how you go about understanding a word such as *indomitable* by analyzing its parts, looking to the prefix for some clue (e.g., *in-* meaning *not*), then the base or root (*domitare* meaning *to tame*, which you note calls to mind the word *dominate*), and finally the suffix (*able*, which means *able to be*), concluding for the class that it means unable to be controlled.

**To have students learn to consult general and specialized reference materials, do the following:**

- Guide your students through different reference works related to vocabulary, including books like *Garner's Modern American Usage*, *The Synonym Finder*, and unabridged and specialized dictionaries for phrases, allusions, etymologies, and aphorisms; these will only be useful if students are engaged in the sort of close, analytical reading that requires such detailed information.

**To have students determine words and phrases with multiple meanings, do the following:**

- Help students learn to identify which words likely have multiple meanings in the context in which they are used; then break out the dictionary and, working in pairs, have them determine which of the eight possible definitions of *fair* apply to the passage where the author uses it repeatedly but never the same way.

**To help your English Language Learners, try this one thing:**

- Confirm that they have access to an appropriate ELL dictionary in their primary language at school and at home; then work with them to develop a set of the most important words for them to know in your class—words the other students are likely to know to varying degrees—and help them learn them as needed.

**Academic Vocabulary:** Key Words and Phrases

**Affixes:** This refers to an extra element attached to the beginning, middle, or end of a word or its root that changes the word's meaning.

**Consult general and specialized reference materials:** This includes everything from a dictionary to usage handbooks such as *Garner's Modern American Usage* or other sources that focus on specialized aspects of words and phrases such as etymologies and allusions, as well as the *Oxford English Dictionary* to examine the word in depth.

**Content:** This refers to texts other than a page of words being "read"; this includes mixed media, as well as digital and visual texts (infographics).

**Context clues:** One makes an informed guess about the meaning of a word after looking at all the words around it, the way it is used (to determine its part of speech), how it is used in this context, and its place in the sentence and/or paragraph.

**Determine and clarify the meaning of unknown and multiple-meaning words:** Students cannot afford to ignore or not know many words in complex texts they read at this level; lacking such understanding, they cannot understand the texts read, especially when these words appear in discipline-specific texts as specialized terms related to a field of study they are trying to learn. As for "multiple-meaning" (polysemic) words they may encounter in literary texts, they must look these up in specialized or unabridged dictionaries with etymologies and the full range of definitions available.

**Inferred meaning:** The meaning we derive from taking what we learn from the text or about the word as it is used in context and adding that to what we already know; this adds up to an inference. That is, what we learn + what we already know = the inferred meaning.

**Parts of speech:** The function a word serves in its context in a given sentence: verb, noun, pronoun, preposition, conjunction, adjective, and adverb as well as a subject or predicate.

**Precise meaning:** When words can be used to mean different things, it is important to determine which, of all the possible meanings, applies to this word as it is being used. **Etymology:** This is the study of a word and its origins, how it has evolved in its meaning across time. This includes examining the word's roots. **Example**: *Character* derives from Middle English *carecter*, meaning imprint on the soul; Old French and Greek *kharacter* meaning to inscribe; and Greek, *kharak-*, which means the pointed end of stick.

**Range of strategies:** The emphasis here is on the *students* knowing and using a "range of strategies": looking up individual words in the context of use, examining those words around the word for clues, skimming to find words they should look up and learn about *before* reading the text, and collecting and looking up words as they read to generate their own definitions of frequently seen and misunderstood words.

**Roots:** This refers to the base unit from which words have been made by adding prefixes or suffixes or by other modification (e.g., *dict, graph*).

**Verify the preliminary determination of the meaning:** After we make an educated guess based on such factors as context and roots, we often need to check the dictionary to confirm our hunch about the word's meaning.

**Word's position or function in a sentence:** Where a word appears in a sentence and how it functions—its part of speech—offers abundant information about its meaning, purpose, and importance.

*Notes*

**Language 5:** Demonstrate understanding of word relationships and nuances in word meanings.

## English Language Arts/History, Social Studies, Science and Technical Subjects

6  Demonstrate understanding of figurative language, word relationships, and nuances in word meanings.

    a. Interpret figures of speech (e.g., personification) in context.

    b. Use the relationship between particular words (e.g., cause/effect, part/whole, item/category) to better understand each of the words.

    c. Distinguish among the connotations (associations) of words with similar denotations (definitions) (e.g., *stingy, scrimping, economical, unwasteful, thrifty*).

7  Demonstrate understanding of figurative language, word relationships, and nuances in word meanings.

    a. Interpret figures of speech (e.g., **literary, biblical, and mythological allusions**) in context.

    b. Use the relationship between particular words (e.g., **synonym/antonym, analogy**) to better understand each of the words.

    c. Distinguish among the connotations (associations) of words with similar denotations (definitions) (e.g., ***refined, respectful, polite, diplomatic, condescending***).

8  Demonstrate understanding of figurative language, word relationships, and nuances in word meanings.

    a. Interpret figures of speech (e.g., **verbal irony, puns**) in context.

    b. Use the relationship between particular words to better understand each of the words.

    c. Distinguish among the connotations (associations) of words with similar denotations (definitions) (e.g., ***bullheaded, willful, firm, persistent, resolute***).

## What the **Student** Does

## English Language Arts/History, Social Studies, Science and Technical Subjects

**6** **Gist:** Show they understand by applying their knowledge about word relationships and nuances in word meaning in three key ways:

a. **Figures of Speech:** Readers determine from context the meaning of such figures of speech as personification.
b. **Relationship Between Words:** Readers determine the meaning of specific words based on the relationship between those words (e.g., cause/effect, part/whole, or item/category).
c. **Connotations:** Readers distinguish among the connotative meanings (associations) of words with common denotative meanings (e.g., *stingy, scrimping, economical, unwasteful,* or *thrifty*).

- Which words or phrases are figures of speech—and what does the context suggest they mean?
- What can you determine about meaning of the words based on the relationship between them?
- Which words share a similar denotative meaning but suggest a distinct connotative meaning?

**7** **Gist:** Show they understand by applying their knowledge about word relationships and nuances in word meaning in three key ways:

a. **Figures of Speech:** Readers determine from context the meaning of such figures of speech as literary, biblical, and mythological allusions.
b. **Relationship Between Words:** Readers determine the meaning of specific words based on the relationship between those words (e.g., synonym/antonym, or analogy).
c. **Connotations:** Readers distinguish among the connotative meanings (associations) of words with common denotative meanings (e.g., *refined, respectful, polite, diplomatic,* or *condescending*).

- Which words or phrases are figures of speech—and what does the context suggest they mean?
- What can you determine about meaning of the words based on the relationship between them?
- Which words share a similar denotative meaning but suggest a distinct connotative meaning?

**8** **Gist:** Show they understand by applying their knowledge about word relationships and nuances in word meaning in three key ways:

a. **Figures of Speech:** Readers determine from context the meaning of such figures of speech as verbal irony and puns.
b. **Relationship Between Words:** Readers determine the meaning of specific words based on the relationship between those words (e.g., cause/effect, part/whole, or item/category).
c. **Connotations:** Readers distinguish among the connotative meanings (associations) of words with common denotative meanings (e.g., *bullheaded, willful, firm, persistent,* or *resolute*).

- Which words or phrases are figures of speech—and what does the context suggest they mean?
- What can you determine about meaning of the words based on the relationship between them?
- Which words share a similar denotative meaning but suggest a distinct connotative meaning?

What the **Teacher** Does

## To help students understand word relationships, do the following:

- Provide them with a set of words from the text that are somehow related. Students reading in a social studies class about American history, for example, might get words such as *liberty, freedom, independence, self-determination,* and *license.* Those reading a novel such as Lowry's *The Giver* might get a list of words such as *dystopia, utopia,* and *eugenics.* In science classes, they would study whatever words were related to the subject of their unit. The task of any such group would be to determine what the relationship is between these different words and how it relates to and affects the meaning of the text when the words are used together.

- Extend the previous activity, or use it in more advanced contexts (upper grades), so that you provide the students with the idea (that the West held out during the Gold Rush the promise of a better life) and then tell them to find words and phrases related to that idea of a Promised Land from the text, presenting them and explaining their connection to this motif.

- Offer more open-ended opportunities at different points in the study of a text or topic. Invite students to generate a group of words that are related by a concept such as fear; this can be done to prepare students to read a text or to enrich their reading of a text that treats this topic in some depth. You can also add conditions, such as all words must be a particular part of speech. Consider trying this same activity using visualthesaurus.com to see what associations it comes up with when a word like *fear* is entered.

- Examine some critical writings about the subject or text you are teaching, looking for the sort of nouns, verbs, and adjectives used to discuss that particular topic. Create a three-column organizer and, as you read, copy the relevant nouns, verbs, and adjectives into the respective columns; if time allows, take verbs such as *character* from the noun column and add *characterize* in the verb column, and *characteristic* and *caricature* to the noun column, and so on. Use these lists as seems appropriate when students are writing about or discussing the topic or texts.

## To have students interpret and analyze figures of speech in context, do the following:

- Develop a graphic organizer that allows students to analyze the associations between the core word and its associated words; for example, you could draw a line and write *Literal* on the top and *Figurative* underneath it, defining a word used figuratively in the text (e.g., the word *swerve* used in a William Stafford poem) first in its literal or denotative meaning; below that, on this two-tier organizer, you would generate with students all the different connotations of the word *swerve* in the figurative, metaphorical sense, and then discuss how these apply to the poem.

- Try a range of other structured activities such as semantic mapping, semantic feature analysis, and concept ladders; a related activity for individual words is to create short sentence templates that allow students to better understand words while practicing their writing. An example of such a template would be something like (the word) is/means (the definition); however, it is not/ does not mean (the antithesis).

## To have students analyze the nuance of words with similar denotations, do the following:

- Draw a continuum on the board and have students place a set of related words (e.g., all words related to *civilized*) along the continuum with *civilized* at one end and the others arranged as students see fit, though they must be prepared to explain the rationale for their placement.

## To help your English Language Learners, try this one thing:

- Do anything you can to make what is very abstract and elusive more visual and concrete for these students.

**Academic Vocabulary:** Key Words and Phrases

**Allusion:** This is a reference intended to evoke in a reader's mind a story (e.g., from Bible, mythology, literature, or history) without mentioning it directly.

**Analogy:** This means to compare things based on similar qualities to explain or clarify an idea.

**Antonym:** This refers to a word that means the opposite of another (e.g., long/short).

**Connotations:** Connotative meanings are the associations and emotions that come to mind in response to certain words; as opposed to *denotations* or *denotative meaning.*

**Denotations:** This refers to the literal or dictionary meaning of a word (as opposed to its connotative meaning, which includes all the more nuanced, subtle meanings of a word as we use and understand them). It is often the nuanced or connotative meaning of words that undermine comprehension, especially for English Language Learners or those without exposure to the other uses of the word.

**Figurative language (figures of speech):** This refers to the use of more visual, associative language to help readers "see" what one is saying or otherwise convey a deeper idea or emotion through such figures of speech as metaphor, simile, analogy, and allusion; clichés and mixed metaphors are also figures of speech, but they are more often weak points the writer should have revised or otherwise rewritten.

**Interpret:** This means to make sense of or explain the meaning of different figures of speech such as those listed here: oxymoron and euphemism.

**Nuance:** Related to connotative meaning (see Denotations), this word reminds us of the subtle meanings of some words as we use and come to know them. In its etymology, the word *nuance* derives from *to shade* something; thus, as readers we discern the veiled or implied meanings of a word and as writers attend to these degrees of meaning as we choose which words to use.

**Personification:** This is the attribution of human characteristics to nonhuman objects or human qualities attributed to abstract ideas (e.g., Dickinson's "Because I could not stop for Death/He kindly stopped for me").

**Pun:** This is a joke based on a play on words meant to exploit the different meanings or common sounds to make a joke (e.g., "being but heavy, I will stand and bear the light," Shakespeare, *Romeo and Juliet*).

**Synonym:** This refers to words or phrases that have an equivalent or similar meaning, though often a different connotation (e.g., *drink* and *swill*).

**Verbal irony:** This is a statement that means other than—or even opposite from—what it means on the surface (e.g., *No other performance came even close to yours tonight*, something one might say when *seeming* to compliment a performer).

**Word relationships:** This refers to how two or more words might be related grammatically, rhetorically, conceptually, or in some other meaningful way as they are used in this text. Included in this category of words are figures of speech such as metaphors, analogies, and similes, which are based entirely on associations and relationships between words and ideas.

*Notes*

**Language 6:** Acquire and use accurately a range of general academic and domain-specific words and phrases sufficient for reading, writing, speaking, and listening at the college and career readiness level; demonstrate independence in gathering vocabulary knowledge when considering a word or phrase important to comprehension or expression.

## English Language Arts/History, Social Studies, Science and Technical Subjects

**6** Acquire and use accurately grade-appropriate general academic and domain-specific words and phrases; gather vocabulary knowledge when considering a word or phrase important to comprehension or expression.

**7** Acquire and use accurately grade-appropriate general academic and domain-specific words and phrases; gather vocabulary knowledge when considering a word or phrase important to comprehension or expression.

**8** Acquire and use accurately grade-appropriate general academic and domain-specific words and phrases; gather vocabulary knowledge when considering a word or phrase important to comprehension or expression.

## What the **Student** Does

## English Language Arts/History, Social Studies, Science and Technical Subjects

**6** **Gist:** Learn and use the language of discourse appropriate to the subject, discipline, or context when reading, writing, or speaking about it, noting that some of these words are specific to the subject being studied; this would include specialized terms such as *personification* (English), *coordinate* (math and economics), *manifest destiny* (history), or *acceleration* (science). Students use other words not so specific to a given discipline but better understood as key academic literacy terms: *analyze, compare, contrast, summarize, synthesize, evaluate*. Students' knowledge of language would include familiarity with certain roots or etymologies (word histories) as alternative ways to make sense of those new words encountered for the first time.

- What are those academic words or phrases you hear most often when writing about or discussing a text or a topic?
- What are the words specific to each subject area—Language Arts, history, science—that you must learn and use accurately when reading, writing about, or discussing the content of those classes?
- What techniques work best for you to gather, learn, and remember words when studying a new or difficult subject?

**7** **Gist:** Learn and use the language of discourse appropriate to the subject, discipline, or context when reading, writing, or speaking about it, noting that some of these words are specific to the subject being studied; this would include specialized terms such as *onomatopoeia* (English), *integer* (math), *charter* (history), or *gravity* (science). Students use other words not so specific to a given discipline but better understood as key academic literacy terms: *analyze, compare, contrast, summarize, synthesize, evaluate*. Students' knowledge of language would include familiarity with certain roots or etymologies (word histories) as alternative ways to make sense of those new words encountered for the first time.

- What are those academic words or phrases you hear most often when writing about or discussing a text or a topic?
- What are the words specific to each subject area—Language Arts, history, science—that you must learn and use accurately when reading, writing about, or discussing the content of those classes?
- What techniques work best for you to gather, learn, and remember words when studying a new or difficult subject?

**8** **Gist:** Learn and use the language of discourse appropriate to the subject, discipline, or context when reading, writing, or speaking about it, noting that some of these words are specific to the subject being studied; this would include specialized terms such as *hyperbole* (English), *prime* (math), *secession* (history), or *oxidation* (science). Students use other words not so specific to a given discipline but better understood as key academic literacy terms: *analyze, compare, contrast, summarize, synthesize, evaluate*. Students' knowledge of language would include familiarity with certain roots or etymologies (word histories) as alternative ways to make sense of those new words encountered for the first time.

- What are those academic words or phrases you hear most often when writing about or discussing a text or a topic?
- What are the words specific to each subject area—Language Arts, history, science—that you must learn and use accurately when reading, writing about, or discussing the content of those classes?
- What techniques work best for you to gather, learn, and remember words when studying a new or difficult subject?

What the **Teacher** Does

**To help students acquire and use academic and specialized words, do the following:**

- Gather a list of words—academic vocabulary words— used in directions, prompts, and assignments for classes or subject areas such as yours; these are words students need to know to do what you assign them and that have often slight but significant differences (e.g., between *evaluate* and *analyze*). These are not the same as specialized academic words, which the Common Core document calls "Tier Three" words, such as *iambic pentameter* (English), *moral hazard* (economics), or other "domain-specific words . . . specific to a domain or field of study (*lava, carburetor, circumference, aorta*) that are key to understanding a new concept within a text" (Common Core State Standards, Appendix A, 33).
- Ask students at the beginning to assess their knowledge of the specialized words important to know in your class; they can do this most efficiently by taking a list of words you prepare and scoring themselves as follows: 1— have never heard or seen it, 2—heard of it, but don't know it, 3—recognize it as somehow related to ____, 4—know it when I read it but not sure I can use it correctly when writing or speaking, or 5—know it and can use it as a reader, writer, speaker, and listener.

**To help students acquire words and phrases for college and career, do the following:**

- Think of these words as arrayed along a continuum with generalization (the ability to define it) on one end and accessibility (the ability to access and use the word with precision and fluency while reading, writing, speaking, thinking, and taking tests) on the other end.
- Focus on what the Common Core calls "Tier Two" words, which it defines as "general academic words . . . [that] are far more likely to appear in written texts than in speech, [including] informational texts (words such as *relative, vary, formulate, specificity,* and *accumulate*), technical texts (*calibrate, itemize, periphery*), and literary texts (*misfortune, dignified, faltered, unabashedly*).

[These] Tier Two words often represent subtle or precise ways to say relatively simple things—*saunter* instead of *walk*, for example" (Common Core State Standards, Appendix A, 33).

**To use these words when reading, writing, speaking, and listening, do the following:**

- Preview the text students will read, write about, and discuss, looking for those words that carry more meaning, more weight in the passage, linked as they are to the central ideas whether literary or informational texts. These are the words *as concepts* in the text that students must know as they are essential to the author's ideas and argument(s).

**To help students acquire and use academic and specialized words, do the following:**

- Use the words as often and in context as you can, incorporating them into assignments, directions, prompts, and your discussion of the content; prompt students to do the same during discussions, restating their observations if necessary so they can hear what they just said in the more precise language of the discipline (e.g., "So what you seem to be saying is that he is a mere caricature rather than a fully formed, dynamic character?").
- Create and incorporate into the class whenever possible sentence templates anchored in and built from these academic words specific to our disciplines (e.g., X argues, through repeated reference to _____, that Y is, in fact, not _____ but _____, which refutes the initial claim that _____.).

**To help your English Language Learners, try this one thing:**

- Check that they always know the essential academic terms needed for that night's homework (e.g., Write a *paragraph* about the *causes* of westward expansion and its *effect* on those who remained, *comparing* the lives of one with the other.).

**Academic Vocabulary:** Key Words and Phrases

**Acquire and use accurately:** The emphasis here is on adding words to one's vocabulary so students are prepared for any text they might read or write about. To "acquire" words, one must attend to the words they see but do not know and then make an effort both to learn and to remember them for future use. The added emphasis on using words *accurately* reminds us that the difference between one word and another is often crucial to full and deeper comprehension.

**College and career readiness level:** Upon entering any postsecondary career or classroom, students immediately realize they are either ready to meet the demands of that situation or not. Those not ready for the demands of college-level reading most often have to take one or more remedial classes, which cost time and money—and often momentum—for those trying to pursue a college degree.

**Comprehension:** It means understanding what you read; full, robust comprehension demands the reader take in *all* the details of a text and examine them in light of the occasion, purpose, and audience to see if there other or deeper meanings to the text.

**Expression:** As it is used here, *expression* refers to writing; it is saying that it is important to know what a word or phrase means before one chooses to include it in something they are writing.

**General academic and domain-specific words:** These are the general words students encounter in all subjects—*analyze, evaluate, describe, compare, contrast*, and so on—and the specialized vocabulary they face in specific course or subject areas—*gravity, force, evolution, inflection point*, and the many words specific to literature and other subject areas.

**Independence in gathering vocabulary knowledge:** For students to grow their vocabulary, they must take pains to look up words and note those meanings so they can draw on them in the future as readers and writers. This independence comes from jotting down and looking up words that either interest or confuse the reader and merit further efforts to understand and distinguish them from others.

**Words and phrases sufficient . . . for college level:** This is similar to the entry for **college and career readiness level**; however, the difference here is the emphasis on being able to use words and phrases appropriate to the college-level classroom. This means using refined, specific, and appropriate language when writing about or discussing a topic in a class. One must learn to master the discourse patterns common to a specific subject area or topic on which the student might be writing or doing research.

*Notes*

# Resources

# Common Core Recommended Reading Lists

The following links take you to places that showed a commitment to building on the initial reading lists provided by the Common Core State Standards document itself. I include this short list to help you explore other sources for rich texts for your students:

Common Core Curriculum Maps

http://commoncore.org/maps

Cooperative Children's Book Center

http://www.education.wisc.edu/ccbc/books/commoncore.asp

North Carolina Department of Public Instruction

http://www.dpi.state.nc.us/docs/acre/standards/common-core-tools/exemplar/ela.pdf

## Official Common Core State Standards 6–8 Text Exemplars

### Grades 6–8 Text Exemplars

**Stories**

Alcott, Louisa May. *Little Women*

Cisneros, Sandra. "Eleven"

Cooper, Susan. *The Dark Is Rising*

Hamilton, Virginia. "The People Could Fly"

L'Engle, Madeleine. *A Wrinkle in Time*

Paterson, Katherine. *The Tale of the Mandarin Ducks*

Sutcliff, Rosemary. *Black Ships Before Troy: The Story of the Iliad*

Taylor, Mildred D. *Roll of Thunder, Hear My Cry*

Twain, Mark. *The Adventures of Tom Sawyer*

Yep, Laurence. *Dragonwings*

**Drama**

Fletcher, Louise. *Sorry, Wrong Number*

Goodrich, Frances and Albert Hackett. *The Diary of Anne Frank: A Play*

**Poetry**

Carroll, Lewis. "Jabberwocky"

Dickinson, Emily. "The Railway Train"

Frost, Robert. "The Road Not Taken"

Giovanni, Nikki. "A Poem for My Librarian, Mrs. Long"

Hughes, Langston. "I, Too, Sing America"

Longfellow, Henry Wadsworth. "Paul Revere's Ride"

Navajo tradition. "Twelfth Song of Thunder"

Neruda, Pablo. "The Book of Questions"

Sandburg, Carl. "Chicago"

Soto, Gary. "Oranges"

Whitman, Walt. "O Captain! My Captain!"

Yeats, William Butler. "The Song of Wandering Aengus"

### Informational Texts: English Language Arts

Adams, John. "Letter on Thomas Jefferson"

Churchill, Winston. "Blood, Toil, Tears and Sweat: Address to Parliament on May 13th, 1940"

Douglass, Frederick. *Narrative of the Life of Frederick Douglass, an American Slave, Written by Himself*

Petry, Ann. *Harriet Tubman: Conductor on the Underground Railroad*

Steinbeck, John. *Travels With Charley: In Search of America*

### Informational Texts: History/Social Studies

Freedman, Russell. *Freedom Walkers: The Story of the Montgomery Bus Boycott*

Greenberg, Jan, and Sandra Jordan. *Vincent Van Gogh: Portrait of an Artist*

Isaacson, Phillip. *A Short Walk Through the Pyramids and Through the World of Art*

Lord, Walter. *A Night to Remember*

Monk, Linda R. *Words We Live By: Your Annotated Guide to the Constitution*

Murphy, Jim. *The Great Fire*

Partridge, Elizabeth. *This Land Was Made for You and Me: The Life and Songs of Woody Guthrie*

United States. Preamble and First Amendment to the United States Constitution. (1787, 1791)

## Informational Texts: Science, Mathematics, and Technical Subjects

California Invasive Plant Council. *Invasive Plant Inventory*

"Elementary Particles." *New Book of Popular Science*

Enzensberger, Hans Magnus. *The Number Devil: A Mathematical Adventure*

"Geology." *U\*X\*L Encyclopedia of Science*

Katz, John. *Geeks: How Two Lost Boys Rode the Internet Out of Idaho?*

Macaulay, David. *Cathedral: The Story of Its Construction*

Mackay, Donald. *The Building of Manhattan*

Peterson, Ivars and Nancy Henderson. *Math Trek: Adventures in the Math Zone*

Petroski, Henry. "The Evolution of the Grocery Bag"

"Space Probe." *Astronomy & Space: From the Big Bang to the Big Crunch*

# Text Complexity Tool

| Title: | | Author: | | Date: | |
|---|---|---|---|---|---|
| Appropriate Grade Level: | | Length: | | Text Type/Genre: | |
| | | **Too Simple** | **Just Right** | **Too Complex** | |

| | Too Simple | Just Right | Too Complex |
|---|---|---|---|
| **QUANTITATIVE FACTORS** | | | |
| **Word Length** | | | |
| ☐ What is the average length of a word in this text? ☐ Do the words tend to have one or many meanings? | | | |
| **Sentence Length** | | | |
| ☐ How long is the average sentence? ☐ Do sentences tend to be all the same length or vary as a function of style? ☐ Do the sentences have a range of syntactical complexity—or do they tend to follow the same pattern? | | | |
| **Word Frequency** | | | |
| ☐ Which words are used frequently? ☐ Are these words known/familiar? | | | |
| **Text Cohesion** | | | |
| ☐ How well does this text hold together or flow (thanks to signal words such as transitions)? ☐ Does the text use other techniques such as repetition, concrete language to improve cohesion? ☐ Does the text lack cohesion as a result of having no signal words? | | | |
| **QUALITATIVE FACTORS\*** | | | |
| **Levels of Meaning or Purpose** | | | |
| ☐ If *literary*, does the text have more than one obvious meaning? ☐ If *informational*, is the purpose explicitly stated or implied? ☐ Does the text explore *more* than one substantial idea? | | | |
| **Text Structure** | | | |
| ☐ Does the text use simple, predictable structures such as chronological order? ☐ Does the text use complex literary structures such as flashbacks or, if informational, sophisticated graphics and genre conventions? ☐ Does the text use other features—layout, color, graphics—in ways that might confuse or challenge some readers? | | | |
| **Language Conventions and Clarity** | | | |
| ☐ Is the language literal, clear, modern, and conversational? ☐ Is the language figurative, ironic, ambiguous, archaic, specialized, or otherwise unfamiliar? | | | |
| **Knowledge Demands** | | | |
| ☐ Does the text make few assumptions about what you have experienced or know about yourself, others, and the world? ☐ Does the text assume you know about this topic or text based on prior experience or study? | | | |
| **READER AND TASK CONSIDERATIONS** | | | |
| **Motivation, Knowledge, and Experience** | | | |
| ☐ How motivated is this student to read this text? ☐ How much does this student know about this topic or text? ☐ How much experience does the student have with this task or text type? | | | |
| **Purpose and Complexity of the Assigned Task** | | | |
| ☐ Is this student able to read and work at the assigned level? ☐ Are these questions the student will know how to answer? ☐ Is the student expected to do this work alone and without any support—or with others and guidance? ☐ Is this text or task appropriate for this student at this time? ☐ Is this text or task as, less, or more complex than the last one? | | | |

Created by Jim Burke. Visit www.englishcompanion.com for more information.

\*The CCSS states that "preference should likely be given to qualitative measures of text complexity when evaluating narrative fiction for students in grade 6 and above" (8).

**Planning Calendar Templates**

## July Planning Calendar

| Sunday | Monday | Tuesday | Wednesday | Thursday | Friday | Saturday |
|---|---|---|---|---|---|---|
| | | | | | | |
| | | | | | | |
| | | | | | | |
| | | | | | | |
| | | | | | | |

# August Planning Calendar

| Sunday | Monday | Tuesday | Wednesday | Thursday | Friday | Saturday |
|--------|--------|---------|-----------|----------|--------|----------|
|        |        |         |           |          |        |          |
|        |        |         |           |          |        |          |
|        |        |         |           |          |        |          |
|        |        |         |           |          |        |          |
|        |        |         |           |          |        |          |

# September Planning Calendar

| Sunday | Monday | Tuesday | Wednesday | Thursday | Friday | Saturday |
|--------|--------|---------|-----------|----------|--------|----------|
|  |  |  |  |  |  |  |
|  |  |  |  |  |  |  |
|  |  |  |  |  |  |  |
|  |  |  |  |  |  |  |
|  |  |  |  |  |  |  |

# October Planning Calendar

| Sunday | Monday | Tuesday | Wednesday | Thursday | Friday | Saturday |
|---|---|---|---|---|---|---|
| | | | | | | |
| | | | | | | |
| | | | | | | |
| | | | | | | |
| | | | | | | |

# November Planning Calendar

| Sunday | Monday | Tuesday | Wednesday | Thursday | Friday | Saturday |
|--------|--------|---------|-----------|----------|--------|----------|
|  |  |  |  |  |  |  |
|  |  |  |  |  |  |  |
|  |  |  |  |  |  |  |
|  |  |  |  |  |  |  |
|  |  |  |  |  |  |  |

# December Planning Calendar

| Sunday | Monday | Tuesday | Wednesday | Thursday | Friday | Saturday |
|--------|--------|---------|-----------|----------|--------|----------|
|        |        |         |           |          |        |          |
|        |        |         |           |          |        |          |
|        |        |         |           |          |        |          |
|        |        |         |           |          |        |          |
|        |        |         |           |          |        |          |

# January Planning Calendar

| Sunday | Monday | Tuesday | Wednesday | Thursday | Friday | Saturday |
|--------|--------|---------|-----------|----------|--------|----------|
|        |        |         |           |          |        |          |
|        |        |         |           |          |        |          |
|        |        |         |           |          |        |          |
|        |        |         |           |          |        |          |
|        |        |         |           |          |        |          |

## February Planning Calendar

| Sunday | Monday | Tuesday | Wednesday | Thursday | Friday | Saturday |
|--------|--------|---------|-----------|----------|--------|----------|
|        |        |         |           |          |        |          |
|        |        |         |           |          |        |          |
|        |        |         |           |          |        |          |
|        |        |         |           |          |        |          |
|        |        |         |           |          |        |          |

## March Planning Calendar

| Sunday | Monday | Tuesday | Wednesday | Thursday | Friday | Saturday |
|--------|--------|---------|-----------|----------|--------|----------|
|        |        |         |           |          |        |          |
|        |        |         |           |          |        |          |
|        |        |         |           |          |        |          |
|        |        |         |           |          |        |          |
|        |        |         |           |          |        |          |

# April Planning Calendar

| Sunday | Monday | Tuesday | Wednesday | Thursday | Friday | Saturday |
|--------|--------|---------|-----------|----------|--------|----------|
|        |        |         |           |          |        |          |
|        |        |         |           |          |        |          |
|        |        |         |           |          |        |          |
|        |        |         |           |          |        |          |
|        |        |         |           |          |        |          |

# May Planning Calendar

| Sunday | Monday | Tuesday | Wednesday | Thursday | Friday | Saturday |
|--------|--------|---------|-----------|----------|--------|----------|
|        |        |         |           |          |        |          |
|        |        |         |           |          |        |          |
|        |        |         |           |          |        |          |
|        |        |         |           |          |        |          |
|        |        |         |           |          |        |          |

# June Planning Calendar

| Sunday | Monday | Tuesday | Wednesday | Thursday | Friday | Saturday |
|--------|--------|---------|-----------|----------|--------|----------|
|  |  |  |  |  |  |  |
|  |  |  |  |  |  |  |
|  |  |  |  |  |  |  |
|  |  |  |  |  |  |  |
|  |  |  |  |  |  |  |

# About the Author

**Jim Burke** currently teaches English at Burlingame High School, a public school where he has worked for more than 20 years. In addition to *The Common Core Companion: The Standards Decoded* (Corwin 2013), Jim is the author of more than 20 books, including an entirely new edition of *The English Teacher's Companion* and *What's the Big Idea?* both published by Heinemann. He is a senior consultant for the Holt McDougal *Literature* program. Jim has received several awards, including the 2000 NCTE Exemplary English Leadership Award. In 2009, he created the English Companion Ning, an online community for English teachers, which has been awarded the Best Social Network for Teachers several times. More recently, he was appointed to the AP English Course and Exam Review Commission and the PARCC Consortium, where he serves on the Content Technical Working Groups, which advise the PARCC Leadership Team and the Operational Working Groups.

# STANDARDS-BASED TEACHING

The key to raising school- and district-wide achievement is purposeful, potent, standards-based instruction—all year long in every classroom. That's where the Your Literacy Standards Companion series can help. Series creator Jim Burke and an all-star team of authors walk you step by step through what the standards mean and how to teach them. Ensure that every student in your district has the critical skills they need to succeed on test day, in school, and in life.

**Grades K–2**
978-1-5063-8682-9

**Grades 3–5**
978-1-5063-8700-0

**Grades 6–8**
978-1-5063-8553-2

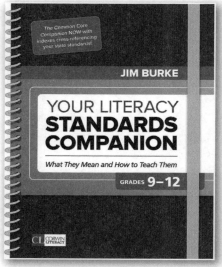

**Grades 9–12**
978-1-5063-8552-5

www.corwin.com/literacy

# BECAUSE ALL TEACHERS ARE LEADERS

**Douglas Fisher, Nancy Frey, John Hattie**
Ensure students demonstrate more than a year's worth of learning during a school year by implementing the right literacy practice at the right moment.

**Grades K–12**
978-1-5063-3235-2

**Douglas Fisher, Nancy Frey, John Hattie, Marisol Thayre**
High-impact strategies to use for all you teach—all in one place. Deliver sustained, comprehensive literacy experiences to Grades 6–12 learners every day.

**Grades 6–12**
978-1-5063-3237-6

**Jeffrey D. Wilhelm, Michael W. Smith**
Through classroom-tested lessons and compelling short excerpts, *Diving Deep Into Nonfiction* helps students read well by noticing the rules and conventions of nonfiction texts.

**Grades 6–12**
978-1-4833-8605-8

**Gretchen Bernabei, Jennifer Koppe**
50 short texts written by famous individuals driven by "an itch" to say something provide students with mentor texts to express their own thoughts.

**Grades 6–10**
978-1-5063-1126-5

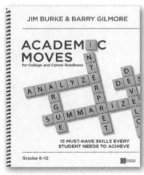

**Jim Burke, Barry Gilmore**
Jim and Barry distill each of fifteen critical reading, writing, and thinking processes into a potent concision that spans subject areas.

**Grades 6–12**
978-1-4833-7980-7

**ReLeah Cossett Lent**
*This Is Disciplinary Literacy* helps content-area teachers put into action the key literacies of their specialties—taking students from superficial understanding to deep content expertise.

**Grades 6–12**
978-1-5063-0669-8

CORWIN
A SAGE Publishing Company

A SAGE Publishing Company

**Helping educators make the greatest impact**

**CORWIN HAS ONE MISSION:** to enhance education through intentional professional learning.

We build long-term relationships with our authors, educators, clients, and associations who partner with us to develop and continuously improve the best evidence-based practices that establish and support lifelong learning.